The Book of
OLD SILVER

The Book of OLD SILVER

English ~ American ~ Foreign

BY SEYMOUR B. WYLER

WITH
ALL AVAILABLE HALLMARKS
INCLUDING
SHEFFIELD PLATE MARKS

PROFUSELY ILLUSTRATED

CROWN PUBLISHERS
NEW YORK

Eighteenth Printing, December, 1963

PRINTED IN THE UNITED STATES OF AMERICA

To

MY MOTHER AND

MY FATHER

AUTHOR'S NOTE

In the preparation of this book I was fortunate in having the counsel and assistance of many friends and the co-operation of many fellow-dealers. I want to thank them all, and especially Mr. Nathan Nathanson of the U. S. Customs; Mr. Ivan Shortt of Ellis & Co. Ltd. of London and New York, from whose great collection of photographs of silver many of the illustrations in this book were made; Mr. Stephen G. C. Ensko and Mr. James Graham, Jr., for permission to incorporate in my tables of American Silversmiths' Marks, their respective compilations of American marks.

SEYMOUR B. WYLER

CONTENTS

LIST OF ILLUSTRATIONS

The Book of
OLD SILVER

I

OLD ENGLISH SILVER

SILVER has always been the most favored of the precious metals for articles of personal or ceremonial ornament and use. Gold, though equal or superior in beauty, malleability, polish and suitability to fine effects, is twice as heavy and therefore much less practical. But the workers in one of these metals almost invariably worked in the other and goldsmithing and silversmithing really constitute one craft. Until recently goldsmith meant a worker in gold and silver.

From the earliest times, and all over the world, this craft of goldsmithing has attracted the best of artists and artisans. The value of the metals compelled a high standard of workmanship and automatically eliminated the inferior producers.

The history of ancient silversmiths is obscured in the fog of time, but since practically none of their silver is available it is not important in the understanding and appreciation of the Old Silver that exists today. It is only when we get to the history of the Art in England, the early customs, regulations and laws, that there is meaning for the amateur or connoisseur of Old Silver.

England produced more fine silver than any other country and the craft had its greatest flowering there. The customs, practices and methods originating in England influenced all other silver producers as English culture and influence spread throughout the world. The "Sterling" standard is an indication of this, though this word owes its origin to a band of immigrant Germans. They called themselves the Easterlings because of the direction in which they lived, and they were first called by King John in approximately 1300 to refine some silver to purity for coinage purposes. In a statute of 1343 the first two letters were dropped from the word "Easterling" and the application of the word "Sterling" to silver commenced.

Silver design, like architecture, followed the great movements and influences of culture and domination. And the periods and styles of silver are on the whole the same as of architecture and furniture.

At the time of the smithing of the first pieces in England, the Church reigned supreme, and the majority of the pieces made were for religious institutions. They were great rarities because of the prohibitive price of the metal in those days. But the shrines, chalices and magnificent altar frontals made for wealthy abbeys were not always the work of monks who worked at goldsmithing. Rather, in many instances, goldsmiths who had reached a high position in their field were admitted to the better abbeys and rapidly promoted because of their artistic skill. The ordinary goldsmith was not a monk vowed to a life relieving him of the normal cares in the struggle for existence, but rather a layman following a highly skilled profession of economic importance and accounted remuneration. Probably at no time during the history of goldsmithing were these men better paid for their labors, and a great number of new craftsmen joined the ranks of this little known industry and apprenticed themselves to the early masters.

The styles of the pieces made then showed a surprising gracefulness of line and proportion, for in those days a silversmith might work on one piece several months in order to complete an object of great beauty. During the Middle Ages goldsmithing was ranked among the highest of the arts, and the work of the various smiths of the time were indeed pieces of great artistic merit. During this period, goldsmiths apprenticed themselves for many years before entering the trade as finished workers. Medieval goldsmiths, however, did not confine themselves only to the production of plate but dabbled as well in many lucrative side-lines. Some were members of the other richer crafts, some often acted as pawnbrokers and they were often especially useful to the Crown. During the twelfth and thirteenth centuries, the machinery of government was becoming steadily more complicated and there were many instances where goldsmiths were called upon to aid in the construction and decoration of royal buildings, as well as the administering of the mints and exchanges.

As time passed and commerce with foreign countries developed, greater quantities of raw silver were brought to England. The English people took largely to the new luxury, and the demand for it increased rapidly. Goldsmiths in the tenancy of the monasteries found they could no longer meet the increased demands for pieces in the precious metals. They wisely took the precaution of forming themselves into guilds or fraternities. The first mention of a goldsmith's company is in the year of 1180, but it appears that this was a voluntary association and carried but little power. As early as the year 1238, many inferior silversmiths immediately took advantage of the trade to make silver of a very much lower standard than was used for government coins, and sold it for the same price as a piece of the correct alloy. With the formation of the first silver guilds in England, a Law of Parliament stated that no silver should be melted unless it had first been assayed by an appointed committee and proved to contain the correct amounts of silver and alloy. In 1335, a second "statutum de Moneta" decreed that each gold- or silversmith must punch on his wares a particular mark of his own, assigned to him by the King. In 1423, an act by Henry VI fixed the price of silver at a definite valuation of twenty-two shillings to the pound. In the succeeding years, this valuation was changed several times. In 1477 a very important law was passed by the London goldsmiths' company, compelling stamping of the leopard's head or crowned leopard's head on every piece of silver of the accepted standard.

In the year 1479, the use of the date letter was first inaugurated. The year of manufacture was to be indicated by stamping a specified letter of the alphabet in a distinctive type of lettering. Thus in the following years we find silver pieces punched with a complete set of hallmarks: the leopard's head, the date letter, the maker's mark.

Although by far the greater portion of silver made during the Gothic period was used and produced for the Church, by no means is it to be thought that plate for use in the private home was overlooked. The birth of secular plate may be said to have been caused by the desires of medieval monarchs to flaunt their power and wealth by displays of magnificent silver and gold objects within their castles. From this arose the inspiration for what is termed domestic silver, as distinguished from that made by the craftsmen of the religious fraternities for use in their ecclesiastical buildings. As we have seen, by the thirteenth century the secular silversmiths had established the foundations of their craft and had developed styles and traditions of distinctly original design. During the thirteenth and fourteenth centuries, silver plate had come into general use in the homes of royalty, and no restrictions were ever placed on the number of articles made for the table. The most popular pieces produced were basins and ewers, ceremonial salts, large dishes, chargers and drinking cups of many varieties. A greater number of drinking articles existed than other pieces, for each man reserved the right to his personal cup. This tradition is found not only among the wealthy but even in the peasant classes, but their drinking cups were made of wood.

Gradually foreign influences entered. During the sixteenth century, domestic plate was greatly influenced in design and style by the influx of foreign silversmiths who came from Italy, France and Germany, in which countries the Italian Renaissance had been fully accepted. The Gothic waned and the Renaissance styles took hold.

Nevertheless there are so few pieces in existence made prior to the sixteenth century that the study of the early goldsmiths can be accurately made only from the libraries of the first silver guilds, and the diaries of prominent persons of the day. The long and bloody Wars of the Roses were undoubtedly responsible for the melting of many magnificent pieces scheduled in ancient inventories. It is for this reason that secular plate from this time is practically unknown. The few remaining examples which unfortunately are not always the representative workings of the better type, are to be found only in private collections and museums. Whenever a piece dating before 1600 is offered at public sale, the price realized is almost fantastic.

This explains the scarcity of secular plate, but what of the pieces carefully stored in the Churches and produced in so much greater profusion? These art treasures carefully protected by the Abbeys were to undergo a fate similar to that of the plate in the homes of royalty and nobility. During the Reformation, the pillage and destruction of practically the whole of the treasures of the Church was effected. However, a further cause for the scarcity of ecclesiastical plate is found in the forced loans which the Tudor and succeeding monarchs commanded from the corporate bodies of the City of London. Many a highly prized specimen was regretfully sacrificed in order to meet the imperious requests of the Sovereign.

During the reign of Elizabeth, internal prosperity resulted in an era of far flung luxury. The stream of art diverted from the Reformation, and from the ecclesiastical channels turned toward domestic and civic comfort and splendor. Wealthy patrons of colleges and universities abundantly endowed their respective Alma Maters with magnificent plate. But the destruction of the majority of this plate was caused by Charles I directly after the Civil War. He borrowed as much money and plate as he could obtain from the leading universities. He promised to repay them for these treasures but did not, and the money was dissipated by this luxury loving monarch. During the Cromwellian era, similar proceedings took place, but during the reign of Charles II the silver business flourished.

Much of the plate had been made from the silver coin of the realm, and in order to prevent the resulting scarcity of coin, the Act of 1696 fixed the standard for plate above that of the silver coinage. The mint had offered a high price for all plate and large quantities were melted down to the ore state.

Laws regulating the silver trade were enacted and especially drastic was the penalty for fraud. In two instances, the penalty for marking inferior silver with the sterling hallmark, was punished by death. It is because of these stringent laws of the English government, upheld today as well as in early times, that practically no forged antique silver is found in Great Britain, for as quickly as the government punished the offender, so it destroyed his wares.

Moreover, the governmental influence on the craft in other ways was so great, that the reasons for many of the features of the craft cannot be understood without a knowledge of the important laws and regulations.

II

LAWS AND REGULATIONS AFFECTING ENGLISH HALLMARKS

A COMPREHENSIVE study of the complete legislation with regard to the ancient art of goldsmithing and silversmithing might well fill several volumes. The laws passed are many, and invariably written in great detail. Here we will attempt merely to give in a very concise form the high-lights or most important acts and laws that influenced the production of old silver.

The year 1180 commemorates the earliest mention of a guild or fraternity with regard to silversmithing. However, little importance is attached to it as the association was purely a voluntary one and had but few laws to govern it. After its inauguration, the founders were fined for being irregularly established without a proper license from the King.

As early as the year 1238, many inferior goldsmiths took advantage of their trade and produced silver of a very much lower standard than was used for government coins. These pieces were marketed for the same price as those of the correct alloy. Because of these numerous frauds, Henry III ordered the Mayor and aldermen of the City of London to choose six of the most discreet goldsmiths to superintend the craft. This order was duly obeyed and in the succeeding years these men were in turn followed by others in the so-called offices of superintendents or wardens.

The wardens were given more and more power as time went on and in 1300 were authorized to assay every silver vessel produced, to ascertain whether or not it contained the correct proportion of silver and alloy. They became known as "gardiens."

In the year 1327 the Guild of London Goldsmiths became regularly incorporated by Royal Charter, under the title of "The Wardens and Commonalty of the Mystery of Goldsmiths of the City of London." The most important legislation enacted by this Congress was that requiring every silversmith to use a particular hallmark of his own.

The second "Statutum de Moneta" in 1335 declared that inasmuch as counterfeit money had been imported by foreigners, plate was not to be exported without official license in order to protect the coin within the realm of the people. It is interesting to note here that the only means of exit from England officially allowed was from

Dover, at which place foreigners were searched and then permitted to depart from England.

A Statute passed in 1363 commanded that no goldsmith should work gold or silver into a wrought article unless it was of the alloy of good sterling. In the succeeding years, numerous by-laws were enacted in regard to the trade, all of varying importance.

The Guild was reincorporated by charter in 1392 with vastly extended powers. In the provinces there is also evidence of the existence of similar guilds. These, however, will be discussed in detail in their proper place.

During the reigns of Henry VIII and Edward VI the silver coinage in England had been scandalously debased to the extent that in 1551, the coin minted consisted of only three ounces of silver to every pound weight of coins. But in 1560, an act of Elizabeth definitely established the Sterling Standard of 11 ounces 2 dwt. This is the equivalent of 92.5 per cent pure silver and this standard has remained until the present time (with the exception of one period from 1697 to 1720). In order to correct the existing evil state of the coinage at this time, all existing base money was recalled by Royal proclamation on February 19, 1560.

In order to stop the melting of coins for use in silverware, a law was passed in 1696 raising the silverware standard above the coin standard to 11 ounces 10 dwt. (95.8%). Pieces made of this standard were to be stamped with a new mark known as Britannia.

But in 1719 the old standard of 11 ounces 2 dwt. was revived since wares of this content were proven to be more durable than the softer Britannia ware and the higher standard did not accomplish its purpose. Silversmiths merely added pure silver to coin silver to increase the standard. The higher or Britannia standard was not abolished but left to the discretion of individual silversmiths. It is interesting to note that the silver standard of 1719 has never changed since. This same act, which was one of the most important recorded in the annals of the Guild, also imposed a tax of sixpence per ounce on all silver made in Great Britain. This is the first known mention of any duty on plate, but because of the ineffectuality of collecting the duty, this act was repealed in 1757. In its place a law was passed which required a license to be purchased by every goldsmith and silversmith, for which a nominal fee was charged.

The duty on plate was reimposed in 1784 and continued until 1890. The head of the reigning sovereign was punched on the piece in order to denote that the full duty had been paid.

In 1890 the duty on silver was repealed, and the use of the sovereign's head was discontinued.

HALLMARKS

Because of the correct and continued use of hallmarks on English silver, the collector and research student of today is enabled to trace the complete ancestry of nearly any piece made subsequent to 1300. However, let it not be thought that hallmarks were ever originally used for any other purpose than to prevent fraud. On all pieces made from the beginning of the fourteenth century, a series of hallmarks was to be impressed denoting the quality of the piece made, and indicative of the individual maker.

The Leopard's Head mark was first established in 1300 and may be said to be the earliest known hallmark on English silver. In 1363 the name was changed and this particular mark was called a King's mark. Through an error in translation from the French, the name leopard was applied to the head as depicted in the hallmark, but actually the figure used was that of the head of a lion. From 1478 to the George II era there was a crown on the leopard's head. After this time, however, the size of the head was diminished and again through an error in reading the original laws of the guild, the crown was omitted.

MAKER'S MARK

This mark is next in chronological order to the leopard's head. The act of 1363 ordained that every Master Goldsmith should have a mark of his own which was to be impressed on each piece after it had been assayed. The first maker's marks were generally flowers, animals, hearts, crosses, or other symbols generally selected in allusion to the maker's name. It is probably because most of the population at this time was illiterate that this form of mark was used. Shops in London of this period were rarely advertised by name since so few people were able to read. Therefore, we may assume that the earliest silversmiths aped the styles of shopkeepers in advertising or hallmarking their own products. This system fell into disuse in the seventeenth century and by the time of Charles II, initials and letters were used. During the years of the Britannia standard many makers used two individual marks, in order to distinguish silver made of one standard from the other. This caused so much confusion that in 1739 a statute decreed that all silversmiths should use the first initials of their Christian name and surname. At this time all previous marks were discontinued.

DATE LETTERS

Although there has been definite proof of the use of the date letter on silver as early as 1500, the first actual mention is in 1629. From this time on, date letters were used with sufficient frequency to enable one to fill in the missing years, and so be able to determine the exact year in which a piece was made. The use of the date letter was arranged in cycles of twenty years using the letters A to U or V, but excluding J. At the end of each twenty years, a different type of letter was used and the cartouche was changed. It must be mentioned here that dates that one often finds engraved on a piece of silver are of but little help in determining the actual year in which a piece was created, as many pieces were given or bequeathed and the date inscribed signified the time of the presentation, not the time of making.

LION PASSANT

This mark was adopted as the official stamp at the Goldsmiths Hall in London in 1544. All London silver made since then must have this mark.

LION'S HEAD ERASED AND "BRITANNIA"

The only importance to be attached to these two marks is that they denoted pieces made of the higher standard and were used for only 23 years, from 1697 to 1720. It is because of the short term of use of these marks that pieces bearing the Britannia are rare and always sought after by collectors.

SOVEREIGN'S HEAD

This mark should be found on all plate assayed in England from 1784 to 1890 as it was required to be used to denote the payment of duty by the silversmith to the Crown. This mark is actually the head in profile of the reigning King or Queen.

Thus the use of these marks enables us to identify the place, year, and maker of old silverware. Complete tables and the method of using them will be found in a separate section of this book.

III

FRAUDS

WE have seen the great and complicated efforts to maintain the regularity and genuineness of silverware. That was because the continued growth of an industry not only produces craftsmen of merit and ability but also individuals who are not content to deal fairly and earn the rewards of honest labor. The establishing of silversmithing as a permanent and lucrative business was the loophole for many dishonest workers to seek unethical methods by which to prosper. The English, being a keen and farsighted people, took precautions as early as 1327 to try and stop any forms of malpractice. In this year, which marks the incorporation of the Goldsmiths Company, the first measures were taken to guard against the counterfeiting of silver. With the passing years, the Goldsmiths Company grew more powerful and for the last five centuries their word has been law in England. Even today, they assay and hallmark all pieces of English origin, and for this reason very little forged silver is to be found there today. Not only did the Company have the right to punish an offender, but they were privileged to confiscate and destroy his wares as well. In early days, the penalties for forging silver were very severe.

There are many ways in which deception may be practiced in the silver trade, and an attempt will be made here to simplify and explain the various means. However, it must be remembered that the actual contact with a fraudulent piece is the most certain way of detecting the deception.

The earliest known fraud was the sale of plated ware, represented to be of the silver standard. The maker hallmarked the pieces himself and thus the payment of duty and all contacts with the Goldsmith Company were avoided. However, legislation and supervision did away with this type of deception. The quality of the silver in a piece may be proved by the application of acid, the resulting reaction on the metal being definite proof of its fineness. This method is used commonly by tradesmen today in dealing with unmarked pieces.

One of the frequently practiced frauds today is that of subtraction which is in effect the removal of a part or parts of an article after it has been hallmarked. For example, let us say that a silver cup of a certain type is wanted, and the nearest thing available is an urn of similar proportion. By removing the spout, the urn becomes a cup and the order is filled. Also, trays are often found which were originally patens. The feet having been removed and the abrasions carefully erased, a more valuable piece has been created. It is safe to say the fraud of subtraction is usually perpetrated only to create a piece of greater saleability.

A similar fraud is that of addition. This is the adding on of a part to an original piece after it has been hallmarked. The law provides that permission must be obtained from the authorities before making an addition, and that if the additional piece increases the weight of the article by more than a third of its original weight, the added silver must be hallmarked. However, it also decreed that an addition could not be performed if it in any way changed the character of the original article. In other words, a foot, a handle or a spout might be put on, but a coffee pot could not be made from a tankard.

Another type of forgery is that of transformation and this is done to turn an original into a piece of greater worth and more character. A tray might be created from a meat platter, as it is far more saleable from the standpoint of the dealer, and definitely more valuable. Although in this type of fraud the hallmark is left untouched, it often becomes twisted and frequently appears upside down or in the wrong place.

More frequent than these frauds is the transposition of the marks from an article that is old into a piece of modern manufacture. As a rule the marks are taken from an old piece of little value and put into an article which if it were old would command a high price. For example, the part of a handle of a teaspoon on which the marks are impressed is removed and transposed on to the side of a coffee pot that is a good reproduction. In this way, new pieces of apparently antique silver are created.

The counterfeiting of marks constitutes the marking of a piece by other than the Goldsmiths Company and the reasons for this deception are easily discerned. Because of the extreme similarity of some new marks to some old ones, this type of fraud is sometimes found. For instance, the fact that the Britannia standard mark is in use today if the piece is of the recognized quality, is reason enough to promote this fraud. As the old standard mark and the new are alike, all the unscrupulous dealer has to do is to have the date letter omitted, and the piece might well be a fine original from the Queen Anne period.

From all the preceding indictment and explanation of fraudulent practices, the innocent bystander might easily remark that with so many varied types of forgery being practiced, it is impossible to purchase a fine original and be completely certain of its authenticity. However, by no means does the author intend to convey the impression that the majority of these frauds cannot be detected. It is a safe practice though, when in doubt to consult an expert, and if necessary pay him for his advice, for in the long run it will be the cheapest investment.

There are many ways in which to detect the forgeries on pieces of silver. Silver can be tested, hallmarks should be properly placed, and the piece must not antedate its introduction. What is meant by the latter is that if tea caddies were introduced during the reign of Queen Anne, one bearing the hallmark of say 1640 must obviously be a spurious piece. It is well also, to consider carefully the period in which the piece was made. More than often it is just such errors as these that lead to the eventual detection of fraudulent pieces. Even the cleverest forger will slip up somewhere, and as a rule it is the lack of knowledge of the history of silver that defeats the counterfeiter.

To an expert, the easiest method of judging the age of a piece is by its color, and although this rule is not infallible, it generally proves true. Silver over a period of years becomes oxidized many times, and this continued action of the elements on the metal gives it a certain softness of texture and color that is known as patina. Frequent cleaning and use in service mellow the piece, and it assumes a certain smoothness that time alone can produce. One often revels in the beauty of old silver, because of its soft bluish color. This is an integral part of the make-up of the patina.

The insertion of an old set of hallmarks in a modern piece, has been said to be the forgery most in use today. This malpractice entails a great deal of labor such as filing, fitting and soldering the marks into place. The heat of the hard soldering discolors the silver, and necessitates the polishing of the piece to hide the defect. After a time, the solder marks will be visible, and it is for this reason that dealers so often blow their breath on the hallmarks. In this way they can sometimes see signs of the transposition. An excellent test is to put the piece in fire and after a few minutes if the marks have been soldered in, the outline will become visible.

Hallmarks on silver are punched in separately and if one finds a set of four salts or a dozen service plates with all the marks perfectly aligned, there is just cause for suspicion.

IV

THE COLLECTION AND CARE OF OLD SILVER

IN purchasing pieces of silver from those who are not absolutely reliable, it is well to beware of these so-called bargains. It is a fairly safe axiom to remember that good things are never too cheap. The reason for this may be explained if one considers that the market for silver is very steady, and purchasers, whether dealers or private people, are almost always ready to increase their collections.

Pieces that have additions such as later chasing or engraving, or badly eradicated hallmarks, can be purchased for very little. However, their worth is little more than that of modern silver, for old means antique, and that in turn may be translated into meaning original.

It is best to buy your silver from an unquestionably reliable dealer. He is more likely to detect a fraud than you and if it is not genuine he won't sell it to you except for what it is. If, however, you are acquiring silverware in one way or another not from a reputable dealer, be careful. First, determine what the piece is supposed to be. Look for the hallmarks. Are they complete, consistent and genuine? The marks must not be too regular. They must not be upside down and each detachable piece must be hallmarked. Then determine where it was made, when and by whom. Consider whether the style of the piece is consistent with the period and whether it has the proper patina for its alleged age. If you are at all uncertain give it the acid test to determine whether it is really silver. Then look for abrasions, rough edges, etc., to see if there has been any subtraction. Look carefully to determine whether by irregular joining, welds, curves, solderings you can detect transformation or addition. And most important check the hallmarking to see whether genuine antique hallmarks have been soldered into a more recent article. The extent of your testing and verification will naturally vary with the price and the importance of the ware.

If the hallmarks are not genuine or not genuinely of the piece, then the ware will not have value as an antique. If the fault is in subtraction or transformation, the piece will have value as an antique, but much less than its apparent value. If the fault is in addition, its value as an antique will be that of a piece without the addition.

The absence or incompleteness of hallmarks does not in itself mean that a piece is worthless as an antique. It merely raises that presumption and makes identification and proof very difficult. In the case of incomplete marks, first be sure that the reading is accurate. The absence of the leopard's head or date letter may mean merely that the piece is not London silver but American or French or the ware of some other country. If the marks that are on the silver do however indicate its origin there may be good and interesting reasons for the omission of the other marks. And the least likely of these reasons would be fraud, because a forger taking the trouble to fake an antique would probably be sure to have his hallmarks complete.

If a piece can be positively identified and proven of standard it will have the same value whether or not the hallmarks are complete because the entire purpose of hallmarks is merely to certify when and by whom a piece of standard silver was made.

Worn, badly erased or eradicated hallmarks are a definite fault. Old silverware, to be worth its true value, must be in good condition and a worn mark besides being an indication of a worn piece makes exact identification impossible.

The relative importance of the imperfection can best be gauged by understanding the factors that determine the value of old silver. First and by far the most important is age or scarcity value. Second is size. As a general principle all other things being equal the bigger the piece the more its worth. But this is not absolutely true. The third factor might be considered to be supply and demand, which is another facet of the scarcity factor. For example, there is very little eighteenth century silver available. Therefore, whatever there is, is very valuable. Of course, a large tray will be worth more than a small tray. But a small coffee pot might be worth more if it happened to be a rare example, or if someone needed it to complete a set. Style, workmanship, the intrinsic beauty of the piece, the maker are other factors that have effect upon the value of the silver.

Nevertheless silver other than antique pieces may have considerable value and may be worthy of collection. Careful selection of low and moderate priced pieces today will probably also bring dividends, in time, to the collector.

Authentic reproductions, any hand wrought ware that is genuine will have in the ordinary course of events important and increasing value. The craft now, as a handcraft is almost non-existent. With the passage of time the absorption into private hands of more and more of this later silverware and the inevitable loss and destruction of pieces, the scarcity and therefore the value will increase. The demand also will increase as the custom and fancy of collecting increases and the standards of living improve.

Silverware has always been a premier investment with ever increasing values and it will continue to be so because the supply of it cannot increase, it must decrease.

Machine made silverware may have a collector's value in time, but only in a limited degree. After all, the chief determining factor is scarcity and machines are used to produce quantities.

However, Jubilee Silver made during 1934-1935 and impressed with the mark of the double sovereigns-head (King George V and Queen Mary) has already risen in value.

THE CARE AND CLEANING OF SILVER

The possession of old silver carries with it a responsibility, as pieces of such rarity must be given great care. Old silver should be cleaned regularly with an accepted standard polish or paste, which will in no way be harmful to the texture of the metal. Inasmuch as the great beauty of antique silver lies in its soft color, it is heartily recommended that all cleaning be done by hand rather than by machine. At no time should silver be left to tarnish to such a degree that it makes it necessary to have it buffed, as in doing this, the hallmarks may be eradicated.

With regard to storage of fine pieces, it is suggested that they be wrapped individually in anti-tarnish flannel bags, which will serve as a means of protection. The author has found from practical experience that many people attempt to have their silver lacquered so as to save work in the house. This is definitely not approved of as the lacquer imparts to the old patina a glaring finish which detracts from the beauty of the piece.

V

FAMOUS ENGLISH GOLDSMITHS

THROUGHOUT the history of silversmithing in England, a few smiths are outstanding for the quality of the work they produced. An attempt is made only to give the highlights in the careers of the most brilliant of these craftsmen.

PAUL LAMERIE

Paul Lamerie was born in Holland April 14, 1688. His family had settled there after escaping from religious persecution in France, one of many of the Huguenots who fled to foreign lands. Because of these family ties of Lamerie which were distinctly French, he is often erroneously thought to have been a French silversmith.

In 1691 Lamerie's father arrived in England and having been of the French aristocracy, would not permit himself to work in a trade. The only profession which embraced manual labor that was acceptable was that of the goldsmith.

At the age of fifteen the young Paul was apprenticed to Peter Platel and it is to this celebrated craftsman that he owes all of his early knowledge of the trade. Very few students were given better opportunity, as Platel's works had been accepted as having reached the zenith of the goldsmith's art. Seven years after his apprenticeship, Lamerie was admitted as a freeman and opened up his first shop. Within a short time his instant success was evidenced by the establishing of a second place of business. In 1717, he was admitted to the livery of the Goldsmiths' Company, and eventually was within reach of the Prime Wardenship of the Guild. During his lifetime he connected himself with the army, and in 1743 attained the rank of Major.

He died in 1751 after a very colorful career. No silversmith throughout English history attained such world-wide fame as did Lamerie, for the quality of his work was distinctly superior to any previously known. As a craftsman, he had a distinct genius for creation and brought many new forms of decoration to the public eye for the first time. It is indeed strange, however, considering his great popularity and success, that he was never appointed as a goldsmith to the crown. Not one article made by Lamerie is to be found in the collection of Royal Plate at Buckingham Palace or Windsor Castle.

Throughout the study of the life of Lamerie, one is apt to be confused by the various spellings of his name. No serious notice need be taken of this if one realizes that that age in which he lived was an illiterate one and people spelled mainly phonetically.

MATTHEW BOULTON

The city of Birmingham is justly proud of Matthew Boulton. Throughout his entire life he was associated with his home city and was one of the earliest of the provincial silversmiths to achieve more than a local reputation. His talents were not confined to silversmithing. During his lifetime he was connected with several other industries, in each of which he left a name well to be remembered. In his younger days, he engaged in the manufacture of hardware and then went into the trade of artistic productions which included articles of Sheffield plate, silver, ormolu and paintings.

Later on he devoted his entire time to the development of Watt's steam engine and made great strides in the field of engineering. In the final stages of his life he brought about numerous improvements in the coining of money, several of which were accepted by the Treasury of England for practical use.

The Boulton family was typical of many known in the seventeenth century, the landed gentry engaged in the manufacturing pursuits. Matthew was born in 1728 and attended school in a suburb of Birmingham. At the age of fourteen he was apprenticed to a trade which he left a short time later to enter business with his father, who was a toy manufacturer. The toy business, as it was then known, was not one in which children's playthings were made, but rather a shop wherein all sorts of trinkets, buckles, seals, boxes and articles of hardware for household purposes were sold. The young Matthew applied himself diligently to this business and before long was entrusted with the entire management of his father's interests. Boulton was married at an early age, but was widowed a short time after. Scarcely a year had elapsed, when his father died and it was this occurrence that brought him into greater prominence than ever before. As his business grew, he became a combined manufacturer and retailer, and was compelled to take in a partner, John Fothergill. Unfortunately, he turned out to be more of a detriment than a help.

Shortly after the discovery of the process known as Sheffield plating, Boulton went to the city of Sheffield better to acquaint himself with this new technique. He realized the tremendous future in store for this new industry and spent several weeks in the work shops of Richard Morton, one of the ablest of the early makers. The earliest mention of a piece of plate by Boulton is in 1762, and he carried the distinction of having the only foundry outside of Sheffield where plate was made. He was one of the first craftsmen to adopt the sterling silver thread edge in place of the plated wire, as he was convinced that this newer process would protect the pieces at the points of hardest wear. Many of the Boulton pieces are stamped with the words: "Silver Borders," in conjunction with his own mark of a sun which he registered in 1784.

After his success in the production of Sheffield plate his thoughts naturally turned to the industry of solid silver making. However, he was faced here with a very serious obstacle, as the silver had to be hallmarked and the nearest assay office was at Chester, seventy-two miles away. The only alternative was to send the pieces to the London assay office, but as this was even further distant, the cost was too great and the likelihood of damage was ever-present. Boulton gave a great deal of thought to this difficulty and soon became determined to appeal to Parliament for the establishment of an assay office at Birmingham. He voiced his opinions on this subject most intelligently and was given a great deal of publicity. Before long, his fellow workmen in the city of Sheffield gave him their whole-hearted support and the two towns requested individual assay offices at the same time. After a great deal of argument, on the part of the Goldsmiths of London, against this measure, permission was granted in 1773, and offices were opened at Birmingham and Sheffield.

Matthew Boulton died in 1809, and conclusive proof of the tremendous success he enjoyed may be gleaned from his will. This provided for the disposition of close to three quarters of a million dollars which in those days was considered a huge fortune. Truly, it may be said that he was successful in every enterprise he undertook, but that in the production of Sheffield plate he achieved a prominence never since equalled by any other craftsman. He produced plate of rare quality, and his works are eagerly sought after today as they are considered among the best specimens of the period in which he lived.

PAUL STORR

Paul Storr was the most celebrated of the late George III silversmiths, and his works showed a degree of skill equalled previously only by Paul Lamerie. Throughout his career he enjoyed the distinction of royal and artistic patronage and executed many important dinner services to special order. He was a great artist and developed many new modes of decoration in his work. During the last ten years his skill has become more appreciated than ever—and today many collectors are specializing in the acquisition of pieces by him.

Paul Storr first entered his name at Goldsmiths Hall in 1792, at which time he was a partner in the firm of Rundell and Bridge. In 1821, in conjunction with John Mortimer, he opened the shop of Storr and Mortimer, which has been carried on to the present time in London under the name of Hunt and Roskell.

ANTHONY NELME

Nelme was one of the earliest smiths to achieve prominence and was extensively patronized throughout his career. He entered his mark in the Hall in 1697. Upon his death in 1722, he was succeeded by Francis Nelme, who adopted Anthony's mark and continued his work in the same style.

PETER PLATEL

Platel was one of the Huguenots who escaped to England where he enjoyed a large and extensive patronage. He produced many magnificent pieces for royalty, but he is probably better known as the tutor of Paul Lamerie.

BATEMAN

The members of the Bateman family, which included Anne, Hester, Jonathan, Peter, and William, were all prominent as silversmiths in the George III era. They were among the most popular smiths of their time and their work portrays clearly the exacting apprenticeship to which each was subjected. The name of Hester Bateman is by far the best known of the five, and the work by this celebrated lady smith is greatly in demand. The delicate craftsmanship which was characteristic of her has influenced greatly present popularity. As only a few pieces bearing her hallmark are available, higher prices are paid than ever before.

Among many other craftsmen who achieved fame were: Simon Pantin, Peter Archambo, David Willaume, Richard Gurney, John Cafe, Henry Chawner, and John Emes.

VI

TEA SERVICES

THE spirit of the tea hour seems to be indelibly associated with England, for in no other corner of the world is this simple function still preserved with such dignity and care.

Tea was originally introduced to the English people through an advertisement that appeared in a London newspaper in 1658. "That excellent and by all Physicians approved China Drink called by the Chinese Tcha, by other nations Tay, alias Tee, is sold at the Sultaness Head, a coffee-house in Sweeting's Rents, by the Royal Exchange, London." It was mentioned again in the diary of Samuel Pepys, who in 1660 wrote of having tasted a new beverage from the East and having found it to his liking. However, it was not until 1664 that tea came to be better known. In that year, the East India Company, one of the largest trading establishments of its day, presented two pounds of this new luxury to His Majesty Charles II. Tea cost over one hundred shillings a pound at that time so that the mention of a gift of two pounds of tea to the reigning king of England, need not seem strange.

Although tea was first considered to be expressly for medicinal purposes, it soon grew to be better known as a refreshment. It is recorded that tea found instant favor with the ladies and gentlemen of the court, and it was not long before it was imported in larger quantity. As the importation increased, so the price was lessened and in about 1720, tea had reached a price level where it could be enjoyed by others than just the select and wealthier classes. Leading figures of the day with sufficient funds to indulge themselves, consumed as many as twenty to twenty-five cups daily.

The introduction of tea into England is responsible for the production of many beautiful silver vessels for use in service, and were it not for the instant popularity which greeted its importation into England, the world might well have lost these splendid examples of superb craftsmanship displayed by the silversmiths in the making of silver tea ware.

TEA POTS

The earliest known silver tea pot was made in 1670, this priceless treasure now being in the possession of the Victoria and Albert Museum in London. The pot bears the arms of the East India Com-

pany, and is engraved with an inscription of presentation as follows: "This Silver Tea-Pott was presented to ye Comtte of ye East India Cumpany be Ye Honoue George Lord Berkeley Castle A member of that Honourable and Worthy Society and a True Hearty Lover of Them 1670." Were it not for this inscription it might well have been thought to have been a coffee pot, for its shape and size were very similar to the accepted style of coffee pot produced since about 1700. Very few silver tea pots of contemporary date are known. During the reign of Queen Anne many fine specimens of pots were executed to special order of the nobility, but in small sizes only for tea was still very expensive. Not until the reign of George II, 1727-1759, were tea pots made of larger size or in greater profusion.

The early tea pots were severely simple in style, but as the demand brought more and more activity to the silversmiths of the day, many of the early masters indulged in fine chasing and gave full expression to their creative ability. Many of the silver pots made were copied from the exquisite Chinese masterpieces fashioned in porcelain by the potters from the East.

Since the time of George I, tea pots have constantly changed in shape and decoration, as silversmiths all over Europe tried to create pieces expressing the individual tastes of their clients.

Tea pots with characteristic spouts first began to appear in the last quarter of the seventeenth century. The Chinese custom of preparing tea differed from that of the English, and this greatly influenced the change in the shape of the pots. The Chinese poured hot water out of the pot on the leaves, while the English infused the tea in the pot. Tea pots of the Queen Anne and George Ist period were very beautiful, as a rule being of a pear shaped body with a domed lid, the outline being either rounded or polygonal. The popular type with the inverted pear shaped body was introduced about 1730. As the demand for silver tea pots increased to the point where practically every home of good standing owned one, styles repeatedly changed. The Adam period was extremely prolific in designs for tea pots. Typical specimens of the time were made with a circular, oval or octagonal drum shape body, usually with a straight spout. Many in this period had stands to match, as the bottoms were constantly burning and scratching the highly polished wood surfaces of the tea table. It is not unusual, however, to find a tea pot by one maker, and a stand to match by a different smith of a few years later date. This was because people did not realize at first how essential the stands were if their fine tables were to be preserved. The tea pot so popular in Scotland for many years, of a globular shape on a tall

foot, remained purely local, and never found much favor south of the Tweed.

TEA CUPS AND SAUCERS

Silver tea cups and saucers are among the rarest known objects in silver, but a few specimens dating from 1684 to 1700 have survived. These, it may be added, are nearly entirely in private collections or on display in leading museums. Both cups and saucers were of the convex fluted style, later copied by leading porcelain factories. All were made without handles, proving beyond doubt that the earliest vessels connected with this beverage were influenced by the Chinese forms.

COFFEE POTS

Coffee first found its way into England during the Commonwealth, 1649 to 1660, so as a beverage, it antedates tea in England. However, it was greatly frowned upon at first, as many thought it to be a drug, and that its constant use would cause the men of the nation to "dwindle into a succession of apes and pygmies." So radical was the feeling against coffee that many bills were introduced into Parliament to prohibit its sale.

The earliest known uses of coffee are traced to Abyssinia, where it was consumed as early as the fifteenth century. Coffee was also used in early Mohammedan religious ceremonies as an antisoporific. However, it was later excluded from these services, as many thought it to be intoxicating, and contrary to the teachings of the Koran.

Eventually, coffee became popular in England and in 1651 the earliest known coffee house was opened by a Syrian, Cirques Jobson, Oxford. However, these places did not meet with the favor of the King, as he considered them a meeting place for political agitators. Years later, after much legislation concerning them, coffee houses were firmly established throughout England. Even today one may find some that are a few centuries old.

The first silver coffee pot is dated 1681, and was less than 10 inches high, being considerably shorter in height than the "tea-pott" of 1670. However, the general shape resembled that of the tea pot, the main difference being that the handle was opposite the spout. The next examples known had the handles placed at right angles to the spout, and this style remained unchanged until the beginning of the George II period. Shortly before 1700, the spout was curved, and as the Queen Anne period progressed a style of coffee pot of octagonal shape was very popular. This was merely an alternative to the regular tapering cylinder. During the George Ist period, the

silversmiths created an object of more beauty, by modifying the tapering cylindrical shape, and curving the base into the spout. The lid became flatter and more deeply moulded, and gradually as the years passed, the accepted style of pot was decidedly dissimilar to the first creations of the earliest craftsmen.

SUGAR BOWLS

Little sugar was imported into England before its use in tea, and consequently the first silver sugar basins were not introduced until the reign of William III, 1695 to 1702. These were originally made with a rounded base, with a saucerlike cover, so very similar to the Chinese tea cup. However, the style was later discarded for a type set on three feet, and many years later were made to match tea pots. Sugar baskets were first made at the time of Queen Anne and reappeared again at the end of the eighteenth century with colored glass linings. About this time, the flair for pierced work found great favor with the silversmiths of the day, and it is for this reason that so many pierced as well as richly embossed sugar bowls are known.

At the time of the production of the first tea services, sugar bowls were decidedly out of proportion in size to the balance of the service. Frequently, they were fully as large as the tea pot. This was because at that time only unrefined sugar was known, the pieces were large and bulky and it was necessary to have a vessel of ample size to contain them.

CREAMERS

The Chinese did not use cream in their tea so that no cream pitchers in silver are known earlier than the time of Queen Anne, when the English adopted their own method of tea drinking, which involved cream and sugar.

The earliest specimens of creamers were made with simple round feet, but this style changed as the shapes of tea pots varied. In later years, as a rule, creamers resembled the general style of the tea pot. The popular type of helmet-shaped creamer was introduced during the George III era and the oval forms of the nineteenth century that followed were called squat creamers.

Various curious shapes were adapted to small creamers. Many eccentric forms are known today, the best known of which is in the shape of a cow. (Such specimens are exceedingly rare and may be confused with the modern Dutch ones that have flooded the market for years.) This was originally a creation of Nicholas Sprimont, a silversmith connected with the Chelsea porcelain factory.

TEA CADDIES

Tea caddies were introduced during the reign of Queen Anne, and specimens from this era are very rare. They were made in greater numbers during the George Ist period. The word caddy is derived from the Malay "kate," which means a weight equivalent to 1 1/15th of a pound. As tea was always sold by the "kate," the name became by transference applied to the case in which it was contained. The word canister, sometimes used instead of caddy, antedated the English adoption of caddy. Its use has been found in an advertisement of 1711.

Caddies were originally made in sets of three and later two, as different blends of tea were used, according to taste preference. It has been suggested that many times the center caddy of a set of three was originally made to be used as a sugar bowl, but this can only be surmised. The earliest known caddies were small, because of the prohibitive prices of tea, but as the beverage became more generally consumed and the price lessened, they were made of a more substantial size. The first caddies were made with a sliding panel and a domed top. The object of the panel was to prevent waste in transferring the tea from the original package, since it was much simpler to insert the tea through the larger opening at the base. Later, caddies were almost invariably made with hinge covers like regular boxes. It is perhaps because of this that so many have been adapted to present day use for cigarette containers.

As a general rule, caddies were placed in an outer case of beautifully decorated wood or shagreen and fitted with a lock and key. However, it is rare to find an original case in use today, as through hard wear and constant usage they were discarded or replaced. Not only were the cases of the caddies supplied with locks and keys but the pieces were, also. Tea was so expensive at that time, that people feared unless it were fully protected, servants might be tempted to steal some of it.

Some of the finest works of celebrated silversmiths are represented in caddies, as specimens of Lamerie and other famous smiths prove. However, the demand for elaborate decoration that came many years later was also transferred to tea caddies. Some of the fantastic and ornate creations applied to caddies are almost unimaginable.

TEA KETTLES

The tea kettle was the natural outcome of the tea pot, for in style it is little more than a tea pot mounted on a base with a spirit lamp for purposes of heating. However, it was not until twenty years after the introduction of tea pots that kettles were made in silver. The earliest known mention of one is in a Royal Warrant of 1687, but no example from that date is known to exist. The earliest one known today is the work of David Willaume executed in 1706, and the next in order, 1709, is the work of the celebrated Anthony Nelme, now owned by the Duke of Portland.

Tea kettles of the first quarter of the eighteenth century follow the lines of the early pear-shaped tea pots, and are circular or polygonal in plan. Later, a globular form was introduced and finally the popular inverted pear shaped type. As a general rule the stands were of delicately pierced work and contained in the center a lamp used for purposes of heating. During the George II era, many richly embossed pieces were created to harmonize with the changing trend towards decorative silver. Kettles of this period were often made with a small triangular stand, which prevented the tea table from being scorched by the heat of the flame of the lamp. In the latter part of the Queen Anne period, occasional mention is made of a huge stand sometimes three feet high on which conveniently to place the kettle next to the table, but only one or two such specimens are extant.

Because of the high cost of tea, the beverage was infused right at the table to prevent waste, and this readily explains the introduction of the tea pot with the lamp. It is very important in purchasing antique silver kettles to note that the hall marks on the bodies and stands match, for over a period of years stands were lost, and replaced by ones of later date. Also, many of the first owners of tea pots had stands made to fit them, to avoid the cost of an extra new piece. These, naturally, are not so desirable nor of value equal to those that are completely hallmarked in stand, body and lamp, and of uniform design as originally made.

URNS

The demand for a larger vessel to be used at social functions caused the silver tea urn to be made. It was usually of immense size and used to contain hot water. Many people actually tried to brew the tea inside these urns, but found upon experiment that the resulting beverage was far from palatable.

Tea urns were introduced about 1760, and at first were made similar to a kettle with a spirit lamp. This was soon altered, and urns were made with a compartment on the inside to hold a heated iron. This was heated in the kitchen and dropped in the compartment. It actually kept the beverage hot for hours. The iron heaters were connected on the inside to the handles.

The styles and shapes were influenced along with other pieces of the day by the contemporary styles. Rarely were they made to match tea services, though, as were kettles.

CHOCOLATE POTS

Although the chocolate pot is not actually a part of the tea service, its history in silversmithing is so closely allied to the coffee pot, it must be mentioned.

Chocolate originated from the West Indies, and was first heard of in England in 1657. As a beverage it grew rapidly in popularity, but being too rich for constant use, vessels for its service were not created in great numbers.

The main difference between a chocolate pot and a coffee pot, is that in the top of the former there is an opening covered by a small hinged lid, rather than a spout. Through this lid, a circular wooden stick was placed to aid in crushing and mixing the chocolate. This was known as a swizzle stick.

As for the changing style and decoration of the chocolate pot, it can only be said that it followed the coffee pot very closely, and was only distinguished by its lack of spout. In later years, as even today, chocolate pots were made with the handle at right angles to the spout.

COFFEE BIGGINS

A biggin, or coffee biggin, is a particular type of coffee pot, conceived by a man of that name. It was in reality a percolator. The coffee was first placed in a separate compartment fitted into a larger vessel, and this larger vessel contained water which was heated from below by an alcohol lamp as used in the kettle.

TEA SERVICES

The first complete tea service incorporated a tea pot, a sugar and a creamer. These three-piece services were made about 1790. A few specimens of prior date are known but are very rare. During the latter part of the George III era, coffee pots to match were added. However, it was not until years later that the complete tea service of six pieces with a kettle and a waste bowl of uniform design was introduced. It may be noted that the waste bowl is comparatively a new note in silversmithing. Judging from the varying styles and profusion of tea services dating later than 1850, it may be safely assumed that afternoon tea was at the height of its popularity during the reign of Queen Victoria. Many of the styles, so popular during the latter part of the Georgian era were reproduced, and are greatly in demand today. It is unfortunate, though, that so many of the earlier models were richly chased and embossed to suit the taste of the hour, for more than often the application of too much ornamentation detracted from the original shapes. It is difficult to realize the tremendous quantity of tea services produced during this era, unless one has viewed the countless different styles copied from the art motifs of foreign countries.

The collection of an antique silver tea service may entail much searching and a great difficulty in matching pieces. However, since no complete services were ever executed, it is within the full right of any collector to own a service of assembled pieces. Many times, makers are asked to make modern matching pieces to an original service of three units. However, a true lover of antique silver will never object to a service that does not match exactly. Rather, it is much more interesting to spend months searching for just that particular coffee or kettle to use with your own service, and finally realize that if you have been fortunate, you have succeeded in accomplishing what every silver dealer is continually trying to do.

VII

MAZER BOWLS

MAZER bowls are among the earliest examples of English domestic silver. They were turned from bird's eye maple wood, which being of a fibrous texture, permitted the bowl to contain liquid without cracking or warping. Frequently the rims were ornamented with precious metals, although many mazers were executed for the poorer classes and were without silver embellishments. Mazer bowls were commonly in use during the thirteenth, fourteenth, and fifteenth centuries. During the reign of Queen Elizabeth they ceased to be made, as other creations of the silversmiths were found to be more useful.

The name "mazer" was probably derived from the German word "mazo," which means a spot. This referred to the speckled nature of the wood; however, the word may have derived from the Dutch "maeser" which means "knot of wood."

Some examples have a silver collar around the rim, which was probably used to conceal the marks of the turning lathe. They may have been copied from the early Roman pottery pieces which had a similar design. Occasionally a mazer was raised on a silver trumpet-shaped stem with a deep foot, ornamented with an open crest for use as a standing cup. In this way, the importance of the piece was often increased.

The usual silver mounts of a mazer were a band around the lip and a circular medallion in the bottom of the inside of the bowl, which was referred to as a "print" or "boss." The early examples are usually deep with narrow lip bands, while the later specimens are shallower with wider bands and an increased capacity. The band was generally used for the purpose of bearing an inscription of presentation or ownership.

Prints on the inside of a mazer were decorated in many varied fashions, although for the most part they consisted of a medallion depicting a religious device, a coat of arms, or a floral motif. Another name occasionally used to describe this medallion is "frounce." Covers for mazer bowls were not unusual although of the sixty examples which have survived to the present day, none is known with its original cover. Although so few mazers have survived the years, at the time of their introduction to English society they were very popular and were made in great profusion. However, by far the greatest number were made of solid wood as each man reserved the right to his personal drinking cup and only a few could afford the luxury of the increased cost of the addition of silver mounts.

The popularity of the mazer may be gathered from the fact that in 1328 there were 182 in the refectory of Christ Church in Canterbury. But eventually silver mounted mazers lost their popularity as pure silver gained in favor.

Mazers were used as early as the twelfth century by the rollicking monks to drink what they called "celestial nectar." One of the most famous is the masterpiece of 1398 in Yorkminster. A most unusual type is John Northwode's mazer of the late fourteenth century at Corpus Christi College, Cambridge. Fixed inside the center of the bowl is a hexagonal pillar with a battlemented top, upon which rests a swan. On the inside of this pillar is a hollow tube, open at both ends and so adapted that the bowl cannot be filled with wine above the top of the tube. Upon reaching that height, the wine begins to flow out, escaping through the end in the bottom of the bowl until empty. A few important mazers are owned by the Harbledown Hospital, one dating from the reign of Edward II.

An interesting allusion is made by Samuel Pepys, in his diary, wherein he describes drinking "In a brown bowl, tip't with silver which I drank off and at the bottom was a picture of the Virgin with the Child in her arms." He refers to the medallion of the sacred subjects found at the bottom of so many mazers.

Mazers were frequently engraved on the silver rims with appropriate inscriptions in Latin and occasionally in English. Many of the early specimens were converted into standing cups by ingenious silversmiths who followed the demand by the wealthy classes for pieces of more importance.

The value of a mazer cannot be measured except by its rarity, and the fact that it is probably the first piece of English domestic plate. The work on them is certainly not representative of first class silversmithing.

DRINKING HORNS

The use of horns for drinking vessels has been recognized from early times, and the medieval silversmiths were quick in adding to their beauty by the addition of fine mountings of silver gilt. Although very few of these early specimens have survived, much curious data has been handed down regarding their use. From remote antiquity comes the superstition and belief in horns as an antidote for poison.

The horn was supposed to vibrate as it came into contact with a substance containing poison. This superstition prevailed as late as the sixteenth century. The medieval member of royalty who possessed a small piece of this horn would attach it to a chain and dip it into the wine before partaking of it, thus reassuring himself. The most prized and theoretically most effective horns were those of the unicorn, an animal which never existed. But the horns of other animals such as the "narwhal" and the rhinoceros were sold by unscrupulous people as genuine unicorn. The form of this fabulous animal of India is well-known as the sinister supporter of the Royal Arms of England.

The influence of the early horn never quite disappeared as many tankards of later years and even of the present day retain the original horn shape. The use of horns, which was widespread in Anglo-Saxon times, steadily decreased and reference to them in later medieval documents is relatively uncommon. The later types of horns were equipped with feet so that they could be set down on the table. Another use of horns was for the purpose of serving as a charter for lands during the middle ages. Accurate proof of this is found in the horn presented to Pusey by King Knute with an inscription confirming the grant of property.

Medieval drinking horns are so rare as to be of little interest to collectors. Actually only five specimens are known. Among these, three important examples are herewith described. The first, now in the possession of Queen's College, Oxford, is engraved with Latin letters on each of three silver gilt bands mounted on the buffalo horn. The second, dating from the first half of the fourteenth century is less ornate, and became the property of Corpus Christi College, Cambridge, in 1352. Another treasure of its type dates from the reign of Henry VII, and is in possession of Christ's Hospital, Horsham.

STEEPLE CUPS, STANDING CUPS AND COVERS

These articles are sequels to the mazer bowl, and they carry certain rites and ceremonies that have been retained to the present time by corporations and fraternities that have rituals dating from the past. Among them is the age-old observance of the taking of wine from a loving cup as a token of friendship. Inasmuch as there were innumerable instances when a foe stabbed an enemy while in the act of drinking, it was not unusual for a guest in a strange house to have a comrade standing by his side while he drank. With dagger drawn, his ally stood ready to defend him in case an attack were made on the drinker. From this sequence we have inherited our present day manner of toasting with regard to loving cups. There are always three people standing; two facing each other and the third behind the person drinking as a safeguard against perfidy.

The standing cup was usually tumbler shaped, resting on a baluster or vase-shaped stem. The cover was slightly domed and surmounted in the usual way by a human figure. Some examples were plain, while others were repoussée with fruits and masks. Sometimes, cups of the early part of the seventeenth century assumed the conical shape with a dome-like cover, surmounted by a high finial, obviously copied from the spires of a church. These so-called steeple cups are generally found in sets of three, one being slightly taller than the other two. They are distinctly peculiar to the reign of James I. Among the many magnificent examples of standing cups and covers that have been handed down to the present time is the "Anathema cup" dating from 1481, and now in the possession of Pembroke College, Cambridge. This is the earliest known hallmarked cup. The second earliest surviving cup is the magnificent Leigh standing cup and cover, dated 1499.

The majority of cups of this type were highly chased with figures in relief and delicate piercings, such as demonstrated in the "Foundress" cup of Christ College, Cambridge. One of the few plain examples is the previously mentioned "Anathema cup." Although simple in form and practically void of decoration, it is by no means lacking in beauty.

Probably more fine specimens of standing cups and covers were executed in Germany than in any other part of the continent. The surviving examples clearly illustrate the importance of the German silversmith of the day. It may be assumed that many of the English cups were the work of German silversmiths who migrated to London.

Two of the finest known cups were sold at the disbursement of the Swaythling collection; one being the Rodney cup and cover of the late fifteenth century which fetched the sum of $38,000, and the other, the Tudor cup bearing the London hallmark of 1500, which was sold for $15,000. These prices readily indicate the appreciation and rarity of these masterpieces of early silversmithing.

COCOANUT CUPS AND OSTRICH CUPS

Many standing cups of the fifteenth and sixteenth centuries were formed of a cocoanut or an ostrich egg mounted in silver and raised on a tall stem. Few early specimens have survived, as the brittle texture of these pieces caused many to be damaged and discarded throughout the years of service. In effect, they were a variation of the standing cup and cover and may be definitely assumed to have been copied from workings of European silversmiths. As a general rule the work was very elaborate and covered a section of the top of the shelf and a part of the base.

Probably the main reason for the use of the cocoanut cup was its great rarity. By owning a specimen of this type, a definite display of wealth could be shown. However, some thought was given to the idea that wine imbibed from these shells contained medicinal properties. In a volume of 1640 they were accredited with having protective powers against colic, rheumatism, and epilepsy.

As early as 1259 a cocoanut cup was mentioned in a will, but no surviving example antedates the middle of the fifteenth century. Evidence of their popularity at the time of their inception may be judged by the inventory plate of Winchester College, in which eleven specimens occurred.

London silversmiths ceased to regard cocoanut shells as curiosities worthy of their skill after the reign of James I. However, for some unexplained reason the fashion was revived about 1770 when large numbers of shells were mounted as cups and goblets with silver lips, linings, and feet. This fashion continued until the early years of the nineteenth century.

Far rarer than the cocoanut cup in England is the ostrich egg cup. A notable example is dated 1592 and is in the possession of Corpus Christi College, Canterbury. The silver garnishings comprise a stem fashioned like the twisted trunk of a tree in the manner of many German cups. The egg of the Ostrich was definitely regarded as worthy of the skill of the greatest silversmiths, as evidenced by the large number of articles such as tankards, cups, ewers and pots fashioned from silver and the egg. Ostrich egg cups appear frequently, although they were usually described as being griffins' egg cups.

The nautilus shell cup, so popular with the silversmiths in Germany in the sixteenth and seventeenth centuries, found little favor in England. Only one specimen has survived, although the delicate character of the shell may account for the destruction of the other examples. This cup is in the form of a melon shell, mounted as a monster of the sea. It was the work of a London silversmith in 1577.

One finds during the medieval times and the Renaissance, numerous objects of little intrinsic value mounted as cups by English silversmiths. It may be, that coming from parts of the earth then little known, these shells were invested with much mystery which enhanced their value and importance. Probably the only reason that any of the early specimens has survived is, that having a small quantity of silver in the mountings, they were hardly of sufficient importance to melt down.

FONT SHAPED CUPS

Another type of cup originating at the beginning of the sixteenth century had a shallow bowl with straight, vertical sides, resting on a wider splayed circular foot, the diameter of the bowl being approximately equal to the height of the cup. These are known as font-shaped cups. The earliest known examples are in the Victoria and Albert Museum and were executed in 1500. Probably the best type known of the few that have survived, is the one owned by the Goldsmiths' Company, which bears the London hallmark of 1503.

As a general rule, font cups are thick and heavy and void of decoration. However, some specimens were embossed as evidenced by the cup of 1515 now in the possession of Corpus Christi College, Oxford. Occasionally these pieces had covers which were almost flat with a knob, and a top suitable for a coat of arms.

BEAKERS

The form of most drinking vessels in use during the middle ages may be classed roughly into two stages: those derived from the beaker and those from the bowl. In all probability the beaker originated from the use of a straight section of ox-horn with one end stopped up. However, it has been impossible to trace either the name or the shape further back than the fourteenth century. It has been suggested that the introduction of the beaker was probably due to traders between England and the Low Country, or to the Protestant refugees, who sought escape from England in the seventeenth century.

Silver beakers were popular as long ago as the Elizabethan era and continued to be made and developed. During the reign of Charles II they were sometimes embossed or ornamented with a band of Acanthus chasing. Otherwise, the majority of these examples differ very little from the early Elizabethan types. They are usually about six inches in height, spread toward the top and made with a molded base. Very few beakers were made in the eighteenth century. A type more popular and differing distinctly from the early examples was that shaped and engraved as a beer barrel. It is curious that so few examples of standing beakers are known with English hallmarks, for on the continent they were by far the most popular type.

By the seventeenth century the original straight table beakers developed a flare in form, and although they remained in use, there is little doubt that they were for the most part replaced by individual cups for drinking. Beakers of the Elizabethan and James I periods were usually embossed in low relief and engraved with foliage. The earliest types were originally made of horn and date back to the middle ages. These shapes were later reproduced by the silversmiths.

Although beakers were reserved for personal use, specimens in silver were indulged in only by the wealthy, and it is for this reason that early examples are very rare and command huge prices. However, as the specimens of the eighteenth and nineteenth centuries were produced in far-flung profusion, they have not yet come to be known as rarities among pieces of Old English silver.

TANKARDS AND MUGS

Certain names applied to silver objects have more or less romantic origins, and such a survival occurs in the word "tankard." Although long since forgotten, the word originally indicated the clumsy hollowed logs bound with iron and used to carry water from city conduits. In later years the name was applied to great wooden mugs bound with metal.

No English silver tankards are known prior to the sixteenth century and generally speaking, many of the earliest specimens displayed some tendency to the natural taper of the early ox-horn. Although made in a vast variety of sizes and shapes, they were all generally of the same tapered type. The exceptions were the few straight cylindrical bodied ones, reproduced from continental models. Many of the earliest tankards were made with bodies of horn or bone which were then mounted with silver covers, neck bands and feet. It was believed that with the bone or horn substance contained therein, the presence of any poisonous substance in the beverage could be immediately detected. Some tankards are found with a body of crystal, for it was generally believed that if the liquid contained any poison it would cloud the crystal on coming in contact with it.

During the James I period the in-curving taper of the horn disappeared in the shape of the tankard, and was replaced by straight sides. During the reign of Charles II, many tankards were produced and while the ornamentation was retained for a short time, molded lips disappeared, covers were made of much simpler style; and the finials of the early types were discarded. Later on in the century, a shorter type of a plain cylindrical body with a flat projecting rim became fashionable. Although tankards were originally made in pint sizes in the beginning of the seventeenth century, they were later made of much larger proportion. Tankards were generally of a uniform shape with an "S" shaped handle. Many are found with encircling bands of silver and these may be said to have survived from the early metal bands on the original wooden receptacles.

Among the types of tankard most sought after by collectors, is "peg" tankard. This type contained a vertical row of pegs fitted on the inside of the body at equivalent distances, and was used to mark the quantity of wine or beer permitted to each man at the passing of the cup. An interesting feature of many of the early tankards was a slot on the under side of the handle. The idea has been suggested that this was used to summon an attendant when a vessel was empty, but whether it was designed for that purpose or rather as a vent to allow the hot air to escape, can only be surmised.

Tankards were made in great profusion throughout England as well as Europe, and the continental influence is easily detected, particularly in those mounted on feet.

During the late 17th century, an offspring of the tankard known as the mug, was introduced. This, in effect, was actually a tankard on a smaller scale, but lacking the cover. These mugs were tremendously popular as beer drinking vessels at the leading universities throughout England.

GOBLETS

Although there is a slight difference between a goblet and a wine cup, they may be classified together as they grew in popularity in the late Tudor period, at which time they replaced the earlier beakers. These were actually vessels made for individual service and numerous examples from the 17th century are available. Goblets date back to very early times and have practically never ceased to be made. After the general adoption of silver wine goblets, the silversmiths lost many of their opportunities for producing varied pieces, as these replaced practically all of the earlier types of drinking equipments. However, with the general importation and use of crystal at the dinner table, wine cups and goblets fell into disuse. It is interesting to note though, that the modern adaptation in crystal for individual service carries out almost perfectly the original design of the goblet or wine cup. Goblets were used for other purposes besides drinking as frequently specimens are found that were made as presentation cups.

TUMBLER CUPS

Originally known as a "bolle," the tumbler cup was introduced during the middle ages for use as a wine vessel. However, no surviving specimen earlier than the end of the 17th century is available. A tumbler cup is quite different from all other drinking vessels in the manner of its construction. It was usually of very heavy silver, the lower part of the bowl being hemispherical and hammered in such a way as to leave a thick bottom. When filled with wine, the round bottom caused the bowl to tumble from side to side, but it was prevented from toppling over by the extra weight of the metal on the under side. Sets of these tumbler cups are found complete rather often because they were usually nested one inside the other. They were quite small in size, being designed, as a rule, to contain only a single drink.

POSSET CUPS, CAUDLE CUPS AND PORRINGERS

The little two-handled cups with covers which came into general use during the second half of the seventeenth century were intended to hold caudle and posset. The squat pear shaped vessels were doubtlessly inspired by objects imported from the Orient. Caudle was made largely of wine, or some alcoholic liquor, to which sugar, spice, and crumbled bread were added. Posset, on the other hand, was somewhat similar to what is known today as porridge, and was composed of bread or oat cakes mixed with curdled milk, combined with wine or beer, and flavored with spice.

These little cups and those referred to as porringers were used for wine and hot drinks. However, from the name porringer which is doubtless a corruption of the word "porridger," it is safe to assume that they were used to serve stews and similar refreshment as well. Porridge, at the time of the making of the little silver containers, was actually a thick soup, while the now obsolete word "pottenger" indicated a maker of pottage, which was a stew of vegetables and meat.

Porringers, as a rule, were made without covers, the bowl usually being less than four inches deep, while caudle and posset cups invariably had lids and were both larger and deeper. Caudle and posset cups, as well as porringers, all appear as early as in sixteenth century inventories, but no examples have survived from this date. Caudle cups were generally decorated in relief with the large animals and fruits characteristic of this period, and sometimes the wide rim of the saucer-like stand in which they were placed, was ornamented, too. Porringers were introduced about 1680 and were popular until about 1715. It is indeed curious that these little vessels have become the most popular of all christening presents as their long association with intoxicating foods and drinks scarcely seems to be congruous with the partaking of nourishment by a child.

BEER JUGS AND CLARET JUGS

Silver beer jugs were made as early as the time of George I, but did not come into general use until the period of about 1770. It is very rare to find original beer jugs as many of the ones sold today have been fashioned from chocolate pots and tankards. Beer jugs resembled in style the water pitcher as known today, while claret jugs were similar to hot water jugs introduced during the early Georgian period.

PILGRIM BOTTLES

Huge pilgrim bottles appeared late in the seventeenth century and continued until the early years of the eighteenth century. As a rule, they were beautifully ornamented, although on many, an over-profusion of decoration is found. The original use of pilgrim bottles was to hold wine for use at large dinners, although they were also made as ornaments for sideboards. There is little doubt but what these massive silver bottles were designed after the outlines of the ancient pilgrim bottles. Earl Spencer owns one of the earliest known pairs, made in 1701, and probably the work of John Goode.

FLAGONS, STONEWARE JUGS AND BLACKJACKS

The word Flagon was definitely derived from the early French "flacon," which denoted a bottle-shaped vessel of leather, having a narrow neck and a plain ovoid body. Closely allied to these flagons were stoneware jugs and blackjacks, which were in use about the middle of the 17th century. Stoneware jugs were popular during the latter half of the sixteenth century, at which time they were imported from Germany and fitted with silver or gold neck bands, feet, and covers, by the English silversmiths. Stoneware is exceptionally hard and non-porous, the surface being glazed by throwing salt into the furnaces while the clay vessels are being baked. The jugs followed the form of the early flagons with the bulbous bodies and narrow necks. The color of the ware varied from a dull gray to a common spotted surface from which was derived the name "tiger Ware." Other rare examples of this type of jug were made of blue glazed earthenware, in the old Lambeth potteries, while occasionally specimens of Rhodian faience come into the market. Examples of these pieces with Elizabethan mounts are extremely rare and fetch high prices at auction.

Blackjacks were vessels of waxed leather used for centuries for carrying and storing liquors. The larger ones became known as bombards, the name being derived from their resemblance to the old cannons of that name. This type was used exclusively for the purpose of storing fine liquors. A smaller type intended for use as a drinking vessel was sometimes mounted with silver and engraved with a coat of arms. The dates of these articles can only be estimated as the silver mounts rarely, if ever, bear any hallmarks.

During the first half of the 17th century, flagons retained the style of decoration which characterized the work of silversmiths of the previous century. The pieces were tall and cylindrical, with feet splayed out into a handle formed by an "S" scroll. Fruits and fishes were commonly the motifs of the design, alternating with other delicately engraved ornamentation. Flagons and stoneware jugs were commonly in use by the churches of England as early as Elizabethan times. They were employed when it was necessary to bring wine to the communion table. Before the middle of the seventeenth century, flagons had developed into vessels of great size and capacity and were frequently made in pairs. As a rule, they were plain and without gilding. The churches of London were particularly rich in such vessels, and a group covering nearly every successive year from 1605 to 1660 is available.

COASTERS AND DECANTER STANDS

The wide use of crystal decanters led to the making of coasters, the commonest type having a wood turned bottom and a solid or pierced silver side. They were introduced during the Adam period while decanter stands were first made during the George I era. However, they were not produced in quantities until nearly forty years later.

Many decanter stands were doubled or tripled, and joined together by a bar and mounted on wheels. These pieces had a small silver handle and resembled the general shape of a cart on wheels, hence the applied name of wine wagon.

A coaster or decanter stand is a clear illustration of the outcome of changing social customs which caused the introduction of many new pieces in silver. As the fashion prevailed to remove the cloth from the dining table for dessert, someone probably conceived the idea of placing the bottle in a stand and coasting it along the table. This explains why the base is covered with baize on the bottom, to prevent any markings on the polished mahogany tables. It is also probable that after the bottles had been refilled several times and the guests had become slightly inebriated, the decanters did not always reach their intended destinations while being passed.

Coasters were made in a wide variety of designs and included examples of delicately pierced work as well as richly embossed specimens. Many were ornamented with a band of grapes and leaves which was appropriate to the wine decanter which it contained. As a rule, coasters were made in pairs or sets of four, six or eight.

EWERS

Many articles in use today were made for entirely different purposes at the time of their conception. These changes are to a large extent due to the refinements which gradually appeared in the social observances connected with the dining table. The common instance, is our practice of washing the hands before sitting down to dinner, which, in effect, is actually a perpetuation of washing the hands at the table. This custom instituted many centuries ago, was symbolized by the use of basins and ewers among the noble families, from the middle ages to the seventeenth century.

Ewers were introduced originally from Italy and quickly rendered the medieval finger bowl obsolete. As a rule they were gilded, and many displayed the graceful forms of the Italian Renaissance. Probably the outstanding creation of the Tudor silversmiths with regard to splendor and magnificence, were their rosewater ewers.

Until the introduction of the fork, the washing ceremony was an essential part of dining, as in those days it was the custom to hold the food in one hand, cut it with the knife, and then lift it to the mouth with the fingers. It was customary for a servant to hold a silver basin in front of each guest. The water was then supplied from a ewer carried by another servant who poured it over the hands of the guest into the basin. At the conclusion of this ceremony, the servant produced a towel with which he dried the hands of the diner. This was recognized as a part of the general etiquette of the dining table, and guests received attention in accordance with their rank.

The custom of using a ewer and basin at the table was not restricted to the wealthy classes as those in more moderate circumstances used specimens made of brass. Although silver ewers and basins were mentioned frequently in wills and inventories, very few have survived to the present day. The amount of precious metal expended on their manufacture rendered them extremely liable to be consigned to the melting pot in time of financial difficulties.

There were three distinct types of ewers made and they are clearly demonstrated by the following examples. An early specimen is that presented to Corpus Christi College, Cambridge, in 1570. This piece has a rounded foot and a swelling octagonal body, the sides of which were alternately engraved with arabesques. Two of the remaining sides were plain and occupied by the angular handle and spout which was attached to the whole of the length of the body.

The second known variety had a vase shaped body and a narrow neck with a spout and scroll handle. It was richly chased and the handle was in the form of a demi-lion. This type is exemplified by one made by Robert Signall, in 1583, which may now be seen in the Victoria and Albert Museum. The third, which appeared during the reign of James I, was, as a rule, undecorated except for heraldic achievements.

The ewers resembled a straight sided goblet with scroll handle and curved spout. The introduction of a vessel so conspicuously lacking in aesthetic charm is typical of a period when silversmiths were seeking originality at all costs. Just previous to 1700 appeared the last standard pattern of ewer. This was known as the helmet shape and was a magnificent example of the proper combination of a good shape with restrained ornamentation. About the middle of the George I period, ewers and basins were discarded and used only as ornaments.

Ewers are very rare and fine specimens fetch fantastic prices. Some are known to have reached a figure at auction of $100,000.

MONTEITH BOWLS, PUNCH BOWLS, AND ACCESSORIES

The magnificence which prevailed in the production of so many silver vessels connected with the ceremony of drinking, is often present in punch bowls. Punch, which was of Oriental origin, consisted of five ingredients: spirits, water, lemon juice, sugar and spice. Thus the assumption is made that the word punch was probably derived from the Hindustani "panch" which meant five. Although the brewing of punch was introduced into England during the reign of Charles I, silver bowls for service do not seem to have been made until after the Restoration.

The earliest known punch bowls were small and of simple design, while those wrought in the later Georgian era were of far greater capacity and generally with a wealth of ornamentation. As early as the Stuart period examples are found with notched rims. However, the type with the removable rim known as the monteith bowl was not introduced until nearly the end of the seventeenth century. The introduction of this type of bowl was attributed to a Scotchman named Monteith, who gained considerable reputation from his ability to brew punch of excellent character. Because of the fact that he wore a cloth coat scalloped in the bottom, much in the same style as were the punch bowls of this time, his name was applied to them. From this time on, all bowls with removable rims were known as monteiths. Many explanations have been advanced regarding the addition of the removable rim, and the most probable of these is that the glasses were placed in the notches to prevent their breakage, when being brought into the dining room by the footman. Another theory advanced was that the bowl was filled with water and the glasses hung from the notches to keep cool.

There seems to be no limit to the sizes of punch bowls, and many were used at important functions. The majority of them have fluted bodies with lion's head ring handles. Monteiths were very popular and a great number were made until the end of the eighteenth century, and may be found today among the plate of most of the corporate bodies who would quite naturally have had frequent opportunities to use them.

Several small accessories necessary to the brewing of punch were introduced by the silversmiths of this time. However, the only one that has survived in any degree is the long handled ladle used for transporting the liquid to the jugs. Occasionally one finds a circular strainer with two wrought handles, which was placed across the jug to strain the punch. Punch ladles were made in a variety of designs and were hammered out of Spanish silver dollars or crown pieces in such a way that the marginal description still appeared on the lip of the ladle. The placing of a coin at the bottom of the bowl was also a common trick.

With the return of entertainment on a larger scale, Georgian drinking accessories have once again come into demand. Because of their low price, punch ladles make ideal items for those interested in old silver.

WINE FOUNTAINS, WINE CISTERNS

These two articles reflect beyond a doubt the indulgence used to achieve the sumptuous display of magnificence in silver but very few examples of wine fountains or cisterns exist now. Wine fountains were actually massive upright vase-shaped covered vessels, fitted with an ice chamber and a small tap from which the wine was drawn into the glasses. Cisterns, on the other hand, were enormous oval bowls, intended to hold water and ice, in which the bottles of wine were placed to cool. Although these pieces were of huge proportions and more than extravagantly covered with ornamentation, they still retained the basic form suggestive of the work of the early silversmiths. The detail of the embossing, usually suggested mermaids, dolphins, or figures of Neptune, and was of the highest quality. Wine fountains are known to have weighed more than 1000 ounces and measured close to four feet in height, while wine cisterns were usually about four feet long and weighed close to 2000 ounces.

The largest piece of English plate known, is an enormous wine cistern made in 1734 by Charles Kandler for the Czar of Russia. The immense proportions will be immediately realized if one notes the excessive weight of nearly 8000 ounces contained in the piece. The actual dimensions of it are five and one half feet long, three and one half feet deep, and three and one half feet wide. In 1672 Charles II presented his mistress with a massive creation weighing over 1000 ounces, but this unfortunately has not survived. The earliest example known today was made two years later, and is now in the collection of the Earl of Rosebery. Although wine cisterns in silver were not made until after the Restoration, specimens of base metal were definitely used during the early part of the seventeenth century.

The wine fountains made during the early part of the eighteenth century were greatly reduced in size and were much more usable. As a general rule they were urn-shaped with a tap at the front and had two or four handles. Shortly after the introduction of silver wine cisterns, practically every home of importance owned one. Further proof of their constant use and even earlier introduction than is originally credited, may be found in many of the early pictures painted by Dutch artists.

WINE COOLERS AND ICE PAILS

The eventual outcome of the early wine cisterns was the smaller and more graceful wine cooler made to contain but a single bottle of wine. The interior was fitted with a removable jacket which held the wine, while the space between the jacket and the wall of the vase formed the ice chamber. These were generally of a vase shape in a single foot and invariably made with two handles. At first wine coolers were very simple in design, but the increasing flair for vessels of excessive ornamentation and richness of design caused the smiths to yield to popular demand. Although most wine coolers were not over twelve inches in height, a few enormous specimens are known. However, as the demand for huge pieces waned, the purchase price was lowered and wine coolers became more and more popular. By the beginning of the nineteenth century, literally thousands of pairs of silver and Sheffield plate had been produced. Also occasionally wine coolers were made with linings of base metal.

The wine cooler was probably an importation from France, as vessels of similar style and shape made in other metals than silver were known there.

Ice pails which were similar in shape to the coolers are known during the eighteenth and nineteenth centuries, and the ornamentation on them was similar to that found on the wine cistern and fountain of a century previous. The main distinction between an ice pail and a wine cooler is that the former was made without an inner jacket and the bottle was not placed in it to cool.

WINE LABELS, WINE FUNNELS, WINE TASTERS

During the reign of George III, the use of small silver labels pierced or engraved with the name of a particular wine, became increasingly popular. These labels were attached to a hanging chain and fitted around the neck of the bottle. It is not unusual to find a complete set of these little gadgets with as many as forty varieties of liquid refreshment included. It is actually necessary to study in detail the various types of wine consumed throughout England, to comprehend the vast number of labels produced. It is rather interesting that only of recent date have labels attracted the attention of the collector. Inasmuch as they require but a small investment, and since many are examples of exquisite workmanship, it is difficult to understand why they have never been appreciated heretofore.

The earliest known funnel for decanting wine is the example of 1661 in the Victoria and Albert Museum. Although these little silver articles were made extensively during the Georgian periods, early examples are scarce. But little attention has been given them, since from the artistic standpoint they are of no great interest. No home in England was considered fully equipped for the service of wine unless it had a funnel and strainer, and for this reason hundreds of later specimens are known today. Inasmuch as funnels are fitted at the base with a detachable strainer many collectors, unable to find suitable tea strainers, have purchased these funnels and retained only the strainer part for use.

The original purpose of the wine taster may be traced back to the time of the middle ages, where it was used on ceremonial occasions by deputised tasters, to see if the beverage contained any poison. In this way the important people who were at the dinner were protected from evil intent. Another use of the wine taster was to aid the vintner in sampling the wine which he was proposing to purchase. For this purpose it was necessary to have a small shallow bowl which would show the clear color of the wine. The vintner's silver taster was a well-known feature in late medieval times, and an example of 1383 appears in the inventory of the owner of a Norwich tavern. The earliest wine tasters were mostly plain saucer shaped articles with a raised dome in the center, the purpose of which was to prove that if the liquid was clear, it could be determined as it passed over the plain surface of the silver. The sides of these tasters were usually embossed with various floral designs or punched with flutes. In the latter half of the sixteenth century, a new type of wine taster was introduced. This was in the shape of a small bowl with a sloping side and a dome bottom, which showed the wine to great advantage. One of the earliest known examples of this type bears the Norwich hall mark of 1573. The next earliest known tasters were the shallow two-handled bowls, about three inches in diameter with wire handles. The early cups used for sipping were generally straight sided on short trumpet shaped feet. There is little doubt that many other vessels of similar type were employed in the tasting of wine, and among these may be mentioned the porringer, or, as it was sometimes called in England, the bleeding bowl. Their use as wine tasters can only be assumed from the few known examples which bear engraving suggestive of that particular service.

Although wine tasters have long since lost their original use, they are popular today for use as ash trays. However, it is most rare to find originals.

VIII

CONDIMENT SETS

THE standing salt was introduced during the middle ages. At the time of its use it was a symbol of social distinction because only a family of great wealth could afford it.

In medieval times, salt was very expensive, it was among the rarest of all table condiments, and for this reason important silver holders were used for it.

Salt has always been regarded with superstition as is evidenced by its uses at rituals among the ancient peoples to whom the "eating of salt" and the "breaking of bread" signified brotherhood. It was the belief that salt was a protection against the evils of witches and today many of us still adhere to the legend that the spilling of salt brings misfortune unless a pinch is thrown over the shoulder. The name saltceller is actually a corruption of the old French "saliere," meaning salt holder.

Originally the master saltcellar was placed in the center of the table at which the master of the house was seated. This particular table was denoted as the high table and distinguished from the others in that it was raised on a dais above the floor level. The position of each person in relation to the master salt was dictated by his social rank and until the seventeenth century, the entire household, from master to servant, ate together in a commonhall. The normal use of salts in the fifteenth and sixteenth centuries may be gathered from the books of "Curtesy" and "Nurture," published in 1508, wherein the passage is quoted: "set your salts on the ryght side where your soverayne shall sytte . . . and at every ende of ye table set a salte sellar . . . and when your soverayne's table, thus arrayed, cover all other bordes with salts, trenchours, and cuppes."

Those sitting at other than the high table were designated as being "below the salt," often causing much ill feeling because of the distinction. In addition to the ceremonial salt were smaller holders known as trencher salts to be placed at varied intervals around the table. The name was derived from the custom of lifting salt from the holder to a wooden trencher with the end of the knife. From descriptions in inventories we note that some of the early salts were often cast of solid gold, beset with jewels. An example of this is known from the diary of Charles I, wherein it is recorded that when he came to the throne in 1625, he sold a gold salt weighing one hundred and fifty ounces that was studded with sapphires, rubies, pearls and emeralds. One of the earliest English standing salts is the Huntsman salt which definitely portrays the Gothic influence in its ornamentation. Although the earliest salts were pieces of great importance in meaning, they were but slight in stature in comparison to the later types, as those known as early as 1313 weighed between six and eleven ounces.

The coming of the Renaissance styles influenced the shapes of standing salts for then they began to assume greater splendor. The early Gothic forms in the sixteenth century were replaced by those known as pedestal salts. In the Tudor period the bodies were rectangular or cylindrical, richly chased or embossed with foliage, fruit and figures. The cover was generally surmounted by a vase which supported a modeled figure. Such ceremonial salts frequently measured sixteen inches in height. Although popular for a considerable time, they were later replaced by the far simpler bell-shaped salt which appeared about 1590. These were made in three sections comprising two salt cellars and a pepper caster, and could be either joined together on ceremonial occasions or used separately. This type which was about eleven inches high was finally superseded by the steeple salts which assumed a greater proportion than ever previously known. Not infrequently steeple salts were made with two bowls.

During the latter part of the seventeenth century the custom of fitting a removable cover to the great salts was discontinued and in its place a bracket was fitted to the rim to support a napkin or plate which protected the salt from dust. These brackets are often mistaken for handles although only rarely does one find examples made with them. During the latter part of the fifteenth century and the first quarter of the sixteenth century standing salts were made in the shape of an hour-glass; ten examples of this type are extant. The finest of this collection is the one given by Walter Hill to New College, Oxford, of which he was Warden from 1475 to 1494. It is one of the unusual types combining beauty in silver work with richly engraved crystal. The use of salts in fancy shapes was very popular during the latter part of the 16th century, and much knowledge of them has been gleaned from the inventories of the royal plate wherein several are mentioned.

One was in the form of a dragon issuing from a shell; another had the shape of a crown falcon, and others were made in the form of men and women holding the receptacles for salt in their hands. These quaint forms of decoration although no longer familiar to us, suggest the fertility of the imagination of the early silversmith. In the will of Edmund, Earl of March, two unique specimens in the shape of dogs are listed. Another interesting example which has survived is known as the Monkey salt and is now in the New College, Oxford.

An early piece which shows the Renaissance influence is an hour glass salt made in 1522, belonging to the Goldsmiths' Company. It is of extreme interest because it is considerably ahead of most of the work of the first fifteen years of the English Renaissance with regard to form. Although the silversmiths in Germany and France greatly influenced the workers in England on much of the domestic plate, the designs for standing salts were original.

During the reign of Queen Elizabeth there was a definite increase in the production of small salts, although some of these are merely reproductions in miniature of the contemporary standing salts. Others which were of circular or triangular shapes were the forerunners of the great variety made in the later periods. The disappearance of the large standing salt is a direct result of the increasing popularity of the individual type. During the Charles II and Queen Anne periods a considerable number were produced which were either faceted or moulded, while those of a few years later assumed more elaborate decoration. From about 1720 to 1740 a salt with a circular bowl and a round foot was much in evidence, many examples of these being attractively decorated with applied leaf work. Towards the middle of the century the prevailing type consisted of a small bowl on three or four feet. Many of these were embossed with floral swage and lion masks above the feet, while others were pierced with rococo designs and fitted with glass liners.

During the Adam period the continued use of pierced work was much in evidence and the use of a blue crystal liner was seen much more frequently. These later salts were made in a wide variety of forms, all of which can be traced back directly in shape and feeling to the trenchers.

Sets of four early Georgian salts are very rare although greatly in demand. However, those of the later period can usually be purchased in their entirety as originally produced.

SALT AND MUSTARD SPOONS

Salt spoons are unknown before the end of the seventeenth century, at which time those made resembled miniature table spoons. The familiar ladle shape appeared at a slightly later date, while those varieties with a shovel shape bowl in use during the George III period as well as a number of eccentric types do not require much description. Mustard spoons, formed like small sauce ladles, date well into the eighteenth century. However, one is mentioned in an advertisement as early as 1678.

CASTERS AND MUFFINEERS

Although white pepper was known for use in England as early as the twelfth century, no form of caster appears among English silver previous to the reign of Elizabeth.

At this time they consisted of a small perforated section attached to bell shaped salts, but as individual articles they were not found earlier than the late Stuart period. The name muffineer was derived from the use of sprinkling salt on buttered muffins and, although, similar in form to casters they were somewhat smaller in size. Those known in the time of Charles II are cylindrical, the top being attached to the body by an elbow joint which consisted of two projection lugs soldered to the lower part of the top. The ears passed two notches in the grooved moulding around the rim of the body, which after being turned slightly, engaged firmly with the top.

Muffineers were made as a rule, in sets of three, one being considerably larger than the other two. The smaller pair were used for pepper, one being for Jamaica and the other for cayenne; while the large one was used for sugar. Casters were made in a variety of shapes and it is not difficult to estimate their approximate date from the form and style of ornamentation. During the Queen Anne period the pear shape, or pyriform, copied from Oriental vases, replaced the cylindrical bodies. This evidently was superseded by an undulating pyriform, with a tapering cover. As a rule, the ornamentation was restricted to bands or engraving around the edge of the cover, the bulging part of the body and the foot. The high domed covers of casters afforded the early silversmiths an opportunity to exercise a branch of their skill soon to become a feature of great importance. This intricate piercing found on so many Georgian casters plus the simplicity of the bodies made them objects of great beauty.

During the first half of the eighteenth century, a small type of caster with a handle, generally known as a kitchen pepper, was introduced. Later in the Georgian era smaller casters in sets of four or six were used to contain pepper and salt for individual service.

CRUET STANDS

Although cruet stands may have existed prior to 1700, the series of surviving pieces seems to begin with the latter part of the reign of Queen Anne. Undoubtedly owing to the difficulty of replacing the fragile contents large numbers were allowed to perish. Cruet stands are important examples of silver work because the finest smiths devoted their full talents to their production. During the medieval times they consisted of glass bottles which were used for vinegar and other flavors, while in the first quarter of the eighteenth century, a combination of bottles and casters fitting into a silver frame was introduced. This type was used on the table and known as a Warwick cruet. Good examples fetch high prices as the rare casters in them increased their value many times. The glass bottles were invariably made with small silver caps which could be placed in the small holes fastened on the sides of the stand. During the eighteenth and nineteenth centuries many varied styles were made among which one of the most popular consisted of a boat shaped stand with handles. In the early part of the nineteenth century, a circular type was introduced and at the same time individual bottles were supplied with the little labels similar to those used on decanters to identify the casters.

MUSTARD POTS

Although mustard was used in England much earlier, there is no evidence of silver containers for it prior to the reign of George I. Specimens from this time are very, very rare and most types obtainable now date from the latter part of the eighteenth century. These were generally made with a cylindrical body and a hinged flat lid, or oval body with domical lid, the sides often pierced and the body fitted with blue glass liners. The earliest known reference to a silver mustard pot appears to be in 1670 in a bill for plate made by Alderman Backwell for Prince Rupert, while the next earliest mention is four years later. One of the most beautiful known examples was executed in 1724 by Paul Lamerie in the shape of a barrel with a scroll handle and domed lid.

IX

FLAT SILVER

FLATWARE SERVICES

GENERALLY speaking, the service of flat silver occupies the throne of honor in the home today, for what bride does not thrill to the thought of possessing her own table silver. In most cases, it is the first purchase in the assembling of the trousseau, and usually the most cherished.

The demand for services in antique silver far exceeds the supply, for flat silver in complete services is distinctly a modern note. However, fine matching services can be collected over a period of time, and for the amateur collector this presents the ideal field of endeavor. A large initial investment is unnecessary, as the chances are that after one has selected a pattern, only a few pieces at a time will be available to purchase. Dealers in old silver are continually buying as much flat silver as possible, for it can be purchased most reasonably in oddments, and yet commands a high price when assembled in a complete service. A few years ago an important collector, well able to indulge herself in the luxuries she wished, wanted to assemble a matched service, all dated prior to the reign of George III. The forks were to be three pronged, the spoons "rat-tail," and the knives pistol handled. Although she allowed "carte blanche" as regards price, it took over four years of diligent searching all over the world in order to complete the set.

For those who are as well pleased by authentic reproductions, the finest patterns have been copied by contemporary silversmiths with great skill.

SPOONS

The spoon was probably suggested by the shells used in prehistoric times for eating liquid foods. In the Middle Ages spoons were made of bone, horn, crystal, and wood. There is also indication that some were fashioned from metals such as pewter and brass, but the earliest silver spoons in England date no further back than the end of the fourteenth century. The first known mention of a spoon made of a precious metal is in the Bible, wherein the Lord instructed Moses to make golden spoons for the Tabernacle. The age old custom of using a spoon for anointing a sovereign at a coronation is also noted in the Bible. It records how Nathan the Prophet anointed Solomon as King of Israel.

The first known English spoons are really only reproductions of the original ones made in bronze by the Romans and Greeks. However, the word spoon was doubtlessly derived from the fact that in early English times spoons were made of wood and the old English word for a splinter of wood is "spon."

The characteristics of these medieval spoons are a long slender polygonal stem tapering towards the head, and an elongated pear-shape shallow bowl. This definitely suggests that they were not used for thin liquids, but for thicker foods such as cream, custard or posset.

During the 250 years that followed the making of the first silver specimens, the basic form of the spoon remained the same, only the ornamentation or shaping being changed or modified. Such variations as occur are restricted to the ornamental knops at the end of the stems, but the oval or fig shape of the bowl was constant until the reign of Charles I.

A further development is noticed in the style of the stem which was changed from a thin round taper to the more robust hexagonal. The flat stem was not introduced until the Commonwealth.

From the latter part of the fourteenth century until the arrival of the flattened stem, different types of knops distinguished more or less definitely the individual periods. The earliest known was the acorn top, while during the fifteenth and sixteenth centuries, the diamond point and maidenhead predominated. With regard to the last mentioned type, it is interesting to note the variation in the style of headdress in the figure depicted, according to the prevailing fashion of coiffure at the time of the making. During the Tudor period, the knop resembled an inverted bunch of grapes, and sometimes was in the shape of a bird. Seal tops and those with the lion sejant are also known and the influence of the continental silversmiths is noticeable in the series of figures at the end of the stems.

A spoon that became common in the seventeenth century, was an absolutely plain type with a flat handle. It became very popular with the Roundheads, and hence was given the name Puritan spoon.

Apostle spoons are interesting. These were originally made in sets of thirteen, comprising a figure of the Lord and twelve disciples. Complete units of Apostle spoons are perhaps among the rarest known articles in silver, as evidenced by the fact that only a few years ago, a set of thirteen dated 1536 was purchased at auction for a sum in excess of $25,000. Other religious types of spoons depicted the figures of saints, cherubs and angels. Apostle spoons are more plentiful today than these other types, due to the custom of presenting one to each child on the occasion of his baptism.

At the time of Charles I, the bowls of spoons became egg shaped, and the stems took on a flat broad rectangular form, the ornamental knops being discarded. After the Restoration in 1660, the stem was flattened with the top cleft in two places to suggest a trifid. Also, at this time, the triangular tongue at the back that covered part of the bowl, appeared. This style was known as the "rat-tail," and enjoyed much popularity.

By the end of the seventeenth century, the spoon began to assume the shape that is commonly accepted and used today. The clefts disappeared from the handle, and were replaced by a rounded end that widened in a concave curve to form the handle. At this time, the bowl was broad and elliptical, although later it took on a more pointed shape. In the following years, the handle was turned upwards towards the face of the bowl and formed a distinct hook. About the middle of the eighteenth century, the more convenient down turn superseded the earlier type, and is the accepted style of handle today.

All manner of engraving and chasing was incised on spoons during various periods, and in some instances the bowls were ornamented with scrolls, foliations and shells. These were often symbolic of either the use of the spoon or else the person for whom it was intended. During the last hundred years or so, other styles have evolved, the most popular being the fiddle-back. This in turn was changed into the fiddle and thread, sometimes surmounted by a shell.

Teaspoons were introduced in the late seventeenth century, and were so small they resembled our present day after dinner coffee spoons. By the time of George I, the proportions had grown though, until they were of similar style to those used now.

The dessert spoon was not popular until after the Restoration, and from then on closely followed the style and shape of the table spoon.

FORKS

Comparatively speaking, forks are very recent to civilization, for although knives and spoons are known to have existed in crude forms, since ancient times, the general use of forks is not found until the end of the fifteenth century. At this period in history, forks were known only in Italy, although a few scattered continental

Dinner Service Paul Storr, London, 1818

Courtesy S. Wyler, Inc.

SHEFFIELD TEA MACHINE — Daniel Holy-Wilkinson and Co., London, 1798

Rosewater
Dish
London, 1569

Rosewater Dish

London, 1680

Courtesy Metropolitan Museum of Art

SILVERGILT MONSTRANCE German, 16th Century

Courtesy Metropolitan Museum of Art

COVERED CUP Salzburg, 16th Century

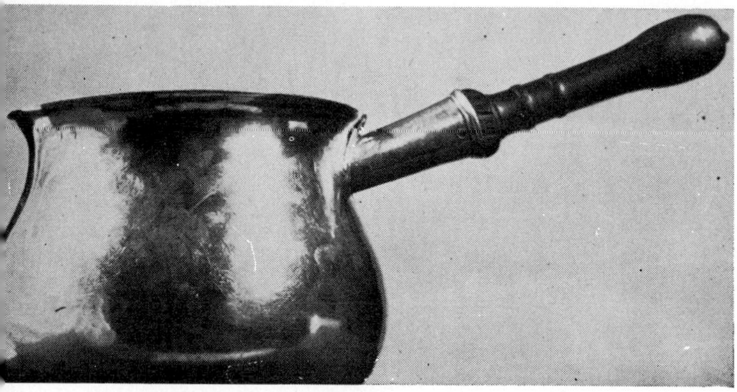

Brandy Sauce Pan — John Boddington, London, 1708

Courtesy J. E. Caldwell & Co.

Porringer — London, 1683

Courtesy J. E. Caldwell & Co.

Goblet — London, 1654

Candlesticks — Wm. Denny and John Barnard, London, 1697-1703

Courtesy Tiffany & Co.

Kettle and Stand — Francis Garthorne, London, 1716

Courtesy Marshall Field & Co.

CENTERPIECE — Paul Storr, London, 1820

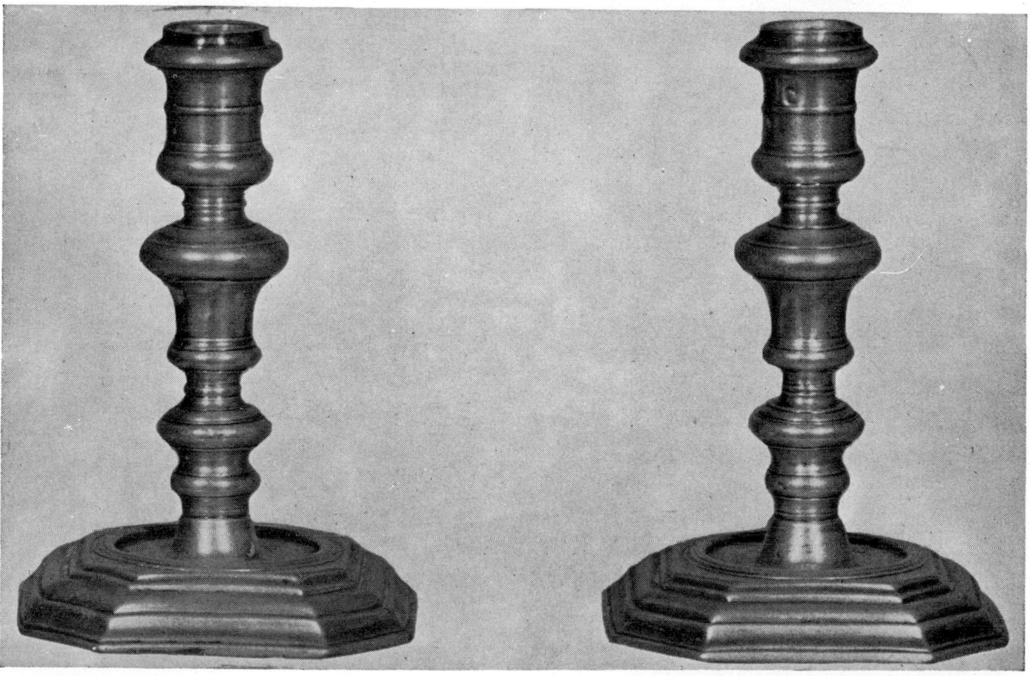

CANDLESTICKS — Anthony Nelme, London, 1723

Courtesy Metropolitan Museum of Art

Coffee Pot — John Burt, Boston, 1712

Courtesy Metropolitan Museum of Art

Chocolate Pot — Edward Winslow

TAZZA Paul Lamerie, London, 1722 *Courtesy Tiffany & Co.*

Courtesy J. E. Caldwell & Co.

Covered Cup — Paul Storr, London, 1813

Bachelor Tea Set — William Kingdon, London, 1821 — *Courtesy S. Wyler, Inc.*

Tea and Coffee Set — London, 1784-1795

Tea Caddy

London,
1752

Courtesy J. E. Caldwell & Co.

Chocolate Pot on Stand

Gabriel Sleath, London, 1714

Courtesy Marshall Field & Co.

Coffee Pot — Peter and Anne Bateman, London, 1791

Courtesy J. E. Caldwell & Co.

Coffee Pot — Hester Bateman, London, 1787

Courtesy S. Wyler, Inc.

KETTLE — Ed. Fennell, London, 1767

Courtesy J. E. Caldwell &

KETTLE AND STAND

Thomas Whipman and Charles Wright, London, 17

Courtesy Tiffany & Co.

TANKARD London, 1677 PAIR OF TUMBLER CUPS London, 1686 WINE TASTER London, 1649

Caudle Cup and Cover
Gerrit Onkelbag, New York, 1670-1733

Courtesy James Graham, Jr.
Mabel Brady Garvan Collection, Yale Museum

John Coney, Boston   Samuel Vernon, Newport   Adrian Bancker, New York   *Courtesy James Graham,*

pieces have survived. They were eventually introduced into England about two centuries later, after having been noticed by English travelers in Italy.

An interesting reference to forks was published in a book called "Crudities," written at the beginning of the seventeenth century. The allusion is the expression of the author, Thomas Coryate, an Englishman traveling in Italy in 1620. "I observed a custom in all those Italian cities and towns through which I passed that is not used in any other country that I saw in my travels, neither do I think that any other nation of Christendom doth use it, but only Italy. The Italian, and also most strangers that are commorant in Italy, do always at their meals use a little fork when they cut their meat . . . their forks being for the most part made on iron or steel, and some of silver, but these are used only by gentlemen. The reason of this their curiosity is because the Italian cannot endure by any means to have his dish touched by fingers, seeing that all men's fingers are not alike clean. Hereupon I myself thought to imitate the Italian fashion by this fork cutting of meat, not only while I was in Italy, but also in Germany, and often-times in England since I came home."

It seems incredible that in a period of English history so famed for its extravagance and luxury, that forks were rarely used. This new display of refinement was indeed slow in being generally accepted, as evidenced by the few specimens made. However, their use may have been retarded somewhat, because ministers contended it was an insult to God not to touch meat with one's fingers. As more and more travelers noted their use and general advantages in the consumption of food, silversmiths produced forks in greater quantities. It was not until late in the eighteenth century, however, that they were in common use.

The earliest forks made were probably used only for serving pieces, as one in the inventory of the Royal Plate of 1399 weighed fifteen and one-half ounces. Another in a will of 1463, was listed as being used for "grene Gynger." Early in the Tudor period, a type of fork which was really a rudely wrought piece of silver with two prongs at one end, and a small spoon bowl at the other, was known. This was used for lifting "suckets" such as plums or other fruits preserved in syrup.

Even after the introduction of forks, it remained customary for dinner guests to provide their own utensils for eating. This undoubtedly explains the ingenious one-piece combinations which were made to serve the purpose of a spoon and fork. The three pronged fork would serve as the handle for a spoon bowl, by fitting the prongs in two loops and fastening it to the back. The handle hinged back to permit folding for convenience when carrying in the pouch. Surviving examples of these of English origin are very rare, and the few known today are all of continental make.

The earliest forks made were for the most part of iron and steel, with a few in silver owned by families of great wealth. Until the early part of the eighteenth century, a gentleman who traveled carried a knife and fork of his own, as the inns were not likely to have them. Visitors to England were continually criticizing the lack of forks, as they thought the English custom most unsanitary. Even after forks attained a fair amount of popularity, rich people did not possess many of them. Hence it has been suggested that the custom of serving a sherbet in the middle of the meal was introduced in order to permit the servants time to wash the forks for the next course.

The introduction of forks caused silver ewers and basins to fall into disuse completely. The earliest known fully hallmarked English fork is dated 1632. It is 7 inches long, two pronged, and bears the interesting crest of the Earl of Rutland. It remains today on exhibition at the Victoria and Albert Museum in London.

There was very little change in the style of the forks made from the beginning, until nearly the middle of the seventeenth century. At this time, a three pronged type with a flat rectangular handle appeared that closely resembled the Puritan spoon. This was probably copied from a contemporary French specimen, as forks are known to have existed in France as early as 1300. Until about 1730, English forks are found having two, three or four prongs. Thus the number of prongs cannot indicate any particular period. While during the Commonwealth, three prongs are common, after the Restoration three or four prongs were in use and dating from the reigns of William III and Queen Anne, many have only two tines.

With the passing of the Puritan austerity, more refined stems began to appear following the design of contemporary spoons. At first, the flat stem had the wide trifid end, but this soon developed into the more graceful trifid shape, although for some time it retained the notches. From then on, the fork was made similar to the spoon, until the introduction of the plain Old English type with the curved back, which has been generally accepted today, as the most useable and graceful. During the Georgian period stems of forks were ornamented with bright cut engraving or feather edging, although retaining the Old English pattern.

Mention must be made of the pistol handled forks, which were made to match the knives of the period. And there was also a type with a steel prong and a handle of thinly stamped silver filled with a resinous substance.

KNIVES

Knives are known in history a great deal earlier than forks, although ones with silver handles were not made prior to the eighteenth century. The origin of the knife may be traced to prehistoric times, at which time those executed were hardly more than pieces of flint. However, as time progressed, they were made of stone, and later of bronze, iron and steel.

The original use of the knife was of course in hunting and as a means of protection, but evidence exists to prove that the early Greeks used knives in the service of food. This was actually only a large serving knife, employed to cut the meat into smaller pieces, but it definitely laid the foundation for the making of individual table knives in later years.

There is no actual date which can be recorded for the introduction of the knife into England. However, Chaucer who died in 1400, speaks of a Sheffield whittle, the English term for knife. Thus, we may assume that they were used from this time on. Before the introduction of the fork, the diner held his food with one hand on the trencher, and cut it with his knife. In early English times, men carried a knife in a sheath. This type often had an ornamented silver handle, and we know it was used both at meal times and for defense. The custom of carrying a sheathed knife continued until the seventeenth century, and by the end of that age, a knife and a fork were encased in a single sheath. These coverings were exemplary of the beautiful silver work of the period, and many were studded with precious stones. By the beginning of the eighteenth century, the use of the sheathed knife at meal times fell into disuse, and the rich man's table at that time was set with silver handled knives.

One of the most popular types of knife was the pistol handled shape, many of which are reproduced today in modern silver. Other types are the "pied-de-biche," and later on the reeded and plain forms with the shell. While Georgian silver table knives are very rare and sought after by collectors, they are not too desirable for present day service, as they are somewhat too heavy and cumbersome.

Much interest is found in the shapes of the blades fitted to various silver handles during the eighteenth century. Many retain influences of former centuries, and these in turn can be traced back to flint instruments of prehistoric times. As silver blades were only introduced at a much later date, all early knives are hallmarked on the handles. However, many times, only a few out of a set were marked, so the collector need not feel discouraged if he cannot obtain a completely marked lot.

In the early part of the George III era, 1760-1820, dessert knives were introduced, usually with a silver blade and an ivory handle. Often the ivory was colored, purely for decorative purposes, and complete sets in good condition are practically unknown.

SKEWERS

Among the late Georgian table plate is the long pointed skewer used to hold joints of meat in shape. Apart from those having ornamental rings or tops, they vary little in style, and are not attractive as examples of the silversmith's art. In present times, they have been adapted for use as letter openers, in which capacity they are more presentable.

MARROW SCOOPS

The marrow scoop was originally a variation of the bowl of a spoon moulded into a long narrow gulley, which would enable one to dig into the inside of a bone in order to remove the marrow. Marrow now being extinct as a delicacy, their use has been given a distinctly modern note, and they are now employed as highball mixers, and drink stirrers. They were introduced at the time of Queen Anne and made in great profusion, because marrow was the epitome of the fastidious diner's art.

SERVING PIECES, LADLES AND SPOONS

A great variety of spoons suitable for serving and stuffing were made during the Georgian eras. Some, such as sauce ladles are rarely found earlier than the George II period, while long handled tasting spoons are known as early as the time of Queen Anne. Fish slicers, introduced about 1735 were very popular and a great variety with delicately pierced bowls were executed.

X

TABLEWARE

EPERGNES AND CENTERPIECES

EPERGNES and centerpieces were introduced during the latter part of the George I era, replacing to a large extent the standing salts which had gone out of use. The word epergne was doubtlessly derived from the French "epaigner," meaning to be thrifty. Inasmuch as the small baskets on the epergnes were used to contain condiments, fruits, nuts and similar luxuries from the Far East, the use of these large objects in the center of the table avoided waste. Each person helped himself from the one main epergne, and in this way, those delicacies not used were left on the table and not extravagantly thrown away with the leavings on the plate.

The first epergne fashioned was long and low with a bowl in the center and sweetmeat dishes on either end. In some instances they contained candle holders as well as casters, although such examples are rare. However, the later models were pieces of great height, elaborately decorated and generally consisted of a fruit or flower dish in the center surrounded by any number of small hanging baskets. Later in the century delicate piercing was introduced, and no article of domestic plate illustrated more clearly the height to which that phase of ability had risen. The hanging baskets were often replaced by small dishes on flat stands which could be adapted to individual use. One of the most popular types during the eighteenth century was made in the shape of a pagoda, the Chinese influence also being discernible in the styles of the pierced lattice work and series of semicircular shapes. In the latter part of the century boat shaped center pieces with smaller ones to match were greatly in demand. Epergnes are also found without the side embellishments and resemble huge flower vases with heavy crystal liners.

The extreme popularity of epergnes is readily understood when one realizes that the leading smiths of the period exerted their full efforts to produce masterful creations in silver. Paul Lamerie produced several of great beauty. They afforded him the opportunity for the lavish display and magnificent ornamentation in which he took so much delight. There was an extraordinary one made by him in 1734 for Count Bobrinsky of Russia, and the electroplated reproduction now in the Victoria and Albert Museum affords ample opportunity for inspection. It was a large piece, fitted with casters, candle brackets and cruet frames surrounding the center body. Because it was impossible to use the entire equipment at one time, the pieces were all removable and could be replaced by ornamental knobs. Another important epergne by the same maker is the specimen executed for the Newdegate family.

The epergne was probably copied from pieces of similar plate made in France at an earlier date. In the nineteenth century crystal dishes were used in place of the silver bowls because of the lower cost. For this same reason many more examples were produced in Sheffield plate than in solid silver. Epergnes, unfortunately are not in great demand today, as the massive proportions hardly blend with the present small dining rooms. It was not unusual for some to weigh as much as one thousand ounces, and specimens of that character are recorded in the inventory of royal plate as early as 1725.

Before the middle of the eighteenth century actual silver centerpieces were introduced in place of epergnes. Many of these large covered fruit bowls were made, but very few escaped the melting pot.

DINNER PLATES AND PLATTERS

Although silver dishes and plates were used as early as the middle ages by royal families but few examples have survived. The predecessors of the modern platter, known as chargers, were used previous to the Tudor period for carrying the joint of meat to the table. Another piece of similar design known as a Voyder was used for collecting the broken food that remained on the trenchers so that it might be distributed for charitable purposes. But enormous quantities of this plate were melted down during the Civil Wars in England and very few examples antedate the Restoration in 1660. However, a magnificent set of twelve bearing the London hallmark of 1567 has survived. The plates were parcel gilt and finely engraved with scenes depicting Hercules performing feats of strength. They were eight inches in diameter with a side rim, and although the center depression was somewhat smaller than in the later plates, they clearly show the evolution from wooden trenchers. The continuation of this shape has remained with silver plates. After the Restoration, plates were produced in great quantity and the former types which had been quite plain with simple moulded edges assumed ornamental mounts for the first time.

The French craftsmen who migrated to England were directly responsible for this new style and for many years rococo shells and elaborate scrolls were applied to the borders. However, with the gradual return to pieces of simpler design, the gadroon or bead edge replaced the more elaborate borders. Some of the early dishes of the latter half of the seventeenth century clearly illustrate again the definite influence of the Orient on English crafts. With the importation and continued popularity of Chinese porcelain in England, the silversmiths were soon reproducing the band of decorations by engraving quaint Oriental scenes and figures on the plain surfaces. Early plates command huge prices today as it is indeed rare to assemble a set of twelve or eighteen with the same date letter and by the same maker. For a time plates were so common that they fetched but little above the silver value, but today they have grown exceedingly scarce and are in constant demand.

With the introduction of the large silver dinner service, oval meat dishes of varied sizes appeared. They measured from the small types of ten inches to the venison dishes often as long as twenty-six inches. Those pieces used to hold the meat were equipped with what is now known as the "well and tree" which was, in effect, a series of small channels which allowed the gravy to run through into a large depression at one end of the dish. In the latter half of the nineteenth century porcelain services for dinner plates had come into general use and silver services of this type were no longer made except upon special occasions.

Soup plates as well as dessert plates closely followed the designs of dinner plates although they generally appear at a slightly later date.

SOUP TUREENS

The name tureen as applied to the containers for soup is said to be derived from the fact that Marshal Turenne of France, on one occasion, used his helmet to hold soup.

The tureen was introduced from France, from whence so much English domestic silver has been taken. During the time that Charles II lived in exile he learned many new customs from the French, among which was the custom of serving soup from a large bowl placed on the dining table or sideboard.

Soup tureens are pieces of large proportion, frequently being 22 inches in height including the cover and that they were considered pieces of notable importance is evidenced from the fine display of ornamentation so perfectly executed by the smiths of the period. Those made in the early Georgian period were large oval bowls generally ornamented in the rococo style and set on massive feet, while those produced a short time later displayed the more dignified forms of the Neo-classic era. Tureens were sometimes accompanied by a standing plateau which was placed directly underneath with the intention of protecting the table from the heat of the tureen containing the hot soup.

The earliest known specimen was made in 1703 by the celebrated Anthony Nelme, and formerly was in the possession of Lord Bateman. Further evidence of the popularity of the silver soup tureen or "soupiere," as it was known, is seen at Windsor Castle where numerous examples include thirteen pairs. Many of these were executed by Paul Storr who probably produced more fine specimens than any other maker. During the George III and George IV periods, soup tureens were considered inseparable adjuncts to the dining table, and during the last few years the old custom of serving soup at the table has been revived.

SAUCE BOATS, SAUCE TUREENS AND ARGYLES

The earliest known sauce boat was made in 1698 by William Scarlett. It was of a type directly copied from the French goldsmiths with a low, plain, oval body with double spouts and handles set on a low molded foot. In the second part of the eighteenth century, these types were discarded for boats on three feet with a single spout directly opposite to the handle. In general they followed the prevailing fashions in decoration and were produced in great quantities until the introduction of sauce tureens which were executed as exact replicas in small size, of the soup tureens. The sauce boat is a natural accompaniment to the dinner table and large services often have as many as four pairs with them.

An unusual type of small vessel used for gravy was introduced about 1750 and was called "argyle." These vessels are supposed to have been named after John, the fifth Duke of Argyll. Actually they were gravy tureens with spouts fitted on either side to hold a piece of hot iron which maintained the heat of the gravy. This style was greatly improved a short time later when a jacket was introduced which contained boiling water. Argyles are very rare and only a limited number were produced.

A curious form was made with a bulbous body and a small foot that served as a special compartment for the hot water, in this way offering a greater capacity for the gravy. Many of the early argyles were later converted into coffee and tea pots for which purpose they were admirably suited.

ENTRÉE DISHES, BACON DISHES, CHAFING DISHES, REVOLVING DISHES, DISH COVERS AND HEATERS

Entree dishes were introduced from France and originally called cover dishes or second course dishes. Similar articles generally referred to as sweetmeat dishes, although they were used to hold hot foods, were in use as early as the reign of Charles II. The custom of using the cover as a second dish was introduced during the Georgian era when the dishes were supplied with a removable handle. The dishes made in the Stuart period were restricted to oval shapes and circular domes with molded borders, while those of the later period were oval, circular, or oblong and generally ornamented with a gadroon, thread or bead or similar mount. Many entree dishes which are found in sets of four, six or eight were furnished with so-called heaters in which hot charcoal or boiling water was placed. Some were made with a heater as a combined part and these generally had a small opening with a screw cap at one end into which the water could be poured.

Another type of dish which was originally used for the serving of marrow was known as a second course dish and these are rarely found with covers. An article known as a bacon dish was furnished with a hot water base directly under the dish. It was generally fashioned with a long wooden handle which screwed into a socket at the back of the dish, the socket serving as the opening through which the hot water could be poured into the base. These were used in the service of eggs and bacon and other breakfast foods and during the past few years have become most popular at cocktail parties to hold hors d'oeuvres. Of little interest are the massive domical shaped, deep covers which have now fallen into complete disuse.

Inasmuch as the kitchens of all large houses were quite a distance from the dining rooms, it was necessary to use these covers to keep the food hot while being carried. The problem of heating food at the table was eventually solved by the introduction of the chafing dish which was, in effect, an entree dish fitted into a stand which contained an alcohol lamp in the center. The earliest known types of these were called braziers and were originally introduced by the colonial silversmiths of America. The bodies were pierced with scrollings and ornamental designs and appear to follow the style of a similar object more commonly used in France than in England.

During the Victorian era, another article known as the revolving tureen was first made. It was in the nature of a vegetable dish with a strainer fitted into a large deep oval stand which contained hot water, and also fitted with a corresponding cover which could be rolled back when the food was ready to be served or else left closed in order to retain the heat and keep the food clean.

As prosperity increased in the second half of the eighteenth century, plate was made heavier and heavier and large dinner services were produced for the first time. Soup tureens, sauce tureens, entree dishes, plates, and platters were incorporated into an enormous set containing hundreds of pieces. Complete services are now very rare as upon the settlement of estates in England, they were usually divided among the heirs. However, now and then a magnificent creation practically in its entirety is seen. Unfortunately many of the large pieces in them are too large, useless and obsolete. Throughout history these massive pieces have, as a rule, been converted into other articles.

XI

LIGHTING APPLIANCES

CANDLESTICKS

THE Bible mentions candlesticks, but these solid gold articles were actually for lamps and not candles. The Romans used a crude sort of candle which resembled a modern torch, but it was not until the third century that candles as they are known today were in use. At first these were used exclusively in churches, and the institution of Candlemas Day by Pope Gelasius in the fifth century, was probably the legal adoption of the candlestick. The large number of candles used is an important feature of the ceremony, and the need of some receptacle in which to place the candles was the cause of the origin of the candlestick. The earliest candlesticks were probably made of wood, but later on precious metals were used.

In the description of gifts given by Bishop Aethalwald to the monastery of Peterborough, in 963, candlesticks are mentioned. During the eleventh century, the Abbot Robert sent as a gift to his fellow countryman, Pope Adrian IV, two wonderful candlesticks of gold and silver, which the Pope admired so much that he had them placed in St. Peter's. During the Tudor period mention is made of a banquet given by Cardinal Wolsey to the French embassy and retinue at Hampton Court. As an example of lavish magnificence and splendor by those nearest the throne, the dinner was outstanding. Candlesticks are noted in the following manner: "and upon the nethermost dish garnished all with plate of clear gold, having two great candlesticks of silver and gilt, most curiously wrought, the workmanship thereof, with the silver, cost three hundred marks, and lights of wax as big as torches burning upon the same."

The earliest candlesticks were the type known as prickets. The pricket was actually a sharp point in the top of the shaft to hold the candle, and usually surrounded by a saucer to catch the wax. Although many of the English cathedrals used pricket candlesticks in the Middle Ages, in the sixteenth century they came to be considered monuments of superstition and were destroyed. The pricket was replaced by the socket which held the candle firmly in place.

Although it is accepted as fairly definite that the date of introduction of the socket candlestick was after the sixteenth century, proof of an earlier existence is found in a German picture of 1560, in which a pair is depicted.

Mention is found in wills and inventories of candlesticks which must have been of enormous value. One extremely important example is the pair of sticks given by Henry VI to Cardinal Beaufort in 1439 which were wrought of solid gold, and set with pearls, rubies, sapphires and emeralds.

Very few candlesticks from before the Restoration have survived. An unusual example of the Elizabethan period formed of silver and rock crystal is known, as well as a pair made in 1618, formerly in the possession of Lord Swaythling. They were of curious design, being set on a tripod base. An important set of four bearing the London hallmark of 1637 actually represent in the fuller sense candlesticks as we know them today. Each had a cylindrical stem and a base in the form of an inverted wine glass, with a wide circular disk in the middle to serve as a grease pan. These were probably inspired by a continental model. A magnificent pair from the Restoration period bearing the London hallmark of 1663 was formerly in the Treasury of the Kremlin, Moscow. They were richly ornate with large floral and animal decorations characteristic of the Charles II period, and were no less than 17½ inches in height.

Candlesticks of the Charles II and Queen Anne periods are found in considerable numbers and of varying design. An early form was of square plate throughout while a variation doubtless suggested by French work was octagonal in design. Closely akin to this was another type which had a round fluted column with a square plinth and abacus rising from a square plain moulded foot. Variations giving way to octagonal members with either plain or gadrooned borders are known. These sticks were generally of hammered silver and varied in height from seven to twelve inches.

The law compelling the use of a higher standard attracted the attention of the craftsman to cast work, the softer metal not lending itself to the hammer. Consequently from 1700 on, numerous sets of cast candlesticks are known. This new type was shorter in height than its predecessor and the form had much in common with the standing cup of the period, with the foot generally enriched with mouldings of gadrooned ornamentation. The whole surfaces of the candlesticks were at first left very plain, so that the reflecting light from the candle would be most brilliant. However, the demand for pieces of increased ornamentation which dominated the George II period, had its effect on candlesticks. With the introduction of the rococo style, a new and heavier type of candlestick, sadly lacking in the simplicity and beauty of the earlier type was wrought. Towards the middle of the century, a return to simplicity is noted, and many new varieties in style were produced. One of the popular types was in the form of a column, copied from the early Greek architecture. By now decanters of unusual design were applied, among the most popular being ram's heads, rosettes, medallions and festoons.

About the year 1760, a great change took place in the production of candlesticks, the pieces being made of thin stamped metal loaded with pitch to give them strength. Although this style would undoubtedly have been repugnant to goldsmiths of the Renaissance, the increased economy over cast sticks was found to be most practical.

Cast candlesticks are very much in demand, as a feature was the unusual weight which was quite natural in view of the larger quantity of silver used. The general practice of preparing a model of the candlestick in wax, and then pouring the molten metal into the mold, continued for many years. This same method was employed in making the more elaborate rococo styles. Here the work was in relief, and the separate ornamentations were cast in molds and soldered to the candlestick.

Sets of four early candlesticks are rare and for this reason many people who need four to complete a formal dinner table, have to be satisfied with owning two similar pairs. This situation is true throughout the collection of old silver, for complete services as needed today are rarely found.

CANDELABRA

In ancient Roman times candelabra were known, but at that time candelabra meant, in most cases, a support for a lamp. They were wrought in many different materials including the precious metals, but most of those that have been excavated were in bronze. Some fifty or sixty years ago, parts of a Roman silver candelabrum were found near the city of Hanover. The piece was probably made about the first century or earlier. The general form of early metal candelabra was similar throughout, the base being composed of three spreading feet with the lamps suspended from the arms. On top of the shaft there was usually a figurine or statuette, and the height ran anywhere from twelve inches to ten feet. The early churches possessed many examples patterned after the early Roman form, but there are no examples known today.

Silver candelabra dating prior to the reign of George III are rare. As prosperity increased during the second half of the eighteenth century, the silver was made heavier and heavier and massive candelabra were not uncommon in the great houses throughout the land. The nineteenth century produced many magnificent specimens with three or five lights, and occasionally one finds an important pair made for a large dining hall with as many as twelve lights.

Candelabra for the most part followed the designs used in candlesticks during the Queen Anne period. The prevailing patterns had three branches radiating from a center stem which was surmounted by a molded finial. During the rococo period, twisted branches were not uncommon and the finial center was frequently replaced by a socket. No doubt because of the excessive cost of silver candelabra many more pairs were made in Sheffield plate. For this reason the most representative work of the silversmiths who specialized in the production of candelabra is found in the plate examples.

CHANDELIERS

Chandeliers are known to have existed as early as the twelfth century when they reposed in churches, and although very common among the more important English families, practically none have survived to this date.

One of the most famous executed in silver is the specimen at Hampton Court. It is a massive piece with twelve branches richly decorated with laurel leaf bands and bosses. The upper part is ornamented with four cartouches containing a rose, thistle, harp and fleur-de-lis, each surmounted by a crown. It dates from the reign of William III. Earlier types combining the acanthus decoration of the Charles II period are also known as well as an important pair with eight branches now at Knole Park, Kent. Perhaps the most magnificent English silver chandeliers are found in Russia and outstanding among those is the pair, made by Paul Lamerie in 1734, which formerly hung in the Treasury of the Kremlin. They were in the best style of Lamerie, combining a wealth of decoration and strap work surmounted by a Russian imperial crown. Each was wrought with sixteen individual branches, so an idea of the immensity may be surmised. During the invasion of Napoleon's troops important pieces made in 1630 for the Cathedral of the Assumption in Moscow were melted down. Although chandeliers are recorded among the pieces of larger plate belonging to Charles II, none from his reign have survived in the world's collection.

SCONCES

During the exile of Charles II in the Low Country, he became familiar with many silver vessels previously unknown in England. Among these were silver sconces and shortly after the introduction of these sconces into England, they became very popular and fashionable. A large number have survived from the late seventeenth century and also from the eighteenth century, and handsome specimens make their appearance quite frequently. It appears that they were known as early as the time of Henry VIII as there is mention of them in the account given by George Cavendish of the reception given by Cardinal Wolsey to the French ambassador in 1527. Further references to their use are found in the inventories of royal plate during the Tudor period. From 1660 until the time of Queen Anne, wall sconces were extremely popular and the scarcity of the early examples can be blamed on the wholesale destruction of plate in later years. From an artistic point of view, sconces are representative of the better work of the silversmith and clearly illustrate the high degree of excellence attained by workers in the late seventeenth century. They were made in a variety of patterns generally with the back plates richly embossed. Three principal types are known, among them being one made in 1665 with a single socket attached to the oblong back plate with a rounded top. It was engraved and embossed with elaborate floral designs. Another type which is somewhat less common has an enriched truss in place of a back plate, and a scroll branch with a socket. However, the most standardized pattern consisted of a richly embossed back plate with either one or two branches with sockets. Among the many variations executed, is one which has in the center of the back plate a human arm, grasping in its hand the branch. Silver-framed, mirrored sconces were once very popular but they are seldom encountered today.

The fashion of lighting rooms by means of sconces was generally known throughout England after the accession of Queen Anne. Illustrative of the type most in demand at that time are a pair made in 1703, now in the Victoria and Albert Museum, and a magnificent set of six by the celebrated Peter Archambo. A splendid collection of early sconces is owned by the royal family, and includes two lovely sets bearing the monogram of William and Mary, surmounted by a royal crown. These were all in high relief with strongly defined ornamentation, the craftsman's intention being to reflect as much light as possible.

CHAMBERSTICKS

Throughout the eighteenth century many types of portable chamber candlesticks were used for lighting the way to one's bedroom through the long dark halls, and also to illuminate the chamber itself. In the royal plate of 1438 mention is made of a "hond candilstikke" which may be considered the ancestor of all chamber candlesticks. Although examples prior to 1700 are very rare, an outstanding chamberstick with a circular pan to match, made in 1688, may now be seen at Exeter College. Also, they are rarely found complete, because over a period of years the snuffers have generally been lost.

An ancient custom which descended from medieval times was an auction sale conducted "by inch of candle." A small piece of candle was lighted and allowed to burn itself out and the final bidder before the flame expired was the successful purchaser of whatever was offered for sale. For this purpose special silver holders were made.

TAPER STICKS

A taper stick is actually a reproduction of a candlestick in miniature and was used for melting wax to seal letters, or when impressing a seal to accompany a signature on a document. Tapersticks date back to the time of William and Mary in 1688 and were in use only until the introduction of the gummed envelope. They were intended for use on the writing desk, but later in the century became an actual part of the silver inkstand. Their development followed closely that of the candlestick.

WAX JACKS

Another implement made in silver and used on the writing desk during the eighteenth century was an article called a wax jack. This was actually a wax taper coiled around a spindle. It passed through a socket enclosed in a sort of openwork bird cage. The earliest specimens which date as far back as 1698, were enclosed in a cylindrical box which had a hole in the center of the lid for the wax to protrude. Although often found in completely enclosed silver units the loveliest types were usually pierced.

SNUFFERS

Requisite to early candlesticks were the small snuffers on trays which were evidently in use as early as the sixteenth century. As candles in the early days burned more slowly and the wax ran down the sides of the candlestick, it was frequently necessary to clip the charred pieces of wick. Snuffers were a household essential before the invention of candle wicks which could be entirely consumed by the flame.

Snuffers resemble in shape a pair of scissors, but differ in that one blade is broad, the solid piece set perpendicularly at the end. Those of the post-Restoration period were generally fitted with a box on one blade and a pressing plate on the other which fitted inside. At this time many were equipped with little pans shaped to the form of the snuffers, but later on these gave way to attractive stands made with little handles so that they could be carried about.

The earliest known reference to a snuffer is in the list of plate at All Souls' College at Oxford in 1448. Several examples are known from the sixteenth century, including the specimen in the British Museum which bears the arms of Henry the Eighth.

XII

BOXES

UNFORTUNATELY silver boxes are not representative, as a whole, of the better workmanship of the English and Irish silversmiths. The finest specimens were executed in European countries. Although hallmarked silver boxes are known to exist from as early a time as the reign of James I, 1603 to 1625, they are far from plentiful, few having survived throughout the years. They were rarely made in great profusion, being almost exclusively for royalty and those in court circles.

They were very small in size and consequently many were lost or buried. But it is just because of this scarcity that early silver boxes are so much in demand. Well-marked specimens of authentic date fetch fantastic prices in sale rooms, and collectors and dealers all over the world are always in the market for the better types.

Nearly all small boxes were originally parts of elaborate toilet services, although a few spice and sweetmeat boxes are known to have existed prior to the making of these handsome toilet sets. It may be said, without a doubt, that silver boxes were considered a luxury, and as a rule, were only made to special order for a chosen few.

FREEDOM BOXES

Among the many styles of silver boxes known in England, were small shallow receptacles known as freedom boxes. In shape they were similar to tobacco boxes. They were originally made to hold the vellum certificate used at the presentation of the freedom of a borough to some important personage. As a general rule, the lid was engraved or embossed with the arms of the borough to which the freeman had been admitted.

Freedom boxes are very rare. However, they are not greatly in demand as they are a poor representation of the work of the English silversmiths. Outstanding among freedom boxes were the two executed in solid gold and given with the freedom of certain Irish towns to the fourth Duke of Devonshire and the fourth Duke of Rutland, both holding the same office of Lord Lieutenant of Ireland. Both examples being unmarked, one can only surmise as to their origin, but data that have been handed down concerning the lives of these two prominent men prove fairly conclusively that they were the work of Dublin goldsmiths. Unfortunately, these two fine examples are no longer in their original state, having been melted down. In 1801 and 1813 the gold in them was made into a salver and a platter by the celebrated Paul Storr.

Cork silversmiths in the eighteenth century were busily engaged in making gold and silver freedom boxes. Outstanding among the fine examples extant today, are the ones originally belonging to the Earl of Shelbourne and Admiral Lord Redding, both the work of the famed Irish silversmith, William Reynolds. An earlier example was made in Cork in 1737, and carried with it the freedom of that city. This box is now in the collection of Dean Swift.

POMANDERS

Pomanders were in general use among the wealthier classes as early as the fourteenth century, but examples from this period are no longer obtainable. Such few as have survived from the sixteenth and seventeenth centuries are now in museums and private collections only.

The pomander is a curious corruption of the French word "pomme d'ambre," which means apple of amber. The amber referred to the ambergris, which, when worn, diffused a pleasant odor. A small bar of ambergris, or musk, was enclosed in a silver container and worn around the neck or hung from a girdle. The original "pomme d'ambre" eventually came to be spelled "pomander" and, as such these little boxes are known today.

Pomanders were originally carried to counteract fever and to protect the olfactory nerves from offensive smells prevalent in the Middle Ages. These small boxes which were originally relics of old silver toilet services were practically a necessity for those who wished, and could afford the luxury of protecting themselves against the existing unsanitary conditions. It is said that the pomander owes its general use to Cardinal Wolsey, who filled an orange with a sponge soaked in vinegar, worm wood, rosemary and spices, and carried it with him everywhere. The silversmiths of the day quickly perceived the need for such an article and produced them profusely.

TOILET SETS

In the study of the history of silver, mention is made of small silver boxes, perfume flasks, and other toilet accessories that were used by Queen Elizabeth, but no complete English toilet service dated prior to the seventeenth century is known. However, it is probable that they were in use many years before that as they are noted in the luxurious domestic appointments which appeared in Spain after she began to obtain quantities of silver from her American colonies.

Full credit, however, must be given to France for the general popularity of the toilet set. They were widely used by the court of Louis XIV, and from there the use spread to England; for the court of Charles II used only typically French ornaments in the gold and silver appointments. The only complete English toilet sets which have survived are all dated after the Restoration, 1660.

These services often comprised as many as from 20 to 35 pieces, including all the toilet implements, table mirrors, silver candlesticks, powder and page boxes, precious salvers, pin-cushions, flasks, and innumerable other small articles which help to complete the lady's toilet.

Probably the finest known toilet service in the world today is the one presented by Charles II to Frances Stuart, Duchess of Richmond, and hallmarked Paris, 1672 and 1680. The King himself paid close to ten thousand pounds for this service when it was made, so one can readily imagine the fantastic value placed on it today by collectors.

Although Irish silver toilet sets are very rare, one made by a Dublin silversmith in 1791 is known. Several noted English silversmiths are regarded as the makers of beautiful and elaborate toilet sets. Among these are: David Willaume, Anthony Nelme, and Paul Lamerie.

Toilet sets are very rare. Recently a partially complete set by Paul Lamerie reached a price close to thirty thousand dollars.

TOBACCO BOXES

Tobacco was originally introduced into England by Ralph Lane, the first governor of Virginia, during the reign of Queen Elizabeth. It was carried in small boxes of either base metal or silver, although the latter were not in general use until the following century. No tobacco box antedating the Restoration is known, and the few remaining examples of the period are merely plain, shallow containers of little beauty and no great importance as examples of the silversmith's art in England.

MULLS

Scotch mulls were large or small horns frequently mounted in silver and used for snuff boxes. They are generally found bearing presentation inscriptions and are in demand today, as Scotch silver of early date is always desirable. One of great historic interest is a five-compartment box which was given to the Perthshire Regiment of Gentlemen and Yeomenry Cavalry by James Hay, Esq., captain of the Cassé troup in 1804.

NUTMEG GRATERS

Small boxes suitable for carrying in the pocket, and used to contain nutmeg were particularly popular during the eighteenth century. At this time nutmeg and other flavors had been introduced from the East and were in great favor throughout England. A nutmeg grater was actually a small silver container fitted with an inner grate attached to the cover on the inside. This permitted the dust to fall through into the box. The graters were made in a great variety of styles and shapes, but the general purpose of all was alike. It is interesting to note that they were in use throughout the first half of the Victorian era.

SPICE AND SNUFF BOXES

Spice and sweetmeat boxes appear to have been fashionable during the sixteenth century, and there is direct evidence of their popularity in court circles in the latter half of the following century. However, few English snuff boxes can compare in detail and workmanship with the masterpieces executed by the French craftsmen. One of the earliest known spice boxes dated 1598, survived from the Elizabethan era. It was recently sold at Christie's for upwards of six thousand dollars. It was in the form of a cockle-shell on four feet, the sides ornamented with arabesque on a matted ground and the handles molded with an egg and tongue border.

Another specimen, an oval box made in 1677, was sold at auction for nearly three thousand dollars. These prices are mentioned merely to indicate the great rarity of such articles.

Probably the best known of all snuff boxes are those associated with the Russian silversmiths. In very few countries in Europe were these superb creations so fully appreciated or expertly conceived as there. Many magnificent specimens in gold and enamel date from the nineteenth century and their popularity today for use as table cigarette boxes is wide. These Russian boxes were covered with niello which was a metallic alloy of sulphur and silver having a deep black color. Pieces were decorated with inside designs filled with niello.

It is interesting to note here the collaboration between makers and decorators of English silver pieces. Conclusive proof that articles were often executed by more than one maker is found in the historic gold tobacco box of 1741, made by Humphrey Payne in London. The piece bears his makers' mark as well as the signature on the inside cover of the engraver, John Ellis. Therefore, it is not unusual to find that, although pieces were often completed by one maker, heraldic devices and other ornamentations were often added by contemporary or later craftsmen.

In the past decade, prices of antique silver snuff boxes have risen tremendously, chiefly because many of these early snuff boxes were of a sufficient size to fit cigarettes used today. In this way a person wishing to assemble a well-appointed table of completely original silver might find the necessary containers for a modern note.

VINAIGRETTES

Silver vinaigrettes were regarded as indispensable until the middle of the nineteenth century, and were carried by as great a number of ladies as might outfit themselves today with compacts. These little silver boxes varied greatly in size and style, but being made exclusively for the feminine interest were all of a pretty and pleasing design. The general construction of all vinaigrettes was generally the same. A perforated inner lid permitted the choice aromatic scents to escape, and diffuse a very pleasant scent. Actually, they are a modern adaptation of the sixteenth century pomander, as their original use was much the same.

Vinaigrettes, as a rule were hallmarked under the lid, and the majority of them are of Birmingham origin. In glancing over a collection of possibly a hundred varied types, one would probably find that over 75 per cent were made there, and that in all probability, not more than seven or eight different makers would be represented in the entire lot.

Vinaigrettes are often found with a ring attachment through which a chain was passed, as very often they were worn as lockets.

Vinaigrettes in general exhibited a finer type of workmanship in the fine piercing of the inner lids and delicate repoussée work, than any other of the small silver boxes. Today they are greatly in demand by collectors the world over and in the past ten years their value has increased many fold. One of the most recent adaptations of the vinaigrette is for use as a pill-box or else as a container for saccharine tablets.

XIII

MISCELLANEOUS PIECES

TRAYS, SALVERS AND PATENS

IN the last half of the seventeenth century, small circular trays were used as stands for large silver tankards, but specimens of these are far from plentiful. The earliest known mention of such a piece is in 1661, wherein it is described as follows: "salver . . . is a new fashioned piece of wrought plate, broad and flat, with a foot under neath, and is used in giving beer, or other liquid thing to save the Carpit or Cloathes from drops."

As a general rule the earliest salvers, now referred to as card trays, were simple in design and void of decoration, as opposed to the later types which combined molded or cast borders with engraving, or heraldic insignia in the center. Occasionally small engraved trays of early date are found, and they are by far the most valuable because of their extreme rarity. The introduction and continued use of the circular salver, many of which assumed massive proportions, was undoubtedly influenced by the early rose water dishes. Although many of the larger salvers weighed as much as 200 ounces, largely because of the heavy rococo mounts, examples displaying the full ability of the silversmith's skill may be seen. These excelled particularly in the manner of the engraved and flat shaped work. Perhaps no other article of domestic plate retained the quiet dignity of Queen Anne's time as fully as the salver. During the George II period when the flair for over-ornamentation was prevalent everywhere, a simple style of tray was introduced known as the "Chippendale." The name was applied to them because the borders were reproduced from the rims of tables designed by that great furniture designer. "Chippendale" as well as other salvers were made in a great variety of styles and shapes, including square, circular, oblong and shaped specimens.

Dating from the beginning, the tea service was placed on what is now known as a tea tray. They were almost indispensable to the serving of tea, and increased in size as more pieces were added to form a service. Although made in a wide variety of sizes and shapes, generally supported on four feet, their beauty was not confined to the work on the borders, for the finest decorative engraving was lavished on the plain surfaces. The ordinary tea tray as we know it measured anywhere in length from eighteen inches to twenty-four inches, and was placed on a large table at tea time. However, in the middle of the eighteenth century, a wooden stand was devised with a top of the same size as the silver tray with sockets to hold the feet. These never attained great popularity though, for the regulation tray with its two easily grasped handles was found to be more convenient.

At the time of the neo-classic vogue, a complete change in ornamentation is noted. The craftsmen used flat chased motifs, generally in a wide band around the edge, with the center left plain for an engraved coat of arms. Other variations noted at this time were the introduction of large oval and oblong waiters with high pierced gallery borders, as well as some with wooden or papier mache bases. Waiters for use in large houses were often made in pairs or sets of three, but are rarely found today.

During the Queen Anne and George I periods the paten was introduced. This was in the nature of a circular waiter standing on a low trumpet mouth foot, the joint of which was frequently masked by a circle of cut-card work. Although generally used by the church for sacred purposes, patens were employed in ordinary life to serve as containers for fruit.

INKSTANDS AND STANDISHES

Inkstands or standishes, as they were called at first, were introduced in the first half of the seventeenth century. As a matter of record, the earliest known hallmarked specimen was made in London in 1630.

Within a short time, silversmiths were producing inkstands of great beauty, and also at all times during the history of their production, simplicity was the keynote. Hardly ever did they assume the fantastic forms and over-ornamentation that influenced the other domestic plate during the rococo period. In time they became essentials of the well-appointed writing table and their popularity never waned during the history of silversmithing in England.

The inkstands or standishes made during the reign of Charles II were fashioned like large plain rectangular boxes with two flat covers and a handle in the middle. A specimen of this rare type dated 1685 is now in the Treasury. As time progressed, inkstands were greatly altered in style, and by the eighteenth century the casket type was introduced. Occasionally, these were fitted with a slide drawer below, to hold the sealing wax. This general style of a rectangular tray with receptacles for ink, sand and wafers prevailed during the century. Slight variations occur in some specimens wherein the wafer box in the center was covered by a hand bell which was used to summon the servant when the letter was ready to be sent. In later years, the bell was replaced by a taperstick which previously had been a separate unit. During the George III era, the silver fitments were replaced by glass receptacles with silver tops fitted on to the tray base. One top was pierced with holes in which to place the quills when not in use, another had finer perforations for use as a sandcaster, while the third well contained the ink. The trays were somewhat larger than the earlier examples, the border being ornamented with a concave depression on either side to hold the wax. Steel pens were introduced in 1805, but were not generally used until many years later. For this reason it is not unusual to find inkstands fitted with sandboxes and quill holders, dating well into the nineteenth century.

There was an early mention of an inkstand in the inventory of the plate of Henry VIII, where two are recorded in 1520. One was of Spanish origin, while the other was probably of English make. The specimen of 1630 belonging to Sir John Noble appears to be the only surviving inkstand of those made before the Civil War. One of the most magnificent and largest inkstands ever made, is the one executed by Paul Lamerie for the Duke of Cumberland. One famous inkstand was used by Sir Joshua Reynolds in many of his portraits.

In the collection and purchase of old inkstands, it is essential to make sure that each individual piece is marked, for over a period of years parts may have been lost and replaced. Also many of the early snuffer stands have been converted into inkstands by the addition of wells. It is well to remember that when parts have been added or alterations made, the value of the piece has been greatly lessened.

BREAD, CAKE, AND SWEETMEAT BASKETS

Oval pierced baskets with handles were introduced during the reign of George II at which time they were used for bread, thereby accounting for the decorative wheat sheaves often noted. The earliest examples were low and very heavy, while the later types were generally pierced and much lighter in feeling. However, towards the end of the eighteenth century the piercing was abandoned and baskets were again made with stands that followed the circular or oblong shapes then in vogue.

Baskets were made in a wide variety of shapes which changed with each successive period. Originally the basket was made with a small handle at either end, but this was replaced later by the large swinging handle. Among the interesting examples known of unusual baskets is a George III specimen with a pierced separation in the center, one side of which was marked "fresh" and the other "stale" to indicate the place for each kind of bread. A very rare type, beautifully pierced with an original wicker work pattern typified the unusual designs created by Paul Lamerie. It was made in 1733 and formed part of the collection of Lord Swaythling. In the George II reign, baskets were often made in the form of a large shell on dolphin feet, an example of 1751 being in the collection of Royal plate at Windsor Castle.

The middle of the eighteenth century showed the popularity of delicately pierced sweetmeat baskets. They were actually reproductions in miniature of the larger cake baskets and carried out to the minutest detail the same character of workmanship found in the larger pieces. A variation of the candy dish was in the shape of an escalloped shell, examples of which are very rare. A magnificent pair, formerly in the possession of Sir Montague, were made by Paul Lamerie in 1732, which date is the earliest known reference to a shell. Shells are among the most desirable pieces of old silver as they fit in perfectly with the table appointments of today.

DISH RINGS

Dish rings are peculiar to the work of Irish silversmiths, in whose country they seem to have first come into use about 1750. From this time on they remained as one of the principal articles of table plate until the latter part of the nineteenth century. The dish ring, as made in Ireland, was always circular and resembled in shape an enlarged napkin ring, while English examples of oval body are known. The dish ring was probably introduced in the attempt to avoid the damaging results of standing hot dishes directly on the table. The ring remained on the table throughout the meal to support in turn the soup bowl, the potato bowl, the dessert bowl, and occasionally the punch bowl. Inasmuch as the fashion in Ireland was to serve potatoes in a large wooden bowl which was placed on top of the silver stand, it is not strange that for years these silver articles have been erroneously termed potato rings.

The earliest type of dish ring made is very shallow, the sides of some being less than three inches deep, and the diameter at the rim being generally identical with that of the base. As a rule, the sides were ornamented with shaped and pierced scrolls and flowers, with chased cartouches framed by scrolls for the armorial insignia. Dish rings often portrayed pastoral and farm scenes. Many rings bore the Oriental influence in the Chinese architecture and native figures, these subjects often being combined with European hunting scenes. Dish rings of this character are greatly in demand as specimens of unusual creation by silversmiths in piercing. The later type of dish ring does not have the same amount of appeal since it lacks the charming decoration of the preceding style.

The earliest known reference to a dish ring is in an anonymous inventory of plate dating from 1697, wherein two are mentioned. An advertisement of the same year refers to two rings for the table, although it can only be assumed that dish rings were meant. However, an example as early as 1704 has survived and it is thought most probable that some specimens may have existed a few years earlier. It is interesting to note that the Irish dish rings retained the elaborate ornamentation of the rococo period long after that style had gone out of fashion in England. Reproductions of these rings are made today and have been improved upon by the addition of a blue glass liner which enables them to serve as attractive flower bowls and centerpieces.

DISH CROSSES

As dish rings fell into disuse, dish crosses were introduced to serve the same purpose. They were a great deal more practical than their predecessors because the supports and the feet were made to slide along the rods of the cross in order to contain various dishes. They were introduced during the time of George II and used extensively throughout England. However, they never grew in popularity in Ireland and the dish ring remained there for many years. Dish crosses were sometimes fitted with spirit lamps which helped to keep the food hot.

SILVER FURNITURE

Previous to the Restoration, nearly all plate made was for domestic use, but with the accession to the throne of Charles II many fantastic objects such as silver furniture were introduced. All of these silver pieces are symbolic of the waste of money fostered by the Merry Monarch, who sought to emulate the costly furnishings he had known at the French court. The prevailing extravagance is noted as early as 1674 when a silver bed was made for Nell Gwyn. Although the bed was the work of a foreigner, John Cooqus, it started a vogue among English smiths. A true picture of the lavish splendor of the period is best recorded by the Duchess of Portsmouth, in 1683, on her return from a visit to the apartment of the king's mistress—"great vases of wrought plate, tables, stands, chimney furniture, sconces, branches, braseras, etc.; all of massive silver and out of number."

However, previous references to silver furniture are noted as early as 1508, when a silver weaving stool appeared in the list of Princess Mary's trousseau and again in 1520 at which time Henry VIII possessed a silver mounting block.

In the Royal collection at Windsor Castle, the remains of three magnificent sets of silver furniture are found. Two of them were presents to Charles II and William III from the city of London, and from descriptions, one table alone weighed over eight thousand ounces. In this furniture, as well as in similarly made pieces, only a minimum of wood and iron were used in the construction. Among the numerous other pieces which reflected the wild orgy of spending, are silver mirrors, andirons, and candlestick stands. Mention must also be made of the existence of silver clocks which are known since the latter half of the sixteenth century. Huge silver vases, specimens of which are very, very rare, were made in these times. As a rule they consisted of a garniture of three pieces which included a vase flanked by two enormous flasks.

There is little likelihood that any of the silver mounted furniture will ever come into the market as most of it is preserved at Windsor Castle, Knole House, Seven Oakes, and Ham House.

BUTTER DISHES

Made in great number chiefly in Ireland butter dishes typified the Celtic love of figures and pastoral scenes. They were usually in the shape of a deep oval box, about seven inches long with a high cover surmounted by the figure of a cow which formed the handle. Butter dishes and dish rings show a decided resemblance in treatment, although the former are by no means as fine.

TABLE BELLS

Silver bells were introduced about the time of Queen Anne, and later accompanied inkstands as the center ornament. They are rarities.

SERVING PIECES

Grape shears and asparagus tongs were introduced during the reign of George II. The former were generally made with a wealth of ornamentation while the latter were, as a rule, very simple in design. Cheese scoops were not made in profusion until the late Georgian periods although a few examples of earlier date have survived. They were often combined with ivory and agate handles and are attractive as well as useful.

XIV

THE ENGLISH PROVINCES

SILVERSMITHING IN YORK

YORK was by far the most important provincial city in England in the Middle Ages and was the first town to receive a touch mark by the Act of 1423. However, it was not until twelve years later that statutory recognition was given to it, according to the ordinance of its Mayor. The law provided that no goldsmith anywhere in England should make silver of lower alloy than sterling, nor offer any article for sale without first impressing it with his own mark. In the following years of the fifteenth century, many references to York goldsmiths are found in wills and inventories. In 1560 it was ordained that all work should be "towched with the pownce of the citie, called the halfe leopard head and halfe flowre-de-luyce," that no silver should be worked of "worse alaye than sterlyng" and anyone working gold or silver below these standards should forfeit double the value of the article.

At the time that the city mark and maker's mark were compulsory, a date letter was introduced, so that all York plate made from about 1560 to 1698 should bear three hallmarks. Upon the reestablishment of the York Assay Office in 1700, the town mark was changed and the arms of the city, a cross charged with five lions passant, were thenceforward used in addition. Pursuant to the terms of the Act of 1700, the lion's head was erased, and the figure of Britannia was struck, thereby increasing the number of compulsory marks to five. It was also decreed at this time that the maker's mark should be formed from the first two letters of the surname, as in the case of London. In 1717 the assaying of plate at York was discontinued, as the two principal goldsmiths of the town entered into an agreement with the Newcastle Goldsmiths Company to have plate assayed there upon payment of an annual fee. For this reason no York-marked plate is known between the years of 1714 and 1779. Many variations occur in date letters as shown in the table of marks. In 1858 the office was finally closed and it is likely that it will never be reopened.

SILVERSMITHING IN NORWICH

It is probable that Norwich plate approaches more closely the date of York work than that found in other provinces. The work of the sixteenth century goldsmiths of Norwich is entitled to the highest rank in all of the English provinces, and many of their Elizabethan pieces are fully equal to those produced in London at that time.

Norwich records show a great many goldsmiths working from the end of the thirteenth century and with few intervals names of prominent makers are known down to the end of the seventeenth century. Norwich was one of the seven cities appointed in 1423 to have a "touch." The town mark consisted of a castle and lion and was practically unchanged from 1565 to 1575. No plate was officially marked before 1565, but from that date on, the compulsory assaying and marking with the arms of the city took effect. Although no mention is made of a date letter, it seems clear from the earliest examples that this practice was also begun in 1565, but no date letter mark between the years 1585 and 1624 has appeared, and in all probability, none was used.

The use of the date letter was again resumed in 1624 but discontinued between 1643 and 1688. Finally in this last year, an effort was made to institute a regular system of hallmarking and, with but few variations, marks show a consistency not previously found. The Act of 1697 prevented the Norwich goldsmiths from continuing to work under the old regime, and it appears that only a few survived to take advantage of the legislation in 1701 which permitted them to reestablish an assay office.

Peter Peterson was the one outstanding Norwich silversmith but towards the end of the seventeenth century the craft of Norwich goldsmiths dwindled and disappeared.

SILVERSMITHING IN EXETER

Judging from the examples of plate which have survived to the present time, the goldsmiths of Exeter were probably next to those of Norwich in order of antiquity. But apparently Exeter did not have an official "touch." No assay office was established until 1701, and consequently no records are available prior to this time. Exeter was too far removed from London, it was not convenient for its goldsmiths to send their plate there to have it assayed, and therefore, we may infer that the goldsmiths of Exeter worked under the privileges of a royal charter, although its existence has never been discovered.

During the sixteenth and seventeenth centuries the Exeter town mark was the Roman letter "X." In some early Elizabethan pieces, the mark varied from that of an "x" with a crown over the letter and a pellet on either side, to an "x" in a circular stamp without surrounding dots. In 1701 the Exeter town mark officially used was composed of the arms of the city which consisted of a triple towered castle.

Although only an inference can be drawn due to the lack of records, it seems most probable that the small letters found on early pieces of about the year 1600, were date letters. With the passing of the Act of 1700, date letters were uniformly incorporated into the marking of silver, and thenceforward were changed annually. Their use continued until 1883, at which time the office was closed.

In the absence of records it is impossible to say what plan was used in testing and assaying Exeter plate prior to 1701. However, as it is likely that masters and wardens were used, each was probably entrusted with the punch for striking the town mark. In those instances where a mark occurs which is neither the town mark nor the maker's mark, it may be safely assumed that it was struck by the master or the warden.

SILVERSMITHING IN NEWCASTLE

The earliest known reference to a Newcastle goldsmith occurs in an ordinance of 1248, wherein two goldsmiths were appointed to be in complete charge of assaying the money coined. In 1423, Newcastle was given a touch mark of its own. No further reference to these smiths appears until 1536 when they were incorporated in a common company with freemen of many other trades. Although no Newcastle plate of earlier date than the middle of the seventeenth century has survived, it is known that the art of the goldsmith flourished during the sixteenth century, and in all probability those pieces made were melted down in the troublous times of Charles I.

The Act of William III, which conferred on the Goldsmiths Company of England the sole rights of assaying, reflected great hardship and inconvenience on the goldsmiths of Newcastle, who were put to great expense, risk and delay in sending their plate to London. This hardship was remedied in 1700, when assay offices were established at Exeter, York, Chester, Norwich and Bristol, but Newcastle was not one of the places where mints had been established to recoin money and it was not included. However, there is little doubt that although it was illegal, much plate was made during this time. After many petitions and entreaties set forth by the goldsmiths of Newcastle, royal assent to reestablish the assay office of Newcastle was granted in 1702. This same act provided that all smiths who were freemen of Newcastle should be incorporated and known as the Company of Goldsmiths of Newcastle-upon-Tyne. At this time it was compulsory for all plate of the required standard to be struck with the maker's mark, which consisted of the first two letters of his surname, the lion's head erased, the Britannia mark, the town mark, and a variable date letter.

Although the goldsmiths of Newcastle had been constituted as an independent corporation, they continued in association with other tradesmen until 1716. In 1844 the Goldsmiths Company of London endeavored to obtain jurisdiction over all the provincial offices, claiming that great illegalities existed in these places with regard to the correct assaying of plate. Through dint of pressure brought to bear by the London Company, silversmithing at Newcastle finally simmered to nothing, and in 1884 it was finally resolved to discontinue the assay office there.

The town mark of Newcastle, which was probably derived from the original arms of the borough, consisted of a single castle, and was used until about the middle of the seventeenth century. In 1670 the mark was changed and the entire coat of arms of Newcastle, which consisted of three castles in a plain heraldic shield, was struck. About ten years later the shape of thc shield was altered and it assumed a more elaborate form. However, the only distinguishing mark is the often repeated use there of the lion passant, "to sinister."

SILVERSMITHING IN CHESTER

The silversmiths of Chester are really entitled to a preference over those of the other provincial guilds, as they are the only ones who still maintain an assay office today. It is fully alive and in constant competition with those of the other large cities in England. It is known that the goldsmiths and money coiners of Chester are recorded as early as 925, which gives them further distinction. From the twelfth to the fifteenth century there is occasional mention of prominent goldsmiths in Chester, but it is not until 1540 that any amount of data is available. From this time on Chester goldsmiths are recorded in a fairly continuous line down to the present day.

Chester was not appointed along with the other provinces in 1423 to have a touch, the reason for it being, that the smiths already had this privilege and had been enjoying it for almost 200 years. Coins were minted in this city as early as the time of Athelestan. Prior to 1573 a maker's mark was not struck, nor was the mark of the assayer used. From this time on, however, all goldsmiths were re-

BOWL Fuller White, London, 1765

BOWL (Pair) W. Fountain, London, 1802

Courtesy S. Wyler, Inc.

TOBACCO BOX Henry Cowper, London, 1792

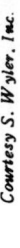

PAIR OF MUGS Henry Cowper, London, 1774 *Courtesy S. Wyler, Inc.*

Sheffield Plate Bowl c. 1800 *Courtesy Black, Starr & Frost-Gorham, Inc.*

One of Pair of Sheffield Soup Tureens *Courtesy Black, Starr & Frost-Gorham, Inc.* T. & J. Creswick, c. 1800

TRAY WITH ARMS OF LORD MACKENZIE — Jno. Crouch, London, 1810

Cruet J. Delmester, London, 1758

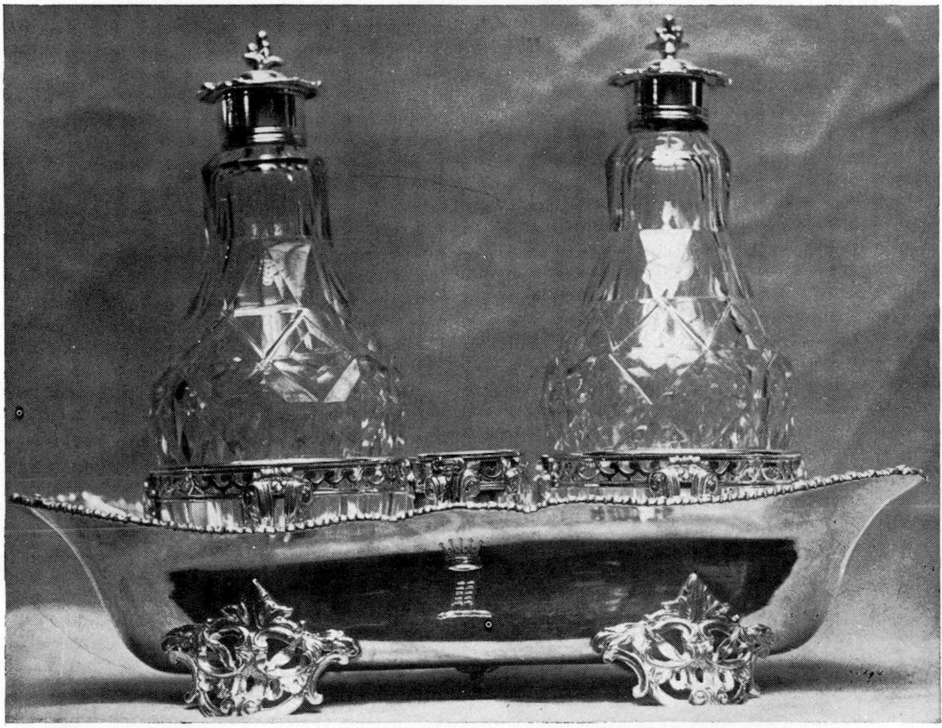

Cruet Andrew Fogelberg, London, 1772

EA SERVICE — Peter de Riemer, New York, 1769 — *Courtesy Robert Ensko, Inc.*

EA SERVICE — Daniel Van Voorhis, New York, 1779 — *Courtesy Robert Ensko, Inc.*

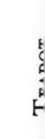

Courtesy James Graham, Jr.

Pitcher — Robert Evans, Boston, 1770

Courtesy Metropolitan Museum of Art

Teapot — John Coney, Boston

Courtesy S. Wyler, Inc.

Teapot — John Jackson, New York, 1736

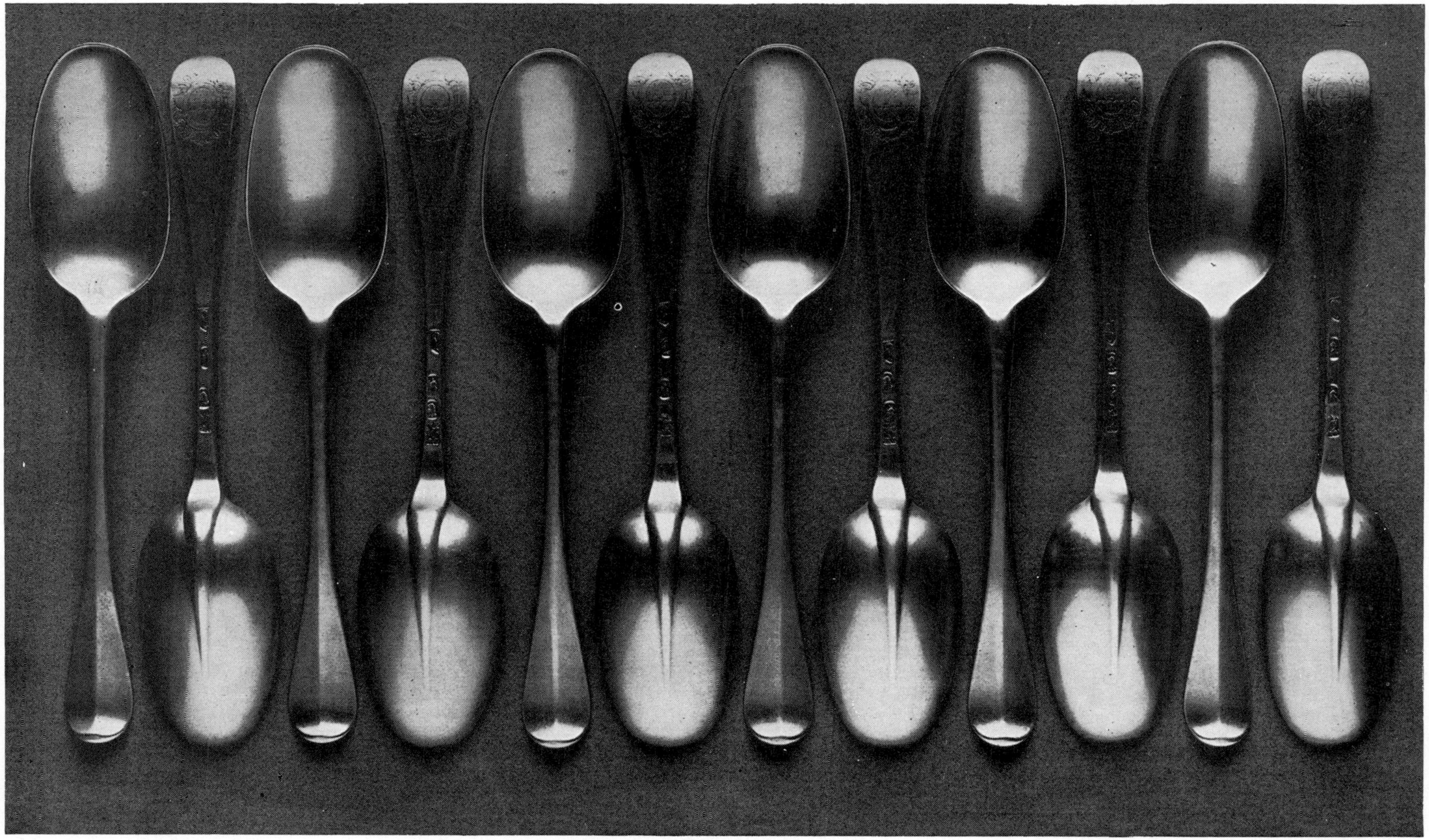

Rattail Spoons — John Ladyman, London, 1715 — *Courtesy Tiffany & Co.*

Soup Tureen — Wm. Fountain, London, 180

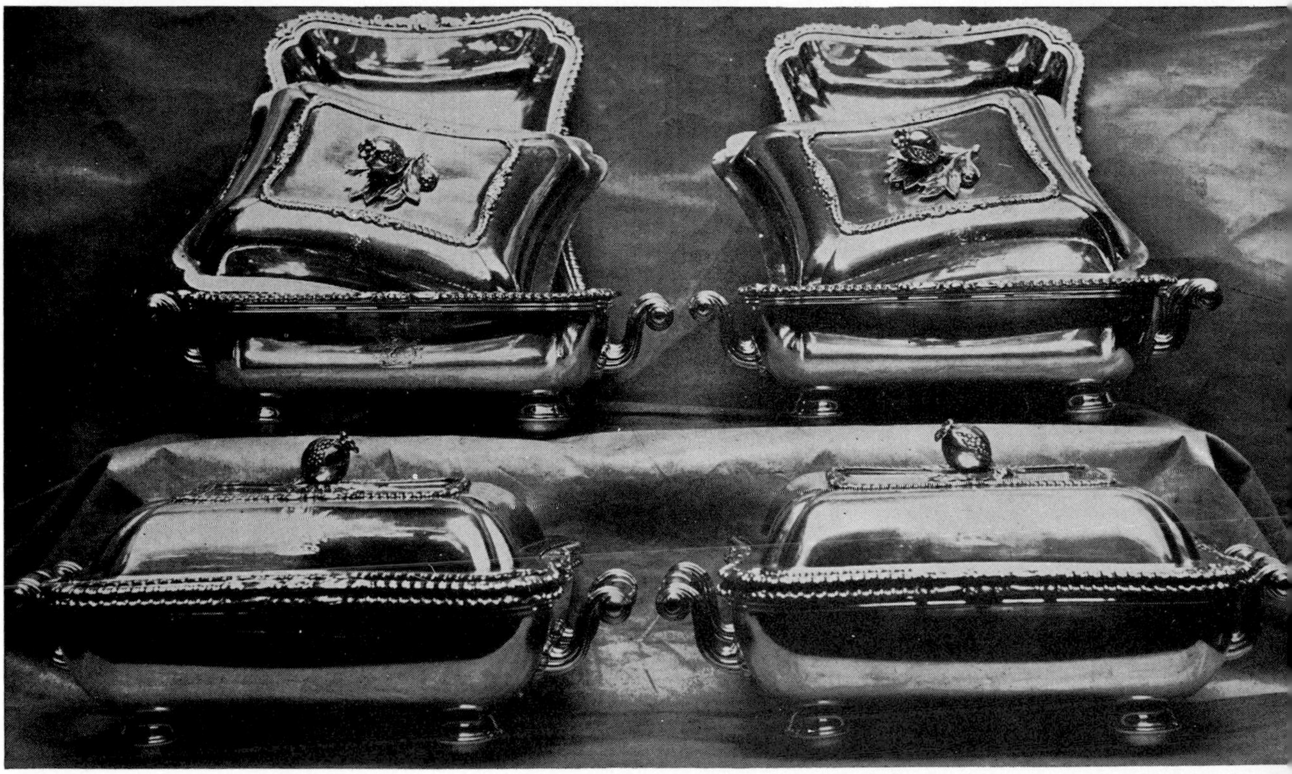

Entree Dishes — Wm. Bateman, London, 181

Candelabra W. Pitts, London, 1808

Chamber Candlesticks — Matthew Boulton

Top: Nathaniel Smith & Co., Sheffield, 1799-1801
Bottom: J. Parsons, Sheffield, 1783

Boulton and Fothergill — Birmingham, 1773

OLD SHEFFIELD TEA TRAY — Circa, 1810

SHEFFIELD INKSTAND — *Courtesy S. Wyler, Inc.* — Watson and Bradbury, London, 1812

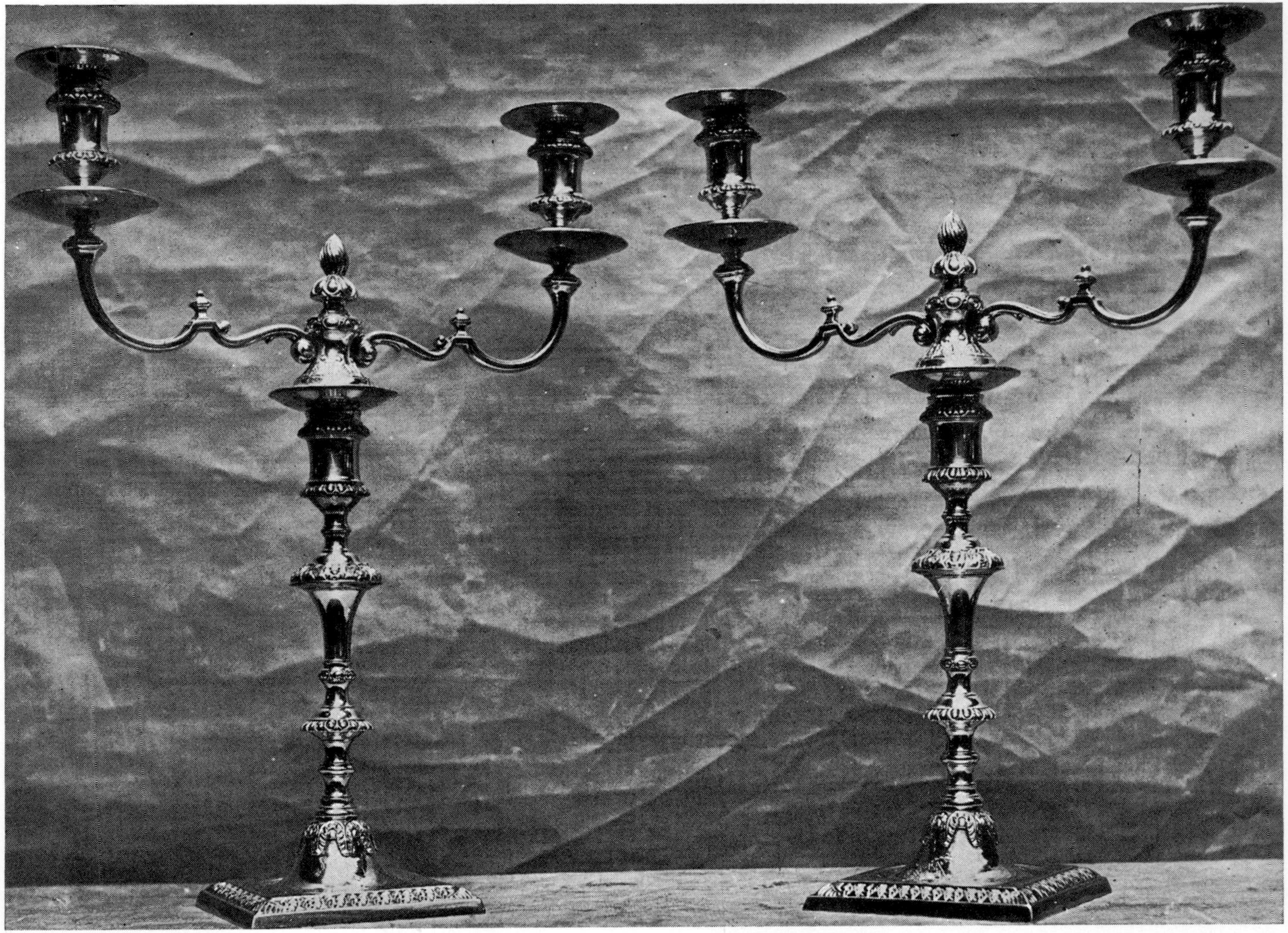

CANDELABRA E. Capper, London, 1767

Covered Cup   Sam. James, Newcastle, 1759   *Courtesy J. E. Caldwell & Co.*

Newcastle, 1800

Cup   Shrewsbury, 1560

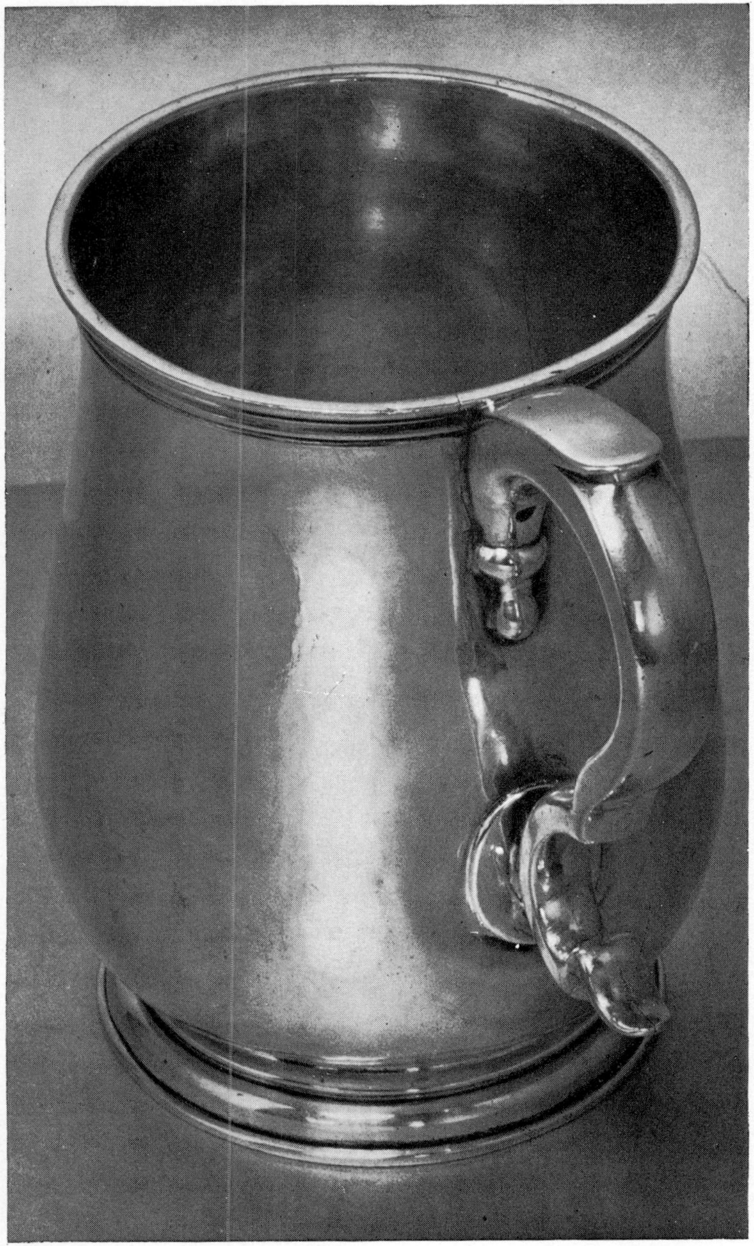

Courtesy Robert Ensko, Inc.

Courtesy Robert Ensko, Inc.

quired to punch their wares and guarantee them to be of the required standard.

In 1685 the city of Chester was granted a charter by James II, and although a diligent search has been made, no evidence has been found to indicate that a town mark or date letter was used before this time. Although much plate disappeared from Chester during the reign of Charles I, it must not be imagined that none remains. It is far more probable that much of it is in private collections today and, unfortunately, cannot be accurately identified, as only a maker's mark was used. The operation of the charter granted by James II was suspended by the Act of 1695. However, in 1701, Chester, being one of the principal cities where mints had been erected, was reestablished as an assay office. Until the present time it has continued to flourish, the work executed there in recent years being greatly in excess of that done in past history.

The word, "sterling," found quite frequently on pieces of Chester plate, was probably used as the maker's guarantee that the piece was of a legal alloy. Date letters are known as early as 1688, but one date letter was often used for two to three years. When, in 1701, the assay office was reestablished, the marks followed those used in all the other English provincial towns—the lion's head erased and Britannia. In addition a new form of the town mark, composed of three lions of England dimidiating the three garbs of the Earldom of Chester in a plain shield, plus the date letter and the maker's mark was used. In 1779, an entirely new set of punches was instituted and the town mark was changed accurately to represent the arms of the city, as formerly used from 1687 to 1692. At this time, two new stamps were obtained for the leopard's head and lion passant, and these continued in use until 1784 when the King's head was impressed. In 1823 the leopard's head first appears uncrowned and a new set of date letters was inaugurated.

SILVERSMITHING IN BIRMINGHAM

The establishment of an assay office at Birmingham in 1773 was mainly due to the efforts of one of the great silversmiths. Matthew Boulton, who was by far the outstanding Birmingham smith of all time, personally prepared, on behalf of himself and the other goldsmiths, a petition which was submitted to the London Goldsmiths Company. In the petition was stated the extreme difficulties suffered by the plate workers in the exercise of their trade because no assay offices were conveniently located. The result was the granting of a charter to both Birmingham and Sheffield, and both offices are now in existence. The Act of 1773 provided that all plate should bear the town mark of an anchor, a distinct variable date letter to be changed annually, the lion passant, the figure of Britannia for plate of the standard of eleven ounces, ten dwt., and the mark of the maker, which should be the first letters of his Christian and surname. Very small wares, incapable of being fully marked without injury being done to them, were excepted. For this reason, one often finds vinaigrettes and the like, struck with only a maker's mark and the anchor. There is no particular reason why the anchor should have been chosen as the town mark for Birmingham except that a great deal of overseas commerce was transacted there.

SILVERSMITHING IN SHEFFIELD

As previously mentioned, the assay office in Sheffield was established in 1773, when this right was conferred on Birmingham. The silversmiths of Sheffield lost no time after the Act was passed to proceed in business, and production flourished on a great scale. The marks required to be stamped on all wrought silver assayed at Sheffield, are the town mark of a crown, a date letter, the standard mark which is either a lion passant or Britannia, according to the alloy, and the maker's mark.

From 1784 to 1890 the duty mark was added, as on London plate. In the marking of many pieces the date letter and town mark were combined in one stamp to save space, but this was discontinued many years ago and never again resumed. From 1815 to 1819 the town mark of the crown was struck upside down and the only reason for this can be to differentiate between similar marks of a few years earlier date. It is curious that Sheffield was one of the few places where gold was never assayed until 1904, though in the other provinces both silver and gold objects were wrought.

SILVERSMITHING IN HULL

The goldsmiths of Hull are mentioned as early as the fifteenth century, but they were never incorporated by statute or charter.

Several examples of the plate have been found in and around Hull, stamped with the letter "h" to indicate the town of manufacture. During the seventeenth century the arms of the borough, "three ducal coronets in pale," were adopted as the town mark. Although there is no evidence of any regular assay office having been established, several attempts were made to introduce a system of marking with date letters. Those examples which have survived, however, clearly indicate that this practice was never continued. Although goldsmiths' names are recorded in the archives of the borough as late as 1774, not more than one example of Hull plate of the Queen Anne period is known. It is most probable that those names listed were of dealers in goldsmiths' work, and not manufacturers.

SILVERSMITHING IN LINCOLN

Practically no information regarding the workings of the goldsmiths in Lincoln has ever been found, outside of the fact that it was one of the seven towns appointed by the Act of 1423 to have a touch. However, records and inventories allude to goldsmiths from the twelfth century onwards, and these references appear down to the year 1708. The arms of the city were used as the distinguishing town mark, and were adopted from the coat of arms of the city which consisted of "argent, on a cross gules, a fleur-de-lys or." Pieces bearing the Lincoln mark are very rare and consist mostly of church plate, or an occasional drinking vessel.

SILVERSMITHING IN SHREWSBURY

Although Shrewsbury was not one of the appointed towns in 1423, goldsmithing is known to have been in practice there during the Middle Ages. The provisions of the Statute of 1300, decreeing that "no manner of vessel or other work of silver should be set to sale without having the mark of a leopard's head upon it," were an aid rather than a hindrance to the Shrewsbury silversmiths because the arms of the town were "azure, three leopards' heads, or." One of these heads would naturally be the mark adopted by the Shrewsbury goldsmiths. Many examples of plate marked solely with an uncrowned leopard's head are wrongly ascribed to London. Some of these pieces are undoubtedly the work of Shrewsbury silversmiths.

SILVERSMITHING IN LEWES

The only information relative to this town is the mark adopted by the goldsmiths in the late fourteenth century. It consisted of "Checky (or and azure) on a conton sinister gules a lion rampant or," and pieces of plate bearing this mark are only rarely found.

SILVERSMITHING IN BARNSTAPLE

The most celebrated of all goldsmiths known to have worked in Barnstaple is Thomas Mathew, examples of whose work have been found in many parishes. Much of the plate wrought by him bears, in addition to his name stamp, the mark of a flower or fruit on a slipped and leaved stalk, which is intended to be a representation of a pomegranate. This device is portrayed in the Tregoney arms and it has been suggested that Mathew used this to denote that he was a native of that place. The town mark of Barnstaple was taken from the borough shield and used until 1624. The shield consisted of a bird in a circular stamp, but in 1625 the mark of a triple-turreted tower was granted to Barnstaple as its arms, and this was used until the end of the seventeenth century.

SILVERSMITHING IN PLYMOUTH

A few pieces of plate impressed with a representation of the arms of the borough of Plymouth are known as early as the beginning of the seventeenth century. The arms are composed of "a saltire between four castles." Certain examples bear the sterling mark indicating the legal standard. A curious form of the Britannia standard mark is known on a lighthouse salt made in 1698, on which the standard is described by the technical term "Britan." This mark suggests, therefore, that the piece was probably made about 1698 immediately after the introduction of the new standard, and it became technically represented by the Britannia mark.

SILVERSMITHING OF BRISTOL

It seems most unusual that no record of any assay office has ever been found in Bristol, nor any allusion to a guild of goldsmiths in a town of such importance. Although mentioned in the Act of 1423 as one of the seven towns appointed to have a touch mark, and again in the Act of 1701 as a place where an assay office could be legally established, no trace of any reference to goldsmithing has appeared. A few pieces of Bristol plate are struck with an oblong punch mark bearing the arms of the city, which consist of a ship issuing from a castle.

SILVERSMITHING IN OTHER PROVINCIAL TOWNS

Examples of the work of medieval goldsmiths are known in many outlying communities. As a general rule only a town mark was impressed and but little data of the history of goldsmiths in these provinces is available.

Dorchester	Salisbury	Coventry	King's Lynn
Sherborne	Colchester	Poole	Taunton
Rochester	Channel Islands	Carlisle	Gateshead
Sandwich	Leicester	Leeds	

CALCUTTA

Gold and silver wares have been wrought in India for centuries, but it was not until the eighteenth century that articles made by workers of British origin are noted. In 1808 the firm of Hamilton and Company was established in Calcutta and numerous fine examples of their work are known. The mark used was that of an elephant.

XV

IRELAND

SILVERSMITHING IN IRELAND

SILVERSMITHING was practically the only art developed to any high degree in Ireland. There were skilled goldsmiths there prior to the date of the Norman Conquest. The Ardagh Chalice found by a peasant while digging near Limerick indicates the high merit of the craftsmanship of this time. Although several other examples of plate have survived to the present time, by far the majority are lost forever to posterity. Ireland then as now was turbulent, constant political upheavals took heavy toll of family silver, and the enthusiastic champions of the various causes cheerfully surrendered their plate in order to finance their parties.

The similarity of basic forms as compared with English silver is always to be noted, but the decorative scheme was for the most part original, rather than copied from the arts of continental Europe. The silversmiths in Ireland were greatly influenced by their environment, and their native whimsicality is reflected in the original designs found in so many pieces of Irish plate. Of particular notice are the pastoral scenes taken from the every-day farm life and its environs so dear to the hearts of the Celtic race. The chasing on pieces of Irish plate is always to be recognized, because the silversmiths apparently did not care to risk the process of flat hammering on the chased articles. Pieces of this particular style are to be found nowhere but in Ireland.

By the middle of the eighteenth century the prevailing rococo styles waned, and the classic influence introduced by the Adam brothers grew in favor. For many years, however, the delicate embossing enclosing escutcheons for crests and coats of arms, was distinctly reminiscent of the earlier elaborate designs.

The craft of the great Irish silversmith was not confined to Dublin. The city of Cork, with its natural silver mines, became a large center for silversmithing, and examples from the seventeenth century are known. Among other provincial towns producing silver in Ireland may be mentioned Limerick, Galway and Youghal. The curious practice of impressing the word, "dollar" on many provincial pieces is noted, thus bearing witness to the custom, prevalent also in America, of melting Spanish dollars for use in the silver craft. Another variation of hallmark often found on pieces of Cork manufacture is the word, "Sterling." In 1710 this mark was often inscribed to indicate that the pieces were equal in quality to that of the English silversmiths. The story of silversmithing in the provinces may be said to end with the year 1848. Very little silver was made from then on, and today practically all Irish plate is Dublin-made.

Irish silver is regarded by collectors throughout the world as most desirable. Because of the loss of so much of the early plate, very few pieces dating from the seventeenth century are encountered, nor are examples prior to the reign of George III plentiful. Many famous silversmiths are known who worked in the leading cities of Ireland, and examples by them fetch tremendous prices today. However, with the steadily decreasing supply of pieces of Celtic origin, it is safe to assume that within a few years all fine specimens will be in private collections or museums.

SILVERSMITHS OF DUBLIN

The earliest known reference to a guild of goldsmiths in Ireland is recorded in the archives of the Dublin Corporation. The guild is mentioned in the reference to the festival of Corpus Christi in 1498, wherein the town goldsmiths were represented. In 1555 the Dublin Goldsmiths presented a petition to the City Corporation stating that the charter which had been previously given to them had been accidentally burned. They wished to enjoy the privileges to which they were entitled, so they applied to the City Assembly for leave to enter a copy of their charter. In 1557 the application was granted.

Throughout the next fifty years, there appears to have been no entry in the records with reference to any marks to be impressed on gold or silver articles. Because of the continued fraudulent practices and abuses, it was resolved in 1605 by the Dublin City Council that henceforth certain marks should be stamped on all wrought plate, which, in quality, had to be equal to the silver standard coin then current. The above legislation, which is the earliest known reference to the marking of Dublin plate, required the use of the figure of a lion, a harp, and a castle, in addition to the goldsmith's own punch. However, not a single example appears to be known bearing these marks, which were supposed to have been used until 1637. At this time the Dublin goldsmiths became dissatisfied with their status under the domination of the City Corporation. They probably felt their inferiority to the London goldsmiths who had full control of all matters pertaining to the assaying and marking of pieces, without interference by civil authorities. A petition to the King was presented, in which they asked to be incorporated by Royal charter. Their petition was favorably received and in 1637 Charles I granted it.

The archives of the Dublin Goldsmiths Company refer to various articles which were brought in to be assayed. These included ewers and basins, caudle cups, sugar boxes, porringers, trencher salts, spoons and candlesticks. The entries of plate continued until 1649 when a break occurs owing to the loss of records and no further entry appears until 1694. Mention must be made of the strict vigilance shown by the Company in the detection of fraudulent pieces. The punishment for these offenses was severe, and Irish goldsmithing was raised to a high plane. Although we know of the use of hallmarks prior to 1637, no example is known bearing them. The charter of 1637 described the use of the crown harp, which was the king's stamp, as well as the standard mark, plus the makers' marks. The first article made under the new law was dated April 6, 1683, and from that time to the present day no article in silver or gold of Dublin make can be legally sold without being so distinguished. The use of the date letter was adopted at this time, in addition to the crown harp and the maker's mark. A fourth mark, the figure of Hibernia was incorporated in 1730 and was used to denote the payment of duty as ordered by the Commissioner of Excise. From 1807 to 1890, a fifth mark, consisting of a representation of the head of the Sovereign was impressed. This superseded the Hibernia stamp, and was applied to all plate wrought in Ireland, as in every other assay office then open in the United Kingdom.

SILVERSMITHS OF CORK

There is good reason to believe that goldsmithing of high merit was practiced in Cork as early as the Middle Ages. Some of the exquisite chalices, patens, and other church pieces are confidently ascribed to this city, although very little is known of the early history, and the records of the guild date no further back than 1656. In 1631, by a charter of Charles II, the Corporation of Cork was granted privileges which included the power to appoint a Clerk of Assay. His duties combined the testing of weights and measures, rather than the assaying of precious metals.

There being no regular assay at Cork, it seems probable that the only test used was that of the touchstone, except when an assay by cupel was required, which necessitated sending the plate to Dublin.

Cork was situated in a direct line with the Spanish peninsula and the west of France. This afforded increased advantages of intercourse with these countries, whence the city received not only its supply of silver, but innumerable emigrant craftsmen who brought with them knowledge of designs applied by European smiths. This accounts for the frequent examples known which resembled the contemporary styles that prevailed on the continent.

The earliest known example of the Cork town mark consists of a ship duplicated, or a ship between two castles; adopted from the arms of the city. There were many variations of this mark and it would appear that each goldsmith adopted his own peculiar town-mark stamp. Early in the eighteenth century the use of this mark was discontinued, and between 1710 and 1719 the word "STERLING" was introduced as a mark for Cork plate. This mark is also found in various forms including abbreviations to STER and STERG. The spelling also varied and specimens are known with impressions as follows: STARLING, STIRLING, STARLIN, and STERLIN. As previously mentioned, indication of the plate having been wrought from Spanish dollars is found in the use of the word, "dollar," just as the sterling stamp indicated the fineness of eleven ounces, two dwt.

Makers' marks in Cork, used in the seventeenth and early part of the eighteenth century, were generally composed of the initials of the maker combined with a heraldic device. These combinations disappeared shortly after 1731 when the Dublin Goldsmiths Company prohibited the use of such ornaments. Here may be seen the complete power of the Dublin Goldsmiths Company to regulate the production of plate throughout all of Ireland. No date letter was ever used on pieces of Cork plate, except those assayed at Dublin, and it is difficult to ascertain the exact year in which a piece was produced. However, a study of the makers' marks plus the style in vogue at the time, helps to approximate the date within a score of years.

SILVERSMITHS OF YOUGHAL

By virtue of a charter granted in 1608 by James I, the Corporation of Youghal was empowered to arrange the various craftsmen into appropriate guilds. But probably never more than a dozen goldsmiths were working in the town at any one time. The mark of a small single masted sail boat by common adoption of the goldsmiths is approximated at about 1620. The boat was commonly known as a yawl, but heraldically speaking, as a lymphad. Several names of prominent goldsmiths have been gleaned from the records and the few marks are reproduced.

SILVERSMITHS OF GALWAY

The goldsmiths of Galway adopted the mark of an anchor, generally found in a shaped cartouche. Only rarely is the name of a Galway silversmith apparent as no plate earlier than 1648 or later than 1730 is known. In the George III era, the names of nine goldsmiths are recorded in the books of the Dublin Goldsmiths Company as required by the Act of 1783.

SILVERSMITHS OF LIMERICK

As in the case of the silversmiths of Galway, many Limerick craftsmen are registered with the Company of Goldsmiths in Dublin. The Limerick marks closely resemble those used in Cork, being a triple towered castle plus the maker's initials. For many years these marks remained unidentified, until the discovery of an old Limerick toll-stamp, bearing a castle of similar form.

The word, Sterling, is often found on pieces made in and around Limerick, and these are frequently confused with plate produced in Cork. No records of the existence of a goldsmiths' guild are known in Limerick, but it may be assumed that associations were formed for protective purposes.

SILVERSMITHS OF OTHER PROVINCIAL TOWNS

Pieces have appeared which indicate clearly the production of plate in many smaller communities throughout Ireland. It is commonly supposed that the mark of a hand erect was the town mark for Belfast. Names of goldsmiths are recorded in Dublin which give sufficient evidence that some plate was wrought there.

References to the existence of guilds which included goldsmiths and silversmiths are known in the records of the towns of Kinsale, Derry, Kilkenny, Tipperary, Newry, and Drogheda. Unfortunately no ascribed marks identifying these towns or their goldsmiths are known.

XVI

SCOTLAND

SILVERSMITHING IN SCOTLAND

THE characteristic traits of a people are often reflected in the quality of their art, and so it is with the history of the early Scotch silversmiths. The austerity and simple tastes of the Scotchman are brought to notice by the work of the earliest craftsmen. The majority of silver articles made were definitely for practical use, rather than for purposes of decoration. Most of the early Scotch silver was used in churches, or else in the gentle art of drinking.

Perhaps the most definitely Scotch of all articles made of silver was the quaich, which was originally a small two-handled bowl, made of wood with silver stripings and used for drinking brandy. However, a few of the more affluent Scotchmen had these quaiches especially made to order in solid silver. Only a limited quantity of these are available, hence they have come to be recognized as the most valuable pieces of Scotch silver to be had. Among the other articles definitely attributed to these silversmiths were mulls which were made of large or small horns mounted in silver and used as snuff boxes. Tankards, caudle cups, flagons, jugs, and mazer bowls are all found among the earliest examples, and to a Scotch silversmith named Monteith, we are indebted for the introduction of what is now called a monteith bowl.

Unfortunately, there is very little early Scotch silver available to the collector today, as even the wealthy lairds and chieftains did not indulge in lavish appointments for the home. Also, due to the fact that much plate was melted during the seventeenth century to foster political causes, but little remains today. Since the early smiths could not find sufficient work in any one town, they led a nomadic existence, making small pieces here and there to order. The careful attitude towards spending money, so often characteristic of the Scotch as a people, had its effect on silversmithing. Complete tea services are practically non-existent because families would add but one piece at a time every few years to their sets. Consequently, to find a Scotch tea service of similar date and maker is almost an impossibility. It is interesting to note that in the earliest days of silversmithing in Scotland, it was the general custom for the client to bring his own silver or gold to the craftsman to be wrought at his order. It appears that dishonest workmen diluted and adulterated the metal, and outrageously cheated the customers. Because of this the amount of alloy permissible was regulated by law. Perhaps in no country was stricter adherence to the legislation of the silver craft demanded, and for this reason nearly all Scotch silver found today is of legal standard. The same laws conceived as early as 1483, regulating the quality of the metal, are still in use today.

From the standpoint of the collector or dealer, the original marks used by deacons in Scotland have been invaluable in determining the approximate dates of the earliest pieces, as date letters were not inaugurated until a much later time. Frequently in the provincial towns as well as Edinburgh and Glasgow, just the name of the city was impressed and therefore dates can only be surmised.

Scotch silver presents a field of high endeavor to the collector, not only because of the rarity of pieces, but also because there is a ready market at all times for good specimens regardless of price.

SILVERSMITHING IN EDINBURGH

Previous to the year 1483, silversmiths in Edinburgh were associated with other hammer-wielding trades under the general description of "Hammermen." At this time they presented a petition to the town council asking for certain privileges which would give them more freedom in the furthering of their craft. Before fifty years had elapsed from the time of this grant, they became an independent corporation, as recorded in the records of the oldest minute book, dated 1525.

A statute of the year 1485 decreed a Deacon and searcher were to be appointed to regulate the marking of all pieces of plate. In 1555, a further act of Parliament ordained that each goldsmith was to use his own mark, and that every piece must bear, in addition to this, a deacon's mark and a town mark. It is important to note that the introduction of the deacon's mark was instituted in order to regulate quality of the wrought metal. In 1586 the "Craft," which included the deacon and the masters of the goldsmiths, was empowered to seize any pieces deficient in the required fineness. Finally, in 1687, the first charter was granted to the silversmiths of Edinburgh, and all privileges previously enjoyed were confirmed in addition to more extensive powers.

With the issuance of this charter, notice was given to the smiths of other Scottish towns directing their attention to the necessity of maintaining their gold and silver work up to the required standard.

At the time of the adoption of the Britannia standard in England, all wrought plate was raised to a fineness of eleven ounces, ten dwt., but this was never operative in Scotland. However, with the union of the English and Scotch Parliaments, the Scotch standard for plate was raised in 1720 to conform with that of the English. This same act imposed a duty of sixpence per ounce on all plate manufactured in, or imported into Great Britain. In 1757 the duty on plate was repealed and in its place a license tax was levied which required every person dealing in gold and silver wares to pay a sum each year for the privilege of trading. The former duty was reimposed in 1784 and twenty-three years later the duty on plate was increased from sixpence to one shilling.

It is probable that no marks were used in Scotland before 1457 when the statute of that year provided for the use of a deacon's mark. These requirements with respect to the marking of plate have enabled us to approximate quite clearly the date of their manufacture. A further aid in identifying silver was the adoption of the town mark which was taken from the arms of the burgh which are "Argent, on a rock proper, a castle, triple towered and embattled, sable." In 1681 a variable annual date letter was adopted mainly for the reason that any manufacturer of plate in fraudulent practice might more easily be detected. From 1681 on it is possible to determine the exact year of any marked piece of Edinburgh plate. With the adoption of the date letter the Edinburgh goldsmiths abolished the deacon's mark and in its place substituted the mark of the assay master, which originally consisted of the initials of the assayer. A further alteration in the marking of plate was instituted in 1759 when the use of the assay master's initials was discontinued, and in their place the mark of a thistle was substituted. With the reimposition of the duty on plate in 1784, a fifth mark which consisted of the sovereign's head was struck on all plate to indicate the payment of the duty. As found in England, this mark continued in use until 1890, when all duties on plate were repealed.

SILVERSMITHING IN GLASGOW

The city of Glasgow, although not always as it is now, the largest and most densely populated town in all Scotland, may well lay claim to the premier place among Scottish provinces in importance as the center of the goldsmiths' craft. As found in Edinburgh the goldsmiths were originally incorporated in a large group under the designation of "Hammermen." But the earliest minute books have been mislaid, and little information is available regarding the progress of the guild. However, no Glasgow plate of earlier date than 1681 is known. At this time a date letter was adopted, but its use was discontinued about 1710, and not found again until 1819. For this reason it is necessary to approximate all pieces made during the interval. Between the years 1730 and 1800, a curious punch which consisted of the letter "s" in various shapes, was generally used. Although no definite explanation of this mark has ever been ascertained, it is probable that it was meant to indicate the word "sterling," to guarantee the piece to be of the accepted standard.

The Glasgow town mark adopted from the arms of the burgh is commonly known as the "fish, tree and bell." The actual heraldic description of it being "Argent, on a mount in base an oak tree proper, the trunk surmounted by a salmon proper with a signet ring in its mouth, or, on the top of the tree a red breast, and on the sinister fesse-point a hand-bell both proper."

There appears to be no evidence of the existence of a regular assay office at Glasgow before 1819, proof of which is derived from the variety in the form of the town mark used by the different makers at the same time. The 1819 statute incorporated the Glasgow Goldsmiths Company, empowered it and placed it under similar regulations to those ascribed to Edinburgh.

SILVERSMITHING IN ABERDEEN

It appears that in early times Aberdeen was divided into two distinct towns, known as Old Aberdeen and New Aberdeen. Each maintained its own distinct guilds and trade privileges, the only similarity being the incorporation of the smiths again under the common title of "Hammermen." In neither burgh was the town mark taken from the arms of the city but it was composed of the first two letters; AB or the first two and fifth letters; ABD. It has been suggested that this curious departure in the adoption of a town mark was taken mainly because the arms of the burgh resembled those of Dundee so much.

New Aberdeen, as it was called, until the extension of its boundaries into the adjoining burgh, records at least two goldsmiths as early as the fifteenth century. We have seen that the town mark was varied from AB to ABD and occasionally the Roman capital A was found struck three times instead. Early in the eighteenth century a new stamp composed of three castles in a shaped shell was used by one silversmith who was, in turn, followed by many others in this respect.

SILVERSMITHING IN DUNDEE

A reference in the year 1550 mentioning one David Stevenson as a goldsmith gives credence to the thought that plate was produced as early as this time. The arms of the town were adopted as the mark and consisted of "azure a pot of growing lillies argent." Further variations were adopted by smiths in the seventeenth and eighteenth centuries and in some instances the word Dundee was impressed as well as a thistle mark.

SILVERSMITHING IN ELGIN

The town mark of this burgh was contracted into ELG or ELN, and is sometimes spelled out. A variation is found on some of the earlier pieces which consisted of the representation of a mother and child in an upright, oblong cartouche. Here, again, a supposed town mark is sometimes noted, as well as a thistle as seen on Dundee plate. There does not seem to have been any incorporation of goldsmiths at Elgin, and the earliest record of any smith is 1701.

SILVERSMITHING IN OTHER PROVINCIAL TOWNS

Throughout Scotland many of the smaller provinces are recognized as having produced plate. These include Arbroath, Banff, Greenock, Inverness, Montrose, Perth, St. Andrews, Stirling, Wick and Tain.

XVII

SHEFFIELD PLATE

THE history of the trade known as Sheffield Plating reads like fiction, for its discovery was purely accidental, and its rise as an industry phenomenal.

In the 18th century silver, as an essential part of the well appointed home, was recognized in England as well as abroad, and workmen were busily engaged in creating new ideas. But the price of silver was still too prohibitive to permit any but the noble and wealthy to indulge themselves. It was the discovery of Sheffield Plate that enabled people of moderate means to own exact replicas of the solid silver domestic articles at a fraction of their cost.

The discovery of plating was an accident, but one of sufficient importance to revolutionize the trade life of a city. In time it became a leading industry in England, and the growth of the city of Sheffield from a London suburb, so to speak, to a great manufacturing center, is attributed to it.

It is unfortunate that so little data on the subject of combining metals is available, for there is evidence to show that many centuries earlier, the Jews and Egyptians worked along these lines with a fair amount of success. The Romans as well keenly appreciated the beautiful gold and silver objects which were produced, but so few have survived, that their methods of plating and gilding are practically unknown. There is no doubt though, that none of the early processes resembled plating as discovered and perfected in England.

In 1742, in the garret of a small building known as Tudor House, a mechanic, one Thomas Boulsover, was repairing the blade of a broken knife. He accidentally fused silver and copper during this operation, and discovered that when these two metals were heated to a certain degree they became inseparable. He immediately realized that this strange occurrence might be turned to good purpose, and upon further experimentation found he was able to manufacture small bits such as buttons, boxes and buckles. These are the earliest known specimens of Sheffield Plate.

However, Thomas Boulsover can hardly be called the father of Sheffield Plate, for although he discovered the process and produced a few pieces, he was soon forced to abandon it. The man he employed to travel on the road to introduce his new product, cheated him outrageously, and before long he was left without sufficient funds to continue.

But during the first few months of Boulsover's experimenting, he apprenticed a young man named Josiah Hancock. This young employee was a lad of great vision, and soon realized that the new industry might grow to huge proportions if properly managed. After diligent work he began to progress rapidly, and within a few years Sheffield Plating became a recognized industry largely because of his efforts. New pieces were created, faithful reproductions of sterling pieces were made and there was an increased demand for them, especially because excessive government taxation had forced the price of wrought silver articles to higher levels. The goldsmiths tried to combat the new industry by burdens of taxation and bothersome regulation but it prospered.

Although the city of Sheffield fostered the production of nearly all the Plate made in England for many years, very few pieces can be found in homes or collections there today. Most of the articles made were marketed in the larger cities and in foreign countries.

The first pieces of Sheffield Plate produced were probably purchased by royalty and families of wealth, as evidenced by the number of old pieces found today bearing original crests and coats of arms. It is for this reason that pieces have survived until today in such fine condition, for it was necessary to plate the articles made with an increasing amount of silver, in order that they might not be ruined by the inscriptions and arms being engraved upon them. The better quality pieces were invariably made with a circular, oval or shaped inset of pure silver, designed expressly for the purpose of cresting. As the industry grew and pieces could be produced for lower prices, the so-called middle class families quickly purchased articles for domestic use and the industry enlarged rapidly.

Plate was produced in foreign countries as well, but the English craftsmen so far excelled their neighbors in workmanship and originality, that they received more than 90% of the business. Ireland was one of the largest consumers of Sheffield Plate and today many outstanding collections are to be found in Dublin and other important cities, though there is no evidence of Irish plating.

During the first twenty years of Sheffield Plating, many beautiful articles were produced, which in design and workmanship often equalled the originals in solid silver. The first manufacturers of Plate quickly sensing the opportunities for deception, impressed hallmarks similar to those on silver articles. Examples showing these are extremely rare. The silver manufacturers immediately protested to the Guild, and the hallmarking of Sheffield Plate was forbidden. But in 1773 Sheffield was granted its own assay office and in 1784 smiths were allowed the privilege of using a maker's mark of their own, providing it had been approved by the Guild.

The history of Sheffield Plating may be divided into two periods. During the years from 1750 to 1780, pieces were made of entirely different style from those which followed in the later period. It is not rare to find many embossed objects, for the original manufacturers knew that with a wealth of design and ornamentation they could easily conceal those defects which so often appeared on the earliest pieces of Plate. This was due solely to their inability to turn out a perfect product, for the corresponding pieces produced in solid silver of that period, were of a much simpler style. But as the years progressed, the ability of the platers reached a higher degree, and for ten years or so delicately pierced objects were made. These, while not so graceful as the contemporary pieces in solid silver, met with much favor. During the first period which might be called probationary, Dish Rings, Baskets, Cups and Covers, Water Jugs, Epergnes, Cream Pails, etc., were produced. And it is easy to recognize pieces from this period by their lack of applied borders, and silver rims. It is practically impossible to find pieces from the first period in fine condition, for the process of plating whereby the silver would not wear through to the copper, had not yet been perfected.

From 1780 until 1820 the finest Sheffield Plate was produced in large quantities. By this time, the majority of leading cutlers in Sheffield had begun to manufacture Plate, and the industry was at its height. With the advent of the Adam Brothers in England, the demand for pieces of extreme simplicity was so pronounced it influenced the designs of Sheffield Plate objects. Many important pieces such as Tea Services, Cruets, Candelabra, Trays and various other household appointments were manufactured in quantity for the first time. As the years passed, the influence of the master silversmiths in vogue in England at the time caused the designs and shapes of Sheffield Plate objects to follow in the footsteps of their creations.

During this, the second period, we find the introduction of a white metal known as German silver, first used as a base. This new process was much favored, as the lasting qualities of Sheffield Plate objects were doubled. This new base would not show through when the silver was worn off, as did the copper. However, German silver was not fully accepted until about 1835. It derived its name from a Mr. Guitike of Berlin, who came over to Sheffield with the first examples of this new compound of nickel, copper, and zinc. The metal itself is of Chinese origin, and was used for centuries in the East before its introduction into England from Germany. The first English smith to avail himself of the new base product was Samuel Roberts. In 1830 he applied for a patent to plate silver on a German silver base.

The process of Sheffield Plating was definitely terminated in 1838, in which year electroplating was discovered by Elkington. Actually, the term Sheffield Plate was the name applied to articles made of copper and coated with silver by fusion. It is not to be confused with the modern silver plate as produced today by means of electrolysis.

Sheffield Plate from the collector's viewpoint, presents an admirable field of endeavor, for as yet prices have not risen to the heights commanded by solid silver articles. However, when one considers the limited supply available and the short period in which it was produced, it seems probable that as time goes on, prices will reach those paid for solid silver articles of similar date. In the past five years, the values of Old Sheffield Plate have doubled, and the farseeing buyer of today will guard carefully those pieces he is fortunate to possess today.

The buyer of Sheffield Plate must be a careful and critical purchaser, as the markets are flooded with semi-old and reproduction pieces that are represented to be genuine. Many brand new pieces are being made now with silver edges and tinned backs that at first seem to be Sheffield Plate. But the connoisseur may detect the fraud mainly by the color of the silver, as the old pieces have a bluish tinge caused by the use of alloy, while pieces that have been electroplated are much whiter. Old Sheffield Plate like old silver should be purchased only from reliable dealers, for even connoisseurs are often misled. Many pieces have worn through over a period of years, and have been replated in order to increase their salability. These pieces should be definitely avoided, as any repairing or replating done to an old piece destroys its value as an original.

XVIII

SILVERSMITHING IN AMERICA

IN direct contrast to silversmithing in England and Europe, the trade in America at the beginning was far from profitable. The early New Englanders were hardy people facing arduous tasks in their struggle for existence and they had little use for the luxury of ornamental silver. At no time was any attempt made to imitate the magnificent baronial silver of England and only pieces for particular use were produced. However, the market was considerably bolstered by the needs of the churches. The Pilgrims of course, were very religious and took great pride in their houses of worship so that much of the early American fine plate was for church use.

It was natural that the first pieces should be reproductions of English pieces which the Colonists had brought with them and from this start a natural evolution took place along the lines of the development of the character of the people.

The simplicity and austerity of their lives caused them to prefer in all things purity of form and a fine sense of proportion to elaboration and bulk. This is true of colonial architecture and furniture as well as of silver.

Much of this early American silver was made in New England but New York and Philadelphia were other important centers of silversmithing. Paralleling the English influence on New England silver, New York silver clearly bore a Dutch influence. Whatever there was of Southern silver perished during the Civil War.

In New England, Newburyport harbored some silversmiths but the city of Boston was the real center for the trade in America. It had the advantage of the first start and was the home of the first known American silversmith.

Boston had built up a flourishing trade with England and the colonial possessions in the West Indies. It was the haven of the wealth and the social life of early America and it was quite natural that the greatest market should harbor also the greatest center of production. It is worthy of note that almost no fraudulent practices prevailed among the colonial silversmiths. Also, living conditions being very stable, very little of the plate was destroyed. Practically the only New England pieces that were melted down were those which were in the hands of Southern families during the Civil War.

An Englishman, John Hull, is generally conceded to be the earliest silversmith in America. He was appointed the first master of the first mint in America. This mint was established in Boston in 1652 by the general court of Massachusetts which disregarded the decision of the higher court in London. Colonists had experienced excessive difficulty in securing a sufficient supply of money to carry on local trade. Their complaints and agitation resulted in this decision of the court which in later years was frequently cited as being a deed of defiance against the Crown.

The Colonists had to do with paper currency and the instability of value of this currency stimulated the demand for silver which was a far better investment than paper money of uncertain value. With this stimulated demand, the establishment of the mint and the availability of English and Scotch artisans who had studied the trade abroad, the craft of silversmithing flowered and produced many outstanding silversmiths and a wealth of fine silverware.

The majority of pieces are a vivid reminder of the fact that early Americans did indulge in tippling. Beer and hard liquor accompanied the Pilgrims from England. No business transaction was consummated, no marriage celebrated and no funeral ceremony performed without the company or spirits. This furthered the production of silver, and tankards, mugs and other drinking accessories are numbered among the best efforts of the Colonial silversmiths. However, the earliest domestic utensil was the spoon, the shape of which underwent many changes from the early "Puritan" types to the early 19th century "Fiddleback." Tea and coffee pots were unknown until the end of the 17th century and few are found antedating 1750. Previous to this though, spout cups are known which were copied from early Chinese models and were undoubtedly the forerunners of tea pots.

Practically the only form of decoration used by American silversmiths was engraving. Chasing and gadrooning are rarely found. The craft flourished until about 1840 when the factories with their machinery for stamping and spinning silver came into general use and the silversmith as a craftsman disappeared.

Many of the early smiths held important civic positions in the community and were generally men of good financial standing. Among the outstanding men who developed the silver trade from its infancy were Jeremiah Dummer, John Coney, John Edwards, and Edward Winslow. They created new styles and pieces, and their fame as superior craftsmen is indelibly associated with Colonial silversmithing. As time went on, the trade became more or less concentrated in the hands of three families: the Burts, the Hurds, and the Reveres. John Burt came to Boston as a young man and was enormously successful, as evidenced by the great value of his inventory. Two sons, Samuel and Benjamin, succeeded him in business, and carried on the traditions of the father in creating many splendid examples. Jacob Hurd, well-known for his military service, enjoyed a brisk business and was finally succeeded by his son, Nathaniel, who eventually became more famous as an engraver of copper plates than as a silversmith.

The most famous American silversmith was Paul Revere, whose works are cherished for their exquisite beauty as well as for the historic association connected with this patriot. His father, originally of French birth, migrated to America where he was apprenticed to John Coney. In 1723, he went into business for himself in Boston, and was so successful that he was able to support a wife and a family of twelve children. Young Paul entered his father's shop at the age of 19, and in the few years that he was connected there, acquired sufficient knowledge and acumen successfully to carry on the business which came to him with the death of his father. Paul Revere, jr., developed great ability as an engraver, which is evidenced by the beautiful crests and armorial designs which adorned many of his pieces. This training enabled him to venture into the realm of copper plating, and eventually this talent caused a great deal of trouble to the Colonies. He frequently published political cartoons in which he derided the British Ministry and these caused no little consternation on the part of the English authorities. One of the most famous pieces of American silver is the magnificent punch bowl ordered by the "Fifteen Sons of Liberty." In this work, Revere reached a degree of excellence rarely attained by any silversmith. The inscription on the side of the bowl is plain-spoken and clearly indicated the feelings of the community at this time: "To the Memory of the Glorious NINETY-TWO Members of the Honorable House of Representatives of the Massachusetts Bay, who, undaunted by the insolent Menaces of Villains in Power, from a strict Regard to Conscience and the LIBERTIES of their Constituents, on the 30th day of June, 1768, voted NOT TO RESCIND."

It has always been difficult to distinguish between the wares of Paul Revere, Sr., and his illustrious son, because in many instances the same maker's marks were used by both.

The Federal, Colonial and state governments did not regulate the craft, set up standards or require date letters. But New York and

Boston each had Societies or Guilds by which the silversmiths themselves regulated their craft and probably other cities also had similar organizations. Baltimore had an assay office with careful supervision by elected silversmiths.

Marks on American silverware consist of the maker's mark which is almost invariably the initials or full name of the maker and occasionally a standard mark. No date letters were used and the dates of pieces can be determined only by other factors, such as engraving, style, etc.

In the collection of American silver one must be careful accurately to identify makers' marks because in many instances English and Irish pieces are misrepresented as American by the removal of all marks except the makers' marks.

XIX

SILVERSMITHING IN EUROPE

AN extensive study of European silver reveals one similarly striking fact with regard to nearly all countries; very little of the early plate remains, even though silversmithing on the continent may be traced back as early as the fifth century. The continual struggle for power and existence, plus the dire need for money caused many art treasures to be consigned to the melting pot. Again, the fact that so much of the early plate was made for use in the churches which were in constant fear of destruction, made it necessary to bury a great deal of the silver in the ground for preservation. Sometimes these pieces were not excavated or brought to light for centuries. However, the amount that has been found in this way is so minute compared to the great quantities that were buried, that one stops to wonder why so much more has not been discovered. The book records of the various townships speak of the large quantities of plate made, and yet very little remains to be viewed today.

Unfortunately, there is but little data available regarding the earliest pieces. This is due to the fact that only a few records have survived, and those that have are generally in such a state of decay that they are practically illegible. Although only a little early plate may now be seen in museums, it definitely proves that many magnificent pieces were wrought as early as the eighth century.

SILVERSMITHING IN AUSTRIA

Although it is known that several small towns in Austria had their goldsmiths, Vienna was by far the most important center wherein the art of the metal worker flourished. From the time of Rudolph IV, this city was the permanent residence of the German emperors, and Court Goldsmiths were appointed. It was thought that these smiths were exempt from guild regulations, and consequently, were not compelled to hallmark their wares. Therefore many pieces which were thought to be of Viennese origin cannot be definitely so assigned.

Wenzel Jamnitzer, one of the most famous goldsmiths of the sixteenth century was born in Vienna, but migrated to Nuremberg in 1534. It is here that he built up his reputation for excellent craftsmanship. Many other great silversmiths were apprenticed in

Vienna and surrounding cities, but for the most part they produced their best work in other countries. A few Austrian silversmiths who achieved recognition in their native country are known, including Erhard Efferdinger, identified from his important Gothic monstrance made in 1524, and Marx Kornblum, whose fame results from a few specimens of enamel and metal combination.

Vienna developed rapidly as the social center of the country, particularly during the brilliant reigns of Charles VI (1712-1740) and Maria Theresa (1740-1780). That period brought work that was definitely under the influence of the French craftsmen, as is proved by the many pieces in the Louis XIV style. A specific example of this work is seen in the magnificent gold toilet services made for the Empress by Anton Mathias Domanek. During the eighteenth century a taste for the pieces of English design was noted by the advertisements of a few London goldsmiths in Austria who carried on an enjoyable and rather brisk trade.

SILVERSMITHING IN THE BALTIC STATES

There is definite proof that plate was wrought for several centuries in the Baltic States. But Reval, the capital of Esthonia, and Riga, the capital of Latvia, were the only towns of importance where gold and silver were worked. Hans Ryssenback, who worked in the last quarter of the 15th century, achieved the greatest prominence as a goldsmith. Although it is supposed that many workers resided in Riga during the sixteenth century, only two names have descended to the present time; Hans Urma and Thomas Smallde. Silver made in Riga is easily distinguished from that made elsewhere in the Baltic States because Riga used a town mark as early as the sixteenth century.

No secular plate has survived from Finland although goldsmiths worked there in medieval times. The national museum at Helsingfors has a few pieces of plate from the late eighteenth century which prove the charming quality of the work of the Finnish silversmiths.

SILVERSMITHING IN BELGIUM

At the beginning of the sixteenth century, Antwerp was at the height of its commercial prosperity. Naturally, it was invaded by many of the greatest artists and an enormous quantity of plate was produced there. However, by the end of the seventeenth century, the era of vast wealth was over and Belgium fell victim to a prolonged depression. During the period of 1466 to 1695, many important pieces were created, and as many of the early records are still available, the student of Belgian silver is enabled to get a clear insight to the workings of the smiths and their craft.

Although Antwerp was the center of prosperity, the city of Bruges was by far the most important as the center of artistic activity. Flemish art reached its zenith during the reign of Charles the Bold when many of the world's most famous craftsmen worked in Bruges, but none of the splendid secular plate for which the Flemish goldsmiths were noted remains today. However, some pieces used by the church for daily and festival services have been preserved.

Although there was no definite legislation with regard to silver previous to 1814, many of the early makers used date letters, which have been an invaluable aid in tracing the exact year in which a particular piece was made. Silver in Belgium was made in two qualities; that of 900 fine being shown by the block letter "A" in an irregular shield, and that of 800 fine being denoted by the same letter in a square shield.

It is interesting to note that many of the early Flemish pictures depict objects of silver, and from them we have gleaned much knowledge. In the National Gallery of London hangs the world-famous picture "Taste" done so beautifully by Gonzales Cozues in 1618. The picture shows a cylindrical caster, definitely proving that this article was known in Flanders earlier than in England.

In the city of Antwerp there was one outstanding silversmith, called Hans of Antwerp, but as his maker's mark has never been positively identified, not one actual piece can be said to have been definitely wrought by him.

As early as the fifteenth century, a guild of goldsmiths was organized in Ghent, and this is the earliest note of any such association in Belgium. An outstanding master in this romantic city was Corneille de Bont, who worked in the 15th century.

Many other cities in Belgium produced silver and gold objects at an early date, and among them were the towns of Mons, Liege, and Tournai.

CZECHOSLOVAKIA

The city of Prague was outstanding as the center of art in Czechoslovakia. Under the encouragement and fostering of Premysl Otakar II, the "gold king of the thirteenth century," the art of the silversmith and goldsmith flourished to a high degree. Even to the present time many pieces have been preserved which are recognized as the work of masters, and from which many later artists on the continent copied their designs. However, the silversmiths of Prague were themselves influenced by craftsmen of foreign lands.

Prague was the center for the carving of semi-precious stones and beautiful ornaments and many of these were surmounted by bands of magnificently chased gold and silver. They reveal the highest degree of workmanship, and a limited number of specimens may be seen today in museums.

The only other city in Czechoslovakia noted as a center for goldsmithing, was Olomuc, known today as Olmutz. Pieces have been traced from here as early as 1575, as the workers registered their marks with a town corporation. Although it is definitely known that many smiths wrought their wares previous to this time, no definite marks or pieces are available.

SILVERSMITHING IN DENMARK

No Scandinavian silver dated previous to the thirteenth century has survived, although pieces were made as early as the eighth century. The demand was mostly for pieces of practical use and so artists from other European countries did not settle there to work. The creators of luxurious silver from other countries could find no ready market for their wares in Denmark, and for this reason the majority of articles found pertain to the necessities of life. Much data regarding the life of the silversmith has been obtained from early records, and as early as 1685 the first ordinances governing the production of silver were introduced. During the Thirty Years War vast quantities of plate were buried in the earth for protection against invading enemies, and only recently have numerous pieces been found, thus making the present day collection of early Danish silver more comprehensive.

A distinctly Danish article was the drinking horn. These horns, originally made of whalebone or some other hardy substance by the early settlers in Iceland, were introduced by fur traders and travellers coming to Denmark to purchase their winter supplies. The Danish silversmiths mounted these horns with bands of plain silver, and an object which had theretofore been purely useful became ornamental.

Shortly after the inauguration of horns and other silver drinking vessels, the demand for pieces of more florid taste is noted. From this time silver was executed only of a heavily embossed nature, as the Danish smiths did not possess the skill necessary to indulge in flat chasing. Therefore, Danish silver with contemporary chasing dated prior to 1700 is most valuable. Perhaps ninety per cent of all silver made in Denmark was wrought into drinking vessels, and extravagant ornaments had little vogue.

The name of Magnus Berg is outstanding, as he gained the greatest recognition throughout Europe in his special field of beautifully carved ivory pieces.

Copenhagen was the center of silversmithing in Denmark and pieces from there bear the town mark "in an ellipse, three towers or minarets above the date." The only other town in Denmark where silver was produced was Odense which registered the town mark of "a fleur-de-lys, joined to two spreading leaves in an ellipse."

SILVERSMITHING IN FRANCE

The earliest known French silver dates back to the time of the Roman invasion when silver and gold were used as decorations on horsetrappings. From 588 to 659 a silversmith known as St. Eloi did more to promote the industry than any other man and he is the patron saint of the French goldsmiths. He organized the first guild and secured from the French government permission for this organization to be its own lawmaking body with full privileges. In no other country in the world was a guild formed as early as in France. The French were the first in Europe by several centuries fully to understand and accept the craft of precious metal working. At the time of St. Eloi the craft was practiced only by the priesthood, and it was not until the beginning of the twelfth century that the craft of silversmithing was secularized.

The first statute that required the use of a town mark was enacted in 1275. And in 1313 the first punch of guarantee was introduced, and was denoted by a fleur de lys in a lozenge. The use of the date letter in conjunction with the town mark was introduced in 1416.

With the introduction of the town mark, definite importance was accorded to the industry. When in 1313 the guarantee mark was used, plus the date letter one hundred years later, the actual system of hallmarking silver in France was established. The mark of guarantee was very similar to that used in other countries to denote the actual fine silver content of a piece. During the reign of Louis XII a new office of Farmer of the Reserve was created. This appointee was required to impress his mark next to the maker's mark to show that duty had been charged on the piece. Then, the law required that this Farmer stamp another symbol as proof of the payment of duty. These peculiar punches were used until the duty was abolished. In 1797 the tax was reimposed, but was levied at the time of the imposition of the first stamp, so the discharge mark was eliminated. Inasmuch as the standard of the silver was proved by the same mark, French silver from that date on was only impressed with the symbol of the maker, the town mark and the duty mark.

A splendid piece of early French silver extant today is the beautiful cup of the Kings of France and England. Originally the work of French silversmiths, it was sent as a gift to the King of England, and later returned to France. It was then sent to Spain but was finally shipped to England where it reposes today in the British Museum. It depicts the life of St. Agnes, and is worked in beautifully executed relief.

In recent times the outstanding name in French silver history is that of Odiot who is credited with being the creator of the style known as Empire. Rivalled in excellence only by the Brothers Adam in England, Odiot's designs spread like wildfire throughout Europe and few styles of any period have enjoyed the lasting compliment as did the Empire. Royalty throughout Europe commissioned Odiot to make magnificent services, and much of his silver is known today.

The finest collections of French plate are not to be found in France. The Royalty of Europe and England, eager to own these fine treasures, collected them carefully, and today the most comprehensive collection of French silver in the world is in the possession of Great Britain's Royal family. French silver is ardently sought after by collectors and its value is great. The pieces are beautifully made, finely proportioned and delicately designed. France is second only to England in the excellence of its silversmithing.

SILVERSMITHING IN GERMANY

Today in Germany there is a wealth of early ecclesiastical plate to be seen, dating back to the twelfth century. Although this nation produced gold and silver objects as early as the fifth century, few of these very early efforts have survived. Among the first known pieces of secular plate are the Ewer of Goslin produced in 1477, and the celebrated Luneburg Horn of silver and ivory, made in 1486. These two historical works of art exemplify the characteristic traits of the German silversmith, wherein a wealth of detail and almost an over-profusion of ornamentation are to be observed. Hardly ever is a definite note of simplicity found, and this includes the silver made in Germany today. The influence of the Renaissance is apparent in the goldsmith's art earlier than in any other craft.

This influence was introduced in 1490, and was firmly established by 1520.

The inheritance by the present generation of a great quantity of old German silver can be laid to the fact that this country suffered practically no great losses of plate. The only noticeable disappearance occurred during the Thirty Years War, when hundreds of magnificent pieces were the target for those who invaded to pillage and plunder.

Until 1884, all legislation governing the production of silver was enacted by each separate state of the empire, and hundreds of minor statutes were passed. It is almost impossible to enumerate the individual ordinances, as over five score towns were producing silver in Germany.

Augsburg and Nuremberg were the chief centers of silversmithing. Here the craft of the goldsmith was stimulated by the opulence of the people, as well as by the patronage of ecclesiastics, princes and nobles. The town mark used for Augsburg was "a pineapple erect." Date letters were impressed which have been most helpful in aiding the collector to arrange a chronological list of pieces.

The city of Nuremberg was second only to Augsburg in the quantities of plate produced, and its silver wares were denoted by the letter "N." At first a capital Roman "N" was used, and during the nineteenth century a capital script "N" in a circle was substituted. After 1760 date letters are noted.

Silver in Germany was made of many different standards and each piece was registered and marked accordingly. Today most of the silver manufactured is 800 fine, which is a lesser degree than our own or the English sterling.

Gold and silver tipped horns were used for drinking as early as the days of Caesar. In the years that followed, these are closely identified with the work of the German silversmiths who took the horns of the bison or ulus for these objects. Later on many of the early specimens were bound with silver worked in beautiful detail.

Beakers were very popular during the sixteenth, seventeenth and eighteenth centuries when they were employed as guild cups. Many examples depict Scriptural and classical scenes in high relief.

Among the most unusual articles produced were the ivory, stoneware, amber, and serpentine tankards, invariably mounted with silver. The use of the metal wherever possible clearly proves the definite flair for silver in the Reich.

Double cups, as well as hunting cups in sets of from six to twenty were also made. The double cups with their familiar bosses are distinctly German and were made nowhere else in Europe. They served as household objects as well as things of beauty, for the smaller tops were reserved exclusively for the ladies of the house, while the master consumed his fill from the three-quarter bottoms. These pieces are often referred to as bridal cups, and were the subject of much wagering and amusement in their usage.

Silver objects of every known description are credited to German smiths during the seventeenth and eighteenth centuries. Germany stands alone as the only country in Europe where pieces for purely decorative purposes were produced. The silversmiths frequently modeled animals of massive proportion and it is not unusual to find a replica of a life sized eagle or a small beast. Nautilus shells and ostrich cups met with great favor in Germany, and a few examples which have been carefully preserved may be seen today. Tea services, vases, candelabra, etc., are all products of this age of silversmithing, and probably more plate was exported from Germany than from all the rest of Europe.

In the study of silversmithing in Nuremberg, the name of Wenzel Jamnitzer is preeminent. Often called the Cellini of Germany, he migrated from Vienna in 1534, and continued to produce pieces of rare quality until his death in 1585. He was one of five sons, each of whom lived to create a reputation in the field of art. Jamnitzer often specialized in the production of silver pieces combined with fine enamel, and his works were purchased by collectors throughout Europe. Today, if an example of his work is sold in the open market, the true appreciation of his ability is found in the huge prices realized.

SILVERSMITHING IN HUNGARY

Judging from the number of magnificent vessels unearthed from graves, it is likely that silver was made in Hungary as early as the Middle Ages. The records also tell of rich endowments of plate given to wealthy brides of the day. However, as most of that has perished, the real history of silversmithing in Hungary may be said to start about 1600. As early as the thirteenth century, goldsmiths held important positions in the realm of power, and under the reign of the Anjou kings, they were even granted arms of their own. Today the churches are filled with objects of costly precious metals, showing the early appreciation of beautiful things in Hungary. The goldsmiths' guilds which were formed in each town greatly encouraged the craft, and today the museums are rich in the art that was produced many centuries before.

As evidenced almost everywhere, drinking articles were made in great profusion. However, the most proficient workmen specialized in the production of unusual enamel and gold pieces often combined with colored crystal. Some of the later pieces have been preserved and a visit to the churches in Hungary will quickly prove the high quality of this work.

Goldsmiths were greatly influenced in their designs by the craftsmen of surrounding countries. In the sixteenth century the German trend is noticed, while in Transylvania the silversmiths who were in constant touch with the East displayed definite traits of Oriental artistry. In the South, a definite Turkish manner is found, which combined with the above gives a varied trend in design to the silver of Hungary.

Silver legislation in Hungary commenced at the beginning of the sixteenth century when an ordinance decreed that no maker should sell an unmarked piece. Not only was it necessary for each article to be impressed with the maker's private mark, but after being subjected to a test of quality, it had to be further marked by two fellow workers who would swear under oath as to the silver content. During the seventeenth and eighteenth centuries the hallmark regularly in use was "a castle with central tower, above the numeral 13 in ellipse or irregular outline." In 1836 the word "PESTH" was introduced, and followed in 1866 by the capital Roman "P" which served as a date letter.

SILVERSMITHING IN HOLLAND

Silver was not particularly in general use in Dutch households until about 1850, when a mild wave of prosperity allowed this extravagance. At this time, as in former days, Holland silversmiths specialized in the production of drinking vessels, ewers and basins and a little ecclesiastical plate. It is indeed strange though that tankards were rarely included among domestic pieces.

Early examples of Dutch silver fetch tremendous prices as very few specimens earlier than the fifteenth century have survived. Amsterdam was the center of silversmithing although examples of work are known from the smaller towns, such as Breda, Dakkum, The Hague, Haarlem, Hertagenbisch, Leeuwarden, Rotterdam, Utrecht and Zwolle.

Van Viamen stands out in Holland as the most prominent silversmith. He came from a family famed all over Europe for their accomplishments in art, and a number of beautiful pieces are attributed to this great craftsman. The only other name of prominence

Tea Set — Dublin, 1822 — *Courtesy S. Wyler, Inc.*

Pair of Beakers — *Courtesy S. Wyler, Inc.* — Dublin, 1715

Bowl — Dublin, c. 1730

SUGAR John Irish, Cork, 1750

JUG Thos. Walker, Dublin, 1718

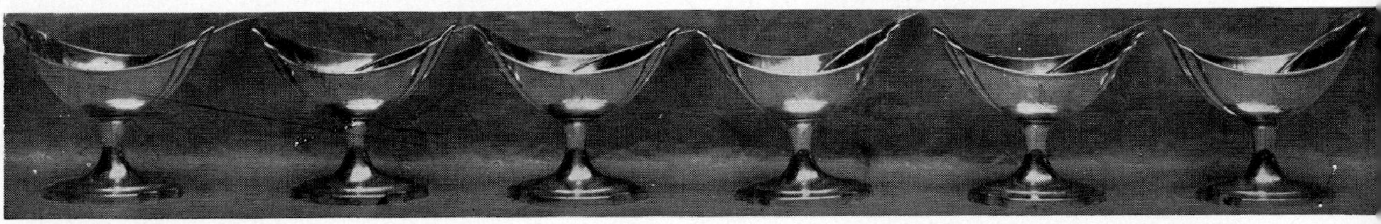

SALTS J. Johnson, Dublin, 180

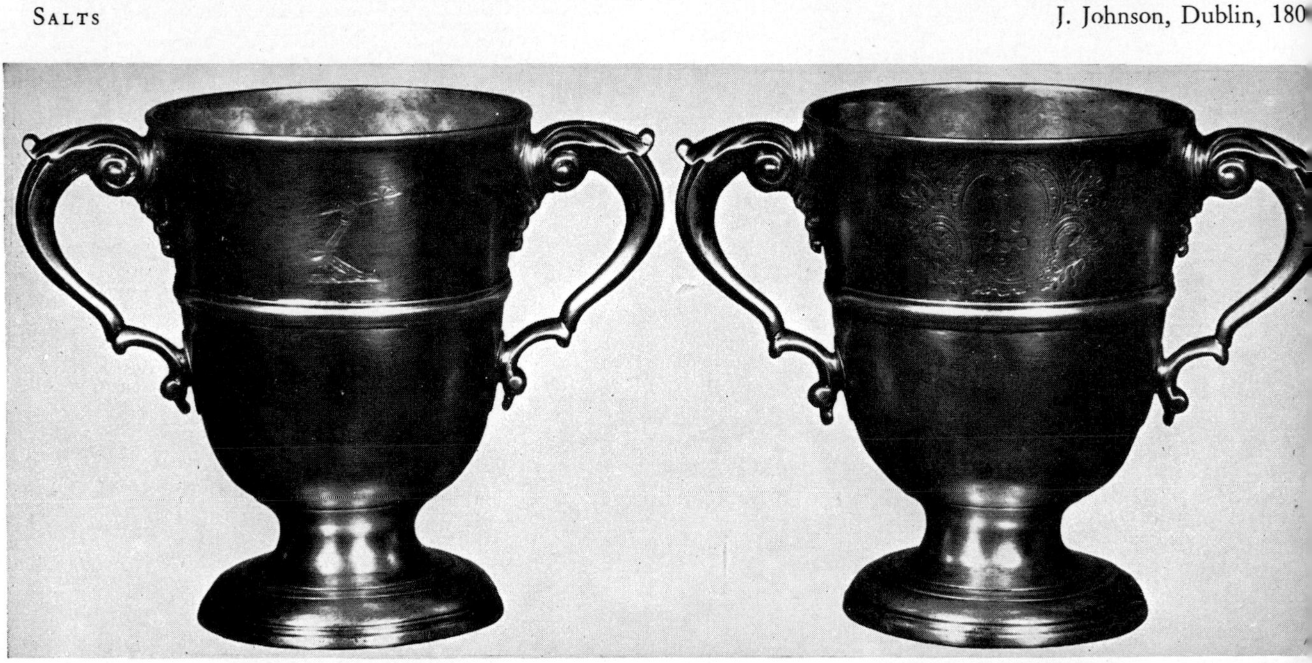

PAIR OF CUPS *Courtesy S. Wyler, Inc.* Dublin, 1736, Robert Calderw

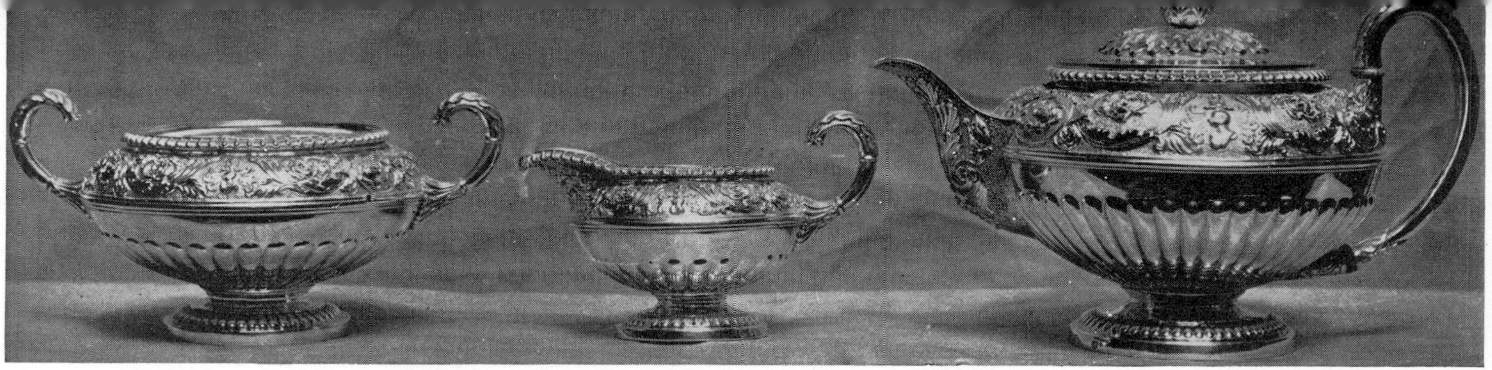

TEA SET — R. Gray & Son, Glasgow, 1819

SUGAR BOWL — Edinburgh, 1784

SALTS — J. McKay, Edinburgh, 1810

PAIR OF BEAKERS — Edinburgh, 1776

CREAM JUG — James Dempster, Edinburgh, 1790

SHEFFIELD SUPPER DISH Nathaniel Smith, 1806

Tea Pot Paul Revere Detroit Museum *Courtesy James Graham, Jr.*

Sugar Bowl and Cream Jug Paul Revere, Boston *Courtesy Metropolitan Museum of Art*

Courtesy James Graham, Jr.

Hebrew Candlestick

Myer Myers, New York, 1760

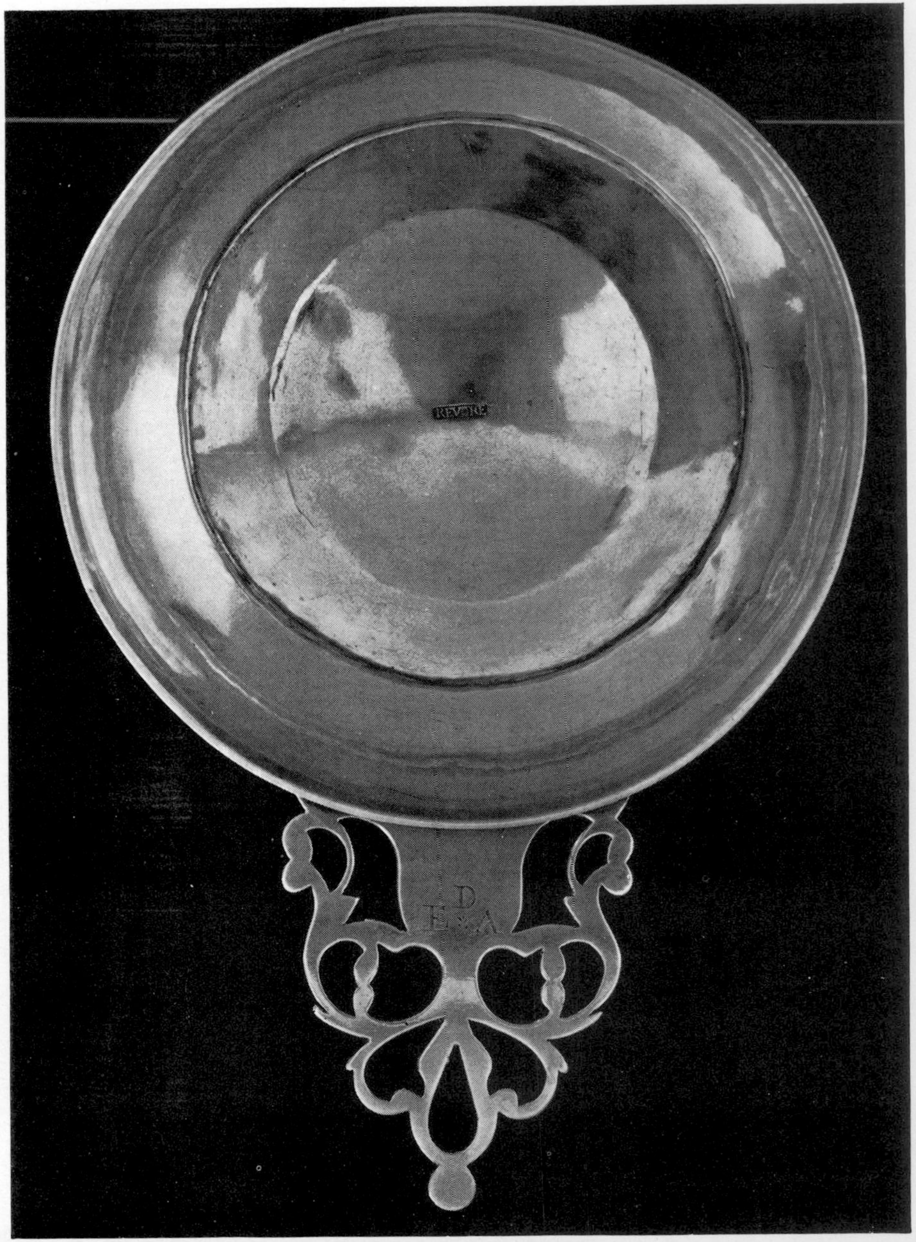

Courtesy Metropolitan Museum of Art

COFFEE POT

Made by F. T. Germain, Paris, (Louis XV) for the King of Portugal

PEG TANKARD Stavanger, 1812

ITALIAN 16th Century

DANISH BEAKER 17th Cent.

SILVER-GILT CASKET by Vianen Flemish, 17th Century

PORTUGUESE PERFUME BURNER 18th Cent.

PORTUGUESE EWER AND BASIN 18th Century

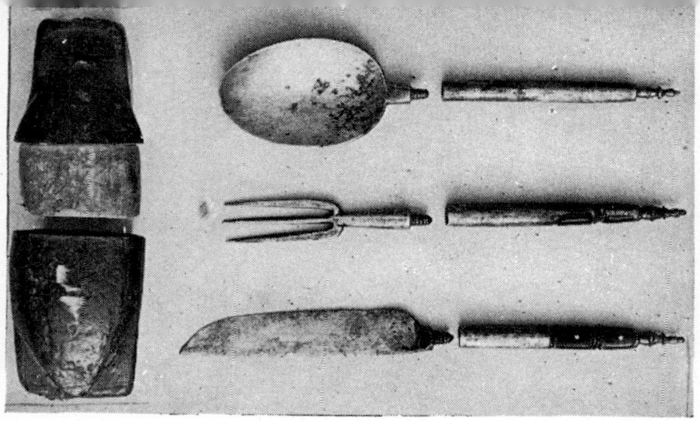

Knife, Fork, and Spoon in Traveling Case
Spanish, 17th Century

One of Set of Four Candlesticks Representing
Four Continents
Paris, 1790

Tobacco Box — Amsterdam, 1796

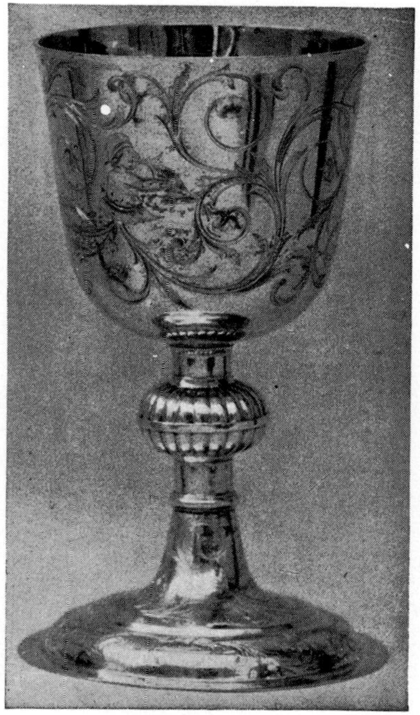

Standing Cup
Niels Jonson, Copenhagen, c. 1720

Snuffers and Stand — Italian, 17th Century

Chalice — Antwerp, 16th Century

COVERED CUP — Fred Kandler, London, 1778

Candelabra Suite — Matthew Boulton, c. 1800

Old Sheffield Soup Tureen — c. 1790 — *Courtesy Marshall Field & Co.*

Sheffield Kettle c. 1785, Coll. Lord Amherst

Venison Dish Matthew Boulton, c. 1800

Rare Sheffield Goblet c. 1760

Sheffield Wine Cooler on Plateau c. 1810

Old Sheffield Globe Ink Stand c. 1770

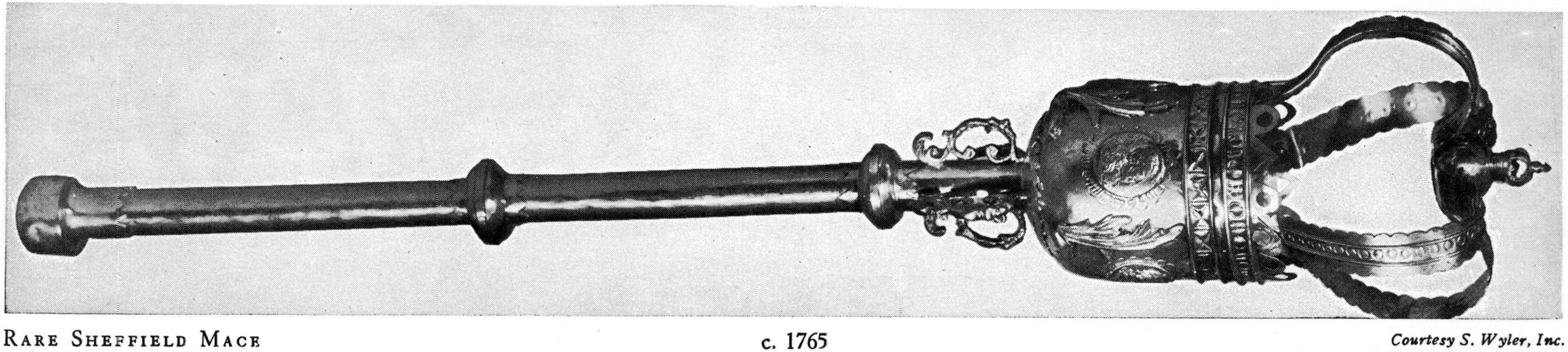

Rare Sheffield Mace c. 1765

Courtesy S. Wyler, Inc.

Old Sheffield Epergne and Plateau c. 1810 *Courtesy S. Wyler, Inc.*

Courtesy S. Wyler, Inc.

CASTER
John Coney, Boston

Courtesy Metropolitan Museum of Art

TEAPOT Josiah Austin, Charlestown

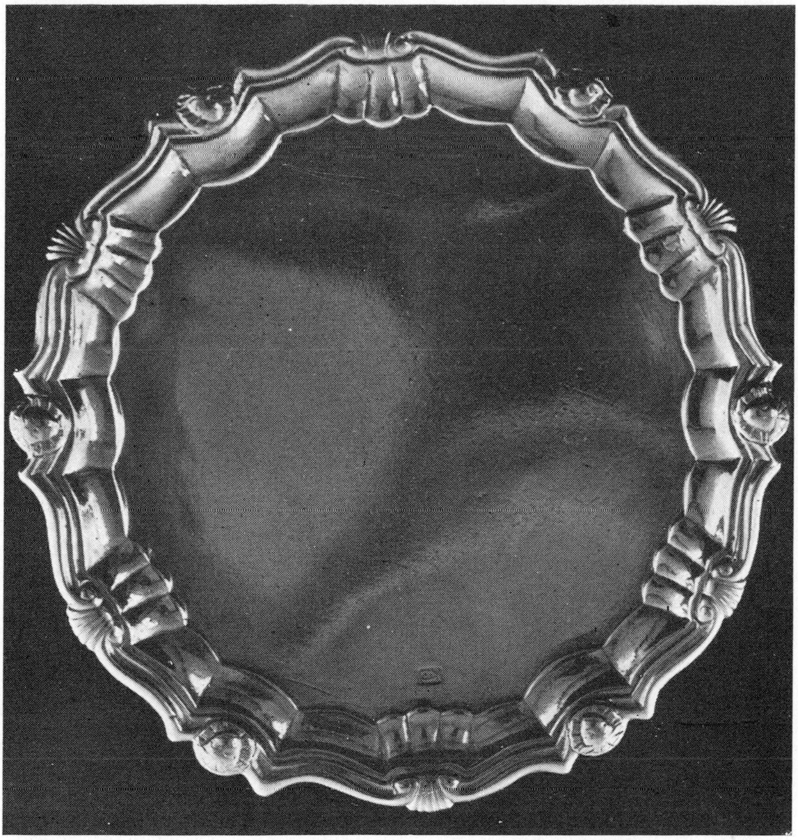

Courtesy James Graham, Jr.

PLATE Keonraet Ten Eyck, Albany, 1716

Snuffer
Cornelius Kierstaede, N.Y.

Candlesticks Jacob Hurd, Boston, 1702-1758 *Courtesy Metropolitan Museum of*

Sauce Boat Joseph Richardson, Philadelphia *Courtesy Metropolitan Museum*

associated with early Dutch silver is that of Johans Lutma, who was the devoted friend of the great Rembrandt. His portrait done by this celebrated artist is well known.

The town mark used by the city of Amsterdam was "a narrow shield, charged with three saltires in pale, and surmounted by an arch bow." The silver standard was indicated by the "head of Perseus," with the letter "a" on his cap, in a circle. All Holland silver bore the duty mark as well as the stamp of the maker.

SILVERSMITHING IN ITALY

No country in all of Europe was richer in ecclesiastical plate than Italy, but in direct contrast it suffered the greatest losses in secular plate. This was not alone due to the results of conflict and invasion but also to intentional destruction. Many of the later artists, lacking a sufficient quantity of metal were forced to remake earlier pieces.

The Renaissance began and had its first flowering in Italy. The city of Florence was the world's center of art, and students from all over the continent came there to be apprenticed. They had to submit a finished work as an example of their skill, and if accepted, they were then known as full-fledged masters. Some of the most beautiful gold and silver work in the world was made in Italy at this time and goldsmithing was raised to a higher standard than ever known before. Royalty from all of Europe sent to Italy for services to be made to special order, and since time was not an important element, the most magnificent results were achieved. As time progressed, the love of luxury, the desire for elegance and splendor so increased that one finds very few pieces of church plate during the sixteenth century. Rather, the finished articles were pieces of wondrous beauty which graced the halls of those so well able to afford extravagances. Much work in the combination of gold and crystal was produced and the most noted of workers who specialized in this field was Valerio Belli, 1468 to 1546. Of course, the most famous goldsmith of all time—Benvenuto Cellini was an Italian. Very rarely has any artist in his field achieved such a high degree of perfection as was displayed in the works of Cellini. Unfortunately less than a dozen pieces of his work exist today, but it is significant that articles wrought by him command higher prices than those of any other silversmith in the world, regardless of date.

Under the pontificate of Nicholas V, 1447 to 1455, the patronage of the arts really commenced, yet, unfortunately, nothing of the work of the period remains. A decided flair for the improvement of original pieces caused the destruction of many. Many of the world's famous painters and sculptors occasionally tried their hands at goldsmithing, but nothing remains of their efforts.

The first goldsmiths' association in Italy is recorded as early as 1035, while in 1314 the city of Florence introduced legislation protecting the industry. Prior to the consolidation of the numerous small Italian states, each section used its own particular markings. The general laws passed which definitely legalized the production of silver in Italy were not introduced and adopted until 1873.

SILVERSMITHING IN NORWAY

The only silver known in Norway prior to 1400 consisted of a few odd pieces of jewelry and seals, and an occasional silver tipped drinking horn. However, from the year 1425, the craft assumed a real importance and until the end of the fifteenth century it was recognized as a major industry among the arts. The two outstanding centers of silversmithing were Christiania and Bergen, the latter being of far greater importance. A few prominent silversmiths are known from each of these places, from examples of their work which have survived. In Christiania, Romanus Moller and Berendt Platt are noteworthy as the two silversmiths who specialized in the production of pieces reproduced along the styles of the English masters. These pieces are unusual for their extreme simplicity, as most of the early Norwegian silver was rather ornate. In Bergen, the most proficient craftsmen known were Martin Finchenberger and Albert Grath.

The silversmith in Norway specialized for the most part in the production of drinking accessories. Beakers of typical Scandinavian design were made in great profusion and were invariably modeled after the Danish pieces made from horn years previously. Of extreme interest to the student of Norwegian silver is a small two-handled bowl called the "oreskall." This article was made exclusively in Norway and only rarely are examples obtainable. Tankards were by far the most popular pieces fashioned from silver. However, the majority of them were of wood, as only a limited number of inhabitants were wealthy enough to indulge in the luxury of silver. This situation is comparable to the one existing in Scotland, when silver quaiches were made for the prosperous and wooden ones for the peasants.

The city of Stavanger was also a thriving silver center after 1593. Here there was a rather unusual procedure in regard to the legislation on silver. Anders Hansen, a local worker built up a reputation as the outstanding silversmith of the town and ruled the industry for years. However, he accomplished this by political influence, rather than by dint of the quality of the work he produced. In this way he was able to create a monopoly, and in 1789, the records list his name as the only smith known in Stavanger. He even went so far as to disallow the practicing of any other silversmith in the town. He himself introduced the fraudulent practice of impressing his maker's mark on all pieces brought to his shop for repair. The competition offered by Jacob Campbell, a smith who finally secured permission to work in Stavanger, caused the exposure of Hansen.

All Norwegian silver was required to be marked with a maker's mark and a standard stamp. The town mark for Bergen, by far the most flourishing silver center of Norway, was a "mosque or domed building, above seven pellets, in outline."

SILVERSMITHING IN POLAND

The general destruction of art in Poland was deplorable, particularly after the invasions of the Mongols in 1241, 1259, and again in 1287. They effected the wholesale slaughter of the efforts of the earliest Polish artists, to the extent that practically no pieces remain. Poland was producing beautiful silver as early as the year 1000, but, unfortunately, all that has been left to posterity are two silver chalices. One of these bears the date 1166, and is considered to be the finest example of early silver known today. For many years after the Mongolian invasions, art suffered a great depression and very few efforts in any artistic direction were attempted. However, under Casimir the Great, the country again evinced a new interest in silversmithing and many unusual statues and reliquaries were made. The forms of monstrances made during the fifteenth century were dominated by the styles of the Gothic architecture, and this lack of originality is found throughout Polish smithing. Until the middle of the fifteenth century, Bohemian influences are noted, but from that time on the characteristics of the Nuremberg craftsmen were predominant. The dynastic connection between Hungary and Poland may be quickly detected in the similarity of their art, and often when pieces of unmarked silver appeared, it was impossible to distinguish the country of origin.

The Stwasz family in Poland exerted great influence on the decoration of ecclesiastical and secular plate, and their ability as masters of their art was finally recognized when they were appointed as goldsmiths to the Polish court. Krakow, the old capital of Poland, attracted many rich merchants and it became widely known as an important gem center. This naturally caused great prosperity among those displaying artistic talents, and it was in this city that Polish silversmithing reached its greatest heights. Nearly all the plate remaining from these times is ecclesiastical as only those pieces stored in churches escaped destruction in the horrible siege of the city of Krakow in 1655 by the Swedes. Lemberg and Vilna are also known as towns where silver was produced, but neither attained the fame of Krakow. Throughout the political history of Poland and its ever-changing government, the influence of foreign artists on the designs in silversmithing is recognized.

SILVERSMITHING IN PORTUGAL

After the rise of Portugal in the fifteenth century to one of the foremost colonizing powers in Europe, a marked development in the taste of the people is noted. The demand for personal luxuries grew by leaps and bounds and before long a ready market for fine gold and silver was established. Likewise, the churches benefited by this cultural ascent, and houses of worship were filled with beautiful pieces fashioned from costly metals. During the reign of Emanual I, the call for plate increased as Portugal enjoyed greater and greater wealth, and during this time some of the most magnificent objets d'art in all of Europe were produced.

During the Portuguese Empire, 1499-1580, social life in Lisbon is said to have equalled that of Rome. This Golden Age of silversmithing was accompanied by the most intensive appreciation of fine art in the history of the country. Shortly after this, a style of architecture, known as the Arte Manuelina, was introduced which influenced the work of the goldsmiths greatly. Unfortunately, this new trend lacked beauty and the pieces of plate can hardly be called artistic.

No native metal could be mined in Portugal so importation was the only means of supply. Eventually trading became more difficult and this resulted in a natural shortage of silver. As the metal became scarcer, pieces were made of a much thinner gauge, and their appearance also suffered. During the sixteenth century, Portuguese plate was prone to over-ornamentation and resembled the work of the Spanish smiths to such a degree that it was impossible to distinguish between the two in the absence of marks.

The beautiful creations of the two previous centuries were replaced by pieces which bore the influence of foreign silversmiths. However, in 1703, the date of the Methuen treaty with England, the styles of the British silversmiths were reproduced almost exclusively. In Lisbon and Oporto, the two main centers of silversmithing in Portugal, the demand for pieces in the English style progressed to the degree where many of the fraudulent workers punched English hallmarks on their wares.

During the reign of John V, 1706-1750, the most serious destruction of plate in the history of Portugal commenced. His extravagances led to enormous debts and he was forced to melt large quantities of plate to pay for these indulgences. In 1755, the earthquake and resulting fires completed the loss.

The earliest record of the legislation for silver in Lisbon is noted in 1460, while in Oporto the mention of assayers occurs as early as 1570. However, a complete system of hallmarking silver was not established in Portugal until the eighteenth century. The national mark used on gold and silver wares was "A capital Roman 'P' beneath a pellet in arched outline." In Lisbon the town mark adopted was "A capital Roman 'L' beneath a crown, in regular outline." Several other towns in Portugal are known for silversmithing and among these Beja, Broga, Setubal, and Evara are to be remembered.

SILVERSMITHING IN RUSSIA

The Russian art is said to date from the time of Vladimir, 956 to 1015. Although the names of no Russian silversmiths survived from the Middle Ages, that of the famous icon painter, Rublev, is remembered from this period. During the sixteenth and seventeenth centuries the splendor of the Czar's plate was the envy and talk of every visitor to the palace, although most of it was executed by foreign smiths. It was said that although the Russian silversmiths were great copyists they could not create originals. Therefore, most of the designs found in Russia were not the work of their own countrymen. The westernization of Russia by Peter the Great created new tastes in art, so that before long the majority of the typically domestic pieces were discarded. The introduction in 1700 of a system of compulsory hallmarking had a great effect on the industry, particularly in Moscow and St. Petersburg, which were the main silver production centers.

The Russian silversmiths created pieces for practical use which were to be found no place else in the world. The most conspicuous of these was the bratma, which was used as a toasting glass at funerals, for blessings, and at every imaginable function. Often the remains of the deceased were cremated, and the ashes put into the bratma to be buried in the grave. They were fashioned from gold, silver, or precious stones and no wealthy home in Russia was without one. Another typically Russian creation in silver was the kaush, which was a small boat shaped vessel with one handle, used for ladling daily drinks. A small brandy cup, known as a charka was also introduced about the year 1800. The discovery of a product known as niello caused great alteration in the general appearance of the silver pieces. Niello was a variety of black inlay enamel which was used on silver either as a form of decoration or as a means of lettering. The popularity of this alloy has never waned. It is still used at the present time.

Russia contributed the icon to the world of art. This was a beautiful painted piece depicting a Scriptural scene, surmounted by a casing of gold or silver. Icons were made in several styles varying from the rich ones encrusted with precious gems to the peasant icons mounted in copper or some other inexpensive metal.

Although Moscow and St. Petersburg are outstanding as silver centers, other places such as Kaluga, Kazan and Kiow, are known. The town marks used by the main cities are as follows:

Moscow—"A double-headed eagle displayed, holding in his dexter claw a sword, and in his sinister a ball, above the letters MOCK above B.A. in outline."

St. Petersburg—"A double-head eagle displayed, holding in his dexter claw a dagger and in his sinister an orb in outline."

SILVERSMITHING IN SPAIN

Conquest in the New World brought vast wealth to Spain, and again from 1556 to 1590, under the rule of Phillip II, the prosperity of the country increased. Phillip, who was one of the chief monarchs of Christendom, adorned the great Escorial with vast quantities of plate and finely jeweled objects, executed by the leading silversmiths of foreign countries as well as by Spanish craftsmen. Never before had the patronage of the goldsmith in Spain increased so materially. The glory of the Spanish Renaissance was surpassed only by Italy's. But this era, although the most scintillating in Spanish history, has left no traces of its magnificence, though ecclesiastical silver from this time has survived.

The defeat of the Armada in 1588 was a stirring blow to material prosperity, and the art of the goldsmith declined. With the accession to the throne of Phillip III, Spanish power began to wane, and the arts in general deteriorated to the lowest point in the history of the country. The practice of looting treasures of a country by invading enemies is evidenced by the amount of Spanish plate found today in France and England. The soldiers of those countries being sufficiently educated to appreciate fine art, realized that these pieces were more valuable in their original form than if melted down. It is interesting to note that during the eighteenth century, although the Spanish silversmiths were influenced by the influx of French art, the demand was great for typically English table appointments, and so we find cruets, inkstands, candelabra, and other articles of domestic plate made at this time.

In the study of Spanish silver notice must be taken of the huge monstrances used to decorate many of the fine buildings. These custodia, as they were termed in Spain, contained beautifully executed silver and gold statuettes and are of importance for the high quality of the work. Two of the outstanding examples known today were created by Enrique d'Arphe, one for Cordoba in 1513, and the other for Toledo in 1524. His son Antonia, greatly influenced by the style of the Renaissance, produced a most unusual type in 1544 at Santiago. Juan d'Arphe who was the best known of this illustrious family is remembered for the great and important custodia created at Valladolid.

Spanish silver from the fifteenth to the seventeenth century was prone to over-elaboration because the silversmiths worked to special order of the wealthy and noble classes.

Peculiar to Spanish silver history was a shallow dish with a short foot, the shape of which was derived from early Valencian pottery.

As early as the thirteenth century, silversmiths were working at Toledo, Saville, and Burgos, while in the fourteenth century the craft spread to Valencia, Valladolid, Guadalupe, Genoa, and other small towns. The most important center of silver production was Madrid, with Barcelona a close second in the quality and quantity of pieces produced. The filigree work closely related to the Spanish silversmiths was conceived in Barcelona, and work in this design was done later at Cordova and Salamanca. Very little data relative to early Spanish hallmarks is available and it is only through book records that have been preserved, that pieces can be accurately dated or identified.

SILVERSMITHING IN SWEDEN

Silversmithing in Sweden first achieved prominence as an art under the patronage of Charles X and Gustavus Adolphus. It was not until the seventeenth century that the smiths produced pieces of any great importance, and then most of them bear the mark of

German influence. Only the few pieces in filigree design are definitely Swedish. It has been very difficult to date the few early pieces which have survived, since no hallmarks were used until the seventeenth century. Pieces were reproduced from century to century, so one can only surmise the time of their creation. Among the most typically Swedish pieces produced were unusual bridal crowns of silver and gold which held great favor throughout the small villages.

The cities of Gothenburg and Stockholm were the only important centers of silversmithing. The mark adopted by the city of Stockholm was "a maiden's head, affronte, in irregular shield." In 1759 a state control mark which consisted of the arms of Sweden was adopted. This was represented by "three crowns, two and one, in ellipse or inverted trefoil."

SILVERSMITHING IN SWITZERLAND

Swiss domestic silver fell victim to the melting pot in time of war, as did the plate in nearly every other country in Europe. Unfortunately, there is no silver left today that illustrated the important art movement that occurred from 1430 to 1530. Drinking articles were produced here in great quantities as well as many other pieces directly copied from the work of the German silversmiths. Not only were German objects reproduced, but all pieces definitely show the Teutonic influence in design. In 1880 the control of silver was regulated by law, and pieces were made with either of the following standards: the standard of 875 fine was represented by a "bear rampant," while those made of the consistency of 800 bore the mark of a "hen contourne, in ellipse." Zurich, the most prosperous city in Switzerland, was easily the main center of silver production, although seventeen other towns were recorded.

HOW TO IDENTIFY HALLMARKS

Bear in mind that the marks must be exact. There is often great similarity between marks of widely differing times, places and makers. The marks must also be complete to insure certainty of identification.

FIRST, DETERMINE THE PLACE OF ORIGIN.

If you know this, refer below to the special instructions for that locality and then to the Tables of Hallmarks for that locality. But if you do not know the origin the following *probabilities* may be helpful.

LEOPARD'S HEAD, LEOPARD'S HEAD ERASED: London.

Other possibilities: Leopard's head erased also used by Provinces, 1697-1719. Also Chester used similar markings to London but Chester is noted chiefly for small pieces.

LION PASSANT: English.

THISTLE: Edinburgh.

HARP: Dublin.

FISH AND TREE: Glasgow.

ONE OR TWO MARKS ONLY: American.

Especially if the marks are names or initials. Possibly English Provincial, Scotch or Irish.

"STERLING"; Irish or American.

"COIN," "DOLLAR," "STANDARD," ETC.: American. Possibly Irish.

ORNATE CAPITAL LETTERS WITH CROWN OR FLEUR DE LIS: French.

HAND: Antwerp. Possibly Belfast.

SPREAD EAGLE: German though there are many other possibilities.

If the marks do not indicate the origin perhaps the character, style or workmanship of the piece may give a clue. If not, a process of elimination must be used.

IF YOU KNOW THAT THE ORIGIN OF THE PIECE IS LONDON. Look for the date letter. Consult the "Marks on London Plate" tables and you will determine the year of manufacture. These tables will also indicate the standard and show what other marks were necessary. The remaining mark will be the maker's mark. Consult the "Index of English, Scotch and Irish Marks" and this will indicate the page on which the maker's mark is listed. Names will be shown for 1697 or later. But maker's names before 1697 cannot be identified though the marks can be verified. Maker's marks may also be found by consulting the "London Goldsmiths Marks" tables for a number of years before and after the date of the piece.

ENGLISH Provincial, Scotch or Irish. If town is known consult the tables for that locality to identify date letter. Then consult "Index of English, Scotch and Irish Marks" for the maker. If town is not known the maker's identification will probably indicate the town. Otherwise a process of elimination is necessary.

SHEFFIELD PLATE. Consult Tables.

AMERICAN. Consult tables which are alphabetically listed according to last names. If mark consists of initials the last letter probably is the initial of the last name.

FRENCH. Consult "French Hallmarks" tables which are arranged according to the character of the marks (Letters, Flowers, etc.)

GERMAN. Consult "German Marks" tables which are in three sections arranged alphabetically by towns (according to the character of the marks). This will give the number of the mark which will be identified in the "Index of German Marks." If you know the town, refer to the proper section. Otherwise, try each section until the mark is found.

OTHER COUNTRIES. Consult "Hallmarks of Other Countries Tables" (arranged according to the character of the marks). This will provide a number which will be identified in the "Index of Hallmarks of Other Countries."

	LEOPARD'S HEAD CROWNED.	DATE LETTER.
EDW. IV 1478-9		
1479-80		B
1480-1		
1481-2		D
1482-3		
RICH. III. 1483-4		
1484-5		
HEN. VII. 1485-6		h
1486-7		
1487-8		
1488-9		L
1489-90		
1490-1	,,	N
1491-2		O
1492-3		
1493-4	,,	Q
1494-5	,,	R
1495-6		
1496-7		T
1497-8		

	LEOPARD'S HEAD CROWNED.	DATE LETTER.
1498-9		a
1499 1500	,,	b
1500-1	,,	c
1501-2	,,	d
1502-3		
1503-4	,,	f
1504-5	,,	g
1505-6		
1506-7		i
1507-8	,,	k k
1508-9		l
HEN. VIII 1509-10		m
1510-1	,,	n
1511-2	,,	o
1512-3	,,	p
1513-4	,,	q
1514-5	,,	r
1515-6		s
1516-7	,,	t
1517-8	,,	v

	LEOPARD'S HEAD CROWNED.	DATE LETTER.
1518-9		A
1519-20		B
1520-1	,,	C
1521-2		D
1522-3	,,	E
1523-4	,,	F
1524-5	,,	G
1525-6	,,	h
1526-7		
1527-8	,,	K
1528-9	,,	L
1529-30	,,	M
1530-1	,,	N
1531-2		O
1532-3	,,	P
1533-4	,,	Q
1534-5	,,	R
1535-6	,,	S
1536-7	,,	T
1537-8	,,	V

	LEOPARD'S HEAD CROWNED.	DATE LETTER.	LION PASSANT. FROM 1544.
1538-9		A	
1539-40		B	
1540-1	,,	C	
1541-2	,,	D	
1542-3			
1543-4	,,	F	
1544-5		G	
1545-6		H	
1546-7	,,	I	,,
EDW. VI. 1547-8		K	
1548-9	,,	L	
1549-50	,,	M	,,
1550-1	,,	N	
1551-2		O o	
1552-3	,,	P	
MARY. 1553-4	,,	Q	,,
1554-5	,,	R	,,
1555-6	,,	S	,,
1556-7	,,	T	,,
1557-8	,,	V	

	LEOPARD'S HEAD CROWNED.	DATE LETTER.	LION PASSANT		LEOPARD'S HEAD CROWNED.	DATE LETTER.	LION PASSANT.		LEOPARD'S HEAD CROWNED	DATE LETTER	LION PASSANT
ELIZ. 1558-9		a		1578-9		A		1598-9		A	
1559-60	,,	b	,,	1579-80	,,	B	,,	1599 1600	,,	B	
1560-1	,,	c c	,,	1580-1	,,	C	,,	1600-1	,,	C	,,
1561-2	,,	d		1581-2	,,	D	,,	1601-2	,,	D	
1562-3		e	,,	1582-3	,,	E	,,	1602-3	,,	E	,,
1563-4	,,	f f	,,	1583-4	,,	F F	,,	JAS. I. 1603-4	,,	F	,,
1564-5	,,	g	,,	1584-5	,,	G	,,	1604-5	,,	G	
1565-6	,,	h	,,	1585-6	,,	H	,,	1605-6	,,	H	,,
1566-7	,,	i	,,	1586-7	,,	I	,,	1606-7	,,	I	
1567-8	,,	k k	,,	1587-8	,,	K	,,	1607-8	,,	K	,,
1568-9	,,	l	,,	1588-9	,,	L	,,	1608-9	,,	L	,,
1569-70	,,	m m	,,	1589-90	,,	M	,,	1609-10	,,	M	,,
1570-1	,,	n	,,	1590-1	,,	N	,,	1610-1	,,	N	
1571-2	,,	o	,,	1591-2	,,	O	,,	1611-2	,,	O	,,
1572-3	,,	p	,,	1592-3		P		1612-3	,,	P	,,
1573-4	,,	q		1593-4	,,	Q	,,	1613-4	,,	Q	,,
1574-5	,,	r	,,	1594-5	,,	R		1614-5	,,	R	,,
1575-6	,,	s s	,,	1595-6	,,	S	,,	1615-6	,,	S	,,
1576-7	,,	t	,,	1596-7	,,	T	,,	1616-7	,,	T	,,
1577-8	,,	u	,,	1597-8	,,	V	,,	1617-8	,,	V	,,

	LEOPARD'S HEAD CROWNED.	DATE LETTER.	LION PASSANT.		LEOPARD'S HEAD CROWNED.	DATE LETTER.	LION PASSANT.		LEOPARD'S HEAD CROWNED.	DATE LETTER.	LION PASSANT.
*1618-9		a		1638-9		a b		1658-9		A	
1619-20	,,	b b	,,	*1639-40	,,	b	,,	1659-60	,,	B B	,,
1620-1	,,	c	,,	1640-1	,,	c	,,	CHAS. II. 1660-1	,,	C	,,
1621-2	,,	d	,,	1641-2	,,	d	,,	1661-2	,,	D	,,
1622-3	,,	e	,,	1642-3	,,	e	,,	1662-3	,,	E	
1623-4	,,	f	,,	1643-4	,,	f	,,	1663-4	,,	F	,,
1624-5	,,	g	,,	1644-5	,,	g	,,	1664-5	,,	G	,,
CHAS. I. 1625-6	,,	h	,,	1645-6	,,	h	,,	1665-6	,,	H	,,
1626-7	,,	i	,,	1646-7	,,	i	,,	1666-7	,,	I	,,
1627-8	,,	k k	,,	1647-8		k		1667-8	,,	K	,,
1628-9	,,	l	,,	1648-9	,,	l	,,	1668-9		L	
1629-30	,,	m	,,	COMWTH. 1649-50	,,	m	,,	1669-70	,,	M	,,
1630-1	,,	n	,,	1650-1	,,	n	,,	1670-1	,,	N	,,
1631-2	,,	o	,,	1651-2	,,	o	,,	1671-2	,,	O	,,
1632-3	,,	p	,,	1652-3	,,	p	,,	1672-3	,,	P	,,
1633-4	,,	q	,,	1653-4	,,	q	,,	1673-4	,,	Q	,,
1634-5	,,	r	,,	1654-5	,,	r	,,	1674-5	,,	R	,,
1635-6	,,	s	,,	1655-6	,,	s	,,	1675-6	,,	S	,,
1636-7	,,	t	,,	1656-7	,,	t	,,	1676-7	,,	T	,,
1637-8	,,	v	,,	1657-8	,,	v	,,	1677-8	,,	V	,,

	LEOPARD'S HEAD CROWNED	DATE LETTER.	LION PASSANT
1678-9		a	
*1679-80	,,	b	
1680-1		c	
1681-2	,,	d	,,
1682-3	,,	e	,,
1683-4	,,	f	,,
1684-5	,,	g	,,
JAS. II. 1685-6	,,	h	,,
1686-7	,,	i	,,
1687-8	,,	k	,,
1688-9	,,	l	,,
WM. & MY. 1689-90		m	
1690-1	,,	n	,,
1691-2	,,	o	,,
1692-3	,,	p	,,
1693-4	,,	q	,,
1694-5	,,	r	,,
WM. III. 1695-6	,,	s	,,
MAY 29, 1696, TO MCH. 27, 1697.	,,	t	,,

	BRITANNIA.	DATE LETTER.	LION'S HEAD ERASED.
*1697 MCH. 27 TO MAY 29		b	
1697-8	,,	b	,,
1698-9	,,	c	,,
1699-1700		d	
1700-1	,,	e	,,
1701-2	,,	f	,,
ANNE. 1702-3	,,	g	,,
1703-4	,,	h	,,
1704-5	,,	i	,,
1705-6	,,	k	,,
1706-7	,,	l	,,
1707-8	,,	m	,,
1708-9	,,	n	,,
1709-10	,,	o	,,
1710-11	,,	p	,,
1711-2	,,	q	,,
1712-3	,,	r	,,
1713-4	,,	s	,,
GEO. I. 1714-5	,,	t	,,
1715-6	,,	u	,,

	BRITANNIA. / LEOPARD'S HEAD CROWNED	DATE LETTER.	LION'S HEAD ERASED. / LION PASSANT
1716-7		A	
1717-8	,,	B	,,
1718-9	,,	C	,,
*1719-20		D	
†1720-1	,,	E	,,
1721-2		F	
‡1722-3	,,	G	,,
1723-4	,,	H	,,
§1724-5		I	
1725-6	,,	K	,,
1726-7		L L	
GEO. II. ‖1727-8	,,	M M	,,
1728-9	,,	N	,,
1729-30		O	
1730-1	,,	P	,,
1731-2	,,	Q	,,
1732-3	,,	R	,,
1733-4	,,	S	,,
1734-5	,,	T	,,
1735-6	,,	V	,,

	LEOPARD'S HEAD CROWNED.	DATE LETTER	LION PASSANT.
1736-7		a	
1737-8	,,	b	,,
*1738-9	,,	c	,,
1739-40	,,	d	,,
1739-40		d	
1740-1	,,	e	,,
1741-2	,,	f	,,
1742-3	,,	g	,,
1743-4	,,	h	,,
1744-5	,,	i	,,
1745-6	,,	k	,,
1746-7	,,	l	,,
1747-8	,,	m	,,
1748-9	,,	n	,,
1749-50	,,	o	,,
1750-1	,,	p	,,
†1751-2		q	
1752-3	,,	r	,,
1753-4	,,	s	,,
‡1754-5	,,	t	,,
1755-6	,,	u	,,

	LEOPARD'S HEAD CROWNED.	DATE LETTER.	LION PASSANT.		LEOPARD'S HEAD CROWNED.	DATE LETTER.	LION PASSANT.	KING'S HEAD.		LEOPARD'S HEAD CROWNED.	DATE LETTER.	LION PASSANT.	KING'S HEAD.
1756-7		A		1776-7		a			1796-7		A		
1757-8	,,	B	,,	1777-8	,,	b	,,		1797-8	,,	B	,,	,,
1758-9	,,	C	,,	1778-9	,,	c	,,		*1798-9	,,	C	,,	,,
1759-60	,,	D	,,	1779-80	,,	d	,,		1799 1800	,,	D	,,	,,
GEO. III 1760-1	,,	E	,,	1780-1	,,	e	,,		1800-1	,,	E	,,	,,
1761-2	,,	F	,,	1781-2	,,	f	,,		1801-2	,,	F	,,	,,
1762-3	,,	G	,,	1782-3	,,	g	,,		1802-3	,,	G	,,	,,
†1763-4	,,	H	,,	1783-4	,,	h	,,		1803-4	,,	H	,,	,,
1764-5	,,	I	,,	†1784-5	,,	i	,,		†1804-5	,,	I	,,	,,
1765-6	,,	K	,,	1785-6	,,	k	,,	,,	1805-6	,,	K	,,	,,
1766-7	,,	L	,,	1786-7	,,	l	,,		1806-7	,,	L	,,	,,
1767-8	,,	M	,,	1787-8	,,	m	,,	,,	1807-8	,,	M	,,	,,
†1768-9	,,	N	,,	1788-9	,,	n	,,	,,	†1808-9	,,	N	,,	,,
1769-70	,,	O	,,	1789-90	,,	o	,,	,,	1809-10	,,	O	,,	,,
1770-1	,,	P	,,	1790-1	,,	p	,,	,,	1810-1	,,	P	,,	,,
†1771-2	,,	Q	,,	1791-2	,,	q	,,	,,	1811-2	,,	Q	,,	,,
1772-3	,,	R	,,	1792-3	,,	r	,,	,,	1812-3	,,	R	,,	,,
1773-4	,,	S	,,	1793-4	,,	s	,,	,,	1813-4	,,	S	,,	,,
1774-5	,,	T	,,	1794-5	,,	t	,,	,,	1814-5	,,	T	,,	,,
1775-6	,,	U	,,	1795-6	,,	u	,,	,,	1815-6	,,	U	,,	,,

	LEOPARD'S HEAD	DATE LETTER.	LION PASSANT.	KING'S HEAD.
1816-7		a		
1817-8	,,	b	,,	,,
1818-9	,,	c	,,	,,
1819-20	,,	d	,,	,,
GEO. IV. 1820-1	,,	e	,,	
1821-2		f		,,
1822-3	,,	g	,,	,,
1823-4	,,	h	,,	,,
1824-5	,,	i	,,	,,
1825-6	,,	k	,,	,,
1826-7	,,	l	,,	,,
1827-8	,,	m	,,	,,
1828-9	,,	n	,,	,,
1829-30	,,	o	,,	,,
WM. IV. 1830-1	,,	p	,,	,,
1831-2	,,	q	,,	
1832-3	,,	r	,,	,,
1833-4	,,	s	,,	,,
1834-5	,,	t	,,	,,
1835-6	,,	u	,,	,,

	LEOPARD'S HEAD	DATE LETTER	LION PASSANT	KING'S HEAD.
1836-7		A		
VICT. 1837-8	,,	B	,,	
1838-9	,,	C	,,	,,
1839-40	,,	D	,,	,,
1840-1	,,	E	,,	,,
1841-2	,,	F	,,	,,
1842-3	,,	G	,,	,,
1843-4	,,	H	,,	,,
*1844-5	,,	I	,,	,,
1845-6	,,	K	,,	,,
1846-7	,,	L	,,	,,
1847-8	,,	M	,,	,,
1848-9	,,	N	,,	,,
1849-50	,,	O	,,	,,
1850-1	,,	P	,,	,,
1851-2	,,	Q	,,	,,
1852-3	,,	R	,,	,,
1853-4	,,	S	,,	,,
+1854-5	,,	T	,,	,,
1855-6	,,	U	,,	,,

	LEOPARD'S HEAD	DATE LETTER.	LION PASSANT.	QUEEN'S HEAD.
1856-7		a		
1857-8	,,	b	,,	,,
1858-9	,,	c	,,	,,
1859-60	,,	d	,,	,,
1860-1	,,	e	,,	,,
1861-2	,,	f	,,	,,
1862-3	,,	g	,,	,,
*1863-4		h		,,
1864-5	*Leopard's head as above*	i	*Lion passant as above*	,,
1865-6	,,	k	,,	,,
1866-7	,,	l	,,	,,
1867-8	,,	m	,,	,,
1868-9	,,	n	,,	,,
1869-70	,,	o	,,	,,
1870-1	,,	p	,,	,,
1871-2	,,	q	,,	,,
1872-3	,,	r	,,	
1873-4	,,	s	,,	,,
1874-5	,,	t	,,	,,
1875-6	,,	u	,,	,,

	LEOPARD'S HEAD	DATE LETTER.	LION PASSANT.	QUEEN'S HEAD.
1876-7		A		
1877-8	,,	B	,,	,,
1878-9	,,	C	,,	,,
1879-80	,,	D	,,	,,
1880-1	,,	E	,,	,,
1881-2	,,	F	,,	,,
1882-3	,,	G	,,	,,
1883-4	,,	H	,,	,,
1884-5	,,	I	,,	,,
1885-6	,,	K	,,	,,
1886-7	,,	L	,,	,,
1887-8	,,	M	,,	,,
1888-9	,,	N	,,	,,
1889-90	,,	O	,,	,,
1890-1	,,	P	,,	
1891-2	,,	Q	,,	
1892-3	,,	R	,,	
1893-4	,,	S	,,	
1894-5	,,	T	,,	
1895-6	,,	U	,,	

	LEOPARD'S HEAD	DATE LETTER.	LION PASSANT.
1896-7		a	
1897-8	,,	b	,,
1898-9	,,	c	,,
1899 1900	,,	d	,,
1900-1	,,	e	,,
EDW. VII. 1901-2	,,	f	,,
1902-3	,,	g	.
1903-4	,,	h	,,
1904-5	,,	i	,,
1905-6	,,	k	,,
1906-7	,,	l	,,
1907-8	,,	m	,,
1908-9	,,	n	,,
1909-10	,,	o	,,
1910-1	,,	p	,,
1911-2	,,	q	,,
1912-3	,,	r	,,
1913-4	,,	s	,,
1914-5	,,	t	,,
1915-6	,,	u	,,

1916	a
1917	b
1918	c
1919	d
1920	e
1921	f
1922	g
1923	h
1924	i
1925	k
1926	l
1927	m
1928	n
1929	o
1930	p
1931	q
1932	r
1933	s
1934	 t
1935	u
1936	A
1937	B

Date.	Maker's Mark.
1479-80	
1481-2	
1488-9	
1490-1	
1491-2	
1493-4	
1494-5	
"	W
"	
1496-7	
"	
"	
1498-9	
1499-1500	

Date.	Maker's Mark.
1500-1	
1501-2	
1503-4	
1504-5	
"	
1506-7	
"	
1507-8	
"	
"	
"	
1508-9	
"	
1509-10	
1510-1	
"	
1511-2	
1512-3	
1513-4	
1514-5	
"	
"	
"	
"	
1515-6	
"	S

Date.	Maker's Mark.
1516-7	
1517-8	
1518-9	
"	
"	D
1519-20	
"	S
"	
1520-1	
1521-2	
"	
"	
"	
1522-3	
"	
1523-4	
"	
1524-5	
"	
1525-6	
"	
"	
"	
1527-8	
"	S
"	

Date.	Maker's Mark.
1527-8	
"	
1528-9	
"	
"	
1529-30	
1530-1	
1531-2	
"	
1532-3	
"	
"	
1533-4	
"	
"	TW
1534-5	
"	
"	S
"	
1535-6	
"	
"	
"	
"	

Date.	Maker's Mark.
1536-7	
1537-8	
1538-9	
1539-40	S
1540-1	
"	
1541-2	S
1543-4	
"	S
"	
1514-5	
"	
1545-6	
"	
"	
1546-7	
1547-8	
1548-9	
"	
"	
1549-50	FB
"	
"	
"	
1550-1	
"	

Date.	Maker's Mark.
1551-2	
"	
"	
"	
1552-3	
1553-4	
"	
1554-5	
"	
1555-6	IF
"	
1556-7	
"	W
1557-8	
"	
1558-9	
"	
1559-60	HW
"	
"	
"	
"	
"	
"	SK
1560-1	
"	
"	

Date.	Maker's Mark.
1561-2	
"	PC
"	
"	
"	
"	RB
"	
1562-3	SR
"	
"	RM
"	WC
"	
"	
"	HK
"	
"	
"	
"	
"	
"	
"	
1563-4	
"	IP
"	HW
"	
"	

Date.	Maker's Mark.	Date.	Maker's Mark.	Date	Maker's Mark.	Date.	Maker's Mark	Date.	Maker's Mark.	Date.	Maker's Mark.	Date.	Maker's Mark.
1563-4		1567-8		1569-70		1571-2	TL	1575-6		1577-8		1581-2	HW
"	BD	"	L	"	RV	"		"		"		1582-3	
1564-5		"		"		"	AB	"		"	AH	"	
"		"		1570-1		"	NR	"	TB	"	WH	"	
"		"		"		1572-3		"	M	"		"	IF
"	IC	"		"		"		"		"	RP	"	
"		"		"		"	HB	"		"		1583-4	RS
"		"	B	"		"	HR	"		1578-9		"	
"		"	B	"		"		1576-7		"		"	IF
"	A	"		"		"		"		"		"	IH
1565-6		"		"	HB	1573-4	B	"	IH	"		1584-5	IC
"	I·P	1568-9	IF	"	M	"	IF	"		"		"	
"		"	M	"		"		"		1579-80		"	
"		"		"	IH	"	IP	"		"		"	
"	HW	"		"		"		"		"		"	
"	RK	"	R	"	RH	"		"		c. 1580		"	RW
1566-7		"	IH	1571-2		"		"		1580-1	SB	1585-6	
"	A	"		"		"		"	WC	"		"	
"		"		"	TA	"	HR	"		"		"	
"		"		"		"		"		1581 2		"	M
"		"	RA	"		"		"		"		1586-7	
"		1569-70		"		1574-5		1577-8	LR	"		"	
"	T	"	F	"		"	CP	"	LR	"	HW	"	
"	WH	"		"		"	VS	"		"	RW	"	T
		"		"		1575-6				"	B	"	
												"	

Date.	Maker's Mark.	Date.	Maker's Mark	Date.	Maker's Mark.	Date	Maker's Mark.	Date.	Maker's Mark.	Date.	Maker Mark.	Date.	Maker's Mark.
1587-8	D	1593-4	CG	1597-8	IB	1601-2		1605-6		1608-9		1610-11	TC
"		"		1598-9	TF	"	TS	"	D	"	FM	"	TA
"		1594-5	IM	"		1602-3		"	G	"	A	"	HS
"	NI	"		"	RP	"	LVM	"	RW	"	WR	"	M
"		"	TH	"	ER	"	D	1606-7	F	"	SO	"	
1588-9	CB	"	WH	1599-1600	BW	"		"	RW	"	IK	"	
"		"		"	IA	"		"	RW	"		1611-12	
"	W	1595-6	IH	"	RC	"	W	"		"	NR	"	WC
"	RF	"		"		"		"	LB	"		"	B
"	WS	"	GS	"	IB	"	AB	"	RS	"		"	
1589-90	D	"	IB	"	T	"	6	"	FS	1609-10	RP	"	
"	IM	"	TN	"		1603-4	IG	"	HB	"		"	IT
"	H	"	CB	"		"	G	"	TH	"	C	"	
1590-1	PW IN	"	GA	1600-1	SO	"	AT	"		"	EW	1612-13	
"		1596-7		"		"		"	GC	"		"	
"		"		"	HD	"	IB	1607-8	Q	"	BXT	"	
"	RM	"		"		"	HI	"		"		"	AB
1591-2	TF	"		"	GB	"		"		"		"	RB
"		"		"	M	1604-5		"		"	W	"	NR
"	NR	"	T	"		"	AB	"		1610-11		"	WC
"	TF	1597-8	IB	1601-2		"	WI	"		"	TP	"	
1592-3	CG	"	IH	"	6	"	IX	"	RS	"	TI	"	WR
"	W	"	ID	"		"	IE	"	IS	"		"	
"	RW	"	IB	"		"	MB	"		"	EM	"	
"	PW	"	RB	"		605-6	HM	1608-9	TC	"	HB		

Date.	Maker's Mark.	Date.	Maker's Mark.	Date.	Maker's Mark.	Date.	Maker's Mark.	Date.	Maker's Mark.	Date.	Maker's Mark.	Date.	Maker's Mark.
1613-14	TC	1615-16		1618-19	AI	1622-3	ER	1625-6	CB	1629-30	BP	1632-3	D
"	MH	"	WF	"	C	"	D	1626-7	PH	"	RC	"	IM
"	W	1616-17	IA	"		"	H	"		"		"	
"	N	"	RN	"	C	"	IF	"	HS	"	IT	"	CB
"	HB	"	IP	"	RC	1623-4		"	HB	"	CG	"	IG
"	RS	"	IA	"	RW	"	WC	"	RB	"	PG	"	IH
"	IM	"		"	WC	"	IM	"	AH WW	1630-1	TB	1633-4	IB
1614-15	RB	"	RW	"	RC	"	RC	"	BY	"	WM	"	WM
"	RC	"	RC	"	IS	"	EH	"	WS	"	RS	"	
"	BF	"	E	1619-20	E	"	RS	"	WS	"	I	"	
"	IM FB	"		"	FM	"	TB	1627-8	SW	"	IM	"	ES
"	SO	"	E	"	AB	"	RS	"	RI	"	IA	"	HB
"	ID	"	IC	"	RK	"	IF	"	WS	"	WC	"	RC
"	RM	1617-18	RW	"	RG	1624-5	IH	"	TB	"	RS	1634-5	RS
"	IM	"	HB	1620-1	IC	"		"	TE	1631-2	RS	"	WM
1615-16	CR	"	IV	"	II	"		"		"	B	"	PG
"	IR	"	RS	"	IS	"	A	"	TV	"	HM	"	RW
"	MH	"	IC	"	AI WT	"	I	1628-9	RM	"	WC	"	DW
"	HS	"	RP	1621-2	EL	"	BY	"		"	DW	"	RC
"	S	"	WC	"	a	1625 6	IE	"	D	"	WR	"	PB
"		"	IF	"	H	"	IV	"		"		1635-6	F
"	TI	"	H	"	B	"	HS	"	BY	"	CB	"	LI
"		"	CC	"	R	"	SW	"	WS	"	VS	"	RS
"	RD	1618-19	IP	"	C	"	HS	"	C	1632-3	EH	"	RH
"		"	WR	1622-3	RD	"	WS	1629-30	DC	"	PB	"	RO
						"	TB	"	RB	"	TE	"	RS

Date.	Maker's Mark.
1635-6	EC
"	IB
"	ER
"	HM
"	RB
"	
1636-7	RW
"	GM
"	RW
"	I
"	RW
"	RH
"	BF
"	CR
"	ES
1637-8	RG
"	RS
"	
"	
,	
"	RB
"	RM
"	RC
"	GS
"	GD
"	WC

Date.	Maker's Mark.
1637-8	WM
"	RG
1638-9	RA
"	IH
"	WT
"	TI
"	TH
"	H
"	SV
"	RC
"	F
"	WM
"	IG
"	IC
"	F
"	RR
"	BE
"	IH
"	WS
1639-40	CP
"	TP
"	HB
"	TD
"	BF
"	
1640-1	DI

Date.	Maker's Mark.
1640-1	TI
"	IM
"	IB
"	RP
"	RW
,	HB
"	W
"	WC
1641-2	WM
"	TH
"	RW
"	IF
"	EI
"	OM
"	TH
"	II
"	WC
"	IT
"	TM
1642-3	IW
"	F
"	RS
"	RC
"	WS
"	RK
1643-4	

Date.	Maker's Mark.
1643-4	TT
"	TM
1644-5	BB
1645-6	DW
"	TG
"	SV
1646-7	WT
"	NW
"	IL
"	CO
"	AF
1647-8	IA
"	RV
"	WM
"	SA
"	
1648-9	
"	II
"	H
"	IG
,	BE
1649-50	
"	M
"	CT
"	

Date.	Maker's Mark.
1649-50	SA
1650-1	IC
"	WM
"	IW
"	HG
"	IG
1651-2	S
"	SV
"	IT
"	IR
"	II
1652-3	IB
"	AF
"	SV
"	RS
"	IB
"	SA
"	RF
"	AF
1653-4	WH
"	HC
"	TC
"	IV
"	ED

Date.	Maker's Mark.
1653-4	RR
1654-5	
"	
"	HN
"	WC
"	IR
1655-6	DR
"	IL
"	RN
"	B
"	RF
"	RW
"	FW
"	IW
"	WG
"	MG
"	WG
"	WG
1656-7	AD
"	CIS
"	EL
"	GD
"	WM
"	B
"	ET
1657-8	
"	TG

Date.	Maker's Mark.
1657-8	KF
"	IG
"	IH
"	AF
"	RW
"	HW
1658-9	HB
"	WC
"	PB
"	I
"	ST
"	GB
"	SA
"	FL
"	GS
"	FL
1659-60	S
"	TG
"	GS
"	AF
"	TA
"	IG
"	M
"	IC
"	SV
"	RD

DATE.
MAKER'S MARK.
1660-1
1661-2
1662-3
1662-3
1663-4
1664-5
1664-5
1665-6
1665-6
1666-7
1667-8
1668-9
1668-9
1669-70
1670-1
1671-2
1671-2
1672-3
1673-4

Date.	Maker's Mark
1673-4	IK
,,	EH
,,	SS
,,	LC
,,	HE
,,	RL
,,	LC
,,	EM
,,	EI
,,	MW
,,	GW
1674-5	EM
,,	TG
,,	GG
,,	[illegible]
,,	TL
,,	RD
,,	GT
,,	HK
,,	WW
,,	EH
,,	WR
,,	M
,,	WS
,,	DW

Date	Maker's Mark.
1674-5	M
	CS
1675-6	GC
,,	FC
,,	RA
,,	N
,,	B
,,	TD
,,	M
,,	TI
,,	IS
,,	AR
,,	IB
,,	IH
,,	IF
,,	TL
,,	IE
,,	S
,,	CW
1676-7	RM
,,	FS
,,	YI
,,	FA
,,	KS
,,	TF

Date.	Maker's Mark.
1676-7	IO
,,	W
,,	TC
,,	AS
,,	WW
,,	CE
,,	SH
,,	SR
,,	OS
,,	IR
,,	B
1677-8	IC
,,	WS
,,	SC
,,	WC
,,	WS
,,	IH
,,	MP
,,	IS
,,	WC
,,	FG
,,	AK
,,	FS
,,	DR
,,	WS

Date.	Maker's Mark.
1677-8	[illegible]
,,	IB
,,	M
1678-9	IB
,,	SR
,,	RN
,,	NC
,,	WN
,,	TR
,,	IA
,,	AR
,,	WS
,,	IB
,,	CK
,,	IP
,,	B
,,	[illegible]
,,	RS
,,	AH
,,	S
,,	NW
,,	IR
,,	TA
,,	KS
,,	E
,,	EC

Date.	Maker's Mark
1678-9	IL
1679-80	TH
,,	IT
,,	M
,,	RH
,,	CK
,,	TC
,,	TA
,,	BP
,,	M
,,	HC
,,	IS
,,	RH
,,	OS
,,	IS
,,	DC
,,	B
c. 1680	[illegible]
,,	FS
1680-1	[illegible]
,,	IH
,,	LC
,,	RS
,,	DG
,,	FG
,,	IB

Date.	Maker's Mark.
1680-1	WI
,,	RK
,,	IS
,,	IH
,,	TA
,,	TI
,,	TL
,,	FN
,,	RL
,,	BW
,,	RH
,,	WF
,,	SE
1681-2	[illegible]
,,	IC
,,	RC
,,	B
,,	SH
,,	FB
,,	IM
,,	PH
,,	MK
,,	TE
,,	LS
,,	II

Date.	Maker's Mark
1681-2	TS
,,	NW
,,	EV
,,	TA
,,	B
,,	IH
1682-3	IS
,,	AD
,,	A
,,	H
,,	AR
,,	FW
,,	EG
,,	PM
c. 1682	A
1682-3	B
1683-4	IH
,,	WF
,,	RL
,,	MH
,,	R
,,	LC
,,	SH
,,	IP
,,	CK

Date.	Maker's Mark.
1683-4	[illegible]
,,	TZ
,,	[illegible]
-	H
,,	TM
,,	WF
,,	III
,,	RP
,,	SH
,,	MP
,,	IS
,,	HE
,,	RI
,,	IW
,,	WS
,,	EB
,,	CK
,,	TE
,,	MK
1684-5	ILY
,,	IS
,,	II
,,	CT
,,	IB

Date.	Maker's Mark	Date.	Maker's Mark	Date.	Maker's Mark	Date.	Maker's Mark	Date.	Maker's Mark	Date.	Maker's Mark	Date.	Maker's Mark
1684-5	WB	1685-6	PK	1686-7	TR	1688-9	IIS	1689-90	RL	1690-1	WB	1692-3	IW
,,	IW	,,	WK	,,	TP	,,	EC	,,	CS	,,	II	,,	SC
,,	DB	,,	BB	,,	IC	,,	ID	,,	S	,,	ID	,,	RT
,,	NG	,,	BM	,,	CK	,,	WM	,,	[illegible]	,,	TH	,,	GG
,,	AY	,,	IS	,,	IC	,,	WN	,,	RE	,,	DG	,,	NL
,,	IS	,,	TB	,,	WC	,,	SD	,,	WP	,,	AH	,,	WE
,,	II	,,	D	,,	YT	,,	OS	,,	SW	1691	MH	,,	IC
,,	TI	,,	GM	,,	DB	,,	II	c. 1690	NG	,,	IC	,,	GF
,,	CD	,,	AF	,,	RI	,,	MS	1690-1	FE	,,	D	,,	IH
,,	TC	,,	IS	,,	Φ	,,	IS	,,	WB	,,	WS	,,	LB
,,	AH	,,	RB	,,	CR	,,	TV	,,	WK	,,	SD	,,	B
,,	[illegible]	,,	[illegible]	1687-8	RH	,,	IF	,,	ID	,,	[illegible]	,,	WG
,,	P	,,	HR	,,	CO	,,	IR	,,	EK	,,	BS	,,	WH
,,	TA	,,	SE	,,	EG	,,	GS	,,	RL	,,	SI	,,	TA
,,	CS	,,	L	,,	RL	,,	TA	,,	RC	,,	IE	,,	DG
,,	EH	,,	WR	,,	IB	1689-90	HG	,,	TOS	,,	IG	,,	CA
,,	IG	,,	M	,,	NG	,,	D	,,	[illegible]	,,	GM	,,	IG
,,	RK	,,	WL	,,	MH	,,	EB	,,	IS	,,	RG	,,	IS
,,	EO	,,	MW	,,	TG	,,	WB	,,	TL	,,	[illegible]	1693-4	IN
,,	IS	,,	IL	,,	FF	,,	II	,,	TA	,,	NG	,,	DA
,,	GG	,,	W	,,	IC	,,	ME	,,	TS	,,	MH	,,	IL
1685-6	D	,,	PM	,,	HT	,,	HH	,,	WM	,,	N	,,	A
,,	WH	1686-7	RS	,,	B	,,	NB	,,	GM	,,	IC	,,	HC
,,	PR	,,	WM	,,	EC	,,	DA	,,	GN	1692-3	[illegible]	,,	[illegible]
,,	TZ	,,	CK	,,	GS	,,	IE	,,	TT			,,	DW
								,,	CS			,,	ME

DATE.	MAKER'S MARK	DATE.	MAKER'S MARK.	DATE.	MAKER'S MARK
1693-4	HP	1695-6	IS	1696-7	TB
"	R	"	PM	"	IB
"	TK	"	IH	"	RW
"	ET	"	MB	"	[illegible]
"	WS	"	WA	"	F
"	RM	"	SY	"	OC
"	IG	"	AG	"	RC
1694-5	EM	"	MM	"	S
"	SL	"	IK	"	TB
"	ST	"	ID	c. 1696-8	Ga
"	AN	"	ETS		
"	RI	"	SL		
"	P	"	SW		
"	FF	"	ME		
"	HB	"	IS		
"	HV	1696-7	WW		
"	ISI	"	GM		
"	J	"	TZ		
"	IR	"	TF		
"	TA	"	TB		
"	MG	"	IC		
"	WH	"	TZ		
"	IF				
1695-6	RG	"	TB		
"	H	"	LI		

Date.	Goldsmiths' Marks and Names.			
1697	Co	Lawrence	Coles	ent. 1697
"	TH	———	Thriscross	" "
"	RO	Alexr.	Roode	" "
"	WE	Mathew	West	" "
"	ED	Jas.	Edgar	" "
"	AM	Andrew	Moore	" "
"	To	Edmd.	Townsend	" "
"	WI	C.	Williams	" "
"	MA	Mathew	Madden	" "
"	Jo	Lawrence	Jones	" "
"	FR	Wm.	Francis	" "
"	H	John	Hodson	" "
"	IR	Edward	Ironside	" "
"	AS	? Thos.	Ash	.. ..
"	GA	Geo. (probably)	Garthorne	" "
"	GA	Daniel (see p. 153)	Garnier	" "
"	DI	Isaac (see p. 155)	Dighton	" "
"	GI	Wm.	Gimber	" "
"	Co	Edwd.	Courthope	" "
"	HO	Sam.	Hood	" "
"	CA	Christr.	Canner	" "
"	GA	Fras.	Garthorne	" "
"	PA	Thos.	Parr	" "
"	DB EA	Wm. John	Denny & Backe	" "

Date.	Goldsmiths' Marks and Names.			
1697	CH	Jas.	Chadwick	ent. 1697
"	Gi	Wm.	Gibson	" "
"	Ba	Name not traced.		
"	AL	Thos.	Allen	" "
"	BR	Moses	Brown	" "
"	GA	Danl.	Garnier	" "
"	Ash	Thos.	Ash	" "
"	AS	"	"	" "
"	AS	"	"	" "
"	AR	Fras.	Archbold	" "
"	BR	Benj.	Bradford	" "
"	BA	Wm.	Bainbridge	" "
"	SM	Jno.	Smithsend	" "
"	WI	———	Wimans	" "
"	Py	Benj.	Pyne	" "
"	SH	Jno.	Shepherd	" "
"	HO	Frances	Hoyte	" "
"	RO	Hugh	Roberts	" "
"	Jo	Ed.	Jones	.. "
"	Br	Wm.	Brett	" "
"	GR	Dorothy	Grant	" "
"	Co	Stephen	Coleman	" "
"	BR	Jno.	Brassey	" "
"	NI	Rich.	Nightingale	" "
"	Ti	Geo.	Titterton	" "
"	LA	Jn'th'n	Lambe	" "

Date.	Goldsmiths' Marks and Names.			
1697-8	BI	Jos.	Bird	ent. 1697.
"	Ov	Chas.	Overing	" "
"	BR	Thos.	Brydon	" "
"	IS	Thos.	Issod	" "
"	PE	Robt.	Peake	" "
"	Sc	Wm.	Scarlett	" "
"	ST	Jos.	Stokes	" "
"	Ro	Philip	Rolles	" "
"	FA	John	Fawdery	" "
"	AS	Thos.	Ash	" "
"	ED	James	Edgar	" "
"	Sy	Richard	Syngin	" "
"	BI	Joseph	Bird	" "
"	AM	Andrew	Moore	" "
"	IS	Joyce	Issod	" "
"	DI	Isaac	Dighton	" "
"	WI	———	Wimans	" "
"	NE	Anthy.	Nelme	" "
"	Co	Geo.	Cox	" 1698
"	Co	John	Cove	" "
"	BV	Wm	Bull	"
1698-9	GA	Geo.	Garthorne	" 1697.
"	MA	Wm.	Mathew	" "
"	BR	Jonath'n	Bradley	" "
"	Yo	Edwd.	Yorke	" 1705.

Date.	Goldsmiths' Marks and Names.		
1698-9	Henry	Collins?	ent. 1698.
"	Richard	Nightingale?	" 1697.
"	Isaac	Dighton (see pp. 152 and 154)	" "
"	Name not traced.		
"	"	"	"
"	Jos.	Sheene.	
"	Benj.	Bentley	" 1698.
"	Wm.	Matthew	" 1697.
"	Wm.	Fawdery	" 1698.
"	John	Ruslen	" 1697.
"	Wm.	Scarlett	" "
"	Jno.	Ladyman	" "
"	Robt.	Cooper	" "
"	Lawrence	Coles	" "
"	John	Sutton	" "
"	John	Hely	" 1699.
"	Job	Hanks	" "
"	Jno.	Porter	" 1698.
"	White	Walsh	" "
"	Benj.	Bentley	" "
1699 1700	Wm.	Lukin	" 1699.
"	Benj.	Traherne	" 1687.
"	John	Cory	" 1697.
"	John	Diggle	" "

Date.	Goldsmiths' Marks and Names.		
1699/1700	Fras.	Singleton	ent. 1697.
"	Sam.	Thorne	" "
"	Isaac	Davenport	" "
"	Jno.	Chartier	" 1698.
"	Sam	Dell	" 1697.
"	Pierre	Platel	" 1699.
"	John	Downes?	" 1697.
"	Isaac	Davenport	" "
"	?	Gould.	
"	John	Leach	ent. 1697.
"	Joseph	Ward	" "
"	John	Cory	" "
"	Richd.	Syngin	" "
"	Andrew	Raven	" "
"	John	Laughton	" "
"	Alex.	Roode	" "
"	Philip	Oyle	" 1699.
"	John	Broake	" "
1700-1	Wm.	Fawdery	" 1700.
"	Jos.	Stokes	as 1697.
"	Sam	Wastell	ent. 1701.
"	Jno.	Jackson	" 1697.
"	Name not traced		
"	Thos.	Jenkins	" "
"	David	Willaume	" "
"	Ralph	Leeke	" "

Date.	Goldsmiths' Marks and Names.		
1700-1	Phillip	Roker	ent. 1697.
"	Mat.	Madden	" "
"	George	Lewis	" 1699.
"	Henry	Aubin	" 1700.
"	Rich.	Biggs	" "
"	Steph.	Edmonds	" "
"	Wm.	Gossen	" "
"	Edm.	Proctor	" "
"	John	Tiffin	" 1701.
"	Alex.	Roode?	" 1697.
1701-2	Frans.	Singleton (see p. 156).	
"	Ed.	Gibson	ent. 1697.
"	Pierre	Harache	" "
"	Benj.	Watts	" 1698.
"	Sam	Hood	" 1697.
"	Sam	Jefferys	" "
"	Henry	Green	" 1700.
"	Wm.	Andrews	" 1697.
"	Thos.	Brydon	" "
"	Wm.	Keatt	" "
"	Willo'by	Masham	" 1701.
"	Name not traced.		
"	Wm.	Keatt	" 1697.
	Sam	Hawkes	" "
"	Fras.	Archbold	" "
"	Josh.	Field	" 1701.

Date.	Mark	Goldsmiths' Marks and Names.	
1701-2	GO	John Goode	ent. 1700.
"	Le	Ralph Leeke	„ 1697.
"	RE	John Read & Danl. Sleamaker	„ 1701.
"	HV	Alexr. Hudson	„ „
"	CO	Stepn. Coleman	„ 1697.
1702-3	GR	Henry Greene	„ 1700.
"	SY	Richd. Syngin	„ 1697.
"	EC	John Eckfourd	„ 1698.
"	GA	Wm. Gamble	„ 1697.
"	CR	Jonath'n Crutchfield	„ „
"	Pa	Humph. Payne	„ 1701.
"	GA	Name not traced.	
"	SA	Thos. Sadler	„ „
"	WA	Jos. Ward	„ 1697.
"	DO	Jno. Downes	„ „
"	CO	Jno. Cope	„ 1701.
"	WA	Thos. Waterhouse	„ 1702.
"	BA	Wm. Barnes	„ „
"	RV	Abm. Russell	„ „
"		Jas. Chadwick	as 1697.
"	Co	Matt. Cooper	ent. 1702.
"	Gr	Hy. Greene	„ 1700.
"	Wh	Name not traced.	
"	AU	Henry Aubin, see 1700. (earliest ment. 1700).	
"	Fr	? Fraillon.	
"	LL	Name not traced.	

Date.	Mark	Goldsmiths' Marks and Names.	
1702-3	MA	Jonathan Madden	ent. 1702.
"	Lo	Robt. Lovell	„ „
"	Co	Matt. Cooper	„ „
1703-4	Ra	Jno. Rand	„ 1704.
"	Je	Thos. Jenkins	„ 1697.
"	GI	Ed. Gibson	„ „
"	AN	Wm. Andrews	„ „
"	FO	Name not traced.	
"	Br	J. Broake.	
"	SO	Soane or Soame.	
"	KI	Jonah Kirke	„ „
"	PL	Gabl. Player	„ 1700.
"	Sm	Saml. Smith	„ „
"	WI	Chas. Williams	„ 1697.
"	SN	Jno. Snelling	„ „
"	Gr	Nat. Greene	„ 1698.
"	RI	Name not traced.	
"	WA	Wm. Warham	„ 1703.
"	CH	Wm. Charnelhouse	„ „
"	AR	Andr. Archer	„ „
"	Pe	Thos. Peele	„ 1704.
"	PE	Wm. Petley	„ 1699.
1704-5	St	Robert Stokes ?	
"	DE	Wm. Denny	„ 1697.
"	LE	Geo. Lewis	„ 1699.

Date.	Mark	Goldsmiths' Marks and Names.	
1704-5	SA	Thos. Saddler	ent. 1701.
"	PE	Henry Penstone	„ 1697.
"	Co	Jno. Cole	„ „
"	EA	Jno. East	„ „
"	Gi	Jno. Gibbon	„ 1700.
"	AD	Chas. Adam	„ 1702.
"	HA	Geo. Havers	„ 1697.
"	MI	Wm. Middleton	„ „
"	HV	Alex. Hudson	„ 1704.
"	Sp	Wm. Spring	„ 1701.
"	Co	Jno. Cooke	„ 1699.
"	BO	Ishml. Bone	„ „
"	FL	Jno. Fletcher	„ 1700.
1705-6	Ti	Robt. Timbrell	„ 1697.
"	FA	Wm. Fawdery	„ „
"	PA	Samuel Pantin	„ 1701.
"	MA	Jon. Madden (see 1702)	„ 1702.
"	LI	Isaac Liger (see below)	„ 1704.
"	PI	Matthew Pickering	„ 1703.
"	FL	Wm. Fleming	„ „
"	Sp	Thos. Spackman	„ 1700.
"	L	Mathw. Lofthouse	„ 1705.
"	WA	Saml. Wastell	„ 1701.
"	RE	Josh. Readshaw	„ 1697.
"	LI	Isaac Liger	„ 1704.

Date.	Goldsmiths' Marks and Names.			
	Mark			
1705-6		Jonah	Clifton	ent. 1703.
,,		Jno.	Corosey	,, 1701.
,,		Wm.	Warham	,, 1705.
,,		Thos.	Corbet	,, 1699.
,,		Natl.	Lock	,, 1698.
,,		John	Barnard	,, 1702.
1706-7		Jos.	Barbitt	,, 1703.
,,		Wm.	Matthew	,, 1700.
,,		Wm.	Juson	,, 1704.
,,		Timothy	Ley	,, 1697.
,,		John	Backe	,, 1700.
,,		Launcelot	Keatt	,, 1701.
,,		Benj.	Pyne	,, 1697.
,,		Jacob	Margas	,, 1706.
,,		Jno.	Ladyman	,, 1697.
,,		Louys	Cuny	,, 1703.
,,		Jno.	Abbot	,, 1706.
,,		Wm.	Spring	,, 1701.
,,		Jno.	Crutcher	,, 1706.
,,		Wm.	Fordham	,, ,,
,,		Name not traced.		
1707-8		Danl.	Sleath	,, 1704.
,,		Wm.	Fleming	,, 1697.
,,		Thos.	Burridge	,, 1706.
,,		John	Leach	,, 1697.
,,		Anthy.	Nelme	,, ,,

Date.	Goldsmiths' Marks and Names.			
	Mark			
1707-8		Pierre	Le Cheaube	ent. 1707.
,,		Richard	Hutchinson	,, 1699.
,,		Philip	Roker	,, 1697.
,,		Benj.	Harris	,, ,,
,,		Chr.	Atkinson	,, 1707.
,,		Phil.	Rainaud	,, ,,
,,		Thos.	Fawler	,, ,,
,,		Jos.	Smith	,, ,,
,,		Samuel	Lee	,, 1701.
,,		Benj.	Pyne	,, 1697.
,,		Saml.	Wastell	,, 1701.
,,		John	Backe	,, 1700.
1708-9		Mary	Matthew	,, ,,
,,		Jos.	Bird	,, 1697.
,,		Thos.	Farren	,, 1707.
,,		Philip	Rolles, Jr.	,, 1705.
,,		Wm.	Warham	,, 1703
,,		Lawrence	Jones	,, 1697.
,,		Chris.	Riley	,, ,,
,,		Alice	Sheene	,, 1700.
,,		Jno.	Read	,, 1704.
,,		Jno.	Bodington	,, 1697.
,,		Wm.	Fawdery	,, 1698.
,,		Henry	Greene	,, 1700.
,,		Anty.	Blackford	,, 1702.

Date.	Goldsmiths' Marks and Names.			
	Mark			
1708-9		Thos.	Wall	ent. 1708.
,,		Jno.	Clifton	,, ,,
,,		Richard	Clarke	,, ,,
,,		John	Chartier	,, 1698.
1709-10		Jno. W. Edw.	Stocker & Peacock	,, 1705.
,,		Jno.	Clifton (?)	
,,		Thos.	Allen	,, 1697.
,,		Fras.	Turner	,, 1709.
,,		Isr'l.	Pincking	,, 1697.
,,		Hy.	Greene	,, 1700.
,,		Laun.	Keatt	,, 1701.
,,		Jno.	Rand	,, 1704.
,,		Simon	Pantin	,, 1701.
,,		Phil.	Rolles	,, 1705
,,		See 1702.		
,,		Wm.	Francis	,, 1697.
,,		Andrw.	Dalton	,, 1708.
,,		Ebenezr.	Roe	,, 1709.
,,		Thos.	Prichard	,, ,,
,,		Hen.	Clarke	,, ,,
,,		Jas.	Wethered	,, ,,
,,		Richd.	Watts	,, 1710.
1710-1		Thos.	Folkingham	,, 1706.
,,		Jno.	Smith	,, 1710.
,,		Wm.	Hinton	,, 1704.
,,		Geo.	Gillingham	,, 1703.

Date.	Goldsmiths' Marks and Names.		
1710-1	Lewis	Mettayer	ent. 1700.
,,	Ed.	Cornock	,, 1707.
,,	Jno.	Wisdom	,, 1704.
,,	Wm.	Pearson	,, 1710.
,,	Wm.	Twell	,, 1709.
,,	Jas.	Beschefer	,, 1704.
,,	Jacob	Margas	. 1706.
,,	Jas.	Rood	,, 1710.
,,	Jno.	Keigwin	,, ,,
,,	Gabriel	Sleath	,, 1706.
,,	Name not traced.		
,,	Jacob	Margas	,, ,,
,,	Jas.	Goodwin	,, ,,
,,	Abm.	Russell (?)	,, 1702.
,,	Robt.	Keble	,, ,,
,,	Jos.	Sheene	,, ,,
,,	Jno.	Stockar	,, ,,
,,	Wm.	Truss	,, ,,
,,	Hezk.	Mountfort	,, 1711.
,,	Isaac	Malyn	,, 1710.
,,	Jno.	Flight	,, ,,
1711-2	Edmd.	Pearce	,, 1704.
,,	Dorothy	Grant	,, 1697.
,,	John	East	,, ,,
,,	Joseph	Barbitt	,, 1703.

Date.	Goldsmiths' Marks and Names.		
1711-2	John	Porter	ent. 1698.
,,	Richard	Williams	,, 1712.
,,	Wm.	Penstone	,, ,,
,,	Ed.	Jennings	,, 1709.
,,	Jno.	Read	,, 1704.
,,	Lewis	Mettayer (probably).	
,,	Nich.	Clausen	ent. 1709.
,,	Ed.	Holaday	,, ,,
,,	Aug.	Courtauld	,, 1708.
,,	Hen.	Greene	,, 1700.
,,	Jno.	Chamberlen	,, 1704.
,,	Isaac	Dalton	,, 1711.
,,	Wm.	Matthew	,, ,,
,,	Jonthn.	Newton	,, ,,
1712-3	Thos.	Sutton	,, ,,
,,	Jno.	Rand	,, 1704.
,,	Seth	Lofthouse	,, 1697.
,,	Isaac	Dalton	,, 1711.
,,	Ed.	Gibson	,, 1697.
,,	Wm.	Lukin	, 1699.
,,	Richd.	Bayley	,, 1708.
,,	Richd.	Raine	,, 1712.
,,	John	Hobson	,, 1697.
,,	Glover	Johnson	,, 1712.
,,	Wm.	Turbitt	,, 1710.
,,	Richd.	Williams	,, 1712.

Date.	Goldsmiths' Marks and Names.		
1712-3	Thos.	Bevault	ent. 1712.
,,	Jno. M.	Stockar	,, 1710.
1713-4	Samuel	Margas	,, 1706.
,,	Ambrose	Stevenson	,, ,,
,,	Natl.	Locke	1698.
,,	Hugh	Roberts	,, 1697.
,,	Gabriel	Sleath	,, 1706.
,,	Mark	Paillet	,, 1698.
,,	Henry	Collins	,,
,,	Edw.	Vincent	(?)
,,	Jno.	Ludlow	,, 1713.
,,	Gundry	Roode	,, 1709.
,,	Thos.	Mann	,, 1713.
,,	Thos.	Ewesdin	,, ,,
,,	Wm.	Looker	,, ,,
,,	John	Bathe	,, 1700.
,,	Wm.	Juson	,, 1704.
,,	Seth	Lofthouse	,, 1697.
1714-5	Robt. Benj.	Timbrell & Bentley }	,, ,,
,,	David	Tanqueray	,, 1713.
,,	Joseph	Fainell	,, 1710.
,,	Thomas	Bevault	,, 1712.
,,	Glover	Johnson	,, ,,
,,	Mich'l	Boult	,, ,,
,,	Name not traced.		

Date.	Goldsmiths' Marks and Names.		
1714-5	EN VA	Wm. England & John Vane	ent. 1714.
"	We	Sam Welder	" "
"	GR	Rich'd Green	" 1703.
"	HO	Jno. Holland	" 1711.
"	HI	Saml. Hitchcock	" 1712.
"	We	Saml. Welder	" 1714.
"	Br	Philip Brush	" 1707.
"	DA	Josiah Daniel	" 1714.
"	BL	Nathl. Bland	" "
"	GI	Richd. Gines	" "
"	BE	Henry Beesley	" "
"	MI	Henry Miller	" "
1715-6	AL	Thos. Allen	" 1697.
"	Kil	David Killmaine	" 1715.
"	PL	Fras. Plymley	" "
"	CO	John Corporon	" 1716.
"	SL	Danl. Sleamaker	" 1704.
"	Pa	Humph. Payne	" 1701.
"	Le	Petley Ley	" 1715.
"	PO	Thos. Port	" 1713.
"	Gr	Richard Greene	" 1703.
"	Io	Edward Jones	" 1697.
"	DA	Josiah Daniel (see 1714)	" 1714.
"	GO	Jas. Goodwin	" 1710.
"	Ye	Danl. Yerbury	" 1715.
"	LA	Geo. Lambe	" 1713.

Date.	Goldsmiths' Marks and Names.		
1715-6	hi	Robt. Hill	ent. 1716.
"	Ho	Thos. Holland	" 1707.
1716-7	HO	John Holland	" 1711.
"	RO	Nat. Roe	" 1710.
"	CL	Jos. Clare	" 1713.
"	Ma	Thos. Mason	" 1716.
"	LA	Paul Lamerie	" 1712.
"	EW	Thos. Ewesdin	" 1713.
"	Se	Jas. Seabrook	" 1714.
"	LE	Petley Ley	" 1715.
"	RO	Phillip Robinson	" 1713.
"	CL	Joseph Clare (see above and 1719)	" "
"	Ne	Anty. Nelme	" 1697.
"	LA	Geo. Lambe	" 1713.
"	BE	Wm. Bellassyse	" 1716.
"	Gr	David Green	" 1701.
"	GU	Jno. Guerrie	" 1717.
"	CV	Danl. Cunningham	" 1716.
"	BE	Jos. Bell	" "
"	Ed	Richd. Edwards	" "
"	Mo	Jas. Morson	" "
"	PE	Wm. Pearson	" 1717.
1717-8	Fr	Jas. (?) Fraillon	" 1710.
"	KE	Robt. Kempton	" "
"	PE	Wm. Penstone	" 1717.

Date.	Goldsmiths' Marks and Names.		
1717-8	Wa	Joseph Ward	ent. 1717.
"	BA	Edward Barnet	" 1715.
"	IA	Chas. Jackson (see 1718 below)	" 1714.
"	PE	William Pearson (see 1716)	" 1710.
"	RI	Isaac Riboulau	" 1714.
"	BA	Edw. Barnet	" 1715.
"	RO	Phil. Robinson	" 1713.
"	HO	Thos. Holland	" 1707.
"	Ha	Jno. Harris	" 1716.
"	ST	Wm. Street	" 1717.
"	SM	Jas. Smith	" 1718.
"	SH	Thos. Shermer	" 1717.
"	WI	Starling Wilford	" "
"	HA	Paul Hanet	" "
"	BU	Thos. Burridge	" "
"	BE	Wm. Bellamy	" "
"	We	Sam. Welder	" "
1718-9	St	Ambrose Stevenson	" 1706.
"	PE	Wm. Petley	" 1717.
"	HA	Paul Hanet	" 1715.
"	Fa	John Farnell	" 1714.
"	IA	Chas. Jackson	" "
"	PA	Thos. Parr	" 1697.
"	BE	Geo. Beale	" 1713.
"	Ho	Ed. Holaday	" 1709.

Date.	Goldsmiths' Marks and Names.		
1718-9	TA	David Tanqueray (see 1714)	ent. 1713.
"	CL	Henry Clarke (see 1709)	,, 1709.
"	Ma	Thomas Mason	,, 1716.
"	TE	Thomas Tearle (see 1719 below)	,, 1719.
"	Ke	John Keigwin	,, 1710.
"	SA	John Sanders	,, 1717.
"		Wm. Fawdery (as 1705)	,, 1697.
"	DA	Wm. Darkeratt	,, 1718.
"	SA	Hugh Saunders	,, ,,
"	BI	John Bignell	,, ,,
"	GI	Geo. Gillingham	,, ,,
"	MI	Jno. Millington	,, ,,
"	LI	Jno. Lingard	,, ,,
"	LI	Do. do. (for O.S.)	,, 1719.
1719-20	TE	Thos. Tearle (see 1718-9)	,, ,,
"	LA	Thos. Langford	,, 1715.
"	HU	René Hudell	,, 1718.
"	SP	Wm. Spackman	. 1714.
"	BO	Geo. Boothby	.. 1720.
"	Wh	John White	.. 1719.
"	SA	John le Sage	.. 1718.
"	BL	Benj. Blakeley	.. 1715
"	Pla	Wm Paradise	,, 1718.
"	IO	Lawrence (?) Jones	,, 1697.

Date.	Goldsmiths' Marks and Names.		
1719-20	Gi	John Gibbons	ent. 1700.
"	SH	Thomas Shermer	,, 1717.
"	DA	Wm. Darkeratt (see 1718)	,, 1718.
"	BA	Edw. Barrett	,, 1715.
"	SM	James Smith	,, 1718.
"	SL	Gabriel Sleath	,, 1706.
"	AL	Thos. Allen (2nd Mark)	,, 1697.
"	MO	Thos. Morse	,, 1718.
"	GI	Edw. Gibbon	,, 1719.
"	SM	Saml. Smith	,, ,,
"	ST	Jos. Steward	,, ,,
"		Jos. Clare,	as 1716-7.
"	Gt	Chris. Gerrard	ent. 1719.
"	HI	Edmd. Hickman	,, ,,
"	WP	Wm. Pearson	,, ,,
"	BR	Geo. Brydon	,, 1720.
"	GL	Thos Gladwin	,, 1719.
"	SW	Starling Wilford	,, 1720.
"	LI	John Lingard	,, 1719.
"	IO	John Jones	,, ,,
"	HA	Paul Hanet	,, 1717.
"	EH	Edwd. Hall	,, 1720.
"	NA	Bowles Nash	,, ,,
"	Ho	—— Hodgkis	,, 1719.
"	PH	Phyllis Phillip	,, 1720.

Date.	Goldsmiths' Marks and Names.		
1719-20	FA	Joseph Fainell	ent. 1710.
"	PP	Phyllis Phillip	,, 1720.
"	RG	Richard Gines	,, ,,
"	WS	Wm. Scarlett (O.S. as before 1697)	,, ,,
"	RO	Mary Rood	,, ,,
"	CG	Christr. Gerrard	,, ,,
1720-1	ED	John Edwards	,, 1697.
"	EV	Thos. Evesdon (see 1721-2)	,, 1713.
"	WL	William Looker	,, ,,
"	LA	Paul Lamerie	,, 1712.
"	CR	Paul Crespin	,, 1720.
"	LA	Geo. Lambe (widow of)	,, 1713.
"	WF	William Fawdery	,, 1720.
"	M·I	Henry Millar	,, ,,
"	FO	Thomas Folkingham	,, ,,
"	LE	Petley Ley (see 1716)	,, 1715.
"	FA	John Fawdery	,, 1697.
"	MC	Matt. Cooper	,, ,,
"	TA	Ann Tanqueray	,, 1720.
"	CI	Chas. Jackson	,, 1714.
"	Ho	Sarah Holaday	,, 1719.
"	R AP O	Hugh Arnett & Ed. Pocock	,, ,,
"	DK	Name not traced.	
"	Ba	Thos Bamford	,, ,,

Date.	Goldsmiths' Marks and Names.		
1720-1	Jno.	Bromley	ent. 1720.
,,	Benj.	Watts	,, ,,
,,	John	Bignell	,, ,,
,,	John	Betts	,, ,,
,,	Michl.	Boult.	,, ,,
,,	Saml.	Hitchcock	,, ,,
,,	Thos.	Sadler	,, ,,
,,	Geo.	Boothby	,, ,,
,,	Phil.	Rolles	,, ,,
,,	Jno.	Hopkins	,, ,,
,,	Do.	do.	,, ,,
,,	Saml.	Welder	,, ,,
,,	*John	Penfold (probably)	,, ,,
,,	Fras.	Turner	,, ,,
,,	Jas.	Morson	,, ,,
,,	Jno.	Millington	,, ,,
,,	Thos.	Folkingham	,, ,,
,,	John	Ludlow	,, ,,
,,	Thos.	Mann	,, ,,
,,	Ed.	Jennings	,, ,,
,,	Do.	do. (O.S.)	,, ,,
,,	Richd.	Watts	,, ,,
,,	Name not traced.		
,,	J.	Burridge	,, ,,
,,	Jno.	Barnard	,, ,,
,,	A'brose	Stevenson	,, ,,

Date.	Goldsmiths' Marks and Names.		
1720-1	Edw.	Feline	ent. 1720.
,,	Jas.	Seabrook	,, ,,
,,	Jos.	Steward	,, ,,
,,	Henry	Miller	,, ,,
,,	Geo.	Squire	,, ,,
,,	Gabl.	Sleath	,, ,,
,,	Phil.	Roker (N.S.)	,, ,,
,,	Do.	do. (O.S.)	,, ,,
,,	Geo.	Brydon	,, ,,
,,	Hen.	Greene	,, ,,
,,	Edwd.	Pearce	,, ,,
,,	Jno.	Brumhall	,, 1721.
,,	Jno.	Newton	,, 1720.
,,	Wm.	Matthew	,, ,,
,,	Saml.	Lee	,, ,,
,,	Henry	Clarke	,, ,,
,,	Jno.	Corosey	,, ,,
,,	Jno.	Farnell	,, ,,
,,	Glover	Johnson	,, ,,
,,	Wm.	Looker	,, ,,
,,	Phil.	Rainaud	,, ,,
1721-2	Ed.	Vincent (probably)	,, ,,
,,	Isaac	Liger	,, ,,
,,	Henry	Jay	,, ,,
,,	Jos.	Clare	,, ,,
,,	M. / Ed.	Arnett & / Pocock }	,, ,,

Date.	Goldsmiths' Marks and Names.		
1721-2	Simon	Pantin	ent. 1717.
,,	John	Wisdome (probably)	,, 1720.
,,	Jane	Lambe	,, 1719.
,,	Ed.	Turner	,, 1720.
,,	Abm.	Buteux	,, 1721.
,,	Saml.	Lee	,, ,,
,,	Geo.	Wickes	,, ,,
,,	Hugh	Spring	,, ,,
,,	Mary	Rood	,, ,,
,,	Gundry	Roode	,, ,,
,,	Wm.	Truss	,, ,,
,,	Do.	do.	,, ,,
,,	Name not traced.		
,,	Sarah	Holaday (see 1720-1)	,, 1719.
,,	Joseph	Bell ?	,, 1716.
,,	Thos.	Evesdon (see 1720-1)	,, 1713.
,,	Edmund	Pearce	,, 1720.
,,	Simon	Pantin (see above)	,, 1717.
1722-3	Bowles	Nash	,, 1721.
,,	Edward	Feline (see 1720)	,, 1720.
,,	Jno. le	Sage	,, 1718.
,,	Ed.	Wood	,, ,,
,,	Benj.	Pyne	as 1706.
,,	Name not traced.		
,,	Anth.	Nelme	as 1716.
,,	Edw.	Jennings	ent. 1720.

Date.	Mark	Goldsmiths' Names	Entered
1722-3	IB	Jno. Bignell	ent. 1720.
„	GU	Natl. Gulliver	„ 1722.
„	DW	David Willaume	„ 1720.
„	IE	Jno. Eckford	„ „
„	IR	Isaac Riboulau	„ „
„	PI	Pere Pilleau	„ „
„	EW	Edw. Wood	„ „
„	GO	Jas. Gould	„ 1722.
„	NC	Nich. Clausen	„ 1720.
„	PR	Phil. Robinson	„ 1723.
„	GO	Phil. Goddard	„ „
„	PG	Do. do.	„ „
„	NG	Natl. Gulliver	„ „
„	CO	Isaac Cornasseau	„ 1722.
„	IC	Do. do.	„ „
„	NI	Michl. Nicholl	„ 1723.
„	CL	John Clarke	„ 1722.
„	GY	Geo. Young	„ „
„	IC	Jno. Clarke	„ „
„	IF	Jas. Fraillon	„ 1723
„	DY	Ed. Dymond	„ 1722.
„	A	Joseph Adams ?	„ „
„	SA	John le Sage	„ 1718.
„	PB	Philip Brush ?	„ 1707.
„	IC	Isaac Cornasseau	„ 1722.
1722-3	RW	Richard Watts	ent. 1720.
„	ED	Ed. Dymond	„ 1722.
„	KI	Jeremiah King	„ 1723.
„	IK	Do. do.	„ „
„	SO	Wm. Soame	„ „
„	WS	Do. do.	„ „
„	IO	John Jones	„ „
„	I·I	Do. do.	„ „
„	HD	Henry Dell	„ 1722.
„	WO	Wm. Owen	„ 1723.
„	IG	John Gibbons	„ „
„	GO	Meshach Godwin	„ 1722.
1723-4	IE	John East	„ 1721.
„	TF	Thos. Farrer	„ 1720.
„	TM	Thos. Morse	„ „
„	CO	Aug. Courtauld	„ 1708.
„	MA	Jnthn. Madden	„ 1702.
„	Pe	Edw. Peacock	„ 1710.
„	RS	Richd. Scarlett	„ 1723.
„	IC	John Chartier	„ „
„	Di	Arte Dicken	„ 1720.
„	LA	Paul Lamerie	„ 1712.
„	IO	John Jones	„ 1719.
„	EG	Edw. Gibbons	„ 1723.
„	WS	Wm. Spackman	„ 1720.
„	RO	Jnthn. Robinson	„ 1723.
1723-4	IB	John Bignell (see 1720 and 1722)	ent. 1718.
„	GS	Geo. Squire	„ 1720.
„	TW	Thos. Wall (?)	„ 1708.
„	Di	Arte Dicken ? or John Diggle	„ 1720. „ 1697.
„	ILM	John Motherby (?)	„ 1718.
„	SH	Sam Hitchcock	„ 1712.
„	FA	Wm. Fawdery ?	„ 1720.
„	IR	Jnthn. Robinson	„ 1723.
„	RE	Richd. Edwards	„ „
„	Φ	John Owing	„ 1724.
„	ED PI	John Edwards & Geo. Pitches	„ 1723.
1724-5	RB	Richd. Bigge (probably)	„ 1700.
„	SC	Richd. Scarlett	„ 1719.
„	DT	David Tanqueray	„ 1720.
„	AB	Abm. Buteux	„ 1721.
„	MG	Meshach Godwin	„ 1722.
„	HP	Humphy. Payne	„ 1720.
„	PC	Paul Crespin	„ „
„	IM	Jacob Margas	„ „
„	DA	Fleurant David	„ 1724.
„	FD	Do do.	„ „
„	M	Mathw. Lofthouse	„ 1721.
„	ED	John Edwards	„ 1724.
„	EC	Edw. Conen	„
„	Io	John Jones	„ 1723.
„	WD	W'sc'mbe Drake	„ 1724.
„	Wh	John White	„ „

Date.	Mark	Goldsmiths' Marks and Names.
1724-5	BV	Jas. Burne ent. 1724.
„	IB	Do. do. „ „
„	HU	Saml. Hutton „ „
„	SH	Do. do. „ „
„	EP	Ed. Peacock „ „
„		John Owing „ „
„	SI	Peter Simon „ 1725.
„	I·G	John Gibbons „ 1723.
„	AC	Aug. Courtauld „ 1708.
„	ID	Josiah Daniel „ 1714.
„	PS	Peter Simon „ 1725.
„	MO	John Motherby „ 1718.
„	PE	John Pero „ 1717.
„	NE	Jnthn. Newton „ 1718.
1725-6		Abm. de Oliveyra „ 1725.
„	EC	John Eckfourd „ „
„	He	Josh. Healy „ „
„	IH	Do. do. „ „
„	RL	Robt. Lucas „ 1726.
„	HP	Harvey Price „ „
„	I·G	John Gorsuch „ „
„	WT	Wm. Toone „ 1725.
„	IB	Jos. Bird „ 1724.
„	HS	Hugh Saunders „ 1718.
„	PH	Paul Hanet „ 1721.
„	FG	Fras. Garthorne „ „

Date.	Mark	Goldsmiths' Marks and Names.
1725-6	MA	Jacob Margas ent. 1720. (see 1724)
„	SW	Starling Wilford (?) „ „ (see 1728 and 1737).
„	EF	Edward Feline „ „ (see also 1722-1729)
„	IG	John Gibbons „ 1723.
„	EV	Edw. Vincent „ „ (see 1729)
„	TM	Thos. Mason „ 1720.
„		Jas. Gould „ 1722.
„	IE	John Edwards „ 1724.
„	G	Geo. Wickes „ 1721.
„	TC	Thos. Clark „ 1725.
„	En	Thos. England „ „
„	WS	Wm. Scarlett „ „
„	TA	Peter Tabart „ „
„	PT	Do. do. „ „
„	CO	Mathew Cooper „ „
„	MC	Do. do. „ „
„	LL	Louis Laroche „ „
„	IF	John Flavill „ 1726.
1726-7	AV	Name not traced.
„	WD	Wm. Darkeratt „ 1724.
„	RG	Richd. Green „ 1726.
„	P	Benj. Pyne (as before 1697).
„	PA	Peter Archambo ent. 1722.
„	F	Wm. Fawdery „ 1720.
„	WA	Wm. Atkinson „ 1725.

Date.	Mark	Goldsmiths' Marks and Names.
1726-7	R·L	Robt. Lucas ent. 1726. (variant of mark of)
„	EV	Thos. Evesdon „ 1713. (see 1720 and 1721)
„		Fras. Nelme „ 1722.
„	BF	Bern'd. Fletcher „ 1725.
„	TB	Thos. Bamford „ 1720.
„	WI	Robt. Williams „ 1726.
„	RW	Do. do. „ „
„	GN	Gawen Nash „ „
„	PE	Chas. Perier „ 1727.
„	CP	Do. do. „ „
„	GB	Geo. Brome „ 1726.
„	PC	Peter le Chaube „ „
1727-8	IR	Isaac Ribouleau „ 1720.
„	IS	* Jas. Smith „ „
„	EW	Edw. Wood „ 1722.
„	EC	Ed. Cornock „ 1707.
„	SB	Saml. Bates „ 1727.
„	TE	Thomas England „ 1725.
„	RP	Richard Pargeter „ 1730.
„	MC	Matt. Cooper „ 1725. (see 1725)
„	AR	?Andrew Raven „ 1706.
„	IS	Jno. le Sage „ 1722.
„	RC	Name not traced.
„	SH	Sarah Holaday „ 1725.
„	IE	John East „ 1721.
„	IC	Jonah Clifton „ 1720.

Date.	Goldsmiths' Marks and Names.		
1727-8	SL	Saml. Laundry	ent. 1727.
"	EB	Edmd. Bodington	" "
"	KA MU	Chas. Kandler & Jas. Murray	" "
"	IM CK	Do. do.	" "
"	EB	Edw. Bennett	" "
"	F	Hester Fawdery	" "
"	TC	Thos. Cooke	" "
"	RH	Richd. Hutchinson	" "
"	KA	Chas. Kandler	" "
"	WE	Geo. Weir	" "
"	GW	Do. do.	" "
"	BE	Name not traced.	
"	AB	Abel Brokesby	" "
"	DI	Dike Impey (probably)	" "
"	BB	Benj. Bentley	" 1728.
"	MI	Mary Johnson	" 1727.
"	IW	I. Wichaller	" 1728.
"	HA	Chas. Hatfield	" 1727.
"	SL	Sam. Laundry	" "
"	CO	Matw. Cooper	" 1725.
"	WI	David Willaume	" 1728.
"	DC	Danl. Cunningham	" 1720.
"	RG	Richd. Gines	" "
"	GG	Geo. Gillingham	" 1721.
"	CH	Chas. Hatfield	" 1727.
"	IF	Jacob Foster	" 1726.

Date.	Goldsmiths' Marks and Names.		
1727-8	GR	Saml. Green	ent. 1721.
"	SH	Wm. Shaw	" 1728.
1728-9	WD	Wm. Darkeratt	" 1720.
"	IG	James Goodwin	" 1721.
"	TL	Tim. Ley (as before 1697)	
"	BF	Blanche Fraillon	ent. 1727.
"	CA	Isaac Callard	" 1726.
"	EG	Name not traced.	
"	IW	James Wilkes	" 1722.
"	AR	Peter Archambo	" 1720.
"	IH	Josh. Holland	" "
"	SP	Simon Pantin (see 1729)	" "
"	IM	John Millington	" 1728.
"	EB	Edward Bennett	" 1727.
"	FR	Ralph Frith	" 1728.
"	RF	Do. do.	" "
"	HO	Geo. Hodges	" "
"	GH	Do. do.	" "
"	IF	John Fawdery	" "
"	IM	John Montgomery	" "
"	RI	? John Richardson	" 1723.
"	WF	? Wm. Fordham	" 1706.
"	SW	Starling Wilford (see 1725 and 1737)	" 1729.
1729-30	IT	John Tuite*	" 1721.
"	TT	Thos. Tearle	" 1720.
"	EV	Ed. Vincent (see 1725)	" "

Date.	Goldsmiths' Marks and Names.		
1729-30	AN	Anthony Nelme	ent. 1722.
"	CM	Chas. Martin	" 1729.
"	EF	Edwd. Feline (see 1722 and 1725)	" 1720.
"	AB	Abel Brokesby (see 1727)	" 1727.
"	SP	Simon Pantin (see 1728)	" 1717.
"	GI	George Jones (see 1735-6)	" 1724.
"	EI	Name not traced.	
"	PL	Paul Lamerie	" "
"	RM	Ralph Maidman	" 1730.
"	RS	Richd. Scarlett (see 1723)	" 1720.
"	M	Name not traced.	
"	II	John Jones	" 1729.
"	SM	Saml. Margas	" 1720.
"	CA	Chas. Alchorne	" 1729.
"	SW	Sam. Welder	" "
"	BG	Benj. Goodwin	" "
"	GM	Name not traced.	
"	EF	Edith Fletcher	" "
"	EG	Eliz. Goodwin	" "
"	IM	Jas. Maitland of the "Grasshopper," Suffolk Street.	" 1728.
1730-1	AC	Aug. Courtauld	ent. 1729.
"	LA	Paul Lamerie	" 1712.
"	IE	Saml. Jefferys	" 1697.
"	GS	Gabl. Sleath	" 1720.

Date.	Mark	Goldsmiths' Marks and Names.	
1730-1	RB	Richd. Bayley	ent. 1720.
"	WB	Wm. Belassyse	" 1723.
"	IC	Isaac Callard	" 1726.
"	WP	Wm. Petley	" 1720.
"	PP	Perè Pilleau	" "
"	CK	Chas. Kandler	" 1727.
"	IW	John White	" 1719.
"	AT	Anne Tanqueray	" 1720.
"	SL	? Saml. Laundry (see also 1727)	" 1727.
"	IC	John Chapman (see 1737)	" 1730.
"	SH	Samuel Hitchcock	" "
"	IJ	Jas. Jenkins	" 1731.
"	WI	Wm. Justus	" "
"	WR	Wm. Reeve	" "
"	AB	Aaron Bates	" 1730.
"	CO	Aug. Courtauld	" 1708.
1731-2	IG	John Gamon	" 1728.
"	EY	Edwd. Yorke	" 1730.
"	GH	Geo. Hindmarsh	" 1731.
"	DW	David Willaume	" 1728.
"	WD	Wm. Darker	" 1731.
"	TE	Thos. England	" 1725.
"	IL	Jane Lambe	" 1729.
"	ML	Mary Lofthouse	" 1731.
"	TM	Thos. Merry	" "
"	IG	Jeffrey Griffith	" "
1731-2	SP	Sarah Parr	ent. 1720.
"	G RA H	Robt. Abercromby & Geo. Hindmarsh	" 1731.
"	WW	Wm. Woodward	" "
"	TC	Thos. Causton	" 1730.
"	ER	Etienne Rongent	" 1731.
"	WD	Wm. Darker (see 1731)	" "
1732-3	R·B	Richd. Beale	" "
"	L S I G	Sam Laundry & Jeffy Griffith	" "
"	I·S	Joseph Smith	" 1728.
"	EP	Edw. Pocock	" "
"	I·S	John Sanders	" 1720.
"	I·F	John Fawdery (see 1728)	" 1728.
"	F·P	Fras. Pages	" 1729.
"	LO	? Matt. Lofthouse	" 1705.
"	DL	Name not traced.	
"	WL	Wm. Lukin	" 1725.
"	FS	Fras. Spilsbury (same mark found in square stamp).	" 1729.
"	TP	Thos. Parr	ent. 1732.
"	WM	Wm. Matthews	" 1728.
"	IS	Jas. Savage	" "
"	IP	John Pero	" 1732.
"	IG	Jas. Gould	" "
"	GS	Geo. Smith	" "
"		R. W. (as 1696).	
"	WS	Wm. Soame	" "
"	CG	Chas. Gibbons	" "
"	SH	Wm. Shaw	" 1728.
1733-4	IE	John Eckfourd, jr.	" 1725.
1733-4	AC	Aug. Courtauld	ent. 1729.
"	IS	Jas. Slater	" 1732.
"	RB	Richd. Bayley	" 1720.
"	HH	* Henry Herbert (of the "Three Crowns")	" 1734.
"	WS	Wm. Soame	" 1732.
"	EB	Eliz. Buteux	" 1731.
"	DC	Danl. Chapman	" 1729.
"	LP	Lewis Pantin	" 1733.
"	CS	Chas. Sprage	" 1734.
"	RA	Robt. Abercromby (see 1734)	" 1731.
"	GB	Geo. Braithwaite? earliest ment.	1728.
1734-5	RM	Ralph Maidman	ent. 1731.
"	CH	Caleb Hill	" 1728.
"	LM	Lewis Mettayer	" 1720.
"	WG	Wm. Gould	" 1732.
"	RA	Robt. Abercromby (see 1733)	" 1731.
"	IN	John Newton	" 1726.
"	MP	Mary Pantin	" 1733.
"	RP	Richd. Pargeter	" 1730.
"	HA	Hugh Arnell	" 1734.
"	AC EF	Alex. Coates & Edw. French	" "
"	IT	John Taylor	" "
"	GO	Wm. Gould	" "
"	IJ	John Jacob	" "
"	IP	John Pollock	" "
"	IM	Jas. Manners	" "

Date.	Mark	Goldsmiths' Marks and Names.	
'34-5	EF	Edw. French	ent. 1734.
"	IB	Jas. Brooker	" "
"	SH	Sam. Hutton	" "
"	WK	Wm. Kidney	" "
'35-6	GI	Geo. Jones	" 1724.
"	RG TC	Richd. Gurney & Thos. Cook	" 1734.
"	EB	Edw. Bennett	" 1731.
"	KA	Fred Kandler	" 1735.
"	BG	Benj. Godfrey (see 1739)	" 1732.
"	GE	Grif. Edwards	" "
"	WS	Wm. Shaw	" 1727.
"	PB	Peter Bennett	" 1731.
"	IW	John White	" 1724.
"	AT	Wm. Atkinson	" 1725.
"	WY	Wm. Young	" 1735.
"	EI	Name not traced, (see 1729-30)	
"	FN	Francis Nelme	" "
"	IB	John Barbe	" "
"	GH	Geo Hindmarsh	" "
"	CH	Christn. Hilland	" 1736.
"	DL	Name not traced	
"	HH	Henry Herbert (of the "Three Crowns")	" 1734.
"	LH	Lewis Hamon	" 1735.
6-7	KV	Name not traced.	
"	WG	Wm. Garrard	" 1735.
"	SW	Sam. Wood	" 1733-7.
1736-7	BW	Benj. West	ent. 1737.
"	RB	Robt. Brown	" 1736.
"	AH	Ann Hill	" 1734.
"	TM	Thos. Mason	" 1733.
"	IJ	John Jones	" "
"	IF	John Fossey	" "
"	BB RT	Bennet Bradshaw & R. Tyrill	" 1737.
"	IK	Jerem. King	" 1736.
"	TM	Thos. Mann	" "
"	DH	David Hennell	" "
"	BW	Benj. West	" 1737.
"	HH	Henry Herbert	" 1734.
"	HP	? Harvey Price	" 1726.
1737-8	IA MF	Joseph Allen & Co.	" 1729.
"	GW	Geo. Weekes	" 1735.
"	IS	Jos. Sanders	" 1730.
"	SB	Saml. Blackborrow	" 1720.
"	TW	Thos. Whipham	" 1737.
"	GH	Geo. Hindmarsh (see 1735-6)	" 1735.
"	SW	Starling Wilford	" 1729.
"	IC	John Chapman (see 1730)	" 1730.
"	RW	Robt Williams	" 1726.
"	RB	Richd. Beale	" 1731.
"	SI	Simon Jouet	" 1723.
"	TI	Thos. Jackson	" 1736.
"	TG	Thos. Gladwin	" 1737.
1737-8	IB	John Barrett	ent. 1737.
"	GB	Geo. Baskerville	" 1738.
"	PP	Philip Platel	" 1737.
"	II	Jas. Jenkins	" 1738.
"	GR	Gundry Roode	" 1737.
"	IR	John Robinson	" 1738.
"	IS	Jas. Schruder	" 1737.
"	WS	Wm. Soame	" 1738.
"	SW	Sam. Wood	" 1737.
"	DW	Denis Wilks	" "
1738-9	RZ	Richd. Zouch	" 1735.
"	TW	Thos. Whipham	" 1739
"	FK	Fred Kandler	" 1735.
"	IR	Jno. Robinson	" 1738.
"	LD	Louis Dupont	" 1736.
"	TR	Thos. Rush	" 1724.
"	BB	Benj. Blakeley	" 1738.
"	HB	Henry Bates	" "
"	PB	Philip Brugier	" "
"	WW	Wm. West	" "
"	FP	Fras. Pages	" 1739.
"	RH	Robt. Hill	" "
"	IL	James Langlois	" 1738.
1739-40	FK	Fred Kandler	" 1735.
"	RB	? Richd. Bayler	" 1739.
"	IP	John Pero (see 1732)	" "

Date.	Goldsmiths' Marks and Names.*		
1739-40	Humphrey	Payne	ent. 1739.
"	Sarah	Holaday	" 1719.
"	Benj. (see 1735)	Godfrey	" 1732.
"	Thos.	Whipham	" 1737.
"	Chas.	Hillan	" 1741.
"	Wm.	Kidney	" 1739.
"	Paul	Lamerie	" "
"	Ben.	Blakeley	" "
"	Isaac	Callerd	" "
"	Jeff.	Griffith	" "
"	Thos.	Tearle	" "
"	Jnthn.	Fossy	" "
"	Paul	Crespin	" "
"	John	Harwood	" "
"	Richd.	Bayley	" "
"	Robt.	Abercromby	" "
"	Lewis	Dupont	" "
"	Wm.	Hunter	" "
"	Wm.	Gwillim	" "
"	Geo.	Boothby	" "
"	Edw.	Aldridge	" "
"	Wm.	Soame	" "
"	Peter	Bennett	" "
"	Henry	Bates	" "
"	John	Tuite	" "

Date.	Goldsmiths' Marks and Names.		
1739-40	Thos.	England	ent. 1739.
"	Robt.	Lucas	" "
"	Ben.	Godfrey	" "
"	Do.	do.	" "
"	Gawen	Nash	" "
"	John	Bryan	" "
"	Richard	Beale	" "
"	John	Cam	" 1740.
"	J.	Barbitt	" 1739.
"	Richd.	Pargeter	" "
"	Marmdk.	Daintry	" "
"	Ed.	Bennett	" "
"	Do.	do.	" "
"	Bennett	Bradshaw & Co.	" "
"	Thos.	Bamford	" "
"	John	Eckfourd	" "
"	Wm.	Shaw	" "
"	John (see 1750)	Jacobs	" "
"	John (see p. 190)	Pero	" "
"	John	White	" "
"	Henry	Herbert	" "
"	Richd.	Zouch	" "
"	Susan'h	Hatfield	" "
"	J.	McFarlane	" "
"	Henry	Morris	" "
"	John	Luff	" "

Date.	Goldsmiths' Marks and Names.		
1739-40	Jessie	McFarlane	ent. 1739.
"	Wm.	Justus	" "
"	Wm.	Young	" "
"	Jas.	Manners	" "
"	John	Harvey	" "
"	Chas.	Jackson	" "
"	Thos.	Rush	" "
"	Thos.	Gilpin	" "
"	Danl.	Chartier	" 1740.
"	Wm.	Shaw	" 1739.
"	Richd.	Gosling	" "
"	Fras.	Spilsbury ‡	" "
"	Louis	Hamon	" "
"	Sam.	Hutton	" 1740.
"	John	Gamon	" 1739.
"	Fras.	Nelme	" "
"	Henry	Morris	" "
"	Thos.	Pye	" "
"	Jas.	West	" "
"	Jas.	Paltro	" "
"	John	Harwood	" "
"	Denis	Wilks	" "
"	Philip	Roker	" "
"	Simon	Jouet	" "
"	Chas.	Clark	" "
"	John le Sage		" "

Date.	Goldsmiths' Marks and Names.		
39-40	Benj.	Sanders	ent. 1739.
"	Abm. de	Oliveyra	" "
"	Thos.	Mason	" "
"	Chas.	Martin	" 1740.
"	Jos.	Steward	" 1739.
"	Geo.	Smith	" "
"	Louis	Laroche	" "
740-1	John	Robinson	" "
"	Griff.	Edwards	" "
"	John	Pollock	" "
"	Jos.	Sanders	" "
"	Benj.	Sanders	" 1737.
"	Wm.	Garrard	" 1735.
"	Gabl.	Sleath	" "
"	Richd.	Gurney & Co	" 1739.
"	Ed.	Wood	" 1740.
"	Chas	Bellassyse	" "
"	Sarah	Hutton	" "
"	Ed.	Lambe	" "
"	Thos.	Mercer	" "
"	John	Barbe	" 1739.
"	Paul	Crespin	" 1740.
"	Isabel	Pero	" "
"	Lewis	Ouvry	" "
"	Jas.	Gould	" 1741.
"	Edwd. (see 1744)	Aldridge	" 1739.

Date.	Goldsmiths' Marks and Names.		
1740-1	? John	Owing	ent. 1724.
"	Name not traced.		
"	Do.	do.	
"	John	Roker	" 1740.
"	Abm. le	Francis	" "
"	Benj.	Gurdon	" "
1741-2	David	Hennell	" 1739.
"	James	Shruder	" "
"	Eliza	Godfrey	" 1741.
"	Saml.	Roby	" 1740.
"	Geo.	Wickes	" 1739.
"	Thos.	Farren	" "
"	Dinah	Gamon	" 1740.
"	John	Newton	" 1739.
"	Thos	Gilpin	" "
"	Chas	Hillan	" 1741.
"	John	Stewart (?)	
"	Peter	Archambo	" 1739.
"	Jas.	Willmott	" 1741.
"	John	Spackman	" "
"	Chas	Laughton	" 1739.
"	Thos	Lawrence	" 1742.
"	Jer'mi'h	King	" 1739.
"	Benj.	Gurdon	" 1740.
"	Robt.	Tyrrill	" 1742.
1742-3	Jno.	Gould	" 1739.

Date.	Goldsmiths' Marks and Names.		
1742-3	Paul	Crespin	ent. 1739.
"	Jos. M'decai	Allen & Fox	" "
"	Robt.	Brown	" "
"	Fras.	Spilsbury	" "
"	Eliz.	Tuite	" 1741.
"	Anne John (see 1745)	Craig & Neville	" 1740.
"	Saml.	Wells	" "
"	Robt.	Abercromby	" 1739.
"	Jas.	Montgomery	" 1742.
"	Jos.	Timberlake	" 1743.
"	Phillips	Garden	" 1739.
"	Paul	Crespin	" "
"	John	Cam	" 1740.
1743-4	Dd.	Williams	" 1739.
"	Benj.	Sanders	" "
"	? Robt.	Abercromby	" "
"	Wm.	Hunter	" "
"	Wm.	Gould	" "
"	Jas.	Wilks	" "
"	Ed.	Feline	" "
"	Aug.	Courtauld	" "
"	Geo.	Jones	" "
"	Jer'mi'h	Ashley	" 1740.
"	Henry	Brind	" 1742.
"	Robt	Abercromby	" 1739.
"	Pere	Pilleau	" "

Date.	Goldsmiths' Marks and Names.	
1743-4	Thos. Whipham	ent. 1737.
"	Name not traced.	
"	Isaac Duke	" 1743.
"	Ed. Malluson	" "
"	Geo Methuen	" "
"	Chas. Johnson	" "
"	Ann Farren	" "
"	Geo. Ridout	" "
"	Robt. Swanson	" "
1744-5	Wm. Soame or Wm. Shaw	" 1723. " 1727.
"	Edwd. Aldridge (see 1740)	" 1739.
"	Ed. Feline	" "
"	Lewis Pantin	" "
"	Robt. Pilkington	" "
"	Chas. Hatfield	" "
"	Peter Archambo	" "
"	John Quantock	" "
"	Aymé Videau	" "
"	John Barbe	" "
"	John Edwards	" "
"	Wm Bagnall	" 1744.
"	Wm Gwillim & Peter Castle	" "
"	Jas. Smith	" "
"	John Neville	" 1745.
"	Thos. Jackson	" 1739.
"	Nich's Sprimont	" 1742.
1744-5	Jas. Morrison	ent. 1740.
1745-6	Benj. West	" 1739.
"	Thos. Whipham & Wm. Williams	" 1740.
"	Ann Craig & John Neville (see 1742)	" "
"	John Holland	" 1739.
"	Ben. Cartwright	" "
"	Fred. Kandler	" "
"	Wm. Cripps	" 1743.
"	Fras. Crump	" 1741.
"	John Higginbotham	" 1745.
"	Geo. Baskerville	" "
"	Jas. Manners, Jr.	" "
"	? Jer'mi'h King	" "
"	John Swift (probably, see 1754-5)	" 1739.
"	Sam Key	" 1745.
"	Robt. Andrews	" "
"	John Harvey	" "
1746-7	Sam Wood	" 1739.
"	Jas. Gould	" 1743.
"	Wm. Hunter	" 1739.
"	Wm. Peaston	" 1746.
"	Jas. Morrison	" 1744.
"	Henry Morris	" 1739.
"	Jos. Barker	" 1746.
"	Ed. Vincent	" 1739.
"	Ann Kersill	" 1747.
1746-7	Ernest Sieber	ent. 1746.
"	Geo. Young	" "
"	Saml. Meriton	" "
"	Henry Herbert	" 1747.
"	Do. do.	" "
"	Simon Jouet	" "
"	Benj. Cartwright	" 1739.
1747-8	Jno. Sanders	" "
"	Wm. Gould	" "
"	Richd. Kersill	" 1744.
"	Wm. Williams	" 1742.
"	Saml. Courtauld (see 1750).	" 1746.
"	Jacob Marsh	" 1744.
"	Thos. Carlton	" "
"	? John Eckfourd	" 1739.
"	? Benj. Griffin or Benj. Gignac	" 1742. " 1744.
"	John Richardson	" 1743.
"	Thos. Parr	" 1739.
"	M'duke Daintry	" "
"	Wm Solomon	" 1747.
"	Saml. Herbert	" "
"	John Fray	" 1748.
"	Ben. Cooper	" "
1748-9	Edwd. Medlycott	" "
"	John Wirgman	" 1745.
"	Hmphy. Payne (see 1739)	" 1739.
"	Elias Cachart	" 1742.

Date.	Goldsmiths' Marks and Names.		
1748-9	MF	M'decai Fox	ent. 1746.
"	WG	Wm. Grundy	" 1748.
"	IC	John Carman	" "
"	GY	Geo. Young	" 1746.
"	IB	John Barbe	" 1739.
"	GH	Geo. Hunter	" 1748.
"	PG	Phillips Garden	" "
"	WS	Wm. Shaw	" 1749.
"	EH	Eliz. Hartley	" 1748.
"	EJ	Eliz. Jackson	" "
"	EO	Eliz. Oldfield	" "
"	ED	Ed. Dowdall	" "
"	DS	Danl. Shaw	" "
"	WB	Walter Brind	" 1749.
1749-50	WG	Wm. Grundy	" 1743.
"	DP	Dan. Piers	" 1746.
"	BC	Benj. Cartwright	" 1739.
"	PC	Paul Crespin	" "
"	EDA	Name not traced.	
"	IKing	Jerem'h King	" "
"	AP	Abm. Portal	" 1749.
"	AL	Abm. le Francis	" 1746.
"	ID	Jabez Daniel	" 1749.
"	WM	Wm. MacKenzie	" 1748.
"	WK	Wm. Kersill	" 1749.
"	AK	Andrew Killick	" "
"	HH	Henry Haynes	" "

Date.	Goldsmiths' Marks and Names.		
1749-50	GB	Geo. Bindon	ent. 1749.
"	TM	Thos. Mann	" 1739.
"	IA	John Alderhead	" 1750.
"	IT	Jas. Tookey	" "
"	WW	Wm. Wooler	" "
"	GM	Geo. Morris	" "
"	TI	Thos. Jeannes	" "
1750-1	IP	John Priest	" 1748.
"	CC	Chas. Chesterman	" 1741.
"	EC	Eben. Coker	" 1739.
"	IR	John Rowe	" 1749.
"	RTGC	Richd. Gurney & Co.	" 1750.
"	HSHB	S. Herbert & Co.	" "
"	LG	Louis Guichard	" 1748.
"	GC	Geo. Campar	" 1749.
"	FW IF	Fuller White & John Fray	" 1750.
"	HB	Henry Bayley	" "
"	IJ	John Jacobs (see 1739)	" 1739.
"	SC	Saml. Courtauld (see 1747 and 1755)	" 1746.
"	PL	Paul Lamerie (see 1729 and 1730)	" 1732.
"	AM	A. Montgomery	" 1750.
"	MW	Michl. Ward	" "
"	GB	Geo. Bindon	" 1749.
"	IH	John Harvey	" 1750.
"	TS	Thos. Smith	" "

Date.	Goldsmiths' Marks and Names.		
1750-1	IB	John Berthelot	ent. 1750.
"	LI	L'r'nce Johnson	" 1751.
"	PG	Phillips Garden	" "
"	MB	Math. Brodier	" "
"	FC	Fras. Crump	" 1750.
"	FC	Do. do.	" "
c. 1750-60	W·F	Name not traced.	
1751-2	IW	? John Wetherell	" 1743.
"	IP	John Payne	" 1750.
"	DW	Denis Wilks	" 1747.
"	FK	Fred Knopfell	" 1752.
"	ST	Saml. Taylor	" 1744.
"	PW	P. Werritzer	" 1750.
"	TM	Thos. Moore	" "
"	WW	Wm. Woodward	" 1743.
"	GSS	G. & S. Smith	" 1751.
"	GM	Geo. Morris	" "
"	NW	Nicks Winkins	" "
"	PP	Paul Pinard	" "
"	ED	Ed. Doweal	" "
"	TB	Thos. Beere	" "
"	PB	Phil. Bruguier	" 1752.
1752-3	RC	Robt. Cox	" "
"	LH	Lewis Haman	" 1739.
"	RC	Robt. Cox (see above)	" 1752.
"	WA	Wm. Alexander	" 1742.
"	IP	John Payne	" 1751.

Date.	Goldsmiths' Marks	and Names.	
1752-3	WH	Wm. Homer	ent. 1750.
"	W W·S P	Wm. Shaw & Wm. Priest	" 1749.
"	IB	John Berthelot	" 1741.
"	IR	John Richardson	" 1752.
"	DP	Danl. Piers	" 1746.
"	CC	Chas. Chesterman	" 1752.
"	IC	John Carman	" "
"	RG	Richd. Goldwire	" 1753.
"	PG	Phillips Garden	" 1751.
1753-4	GH	Geo. Hunter	" 1748.
"	DP	Danl. Piers	" "
"	T&W	Turner & Williams	" 1753.
"	RG	Richd. Gosling	" 1739.
"	RH	Robt. Hennell	" 1753.
"	IC	John Cafe	" 1742.
"	AI	Alex. Johnston	" 1747.
"	FW	Fuller White	" 1744.
"	DW IF	Denis Wilks & John Fray	" 1753.
"	WB	Wm. Bond	" "
"	TT	Thos. Towman	" "
"	IE	John Edwards	" "
"	F G·S C	Gabl. Sleath & Fras. Crump	" "
"	DCF	D. C Fueter	" "
"	DS	Dorothy Sarbit	" "
"	EA	Edward Aldridge (see 1740 and 1744)	" 1743.
"	E I A S	Edwd. Aldridge & John Stamper	" 1753.
1753-4	TR	Thos. Rowe	ent. 1753.
"	SS	Saml. Smith	" 1754.
"	SL	Simon Le Sage	" "
"	HC	Henry Corry	" "
"	BC	* Benj. Cartwright	" "
"	SB	Sarah Buttall	" "
1754-5	P P*A M	Peter Archambo & Peter Meure	" 1749.
"	RP	? Robt. Perth.	
"	WC	Wm. Cripps	" 1743.
"	I·Q	John Quantock	" 1754.
"	E I A S	Ed. Aldridge & John Stamper	" 1753.
"	PG	Phillips Garden	" "
"	IM	John Munns	" "
"	DM	Do'thy Mills	" 1752.
"	IH	John Holland	" 1739.
"	IS	John Steward	" 1755.
"	TC	Thos. Collier	" 1754.
"	HD	Henry Dutton	" "
"	W·B	Walter Brind	" 1749.
"	GB WS	Geo. Baskerville & Wm. Sampel	" 1755.
"	DPW	Dobson Prior & Williams	" "
"	D	John Delmester	" "
"	W·I	? Wm. Justus	" 1739.
"	IS	John Swift (see 1745 and below)	" "
"	H·M	Henry Miller	ent. 1740.
1755-6	IS	John Swift	" 1739.
1755-6	WS	Wm. Sanden	ent. 1755.
"	SL	Simon Le Sage	" 1754.
"	MF	Magd'n Feline	" 1753.
"	TW	? Thos. Wright	" 1754.
"	S·C	Saml. Courtauld (see 1750)	" 1746.
"	PC	Paul Crespin (see 1749)	" 1739.
"	W·B P	Wm. Bond & John Phipps	" 1751.
"	WT	Wm. Turner	" "
"	WB	Wm. Bond	" 1753.
"	II	Jas. Jones	" 1755.
"	PT	Peter Taylor	" 1740.
"	FV	Fred Vonham	" 1752.
"	SS	Saml. Siervent	" 1755.
"	IW	John Wirgman	" 1745.
"	RM	Richd. Mills	" 1755.
"	B·B	Benj: Brewood	" "
"	ED	Ed. Doweal	" 1751.
"	RCox	Robt. Cox	" 1755.
"	R·C	Do. do.	" "
"	TB	Thos. Beezley	" "
"	AS	Albert Schurman	" 1756.
"	IR	John Robinson	" 1739.
1756-7	S·W	Saml. Wheat	" 1756.
"	P·G	Pierre Gillois	" 1754.
"	WR	Wm. Robertson	" 1753.
"	WC	Wm. Caldecott	" 1756.

Date.	Goldsmiths' Marks	and Names.	
1756-7	TG	? Thos. Gilpin	ent. 1739.
"	TH	Thos. Heming	" 1745.
"	R W P P	Name not traced.	
"	MR	Mathew Roker	" 1755.
"	PC	Paul Callard	" 1751.
"	IE	John Edwards	" 1753.
"	WG	Wm. Gould	" "
"	T·D W·W	T. & W. Devonshire Watkins	" 1756.
"	BC	Ben. Cartwright	" "
"	EJ	Edw. Jay	" 1757.
1757-8	D·H	David Hennell	" 1736.
"	CL ARE	Joseph Clare (see 1716)	" 1713.
"	EG	Eliza Godfrey	" 1741.
"	IJ	John Jacobs	" 1739.
"	R W P P	W. & R. Peaston	" 1756.
"	ED	Ed. Darvill	" 1757.
"	RI	Robert Innes	" 1742.
"	SA	Stephen Ardesoif	" 1756.
"	EB	Ed. Bennett	" 1739.
"	IK TG	John Kentenber & Thos. Groves	1757
"	IF	John Frost	" "
"	IF	Do. do.	" "
"	H I S C	John Hyatt & Chas. Semore	" "
"	AA	Arthur Annesley (see 1761)	" 1758.
"	RB	Robt. Burton	" "

Date.	Goldsmiths' Marks	and Names.	
1757-8	IS	John Schuppe	ent. 1753.
"	WC	Wm. Cafe	" 1757.
1758-9	FN	Fras. Nelme	" 1722.
"	ST	Saml. Taylor	" 1744.
"	WC	Wm. Cripps	" 1743.
"	S·C	Name not traced.	
"	W W S P	Wm. Shaw & Wm. Priest	" 1749.
"	CB	Name not traced.	
"	I·H	John Hague	" 1758.
"	WB	Wm. Bell	" 1759.
"	F L H B	Lewis Herne & Francis Butty	" 1757.
"	I·BELL	Jos. Bell	" 1756.
"	I B S A	Name not traced.	
1759-60	H S H B	S. Herbert & Co.	" 1750.
"	FK	Fred. Kandler	" 1739.
"	I·D	John Delmester	" 1755.
"	I·P	John Perry	" 1757.
"	S·W	Saml. Wood, 2nd mk.	" 1739.
"	IBBOT	Geo. Ibbott	" 1753.
"	I·P	John Perry	" 1757.
"	SL	Simon Le Sage	" 1754.
"	WB	? Walter Brind	" 1749.
"	WC	Wm. Cripps	" 1743.
"	IH	John Hyatt	" 1748.
"	HB	Henry Bayley (probably).	

Date.	Goldsmiths' Marks and Names.		
1759-60	SW	? Saml. Wheat	ent. 1756.
"	S WI A	Stephen Abdy & Wm. Jury	" 1759.
"	AB	Alex. Barnett	" "
"	TC	Thos. Congreve	" 1756.
"	TD	Thos. Doxsey	" "
"	WM	Wm. Moody	" "
"	WD	Wm. Day	" 1759.
"	SE	Saml. Eaton	" "
"	JK	? Jno. Kentenber	
1760-1	RR	Robt. Rew	" 1754.
"	EW	Edwd. Wakelin	" 1747.
"	CD	Name not traced.	
"	FW	Fuller White	" 1758.
"	AS	Alex. Saunders	" 1757.
"	IM	John Moore	" 1758.
"	CT	C'nst'ne Teulings	" 1755.
"	WH	Wm. Howard	" 1760.
"	GM	Geo. Methuen	" 1743.
"	IE	John Eaton	" 1760.
c. 1760-1	WL	Name not traced.	
"	Lee	Jeremy Lee	" 1739.
1761-2	RR	Richd. Rugg	" 1754.
"	WP	Wm. Plummer	" 1755.
"	F LH B	Louis Herne & Fras. Butty	" 1757.
"	FB ND	Fras. Butty & Nicks. Dumee	" "
"	WS	Wm. Shaw	" 1749.

Date.	Goldsmiths' Marks and Names.		
1761-2	IH	John Horsley.	
"	IG	John Gorham	ent. 1757.
"	AA	Arthur Annesley (see 1757)	" 1758.
"	GH	Geo. Hunter	" 1748.
"	MF	Magdalen Feline	" 1753.
"	TH	Thomas Heming (see 1756)	" 1745.
"	MP	Mary Piers	" 1758.
"	TP	Thos. Powell	" "
1762-3	II	Jas. Jones	" 1755.
"	WT	Wm. Tant (probably)	" 1773.
"	WS	Wm. Sampel	" 1755.
"	LB	Louis Black	" 1761.
"	C TW	Thos. Whipham & Chas. Wright	" 1757.
"	GI	Geo. Ibbott	" 1753.
"	SD	Saml. Delamy	" 1762.
"	D WI	W. & J. Deane	" "
"	IB	Jos. Bell	" 1756.
"	E EA A	Edwd. Aldridge & Co.	
"	WD	Wm. Day	" 1759.
"	W Wa	Wm. Watkins	" 1756.
"	E*A	Edward Aldridge	" 1739.
"	R*P	R Peaston	" 1756.
1763-4	RT	Richd. Thomas	" 1755.
"	TD	Tmpsn. Davis	" 1757.
"	EA	Edward Aldridge	" 1739.
"	C TW W	Thos. Whipham & Chas. Wright	" 1758.

Date.	Goldsmiths' Marks and Names.		
1763-4	DS RS	Danl. Smith & Robt. Sharp	
"	T WC C	T. & W. Chawner (probably).	
"	EC	Ebenezer Coker	"
"	PV	Phil. Vincent	ent. 1757.
"	WK	Wm. King	" 1761.
"	IB	John Buckett.	
"	IA	John Aspinshaw	" 1763.
"	IL	John Lamfert	" 1748.
c. 1763-4	NH	Name not traced.	
"	TE GS	Do. do.	
1764-5	R DH H	D. & R. Hennell	" 1768.
"	TH RM	? Thos. Hannam & Rich. Mills	
"	CM	Name not traced.	
"	WP RP	W. & R. Peaston (probably).	
"	I WV L	Names not traced.	
"	H IS C	John Hyatt & C. Semore	ent. 1757.
"	AL	Aug. Le Sage	" 1767.
"	TF IM	Thos. Freeman & J. Marshall	" 1764.
"	AC	Anthy. Calame	" "
"	IAC	J. A. Calame	" "
"	II	John Innocent (probably).	
"	WP RP	W. & R. Peaston (see above)	"
"	WC	Wm. Cafe	ent. 1757
"	ER	Name not traced.	
"	BM	Do. do.	
"	C TW	Thos. Whipham & Chas. Wright	" 1758

Date.	Goldsmiths' Marks and Names.	
1765-6	I W V L	Names not traced.
"	GS	Do. do.
"	WC	Wm. Caldecott ent. 1756.
"	EC	Eben. Coker (probably).
"	WF	Name not traced.
"	ER	Emick Romer "
"	BM	Name not traced.
"	R·P	? R. Peaston.
"	IA	John Allen ent. 1761.
"	SH	Sam. Howland " 1760.
"	GH	Geo. Hunter " 1765.
"	T·C W·C	T. & W. Chawner (probably).
1766-7	LH	Name not traced.
"	LC	Louisa Courtauld.
"	JL	John Lampfert ent. 1748.
"	I I L S	John Langford & John Sebille
"	MF	Matthew Ferris " 1759.
"	T·H I·C	Thos. Hannam & John Crouch
"	FC	Fras. Crump " 1756.
"	GA	Geo. Andrews " 1763.
"	TD	Thos. Dealtry " 1765.
"	CM	Chas. Miegg " 1767.
"	DM	Dorothy Mills (probably).
"	TW	Thos. Wynne ent. 1754.
1767-8	JR	Jno. Richardson " 1752.
"	I W F K	Names not traced.

Date.	Goldsmiths' Marks and Names.	
1767-8	O TB I	Thos. Bumfries & Orlando Jackson } ent. 1766.
"	H S H B	S. Herbert & Co. " 1750.
"	CB	Name not traced.
"	WA	Wm. Abdy " 1767.
"	G·F	Geo. Fayle " "
"	W·T	Wm. Tuite (probably).
"	JE	Name not traced.
1768-9	I·P E·W	John Parker & Edwd. Wakelin
"	I·H	James Hunt ent. 1760.
"	W T C C	T. & W. Chawner (probably).
"	R D S S	Dan. Smith & Robt. Sharp
"	W A L	Name not traced.
"	FS	Fras. Spilsbury, Jr.
"	ET	? Eliz. Tuite (see 1742) ent. 1741.
"	WJ	Name not traced.
"	EC	Edward Capper (probably).
"	FC	Fras. Crump ent. 1756.
"	WP JP	W. & J. Priest.
"	JL	John Lamfert " 1748.
"	BB	Benj. Blakeley " 1739.
"	ID	John Darwall " 1768.
1769-70	JN	John Neville (probably).
"	H C A G	Chas. Aldridge & Henry Green
"	FC	Fras. Crump ent. 1756.
"	GS	Geo. Seatoun.
"	CW	Chas. Woodward.

Date.	Goldsmiths' Marks and Names.	
1769-70	I·K	John Kentenber ent. 1757.
"	AL	Aug. Le Sage " 1767.
"	EL	Edwd. Lowe " 1777.
"	WB	Walter Brind " 1757.
"	WG	Wm. Grundy " 1748.
"	SC IC	Septimus & James Crespell }
"	TI	Thos. Jackson " 1769.
"	LC GC	Louisa & Geo. Courtauld Cowles.
"	RR	Robt. Rogers " 1773.
"	JB	John Baker " 1770.
1770-1	B·G	Benj. Gignac " 1744.
"	TH	Thos. Heming " "
"	JA	Jas. Allen " 1766.
"	SC IC	Septimus & James Crespell } see 1769.
"	T·P	? Thos. Powell ent. 1756.
"	TA	Thos. Arnold " 1770.
"	IB	John Baxter " 1773.
"	CW	Chas. Wright.
"	I·B	? John Buckett " 1770.
"	I I L S	John Langford & John Sebille
"	G·S	Name not traced.
"	ER	E. Romer (probably).
"	OJ	Orlando Jackson ent. 1759.
"	fW	Sam. Wheat " 1756.
"	W I G V	John Gimblett & Wm. Vale } " 1770.
"	I·B	J. Bassingwhite " "
1771-2	I·C T·H	John Crouch & Thos. Hannam

Date.	Mark	Goldsmiths' Marks and Names.	
1771-2	TF	Thos. Foster	ent. 1769.
,,	DB	David Bell	,, 1756.
,,	R I·S	? Robt. & Jno. Schofield	,, 1776.
,,	T I·D D	Thos. & Jabez Daniel	
,,	S·B	? Sarah Buttall	,, 1754.
,,	JA	Jonathan Alleine.	
,,	WP	Wm. Penstone.	
,,	W·S	Wm. Sheen	,, 1755.
,,	T·C	Thos. Chawner.	
,,	S·H	Saml. Howland	,, 1760.
,,	A·U	A. Underwood.	
,,	CC	Chas. Chesterman	,, 1771.
,,	EI	Edwd. Jay	,, 1757.
,,	T·T	Thos. Towman (probably).	
,,	WT	Wm. Tuite	ent. 1756.
,,	I·R	John Romer	ent before 1773.
1772-3	I·C	John Carter	,, ,,
,,	TC	Thos. Chawner	,, ,,
,,	ET	Eliz Tookey	,, ,,
,,	WF	Wm. Fearn	,, ,,
,,	BD	Burrage Davenport	,, ,,
,,	I·A	John Arnell	,, ,,
,,	J·S	John Swift	,, ,,
,,	P·N	Philip Norman,	,, ,,
,,	CW	Chas. Wright	,, ,,
,,	P·D	Peter Peter Desergnes or Devese.	
,,	Wa	? Wm. Watkins	,, 1756.
1772-3	HH	Henry Hallsworth.	
,,	A·F	Name not traced.	
,,	I·F	John Fayle	ent. 1772.
,,	WE	Wm. Eley (probably).	
1773-4	R D·S S	Dan. Robt. Smith & Sharp	ent. before 1773.
,,	OI	Orlando Jackson	,, 1759.
,,	JH	John Harvey	,, 1739.
,,	TS	Thos. Smith	,, 1750.
,,	LV	Name not traced.	
,,	AB LD	Abr'm Lewis Barrier & Ducornieu	
,,	WS	Wm. Sheen	,, 1775.
,,	T I·D D	Jabez & Thos. Daniel	see 1771.
,,	BD	Burrage Davenport.	
,,	SW	Saml. Wood (probably).	
,,	PF	P. Freeman	ent. 1773.
,,	MM	Mary Makemeid	,, ,,
,,	TT	Thos. Tookey	,, ,,
,,	LD	Louis de Lisle	,, ,,
,,	WLB	Wm. Le Bas	,, ,,
1774-5	IS	Jas. Stamp	,, 1774.
,,	WP	Wm. Penstone	,, ,,
,,	E·T	Eliz. Tookey	,, 1773.
,,	T·E	Thos. Evans	,, 1774.
,,	IY OI	Jas. Orlando Young & Jackson	,, ,,
,,	I·D	John Deacon	,, 1773.
,,	TD	Thomas Daniel (probably).	
1774-5	PF	P. Freeman	ent. 1774.
,,	WF	Wm. Fennell.	
,,	IY	Jas. Young	1775.
,,	IS	Jas. Stamp	,, 1774.
1775-6	W·T	Walter Tweedie	ent. before 1773.
,,	EC	? Ed. Capper	(see 1776).
,,	WC	? Wm. Cox.	
,,	IK	? John Jas. Jas. Kentish King or Kingman	ent. 1773.
,,	WS RC	Wm. Richd. Sumner & Crossley	,, 1775.
,,	IY	Jas. Young	,, ,,
,,	TL	Thos. Langford	(probably)
,,	I·E W·F	? John Wm. Wm. Easton & Fearn or Fennell, etc.	
,,	RR	Robt. Ross	ent. 1774.
,,	MC	Mark Cripps	,, 1767.
,,	CW	Chris. Woods	,, 1775.
,,	RR	Richd. Rugg	,, ,,
,,	RI	Robt. Jones	,, 1776.
,,	T G·B M	Geo. & T Baskerville Morley	,, 1775.
,,	RP	Robt. Piercy	,, ,,
,,	LD	Louis Ducomieu	,, ,,
,,	BS	Ben Stephenson	,, ,,
1776-7	CH	Name not traced.	
,,	HS	Henry Sardet,	
,,	RP	Robt. Piercy	,, ,,
,,	AB	Alexr. Barnet	,, 1759.
,,	N·D	Nich. Dumee	,, 1776.
,,	W G·H C	Geo. Heming & Wm. Chawner	,, 1774.

Date.	Goldsmiths' Marks	and Names.	
1776-7	I·L	John Lautier	ent. 1773.
"	I·W WT	John Wakelin & Wm. Taylor	" 1776.
"	H C A G	Chas. Aldridge & Henry Green	" 1775.
"	A·C	A. Calame	" 1764.
"	EC	Edwd. Capper or Edwd. Cooke	" 1773.
"	A·L	Aug. Le Sage	" 1767.
"	PR	Phil. Roker	" 1776.
"	ER	Eliz. Roker	" "
1777-8	HG	Henry Greenway	" 1775.
"	JA	Jon'th'n Alleine.	
"	RM RC	Robt. & Richd. Makepeace Carter	" 1777.
"	I·H	Joseph Heriot	" 1750.
"	WH	Wm. Holmes	" 1776.
"	WP	Wm. Potter	" 1777.
"	W WH C	Wm. Howe & Wm. Clark	" "
"	WG	Wm. Grundy	" "
"	GN	Geo. Natter	" 1773.
"	RI IS	Robt. Jones & John Schofield	" 1776.
"	GN	Name not traced.	
"	TD	T. Daniel	" 1774.
1778-9	H C A G	Name not traced.	
"	AF	Andrew Fogelberg.	
"	JD	J. Denzilow.	
"	WE	Wm. Eley.	
"	HB	Hester Bateman.	" 1774.
"	WH ND	Wm. Holmes & Nichs. Dumee	" 1773.
1778-9	NH	Nichs. Hearnden	ent. 1773.
"	ED	Ed. Dobson	" 1778.
"	RC DS RS	Rich. Carter, Danl. Smith & Robt. Sharp	" "
"	WE GP	Wm. Eley & Geo. Pierpoint	" 1778.
"	ID	John Deacon	" 1776.
"	CK	Chas. Kandler	" 1778.
"	EL	Ed. Lowe	" 1777.
"	GR	Geo. Rodenbostel	" 1778.
"	TW	Thos. Wallis	" 1773.
1779-80	I·S	John Schofield	" 1778.
"	EF d	Edith Fennell	" 1780.
"	W GH C	Geo. Heming & Wm. Chawner (see also 1781)	" 1774.
"	HB	Hester Bateman	" 1774.
"	T·S	Thos. Satchwell	" 1773.
"	TP RP	Thos. & Richd. Payne	" 1777.
"	WF	W. L. Foster	" 1775.
"	E WG F	Wm. Grundy & Ed. Fernell	" 1779.
"	LC SC	Louisa & Samuel Courtauld	" 1777.
1780-1	FS	Fras. Stamp	" 1780.
"	WG	Wm. Garrard (probably).	
"	R J·D M	Jane Dorrell & Rich. May	ent. 1771.
"	I·S	Jas. Sutton	" 1780.
"	WV	Wm. Vincent	" 1773.
"	IM WH	Jas. Mince & Wm. Hodgkins	" 1780.
"	TB AH	T. P. Boulton & Arthur Humphreys	" "
"	IL IR	John Langlands & John Robertson of Newcastle	" "
1780-1	HP	Name not traced.	
"	IP	Joseph Preedy.	
"	IK	John Kidder	ent. 1780.
1781-2	TP AH	T. B. Pratt & Arthur Humphreys	" 1773.
"	C·W	Chas. Wright	" 1775.
"	RC	Robt. Cruickshank	" 1773.
"	IC TH	John Crouch & Thos. Hannam	" "
"	I·L	Josh. Lejeune	" "
"	LK	Luke Kendall	" 1772.
"	GH WC	Geo. Heming & Wm. Chawner	" 1781.
"	WP WW	Wm. Playfair & Wm. Wilson	" 1782.
"	TD IW	Thos. Daniel & John Wall	" 1781.
1782-3	GS	Geo. Smith	" 1782.
"	JW	John Wren	" 1777.
"	GG	George Giles (probably).	
"	AF SG	Andr. Fogelberg & Steph. Gilbert	ent. 1780.
"	RH	Robt. Hennell	" 1773.
"	WB	Wm. Bayley.	
"	N A A	This mark is A N S A. Name not traced.	
"	AP PP	Abm. Peterson & Peter Podie	" 1783.
1783-4	I·L	John Lamb	" "
"	IS IB	Jas. Sutton & Jos. Bult	" 1782.
"	WT	Wm. Tant	" 1773.
"	WB	Wm. Brown (probably).	
"	SB	? Saml. Bradley.	
"	A·F S·G	Name not traced	

Date.	Mark	Goldsmiths' Marks and Names.	
1783-4	E·F	Ed. Fennell	ent. 1780.
„	SW	Saml. Wintle	„ 1783.
„	WS (script)	Wm. Sumner	„ 1782.
„	IH (script)	Name not traced.	
„	I·T	John Townshend	„ 1783.
„	TC	Thos. Chawner	„ 1773.
„	IT	John Tayleur	„ 1775.
„	I·S	John Schofield	„ 1778.
1784-5	LI	Name not traced.	
„	BM	Do. do.	
„	CH	Chas. Hougham	„ 1785.
„	HG	Hen. Greenway	„ 1775.
„	SA	Stephen Adams	„ 1760.
„	SG	Saml. Godbehere	„ 1784.
„	WS	Wm. Simmons	„ 1776.
„	PG	Peter Gillois	„ 1782.
„	RI	Robt. Jones	„ 1778.
1785-6	WA	Wm. Abdy	„ 1784.
„	I·MF	Name not traced.	
„	HV	Do. do.	
„	B·L	Ben. Laver	„ 1781.
„	W·T	Walter Tweedie	„ 1775.
„	TW	Thos. Wallis	„ 1778.
„	TD	Thos. Daniel	„ 1774.
„	I·K	John Kidder	„ 1780.
„	TS	Thos. Shepherd	„ 1785.
„	AB	Abm. Barrier	„ 1775.
1786-7	SG EW	Saml. Godbehere & Edwd. Wigan	ent. 1786.
„	TP·AH	T. Pratt & Arth. Humphreys	„ 1780.
„	W·S	Wm. Sutton	„ 1784.
„	WR	Wm. Reynolds	„ 1773.
„		Robt. Hennell	as 1782.
„	HC	Henry Chawner	ent. 1786.
„	GG	Name not traced.	
„	CA	Chas. Aldridge	„ 1786.
„	TD	Thos. Daniel	„ 1774.
„	DD	Danl. Denny	„ 1782.
„	WP	Wm. Pitts	„ 1786.
1787-8	SM	Saml. Massey (probably).	
„	IH (script)	Name not traced.	
„	WE	Wm. Eley.	
„	TM	Thos. Mallison	ent. 1773.
„	DS RS	Danl. Smith & Robt. Sharp	„ 1780.
1788-9	EI	Edwd. Jay	„ 1773.
„	IC	John Carter	before „
„	TP	Thos. Powell, probably	1770.
„	GB	Geo Baskerville (probably).	
„	HC	Henry Cowper	ent 1782.
„	CB	Cornls. Bland	„ 1788.
„	TO	Thos. Ollivant	„ 1789.
1789-90	HB (script)	Hester Bateman	„ 1774.
„	HG	Henry Greenway	„ 1775.
„	IT	John Thompson	„ 1785.
„	IE	John Edwards	„ 1788.
1789-90	TW	Thos. Willmore	ent. 1790
„	PC	Name not traced.	
1790-1	P·P	Peter Podie	„ 1783
„	TP ER	T. Phipps & E. Robinson	
„	GS WF	Geo. Smith & Wm. Fearn	„ 1786
„	RH	Robt. Hennell	„ 1773
„	PB IB	Peter & Jonath'n Bateman	„ 1790
„	SD	Saml. Davenport	„ 1786
„	WA	Wm. Abdy	„ 1784
„	AP	Abm. Peterson	„ 1790
1791-2	WP JP	Wm. Pitts & Jos. Preedy	„ 179
„	GB	Geo. Baskerville	(probably
„	GS	Geo. Smith	ent. 1773
„	RS	Robt. Salmon	„ „
„	WF DP	Wm. Fountain & Danl. Pontifex	„ 179
„	IB EB	Jas. & Eliz. Bland	„ „
„	JL	John Lamb	„ 178
„	TS	Thos. Streetin	„ 179
„	EB	Name not traced.	
„	SG RW	Do. do.	
1792-3	W·L	Do. do.	
„	W·P I·P	Wm. Pitts & Jos. Preedy	(see above)
„	HC	Henry Chawner	ent. 178
„	TH	Thos. Howell	„ 179
„	TN	Thos. Northcote.	
„	GS TH	Geo. Smith & Thos. Hayter	ent. 179

Date.	Mark	Goldsmiths' Marks and Names.	
1792-3	WF PS	Wm. Frisbee & Paul. Storr	ent. 1792.
"	IF	John Fountain	" "
"	TG	Thos. Graham	" "
"	EI	Edwd. Jay	" "
1793-4	I·W R·G	J. Wakelin & Robt. Garrard	" "
"	IM	John Moore	" 1778.
"	I·S	John Schofield	" "
"	PB AB	Peter & Ann Bateman	" 1791.
"	RM TM	Robt. & Thos. Makepeace	" 1794.
"	DU NH	Duncan Urquhart & Naphtäli Hart	" 1791.
"	I·F I·B	John Fountain & John Beadnall	" 1793.
"	W·F I·F	Wm. & John Fisher	" "
1794-5	WF	Wm. Frisbee	" 1792.
"	I·K	John King	" 1785.
"	MB	? Mark Bock (see 1798).	
"	F·T	? Francis Thurkle.	
"	IR	John Robins	ent. 1774.
"	IW	John Wren	" 1777.
"	MP	Michl. Plummer	" 1791.
"	WF	W. Fountain	" 1794.
"	TN GB	Thos. Northcote & Geo. Bourne	" "
1795-6	RG	Richd. Gardner or Robt. Gaze	" 1773. " 1795.
"	TE	Thos. Ellis	" 1780.
"	RM	Robt. Makepeace	" 1795.
"	PB AB	Peter & Ann Bateman	" 1791.
"	TP AH	T. B. Pratt & Arthur Humphreys	" 1780.
"	WE	Wm. Eley.	

Date.	Mark	Goldsmiths' Marks and Names.	
1795-6	SH	Name not traced.	
"	IP IP	J. & J. Perkins	ent. 1795.
"	HN	Henry Nutting	" 1796.
1796-7	SP	Name not traced.	
"	RH DH	Robt. & David Hennell	" 1795.
"	IM	John Mewburn	" 1793.
"	IBO	Jos. B. Orme	" 1796.
"	WEH	Wm. Hall	" 1795.
"	HC IE	Hy. Chawner & Jno. Eames	" 1796.
1797-8	RC	Richd. Crossley	" 1782.
"	HC IE	Henry Chawner & John Emes	" 1796.
"	GC	Geo Cowles	" 1797.
1798-9	EM	E. Morley.	
"	IP	Jos. Preedy	" 1777.
"	IB	John Beldon	" 1784.
"	WE WF	Wm. Eley & Wm. Fearn	" 1797.
"	GS	Geo. Smith.	
"	IH TL	Jos. Hardy & Thos. Lowndes	" 1798.
"	M·B	? Mark Bock.	
"	IE	John Emes.	
"	T·D	Thos. Dealtry	" 1765.
1799/1800	WP	Wm. Pitts	" 1781.
"	WB	Wm. Bennett	" 1796.
"	WP	Wm. Pitts	" 1799.
"	RC	Richd. Cooke	" "
"	AF	Andrew Fogelberg	" 1776.
"	IH	John Hutson	" 1784.
"	W.F.	Name not traced.	

Date.	Mark	Goldsmiths' Marks and Names.	
1799/1800	IP	Jos. Preedy	ent. 1800.
1800-1	P·S	Paul Storr	" 1793.
"	I·W R·G	J. Wakelin & Robt. Garrard	" 1792.
"	WH	Wm. Hall	" 1795.
"	SG EW IB	Saml. Godbehere, Ed Wigan & J. Bult	" 1800.
"	TH IC	Thos. Hannam & John Crouch	" 1799.
1801-2	RG	Robt. Garrard	" 1801.
"	I·P	John Parker.	
"	IE	John Emes	" 1796.
"	PB AB WB	Peter, Ann & Wm. Bateman	" 1800.
"	GS TH	Geo. Smith & Thos. Hayter	" 1792.
"	RH DH SH	Robert, David & Saml. Hennell	
1802-3	IH	John Harris	" 1786.
"	DS BS	Digby Scott & Benj. Smith	" 1802.
"	WB	Wm. Burwash	" "
"	PB AB WB	Peter, Ann & Wm. Bateman	" 1800.
"	AB GB	Alice & George Burrows	" 1802.
"	CB TB	Christr. & T. W. Barker	" 1800.
1803-4	B·L	Benj. Laver	" 1781.
"	TH	Thos. Holland	" 1798.
"	GB TB	G. & T. Burrows.	
"	SG W	Saml. & George Whitford	" 1802.
"	AJ	Name not traced.	
"	IR	John Robins (probably).	
"	TR	? Timothy Renou.	
"	IA	John Austin.	
1804-5	W·P	Wm Purse.	

Date.	Mark	Goldsmiths' Marks and Names.
1804-5	S·B	Name not traced.
"	(crown) RB&R	Rundell, Bridge & Rundell.
"	GW	Geo. Wintle ent. 1804.
"	RG	Robt. Garrard " 1802.
"	I·H	Jos. Hardy " 1799.
"	HN	Hannah Northcote " 1798.
1805-6	DP	Danl. Pontifex " 1794.
"	J·E	John Emes.
"	TA	? T. Ash.
"	W·B R·S	Wm. Burwash & Richd. Sibley } " 1805.
"	TS	Name not traced.
1806-7	RH SH	R. & S. Hennell " 1802.
"	PB WB	Peter & Wm. Bateman " 1805.
"	JS	John Sanders (probably).
"	CF	Crespin Fuller "
"	IS	John Salkeld "
"	TR	Thos. Robins "
"	WF	Wm. Fountain ent. 1794.
1807-8	TG IG IC	T. & J. Guest & Josh. Cradock } " 1806.
"	PB WB	P. & W. Bateman " 1805.
"	SW	Saml. Whitford " 1807.
"	T·H	Thos. Halford " "
"	BS	Name not traced.
"	TR	T Robins " "
"	IWS	? J. W. Storey.
1808-9	I·C	John Crouch " 1808.
"	RE WE	Name not traced.

Date.	Mark	Goldsmiths' Marks and Names.
1808-9	TM	? T. W. Matthews.
"	I·C	John Crouch ent. 1808.
"	E·M	E. Morley.
"	WE WF WC	Wm. Eley, Wm. Fearn & Wm. Chawner } " "
"	HN RH	Henry Nutting & Robt. Hennell } " "
"	RC GS	Richard Crossley & Geo. Smith } " 1807.
"	W·S	Wm. Sumner " 1802.
"	JC	John Crouch " 1808.
1809-10	CH	Chas. Hougham " 1785.
"	TW	Thos. Wallis " 1792.
"	DW	David Windsor (probably).
"	TJ	Thomas Jenkinson "
"	SJ	Name not traced.
1810-1	TH SH	Do. do.
"	RC	? Richd. Cooke ent. 1799.
"	BS IS	Benj. Smith & Jas. Smith. }
"	TP ER	T Phipps & E. Robinson }
"	SB IB	Name not traced.
"	TW JH	Thos. Wallis & Jonath'n Hayne } " 1810.
"	IC TH	John Cotton & Thos. Head } " 1809.
1811-2	JB	James Beebe " 1811.
"	BS IS	Benj. & Jas. Smith.
"	WK	Wm. Kingdon (probably).
"	RR	Robt. Rutland ent. 1811.
"	SH	Saml. Hennell " "
"	DS BS IS	Digby Scott, Benj. Smith, Jas. Smith } (probably).

Date.	Mark	Goldsmiths' Marks and Names.
1812-3	TB	? T. Barker.
"	IS	? John Sanders.
"	TI	Thos. Jenkinson (probably).
"	RE EB	Rebecca Emes & Edwd. Barnard } ent. 1808.
"	GS	Geo. Smith " 1812.
"	MS ES	Mary & Eliz. Sumner " 1809.
1813-4	IC WR	Jos. Craddock & Wm. Reid } " 1812.
"	PS BRITANNIA	Paul Storr " 1793.
"	IWS WE	J. W. Story & W. Elliott } " 1809.
1814-5	SH	Saml. Hennell " 1811.
"	RE EB	Emes & Barnard " 1808.
"	SA	Stephen Adams, junr.
"	W·B	Wm. Bell (probably).
"	W·E	Wm. Elliott ent. 1810.
"	I.L WA	Name not traced.
"	SH IT	S. Hennell & J. Taylor } (probably).
1815-6	TP ER JP	Name not traced.
"	JE EF	Do. do.
"	I·P G·P	Do. do.
"		Emes & Barnard as above.
"	RG	Robt Garrard ent. 1801.
"	CR DR	Christ'n Reid & ano'r of Newcastle " 1815.
1816-7	WB	Wm. Burwash " 1813.
"	IL	Jas. Lloyd.
1817-8	S S R ILD	Name not traced.

Date.	Goldsmiths' Marks and Names.	
1817-8	WB	Wm. Bateman ent. 1815.
"	M·S	Name not traced.
"	WC	Wm. Chawner " "
"	TR	T. Robins (probably).
"	WC	Wm. Chawner ent. 1815.
"	GP	Geo. Purse.
1818-9	GW	Geo. Wintle " 1813.
"	IW	Joseph Wilson.
"	RG	Robt. Garrard " 1801.
1819-20	SR ID	Name not traced.
"	A·H	Do. do.
"	HN	Henry Nutting " 1809.
"	WS	Wm. Stevenson (probably).
"	TI	See 1812-3 above.
"	PR	Philip Rundell ent. 1819.
1820-1	W·B	Wm. Bateman " 1815.
"	I·L H·L	John & Henry Lias " 1819.
1821-2	TB	Thos. Baker " 1815. or Thos. Balliston " 1819.
"	IET	? J. E. Terry & Co. " 1818.
"	ICF	? John Foligno.
"	TUTU	An Exeter maker (probably).
"	JA IA	J. & J. Aldous "
1822-3	PS	Paul Storr "
"	WA	William Abdy "
"	WT	Wm. Trayes ent. 1822.
1823-4	IS	Name not traced.
"	JA	John Angell (probably).

Date.	Goldsmiths' Marks and Names.	
1823-4	I·B	John Bridge ent. 1823.
"	BS	Benj. Smith.
1824-5	TH GH	Thos. & Geo. Hayter " 1816.
"	SC	Name not traced.
"	R·H	Robt. Hennell.
"	FF	Name not traced.
"	WE CE IE	Do. do.
"	GK	Geo. Knight (probably).
"	WE	Wm. Edwards (").
1825-6	TC	James Collins (").
"	IB	John Bridge ent. 1823.
"	RP	R. Peppin (probably).
"	CE	C. Eley (").
"	FH	Fras. Higgins (").
1826-7	IL HL CL	John, Henry & Chas. Lias ent. 1823.
"	A·B·S	A. B. Savory " 1826.
"	RC	Randall Chatterton " 1825.
1827-8	BP	Name not traced.
"	T·C·S	T. Cox Savory " 1827.
"	JW	Jacob Wintle " 1826.
"	ME	Moses Emmanuel (probably).
1828-9	WS	Wm. Schofield (").
"	ES	E. S. Sampson (").
1829-30	JH	Jas. Hobbs (").
"	EE	Edward Edwards.
"	RG	Robt. Garrard ent. 1801.
1830-1	CP	Chas. Plumley (probably).

Date.	Goldsmiths' Marks and Names.	
1830-1	T·D	Thos. Dexter (probably).
"	RA WS	Name not traced.
1831-2	W·H	" "
"	RH	R. Hennell.
1833-4	PS	Paul Storr ent. 1793.
"	AS JS AS	Adey, Joseph & Albert Savory " 1833.
1834-5	N·M	N. Morrison (probably).
"	IF	Jas. Franklin "
"	WB	W. Bellchambers "
"	RP CP	Name not traced.
"	T·E	T. Eley.
1835-6	CF	Chas. Fox ent. 1822.
"	J.C.E	J. Chas. Edington " 1828.
"	CR GS	Reily & Storer (probably).
1836-7	CF	See 1835-6.
"	EB EB JB WB	Edwd. Barnard, Edwd. Barnard, jr., John Barnard, & Wm. Barnard ent. 1829.
1837-8	WE	Wm. Eaton.
"	RS	Richard Sibley (probably).
"	GW	George Webb "
"	RG	Robert Garrard ent. 1821.
"	MC	Mary Chawner.
1838-9	WT RA	Wm. Theobalds & Robt. Atkinson " 1838.
"	CR GS	Rawlins & Sumner.
1839-40	WB DB	Wm. Bateman & Danl. Ball " 1839.
"	FD	Francis Dexter " "
"	WC	Wm. Cooper (probably).
"	I·T	Jos. Taylor "

Date.	Goldsmiths' Marks	and Names.	
1839-40	EE	Ed.	Edwards (probably).
1840-1	GL	Name not traced.	
„	TC	Thos.	Cording „
„	GA	Geo. W. Adams	ent. 1840.
„	JA JA	J. & J.	Aldous.*
„	MC GA	Mary Geo. W. Adams	Chawner & } „ „
1841-2	JS AS	Jos. & Albert	Savory „ „
„	JL	John John	Lacy or Law } (probably).
1842-3	JCE	J. Chas.	Edington ent. 1828.
„	R·H	R.	Hennell.
„	WB WS	Brown &	Somersall (probably).
1843-4	WKR	Wm. K.	Reid.
„	WB	Wm.	Brown (possibly).
„	J·A J·A	Joseph & John	Angel see 1844.
„	RS	Richd.	Sibley ent. 1837.
1844-5	R·G	R.	Garrard „ 1801.
„	J·A & J·A	Joseph & John	Angel.
„	RGH	R. G.	Hennell.
„	BS	Benj.	Smith (probably).
1845-6	ISH	John S.	Hunt ent. 1844.
„	CTF GF	Chas. T. Geo.	Fox & } Fox.
1846-7	GFP	G. F.	Pinnell.
„	H·H	Hyam	Hyams.
„	EJ B &W	E. J. & W.	Barnard.
1847-8	IL HL	John & Henry	Lias.
„	RP GB	R. G.	Pearce & } Burrows.

Date.	Goldsmiths' Marks	and Names.	
1847-8	EE	Eliz.	Eaton.
1848-9	EJ BW	E. J. & W.	Barnard. }
„	RH	R.	Hennell.
„	JW	Jacob	Wintle (probably).
1849-50	C.T.F G.F.	Chas. T. Geo.	Fox & Fox }
„	FD	Frans.	Douglas.
„	WRS	W. R.	Smily.
1850-1	IK	John	Keith.
„	GI	George	Ivory.
1851-2	EB JB	E. & J.	Barnard.
1852-3	JE	James	Edwards (probably).
„	IF	I.	Foligno.
1853-4	EB & JB	E. & J.	Barnard.
1854-5	WR S	W. R.	Smily.
1855-6	GA	George	Angell.
1856-7	CTF GF	Chas. T Geo.	Fox & Fox }
1857-8	HW	Henry	Wilkinson of Sheffield.
1858-9	J·A	Joseph	Angell.
„	W·M	W.	Mann.
„	GR EB	Roberts &	Briggs.
1859-60	GA	George	Angell.
1860-1	EE JE	Messrs.	Eady.
„	CR WS	Rawlins &	Sumner.
1861-2	RH	Robt.	Harper.
1862-3	R·H	Richard	Hennell.
1863-4	GF	Geo.	Fox.
1864-5	GA	Geo.	Angell.

Date.	Goldsmiths' Marks	and Names.	
1864-5	EKR		
1865-6	IJK	I. J.	Keith.
„	R·H	Richd.	Hennell.
1866-7	GE GF		
1867-8	GM HD	Macaire &	Dewar.
„	ML HL		
1868-9	AS		
„	CS H	Chas. Stuart	Harris.
1869-70	J EBW J	J., E., W., & J. Barnard.	
1870-1	WS	Wm.	Smiley.
1871-2	HE W	H. E.	Willis.
1872-3	RS	Richd.	Sibley.
1873-4	RM EH	Martin	Hall & Co. of Sheffield.
1874-5	JEM GW	Mappin &	Webb.
1875-6	[illegible]		
1876-7	CFH	Messrs.	Hancock.
1877-8	”	„	„
„	RJL		
„	TJ		
1878-9	SS	Stephen	Smith.
1879-80	DH CH	Hands &	Son.
1880-1	JWD	J. W	Dobson.
„	EYI		
„	WIS		
1881-2	FH	Francis	Higgins.
1882-3	CS H	Chas. Stuart	Harris.

Date.	Goldsmiths' Marks and Names.		
1882-3	JA JS		
1883-4	JNM		
"	J ASM F		
"	PW		
1884-5	JRH	J. R.	Hennell.
1885-6	JW J		
"	CFH	Messrs.	Hancock.
"	J.W F.C.W	J. F. C.	Wakley & Wheeler.
1888-9	D&C		
"	WD		
1889-90	CFH	Messrs.	Hancock.
1891-2	EH		
1892 3	E·H		
"	WC	W.	Comyns.
1893-4	SWS	S. W.	Smith & Co. (of Birmingham).
"	ST		
1894-5	IG CL		
"	JB ER	Brownell & Rose.	
"	WBJ	Messrs.	Barnard.
1895-6	J.S		
"	JNN		
1896 7	S.H C &	W.	Hutton & Sons, Ltd.
1897-8	JBC	Messrs.	Carrington.
1898-9	GG		
1899 1900	ECP	E. C.	Purdee.
"	RP		

Date.	Goldsmiths' Marks and Names.		
1900-1	CCP	C. C.	Pilling.
1901-2	C.K	C.	Krall.
1902-3	WC	W.	Comyns & Sons.
1903-4	WBJ MBS RD	Edward	Barnard & Sons, Ltd.
"	HL	H.	Lambert.
"	J W		
"	JW ECW		
1904-5	WJ		
1905-6	TB	Thos.	Bradbury of Sheffield.
"	A&H	Alstons &	Hallam.
1906-7	C&Co	Carrington & Co.	
1907-8	J&S		
"	LG		
1908-9	TB &S	Thos. Sheffield.	Bradbury & Son of
"	HSP LD		
"	& WW	Wakeley &	Wheeler.
1909-10	IMS	John	Marshall.
1910-1	SJP	S. J.	Phillips.
1911-2	C T H J W	Thomas &	Co., Bond Street.
1912-3	H&C LTD	Heming &	Co., Ltd.
1913-4	AP FP	A. & F.	Parsons, (of Edward Tessier).
"	SG		
1914-5	D&J W	D. & J.	Welby.
1915-6	PH D CW	Dobson &	Sons.
"	SJP	S. J.	Phillips.
1916-7	LAC	Crichton	Bros.
1917-8	HSP		
1918-9	C&R C	Chas. & Richard	Comyns.

	TOWN MARK.	DATE LETTER.	MAKER'S MARK.	MAKER'S NAME.		TOWN MARK.	DATE LETTER.	MAKER'S MARK.	MAKER'S NAME.
ELIZ. 1559-60		A		... ...	1583-4		a	WR	Wm. Rawnson.
1560-1		B		... ...	1584-5		b	"	" "
1561-2		C		... ...	1585-6		c		... ...
*1562-3		D	RG	Robert Gylmyn.	1586-7		d		... ...
1563-4		E		... ...	1587-8	"	e	GK	Geo. Kitchen.
1564-5		F	M	... ...	1588-9		f		... ...
1565-6		G		... ...	1589-90		g		... ...
1566-7		H	CH	Christopher Hunton.	1590-1	"	h	CK	Geo. Kitchen.
1567-8		I		... ...	1591-2		i		... ...
1568-9		K	RB TS	Robert Beckwith. Thomas Symson.	1592-3		k	WR RG	Wm. Rawnson. Robt. Gylmyn.
1569-70		L	RG	Robert Gylmyn.	1593-4	"	l	WH	? Wm. Hutchinson.
1570-1		M		Name not traced.	1594-5	"	m	GK	Geo. Kitchen.
1571-2		N		... ...	1595-6		n		... ...
1572-3		O	 WF	John Lund. William Foster.	1596-7		o		... ...
1573-4		P		... ...	1597-8	"	p	CH	Chris. Harrington.
1574-5	"	Q	GK	George Kitchen.	1598-9		q		... ...
1575-6		R	"	" "	1599/1600	"	r	FT	Fras. Tempest.
1576-7		S	TW	Thomas Waddie.	1600-1		s		... ...
1577-8	"	T		Indistinguishable.	1601-2	"	t	"	" "
1578-9		V		... ...	1602-3		u		... ...
1579-80		W		... ...	JAS. I. 1603-4		w		... ...
1580-1		X		... ...	1604-5	"	x	CH	Chris. Harrington.
1581-2		Y		... ...	1605-6		y		... ...
1582-3	"	Z	WR	William Rawnson.	1606-7		z		... ...

	TOWN MARK.	DATE LETTER.	MAKER'S MARK.	MAKER'S NAME.	
1607-8		A	IM	John	Moody ?
			RC	Robt.	Casson.
1608-9		B	PP	Peter	Pearson.
1609-10	,,	C	FT	Fras.	Tempest.
1610-1	,,	D	PP	Peter	Pearson.
			,,	,,	,,
1611-2	,,	E	CH	Chris.	Harrington.
1612-3	,,	F	FT	Fras.	Tempest.
1613-4		G	PP [with small mark]	Peter	Pearson.
1614-5	,,	H	,,	,,	,,
1615-6		I	CM	Chris.	Mangy.
			FT	Fras.	Tempest.
1616-7	,,	K	,,	,,	,,
1617-8		L		...	... ...
1618-9	,,	M	SC	Sem.	Casson.
1619-20	,,	N	PP	Peter	Pearson.
1620-1	,,	O	SC	Sem.	Casson.
1621-2	,,	P	PP	Peter	Pearson.
1622-3		Q	,,	,,	,,
1623-4		R	RW	Robt.	Williamson.
			D	...	... ...
1624-5		S	TH	Thos.	Harrington.
CHAS. I 1625-6		T	RH	Robt.	Harrington.
1626-7	,,	U	[shield device]	?	
1627-8	,,	V	IP	James	Plummer
1628-9		X		...	... ...
1629-30	,,	Y	CM	Chris.	Mangy.
1630-1	,,	Z	W	Thomas	Waite.

	TOWN MARK.	DATE LETTER.	MAKER'S MARK.	MAKER'S NAME.	
1631-2		a	SC	Sem.	Casson.
1632-3		b	,,	,,	,,
1633-4	,,	c	RH	Robt.	Harrington.
1634-5	,,	d	TH	Thos.	Harrington.
1635-6	,,	e	IT	John	Thomason or Thompson.
1636-7		f	RH	Robt.	Harrington.
1637-8		g	TH	Thos.	Harrington.
1638-9	,,	h	RW	Robt. or Richd.	Williamson, Senr. Waite.
1639-40	,,	i	FB	Francis	Bryce.
1640-1		j		...	... ...
1641-2	,,	k	IT	John	Thomason.
1642-3	,,	l	TH	Thos.	Harrington.
1643-4	,,	m	IT	John	Thomason.
1644-5		n		...	... ...
1645-6	,,	o	CM	Chris.	Mangy.
1646-7		p		...	... ...
1647-8		q		...	... ...
1648-9		r		...	... ...
COMWTH. 1649-50		s	IP	James	Plummer.
1650-1		t	,,	,,	,,
1651-2	,,	u	,,	,,	,,
1652-3	,,	v	,,	,,	,,
1653-4		w		...	... ...
1654-5	,,	x	TW	Thomas	Waite.
1655-6	,,	y	,,	,,	,,
1656-7	,,	z	PM	Philemon	Marsh.

	Town Mark.	Date Letter	Maker's Mark	Maker's Name.	
1657-8		A	IP	John	Plummer.
1658-9		B	,,	,,	,,
1659-60		C	WW IT	Wm. John	Waite. Thomason.
1660-1	,,	D	IP	John	Plummer.
1661-2	,,	E	,,	,,	,,
1662-3		F	,, GM	,, George	,, Mangy.
1663-4		G	MB	Marmaduke	Best.
1664-5	,,	H	RW	Robt.	Williamson.
1665-6	,,	I	IP	John	Plummer.
1666-7		K	TM	Thos.	Mangy.
1667-8	,,	L	MB	Marmaduke	Best.
1668-9	,,	M	PM	Philemon	Marsh.
1669-70	,,	N	TM	Thomas	Mangy.
1670-1		O	MB	Marmaduke	Best.
1671-2	,,	P	,, RK	,, Roland	,, Kirby.
1672-3		Q	IT	John	Thompson.
1673-4	,,	R	MB	Marmaduke	Best.
1674-5	,,	S	RW TM	Robt Thos.	Williamson. Mangy.
1675-6	,,	T	WM	Wm	Mascall.
1676-7	,,	U	HL	Henry	Lee.
1677-8	,,	V	WB	Wm.	Busfield.
1678-9	,,	W	IP	John	Plummer.
1679-80		X	IT	John	Thompson.
1680-1	,,	Y	WB	Wm.	Busfield.
1681-2	,,	Z	TM	Thos.	Mangy.

	Town Mark.	Date Letter.	Maker's Mark.	Maker's Name.	
1682-3		A	GG	George	Gibson.
*1683-4	,,	B	WB	Wm.	Busfield.
1684-5 JAS. II.		C	IC IP	John John	Camidge. Plummer.
1685-6		D	RC	Richd.	Chew.
1686-7	,,	E	IS	John	Smith.
1687-8	,,	F	IO	John	Oliver.
1688-9	,,	G	CW	Chris.	Whitehill.
WM. & MY. 1689-90	,,	H	WB	Wm.	Busfield.
1690-1		I	RW	Robt.	Williamson.
1691-2		K	CR	Charles	Rhoades.
1692-3	,,	L	CW	Chris.	Whitehill.
1693-4	,,	M	MG	Mark	Gill.
1694-5		N	WB	Wm.	Busfield.
1695-6		O	CR	Clement	Reed.
WM. III. 1696-7	,,	P	WB	Wm.	Busfield.
1697-8	,	Q	IS	John	Smith.
1698-9	,,	R		Wm.	Busfield as above.
1699/1700		S		...	... ...

	Town Mark.	Britannia.	Lion's Head Erased.	Date Letter.	Maker's Mark.	Maker's Name.
1700-1				A	CG	Chas. Goldsborough (probably)
1701-2				B	Tu BE	Danl. Turner. John Bes..
ANNE. 1702-3	,,	,,	,,	C	Bu	Wm. Busfield.
1703-4	,,	,,	,,	D	LA	John Langwith.
1704-5						
1705-6	,,	,,	,,	F	,,	,, ,,
1706-7	,,	,,	,,	G	RH	Chas. Rhoades.
1707-8					LA	John Langwith.
1708-9	,,	,,	,,	H	WI WW	Wm. Williamson.
1709-10						
1710-11						
1711-2	,,	,,	,,	M	LA	John Langwith,
1712-3						
1713-4	,,	,,	,,	O	,,	,, ,,
GEO. I. 1714-5						
1715-6						
1716-7						

	Town Mark.	Lion Passant.	Leopard's Head Crowned.	Date Letter.	King's Head.	Maker's Mark.	Maker's Name.
1776-7				A			... ...
1777-8				B			... ...
1778-9				C			... ...
1779-80				D		IH IP	J. Hampston & J. Prince
1780-1				E			... ...
1781-2		..	..	F		..	,, ,,
1782-3	..	..	.	G		..	,, ,,
1783-4	..	..	..	H		.. IH IP	,, ,,
1784-5	..	..	..	J		.. H&P	,, ,, Hampston & Prince.
1785-6				K			. ...
1786-7				L			... ...

	Town Mark.	Lion Passant.	Leopard's Head Crowned	King's Head.	Date Letter	Maker's Mark.	Maker's Name.		Town Mark.	Lion Passant.	Leopard's Head Crowned.	King's Head.	Date Letter.	Maker's Mark.	Maker's Name.
1787-8					A	I H P	J. Hampston & J. Prince.	*1812-3					a	JB WW	James Barber & Wm. Whitwell
1788-9					b		... ...	1813-4					b		... ...
1789-90	"	"	"	"	c	"	" "	1814-5					c		... ...
1790-1	"	"	"	"	d	"	" "	1815-6	"	"	"	"	d	"	" "
1791-2	"	"	"	"	e	"	" "	1816-7					e		... ...
1792-3					f		... ...	1817-8	"	"	"	"	f	"	" "
1793-4	"	"	"	"	g	"	" "	1818-9	"	"	"	"	g	"	" "
1794-5					h		... ...	1819-20					h		.. ..
1795-6	"	"	"	"	i	I H P	" "	GEO. IV. 1820-1		"	"	"	i	"	" "
1796-7	"	"	"		k	"	" "	1821-2		"	"	"	k	"	" "
1797-8					l or L		... .	1822-3					l		... ...
1798-9	"	"	"	"	M	HP &Co	H. Prince & Co.	1823-4					m		... ...
1799 1800	"	"	"	"	N	"	" "	1824-5	"	"	"	"	n	JB &Co	Jas. Barber & Co.
1800-1	"	"	"	"	O	HP&C	" "	1825-6	"	"	"	"	o	JB &N	Jas. Geo. Wm. Barber, Cattle & North
1801-2	"	"	"	"	P	HP &C	" "	1826-7		"	"	"	p	"	" "
1802-3	"	"	"	"	Q	"	" "	1827-8					q		... .
1803-4	"	"	"	"	R	"	" "	1828-9	"	"	"	"	r	"	" "
1804-5	"	"	"	"	S	"	" "	1829-30	"	"	"	"	s	JB GC WN	" "
1805-6	"	"	"	"	T	"	" "	WM. IV. 1830-1		"	"		t	JB GC WN	" "
1806-7					U			1831-2		"	"	"	u	"	" "
1807-8	"	"	"	"	V	RC JB	Robt. Cattle & J Barber.	1832-3					v		.. ..
1808-9		"	"	"	W	"	" "	1833-4					w		... ...
1809-10		"	"	"	X	"	" "	1834-5					x		... ...
1810-1	"	"	"	"	Y	"	" "	1835-6					y		... ...
1811-2					Z		... .	1836 7					z		.. ..

	TOWN MARK.	LION PASSANT.	LEOPARD'S HEAD CROWNED. TILL 1848	QUEEN'S HEAD.	DATE LETTER.	MAKER'S MARK.	MAKER'S NAME.
VICT. 1837-8					A	JB WN	Jas. Wm. Barber & North
1838-9	"	"	"	"	B	"	" "
1839-40	"	"	"	"	C	"	" "
1840-1	"	"	"		D	"	" "
1841-2	"	"	"	"	E	"	" "
1842-3	"	"	"	"	F	"	" "
1843-4	"	"	"	"	G	"	" "
1844-5	"	"	"	"	H	"	" "
1845-6	"	"	"	"	I	"	" "
1846-7					K		... ...
1847-8	"	"	"	"	L	"	" "
1848-9	"	"		"	M	JB	James Barber
1849-50	"	"		"	N	"	" "
1850-1	"	"		"	O	"	" "
1851-2					P		... ...
1852-3					Q		... ...
1853-4					R		.. ..
1854-5					S		. ...
1855-6					T		... .
1856-7	"	"		"	V	JB	James Barber

	CASTLE OVER LION.	DATE LETTER	MAKER'S MARK.
1565-6		A	
1566-7	,,	B	
1567-8		C	
1568-9		D	
1569-70		E	
1570-1		F	,,
1571-2	,,	G	
1572-3		H	
1573-4	,,	I	
1574-5	,,	K	
1575-6		L	
1576-7		M	
1577-8		N	
1578-9		O	
1579-80		P	
1580-1		Q	
	ROSE CROWNED.		
1581-2		R	
1582-3		S	
1583-4		T	
1584-5		V	

DATE (ABOUT).	MARKS.			
1590				
1595				
1600-10				
1610				
1620				
,,		,,		
,,	,,		,,	
1620-40				
1624				

	CASTLE OVER LION.	ROSE CROWNED.	DATE LETTER.	MAKER'S MARK.
1624-5			A	
1625-6	,,	,,	B	
1626-7		,,	C	
1627-8	,,	,,	D	
1628-9		,,	E	
1629-30			F	
1630-1	,,		G	
1631-2			H	
1632-3	,,	,,	I	
1633-4	,,	,,	K	
1634-5	,,	,,	L	
1635-6			M	
1636-7			N	
1637-8			O	
1638-9	,,	,,	P	
1639-40			Q	
1640-1	,,	,,	R	
1641-2	,,	,,	S	
1642-3	,,	,,	T	
1643-4			V	

DATE (ABOUT)	MARKS.			
1645				
„				AH
1653				AH
1661				AH
„				WL
1670				AH
„	„	„		AH
„				AH
„			AH	
1675				TH
1676	„	„		„
1679	„	„		„
„	„	„	„	
1680				MH
1685			TH	

	ROSE CROWNED.	CASTLE OVER LION.	DATE LETTER.	MAKER'S MARK.	MAKER'S NAME.
1688			a	EH	... ...
1689			b	TH	Thomas Havers.
1690			C		... ...
1691	„	„	d	„	Thomas Havers.
	„	„	„	ID	James Daniel.
	„	„	„	EH	... ...
	„	„	„	LG	... ...
1692			E		... ...
1693			F		... ...
1694			G		.. ..
1695			H		... ...
1696	„	„	I	ID	James Daniel.
1697	„	„	K	PR	... ...
			„	EH	... ...

DATE.	MARKS.	MAKER'S NAME.	DATE.	MARKS.	MAKER'S NAME.
c. 1544-98	RH	Richard Hilliard.	1600	OSBORN	Richd. Osborn.
c. 1562/1607	RO	Richard Osborne.	„	„ RH HERMAN RH	R. Herman.
c. 1568-74	I NORTH	John North.	„		No maker's mark.
c. 1570	HH	Henry Hardwicke.	c. 1600	RO	Richd. Osborn.
1570-3	I IONS	John Ions (Jones).	1606	OSBORN	„ „
„	I IONS	Do. do do.	c. 1610-20	BW BW a	William Bartlett. (1597-1646).
c. 1570/1600	S MORE	Steven More.	1620	„ „ „ b	„ „
1571	I N	John North.	„	„ EA	Edward Anthony (1612-67).
„	I N	Do. do.	„	EA	„ „
„	I IONS	John Jons.	„		
1572	IW	John Withycombe.	c. 1630	WB WB	Wm. Bartlett (probably).
1575	I IONS	John Jons.	„	T T	Anthony mark, &c.*
„	„ „ „	Do. do.	c. 1635	IL IL	John Lavers.
„	I „ A	Do. do.	„	IP	I. P.
„	„ IO „ „	Do. do.	c. 1635-8	IL	John Lavers.
1576	I IONS B	Do. do.	c. 1640	a	... ...
„	VI	... ...	„	HP HP	H. P.
1580	HORWOOD	Wm. Horwood.	„	IR RADCLIFF	Jasper Radcliffe.
c. 1580	I YEDS	John Eydes.	„	LM „	I. M.
1582	C ESTON	C. Eston.	„	R „ „	Jasper Radcliffe.
„	EASTON	C. Easton.	„	OSBORN „	Richd. Osborn.
1585	BENTLY	— Bently.	„	IL IL IL	John Lavers.
„	HERMAN	R. Herman.	„		No maker's mark.
1590	ESTON N	C. Eston.			
1592	C ESTON P	Do. do.			

DATE.	MARKS.	MAKER'S NAME.
c. 1640-50	I·E A	John Elston / Anthony Tripe
,,	PR PR	P. R.
,,	B	Thomas Bridgeman.
,,	EA	Edward Anthony.
,,		Do. do.
c. 1646-98	IF	I. F.
c. 1670	X IR	Jasper Radcliffe.
1676		M. W.
,,		— S.
c. 1680	XON IV	... ...
,,		No maker's mark.
,,	,, IS	I. S.
1690	M EX ON	John Mortimer.
c. 1690	IS	Daniel Slade.
,,	,, WE	Wm. Ekins.
,,	,, WE	Do. do.
,,	M	John Mortimer.
,,		.. ..
,,	I·P	I. P. (See Barnstaple, p. 459 *infra*).
,,	X IP	I. P.
1694	EX NB ON	Nichs. Browne.
1698	X	No maker's mark.

	CASTLE.	BRIT-ANNIA.	LION'S HEAD ERASED.	DATE LETTER.	MAKER'S MARK.	MAKER'S NAME.
1701-2				A	EI	J. Elston.
ANNE. 1702-3		,,	,,	B	,, / FO	Thos. Foote.
1703-4		,,	,,	C	Mu / Av	Hy. Muston. / John Audry.
1704-5	,,	,,	,,	D	Br	Wm. Briant.
1705-6	,,	,,	,,	E	FR	Richd. Freeman.
1706-7	,,	,,	,,	F	RE	Thos. Reynolds.
1707-8	,,	,,	,,	G	WI / SA	Richd. Wilcocks. / Thos. Salter.
1708-9		,,	,,	H	PL	Richd. Plint.
1709-10		,,	,,	I	FV	Name not traced.†
1710-1	,,	,,	,,	K	Ri	Ed. Richards.
1711-2	,,	,,	,,	L	TR / SW	Geo. Trowbridge. / Ed. Sweet.
1712-3	,,	,,	,,	M	Ri	Ed. Richards.
1713-4		,,	,,	N	SL	Danl. Slade.
GEO. I. 1714-5	,,	,,	,,	O	To / Mo	—— Tolcher. / John Mortimer.
1715-6	,,	,,	,,	P	TR	Geo. Trowbridge.
1716-7	,,	,,	,,	Q	Sy / Lo	Pent. Symonds. / Ab'm. Lovell.
1717-8	,,	,,	,,	R	Sp	Pent. Symonds.
1718-9	,,	,,	,,	S	AR	Peter Arno.
1719-20	,,	,,	,,	T	WO	Andr Worth.
1720-1	,,	,,	,,	V	BL / I·E	Saml. Blachford / J. Elston.
1721-2				W	TS	Thos. Sampson.
1722-3				X	SB	Saml. Blachford
1723-4	,,	,,	,,	Y	IE	J. Elston.
1724-5	,,	,,	,,	Z	IW	Jas. Williams.‡

	CASTLE.	LEOPARD'S HEAD CROWNED.	LION PASSANT.	DATE LETTER.	MAKER'S MARK.	MAKER'S NAME.
1725-6				a	SB	Saml. Blachford.
1726-7	„	„	„	b	TS	Thos. Sampson.
GEO. II. 1727-8	„	„	„	c	IC / PE	Joseph Collier. / Philip Elliott.
1728-9	„	„	„	d	IE	John Elston, jr.
1729-30	„	„	„	e	„ / IS	Do. do. / James Strang.
1730-1	„	„	„	f	IB	John Burdon.
1731-2	„	„	„	g	PE	Peter Elliott.
1732-3	„	„	„	h	IC	Joseph Collier.
1733-4	„	„	„	i	IE	John Elston, jr.
1734-5	„	„	„	k	SB	Sampson Bennett.
1735-6	„	„	„	l	PE	Philip Elston.
1736-7	„	„	„	m	IS	James Strang.
1737-8	„	„	„	n	PE	Philip Elston.
1738-9	„	„	„	o	PS	Pent. Symonds.
1739-40	„	„	„	p	IB	John Burdon.
1740-1	„	„	„	q	IB	Do. do.
1741-2	„	„	„	r	Sy	Pent. Symonds.
1742-3	„	„	„	s	IF	Name not traced. J. Freeman ?
1743-4	„	„	„	t	IB	John Babbage ?
1744-5	„	„	„	u	„	Do. do.
1745-6	„	„	„	w		
1746-7	„	„	„	x	PS	Pent. Symonds.
1747-8	„	„	„	y	TB	Thos. Blake.
1748-9	„	„	„	z	IS	Jas. Strang.

	CASTLE	LEOPARD'S HEAD CROWNED.	LION PASSANT.	DATE LETTER	MAKER'S MARK.	MAKER'S NAME.
1749-50				A	TB	Thomas Blake.
1750-1	„	„	„	B	„	„ „
1751-2	„	„	„	C	„	„ „
1752-3	„	„	„	D	WP	W. Parry.
1753-4	„	„	„	E	DC	Danl. Coleman.
1754-5	„	„	„	F	WP	W. Parry.
1755-6	„	„	„	G	„	„ „
1756-7	„	„	„	H	TB	Thomas Blake.
1757-8	„	„	„	I	„	„ „
1758-9	„	„	„	K		
1759-60	„	„	„	L	SF	Name not traced.
GEO. III. 1760-1	„	„	„	M		
1761-2	„	„	„	N		
1762-3	„	„	„	O	MS	Mat'w Skinner.
1763-4	„	„	„	P		
1764-5	„	„	„	Q		
1765-6	„	„	„	R		
1766-7	„	„	„	S	RS	Richard Sams.
1767-8	„	„	„	T	„	„ „
1768-9	„	„	„	U	IH	James Holt.
1769-70	„	„	„	W	TC	Thomas Coffin.
1770-1	„	„	„	X	IF	J. Freeman.
1771-2	„	„	„	Y	RS	Richard Sams.
1772-3	„	„	„	Z		... ...

	CASTLE.	LEOPARD'S HEAD CROWNED	LION PASSANT.	DATE LETTER.	MAKER'S MARK.	MAKER'S NAME.
1773-4				A	RS	Richd. Sams.
1774-5	,,	,,	,,	B		
1775-6	,,	,,	,,	C	{ TE / WW	Thos. Eustace. William West of Plymouth.
1776-7	,,	,,	,,	D		
1777-8	,,	,,	,,	E		
1778-9	,,			F	,,	Thos. Eustace.
1779-80	,,		,,	G	,,	,, ,,
1780-1	,,		,,	H		
1781-2-3	,,		,,	I	,,	,, ,,
1783-4	,,	KING'S HEAD	,,	K	WP	W. Pearse.
1784-5	,,		,,	L		Thos. Eustace (as 1775-6).
1785-6	,,		,,	M	TE	Thos. Eustace.
1786-7	,,		,,	N	JH	Joseph Hicks.
1787-8	,,	,,	,,	O	,,	,, ,,
1788-9	,,	,,	,,	P	,,	,, ,,
1789-90	,,	,,	,,	q	JP	J. Pearse.
1790-1	,,	,,	,,	r		
1791-2	,,	,,	,,	ſ	JH	Joseph Hicks.
1792-3	,,	,,	,,	t		
1793-4	,,	,,	,,	u		
1794-5	,,	,,	,,	w		
1795-6	,,	,,	,,	x	RF	Richd. Ferris.
1796-7	,,	,,	,,	y		

	CASTLE.	LION PASSANT.	DATE LETTER.	KING'S HEAD.	MAKER'S MARK.	MAKER'S NAME.
1797-8			A		RF	Richd. Ferris.
1798-9	,,	,,	B	,,	,,	,, ,,
1799 / 1800	,,	,,	C		JH / WW	Joseph Hicks. / W. Welch.
1800-1	,,	,,	D	,,	JH	Joseph Hicks.
1801-2	,,	,,	E	,,	,,	,, ,,
1802-3	,,	,,	F	,,	,,	,, ,,
1803-4	,,	,,	G	,,	TE	Thos. Eustace.
1804-5	,,	,,	H	,,	RF	Richd. Ferris.
1805-6			I	,,	,,	,, ,,
1806-7	,,	,,	K	,,	,,	,, ,,
1807-8	,,	,,	L	,,	,,	,, ,,
1808-9	,,	,,	M	,,		
1809-10	,,	,,	N	,,	JL	J. Langdon
1810-1	,,	,,	O	,,	WW	W. Welch.
1811-2	,,	,,	P	,,	JH	Joseph Hicks.
1812-3	,,	,,	Q	,,	,,	,, ,,
1813-4	,,	,,	R	,,	GT	G. Turner.
1814-5	,,	,,	S	,,	,,	,, ,,
1815-6	,,	,,	T	,,	,,	,, ,,
1816-7	,,	,,	U	,,	GF	Geo. Ferris.

	Castle.	Lion Passant.	Date Letter.	King's Head.	Maker's Mark	Maker's Name.
1817-8			a		GF	Geo. Ferris.
1818-9	”	”	b	”	”	” ”
1819-20	”	”	c	”	JH	Joseph Hicks.
GEO. IV. 1820-1	”	”	d	”	”	” ”
1821-2	”	”	e	”	”	” ”
1822-3	”	”	f		GF	Geo. Ferris.
1823-4	”	”	g	”	”	” ”
1824-5	”	”	h	”	”	” ”
1825-6	”	”	i	”	IE	John Eustace.
1826-7	”	”	k	”	GM	Name not traced.
1827-8	”	”	l	”	JO	J. Osmont.
1828-9	”	”	m	”	”	” ”
1829-30	”	”	n	”	JH	Joseph Hicks.
WM. IV. 1830-1	”	”	o	”	”	” ”
1831-2			p		WS	W. Sobey.
1832-3	”	”	q	”	J·S	John Stone.
1833-4			r	”	W·P	Wm. Pope.
1834-5	”	”	s		J·O	J. Osmont.
1835-6	”	”	t	”	WRS	W. R. Sobey.
1836-7	”	”	u	”	WW	William Welch.

	Castle.	Lion Passant.	Date Letter.	Queen's Head.	Maker's Mark.	Maker's Name.
VICT. 1837-8			A		SOBEY	W. R. Sobey.
1838-9	”	”	B		J·O	J. Osmont.
1839-40	”	”	C		TB	Thos. Byne.
1840-1	”	”	D	”	J·S	J. Stone.
1841-2		”	E	”	RAM SEY	— Ramsey.
1842-3	”	”	F	”	SOBEY	W. R. Sobey.
1843-4		”	G	”	”	” ”
1844-5	”	”	H	”	WRS	” ”
1845-6	”	”	I	”	” SOBEY	” ” ” ”
1846-7	”	”	K	”	”	” ”
1847-8	”	”	L	”	W W W	? Williams.
1848-9	”	”	M	”	J·S	J. Stone.
1849-50	”	”	N	”	WRS	W. R. Sobey.
1850-1	”	”	O	”	”	” ”
1851-2	”	”	P	”	J·O	J. Osmont.
1852-3	”	”	Q	”	”	” ”
1853-4	”	”	R	”	IP	Isaac Parkin.
1854-5	”	”	S	”	”	” ”
1855-6	”	”	T	”	”	” ”
1856-7	”	”	U	”	J·S	J. Stone.

	Castle	Lion Passant	Date Letter	Queen's Head	Maker's Mark	Maker's Name		Castle	Lion Passant	Date Letter	Queen's Head	Maker's Mark	Maker's Name
1857-8			A		J·S	J. Stone.	1870-1	..	..	O	..		... ...
1858-9	..	..	B	..	,,	.. ..	1871-2	..	..	P	..		.. ..
1859-60	..	..	C	..		. ... ..	1872-3	..	..	Q	..		.. ..
1860-1	..	..	D	..	PO	Name not traced.	1873-4	..	..	R	..		... ...
1861-2	..	..	E	..	JW	Jas. Williams.	1874-5	..	..	S	..		... ...
1862-3	..	,,	F	..		... ...	1875-6	..	..	T	..		... ...
1863-4	..	..	G	..		.. ..	1876-7	..	..	U	..		... ...
1864-5	..	..	H	..		.. ...	1877-8			A		JW & Co	J. Whipple & Co.
1865-6	..	..	I	..		. ..	1878-9	..	..	B	..		... ...
1866-7	..	..	K	..		...	1879-80	..	..	C	..		.. ..
1867-8	..	..	L	..		. ..	1880-1	..	..	D	..		.. ..
1868-9	..	..	M	..	HL	Henry Lake.	1881-2	..	..	E	..		. ...
1869-70	..	,,	N	..		.. ..	1882-3	,,	,,	F	..	WE FD JT	Ellis, Depree & Tucker

SUPPLEMENTARY LIST OF MARKS OF GOLDSMITHS

Impressed at Exeter, but not illustrated in the preceding tables :—

Date	Mark	Name		Date	Mark	Name	
1701	SL	Danie	Slade.	1722	PS	Pentecost	Symonds.
c 1706	IO	Peter	Jouett.	1728	TC	Thomas	Coffin.
1707	Sa	Thos.	Sampson.	1730	IR	John	Reed
1708	W	Richard	Wilcocks.	1732	TC	Thomas	Clarke
1709	SY	Pentecost	Symonds.	,,	IS	John	Suger
1710	Pi	John	Pike.	1741	MM	Micon	Melun.
,,	BE	Joseph	Bennick.	1771	RB	Richd.	Birdlake (Plymouth).
1713	Su	John	Suger.	1825	SL	Simon	Lery
1714	T	Anthony	Tripe.	1830	IP	Isaac	Parkin.
1717	WI	Zacariah	Williams.	1835	GT	G. Turner & partner (? Son).	
1719	BE	Joseph	Bennick.	1845	IG	J.	Golding (Plymouth).
1721	ER	Edward	Richard.	1847	HE	Henry	Ellis.
	IM	John	March.	1850	IP GS	Isaac Geo.	Parkin & Sobey.

DATE (ABOUT).	MARKS.	MAKER'S NAME.
1658	W W	John Wilkinson.
1664	W W	,, ,,
1668	W ,,	,, ,,
1670	,, ID	John Dowthwaite.
1672	,, ,, ID	,, ,,
,,	WR	Wm. Ramsay.
1675	,, ,,	,, ,,
,,	WR ,, ,, ,,	,, ,,
1680	,, ,,	,, ,,
1684	WR WR ,,	,, ,,
,,	,, ,,	,, ,,
,,	WR	,, ,,
1685	WR	Wm. Robinson.
,,	WR WR	,, ,,
1686-7	EB EB	Eli Bilton.
1686-8	WR WR	Wm. Robinson.
1690	,,	,, ,,
1692	WR WR	,, ,,
1694	RS	Robt. Shrive.
,,	EB EB	Eli Bilton.
,,	FB	,, ,,
1695	WR WR	Wm. Robinson.
1697	TH TH	Thos. Hewitson.
1698	,, TH TH	,, ,,
1698-9	EB EB	Eli Bilton.
1700	EB EB	,, ,,
,,	IR IR IR	John Ramsay.
1701	Bi	Eli Bilton.

	THREE CASTLES.	BRITANNIA.	LION'S HEAD ERASED.	DATE LETTER.	MAKER'S MARK.	MAKER'S NAME.
ANNE. 1702-3				A	Ra	John Ramsay.
1703-4	,,	,,	,,	B	Ba	Fras. Batty.
1704-5	,,	,,	,,	C	Sh	Robt. Shrive.
1705-6	,,	,,	,,	D	Bi	Eli. Bilton.
1706-7	,,	,,	,,	E	,,	,, ,,
					Yo	John Younghusband.
1707-8		,,	,,	F	Yo	,, ,,
					Fr	J'nath'n French.
1708-9	,,	,,	,,	G	Bv	John Buckle of York.
1709-10	,,	,,	,,	,,	Ki	James Kirkup.
1710-11						
1711-2					Bi	Eli. Bilton.
1712-3				M	Ho	Richd. Hobbs.
1713-4					LA	John Langwith.
					Fr	J'nath'n French.
GEO. I. 1714-5		,,	,,	M	Ba	Fr. Batty, jr.
1715-6					Sh	Nathl. Shaw.
1716-7						
1717-8	,,	,,	,,	P	BV	Joseph Buckle.
1718-9	,,	,,	,,	M	Ba	Fras. Batty, as above.
					Ki	James Kirkup.
1719-20	,,	,,	,,	D	Ma Ba	R. & F. Makepeace Batty.
					Ca	John Carnaby.
1720-1	,,	,,	,,	E	Wh	Wm. Whitfield.

	THREE CASTLES.	LION PASSANT.	LEOPARD'S HEAD CROWNED.	DATE LETTER.	MAKER'S MARK.	MAKER'S NAME.
1721-2				a	FB IR	Fras. Batty, jr. John Ramsay, jr.
1722-3			,,	B	RM I·K	Robt. Makepeace. Jas. Kirkup.
1723-4	,,		,,	C	IF	Jthn. French.
1724-5	,,	,,	,,	D	IC TP	John Carnaby. Thos. Partis.
1725-6				E	IR	Fras. Batty, jr.
1726-7	,,	,,	,,	F	WW IB	Wm. Whitfield. John Busfield of York. ?
GEO. II. 1727-8		,,		G	I·C	Isaac Cookson.
1728-9	,,		,,	H	GB WW WD	Geo. Bulman. Wm. Whitfield. Wm. Dalton.
1729-30	,,	,,	,,	I	GB	Geo. Bulman.
1730-1	,,	,,	,,	K	WD	Wm. Dalton.
1731-2	,,	,,	,,	L	TG IF	Thos. Gamul ? Jon. French.
1732-3	,,	,,	,,	M	TM IB	Thos. Makepeace. John Busfield of York. ?
1733-4	,,	,,	,,	N	IC	Isaac Cookson.
1734-5	,,	,,	,,	O	TP	Thos. Partis.
1735-6	,,	,,	,,	P	GB	Geo. Bulman.
1736-7	,,	,,	,,	Q	WP	Wm. Partis.*
1737-8	,,	,,	,,	R	IC	Isaac Cookson.†
1738-9	,,	,,	,,	S	WB IB	Wm. Beilby&Co.
1739-40	,,	,,	,,	T	IC R·M	Isaac Cookson. Robt. Makepeace.

	THREE CASTLES.	LION PASSANT.	LEOPARD'S HEAD CROWNED.	DATE LETTER.	MAKER'S MARK.	MAKER'S NAME.
1740-1				A	S·B I·K	Stephen Buckle. James Kirkup.
1741-2	,,	,,	,,	B	WB IB	W. Beilby & Anor. Perhaps Jno. Busfield (of York.)
1742-3	,,	,,	,,	C	IC	Isaac Cookson.
1743-4	,,	,,	,,	D	TS WP	Thomas Stoddart. William Partis.
1744-5	,,	,,	,,	E	FM	F. Martin (probably).
1745-6	,,	,,		F	TB	Thomas Blackett (probably).
1746-7				G	IC	Isaac Cookson.
1747-8	,,	,,	,,	H	IW	John Wilkinson of Sheffield (probably).
1748-9	,,	,,	,,	I	TR	? Thos. Reid of York.
1749-50	,,	,,	,,	K	RG R·M	R. Gillson (of Sunderland). Robert Makepeace.
1750-1	,,			L	TP WB	Thos. Partis II. (of Sunderland). William Beilby.
1751-2	,,	,,	,,	M	WP	William Partis.
1752-3	,,	,,	,,	N	WD I·B	William Dalton. Perhaps John Barrett (of Sunderland).
1753-4	,,	,,	,,	O	IC	Isaac Cookson.
1754-5	,,	,,	,,	P	IL IG	Langlands & Goodriche.
1755-6	,,	,,	,,	Q	IK	John Kirkup.
1756-7	,,	,,	,,	R	I·L	John Langlands.
1757-8		,,		S	IL IL	,, ,, ,, ,,
1758-9				T	RB	Ralph Beilby.

	THREE CASTLES.	LION PASSANT.	LEOPARD'S HEAD CROWNED.	DATE LETTER.	KING'S HEAD.	MAKER'S MARK.	MAKER'S NAME.
1759-60				A		SI	Samuel James.
GEO. III. 1760-8	„	„	„	B		SJ IB	Saml. Thompson. John Barrett of Sunderland.
1769-70	„		„	C		SI RP	Saml. James; Robt. Peat.
1770-1		„		D		I·K	John Kirkup.
1771-2	„	„	„	E		I·F I·L	John Fearny of Sunderland. John Langlands.
1772-3		„	„	F		IC	James Crawford.
1773-4	„	„	„	G		JJ I·H	John Jobson. Jas. Hetherington
1774-5	„	„	„	H		W·S I·M	Stalker & Mitchison.
1775-6	„	„	„	I		I·H H·E FS	Hetherington & Edwards Francis Solomon of Whitehaven.
1776-7	„	„	„	K		H&E	Hetherington & Edwards
1777-8	„	„	„	L		J·H DC	James Hetherington David Crawford.
1778-9	„	„	„	M		I·L I·R	Langlands & Robertson.
1779-80	„			N		DC	David Crawford.
1780-1	„	„	„	O		RP RS	Pinkney & Scott.
1781-2	„	„	„	P		I·L I·R	Langlands & Robertson (as below).
1782-3	„	„	„	Q		I·S BD	John Stoddart. Ben. Dryden.
1783-4	„	„	„	R		JS	John Stoddart.
1784-5	„	„	„	S		RP RS	Pinkney & Scott.
1785-6	„	„	„	T	„	I·M	John Mitchison.
1786-7	„	„	„	U		„	„ „
1787-8	„			W	„	TG L&P	Name not traced. Langlands & Robertson.
1788-9	„		„	X	„	C·R	Chrstn. Reid.
1789-90	„	„	„	Y	„	P&S	Pinkney & Scott.
1790-1	„	„	„	Z	„	I·M	John Mitchison.

	LION PASSANT.	THREE CASTLES.	LEOPARD'S HEAD CROWNED.	KING'S HEAD.	DATE LETTER.	MAKER'S MARK.	MAKER'S NAME.
1791-2					A	IL IR	Langlands & Robertson.
1792-3	„	„	„	„	B	R·S	Robert Scott.
*1793-4	„	„	„	„	C	AH	Anth. Hedley.
1794-5	„	„	„	„	D	MA GW	Mary Ashworth of Dur. G. Weddell.
1795-6	„	„	„	„	E	I·R D·D	Robertson & Darling.
1796-7	„	„	„	„	F	TW R&D	Thos. Watson. Robertson & Darling.
1797-8	„	„	„		G	GL JW	Geo. Laws & John Walker. ?
1798-9	„	„	„	„	H	CR I·R	Chrstn. Reid. John Robertson.
1799/1800	„	„	„	„	I	JR SC	„ „ Sarah Crawford.
1800-1					K	IL	John Langlands, jr.
1801-2	„	„	„	„	L	TW A·R	Thos. Watson. Ann. Robertson.
1802-3	„	„	„	„	M	D·D CR DR	David Darling. Chrstn. K. Reid & David Reid.
1803-4		„	.		N	A·K	Alexr. Kelty.
1804-5	„	„	„	„	O	IL	John Langlands, jr.
1805-6	„	„	„	„	P	GM	George Murray.
1806-7	„	„	„	„	Q	T·W	Thos. Watson.
1807-8	„	„	„	„	R	„	„ „
1808-9	„	„	„	„	S	DD TB	Darling & Bell.
1809-10					T	I·L	John Langlands.†
1810-1	„	„	„	„	U	T·W	Thos. Watson.
1811-2	„	„	„	„	W	D·L IR IW	Drthy. Langlands. Robertson & Walton.
1812-3	„	„	„	„	X	RP M&R	Robert Pinkney. Name not traced.
1813-4	„	„	„	„	Y	CR DR CR	Chrstn. Ker Reid, David. Reid, & Chrstn. Bruce Reid.
1814-5	„	„	„	„	Z	IW	John Walton.

	DATE LETTER	KING'S HEAD	LION PASSANT	THREE CASTLES	LEOPARD'S HEAD CROWNED	MAKER'S MARK	MAKER'S NAME.
1815-6	A					TW	Thos. Watson.
1816-7	B	„	„	„	„	TW	„ „
1817-8	C	„	„	„	„	CD	Christ'r. Dinsdale, of Sunderland.
1818-9	D	„	„	„	„	IR IW	Robertson & Walton.
1819-20	E	„	„	„	„		
GEO. IV. 1820-1	F	„	„	„	„	TW	Thos. Watson.
1821-2	G		„	„	„	„	„ „
1822-3	H	„	„	„	„	„	„ „
1823-4	I	„	„	„	„	„	„ „
1824-5	K	„	„	„	„	TW	„ „
1825-6	L	„	„	„	„		
1826-7	M	„	„		„		
1827-8	N	„	„	„	„		
1828-9	O	„	„	„	„		
1829-30	P	.	„	„	„		
WM. IV. 1830-1	Q	.	„		„		
1831-2	R	„	„	„	„		
1832-3	S		.	„	.	„	Thos. Watson.
1833-4	T	„	„	„			
1834-5	U	.	„	.	„	WL	Wm. Lister.
1835-6	W	„	„	„	„		
1836-7	X		„	„			
VICT. 1837-8	Y		„	„	„	TW	Thos Watson.
1838-9	Z	„	„	„	„	WL CL WL	Lister & Sons.

	KING'S HEAD.	LION PASSANT.	THREE CASTLES.	LEOPARD'S HEAD CROWNED.	DATE LETTER.	MAKER'S MARK.	MAKER'S NAME.
1839-40					A	IW	John Walton.
1840-1	„	„	„	„	B	„	„ „
1841-2		„	„	„	C	TW	Thos. Watson.
1842-3	„	„	„	„	D	„	„ „
1843-4	„	„	„	„	E		
1844-5	„	„	„	„	F		Lister & Sons (as 1838-9).
1845-6	„	„	„	„	G		
1846-7	„				H	GG	Name not traced.
1847-8	„	„	„	„	I		
1848-9	„	„	„	„	J		
1849-50	„	„	„	„	K		
1850-1	„	„	„	„	L		
1851-2	„	„	„	„	M		
1852-3	„	„	„	„	N		
1853-4	„	„	„	„	O		
1854-5	„	„	„	„	P		
1855-6	„	„	„	„	Q		
1856-7	„	„	„	„	R		
1857-8	„	„	„	„	S		
1858-9	„	„	„	„	T		
1859-60	„	„	„	„	U		
1860-1	„	„	„	„	W		
1861-2	„	„	„	„	X		
1862-3	„	„	„	„	Y		
1863-4	„	„	„	„	Z		

Impressed at Newcastle from c. 1750 to c. 1880, but not illustrated in the preceding tables :—

MARK.	NAME.	MARK.	NAME.	MARK.	NAME.
GL	Name not traced.	L&SONS	Lister & Sons.	I·M	John Miller.
WF	" "	L&S	" "	CD	Cuthbert Dinsdale.
WB	Mr. Bartlett ?	I·B	John Brown.	GL	Geo. Sam. Lewis.
SI	Samuel Jones.	J·B	" "	MY&SONS	M. Young & Sons.
PI	Peter James.	JB	" "	SJ	Simeon Joel.
H I I I	Name not traced.	WS	Wm. Sherwin.	J.C	John Cook.
F·S	F. Somerville or Summerville, Sen., and F. S. Junr.	J·D	James Dinsdale.	RD	R. Duncan of Carlisle.
P·B	Peter Beatch.	JS	Name not traced.	J&IJ	Joseph and Israel Jacobs.
I·T	Name not traced.	CJR	Chrstn. J. Reid.	J·F	James Foster.
R·D	" "	RR	Robert Rippon.	W&JW	Wm. and Jno. Wilson.
R·W	Robt. Wilson.	JS	John Sutler.	TR	Thos. Ross of Carlisle ?
D&B	Darling & Bell.	J.W	John White.	TALBOT	A. Y. Talbot of Crook, Darlington.
T·H	Thos. Huntingdon.	DR	David Reid.	TS	Thos. Sewill.
H·B	Hugh Brechinridge.	BUXTON	Wm. Buxton of Bishop Auckland.	IR	Name not traced.
PL	Peter Lambert of Berwick.	I·D	John Deas ?	E.J.C	" "
CR DR	Chrstn. K. Reid & David Reid.	OSWALD	Robt. Oswald of Durham.	WR	" "
CAM ERON	Alexr Cameron of Dundee.	OY	Oliver Young.	E·O	" "
J·R	John Robertson.	IC	John Cook.	RO	" "
		WW&SONS	W. Wilson & Sons.	IH HB	" "
		LP	L. Pedrine of Carlisle.		
		A&S	Alder & Sons of Blyth.		

	DATE LETTER
1864-5	a
1865-6	b
1866-7	c
1867-8	d
1868-9	e
1869-70	f
1870-1	g
1871-2	h
1872-3	i
1873-4	k
1874-5	l
1875-6	m
1876-7	n
1877-8	o
1878-9	p
1879-80	q
1880-1	r
1881-2	s
1882-3	t
1883-4	u

DATE.	MAKER'S MARK, TOWN MARK AND DATE-LETTER.	MAKER'S NAME.
1668	GO	George Oulton.
c. 1683	RW STERLING RW	Ralph Walley.
"	NB	Nathanl. Bullen.
c. 1685	NB Sterl:	" "
"	NB	" "
1686-90	AP	Alexand'r Pulford.
"	E	Peter Edwards.
"	E	" "
"	RW	Ralph Walley.
1690-2	RW	" "
"	PP " " "	Peter Pemberton.
"		" "
"	PP	" "
c. 1692	PP	"
1692-4	PP STERLING STERLING	" "
1695-1700	BB STERLING BB	Name not traced.
1695	D	... ...
1696	E	... ...
1697	F	... .

	BRITANNIA.	LION'S HEAD ERASED.	DATE LETTER.	TOWN MARK.	MAKER'S MARK.	MAKER'S NAME.
1701-2			A		Ri	Richd. Richardson.
ANNE. 1702-3	"	"	B	"	Bi	John Bingley.
1703-4	"	"	C	"	Bu Bi	Nath. Bullen. Chas. Bird.
1704-5	"	"	D	"	Ri	Richd. Richardson.
1705-6	"	"	E	"	Pe Ho	Peter Pemberton. Name not traced.
1706-7	"	"	F	"	Ha	" "
1707-8	"	"	G	"	Ro	Thos. Robinson.
1708-9	"	"	H	"	Gi	Name not traced.
1709-10	"	"	I	"	Co	" "
1710-11	"	"	K	"	Ic	" "
1711-2	"	"	L	"	Sa	" "
1712-3	"	"	M	"	Ta	Tarleton.
1713-4	"	"	N	"	Ri	Richd. Richardson.
GEO. I. 1714-5	"	"	O	"	Ri	" "
1715-6	"	"	P	"	Du	Barth. Duke.
1716-7	"	"	Q	"	Ma Ma	Thos. Maddock. " "
1717-8	"	"	R	"	Ri	Richd. Richardson.
1718-9	"	"	S	"	"	" "
	LION PASSANT.	LEOP'S HEAD CR.				
1719-20			T	·	Ri	" "
1720-1	"	"	U	"	Ma	Thos. Maddock.
1721-2	"	"	V	"	Ri	Richd. Richardson.
1722-3	"	"	W	"	Ri	" "
1723-4	"	"	X	"	Ri	" "
1724-5	"	"	Y	"	Ri "	" " " "
1725-6	"	"	Z	"	JM	John Melling.

	LION PASSANT.	LEOPARD'S HEAD CROWNED.	TOWN MARK.	DATE LETTER.	MAKER'S MARK.	MAKER'S NAME.
1726-7				A	BP	Benj'n Pemberton.
GEO. II. 1727-8	"	"	"	B	BP	" "
1728-9	"	"	"	C	RR	Richd. Richardson.
1729-30	"	"	"	D	RP	Richd. Pike.
1730-1	"	"	"	E	WR	Wm. Richardson.
1731-2	"	"	"	F		R.R. conjoined as at 1728 above.
1732-3	"	"	"	G	RR	Richd. Richardson.
1733-4	"	"	"	H	RR	" "
1734-5	"	"	"	I	"	" "
1735-6	"	"	"	K	" RR	" " " "
1736-7	"	"	"	L	"	" "
1737-8	"	"	"	M	RR	" "
1738-9	"	"	"	N	"	" "
1739-40	"	"	"	O	WR	Wm. Richardson.
1740-1	"	"	"	P	BP	Benj'n Pemberton.
1741-2	"	"	"	Q	RR	Richd. Richardson.
1742-3	"	"	"	R	TM	Thos. Maddock.
1743-4	"	"	"	S	RR	Richd, Richardson.
1744-5	"	"	"	T	"	" "
1745-6	"	"	"	U		... ...
1746-7	"	"	"	V		... ...
1747-8	"	"	"	W		Thos. Maddock as above.
1748-9	"		"	X	RR	Richd. Richardson.
1749-50	"	"	"	Y	"	" "
1750-1		"	"	Z	RR	" "

	LION PASSANT.	LEOPARD'S HEAD CROWNED.	TOWN MARK.	DATE LETTER.	MAKER'S MARK.	MAKER'S NAME.
1751-2				a	RR	Richd. Richardson.
1752-3	"	"	"	B or b		
1753-4	"	"	"	C	"	" "
1754-5	"	"	"	D or d		
1755-6	"	"	"	e	"	" "
1756-7	"	"	"	F or f		
1757-8	"	"	"	G	RR	" "
1758-9	"	"	"	h	RR	" "
1759-60	"	"	"	I or i		
GEO. III. 1760-1	"	"	"	K or k		
1761-2	"	"	"	L or l		
*1762-3	"	"	"	m	RR RR	" " " "
1763-4	"	"	"	n	RR	" "
1764-5	"	"	"	O	RR	" "
1765-6	"	"	"	P	"	" "
1766-7	"	"	"	Q or q		
*1767-8	"	"	"	R	RR	" "
1768-9		"	"	S	"	" "
1769-70	"	"	"	T	B W F	Bolton & Fothergill, Birm.
†1771-2	"	"	"	U	I·W	Joseph Walley.
1773	"	"	"	V	GW I*D	Geo. Walker. James Dixon or Jos. Duke.
1774	"	"	"	W	ID	" "
1775	"	"	"	X	GW	Geo. Walker.
1775-6	"	"	"	Y	RR	Richd. Richardson, jr.

	Lion Passant.	Leopard's Head Crowned.	Town Mark.	Date Letter.	King's Head.	Maker's Mark.	Maker's Name.
1776-7				a		RR	Richd. Richardson.
1777-8	,,	,,	,,	b		GW	George Walker.
1778-9	,,	,,	,,	c		RR	Richd. Richardson.
1779-80				d		,, IW	,, ,, Joseph Walley.
1780-1	,,	,,	,,	e		,,	,, ,,
1781-2	,,	,,	,,	f		GW	George Walker.
1782-3	,,	,,	,,	g		,,	,, ,,
1783-4	,,	,,	,,	h		JA	John Adamson.
1784-5	,,	,,	,,	i		RF	Richd. Richardson.
				i		RR	,, ,,
1785-6	,,	,,	,,	k	,,	JC	J. Clifton or James Conway.
1786-7	,,	,,	,,	l		TP	T. Pierpoint.
1787-8	,,	,,	,,	m	,,	RB	Robt. Boulger.
1788-9	,,	,,	,,	n	,,	IG RI	John Gilbert. Robert Jones.
1789-90	,,	,,	,,	o	,,	WH	Wm. Hull.
1790-1	,,	,,	,,	p	,,	WT WT	Wm. Tarlton.* ,, ,,
1791-2	,,	,,	,,	q	,,	IB	James Barton.
1792-3	,,	,,	,,	r	,,	EM	E. Maddock.
1793-4	,,	,,	,,	s	,,	TA	Thos. Appleby.
1794-5	,,	,,	,,	t	,,	TH	Thos. Hilsby.
1795-6	,,	,,	,,	u	,,	TM	Thos. Morrow.
1796-7	,,	,,	,,	v	,,	IA&S	John Adamson & Son.

	Lion Passant.	Leopard's Head Crowned.	Town Mark.	Date Letter.	King's Head.	Maker's Mark.	Maker's Name.
1797-8				A		GL	George Lowe.
1798-9	,,	,,	,,	B	,,	R·I	Robt. Jones.
1799 1800	,,	,,	,,	C	,,	RG	Robert Green.
1800-1	,,		,,	D	,,	NC	Nicholas Cunliffe.
1801-2	,,	,,	,,	E	,,		Maker's mark indistinct.
1802-3	,,	,,	,,	F	,,	GW	George Walker.
1803-4	,,	,,	,,	G	,,		,, ,,
1804-5	,,	,,	,,	H	,,	I·E	Name not traced.
1805-6	,,	,,	,,	I	,,	NL	Nicholas Lee.
1806-7	,,	,,	,,	K	,,		,, ,,
1807-8	,,	,,	,,	L	,,	GL	George Lowe.
1808-9	,,	,,	,,	M	,,		Mark indistinct.
1809-10	,,	,,	,,	N	,,	WJ	Name not traced.
1810-1	,,	,,	,,	O	,,	IW	John Walker.
1811-2	,,	,,	,,	P	,,	WP	William Pugh (of Birmingham).
1812-3	,,	,,	,,	Q	,,	A&I	Abbott & Jones.
1813-4	,,	,,	,,	R			,, ,,
1814-5	,,	,,	,,	S	,,	JM	Jas. Morton.
1815-6	,,	,,	,,	T	,,		,, ,,
1816-7	,,	,,	,,	U	,,	HA	Hugh Adamson.
1817-8	,,	,,	,,	V	,,	JA	John Abbott.

	LION PASSANT.	LEOPARD'S HEAD.	TOWN MARK.	DATE LETTER.	KING'S HEAD.	MAKER'S MARK	MAKER'S NAME.
1818-9				A		J.W	J. Walker.
1819-20	"	"	"	B	"	V&R	Vale & Co.
GEO. IV. 1820-1	"	"	"	C	"	I&R	Jones & Reeves.
1821-2-3	"	"	"	D	"	HA	Hy. Adamson.
1823-4	"		"	E		MH	Mary Huntingdon.
1824-5	"	"	"	F	"	JT	John Twemlow.
1825-6	"	"	"	G	"	JM	J. Morton.
1826-7	"	"	"	H	"	GL	Geo. Lowe.
1827-8	"	"	"	I	"	RB	Robt. Bowers.
1828-9	"	"	"	K	"	TN	Thos. Newton.
1829-30	"	"	"	L	"	JH JH	John Hilsby, L'pool. " " "
WM. IV. 1830-1	"	"	"	M	"	JC	John Coakley.
1831-2	"	"	"	N	"	JP	John Parsonage.
1832-3	"	"	"	O	"	TW	Thos. Walker or Thos. Woodfield }
1833-4	"	"	"	P	"	RL	Robt. Lowe.
1834-5	"	"	"	Q	"	RL	Richd. Lucas.
1835-6	"	"	"	R		IW	John Walker.
1836-7	"	"	"	S	"	ILS	Jos. L. Samuel.
VICT. 1837-8	"	"	"	T	"	JS	John Sutters.
1838-9	"	"	"	U	"	H.C	Henry Close.

	LION PASSANT.	TOWN MARK.	DATE LETTER.	QUEEN'S HEAD.	MAKER'S MARK.	MAKER'S NAME.
1839-40			𝔄		I.L T.L	J. & Thos. Lowe.
1840-1	"	"	𝔅	"	I&TL	" " "
1841-2	"	"	ℭ	"	H.A	Henry Adamson.
1842-3	"	"	𝔇	"	PL	P. Leonard.
1843-4	"	"	𝔈	"	WS	Wm. Smith.
1844-5	"	"	𝔉	"	RS	Ralph Samuel.
1845-6	"	"	𝔊	"	AB WC	Adam Burgess. Wm. Crofton.
1846-7	"	"	ℌ	"	JB	J. Burbidge.
1847-8	"	"	𝔍	"	IFW	John F. Wathew.
1848-9	"	"	𝔎	"	CJ	Christr. Jones.
1849-50	"	"	𝔏	"	TW	T. Wilson.
1850-1	"	"	𝔐	"	EK	E Kirkman.
1851-2	"	"	𝔑	"	GW	Geo. Ward.
1852-3	"	"	𝔒	"	TC	T. Cubbin.
1853-4	"	"	𝔓	"	RA GCL	Richard Adamson. G. C. Lowe. (Manchester).
1854-5	"	"	𝔔	"	TW	Thos. Wooley.
1855-6	"	"	ℜ	"	AGR	A. G. Rogers.
1856-7	"	"	𝔖	"	JL	John Lowe.
1857-8	"	"	𝔗	"	JM	Joseph Mayer.
1858-9	"	"	𝔘	"	EJ	Edwd. Jones.
1859-60	"	"	𝔙	"	EN	Elias Nathan.
1860-1	"	"	𝔚	"	GR	Geo. Roberts.
1861-2	"	"	𝔛	"	HF	H. Fishwick.
1862-3	"	"	𝔜	"	HS	H. J. Stuart.
1863-4	"	"	ℨ	"	FB	Francis Butt.

	LION PASSANT.	TOWN MARK.	DATE LETTER.	QUEEN'S HEAD.	MAKER'S MARK.	MAKER'S NAME.
1864-5			a		WD	Wm. Dodge.
1865-6	,,	,,	b	,,	IR	John Richards.
1866-7	,,	,,	c	,,	SW	Saml. Ward, Manchester.
1867-8	,,	,,	d	,,	GL	Geo. Lowe, junr.
1868-9	,,	,,	e	,,	HT HT	Henry Tarlton, Liverpool.
1869-70	,,	,,	f	,,	WR	W. Roskell, Liverpool.
1870-1	,,	,,	g	,,	S.Q	S. Quilliam.
1871-2	,,	,,	h	,,	GR	Geo. Roberts.
1872-3	,,	,,	i	,,	RO	Robt. Over.
1873-4	,,	,,	k	,,	TR	Thos. Russell.
1874-5	,,	,,	l	,,	HG	Hugh Green.
1875-6	,,	,,	m	,,	S&R	Samuel & Rogers.
1876-7	,,	,,	n	,,	AC	A. Cruickshank.
1877-8	,,	,,	o	,,	SQ	S. Quilliam.
1878-9	,,	,,	p	,,	GFW	Geo. F. Wright, Liverpool.
1879-80	,,	,,	q	,,	JK	Joseph Knight, Birmingham.
1880-1	,,	,,	r	,,	TP &S	T. Power & Son, Liverpool.
1881-2	,,	,,	s	,,	B.N	Benge Nathan.
1882-3	,,	,,	t	,,	WS	Wm. Smith, Liverpool.
1883-4	,,	,,	u	,,	AR	A. Rogers, Liverpool.

	LION PASSANT.	TOWN MARK.	DATE LETTER.	QUEEN'S HEAD.	MAKER'S MARK.
1884-5			A		NBS
1885-6	,,	,,	B	,,	A.B
1886-7	,,	,,	C	,,	JT&S
1887-8	,,	,,	D	,,	A&M
1888-9	,,	,,	E	,,	W.T
1889-90	,,	,,	F	,,	E.W
1890-1	,,	,,	G		J.W
1891-2	,,	,,	H		T.C
1892-3	,,	,,	I		JH AH
1893-4	,,	,,	K		H.W
1894-5	,,	,,	L		JD WD
1895-6	,,	,,	M		A.M
1896-7	,,	,,	N		W.N
1897-8	,,	,,	O		H.K
1898-9	,,	,,	P		W.A
1899 1900	,,	,,	Q		T.P.B
1900-1	,,	,,	R		GN RH
EDW. VII. 1901-2	,,	,,	A		J.F
1902-3	,,	,,	B		B.B

MARKS ON CHESTER PLATE.

DATE.	LION PASSANT.	TOWN MARK.	DATE-LETTER.
1903-4			C
1904-5	,,	,,	D
1905-6	,,	,,	E
1906-7	,,	,,	F
1907-8	,,	,,	G
1908-9	,,	,,	H
1909-10	,,	,,	I
1910-1	,,	,,	K
1911-2	,,	,,	L
1912-3	,,	,,	M
1913-4	,,	,,	N
1914-5	,,	,,	O
1915-6	,,	,,	P
1916-7	,,	,,	Q
1917-8	,,	,,	R
1918-9	,,	,,	S
1919-20	,,	,,	T
1920-1	,,	,,	U
1921-2	,,	,,	V

MARKS ON LINCOLN PLATE.

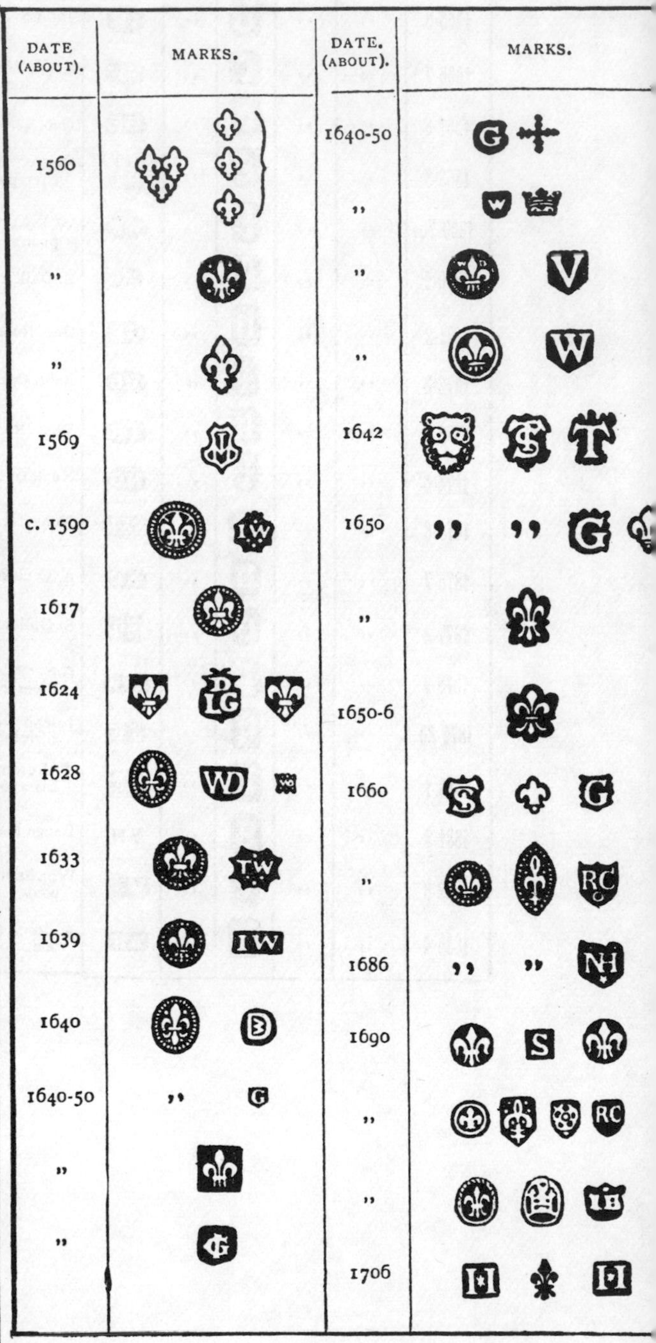

DATE (ABOUT).	DATE. (ABOUT).
1560	1640-50
,,	,,
,,	,,
1569	,,
c. 1590	1642
1617	1650
1624	,,
1628	1650-6
1633	1660
1639	,,
1640	1686
1640-50	1690
,,	,,
,,	,,
	1706

	Lion Passant.	Anchor.	Date Letter.	King's Head	Maker's Mark.	Maker's Name.
1773-4			A		MB IF	Matthew Boulton & John Fothergill.
1774-5	,,	,,	B		,, ,,	,, ,,
1775-6	,,	,,	C		CF	Charles Freeth.
1776-7	,,	,,	D		,,	,, ,,
1777-8	,,	,,	E		RB CF MB IF	Richard Bickley, Charles Freeth. Boulton & Fothergill.
1778-9	,,	,,	F		,, ,,	,, ,,
1779-80	,,	,,	G		TW	T. Willmore & Alston.
1780-1	,,	,,	H			... ...
1781-2	,,	,,	I			... ...
1782-3	,,	,,	K		TW	T. Willmore & Alston.
1783-4	,,	,,	L		,,	,,
1784-5	,,	,,	M		SP	Samuel Pemberton.
1785-6	,,	,,	N	,,	HH	Henry Holland.
1786-7	,,	,,	O		SP	Samuel Pemberton.
1787-8	,,	,,	P	,,	IT	Joseph Taylor.
1788-9	,,	,,	Q	,,	,,	,, ,,
1789-90	,,	,,	R	,,	T·W	Thos. Willmore.
1790-1	,,	,,	S	,,	MB	Mathw. Boulton.
1791-2	,,	,,	T	,,	SP	Samuel Pemberton.
1792-3	,,	,,	U	,,	,,	,, ,,
1793-4	,,	,,	V	,,	MB	Mathw. Boulton.
1794-5	,,	,,	W	,,	IT	Joseph Taylor.
1795-6	,,	,,	X	,,	IS	John Shaw.
1796-7	,,	,,	Y	,,	T·W	Thos. Willmore.
1797-8	,,	,,	Z		,,	,, ,,

	Lion Passant.	Anchor.	Date Letter.	King's Head	Maker's Mark.	Maker's Name.
1798-9			a		TW	Willmore & Alston.
1799. 1800	,,	,,	b	,,	SP	Samuel Pemberton.
1800-1	,,	,,	c	,,	F&W	Forrest & Wasdell.
1801-2	,,	,,	d	,,	IT T·W	John Turner ? Thos. Willmore ?
1802-3	,,	,,	e	,,	MB	Matthew Boulton.
1803-4	,,	,,	f	,,	IS	John Shaw.
1804-5	,,	,,	g	,,	IT	Joseph Taylor.
1805-6	,,	,,	h	,,	ML WP	Matthew Linwood. William Pugh.
1806-7	,,	,,	i	,,	J·W C&B	Joseph Willmore. Cocks & Bettridge.
1807-8	,,	,,	j	,,	WP	William Pugh.
1808-9	,,	,,	k	,,	MB	Matthew Boulton.
1809-10	,,	,,	l		IS	John Shaw.
1810-1	,,	,,	m	,,	T&T	Thropp & Taylor.
1811-2	,,	,,	n	,,	S&S	T. Simpson & Son.
1812-3	,,	,,	o		,, IT	,, ,, Joseph Taylor.
1813-4	,,	,,	p	,,	C&B	Cocks & Bettridge.
1814-5	,,	,,	q	,,	L&C	W. Lea & Co.
1815-6	,,	,,	r	,,	,,	,, ,,
1816-7	,,	,,	s	,,	SP W&K	Samuel Pemberton. Wardell & Kempson.
1817-8	,,	,,	t	,,	ET	Edward Thomason.
1818-9	,,	,,	u	,,	J·W	Joseph Willmore.
1819-20	,,	,,	v	,,	,,	,, ,,
GEO. IV. 1820-1	,,	,,	w	,,	ML	Matthew Linwood & Son.
1821-2	,,	,,	x	,,	L&C	Lea & Clark.
1822-3	,,	,,	y	,,	L&Co	John Lawrence & Co.
1823-4	,,	,,	z	,,	J·W	Joseph Willmore.

	LION PASSANT.	ANCHOR.	DATE LETTER.	KING'S HEAD.	MAKER'S MARK.	MAKER'S NAME.
1824-5			A		TP C·J	T. Pemberton & Son. Charles Jones.
1825-6	,,	,,	B	,,	LV&W T·S	Ledsam, Vale & Wheeler. Thomas Shaw.
1826-7	,,	,,	C		L&Co NM	John Lawrence & Co. Nathaniel Mills.
1827-8	,,	,,	D	,,	U&H MB	Unite and Hilliard M. Boulton & Plate Co.
1828-9	,,	,,	E	,,	J·W ET WF	Joseph Willmore. Edward Thomason. William Fowke.
1829-30	,,	,,	F		IB LV&W	John Bettridge. Ledsam, Vale & Wheeler.
WM. IV. 1830-1	,,	,,	G	,,	TR&S MB	Thos. Ryland & Sons. M. Boulton & Plate Co.
1831-2	,,	,,	H		JW	Joseph Willmore.
1832-3	,,	,,	I	,,	,,	,, ,,
1833-4	,,	,,	K	,,	ES VR	Edward Smith. Vale & Ratheram.
1834-5	,,	,,	L		T&P WP	Taylor & Perry. William Phillips.
1835-6	,,	,,	M	,,	GW	Gervase Wheeler.
1836-7	,,	,,	N	,,	FC J&Co	Francis Clark. Joseph Jennens & Co.
VICT. 1837-8	,,	,,	O	,,	T·S R.E.A	Thomas Spicer. Robinson, Edkins & Aston.
1838-9	,,	,,	P	,,	GU N·M	George Unite. Nathaniel Mills.
1839-40	,,	,,	Q	,,	N&R	Neville & Ryland ?
1840-1	,,	,,	R	,,	,,	,, ,,
1841-2	,,	,,	S	,,		... ...
1842-3	,,	,,	T	,,	R.E.A	Robinson, Edkins & Aston.
1843-4	,,	,,	U	,,	ES	Edward Smith.
1844-5	,,	,,	V	,,	N·M	Nathaniel Mills.
1845-6	,,	,,	W	,,	W&ET	Wm. & Ed. Turnpenny.
1846-7	,,	,,	X	,,	Y&W N·M	Yapp & Woodward. Nathaniel Mills.
1847-8	,,	,,	Y	,,	,,	,, ,,
1848-9	,,	,,	Z	,,		... ...

	LION PASSANT.	ANCHOR.	DATE LETTER.	QUEEN'S HEAD.	MAKER'S MARK.	MAKER'S NAME.
1849-50			A		N·M	Nathaniel Mills.
1850-1	,,	,,	B	,,	,, ES	,, ,, Edward Smith.
1851-2	,,	,,	C	,,	,,	,, ,,
1852-3	,,	,,	D	,,		Nathl. Mills, as 1849.
1853-4	,,	,,	E	,,		... ...
1854-5	,,	,,	F	,,		... ...
1855-6	,,	,,	G	,,	GU	George Unite.
1856-7	,,	,,	H	,,		... ...
1857-8	,,	,,	I	,,		... ...
1858-9	,,	,,	J	,,		... ...
1859-60	,,	,,	K	,,	GU	George Unite.
1860-1	,,	,,	L	,,		... ...
1861-2	,,	,,	M	,,		... ...
1862-3	,,	,,	N	,,		J. H. & Co., as on page 414.
1863-4	,,	,,	O	,,		... ...
1864-5	,,	,,	P	,,	JM&Co	Names registered after 1850 not disclosed.
1865-6	,,	,,	Q	,,		... ...
1866-7	,,	,,	R	,,		... ...
1867-8	,,	,,	S	,,	JG	... ...
1868-9	,,	,,	T	,,		... ...
1869-70	,,	,,	U	,,		... ...
1870-1	,,	,,	V	,,		... ...
1871-2		,,	W	,,	JT	Crown and 18 instead of lion passant.
1872-3	,,	,,	X	,,		... ...
1873-4	,,	,,	Y	,,		... ...
1874-5	,,	,,	Z	,,		... ...

	Lion Passant.	Anchor.	Date Letter.	Queen's Head.	Maker's Mark.
1875-6			a		TP&S
1876-7	,,	,,	b	,,	,,
1877-8	,,	,,	c	,,	H&T
1878-9	,,	,,	d	,,	
1879-80	,,	,,	e	,,	
1880-1	,,	,,	f	,,	
1881-2	,,	,,	g	,,	
1882-3	,,	,,	h	,,	H&T
1883-4	,,	,,	i	,,	,,
1884-5	,,	,,	k	,,	
1885-6	,,	,,	l	,,	
1886-7	,,	,,	m	,,	
1887-8	,,	,,	n	,,	
1888-9	,,	,,	o	,,	
1889-90	,,	,,	p	,,	N&H
1890-1	,,	,,	q		T.W.D
1891-2	,,	,,	r		N&H
1892-3	,,	,,	s		J.M.B
1893-4	,,	,,	t		SWS
1894-5	,,	,,	u		L.G
1895-6	,,	,,	v		T.H
1896-7	,,	,,	w		H M
1897-8	,,	,,	x		HH&Co JHW
1898-9	,,	,,	y		A& JZ
1899 1900	,,	,,	z		JS SS

Date.	Anchor.	Lion Passant.	Date Letter.	Maker's Mark.
1900-1			a	E&CoLd
1901-2	,,	,,	b	H.W.Ld
1902-3	,,	,,	c	IS G
1903-4	,,	,,	d	L&Co
1904-5	,,	,,	e	H&F
1905-6	,,	,,	f	
1906-7	,,	,,	g	
1907-8	,,	,,	h	
1908-9	,,	,,	i	
1909-10	,,	,,	k	
1910-1	,,	,,	l	
1911-2	,,	,,	m	
1912-3	,,	,,	n	
1913-4	,,	,,	o	
1914-5	,,	,,	p	
1915-6	,,	,,	q	
1916-7	,,	,,	r	R&TW
1917-8	,,	,,	s	
1918-9	,,	,,	t	
1919-20	,,	,,	u	
1920-1	,,	,,	v	
1921-2	,,	,,	w	
1922-3	,,	,,	x	
1923-4	,,	,,	y	
1924-5	,,	,,	z	

SUPPLEMENTARY LIST OF ADDITIONAL MARKS OF GOLDSMITHS,

Impressed at Birmingham, not illustrated in the preceding tables.

Date.	Mark.	Maker's Name.
1776-7	JA&S	Jos. Adams & Son.
1778-9	E.S	Edward Sawyer.
1783-4	SP	Samuel Pemberton.
1804-5	W	... ...
1806-7	H&Co.	... ...
1807-8	M	... ...
1811-2	W	... ...
1814-5	J.L	... ...
1820-1	T.N	Thos. Newbold.
1822-3	SP	... ...
1826	T&K	Geo. Tye & Jas. Kilner.
1832-3	G.T	Geo. Tye.
1876-7	TT &Co	... ...
1862-3	JH&Co	... ...
1892-3	HW	... ...

	Lion Passant.	Crown.	Date Letter.	King's Head from 1784	Maker's Mark.	Maker's Name.
1773-4			E		R·M &Cº SR&Cº MF &Cº	Rich'd. Morton & Co. S. Roberts & Co. Mat'w. Fenton & Co.
1774-5	"	"	F		GA &Cº	Geo. Ashforth & Co.
1775-6	"	"	N		IW&Cº	John Winter & Co.
1776-7	"	"	R		W·D	Wm. Damant.
1777-8	"	"	H		HT TL MF RC	Tudor and Leader. Fenton Creswick & Co.
1778-9	"	"	S		I·S	John Smith ?
1779-80	"	"	A		"	" "
1780-1	"	"	C		NS&Cº	Nath'l. Smith & Co.
1781-2	"	"	D		MF RC	Fenton Creswick & Co.
1782-3	"	"	G		IW&Cº	John Winter & Co.
1783-4	"	"	B		DH&Cº I·P&Cº	Danl. Holy & Co. John Parsons & Co.
1784-5	"	"	I		"	" "
1785-6	"	"	y	"	R·M	Richd. Morton & Co.
1786-7	"		k		I·P&Cº	John Parsons & Co.
1787-8	"	"	T	"	"	" "
1788-9	"	"	W	"	ITY&Cº	John Younge & Sons.
1789-90	"	"	M	"	RS	R. Sutcliffe & Co. (?)
1790-1	"	"	L	"	I·P&Cº	John Parsons & Co.
1791-2	"	"	p	"	ITY&Cº	John Younge & Sons.
1792-3			u	"	IP&Cº	John Parsons & Co.
1793-4	"	"	O	"	TL	Thos. Law.
1794-5	"	"	m	"	IG&Cº	John Green & Co.
1795-6	"	"	q	"	ITY&Cº	John Younge & Sons, as above.
1796-7	"	"	Z	"	GE &Cº	Geo. Eadon & Co.
1797-8	"		X		T·LAW	T. Law.
1798-9	"	"	V		SR GC &Co	Saml. Roberts, jr. Geo. Cadman & Co.

	Lion Passant.	Crown.	Date Letter.	King's Head	Maker's Mark.	Maker's Name.
1799 1800			E		IL&Cº IG&Cº	John Love & Co. John Green & Co.
1800-1	"	"	N	"	GA &Cº IG&Cº	Geo. Ashforth & Co. John Green & Co.
1801-2	"	"	H	"	" TW&Cº	" " Thos. Watson & Co.
1802-3			M	"	TL DL R·M	Thos. & Danl. Leader. Richd. Morton & Co.
1803-4	"	"	F	"	N·S&Cº	Nathan Smith & Co.
1804-5	"	"	G	"	IE&Cº	Jas. Ellis & Co.
1805-6	"	"	B	"	AG&Cº	Alexr. Goodman & Co.
1806-7	"	"	A	"	ITY &Cº	J. T. Younge & Co.
1807-8	"	"	S	"	WT&Cº	W. Tucker & Co.
1808-9	"	"	P	"	T·B &Cº	Thos. Blagden & Co.
1809-10	"	"	K	"	I·R&Cº	John Roberts & Co.
1810-1	"		L	"	" GE &Cº	" " Geo. Eadon & Co.
1811-2	"	"	C			John Roberts & Co., as 1809-10 above.
1812-3	"	"	D	"	ST N&H	Smith, Tate & Co. (Nicholson & Holt).
1813-4	"	"	R	"	I·K·I·W&Cº	Kirkby, Waterhouse & Co.
1814-5	"		W	"	I·L	John Law
1815-6	"	"	O	"	JE&Cº	J. Ellis & Co. (?)
1816-7	"	"	T	"	I·W	John Watson.
1817-8	"	"	X	"	" I&T.S.	" " John and Thos. Settle.
1818-9	"	"	I	"	SCY &Cº	S. C. Younge & Co.
1819-20		"	V v	"	T.J.C IK·IW &CO GC&Cº	Thos. and Jas. Creswick Kirkby, Waterhouse & Co. G. Cooper & Co.
GEO. IV. 1820-1	"	"	Q	"	ST H&T	Smith, Tate, Hoult & Tate.
1821-2	"	"	Y	"	JL	Joseph Law
1822-3	"	"	Z	"	IG&Cº	John Green & Co.
1823-4	"	"	U	"	W·B	Wm. Briggs.

	LION PASSANT	CROWN.	DATE LETTER.	KING'S HEAD	MAKER'S MARK.	MAKER'S NAME.
1824-5			a		S.C.Y &Co WB&Co	S. C. Younge & Co. Wm. Blackwell & Co.
1825-6	,,		b	,,	I&IW &Co	Waterhouse, Hodson & Co.
*1826-7	,,	,,	c	,,	BH &H	Battie, Howard & Hawksworth.
1827-8	,,		d	,,	TI NC	T. J. & N. Creswick.
1828-9	,,	,,	e	,,	BH &H	Battie, Howard & Hawksworth.
1829-30	,,		f	,,	IS HW	John Settle & Henry Williamson.
WM. IV. 1830-1	,,		g	,,	TI NC	T. J. & N. Creswick.
1831-2	,,	,,	h		JB	Jas. Burbury.
1832-3	,,	,,	k	,,	S&N A&O	Stafford & Newton. Atkin & Oxley.
1833-4	,,		l	,,	T·I NC WA&Co	T. J. & N. Creswick. Wm. Allanson & Co.
1834-5	,,		m	,,	I&IW &Co	Waterhouse, Hodson & Co.
1835-6	,,		p		H&H	Howard & Hawksworth.
1836-7	,,	,,	q	,,		.. ..
VICT. 1837-8	,,		r	,,	HW &Co	Hy. Wilkinson & Co.
1838-9	,,		s	,,	HW &Co	,, ,, ,,
1839-40	,,	,,	t	,,	SH	Samuel Harwood.
1840-1	,,	,,	u		,,	,, ,,
1841-2	,,	,,	v	,,		...
1842-3	,,		x	,,	HE &Co	Hawksworth, Eyre & Co.
1843-4	,,	,,	z	,,		.. .. ..

	CROWN.	DATE LETTER.	LION PASSANT.	QUEEN'S HEAD.	MAKER'S MARK.	MAKER'S NAME.
*1844-5		A			HE &Co	Hawksworth, Eyre & Co.
1845-6	,,	B	,,	,,		... .
1846-7	,,	C	,,	,,		... ...
1847-8	,,	D	,,	,,		... ...
1848-9	,,	E	,,	,,		... ...
1849-50	,,	F	,,	,,	,,	Hawksworth, Eyre & Co.
1850-1	,,	G	,,	,,		... .
1851-2	,,	H	,,	,,		... ...
1852-3	,,	I	,,	,,		... ...
1853-4	,,	K	,,	,,		... ...
1854-5	,,	L	,,	,,		... ...
1855-6	,,	M	,,	,,		... ...
1856-7	,,	N	,,	,,		.. ..
1857-8	,,	O	,,	,,		... ...
1858-9	,,	P	,,	,,		... ...
1859-60	,,	R	,,	,,	MH &Co	Martin Hall & Co.
1860-1	,,	S	,,	,,		... ...
1861-2	,,	T	,,	,,		... ...
1862-3	,,	U	,,	,,	HH	Harrison Bros. & Howson.
1863-4	,,	V	,,	,,		... ...
1864-5	,,	W	,,	,,	FBros	Fenton Bros.
1865-6	,,	X	,,	,,	HA	Hy. Archer & Co.
1866-7	,,	Y	,,	,,	RM EH	Martin Hall & Co., Ltd.
1867-8	,,	Z	,,	,,		... ...

	CROWN.	LION PASSANT.	DATE LETTER.	QUEEN'S HEAD.	MAKER'S MARK.	MAKER'S NAME.
1868-9			A		R M E H	Martin Hall & Co., Ltd.
1869-70	,,	,,	B	,,		
1870-1	,,	,,	C	,,		... .
1871-2	,,	,,	D	,,		... ...
1872-3	,,	,,	E	,,		... .
1873-4	,,	,,	F	,,	I H	John Harrison & Co., Ld.
1874-5	,,	,,	G	,,		... ...
1875-6	,,	,,	H	,,		... ...
1876-7	,,	,,	J	,,		... .
1877-8	,,	,,	K	,,		... .. .
1878-9	,,	,,	L	,,		... .. .
1879-80	,,	,,	M	,,		.. .. ..
1880-1	,,	,,	N	,,		. .. .
1881-2	,,	,,	O	,,		.. .. ..
1882-3	,,	,,	P	,,		.. .. .
1883-4	,,	,,	Q	,,		. .. ..
1884-5	,,	,,	R	,,		. ..
1885-6	,,	,,	S	,,		. . .
1886-7	,,	,,	T	,,		.. . .
1887-8	,,	,,	U	,,		... . .
1888-9	,,	,,	V	,,	J·K·B	Hawksworth, Eyre & Co., Ltd.
1889-90	,,	,,	W	,,	W B J A	W. Briggs & Co.
1890-1	,,	,,	X	,,	RM EH	Martin Hall & Co., Ltd.
1891-2	,,	,,	Y	,,	J·D&S	Jas. Dixon & Sons.
1892-3	,,	,,	Z	,,	H·S	Henry Stratford.

	CROWN.	LION PASSANT.	DATE LETTER.	MAKER'S MARK.	MAKER'S NAME.
1893-4			a	J D & S	James Deakin & Sons.
1894-5	,,	,,	b	JR	John Round & Son, Ltd.
1895-6	,,	,,	c	J D W D	Jas. Deakin & Sons.
1896-7	,,	,,	d	M&W	Mappin & Webb.
1897-8	,,	,,	e	W F A F	Fordham & Faulkner.
1898-9	,,	,,	f	H.W	Lee & Wigfull.
1899/1900	,,	,,	g	H A	Atkin Brothers.
1900-1	,,	,,	h	W&H	Walker & Hall.
EDW. VII. 1901-2	,,	,,	i	R&B	Roberts & Belk.
1902-3	,,	,,	k	GH	Harrison Bros. & Howson.
1903-4	,,	,,	l		... ...
1904-5	,,	,,	m		... .
1905-6	,,	,,	n		... ...
1906-7	,,	,,	o		.. ..
1907-8	,,	,,	p		.. .. ..
1908-9	,,	,,	q		.. .. .
1909-10	,,	,,	r		. ... -
1910-1	,,	,,	s		. .. .
1911-2	,,	,,	t		.. .. .
1912-3	,,	,,	u		. .. ...
1913-4	,,	,,	v		.. .. .
1914-5	,,	,,	w		.. . ...
1915-6	,,	,,	x		. . ..
1916-7	,,	,,	y		.. ..
1917-8	,,	,,	z		.. ..

SUPPLEMENTARY LIST OF MARKS OF GOLDSMITHS

Impressed at Sheffield, not illustrated in the preceding tables, from 1773 to 1905 :—

DATE.	MARKS.	MAKER'S NAME.
1773	W·H I·R	W. Hancock & J. Rowbotham.
"	WB &Co	W. Birks & Co.
"	TL STERLING	T. Law.
"	LAW STERLING	" "
"	WB &Co STERLING	W. Birks & Co.
"	IR "	J. Rowbotham ?
"	IL "	J. Littlewood.
"	SO "	Name not traced.
"	IK&Co	John Kay & Co.
"	JN WN	J. Nowill. W. Nowill.
1774	I·M	J. Mappin.
"	WM &Co	W. Marsden & Co.
"	S·R	S. Roberts.
1775	I·R·Co	J. Rowbotham & Co.
"	R·K	R. Kippax.
"	I M&Co	J. Mappin & Co.
1776	I·H	T. Hoyland.
"	I T	J. Tibbitts.
1777	I H Co	J. Hoyland & Co.
"	I H&Co	" "
1778	S·W	S. Warburton.
"	DH	D. Holy.
1779	M&T	Madin & Trickett
1780	Y·G&H	Young, Greaves & Hoyland.
"	N·S	N. Smith & Co.
1781	I·D	J. Dewsnap.
1783	S·K	S. Kirkby.

DATE.	MARKS.	MAKER'S NAME.
1784	T·F&Co	T. Fox & Co.
1788	P·S	P. Spurr.
1789	W·J	W. Jervis.
1790	RS	R. Sporle.
1791	I·B	J. Bailey.
"	MF &Co	M. Fenton & Co.
1792	L·P &Co	? Luke, Proctor & Co.
1796	G·A &Co	G. Ashforth & Co.
1797	CP	C. Proctor.
"	EG	E. Goodwin.
"	IC	J. Creswick.
"	H·T&Co	Mark of Henry Tudor & Co.
1798	GG&Co	Goodman, Gainsford & Co.
"	SK&Co	S. Kirkby & Co.
1799	R·J	R. Jewesson.
1801	TP	T. Poynton.
1804	[illegible]	Name not traced.
"	IS	J. Staniforth.
1807	W.T.&Co	W. Tucker & Co.
1808	J·W	J. Watson.
1810	G·W	G. Wostenholme
1811	IS TS	J. Staniforth & Co.
"	RG	R. Gainsford.
1813	I·R	J. Rogers.
1817	RG	R. Gainsford.
1818	B·R	B. Rooke & Son.
"	W·W	W. Wrangham
1820	TJ&NC	T. J. & N. Creswick.
1822	T&IS	T. & J. Settle.

DATE.	MARKS.	MAKER'S NAME.
1822	A·H	A. Hadfield.
1824	CHS	C. Hammond & Co
1825	RG	R. Gainsford.
1828	GH	G. Hardesty.
1829	D&S	J. Dixon & Son.
1833	JM	J. Mappin & Son.
1836	K&W	Kitchen & Walker.
1840	L&M	Lee & Middleton.
"	WK &Co	Walker, Knowles & Co.
1843	W&S	Waterhouse & Co
1844	BW&A	Badger Worrall & Co.
1846	R&S	Roberts & Slater.
1847	P·P &Co	Padley, Parkins & Co.
1853	JC NC	J. & N. Creswick.
1856	WS HS	W. & H. Stratford.
1857	F&A	Fenton & Anderton.
1858	WH	W. Hutton.
"	WS GS	W. & G. Sissons.
1859	MB	Mappin Bros.
"	EM&Co	Elkington Mason & Co.
1861	WWH	W W. Harrison.
1862	W&H	Walker & Hall.
1863	LB	Levesley Bros.
1864	M W&Co	Mappin & Webb.
1866	W& MD	W. & M. Dodge.
1867	J·H·S	J. Slater & Son.
1868	CL TL	Levesley Bros.
1869	AB	A. Beardshaw.
1905	IE &S	Name not traced.

HULL

DATE.	TOWN MARK.	MAKER'S MARK.	TOWN MARK.	MAKER'S MARK.	MAKER'S NAME.
1580	H	PC			Peter Carlille.
1587		I.C	H		James Carlille.
1621		IC	RR	HB	" " *
1629	H	RR	H		Robt. Robinson.
1635		RR	"		" "
1638	H	CW	H		Chr. Watson.
1651		IB			James Birkby.
1666		EM		DATE LETTER.	Edwd. Mangie or Mangy.
1666-70		TG		E	Name not traced.
1670-80	"	"		K	" "
"		EM		A	Edwd. Mangie or Mangy.
1680	"	EM			" "
"	"	EM	"	D	" "
1680-97		KM	"	E	Kath. Mangy.
"		KM			" "
"	..	EM	"	F	Edwd. Mangy.
1689	"	TH	"		Thos. Hebden.
1690-7'		KM			Kath. Mangy.
1697		KM			" "
1706		AB	"		Abm. Barachin.

SHREWSBURY

DATE.	MARKS.
1530	
1560	
"	

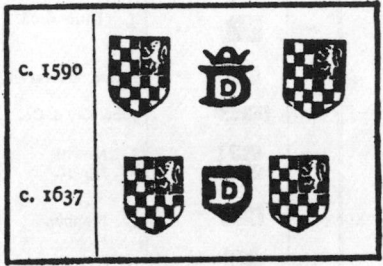

LEWES.

c. 1590	D
c. 1637	D

ROCHESTER

DATE.	MARKS.
1560	R R
c. 1640	R

Sandwich.

BARNSTAPLE

DATE (ABOUT).	MARKS.	MAKER'S NAME.
1568-1601	IC	John Coton.
c. 1570-75	TM	Thos. Mathew.
1576	T MATHEV	" "
1578	D COTON	J. Coton.
1580	TM MATHEV	T. Mathew.
"	IC	*J. Coton.
1584	I COTON	" "
c. 1650	I·P	John Peard
1670-80	IP BAR I P VM IP	" "
1680	IP	" "
1687	IP	" "
1695	I·P	" "

TRURO

DATE (ABOUT).	MARKS.
1560 / 1600	R
"	R T T
"	" "
1600	
1620	R T T
"	
"	R T T
1630	R "

DEVON AND CORNWALL

DATE (ABOUT).	MARKS.
1576-80	WZ
"	
1580	IN W
? c. 1600	HP
c. 1600-30	IS
"	B
"	P·T· PT
"	IW
"	IP Fal mo uth
"	
1610	CF CF
1610-50	RA
1630	WR
1641	
1650 / 1700	MV MV
1675	IP
1680-5	RA
1690	DD
1695	IH
"	TL
1700	RH B
1715	RP

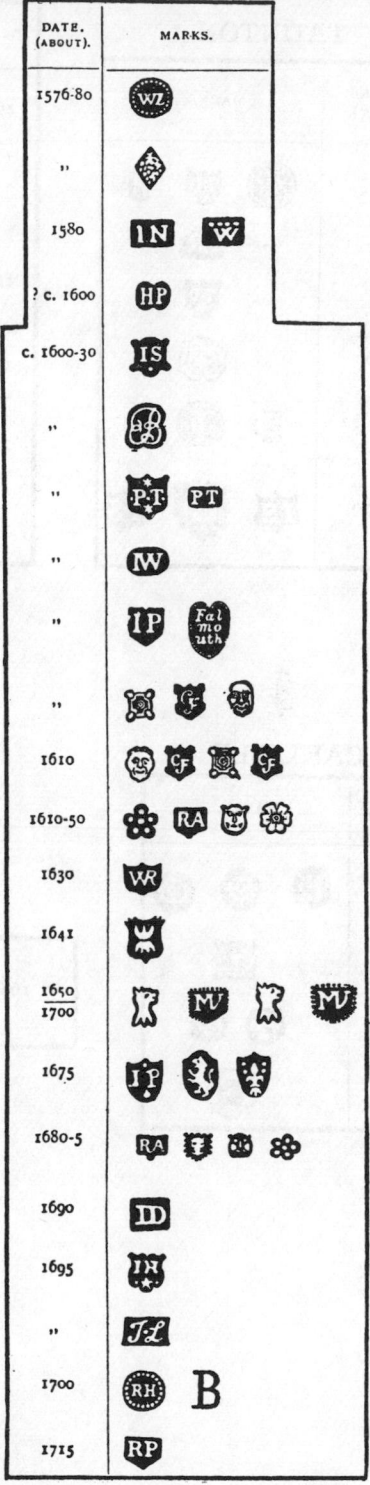

TAUNTON

DATE (ABOUT).	MARKS.
1645	
"	" 
"	
1660	
1676-82	
1689	

LEEDS

DATE.	MARKS.
1650	
TO	
1702	
"	" "
1660	
1680	 " 
1690	
"	 "

KING'S LYNN

DATE.	MARKS.
1632	
1635	 " 
1640	 "

CARLISLE

DATE.	MARKS.
1571	
1630	
"	
1670	

GATESHEAD

c. 1680	

LEICESTER

DATE.	MARKS.
1540	
1590	
1600	
"	
1575 to 1600	
1630	
"	

PLYMOUTH

DATE.	MARKS.
c. 1600	
1690-5	
1695-9	
,,	
c. 1694	
1698	
to	
1700	

SALISBURY

DATE.	MARKS.
c. 1596	
,,	
c. 1620	
,,	
c. 1627	
c. 1629	
,,	

COLCHESTER

DATE.	MARKS.
c. 1723	

JAMAICA

DATE.	MARKS.
c. 1800	

DORCHESTER

Mark of Lawrence Stratford, of Dorchester.	

SHERBORNE

Mark of Richard Orenge (probably).	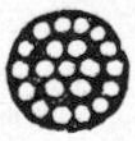
Marks of Richard Orenge.	

CHANNEL ISLANDS

DATE (ABOUT).	MARKS.
GUERNSEY, c. 1690-1730	GH R
c. 1740	
c. 1750	IH
"	IA
"	IH
"	IA
JERSEY, c. 1760	GB
c. 1780	GM
"	J LG J
c. 1790	PN
c. 1800	CWQ
"	IQ
"	J.Q
c. 1830	I.DG J.LG

POOLE.

DATE.	MARKS.
c. 1540	
"	RS
c. 1560	
c. 1580	AA AA
"	IA IA
c. 1620	

CALCUTTA.

DATF.	MARKS.
c. 1810	H&Co A
"	A P &Co

BRISTOL

DATE.	MARKS.
c. 1730	RG A
c. 1731	" B " " "
c. 1780-90	FEI COX SALMON

DATE (ABOUT).	MARKS.	DATE (ABOUT).	MARKS.	DATE (ABOUT).	MARKS.
1500		1570-7		1590	HP
"		"	A	"	
1510		"		"	
1520	S	"	N G	1600	
1530		"		"	N
"		1570-80	RI	"	
1550	R·C	"	PD	"	W
"	I	"	RM	"	
1560	NH	"	RM	"	RW
"	RI	"	H	"	
1570	GARET	1576	IW	"	N
"	W	1580	DR DR	"	K
"	TI	"	P QVICK	"	RW
1570	DV	"	IE	"	
		"	ZB	"	
		"		"	
		1590		"	
		"		"	PARM^r^ R
		"		"	
		"		"	
		"	HL	"	
		"	PARR	"	

DATE (ABOUT).	MARKS.
1600	
"	
"	
1600-50	
1609	
1610	
"	
"	
"	
"	
"	
"	
"	
1620	
"	
"	
"	
"	
"	
"	
"	

DATE (ABOUT).	MARKS.
1620	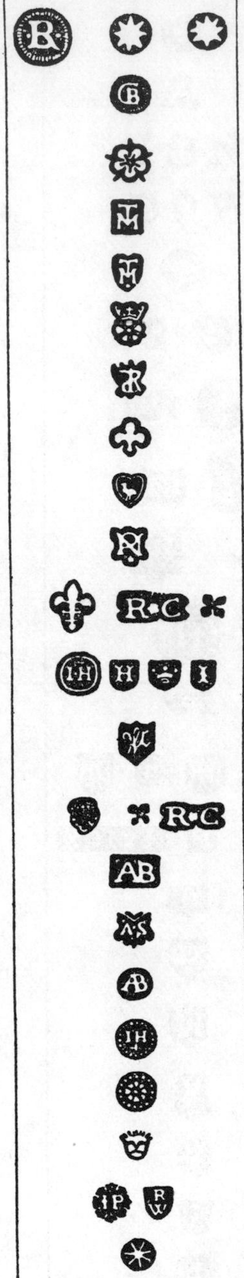
1623	
1625	
1630	
"	
"	
"	
"	
"	
"	
"	
"	
"	
"	
1630-5	
"	
"	
"	
"	
"	
"	
"	

DATE (ABOUT).	MARKS.
1630-5	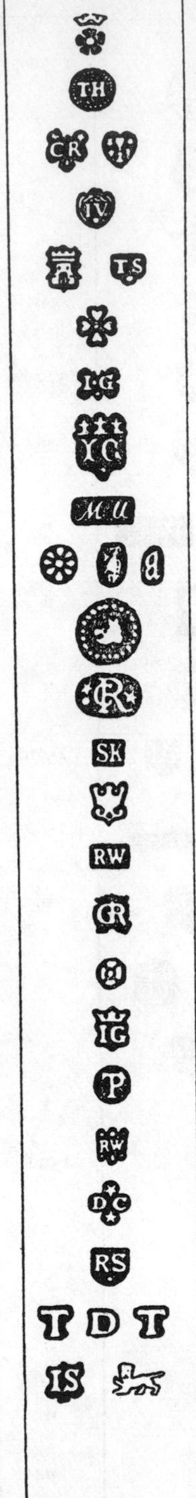
"	
"	
"	
"	
"	
1637	
"	
1638	
1640	
"	
"	
"	
"	
"	
"	
"	
"	
"	
"	
"	
"	
"	
"	

DATE (ABOUT).	MARKS.
1640	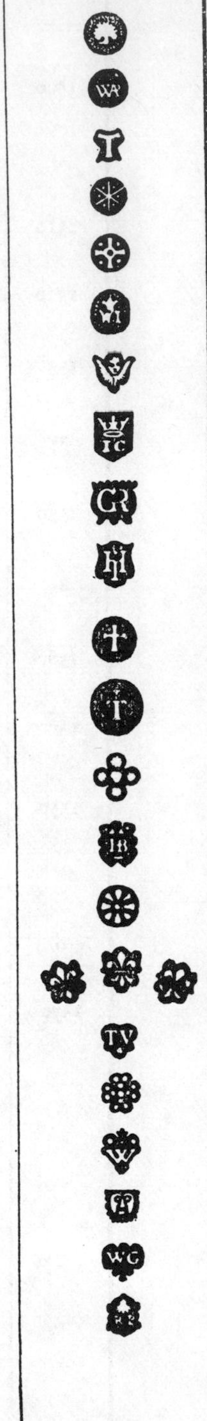
"	
"	
"	
"	
1640-8	
1640-50	
"	
"	
"	
1650	
"	
"	
"	
"	
"	
"	
"	
"	
"	
"	
"	

DATE (ABOUT).	MARKS.	DATE (ABOUT).	MARKS.	DATE (ABOUT).	MARKS.
1650	RR	1674	TM	1680	
"	RH	1675	TG	"	IB
"	IG	"	RH	"	SH
1658	RM	1677	WG	"	
1660	F L S	"	GL	1680-5	RS RS
"	GG	1680	VC	"	
"	RP	"	VC	"	WG
"	HC	"	MR	"	HS
"	RI	"	HW	"	HH
"	WW	"	H	"	ES
"	WR	"	SS	"	
1660-70	DS	"	NB M NB	"	
"		"	PD	"	
1667	T	"	BW	"	IL
1670		"	IF	"	PD
"	H	"	SS	"	NG
1670-4	WR	"		"	AC
"	S TC	"	R	"	RP
1674	,,	"	RS	1682	FB
"	RO	"	IC	1684-5	H
"	IP	"		"	IVB
				"	MC

DATE (ABOUT).	MARKS.
1685	IG
1687	I
1690	IR Ster ling IR
"	IM
"	RH RH Ster ling
"	HA
"	MB
"	IR IR
1690-1	h SS SS
1690-5	FH
"	RS
"	I·K
"	I·C
"	IW
"	GF
"	TS
"	RH
"	WC GM
"	WH I·A
1690-9	WW
"	
1693	

DATE (ABOUT).	MARKS.
1695	I·D
"	HE
"	GM
"	WP
"	SM
1700	AH
"	MI
1700-5	AD
"	WC
1700-40	PS
1702	GL MW DSR 1702
1706-9	La
"	GF
"	GV
1710	SR AR b
"	SR AB b
1720-5	A·I
1720-30	LL
1725-30	I·D
"	IT
"	CR
1730	T·B&C^o

DATE (ABOUT).	MARKS.
1730	A PF
"	
"	GBC
"	TW
1730-4	CI
1730-40	MC MC
"	TM STER LING TM
"	GS Y
"	L+H
"	GT GT
"	IT S S IT
"	L DF
1740	I·D F
1750	RS MG
1750-60	AD
c. 1760	A·T

DATE.	MAKER'S NAME.	MAKER'S MARK	TOWN MARK CASTLE	DEACON'S MARK	DEACON'S NAME.
1552-62	Alex. Auchinleck				Thos. Ewing.
1563-4	Henry Thompsone (1561)		..		James Cok.
c. 1570	(*Mark indistinct.*)		..		George Heriot, senr.*
1576	Adam Craige				James Mosman.
1585-6	John Mosman (1575)		..		John Mosman.
1590-1	Adam Allane, jr. (1589)				Geo. Heriot, senr.*
1591-2	James Craufuird		..		Do. do.
1591-4	David Gilbert (1590)		..		Wm. Cok (Cokie).
,,	James Craufuird (1591)				Do. do.
1596/1600	Hugh Lindsay (1587)		..		David Heriot.
1609-10	Gilbert Kirkwood (1609)		..		Robert Denneistoun.
1611-3	Robert Denneistoun (1597)				David Palmer.
,,	George Craufuird, jr. (1606)		..	..	Do. do.
1617-9	Do. do.	..			John Lindsay.
,,	John Lindsay (1605)		..	..	Do do.
,,	George Robertsone (1616)		..	..	Do. do.
,,	Thos. Thompson (1617)		..	..	Do. do.
c. 1617	Hew. Anderson		..		George Craufuird.
1613-21	Gilbert Kirkwood (1609)				James Denneistoun.
1616-35	George Robertsone (1616)		..		George Craufuird.
1633	Adame Lamb (1619)		..	..	Do. do.
,,	Thos. Kirkwood (1631)		..	..	Do. do.
1633 (?)	(*Mark indistinct.*)				Alexr. Reid (probably).

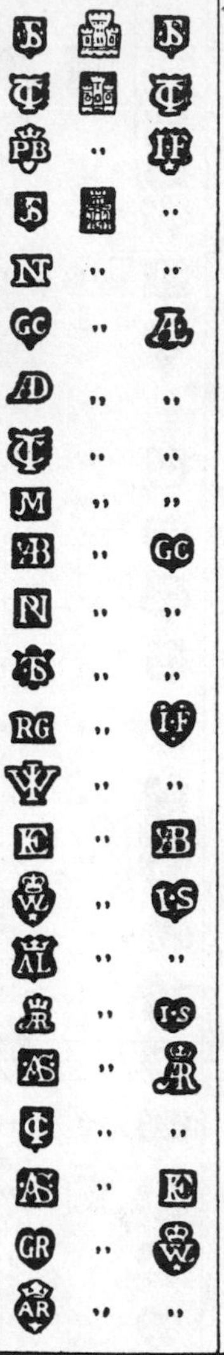

DATE.	MAKER'S NAME.	MAKER'S MARK	TOWN MARK. CASTLE	DEACON'S MARK.	DEACON'S NAME.
1637-9	Jon Scott Adm. (1621)				Jon Scott.
1640-2	Thos. Clyghorne (1606)				Thos. Clyghorne.
1642	Patrick Borthwick (1642)		..		John Fraser.
1643	Jon Scott (1621)			..	Do. do.
,,	Nicoll Trotter (1635)		..	..	Do. do.
1644-6	George Cleghorne (1641)		..		Adam Lamb.
,,	Andro Denneistoun (1636)		..	..	Do. do.
,,	Thos. Clyghorne (1606)		..	..	Do. do.
1644	{John Myln or / Jas. McAulay		..	..	Do. do.
1649	Andro Burrell (1642)		..		George Cleghorne.
1648-57	Peter Neilsone (1647)		..	..	Do. do.
1650	Thos. Scott (1649)		..	..	Do. do.
1651-9	Robert Gibsoune (1627)		..		James Fairbairne.
1657	John Wardlaw (1642)		..	..	Do. do.
1660	Edwd. Cleghorne (1649)		..		Andro Burrell.
1665-7	Wm. Law (1662)		..		James Symontoun.
,,	Andrew Law (c. 1665)		..	..	Do. do.
1665	Alexr. Reid		..		Do. do.
1669-75	Alexr. Scott (1649)		..		Alexr. Reid (2nd)
1674	James Cockburne (1669)		..	..	Do. do.
1663-81	Alexr. Scott (1649)		..		Edwd. Cleghorne.
1675-7	George Rolland (1675)		..		Wm. Law.
1677	Alexr. Reid (3rd) (1677)		..	..	Do. do.

MAKER'S NAME.	MAKER'S MARK.	TOWN MARK. CASTLE	ASSAY MASTER'S MARK	DATE LETTER.	DATE.	ASSAY MASTER'S NAME.
Alexr. Reid (Adm. 1660)	AR		B	a	1681-2	John Borthwick.
Edwd. Cleghorne (1649)	EC					
Andrew Law (c. 1665)	AL	,,	B	b	1682-3	,,
Wm. Law (1662)	WL					
Thos. Yorstoun (1673)	TY	,,	,,	c	1683-4	,,
John Lawe (1661)	IL	,,	,,	d	1684-5	,,
James Penman (1673)	P	,,	,,	e	1685-6	,,
Do. do.	,,	,,	,,	f	1686-7	,,
James Cockburne (1669)	IC	,,	,,	g	1687-8	,,
George Scott (1677)	GS	,,	,,	h	1688-9 WM. & MY.	,,
Wm. Scott (1686)	WS	,,	,,	i	1689-90	,,
James Cockburne (1669)	IC	,,	,,	k	1690-1	,,
Robert Bruce (1687)	RB	,,	,,	l	1691-2	,,
Robert Inglis (1686)	RI	,,	,,	m	1692-3	,,
James Sympsone (1687)	IS	,,	,,	n	1693-4	,,
Geo. Yorstoune (1684)	GY	,,	,,	o	1694-5 WM. III.	,,
Alexr. Forbes (1692)	AF	,,	,,	p	1695-6	,,
James Sympsone ? (1687)	IS	,,	P	q	1696-7	James Penman.
(Not identified).	WI	,,	,,	r	1697-8	,,
Thos. Ker (1694)	TK		,,	s	1698-9	,,
Alexr. Kincaid (1692)	AK	,,	,,	t	1699 1700	,,
Colin McKenzie (1695)	MK	,,	,,	v	1700-1	,,
Geo. Scott, jr. (1697)	GS	,,	,,	w	1701-2 ANNE.	,,
Mungo Yorstoun (1702)	MY	,,	,,	x	1702-3	,,
Thos. Cleghorne (1689)	TC	,,	,,	y	1703-4	,,
James Sympson (1687)	IS	,,	,,	z	1704-5	,,
Patrick Murray (1701)	PM					

MAKER'S NAME.	MAKER'S MARK.	TOWN MARK. CASTLE.	ASSAY MASTER'S MARK.	DATE LETTER.	DATE.	ASSAY MASTER'S NAME.
Patrick Murray (Adm. 1701)	PM		P	A	1705-6	James Penman.
James Tait (1704)	T					
Walter Scott (1701)	WS	,,	,,	B	1706-7	,,
Wm. Ged (1706)	WG	,,	EP	C	1707-8	Edward Penman.
John Penman, jr. (1703)	IP					
Harry Beathune (1704)	HB	,,	,,	D	1708-9	,,
John Seatoune (1688)	IS	,,	,,	E	1709-10	,,
James Mitchellsone (1706)	IM	,,	,,	F	1710-1	,,
Patrick Turnbull (1689)	PT	,,	,,	G	1711-2	,,
Robert Ker (1705)	RK	,,	,,	H	1712-3	,,
Robert Inglis (1686)	RI	,,	,,	I	1713-4 GEO. I.	,,
Mungo Yorstoun (1702)	MY		,,	K	1714-5	,,
,, ,,	MY					
Thos. Ker (1694)	TK	,,	,,	L	1715-6	,,
Harry Beathune (1704)	HB	,,	,,	M M	1716-7	,,
John Seatoun (1685)	IS					
Chas. Dickson (as 1721)	CB	,,	,,	N N	1717-8	,,
Chas. Blair (1707)						
Wm. Ure (1715)	WU		EP	N	,,	,,
James Mitchellsone (1706)	IM	,,	,,	O	1718-9	,,
Mungo Yorstoun (1702)	MY	,,	,,	P P	1719-20	,,
Alexr. Sympsone (1710)	AS					
Jas. Inglis (1720)	II	,,	EP	P	,,	,,
,, ,,		,,	,,	Q	1720-1	,,
David Mitchell (1700)	DM					
Chas. Dickson (1719)	CD	,,	,,	R	1721-2	,,
James Clarke (1710)	IC					
Colin Campbell (1714)	CC	,,	,,	S	1722-3	,,
Ken'th McKenzie (1714)	KM	,,	,,	T	1723-4	,,
Chas. Blair (1707)	CB					
Alexr. Edmonstoune (1721)	AE	,,	,,	U	1724-5	,,
Archd. Ure (1715)	AU	,,	,,	V	1725-6	,,
James Taitt (1704)	T	,,	,,	W	1726-7 GEO. II.	,,
Harry Beathune (1704)	HB	,,	,,	X	1727-8	,,
Patrick Graeme (1725)	PG	,,	,,	Y	1728-9	,,
Wm. Aytoun (1718)	WA	,,	,, AU	Z Z	1729-30	Archibal Ure
Wm. Jameson (1729)	WI					

MAKER'S NAME.	MAKER'S MARK.	TOWN MARK. CASTLE.	ASSAY MASTER'S MARK.	DATE LETTER	DATE.	ASSAY MASTER'S NAME.
James Anderson Adm. (1729)	IA	castle	AU	A	1730-1	Archibald Ure.
Hugh Gordon (1727)	HG	"	"	B	1731-2	"
George Forbes (1731)	GF	"	"	C	1732-3	"
John Main (1729)	IM	"	"	D	1733-4	"
Edw'rd Lothian (1731)	EL (crowned)	"	"	E	1734-5	"
John Rollo (1731) (afterwards Lord Rollo).	IR	"	"	F	1735-6	"
Hugh Penman (1734)	HP	"	"	G	1736-7	"
Alexander Farquharson (1734)	AF	castle	"	H	1737-8	"
James Ker (1723) Dougal Ged (1734)	I·K GED	"	"	I	1738-9	"
James Ker (1723)	I·K	"	"	K	1739-40	"
" " (1737)	"	"	"			"
Ebenr. Oliphant (1737)	EO	"	GED	L	1740-1	†
Law'ce Oliphant (1737) William Aytoun (1718)	LO WA	"	"	M	1741-2	†
Robert Gordon (1741)	RG	"	EL (crowned)	N	1742-3	†
Edwd. Lothian (1731)	EL (crowned)	"	"	O	1743-4	†
Chas. Dickson (1738)	CD	castle	HG	P	1744-5	Hugh Gordon.
Ebenr. Oliphant (1737)	EO	"	"	Q	1745-6	"
ohn Kincard (1726)	IK	"	"	R	1746-7	"
(*Not identified.*)	CL	"	"	S	1747-8	"
William Gilchrist (1736)	WG	"	"	T	1748-9	"
Edward Lothian (1731)	EL (crowned)	"	"	U	1749-50	"
Robert Lowe (1742)	LOW	"	"	V	1750-1	"
" " " " Ebenr. Oliphant (1737)	EO	"	"	W	1751-2	"
ames McKenzie (1747)	IM	"	"	X	1752-3	"
ames Weems (1738) ohn Edmonston (1753)	IW IE	"	"	Y	1753-4	"
Wm. Davie (1740)	WD	"	"	Z	1754-5	"

MAKER'S NAME.	MAKER'S MARK.	TOWN MARK. CASTLE.	ASSAY MASTER'S MARK.	DATE LETTER	DATE.
Ker & Dempster.	K&D	castle	HG	A	1755-6
Rbt. Gordon Adm. (1741)	RG	"	"	B	1756-7
Wm. Taylor (1753) John Clark (1751)	WT CLARK	"	"	C	1757-8
Lothian & Robertson. James Welsh (1746)	L&R IW	"	"	D	1758-9
James Gilsland (1748)	IG	"	THISTLE	E	1759-60
Alexr. Aitchison (1746) Jas. Somervail (1754)	AIT IS	"	"	F	GEO. III. 1760-1
John Robertson (1758) Wm. Dempster (1742)	JR WD	"	"	G	1761-2
" " John Welsh (1742)	IW	"	"	H	1762-3
John Taylor (1760) James Hill (1746)	IT JH	"	"	I	1763-4
Milne & Campbell?	M&C	"	"	K	1764-5
Rbt. Clark (1763) Wm. Drummond (1760)	RC WD	"	"	L	1765-6
John Stirling? (1757)	IS	"	"	M	1766-7
Benjn. Tait (1763) Gillsland & Ker.	TAIT G&K	"	"	N	1767-8
Patk. Robertson (1751)	PR	"	"	O	1768-9
" " Daniel Ker. (1764)	" DK	"	"	P	1769-70
(*not identified.*) James Gilsland (1748)	JB IG	"	"	Q	1770-1
Wm. & Jno. Taylor.	WT IT	"	"	R	1771-2
Wm. Davie (1740)	WD	"	"	S	1772-3
" " Alexr. Gairdner (1754)	AG	"	"	T	1773-4
James Welsh (1746)	IW	"	"	U	1774-5
.. ..		"	"	V	1775-6
Wm. Davie (1740)	WD	"	"	W	1776-7
James Dempster (1775)	ID	"	"	X	1777-8
Patk. Robertson (1751)	PR	"	"	Y	1778-9
James Hewitt (1750)	JH	"	"	Z	1779-80

MAKER'S NAME.	Adm.	MAKER'S MARK.	KING'S HEAD.	TOWN MARK CASTLE	THISTLE	DATE LETTER	DATE.
W. & P. Cunningham.		WP PC				A	1780-1
David Downie	(1770)	DD		"	"	B	1781-2
Fras. Howden	(1781)	FH		"	"	C	1782-3
Robt. Bowman	(1780)	RB		"	"	D	1783-4
Alex. Edmonston	(1779)	AE		"	"	E	1784-5
David Marshall	(1782)	DM	"	"	"	F	1785-6
James Dempster	(1775)	ID		"	"	G	1786-7-8
Thos. Duffus	(1780)	TD	"	"	"	H	1788-9
Alex. Gairdner James Douglas	(1754) (1785)	AG JD	"	"	"	I J	1789-90
W. & P. Cunningham.		WP PC	"	"	"	K	1790-1
Geo. Christie	(1791)	GC	"	"	"	L	1791-2
Alex. Zeigler	(1782)	AZ	"	"	"	M	1792-3
Peter Mathie	(1774)	PM	"	"	"	N	§1793-4
Wm. Robertson	(1789)	WR	"	"	"	O	1794-5
Alex. Henderson	(1792)	AH	"	"	"	P	1795-6
Geo. Christie Alex. Spence	(1791) (1783)	GC AS	"	"	"	Q	1796-7
W. & P. Cunningham.		WPC		"	"	R	1797-8
Thos. Duffus	(1780)	TD	"	"	"	S	1798-9
Alex. Graham & Co. ? W. & P. Cunningham.		AG&C WPC	"			T	1799 1800
John Zeigler	(1798)	IZ	"	"	"	U	1800-1
Fras. Howden	(1781)	FH	"	"	"	V	1801-2
Matt. Craw.		MC	"		"	W	1802-3
Wm. Auld	(1788)	WA	"	"	"	X	1803-4
Simon Cunningham	(1800)	SC	"	"	"	Y	1804-5
(Not identified).		M&R	"	"	"	Z	1805-6

MAKER'S NAME.	MAKER'S MARK.	KING'S HEAD.	TOWN MARK. CASTLE	THISTLE.	DATE LETTER.	DATE.
R. Green or R. Grierson.	RG				a	1806-7
Cunningham & Simpson. *(Not identified).*	PC &S D&M	"	"	"	b	1807-8
Do. do. *	IH	"	"	"	c	1808-9
George Fenwick. John McDonald.	GF IMD	"		"	d	1809-10
Robt. Gray & Son (of Glasgow).	RG &S	"	"	"	e	1810-1
Math. Craw.	MC	"	"	"	f	1811-2
Alexr. Henderson.	AH	"	"	"	g	1812-3
J. McKay.	JM	"	"	"	h	1813-4
Frs. Howden.	FH	"	"	"	i	1814-5
R. K. (a Perth maker). Wm. Zeigler.	WZ	"	"	"	j	1815-6
Js. & Wm. Marshall. Chas. Dalgleish.	J&WM CD	"	"	"	k	1816-7
J. McKay. Do. do.	JM	"	"	"	l	1817-8
Redpath & Arnot.	R&A	"	"	"	m	1818-9
J'n'th'n Millidge ?	JM	"	"	"	n	1819-20
Frs. Howden.	FH	"			o	GEO. IV. 1820-1
Do. do.	"	"	"	"	p	1821-2
Redpath & Arnot.	R&A	"	"	"	q	1822-3
Alexr. Zeigler.	AZ		"	"	r	1823-4
Marshall & Sons.	M&S	"		"	s	1824-5
J. McKenzie ? †	Mc	"	"	"	t	1825-6
J. McKay.	JMc	"		"	u	1826-7
Leon'd Urquhart.	LU	"	"	"	v	1827-8
(Not identified).	WC	"	"	"	w	1828-9
J. McKay.	JMc	"	"	"	x	1829-30
Do. do.	"	"	"	"	y	WM. IV. 1830-1
Peter Sutherland.	PS	"	"	"	z	1831-2

MAKER'S NAME.	MAKER'S MARK.	KING'S HEAD.	TOWN MARK CASTLE.	THISTLE.	DATE LETTER	DATE.
Iarshall & Sons.	M&S				A	1832-3
as. Nasmyth.	JN	"	"	"	B	1833-4
(*Not identified*).	GB	"	"	"	C	1834-5
Ilder & Co.	E&C°	"	"	"	D	1835-6
R. & R. Keay, of Perth.	R&RK	"	"	"	E	1836-7
. McKay.	JMc	"	"	"	F	VICTORIA. 1837-8
.D. (see the Arbroath Marks).		"	"	"	G	1838-9
as. Howden & Co.	JH&C°	"	"	"	H	1839-40
as. Nasmyth & Co.	JN&C	"	"	"	I	1840-1
eo. Jameson, of Aberdeen.	GJ	QUEEN'S HEAD 	"	"	K	1841-2
Iarshall & Sons.	M&S	"	"	"	L	1842-3
.. ..		"	"	"	M	1843-4
McKay.	JMc	"	"	"	N	1844-5
.. ..		"	"	"	O	1845-6
D G as Canongate c. 1836 (page 514).		"	"	"	P	1846-7
Iarshall & Sons.	M&S	"	"	"	Q	1847-8
Hay.	JH	"	"	"	R	1848-9
Iackay & Chisholm.	M&C	"	"	"	S	1849-50
Do. do.	"	"	"	"	T	1850-1
... ...		"	"	"	U	1851-2
.. ..		"	"	"	V	1852-3
... ...		"	"	"	W	1853-4
has. Robb.	CR	"	"	"	X	1854-5
Hay.	JH	"	"	"	Y	1855-6
(*Not identified*).	RN	"	"	"	Z	1856-7

MAKER'S NAME.	MAKER'S MARK.	QUEEN'S HEAD.	TOWN MARK. CASTLE.	THISTLE.	DATE LETTER	DATE.
J. & W. Marshall.	J&WM				A	1857-8
Jonthn. Millidge?	JM	"	"	"	B	1858-9
(*Not identified*).	JU	"	"	"	C	1859-60
Alex. Hay.	AH	"	"	"	D	1860-1
J. Asherheim.	JA	"	"	"	E	1861-2
R. L. Christie. J. E. Vernon.	RLC JEV	"	"	"	F	1862-3
Wm. Crouch.	WC	"	"	"	G	1863-4
D. Blackley. W. J. McDonald.	DB WJM'D	"	"	"	H	1864-5
Wm. Marshall.	RMC WM DMcG	"	"	"	I	1865-6
Elder & Co.	E&C JM	"	"	"	K	1866-7
J. Smith or Scott. D. & J. Sanderson. Cockburn & McDonald.	JS D&JS COCKBURN	"	"	"	L	1867-8
Geo. Edwards & Son.	GE&S	"	"	"	M	1868-9
J. Hamilton & Son.	JH&SON GEO. ST	"	"	"	N	1869-70
George Laing. Walter Neil.	GL WN	"	"	"	O	1870-1
Wm. Carstairs. Carlisle & Watt.	WC C&W	"	"	"	P	1871-2
W. Fraser. Jas. Aitchison.	WF AITCHISON	"	"	"	Q	1872-3
J. Johnston. Jas. Hamilton.	JJ HAMILTON	"	"	"	R	1873-4
	JH&C° M&CS J CRICHTON	"	"	"	S	1874-5
John Crichton. M. Crichton.	JH&C MC JG&C	"	"	"	T	1875-6
Robb & Whittet.	R&W J&WM	"	"	"	U	1876-7
C. or J. Gray.	GRAY	"	"	"	V	1877-8
Mackay & Chisholm.	M&C	"	"	"	W	1878-9
J. Crichton.	JC	"	"	"	X	1879 80
Hamilton & Inches.	H&I	"	"	"	Y	1880-1
... ...		"	"	"	Z	1881-2

MAKER'S NAME.	MAKER'S MARK.	QUEEN'S HEAD.	TOWN MARK. CASTLE.	THISTLE.	DATE LETTER	DATE.
... ...	CS				a	1882-3
Wm. Knaggs.	WK	,,	,,	,,	b	1883-4
Hamilton & Inches.	H&I	,,	,,	,,	c	1884-5
... ...	,,	,,	,,	,,	d	1885-6
Mackay & Chisholm.	M&C	,,	,,	,,	e	1886-7
Jas. Duncan.	JD	,,	,,	,,	f	1887-8
Milne of Aberdeen.	MILNE ABDN	,,	,,	,,	g	1888-9
W. Crouch & Sons.	WC&S	,,	,,	,,	h	1889-90
Hamilton & Inches.	H&I		,,	,,	i	1890-1
J. Crichton & Co. Jas. Duncan.	JC&Co JD		,,	,,	k	1891-2
Brook & Son.	B&S		,,	,,	l	1892-3
J. Crichton & Co.	JC&Co		,,	,,	m	1893-4
Lewis Cohen. Latimer & Sons. Jas. Duncan.	LC L&SONS JD		,,	,,	n	1894-5
D. Crichton.	DC				o	1895-6
J. Crichton & Co.	J.C&Co		,,	,,	p	1896-7
McDonald & Horne. J. Hardy & Co.	M&H H&C C&K		,,	,,	q	1897-8
W. Crouch & Sons.	WC&S		,,	,,	r	1898-9
W. & J. Milne. Hamilton & Inches.	W&JM H&I		,,	,,	s	1899/1900
Thos. Johnston. Young & Tatton.	TJ Y&T		,,	,,	t	1900-1
Jas. Robertson.	JR		,,	,,	u	EDW. VII. 1901-2
Brook & Son.	B&S		,,	,,	v	1902-3
... ...			,,	,,	w	1903-4
... ...			,,	,,	x	1904-5
... ...			,,	,,	y	1905-6
... ...			,,	,,	z	1906-7

TOWN MARK. CASTLE.	THISTLE.	DATE LETTER	DATE.
		A	1907-8
,,	,,	B	1908-9
,,	,,	C	1909-10
,,	,,	D	1910-1
,,	,,	E	1911-2
,,	,,	F	1912-3
,,	,,	G	1913-4
,,	,,	H	1914-5
,,	,,	I	1915-6
,,	,,	K	1916-7
,,	,,	L	1917-8
,,	,,	M	1918-9
,,	,,	N	1919-20
,,	,,	O	1920-1
,,	,,	P	1921-2

DATE.	MAKER'S MARK.	TREE, FISH & BELL.	MAKER'S MARK.	DATE LETTER	MAKER'S NAME.
1681-2	T·M		T·M	a	Thos. Moncrur (1665)
1682-3				b	... ...
1683-4	RB		RB	c	Robt. Brook (1673)
1684-5				d	... ...
1685-6	,,	,,	,,	e	Robert Brook (1673)
1686-7				f	... ...
1687-8				g	... ...
1688-9				h	... ...
1689-90	IS		IS	i	Jas. Stirling (1686)
1690-1	,,	,,	,,	k	Do. Do.
1691-2				l	... ...
1692-3				m	... ...
1693-4				n	... ... ,,
1694-5	RB		RB	o	Robt. Brook (1673)
1695-6				p	... ...
1696-7	RB	,,	RB	q	Robert Brook (1673)
1697-8				r	... ...
1698-9	W.C		W.C	s	Wm. Clerk (1693)
1699/1700	RB		RB	t	Robert Brook (1673)
1700-1	IL		IL	u	John Luke
1701-2	IL	,,	IL	v	James Luke (1692)
1702-3				w	... ...
1703-4				x	... ...
1704-5	TC IL	,, ,,	TC IL	y	Thos. Cumming (1682) John Luke, jr. (1699)
1705-6	,,	,,	,,	z	Do. do. do.

DATE (ABOUT.)	MAKER'S MARK.	TREE, FISH & BELL.	MAKER'S MARK.	LETTER	MAKER'S MARK.
1706-7				A	... ...
1707-8	IL		IL	B	John Luke, jr. (1699)
1709-10	,,	,,	,,	D	Do. do. ,,
	WC		WC	,,	William Clerk (1693)
1709-20	IF		IF		John Falconer (1709)
,,	JL	,,	JL		James Lockhart (1707)
1717-49	IB	,,	IB		Johan Got-helf-Bilsings (1717)
1728-31	,,	,,	,,	S	Do. do. ,,
1725-35	RL	,,	RL	S	Robert Luke (1721)
1743-52	IG		IG	S	James Glen (1743)
,,	GLN	,,	GLN	,,	Do. do. ,,
1747-60	ST		ST	S	Saml. Telfer (1747)
1756-76	DW	,,	DW	S	David Warnock (1756)
,,		,,		S	*(No maker's mark).*
1757-80	IC		IC		John Campbell (1757)
,,	JL		JL		*(Not identified.)*
,,	J·S		J·S	,,	Do. do.
1758-65	WN	,,	WN		Wm. Napier (1758)
,,	B&N	,,	B&N	S	Bayne & Napier.

DATE (ABOUT).	MAKER'S MARK.	TREE, FISH & BELL.	MAKER'S MARK.	LETTER.	MAKER'S NAME.
1763-70	AG		AG		Adam Graham (1763)
"	"	"	"	E	Do. do.
"	"	"	"	F	Do. do.
1773-80	IT	S	IT	S	James Taylor (1773)
1776-80	M&C			O	* Milne & Campbell.
"	M&C		M&C	O	* Do. do.
"	RG		RG		Robert Gray (1776)
"	RG		RG	S	Do. do. "
1783	T&H		T&H		Taylor & Hamilton.
"	J·Mc		J·Mc	"	James McEwen (1783)
1777-90	WL	"	WL	"	Wm. Love (1777)
1782-92	J·W		J·W		James Wright (1782)
1785-95	ID		ID	S	John Donald (1785)
"	"	"	"	O	Do. do. "
1781/1800	MF		MF	S	Patrick McFarlane (1781)
		LION RAMPANT.			
1811-3	MF				Archibald McFadyen (1811)

	TREE, FISH & BELL.	LION RAMPANT.	DATE LETTER.	KING'S HEAD.	MAKER'S MARK.	MAKER'S NAME.
1819-20			A		B.SCOTT / M&R.	B. Scott. (*Not identified.*)
GEO. IV. 1820-1		"	B	"	LFN / JD	Luke F. Newlands (1816) / Jas. Downie (1812)
1821-2	"	"	C	"	RG &S	Robt. Gray & Son (1819)
1822-3	"	"	D	"	RD	Robt. Duncan (1813)
1823-4	"	"	E	"	JB	John Bruce (1815)
1824-5	"	"	F	"	M&S	(*Not identified.*)
1825-6	"	"	G	"	AM	Alexr. Mitchell (1822)
1826-7	"	"	H	"	AMcD	Angus McDonald (1824)
1827-8	"	"	I	"	PA	Peter Arthur (1808)
1828-9	"	"	J	"	EB	Edwd. Bell (1827)
1829-30	"	"	K	"	JB CO	Jas. Burrell & Co. (1825)
WM. IV. 1830-1	"	"	L	"	DR	Danl. Robertson (1829)
1831-2	"	"	M	"		John Mitchell ... (as 1835-6 below).
1832-3	"	"	N		RG &S	Robt. Gray & Son (1819)
1833-4	"	"	O	"	PA	Peter Arthur (1808)
1834-5	"	"	P	"	DCR	D. C. Rait (1832)
1835-6	"	"	Q	"	JM	John Mitchell (1834)
1836-7	"	"	R	"	DCR / JW	D. C. Rait (1832) (*Not identified.*)
VICT. 1837-8	"	"	S	"	WP	W. Parkins (1835)
1838-9	"	"	T	"	RG &S	Robt. Gray & Son (1819)
1839-40	"	"	U	"	"	Do. do. "
1840-1	"	"	V	"	JM	John Mitchell (1834)
1841-2	"	"	W		HM	*Henry Muirhead (1838
1842-3	"	"	X		HD	*Henry Downs (1831
1843-4	"	"	Y		DCR	*D. C. Rait (1832
1844-5	"	"	Z		CB	*Chas. Bryson (1834

	TREE, FISH & BELL.	LION RAMPANT.	DATE LETTER.	QUEEN'S HEAD.	MAKER'S MARK.
1845-6			A		WB
1846-7	,,	,,	B	,,	RG &S
1847-8	,,	,,	C	,,	
1848-9	,,	,,	D	,,	JR
1849-50	,,	,,	E	,,	PA J[R]
1850-1	,,	,,	F	,,	J&WM
1851-2	,,	,,	G	,,	
1852-3	,,	,,	H	,,	RG&S
1853-4	,,	,,	I	,,	
1854-5	,,	,,	J	,,	AM
1855-6	,,	,,	K	,,	RS
1856-7	,,	,,	L	,,	
1857-8	,,	,,	M	,,	AM[c]D
1858-9	,,	,,	N	,,	WA&S
1859-60	,,	,,	O	,,	
1860-1	,,	,,	P	,,	
1861-2	,,	,,	Q	,,	
1862-3	,,	,,	R	,,	JM
1863-4	,,	,,	S	,,	
1864-5	,,	,,	T	,,	
1865-6	,,	,,	U	,,	
1866-7	,,	,,	V	,,	
1867-8	,,	,,	W	,,	
1868-9	,,	,,	X	,,	
1869-70	,,	,,	Y	,,	
1870-1	,,	,,	Z	,,	

	TREE, FISH & BELL.	LION RAMPANT.	DATE LETTER.	QUEEN'S HEAD.
1871-2			A	
1872-3	,,	,,	B	,,
1873-4	,,	,,	C	,,
1874-5	,,	,,	D	,,
1875-6	,,	,,	E	,,
1876-7	,,	,,	F	,,
1877-8	,,	,,	G	,,
1878-9	,,	,,	H	,,
1879-80	,,	,,	I	,,
1880-1	,,	,,	J	,,
1881-2	,,	,,	K	,,
1882-3	,,	,,	L	,,
1883-4	,,	,,	M	,,
1884-5	,,	,,	N	,,
1885-6	,,	,,	O	,,
1886-7	,,	,,	P	,,
1887-8	,,	,,	Q	,,
1888-9	,,	,,	R	,,
1889-90	,,	,,	S	,,
1890-1	,,	,,	T	,,
1891-2	,,	,,	U	,,
1892-3	,,	,,	V	,,
1893-4	,,	,,	W	,,
1894-5	,,	,,	X	,,
1895-6	,,	,,	Y	,,
1896-7	,,	,,	Z	,,

	TREE, FISH & BELL.	LION RAMPANT.		DATE LETTER.
1897-8				A
1898-9	,,	,,		B
1899/1900	,,	,,		C
1900-1	,,	,,		D
EDW. VII. 1901-2	,,	,,		E
1902-3	,,	,,		F
1903-4	,,	,,		G
1904-5	,,	,,		H
1905-6	,,	,,		I
1906-7	,,	,,		J
1907-8	,,	,,		K
1908-9	,,	,,		L
1909-10	,,	,,		M
1910-1	,,	,,		N
1911-2	,,	,,		O
1912-3	,,	,		P
1913-4	,,	,,		Q
1914-5	,,	,,		R
1915-6	,,	,,	,,	S
1916-7	,,	,,	,,	T
1917-8	,,	,,	,,	U
1918-9	,,	,,	,,	V
1919-20	,,	,,	,,	W
1920-1	,,	,,	,,	X
1921-2	,,	,,	,,	Y

1848 TO 1903.

THE DATE WHEN EACH MARK WAS FIRST USED IS NOT RECORDED.

MARK.	NAME.
JR	J. Russell.
WG	W. Gordon.
VL&Co	V. Levy & Co.
SK	D. Sprunt.*
JDD	J. D. Davidson.
M&A	Muirhead & Arthur.
M&A	Do. do.
GA	G. Alexander.
JB&S	J. Ballantyne & Son.
WR	W. Russell.
WC	W. Corbett.
A&T	Aird & Thompson.
T.S.&S	T. Smith & Son.
TS&S	Do. do.
R&WS	R. & W. Sorley.
RS WS	Do. do.
GE GE	Geo. Edward & Son.
DF GE	Do. do.
P&Co.	Parr & Co.
GWS	G. W. Stratton.
KELLY DUBLIN	Kelly & Co., Dublin.
HOWELL	A. Howell.
DS	D. Simpson.
GM	G. Mitchell.
J.E.A.	J. E. Ainsley.
J.H.&Co	Jos. Haywood & Co.
P.G	(*Not identified*).
WG	W. Gordon.
K.C.B	(*Not identified*).
G.E.R	G. E. Rattray.
T.C.G.	T. C. Garstang.
D.M.C	D. M. Cameron.
DM	D. Munro.
F.& J.S.	F. & J. Smith.
MF	M. Friedlander.
M.F	Do. do.
JR	J. Reid.
JF	J. Ferrier.

MARK.	NAME.
JH	J. Hall.
J.R.&W.L.	J. R. & W. Laing.
LAING	Do. do.
M&M	McIntosh & McCulloch.
AB	A. Brown.
RK	Robt. Kerr.
CCM	C. C. McDonald.
HL	H. Low.
J.W	Jas. Weir.
WEIR	Do. do.
J.E	J. Easton
J.P.C	J. P. Campbell.
S&McL	S...... & McLellan.
JHS	J. H. Storer.
M.G	Mungo Guthrie.
H&L	Hamilton & Laidlaw.
W.A	W. Allan.
A.L.B	A. L. Boston.
D&M	Duff & Millar.
J.ADAIR DUMFS	John Adair (Dumfries).
L&Co	Lawson & Co.
JR	J. Riddoch.
D.T	D. Todd.
D.F.T	D. F. Turnbull.
J.D	Jas. Douglas.
T.F	T. Fyfe.
M&Co	Mitchell & Co.
R.S	Robt. Scott.
SCOTT	Do. do.
D.C.R.&S	D. C. Rait & Son.
DD	David Dow.
W.J	W. Jenkins.
T&W	Thomson & Williamson.
WR	Wm. Russell.
MACFARLANE PARTICK	—— Macfarlane (of Partick).
HC	Hector Gollun.
MW	Mark Wilks & Co.
J.C	Jas. Crichton.

MARK.	NAME.
T.SMITH & SON GLASGOW	T. Smith & Son.
T.S&S	Do. do.
MF JBM	(*Not identified*).
A.W.P	A. W. Peden.
R&AA	R. & A. Allen.
D.T	D. Todd.
W.S.&Co	W. Scott & Co.
J.W.	J. Wallace.
T.W.C	T. W. Crawford.
AWA	A. W. Allison.
W.W	W. Warrington.
MVW	M. V. Wilks.
JM	J. Moir.
K&P	Kerr & Phillips.
M&A	Muirhead & Arthur.
A.McD	A. McDonald.
G.JEFFREY	G. Jeffrey.
H&M	Hyslop & Marshall.
W.G.T	W. G. Taylor.
T.M	Thos. Mutter.
ALEXR & SN	Alexr. & Son.
J.M	J. Mark.
F&F	Finlay & Field.
WP	W. Paul.
JP	Jas. Porter.
GMcP	Geo. McPherson.
T.S.	Thos. Stewart.
JF	J. Fettes.
D.F.	Duncn. Ferguson.
WVJ	W. V. Jackson.
G.J.	Geo. Jackson.
T.R&S	Thos. Ross & Sons.
R.T	R. Tennent.
DMcC	D. McCallum.
J.D	John Donald.
D.S	Danl. Sutherland.
J.M	Jas. Myres.
JB&S	J. Blond & Son.

MARK.	NAME.	MARK.	NAME.	MARK.	NAME.
W.S	W. Semple.	B&M	Brown & Miller.	J.N	J. Neville.
J.D.R	J. D. Reid.	JS	Jas. Simpson.	D&S	Davis & Son.
WR&S	Wm. Russell & Sons.	J.R	Jas. Ross.	LM&Cº	Lorimer, Moyes & Co.
R·MC·I	R. McInnes.	J&Cº	Johnston & Co.	AA	Andrew Allison.
W.&W.LOGAN	W. & W. Logan.	L&L	Lyle & Lock.	AF	A. Ferrier ?
D&M	Duff & Miller.	J.LYL	J. Lyle.	J.MJR	J. Muir, jr. ?
J.S	Jas. Smith.	J.M.B.&C	J. M. Ballantyne & Co.	H.T	H. Tennant.
J.F	Jas. Forrest.	G.D&Cº	Geo. Drummond & Co.	GD	Geo. Drummond.
J.H.G.	(*Not identified.*)	M&T	Miller & Thompson.	W&S	Wilson & Sharp, Edinbro.
J.STEVENSON	J. Stevenson.	AT&S	A. Taylor & Son.	M.BROS	Mitchell Bros.
R&F	Ross & Ferrier.	W.M&Cº	W. Miller & Co.	F.N	F. Neville.
R.R	Robt. Ross.	H&I	Hamilton & Inches, Edinbro.	L.K	L. King.
WJ	W. Jaffray.	G.W	George White (or Wilson).	RKM	R. K. Muirhead.
W.J	Do. do.	W.M	W. Mitchell.	AAP	Anton Pfaff.
PM	Peter Martin.	J.MCA	J. McArthur.	R.L.R	R. L. Rawson.
R.B.F.	R. B. Forrest.	RA	Robt. Arthur.	J&AH	J. & A. Howell.
J&AK	Jas. & Andrew Kelly.	R&G	Reed & Garrick.	G&S	Guthrie & Shear.
T&D	Taylor & Downes.	G.T	Geo. Thomson.	TLL	T. L. Leck.
JM&S	J. Muirhead & Sons.	GL	(*Not identified.*)	DH	D. Howie.
G.I	Geo. Innes.	R.B	Robt. Buchanan.	S&R	Smith & Rait.
SB GG	Barclay & Goodwin.	J.HERON	J. Heron.	ABA	Alex. B. Arthur.
D.S &Cº	Dl. Sutherland & Co.	J.MᶜD	J. McDonald.	AW	Alex. Wotherspoon.
JL	J. Laing.	T.F	T. Finlayson.	HD	Hugh Downs.
J&WM	J. & W. Mitchell.	D.T	David Taylor.	J.B	J. Brown.
WA	W. Allan.	TR	Thos. Ross.	AS	A. Sterling.
YOUNG	—— Young.	WB	Walter Baird.	CCC	Colin C. Campbell.
G&W	Gilmore & Watson.	ARS	A. & R. Stewart.	AL	Alex. Lucas.
L&P	Lindsay & Paisley.	RH	Robt. Hyslop.	MM	M. Michael.
LH	L. Hymens.	LA	Lawrence Aitchison.	W.N	W. Noble
W.C	Wm. Coghill.	WCM	(*Not identified.*)	J.C.S	(*Not identified*)
J.MCI	J. McInnes.	W&P	Watson & Pozzie.	JAF	John A. Fetter.
W.S	Wm. Sharp.	D.MᶜD	D. McDonald.	J.F	Do. do.
JMG	J. McGregor.	RD	Robt. Duncan.	R.B.G	(*Not identified.*)
P&Cº	Panton & Co.	AC	A. Coghill.	RGL	Do. do.
RL	R. Laing.	T.C	Thos. Chapman.	M&H	Do. do.
T&Cº	Tennent & Co.	M'K&Cº	McKenzie & Co.	GL	Do. do.
J&WB	J. & W. Boyd.	WSR	(*Not identified.*)	W&D	Do. do.
RRK	Robt. Rankin.	L&M	Lorimer & Moyes.	MᶜH&S	Do. do.
J.C	Jas. Crichton.	L.G&Cº	Leckie, Graham & Co.	R.W.F	Do. do.
		AMC	(*Not identified.*)	S&R	Smith & Rait.
		G.S.B	Do. do.		

DATE (ABOUT).	MARKS.	MAKER'S NAME.
1600-25	AB	... ...
"	,,	... ...
"	AB	... ...
1650	M ABD M	Thomas Moncrur (1649)
"	ABD TM	Do. do. "
"	WM VM ABD	Walter Melvil (1650)
1660-70	AB AB	*(Not identified.)*
1670-7	WS WS	Wm. Scott (1666)
1672-8	A·G AG	Alexr. Galloway (1671)
1690	AB	*(Not identified.)*
1691-7	GW ABD D	Geo. Walker (1685)
1703	GW ABD D	Do. do. "
1708-14	GR ABD GR	Geo. Robertson (1708)
1710-20	GR GR C	Do. do. "
1718-27	IW IW	John Walker (1713)
1730	J WALKER	Do. do. "
"	GC GC C	George Cooper (1728)
"	AF B	Alexr. Forbes (1728)
"	GC	George Cooper (1728)
"	" "	Do. do. "
1734-51	JA	Jas. Abercrombie (1734)
1748-67	CA ABD	Coline Allan (1748)
1750	CA ABD	Do. do. "
1763-70	IW	James Wildgoose (1763)
"	IW ABD	Do. do. "

DATE (ABOUT).	MARKS.	MAKER'S NAME.
1760	BL ABD	*(Not identified.)*
"	B·L B·L	Do. do.
1766-79	IG ABD	Jas. Gordon (1766)
	IG ABD	Do. do.
	"	Do. do.
1772-7	AT ABD	Alexr. Thompson (1772)
1777-8	IL ABD	Jas. Law (1777)
	" "	Do. do.
1782-96	I·L	Do. do.
	IL ABD	John Leslie (1782)
	I·L ABD	Do. do.
	IL	*Do. do.
	" "	Do. do.
	" "	Do. do.
1783-90	J·S A B D	Jas. Smith (1783)
	JS ABD	Do. do.
	JS	Do. do.
1785-95	PR A B D	*(Not identified.)*
1786 to 1818	NG	Nathl. Gillet (1786)
	"	Do. do.
	NG	Do. do.
1790 to 1800	NG Z	Do. do.
	" " N	Do. do.
1796 to 1820	E AA	James Erskine (1796)
	" "	Do. do.
	JE	*Do. do.
	JE	Do. do.
	R&S A B D	*(Not identified.)*

MARKS ON ABERDEEN PLATE—

DATE (ABOUT).	MARKS.	MAKER'S NAME.
1800	WB	(*Not identified.*)
	DOUGLAS ID	J. Douglas (?)
	JA AB	John Allan (1797)
	J.A	Do. do.
	ID	J. Douglas (?)
1800	I·D	Do. do.
TO	GB ABD	(*Not identified.*)
1830	GB AB GB AB	Do. do.
	G.B A B D N	Do. do.
	WJ ABD WJ	Do. do.
	WJ A B D WJ	Do. do.
	A A A	Do. do.
1820	IB ABD	Do. do.
1830	WJ A B D	Do. do.
1841	GJ ABDN	Geo. Jamieson
1850	W·W A B D N	(*Not identified.*)
	WW ABD WW	Do. do.
1871	GS ABD	Do. do.

BANFF

DATE (ABOUT).	MARKS.	MAKER'S NAME.
1680	WS ABC	Wm. Scott.
1698	WS BANF D	Do. do.
1720	WS WS	Wm. Scott, junr.
1725	PS PS BANF	Patk. Scott.
1732-41	PG BANF B	Patrick Gordon.
1750	AS BAF AS	Alexr. Shirras.
1775	BA IA	John Argo.
1780	JA BANF	Do. do.
1785	WB BANF	Wm. Byres.
1795	R IK B	John Keith.
"	B IK H	Do. do.
1800-20	B IK F	Do. do.
"	B IK BANF	Do. do.
"	B IK	Do. do.
"	IK BANF	Do. do.
"	IK B H	Do. do.
"		Do. do.
"	S·A	(*Not identified.*)
1820	GE B	Geo. Elder.
1835	BA McQ	John McQueen.
1850	WS H B	Wm. Simpson.
"	" "	Do. do.

ELGIN

DATE (ABOUT.)	MARKS.	MAKER'S NAME.
1728	WL ELG O	Wm. Livingston.
1730	ER ER	E. R.........
1754	IH ELN A	James Humphrey.
		(E on its back and LN for Elgin).
1760	IH	James Humphrey.
1770	J P ELN RS	... ...
1790 to 1820	CF ELN	Chas. Fowler.
	" "	Do. do.
	CF ELGIN "	Do. do.
	WF "	W. F.........
1830	TS ELN	Thos. Stewart (see Inverness, p. 549).

CANONGATE

DATE (ABOUT).	MARKS.	MAKER'S NAME.
1680	GC XI·D	... ...
"	GC KI·D	... ...
"	MZ MZ	... ...
1696	G·Z G·Z	... ...
1700	P XI	... ...
	ASH	
"	P XI FIS XI	... ...
1760	CM CM	... ...
1763	WC WC	... ...
1780-90	F GIG CA	.. ..
1790 to 1820	PC PC	... ...
	K	.. ..
	K HINCHSLIFFE M	M. Hinchsliffe.
	e IP	... ...
		... ...
1836	K DG	‡David Greig (?)

GREENOCK

DATE (ABOUT).	MARKS.	MAKER'S NAME.
1750	WL WL S	W. L........
1765	JO S G	Jonas Osborne, of Glasgow.
	,, ,, ,,	Do. do.
	,, ,, ,,	Do. do.
	JO	Do. do.
1780	IT IT S	James Taylor, of Glasgow.
	GB G	G. B........
	WC ,, C	W. C........
,,	MC W	M. C.
1790	BC ,, O	B. C.
,,	NH	N. H.
1800	J·H	J. H.
,,	RN G	R. N.
,,	PH S	P. H.
1800	JH C	John Heron.
	,, ,, ,,	Do. do.
	TD ,, ,, ,, ,,	Thos. Davie.
	,, ,, ,, ,,	Do. do.
	IH ,, ,, ,, ,,	John Heron.
1800 TO 1830	I&GH	J. & G. Heron?
	I&GH I&GH	Do. do.
	WHT C +	W. H. T........
1820	WHT C	Do. do.
,,	WS PHD	Peterhead and Greenock mark.

MONTROSE

DATE (ABOUT).	MARKS.	MAKER'S NAME.
1670	WL	Wm. Lindsay (probably).
1671	WL	Wm. Lindsay.
	,, ,, ,, E	Do. do.
1680-3	WL	Do. do.
1710	H	... ...
1752	TI B	Thos. Johnston.
1788	BL	Benj. Lumsden (admitted 1788).
1811	WM	Wm. Mill (1811)

ARBROATH

DATE (ABOUT).	MARKS.
1830	AD
1838	AD
1830-9	AD AD
,,	AD

THE ARBROATH BURGH SEAL.

DATE (ABOUT).	MARKS.	MAKER'S NAME.
1640	MK INS	M. K......
1643	„ „ T	Do. do.
1680	MR INS	M. R......
1708	M „ M	M. L......
1715	M „	—— M......
1720	RI INS A	R I......
1730	IB FB	John Baillie (and another)
„	I·B FB A	Do. do.
1740	IB INS	John Baillie
„	TB INS	Thos. Baillie
1770	AS INS	Alexr. Stewart
1780	RA G INS	Robert Anderson
1790	AS INS	Alexr. Stewart, jr.
„		(*No maker's mark.*)
„	H&Cº A	Hamilton & Co.
„	JA „ A	J. A.
„	T&Cº	T. & Co.
„	AS	Alexr. Stewart, jr.
1800	CJ INS	Chas. Jamieson

DATE (ABOUT).	MARKS.	MAKER'S NAME.
1800	J&N INS	Jameson & Naughton.
„	MAC MAS „	—— Macmas.
„	DF INS	Donald Fraser.
1810	C·J INS C·J	Charles Jamieson.
„	„ „ „	Do. do.
„	J.McR INS	J. McR.
1815	RN INS J RN	Robt. Naughton.
„	RN	Do. do.
1820	A.M. INS	Alexr. MacLeod.
„	AMcL INS	Do. do.
1830	TS INS	Thos. Stewart.
„	D·F INS	Donald Fraser.
„	A·S INS	Alexr. Stewart.
1840		... ...
1857	F BROS	Ferguson Brothers.
1880	F&M INVS	Ferguson & MacBean.

DUNDEE

DATE (ABOUT.)	MARKS.	MAKER'S NAME.
1628	AL AL	Alexr. Lindsay (1628)
1631	RG	Robt. Gairdine (mentioned 1683)
1643	RG RG	Do. do.
1648	RG RG	Do. do.
1667	TL TL	Thos. Lindsay (1662)
1722	CD CD E	Chas. Dickson (1722)
1730	IS IS M	John Steven (mentioned 1764)
1742	AI ,, AI K	Alexr. Johnston (1739)
1764	JS	John Steven (1764)
1776	WS ,, WS W	Wm. Scott (1776)
,,	,, ,, M	Do. do.
	AC C	Alexr. Cameron (1818)
	EL ,, D ,,	Edwd. Livingstone (1809)
	CAMERON ,, C ,, DUNDEE	Alexr. Cameron (1818)
	RN	Robt. Naughton? (see Inverness, p. 549)
1800	T.S ,, ,,	Thos. Stewart? (see Inverness, p. 549)
TO	WC ,, ,,	Wm. Constable (1806)
1840	RH S DUNDEE	*(Not identified.)*
	EL EL m	Edwd. Livingstone (1809)
	WK DUNDEE	*(Not identified.)*
	DM DM	David Manson (1809)
	DM ,, DM	Do. do.
1809	WY D	Wm. Young (1809)

PERTH

DATE (ABOUT).	MARKS.	MAKER'S NAME.
1675	WM B	W. M......
1680	RG B	Robert Gardiner (1669)
1687	RG RG	Do. do. do.
1710	W·S S	William Scott, of Banff
1750	H 3	... ...
1772	IC IC	James Cornfute (1772)
1780	TF ,, TF ,,	T. F......
,,	RK RK	Robert Keay (1791)
,,	JJ ,,	J. J.
1791	RK RK	Robert Keay (1791)
1800	WR WR	William Ritchie (1796)
1810	IS O	John Sid (1808)
,,	R&RK ,, R&RK	R. & R. Keay
1815	DG DG	David Greig (c. 1810)
1816	CM CM	Charles Murray (1816)
,,	S	*(No maker's mark.)*
,,	RMcG ,, RMcG	R. McG.
,,	IH ,, IH	I. H.
1820	RG ,,	Robert Greig (1817)
1830	RK RK	Robert Keay, jr. (1825)
,,	AM AM	A. M......
,,	P S	John Pringle (1827)
,,	,, RK	Robert Keay, jr. (1825)
,,	I·P I·P	John Pringle (1827)
1830 TO 1850	IK ,,	J. K......
	RD ,,	R. D.....
1856	DG ,,	David Greig, jr.

UNASCRIBED SCOTTISH MARKS

DATE (ABOUT).	MARKS.
1500	IB
1690	DK
1700	IB
"	HR SD
1720	G&Mc
1730	AL
1750	JS
"	GG
"	IM
"	IC IC
"	JB
"	C&H C&H
1760	S
"	T.COLGAN
"	G
1770	INCE
"	MK

DATE (ABOUT).	MARKS.
1780	JW
"	CF
1790	R&S b
"	AR
"	LM
"	F G
1800	T·H Q
"	EW
"	RR ,,
"	RB ,,
"	CM
1816	1816 F.D
1800-20	JG
"	DI
"	WA AM

TAIN.

MARKS.
HR SB A
H·R TAIN SB L
A·S TAIN
RW ,,
W.I. TAIN ,,

ST. ANDREWS.

PG PG

STIRLING.

GR S

HL

WICK.

JS WICK

	HARP CROWNED.	DATE LETTER.	MAKER'S MARK.	MAKER'S NAME.
CHAS. I. 1638-9		A	VB	James Vanderbeck,
1639-40		B	IT	John Thornton.
			ETC	Edwd. Chadsey.
1640-1	,,	C	IT	John Thornton.
1641-2	,,	D	WC	Wm. Cooke.
1642-3		E		... ...
1643-4		F		... ...
1644-5		G		... ...
1645-6		H		... ...
1646-7		I	B	John Burke (or John Banister).
1647-8		K		... ...
1648-9		L		... ...
COMWTH. 1649-50		M		... .
1650-1		N		... ...
1651-2		O		... .
1652-3		P		.. ..
1653-4		Q		... .
1654-5		R		.. . .
1655-6		S	DP	Daniel Bellingham.
1656-7	,,	T	IS	Joseph Stoaker (or John Slicer).
1657-8		U		... ...

1639-40		B	GG	George Gallant.

	HARP CROWNED.	DATE LETTER.	MAKER'S MARK.	MAKER'S NAME.
1658-9		a		... ...
1659-60		b	IS	Joseph Stoaker.
			IS	Do. do.
CHAS. II. 1660-1		c		... ...
1661-2		d		... ...
1662-3		e		... ...
1663-4		f	IS	Joseph Stoaker.†
1664-5	,,	g	AR	Abel Ram.‡
1665-6		h		... ...
1666-7		i		... .
1667-8		k		... ...
1668-9		l		... ...
1669-70		m		... ...
1670-1		n		... ...
1671-2		o	IS	Joseph Stoaker.†
1672-3		p		... ...
1673-4		q		... ...
1674-5		r		... .
1675-6		s		... ...
1676-7		t		... ...
1677-8		u		... .

	HARP CROWNED.	DATE LETTER.	MAKER'S MARK	MAKER'S NAME.
1678-9		A		... ...
			TB	Timothy Blackwood.‡
1679-80		B	SM	Samuel Marsden.
			IK	James Kelly.
			AG	Andrew Gregory.
1680-1		C	,,	Do. do.
			IP	John Phillips.
			WL	Wm. Walter Lucas or Lewis.
1681-2	,,	D	ES	Edwd. Swan.
1682-3	,,	E	IK	James Kelly.
1683-4		F		... ...
JAS. II. 1685-6 7	,,	G	IF	John Farmer.
			ITC	John Cuthbert.
			RN	Robert Nevill.
			IH	John Humphrys.
1688 to 1692		H	DK	David King.
			RS	Robt. Smith (warden 1701).
		I		... ...
WM. III. 1693-4-5		K	IW	Joseph Walker.
			WD	Wm. Drayton.
			WM	Wm. Myers.
			AS	Ant'ny Stanley.
			B	Thos. Bolton.
1696-9	,,	L	IP	John Phillips.
			DK	David King.
			IW	Joseph Walker.
			IH	John Humphrys.
			AS	Anth'y Stanley.

	HARP CROWNED.	DATE LETTER.	MAKER'S MARK.	MAKER'S NAME.
* 1699/1700		M		Ant'ny Stanley (as 1693-4-5.)
			EW	Edward Workman.
1700-1	,,	N	S	Alexr. Sinclair.
* 1701-2		O	IW	Joseph Walker.
				... ...
			B	Thomas Boulton.
ANNE. * 1702-3		P	B	Do. do.
1703-4	,,	Q	,,	Do. do.
1704-5-6		R	HM	Henry Matthews.
			IW	Joseph Walker.
1706-7-8		S	DK	David King.
			EB	Edward Barrett.
			B	Thomas Bolton.
1708-9-0	,,	T	,,	Do. do. (*Maker's mark indistinct*)
1710-1-2		U	DK	David King. (*Maker's mark indistinct*)
1712-3-4		W	EW	Edward Workman.
			WA	Walter Archdall.
			IC	John Clifton.
GEO I. 1714-5	,,	Y	WA	Wm. Archdall.
1715-6		Y	IT	John Tuite.†
			IC	John Cuthbert, jun.
			IW	Joseph Walker. David King (as 1706 above).
1716-7		Z		... ...

	HARP CROWNED.	DATE LETTER.	MAKER'S MARK.	MAKER'S NAME.
1717-8		A	IW	Joseph Walker.
			CT	Christr. Thompson.
			WC	Wm. Clarke (of Cork).
			IH	John Hamilton.
			Sa	John Savage?
„		„	TP	Thos. Parker.
1718-9	„	B	EC	Erasm's Cope.
1719-20		C	HD	Henry Daniell.
			IC	John Clifton, jr.
„		C	IC	John Clifton, sr.
1720-1		A	IH	John Hamilton.
1721-2	„	B	„	Do. do.
			TS	Thos. Sutton.
1722-3	„	C	IC	John Clifton, sr.
			EB	Edwd. Barrett.
1723-4	„	D	RH	Robert Harrison.
			TW	Thos. Walker.
			WD	Wm. Duggan.
1724-5		E	TS	Thos. Slade.
			IT	John Taylor.
			B	Thos. Bolton.
1725-6	„	F	MW	Mathw. Walker.
			MH	Michl. Hewitson.,
			MW	Mathw. Walker.
1726-7	„	G	NV	Noah Vialas.
			PK	Philip Kinnersly.
GEO. II. * 1727-8		H	RC	Robert Calderwood.
			IK	John King.
			WC	Wm. Clarke. (of Cork).
1728-9	„	I	IR	John Robinson.
			BC	Bolton Cormick.
1729-30		K	RC	Robert Calderwood.
			IM	John Moore.
			WA	Wm. Archdall.
1730-1	„	L	DK	David King.

	HARP CROWNED.	DATE LETTER.	HIBERNIA.	MAKER'S MARK.	MAKER'S NAME.
1731-2		L		EF	Esther Forbes.
				EC	Erasmus Cope?
1732-3	„	M		AL	Anthony Lefebure.
				ID	James Douglas.
1733-4	„	N	„	WW	Wm. Williamson.
				CL	Charles Lemaitre.
				IT	John Taylor.
				WT	Wm. Townsend.
1734-5		O		CL	Chas. Leslie.†
				TW	Thos. Williamson.
1735-6	„	P	„	BM	Barth Mosse.
				AB	Alexr. Brown.
1736-7	„	Q	„	IW	John Williamson.
				IW	John Wilme.
				AG	Andrew Goodwin.
				IT	James Taylor.
1737-8	„	R	„	DK	David King?
1738-9	„	S	„	SW	Samuel Walker.
				MW	Matthew Walker.
1739-40	„	T	„	AG	Andrew Goodwin.
				FW	Francis Williamson.
				IW	John Walker.
1740-1	„	U	„	IM	John Moore.
				AR	Alexr. Richards.‡
1741-2-3		W	„	ID	Isaac D'Olier.
		W	„	IL	John Laughlin.
1743-4	„	X	„	CL	Christr. Locker.
				RH	Robt. Holmes.
				Let	John Letablere.
1745	„	Y	„	IW	James Whitthorne.§
				M	John Moore.
1746	„	Z	„	W	Jas. Whitthorne. (see 1745).§

	HIBERNIA.	DATE LETTER.	HARP CROWNED.	MAKER'S MARK.	MAKER'S NAME.
1747		A		WW	Wm. Williamson.
				CF	C. Fox.
				WW	Will. Walsh.
1748	,,	B	,,	W·B	Will. Beates.
				IC	John Christie.
1749	,,	C		IL	John Laughlin.
				M·B	Mathias Brown.
1750	,,	D	,,	ID	Isaac D'Olier.
				I·P	John Pittar.
1751-2	,,	E E		WR	William Ring.
1752-3	,,	F	,,	MH	Mich'el Homer.
				W·T	Wm. Townsend.
1753-4	,,	G	,,	AR	Aléxr. Richards.
1754-5	,,	H	,,	CS	Christr. Skinner.
1757	,,	I	,,	A	Matt'w Alanson.
				D·P	Daniel Popkins.
1758	,,	K		MS	(*Not identified.*)
1759	,,	L	,,	SW	Saml. Walker.
				IP	J'nth'n. Pasley.
GEO. III. 1760	,,	M	,,	R·C	Robt. Calderwood.
				GH	Geo. Hill.
1761	,,	N	,,	TJ	Thos. Johnston.
				,,	Do. do.
1762	,,	O		A	Matt'w Alanson.
1763	,,	P	,,	DP	David Peter.
				W·C	Wm. Currie.
1764	,,	Q	,,	WH	Wm. Homer.
				FI	Francis Jones.
1765	,,	R	,,	IC	Joseph Cullen.
1766	,,	S	,,	M·C I·L	{ M. J. } Cormick & Locker.
				F&K	French & Keating.
1767	,,	T		JW	John West.
				R·W	Richd. Williams.
1768	,,	U	,,	RT	Richd. Tudor.
				ID	Jer'm'h D'Olier.
1769		W		J·S	John Shields.
				IG	James Graham.
1770	,,	X	,,	I·L	John Locker.
				C·H	Christr. Haines.
				T·K	Thos. Kinsela.
1771	,,	Y		JL	John Lloyd.
				CT	Chas. Townsend.
1772	,,	Z	,,	CM	Chas. Mullin.

	HIBERNIA.	DATE LETTER.	HARP CROWNED	MAKER'S MARK.	MAKER'S NAME.
1773		A		JW	John Walker.
				WH	Wm. Hughes.
1774	,,	B	,,	I·C	John Craig.
				AB	Ambrose Boxwell.
1775	,,	C	,,	RW	Richd. Williams.
				CT	Chas. Townsend.
1776	,,	D		MW	Matthew West.
				HA	Hay Andrews.
				DK	Darby Kehoe.
1777	,,	E	,,	SW	Stephen Walsh.
				MH	Michael Homer.
1778	,,	F	,,	J·P	John Pittar.
1779	,,	G	,,	I·I	Jos. Jackson.
				MK	Michael Keating.
1780	,,	H	,,	MW	Michael Walsh.
				J·B	John Bolland.
1781	,,	I	,,	IK	John Kelly.
				I·I	Jos. Jackson.
				TJ	Thomas Jones.
1782	,,	K	,,	W·W	Wm. Ward.
1783	,,	L	,,	JL	John Laughlin, jr.
				RW	Robert Wyke.
1784	,,	M	,,	W·T	Wm. Thompson.
				MW	Matthew Walsh.
1785	,,	N	,,	GH	Christr. Haines.
				W·S	Wm. Supple.
1786	,,	O	,,	WJ	Wm. Johnson.
				L&B	(*Not identified.*)
1787		P		J·P	John Pittar.‡
				MW	Matthew West.
1788	,,	Q	,,	MK	Michael Keating.
				I·S	John Stoyte.
1789	,,	R	,,	WL	Wm. Law.
				RW	Robt. Williams.
1790	,,	S	,,	AC	Arthur Clark.
				AON	Arthur O'Neill.
1791	,,	T	,,	BT	Benjn. Tait.
				TJ	Thos. Jones?
1792	,,	U	,,	RS	Robt. Smith.
				WB	Wm. Bond.
				I·K	James Keating.§
1793	,,	W	,,	MK	Michael Keating.
				JP	John Power.
				GW	George West.
1794		X		L&B	(*Not identified.*)
1795	,,	Y	,,	I·L	John Laughlin, jr.
1796	,,	Z	,,	IE	James England.
				GW	Geo. Wheatley.
				FB	Fredk. Buck.

	HIBERNIA.	DATE LETTER.	HARP CROWNED.	KING'S HEAD.	MAKER'S MARK.	MAKER'S NAME.
1797		A			J·R	John Rigby. Geo. West (as 1794.)
1798	„	B	„		J·K JD	John Keene. John Daly.
1799	„	C	„		I·K WEST IS	James Keating.† James Scott.
1800	„	D	„		JK WP	John Kearns. Walter Peter.
1801	„	E	„		IC JP	Jas. Connor. John Power.
1802	„	F	„		RS WH	Richd. Sawyer. Wm. Hamey.
1803	„	G	„		A O N IB	Arthur O'Neil. J. Brady.
1804	„	H	„		RB DE	Robt. Breading. Danl. Egan.
1805	„	I	„		W·D DM	Wm. Doyle. *(Not identified.)*
1806	„	K	„	KING'S HEAD.	S·N T&W W·W	Samuel Neville. Tudor & Whitford. Wm. Ward.
1807	„	L	„		GB	Gust'v's Byrne.
1808	„	M	„	„	CT IW SN	Terry & Williams (of Cork). Saml. Neville.
1809	„	N N	„		JJ RB	Joseph Johnson. Robt. Breading.
1810		O O		„	I·L·B T·R	Jas. Le Bass. *(Not identified.)*
1811	„	P	„	„	C·S W·N	Chas. Stewart. W. Nowlan.
1812	„	Q	„	„	HAMY R·S PM	W. Hamy & R. Smith. P Moore.
1813	„	R	„	„	WR J·P	Wm. Rose. John Pittar.
1814	„	S	„	„	I·S LAW I·N	Jas. Scott. Wm. Law. John Nicklin.
1815	„	T	„	„	PG SB	Phineas Garde (Cork). S. Bergin.
1816	„	U	„	„	DE RC	Danl. Egan. Randall Cashell.
1817	„	W	„	„	J·M WC NWB	James Moore. W. Cummins. Sir N. W. Brady.
1818	„	X	„	„	T·R I·B	T. Read. J. Buckton.
1819	„	Y	„	„	ILB IF WEST	Jas. Le Bass. Jas. Fry.†
GEO. IV. 1820	„	Z	„	„	JS EM	J. Salter (Cork). Edwd. Murray.

	HIBERNIA.	DATE LETTER.	HARP CROWNED.	KING'S HEAD.	MAKER MARK.	MAKER'S NAME.
1821		A			MW&S WM	M. West & Sons. Wm. Morgan.
1822	„	B	„		EC I·B LAW	E. Crofton. J. Buckton. Wm. Law.
1823	„	C	„	„	EP IF	Edwd. Power. Jas. Fray.
1824	„	D	„	„	SN SB	Saml. Neville. Saml. Beere.
1825-6	„	E e	„		WT R·G	Wm. Teare.? Richd. Garde (Cork).
1826-7	„	F	„		W&Co J·S	Ald'm'n West (& Co.). J. Smith.
1827-8		G			CM I·R	Chas. Marsh. J. Read.
1828-9		H			TWY+ HF	Edwd. Twycross. Hy. Flavelle.
1829-30		I I			LN C·M	L. Nowlan. Chas. Marsh.
WM. IV. 1830-1		K			M & G S&G	D. Moulang & W. Gibson. Smith & Gamble.
1831-2		L			E·J R·S TF	Edmd. Johnson. Richd. Sawyer, jr. T. Farnett.
1832-3	„	M	„	„	PM HF	P. Moore. Hy. Flavelle.
1833-4		N N		„	TM EJ	Thos. Meade. Edmd. Johnson.
1834-5		O O			LN WS	L. Nowlan? Wm. Sherwin.
1835-6	„	P P	„	„	PW I·M	P. Weeks? J. Moore.
1836-7	„	Q Q	„	„	WS R·G	Wm. Sherwin. Richd. Garde (Cork).
VICT. 1837-8	„	R R	„	„	IL S&G	Josiah Low. Smith & Gamble.
1838-9	„	S	„		H&F	Hughes & Francis.
1839-40		T		„	PW	Peter Walsh.
1840-1	„	U U	„	„	E&JJ LN	E. & J. Johnson. L. Nowlan.
1841-2	„	V	„	„	GA	G. Alcock.
1842-3		W		„	IW I·L·B	John Warren. Jas. Le Bass.
1843-4	„	X	„	„	IF GW	J. Francis. Geo. West?
1844-5		Y		„	MN	Michl. Nowlan.
1845-6		Z		„	JG JJ20	J. Gamble. ‡ Joseph Johnson.

	HIBERNIA.	DATE LETTER.	HARP CROWNED.	QUEEN'S HEAD.	MAKER'S MARK.	MAKER'S NAME.
1846-7		a			JJ	Joseph Johnson.
1847-8	,,	b	,,	,,	J.M TM	J. Mahoney. Thos. Mason.
1848-9	,,	c	,,	,,	CC WL RS	C. Cummins, jr. Wm. Lawson. R. Samuel.
1849-50	,,	d	,,	,,	D&W	Donegan & Co.
1850-1	,,	e	,,	,,	J.G HF	J. Gamble. Henry Flavelle.
1851-2	,,	f f	,,	,,	IN AC	Joseph Needham. Ann Cummins.
1852-3	,,	g g	,,	,,	GARDNER JS	— Gardner. J. Smyth.
1853-4	,,	h h	,,	,,	RS T&W	R. Sherwin. Topham & White.
1854-5	,,	j	,,	,,	M.K	Michael Keating.
1855-6	,,	k	,,	,,	CC	C. Cummins.
1856-7	,,	l	,,	,,	W.A	W. Atcheson.
1857-8	,,	m	,,	,,	D&W AJ	Donegan & Co. Arthur Johnson.
1858-9	,,	n	,,	,,	J.R.N NEILL	J. R. Neill. Do. do.
1859-60	,,	o	,,	,,	S.L.B	Samuel Le Bass.
1860-1	,,	p	,,	,,	WP W&IP	Wm. Percival. W. & I. Percival.
1861-2	,,	Q	,,	,,	EP	E. Powell.
1862-3	,,	r	,,	,,	JK EJ&JJ	J. Keating. E. & J. Johnson.
1863-4	,,	s	,,	,,	J.S	John Smyth.
1864-5		t	,,	,,	IS RYAN & CO	J. Scriber. Ryan & Co.
1865-6	,,	u	,,	,,	I.W WATERHOUSE FM	Jas. West. Waterhouse & Co. Francis Martin.
1866-7	,,	v	,,	,,	AH BRUNKER DUBLIN	A. Hutton. Thos. Brunker.
1867-8	,,	w	,,		PD WL	Patk. Donegan. Wm. Lawson.
1868-9	,,	x	,,	,,	EJ MT	Edmd. Johnson, jr. Mars. Trench.
1869-70	,,	y	,,	,,	WL	Wm. Lawson.
1870-1	,,	z	,,	,,	TDB	T. D. Bryce.

DATE.	MARKS.				MAKER'S NAME.
1663-4			f	AR	Abel Ram.
1708-10			T	PT	Philip Tough.
1715-6			V	WA	Wm. Archdall.
1731			L	S	——— Sutton ?
1739			T	RH	Robert Holmes.
1740			T	WW JD	Will. Walsh. Jane Daniell.†
,,	,,	,,	,,	Su	——— Sutton ?
c. 1750					

1660	Æ	Andrew Edwards.
1704	AV	Abraham Voisin.
,,	RS	Robert Smith.

1704	IG	John Garrett.
,,	IW	James Walket.

	HIBERNIA.	DATE LETTER.	HARP CROWNED.	QUEEN'S HEAD.	MAKER'S MARK.	MAKER'S NAME AND DATE OF REGISTRATION OF MARK.		
1871-2		A			J.W W&R	J. Weir	Wickham. & Rogers.	(1871). ,,
1872-3	,,	B	,,	,,	JD	John	Donegan.	(1872).
1873-4	,,	C	,,	,,	EGAN CORK	Wm.	Egan & Son (of Cork).	,,
1874-5	,,	D	,,	,,	IC	Ignatius	Cummins.	(1874).
1875-6	,,	E	,,	,,	McD BROS	McDowell	Bros.	(1875).
1876-7	,,	F	,,	,,	MDB	Do.	do.	,,
1877-8	,,	G	,,	,,	W&S	West	& Son.	(1877).
1878-9	,,	H	,,	,,	JR	J.	Redmond.	(1876).
1879-80	,,	I	,,	,,	W&S	West	& Son.	(1879).
1880-1	,,	K	,,	,,	OC &D	O'Connor	& Dillon.	(1880).
1881-2	,,	L	,,	,,	E.JOHNSON EJ	Edmond Do.	Johnson. do.	(1881). (1882).
1882-3	,,	M	,,	,,	WC HH	Wm. Henry	Carty. Hopkins.	(1881). (1883).
1883-4	,,	N	,,	,,	DM	Danl.	Moulang.	,,
1884-5	,,	O	,,	,,	W&L	Winder	& Lamb.	,,
1885-6	,,	P	,,	,,	FBs	Frengley	Bros.	(1885).
1886-7	,,	Q	,,	,,	A&Co	Austin	& Co.	(1886).
1887-8	,,	R	,,	,,	MA JEP	M. Jas. E.	Anderson. Pim.	(1887). ,,
1888-9	,,	S	,,	,,	TB FH	Thomas Fredk.	Barton. Hill.	(1871). (1889).
1889-90	,,	T	,,	,,	WQ J·F	Wm. Joseph	Quinlan. Fray.	(1888). (1889).
1890-1	,,	U	,,		HLS	Henry L.	Stewart (of Limerick).	,,
1891-2	,,	V	,,		S.D.NEILL	Sharman D.	Neill (of Belfast).	(1890).
1892-3	,,	W	,,		H&H MOSLEY	Hopkins Jas.	& Hopkins. Mosley (Waterford).	(1883). (1892).
1893-4	,,	X	,,		CH EJ	C. Edmond	Harris (Coventry). Johnson.	(1893). ,,
1894-5	,,	Y	,,		C.H.L K&G RD	Chas. Howard Kane Richard	Lawson. & Gunning Dillon (Waterford).	(1894). ,, ,,
1895-6	,,	Z	,,		CL C&S	Charles Chancellor	Lamb. & Son.	(1893). (1895).

	HIBERNIA.	DATE LETTER.	HARP CROWNED.	MAKER'S MARK.	MAKER'S NAME AND DATE OF REGISTRATION OF MARK.	
1896-7		A		R&W	Richards & Walsh.	(1895).
				J·M	John Morton.	(1896).
1897-8	,,	B	,,	G Ld	Gibson, Ltd. (Belfast).	(1897).
1898-9	,,	C	,,	R·K	Robert Knaggs.	(1898).
				M&C	Moore & Co.	,,
				RV	Robert Valentine.	,,
1899 1900	,,	D	,,	W.J.G	W. J. Gethings.	,,
				LAWSON DUBLIN	Chas. Howard Lawson.	(1900).
1900-1	,,	E	,,	LAW	Langley Archer West.	,,
EDW. VII. 1901-2	,,	F	,,	H&T	Henderson & Thompson (Belfast).	,,
				McC&D	McCutcheon & Donaldson (Belfast).	(1901).
1902-3	,,	G	,,	W&S	West & Son.	(1902).
1903-4		H		JEB	J. E. Byrne (Belfast).	(1909).
1904-5	,,	I	,,	JAMESON	—— Jameson.	,,
1905-6	,,	K	,,	RLTD	Russell Ltd. (Manchester).	,,
1906-7	,,	L	,,	A.DUFFNER TIPPERARY	A. Duffner (Tipperary).	(1907).
1907-8	,,	M	,,	FSLD	Finnegans Ltd. (Manchester).	(1912).
1908-9	,,	N	,,	E&Co	Elkington & Co. (Birmingham).	,,
1909-10	,,	O	,,	W.E&SNS LTD	W. Egan & Sons (Cork).	(1910).
1910-1	,,	P	,,	N	—— Neill (Belfast).	(1906).
1911-2	,,	Q	,,	YAMW	Youghal Art Metal Works Co.	,,
1912-3	,,	R	,,	FALLER GALWAY	—— Faller (Galway).	,,
1913-4	,,	S	,,	J.McD	J. McDowell.	,,
1914-5	,,	T	,,	C.CROMER LIMERICK	C. Cromer (Limerick).	(1907).
1915-6	,,	U	,,	W&W	Wakeley & Wheeler (London).	(1909).

	HIBERNIA.	DATE LETTER.	HARP CROWNED.	MAKER'S MARK.	MAKER'S NAME AND DATE OF REGISTRATION OF MARK.	
1916-7		a		WS	Will Stokes.	(1910).
1917-8	,,	b	,,	WALDRON SKIBBEREEN	M. Waldron (Skibbereen).	,,
1918-9	,,	c	,,	JR	Jas. Ramsay (Dundee).	(1912).
1919-20	,,	d	,,	RS	R. Sharman.	(1908).
1920-1	,,	e	,,	LAC	Crichton Bros. (London).	(1912).

SUPPLEMENTARY LIST OF MARKS OF GOLDSMITHS,

impressed at Dublin but not illustrated in the preceding tables.

DATE.	MARK.	MAKER'S NAME.
1636	IW	John Woodcocke.
1663-4	FC	Francis Coffee or Clifton.
1679	ES	Edward Swan.
1680	ES	" "
"	LS	Lawrence Salmon.
"	IS	John Seager.
1685	I★P	John Phillips.
1685-7	IC	John Cuthbert.
1696-7	DM	*(Not identified.)*
1698	AS	A. Stanley?
1699	CM P	Cyriac Mallory.
"	GL	George Lyng.
1700	AM	Alexr. Mackay.
1701-2	T·S	Thos. Sumpner.
"	ATS	... ...
1702-3	EB	Edward Barrett.
"	TH	Thos. Hartwell.
1703-4	D	... ...
"	K	David King.
1706	RF	Robt. Forbes.

DATE.	MARK.	MAKER'S NAME.
1706	TB	Thos. Bolton.
1710	HS	Henry Sherwin.
1710-2	TB	Thos. Bolton?
"	T	J. Pennyfather or J. Palet?
1712-4	ED	... ...
1715	GS	Geo. Smart.
"	E+D	Ed. Dowdall.
1715-6	MT	Mark Twelves.
1716-7	Z IW	... ...
1717-8	WB	W. Bell.
1718-9	TW	Thos. Walker.
1719-20	AW	Arthur Weldon.
1720	TR	Thos. Racine.
1722-3	E·F	Ed. Fitzgerald.
1723-4	D WS	... ...
1724-5	PK	Phillip Kinnersly.
1725-6	SA	John Sale.
"	RP	Robt. Pilkington.
"	MC	Matt. Copeland.

DATE.	MARK.	NAME OF MAKER.
1725-6	MB	Mary Barrett.
"	TW	Thos. Wheeler.
1726-7	PR	Peter Racine.
1728-9	S+C	... ...
1729	EF	Esther Forbes.
"	TS	Thos. Sutton.
1730-1	GC	George Cross.
"	GC	Geo. Cartwright.
"	D·M	Dorothy Monjoy.
1731	A	Matthew Alanson.
1732-3	EC	Erasmus Cope.
1734	I·G	John Gumly.
1735	D	Isaac D'Olier.
1736-7	TM	Thos. Maculla?
"	A	Anthony Lefebure.
"	R·W	Ralph Woodhouse.
"	Q S★	... ...
1737-8	I·F	John Freebough.

SUPPLEMENTARY LIST OF MARKS OF GOLDSMITHS

DATE.	MARK.	NAME OF MAKER.
1737-8	TD	Thos. de Limarest.
1740-1	PD	Peter Desenard.
"	MR	... ...
"	I·C	Jas. Champion ?
"	PD	... ...
"	IL	John Letablere.
"	T·B	Thos. Burton.
"	SU	Thos. Sutton.
c. 1740	HJ	? Henry Jago.
1743-4	WB	Wm. Bonynge.
"	R·C	Robt. Calderwood.
1745	G·B	George Beere.
"	RG	Robt. Glanville.
1746	I H	John Hamilton ?
"	W·F	Wm. Faucett ?
"	B·S	Bart'mew Stokes.
"	WW	Wm. Walsh.
c. 1750	IT	Joseph Taafe.
1751	NM	Nathan Murray.
"	I·P	J. Pittar.
"	WB	Wm. Betagh.

DATE.	MARK.	MAKER'S NAME.
1752	ER	Edward Raper.
1754	R·C	Robt. Calderwood or Cope.
"	H·W	Hy. Waldron.
1757	M·F	Michael Fowler.
1758	WW	Wm. Williamson.
"	CS	Christr. Skinner.
c. 1760	H·W	See 1754 above.
1762	I·M	John Moore, Jr.
1764	ID	John Dawson.
"	FJ	... ...
1766	RV	Ralph Vizard ?
1767	W·F	Wm. French.
c. 1767	WT	Wm. Townsend.
1768	JW	Jno. Williamson.
"	B·W	Benj. Wilson.
"	A·T	Abraham Tuppy.
1769	W·T MC	.. ..
"	GH	George Hall.
1770	KAR	John Karr.
1776	I·B	... ...
1779	TL	John Locker ?
"	MS	... ...

DATE.	MARK	MAKER'S NAME.
1780	HO	Hugh O'Hanlon or Owen Hart ?
c. 1780	O·C	Owen Cassidy.
"	AB	Alex. Barry ?
1780-5	BD	Barnaby Delahoyde ?
1785	D·E	Dan. Egan ?
1792	MH	Michael Homer ?
1795	J·ASK	J. R. Ash.
c. 1795	I·W	... ...
c. 1797	TT	Thos. Tudor.
1798	IB	John Brooks ?
1800	S·T	Saml. Teare.
1800-1	JB	John Bolland.
"	G&PW	... ...
1802	JD	John Daly ?
1807	C&W	Clarke & West.
"	ÆR	Æneas Ryan.
1810	RS	Richard Sawyer.
"	IT	John Teare.
1811	JK RF	... .. .
1812	JH	J. Henzell ?
"	JK	... ...
1815	RW	Richard Whitford.

The marks illustrated below are reproduced from a plate of pewter preserved at the Dublin Assay Office, in which marks in use at various dates, from about 1765 to 1812, have been stamped. The plate contains a number of other marks which it is unnecessary to illustrate here, as they appear in the preceding tables.

MARK.	NAME.	MARK.	NAME.	MARK.	NAME.
RA	Robt. Atkinson?	JSB		WG	
ET		EB		I·T	
RID	Richard & Jeremiah } D'Olier.	C·F		W·S	Will. Stafford?
GM		JN	Joseph Nixon.	I·E	John Ebbs.
J·A	John Austin.	RB	Robert Breading.	TA	
JC	John Clarke.	BH		EC BC	
T·F	Thos. Farley.	J·E	Joshua Emerson.	GN	George Nangle.
II	Joseph Jackson.	SR	Saml. Reily (Cork).	IH	James Hadmill.
TS		R·L		G·ALLEY	Geo. Alley.
W·D	Will. Digby?	G·T	Geo. Thompson.	IK	James Kenzie.
JK	John Keene.	J·J	James Jones.	IA	Jerome Alley?
G&B		PM		I·D	John Dalrymple.
TW	Thos. Williamson.	M:CL	Mark M'Cloughlin.	WS	
WB	Will Beere.	WFG	Wm. Fitzgerald (Limerick).	PS	
TP		HL		TM	Thos. Martin.
JC	John Coleman.	TN		WJ	Will. Johnson.
MB	Michael Byrne.	AN	Ambr'se Nicklin.	AT	Alex. Ticknell.
WP	Walter Peter.	O M·N		JO	John Osborne.
CD	Chas. Dowdall.	HM		HN	Henry Nicholson.
T·C	Thos. Cooksey.	NICOLSON	J. Nicolson (Cork).	RT	
J·J	James Jones.	JA		WS	
IP		WK	Wm. Keene.	S·R	Saml. Reily (Cork).
GW		JJ	James Jones?	H&H	Hopper & Hannay.
CC	Christr. Clarke?	I·N		JG	
I·W	Jacob West.	LM	La'rence Martin (Kilkenny).	TH	Thos. Hunt?
I·M		C°G		GN	George Nangle.
L·A				PF	

DUBLIN GOLDSMITHS' MARKS, 1765 TO 1812—

MARK.	NAME.	MARK.	NAME.	MARK.	NAME.
LH		WW		FB	Fredk. Buck.
W·H	Will. Hughes?	BT	Benjn. Tait.	ST	Samuel Taylor.
CK		PW	Peter Wingfield.	RC	Randall Cashell?
WG	Will. Gethin?	TA	Thos. Adams.	W·H	Wm. Hannay?
I·T	John Tweedie?	HM		I·C	
RS	Robt. O'Shaughnessy (Limerick).	TR	Thos. Rourke.	JL	John Lloyd.
I·H·	James Hewitt?	DP		E&B	
IW	John West?	RC	Randall Cashell?	WF	Will French.
JR	J'n'th'n Robinson?	GIBSON	Joseph Gibson (Cork).	W·W	Will Ward.
SLY	Thos. Sly.	GR		AM	Arthur Murphy.
G&PW		JJ	Joseph Johnson.	W·L	
MS		JC	James Campbell?	RD	
TE		D·P		BP	
I·M	James Mills?	ID	Isaac Davis?	J·T	
WL	Wm. Law?	MW&S	Matt. West & Son.	I·G	
WH	Will. Hamey?	I·C	Jas. Connor?	WH	
T·B	Thos. Baker?	B·B		IB	John Bolland?
W·F		SINGLETON	—— Singleton.	TSW	
FR		T·T	Thomas Townsend.		

THE FOLLOWING MARKS, WHICH ARE STAMPED ON A COPPER-PLATE OF LATER DATE, RANGE FROM ABOUT 1813 TO ABOUT 1850.

MARK.	NAME.	MARK.	NAME	MARK.	NAME.
WG		GF		LK	
TK JF		TT		GW WM	
TK		EM		GA	
HL	Henry Lazarus.	IH		JT	John Townsend.
DM		WHT	Wm. H. Townsend.	W·N	Wm. Nelson.
S&W		SB	S. Bergin.	K&F	
J·M & E·M		J·MOORE	James Moore.	RE	
IM	J. Moore.	WC		TO	
BOYLE	—— Boyle.	FM &S		GRAYS	—— Grays.
EM	Edwd. Murphy.	LEE		PG	
		RWS	R. W. Smith.	IS	

DATE.	MARKS.	MAKER'S NAME.
1662	IR	James Ridge.
1663	HB	(*Not identified*).
1670	WB WB	Walter Burnett.
1673	IR IR IR	James Ridge.
1679	RS RS	Richard Smart.
1680	SP SP	Samuel Pantaine.
”	W·B W·B	Walter Burnett.
”		(Both marks repeated).
”	IH IH IH	John Hawkins.
1691	IH IH IH	Do. do.
1683	RG RG RG	Robert Goble.
1686	RG	Do. do.
1690	” RG ” RG	Do. do.
1692	CW CW	Caleb Webb.
”	RG	Robert Goble.
1696	RG ”	Do. do.
”	WB ”	Walter Burnett.
”	RG	Robert Goble.
”	” RG ”	Do. do.
1697	CB CB	Charles Bekegle.
1700	RG	Robert Goble.
”	AS	Anthony Semirot.
1705	RG RG	Robert Goble.
1709	WC	William Clarke.

DATE.	MARKS.	MAKER'S NAME.
1709	AB AB AB	Adam Billon.
1702-29	GB	George Brumley.
1709	IW	John Wigmore.(?)
1710	WC WC	Wm. Clarke.
”	RG STERLING	Robert Goble.
1710-20	I·R STERLING	John Rickotts
1712	RG	Robert Goble.
1715-25	RG STERLING	Robert Goble, Junr
”	” IM	” ”
”	WC STERLING WC	William Clarke
”	WC ” WC	” ”
1719	CR CR CR	Caleb Rotheram
”	WC Sterling	William Clarke.
1720	WC STERLING	” ”
”	BB STERLING	Bernald Baldwin.
”	M·S STERLING	
1720-30	TM STERLING	} Wm. Newenham
”	W·N STERLING	} Wm. Newenham
”	ED STERLING ED	Edward Dunsterfield.
1720-34	WN	William Newenham
”	WN	” ”
”	E·I	(*Not identified—perhaps not Cork*).
1722	ER	... ...

DATE.	MARKS.	MAKER'S NAME.
1724	THO·LILLY STER LING	} Thomas Lilly.
1725-6	R M STERLING	Reuben Millard.
1730	WN STERLING	Wm. Newenham.
„	WN STERLING	„ „
1730-40	W★B STER LING	William Bennett.
„	I H STERLING I H	John Harding ?
„	CR STE RLING CR	Caleb Rotheram.
„	STERLING I·H	John Harding ?
„	R·G	Robt. Goble, jr. ?
„	CP CP CP	Christr. Parker.
1720-37	W·MARTIN	William Martin.
„	W·MARTIN	Do. do.
„	W·M	Do. do.
„	R★M	Reuben Millard.
1730-40	WB STERLING WB	William Bennett or Wm. Bentley.
1731	T.BULL	Thomas Bull.
1740	G·H STERLING	George Hodder.
„	G·H G·H	Do. do.
„	WB WB	William Bennett or Wm. Bentley.
1740-50	R A	.. ...
„	A·S STERLING	} Anthony Semirot.
1745-70	STARLING G·H	George Hodder.
„	GH STERLING GH	Do. do.
„	STARLING GH	} Do. do.
„	G★H GH GH G†H	Do. do.

DATE.	MARKS.	MAKER'S NAME.
c. 1750	STERLING SB	} Stephen Broughton.
1750-70	R·P STERLING	Robt. Potter.
„	I I I·IRISH I I	John Irish.
„	I I STERLING	Do. do. (?)
1757-80	M D DERMOTT	Michael McDermott.
„	MD STER	Do. do.
„	MD STERLING MD	Do. do.
„	WR „	William Reynolds.
„	WR „	Do. do.
„	WR	Do. do.
„	WR STERLING	Do. do.
„	„ STERLING	Do. do.
„	WR	Do. do.
„	WR WR	Do. do.
„	WR WR	Do. do.
„	McD STERLING	Michael McDermott.
„	MD „	Do. do.
1760	L★R STARLING L★R	... ...
„	IA STERLING IA	... ...
1760-80	WALSH SW STERLING	} Stephen Walsh.
„	C·B STERLING	Croker Barrington.
„	SW WALSH STERLING	} Stephen Walsh.
„	SW STERLING	Do. do.
„	WALSH STERLING	} Do. do.
„	SW WALSH STERLING	Do. do.
„	SW „	Do. do.
„	SM „	Stephen Mackrill.

DATE.	MARKS.	MAKER'S NAME.
1760-80	STERLING DMC	Daniel McCarthy?
"	DMC STER	Do. do.
"	STARLING C·B	Croker Barrington.
"	C·B DOLLAR	Do. do.
1760-85	IH STERLING	John Hillery
1765-95	CT " CT	Carden Terry.
1770	IRH STER	John Irish.
"	TA STERLING TA	... ...
"	McD Sterling	Michael McDermott.
"	MD STERLING	Do. do.
1770-88	STER JW STER	John Whitney (free 1775).
1770-99	IN STERLING	John Nicolson.
"	IN STERLING	Do. do.
"	JN "	Do. do.
"	" NICOLSON	Do. do.
1777/1820	PW STERLING	Peter Wills.
1780	C·T STERLING	Carden Terry.
"	IH STERLING IH	John Humphreys
"	I·H "	Do. do.
"	JK STERLING	Joseph Kinselagh.
"	I·H STERLING	John Hillery.
"	CT STERLING	Carden Terry.
"	SC STERLING	(*Not identified.*)
"	SR "	Samuel Reily.
"	JSN "	Jno. & Sam. Nicolson.
"	TC STIRLING	Thomas Cumming.
1770-80	WM STERG	W. Morrisey.
1770-99	NICOLSON STERLING	John Nicolson.
1777/1810	S.R STERLING	Samuel Reily.
"	S·R STERLING	Do. do.
"	SR STERLG	Do. do.
"	REILY STERLING	Do. do.
1783-95	W·ROE STERLING	William Roe.
"	TG STERLING TG	... ...
1786-95	TH STERLING	Thos. Harman.
1787-95	TC STERLG TC	Tim. Conway.
1787	TD STERLING	Thomas Donnallan.
1787-95	JS "	John Sheehan.
"	IG STERLING	Joseph Gibson.
1787-99	R·S STERLING	Richard Stevens.
"	R-S STERLING	Do. do.
"	I·S " I·S	John Sheehan.
"	STERLING SHEEHAN	Do. do.
"	SHEEHAN STERG	Do. do.
"	SHEEHAN STERLING	Do. do.
"	R·S STERLING	Richard Stevens.
1790/1800	JMcN STERLING	(*Not identified.*)
"	RI STERLING	Do. do.
1795	WT STERLG	Wm. Teulon.
"	W.T STERLING	Do. do.
"	WT STERLING	Do. do.
"	" STERLG	Do. do.

DATE.	MARKS.	MAKER'S NAME.
1795		John Supple.
,,	WT STERLING	William Teulon.
,,	WT STERLING	Do. do.
,,	HSM STERLING	*(Not identified.)*
,,	WT ,,	William Teulon.
,,	TJB STERLING	*(Not identified.)*
1791	IW ,,	John Warner
1780-99	,, STIRLING	Do. do.
1795	IW STERLING	John Williams.
,,	I·W STER	James Warner.
,,	I·W STERLING	Do. do.
,,	I·W STERLG	Do. do.
,,	{ STERLING TOLLAND STERLING }	—— Tolland.
1796	I·H STERLING	James Heyland.
,,	RD STERLING	... ...
,,	HEYLAND STERLING	} James Heyland.
,,	JK STERLING	Jos. Kinselagh.
,,	JM[d]	... ...
1800	IT TOLEKEN	John Toleken.
,,	TWM STERLING	*(Not identified.)*
1800-20	{ GIBSON STERLING GIBSON }	Joseph Gibson.
,,	WHELPLEY STERLING	John Whelpley.
,,	,, WHELPLY	Do. do.
,,	K ,, WHELPLY	Do. do.

DATE.	MARKS.	MAKER'S NAME.
1800-20	GIBSON STERLING	Joseph Gibson.
,,	HEYLAND ,,	William Heyland.
,,	,, TOLEKEN	John Toleken.
1795 / 1807	T&W ,,	{ Carden John Terry & Williams. }
1805	SG STIRLING	Samuel Green.
1805-14	SG STERLING SG	} Do. do.
,,	C·T & I·W STERLING	Terry & Williams.
,,	T.MONTJOY ,,	Thomas Montjoy.
,,	IN NN ,,	John & Nicholas } Nicolson.
1807-21	CT IW STERLING	{ Carden Jane Terry & Williams.
1808-20	·CORBETT· STERLING	Daniel Corbett.
1809-30	JS STERLING	James Salter.
,,	R·G ,,	Richard Garde.
1810	T·MONTJOY STERLING	Thos. Montjoy.
,,	CONWAY STERLING	} James Conway.
,,	IE STERLING	John Egan.
,,	P.W STERLING	Peter Wills.
1810-20	WS STERLING	—— Steele ?
,,	I SOLOMON STERLING	Isaac Solomon.
,,	IS STERLING	John Seymour.
,,	I·SOLOMON ,,	Isaac Solomon.
,,	F·S ,,	*(Not identified.)*
,,	PG STERLING	Phineas Garde.
1810-40	IS ,,	{ Isaac John Solomon, or Seymour.
1812	GARDE STERLING	Phineas Garde.
1820	SEYMOUR STERLING	John Seymour.
1820-40	KM ,,	Kean Mahony.
,,	EH ,,	Edward Hawkesworth.
1824	OBRIEN STERLING	Francis O'Brien'
,,	MAHONY STERLING	} Kean Mahony.
1838	M&B STERLING	*(Not identified.)*

YOUGHAL

DATE (ABOUT).	MARKS.	MAKER'S NAME.	
1620	ML	Morrish	Lawless.
„	IS	John	Sharpe.
1644	IG	John	Green.
1650	IG	Do.	do.
1683	BF	Bartholomew Fallon of Galway.	
1702	F	(*Not identified*, but possibly Bartholomew Fallon as above.)	
1712	EG	Edward	Gillett.
1720	„ AB	Austin	Beere.

BELFAST

APPROXIMATE DATE.	MARKS.	MAKER'S NAME.
1780	M GC	... ...
„	M AN. NA.	... ...
1790	MB	*Matthew Bellew ?
1800	M GF	... ...
„	R G	... ...

GALWAY

DATE (ABOUT).	MARKS.	MAKER'S NAME.
1648	RI	R. Joyes, sen. (?)
1666-1684		. . . .
1695	RI RI	Richard Joyes.
1700	RI RI	Do. do.
„	EG	... ...
„	TP	... ...
1720	TL	... ...
1725	RI RI	Richard Joyes.
1730	MF	Mark Fallon.
„	MF	Do. do.
1743-5	PI	... ...

DATE. (ABOUT).	MARKS.	MAKER'S NAME.
1710	I·B I·B	J. Buck, senr. (?)
1718	AB	Adam Buck.
1730-40	I·B STERLING	Jonathan Buck. (free 1731)
"	STERLING IB	Do. do.
1730-62	STERLING	Do. do.
"	" IB "	Do. do.
"	STERLING IB	Do. do.
"	STERLING IB	Do. do.
1730-75	STERLING	Joseph Johns.
"	STERLIN	Do. do.
"	"	Do. do.
1749-50	I·I	? Joseph Johns.
1750	S.J STARLING	Samuel Johns.
1760-85	GM STERLING	George Moore.
"	GM STARLING	Do. do.
1768-80	GFG STERLING GFG	Garret Fitzgerald.
1770	GM	George Moore.
1780	TW	(*Not identified.*)
"	TW STER LING	Do. do.
1784	P.C Ster P.C	Patrick Connell.
"	P.C STER P.C	Do. do.
1784	P·C STER P·C	Patrick Connell.
"	" STERLING "	* Do. do.
"	MFG " MFG	Maurice Fitzgerald.
"	MFG MFG MFG	Do. do.
"	MFG STERLING	Do. do.
"	STER TB STER	Thomas Burke.
"	TB STERLING TB	Do. do.
"	TB STER TB	Do. do.
"	TB STERLING	Do. do.
"	TB STERLING	Do. do.
"	MW STERLING	Matt. Walsh.
"	MW STERLING	Do. do.
1786	DL STERLING DL	Daniel Lysaght.
"	DL STERLING	Do. do.
"	DL "	Do. do.
1798	WW STER WW	Wm. Ward.
1800	WFG STERLING WFG	Wm. Fitzgerald.
"	WFG STERLING	Do. do.
"	RoS RoS	Robt. O'Shaughnessy.
"	RoS STERLG	Do. do.
"	WW WW	Will. Ward.
"	WW STERLING	Do. do.
"	M C	... ...
1810-20	S★P STERLING	Samuel Purdon.
"	"	Do. do.
1800-13	IP	John Purcell.

UNASCRIBED IRISH PROVINCIAL MARKS.

DATE (ABOUT).	MARKS.
1611	
1650	CK
1652	AN
1666	AR
1673	ES
1680	IH
,,	HC HC
1682	WH
,,	WT
1690	MK
1700	W W
1705	I*B
1710	WS
,,	W
1720	IR
1720-40	MC
1726	AW
,,	CM
1750	WL
1756	I·S T I
1760	EC
,,	CK H
1780	G·M
,,	I+F
,,	WG

UNASCRIBED MARKS

DATE (ABOUT).	MARKS.
1574	
1590	COK
1660	
1680	SW
,,	RW
1700	GB
,,	A
1730	R Sta
1740-50	WD A·D WD
,,	CA C·W
1770	I*S
1780	TB T·B·BROWN HX
1800	H·FOSTER

INDEX

ENGLISH, SCOTTISH AND IRISH MARKS

Name of Firm.	Maker's Marks.	Date.
Ashforth G. & Co. ...		1784
Fox T. & Co.		1784
Green W. & Co.		1784
Holy D., Wilkinson & Co.		1784
Law T. & Co.		1784
Parsons J. & Co.		1784
Smith N. & Co.		1784
Staniforth, Parkin & Co.		1784
Sykes & Co.		1784
Tudor, Leader & Nicholson		1784
Boulton M. & Co. ...		1784
Dixon T. & Co.		1784
Holland H. & Co. ...		1784
Moore J.	 §	1784
Smith & Co.		1784

Name of Firm.	Maker's Marks.	Date.
Beldon, Hoyland & Co. ..	BELDON HOYLAND & Co	1785
Brittain, Wilkinson & Brownill	BRITTAIN.WILKIN SON & BROWNILL.	1785
Deakin, Smith & Co. ...	DEAKIN SMITH & Co	1785
Love J. & Co. ... ... (Love, Silverside, Darby & Co.)	I.LOVE & Co	1785
Morton R. & Co. ...	MORTON & Co	1785
Roberts, Cadman & Co.		1785
Roberts J. & S.	I & S. ROBERTS	1786
Sutcliffe R. & Co. ...		1786
Bingley W.	W.BINGLEY	1787
Madin F. & Co.	F.MADIN & Co	1788
Jervis W.	WJER VIS	1789
Colmore S.	SC Colmore Patent	1790
Goodwin E.	E.GOODWIN	1794
Watson, Fenton & Bradbury	WATSON & Co	1795
Froggatt, Coldwell & Lean	FROGGATT COLDWELL & LEAN	1797
Green J. & Co.	I.GREEN & Co	1799
Goodman, Gainsford & Fairbairn	A.GOODMAN & Co	1800
Ellerby W	ELL ER BY	1803
Garnett W.	GARNETT	1803
Holy D., Parker & Co. ...	DAN HOLY PARKER & Co	1804
Newbould W. & Son ...	Wm NEWBOULD & SONS	1804
Drabble I. & Co. ...	I.DRABBLE & Co	1805
Coldwell W.	W.COLDWELL.	1806
Hill D. & Co.	HILL / HILL & Co	1806
Law J. & Son	LAW & SON	1807
Butts T.	TB S B	1807
Green J.	GREEN	1807
Hutton W.	Hutton	1807
Law R.	R.LAW.	1807
Linwood J.	I.LINWOOD	1807
Linwood W.	W.LINWOOD	1807
Meredith H.	MERE DITH	1807
Peake	PEAKE	1807
Ryland W & Son ...	RYLAND	1807
Scot W		1807
Silkirk W	Sil-kirk?	1807
Thomason E. & Dowler...	MANUFACTURED BY E THOMASON & Co / THOMASON	1807
Tonks Samuel	TONKS	1807

Name of Firm.	Maker's Marks.	Date.
Waterhouse & Co. ...	WATERHOUSE&Co	1807
Wilmore Joseph ...	J W; PATENT WILLMORES & WILKES	1807
Gainsford R.	GAINSFORD; GA	1808
Hatfield A.	A H J H	1808
Banister W.	BANI STER	1808
Gibbs G.	GIBBS; GIB BS	1808
Hipkiss J.	HIPKISS	1808
Horton D.	D·HORTON	1808
Lea A. C.	A·CLEA	1808
Linwood M & Sons ...	LIN WOOD	1808
Nicholds J	J·NICHOLDS	1808
Beldon G.	BEL DON	1809
Wright J. & Fairbairn G.	WRIGHT FAIRBAIRN	1809
Cheston T ...	Ches ton	1809
Harrison J	HARRI SON	1809
Hipwood W	WHIP WOOD	1809
Horton J	HOR TON	1809
Silk R.	S I L K	1809
Howard S. & T.	S H & Co; How ard	1809
Smith, Tate, Nicholson & Hoult	SMITH&Co	1810
Dunn G B	DUNN	1810
Hanson M.	HAN SON	1810
Pimley S.	[illegible]	1810
Creswick T. & J. ...	[illegible]	1811
Stot B.	Stot	1811
Watson, Pass & Co. (late J. Watson)	WATSON PASS &Co	1811
Lees G.	I I I; LEES	1811
Pearson R.	PEAR SON	1811
White J. (White & Allgood)	WHITE	1811
Kirkby S.	KIRKBY FOR·USE	1812
Allgood J	ALL GOOD	1812
Allport E	All port	1812
Gilbert J	G PS; Gil bert	1812
Hinks J.	HINKS	1812
Johnson J	JOHN SON	1812
Small T	SMALL	1812
Smith W	SM ITH	1812
Younge S. & C & Co. ...	S.C.YOUNGE &Co	1813
Thomas S.	THO MAS	1813
Tyndall J	TYN DALL	1813
Best H.	BEST	1814
Cracknall J.	CRACK NALL	1814
Jordan T.	JOR DAN; Jor dan	1814

Name of Firm.	Maker's Marks.	Date.
Woodward W.	WOOD WARD WOOD WARD	1814
Lilly John	LILLY	1815
Best & Wastidge	BEST	1816
Ashley	ASH LEY	1816
Davis J.	DAVIS	1816
Evans S.	S·EVANS	1816
Freeth H.	FREETH HF	1816
Harwood T.	Har wood Har wood Har wood	1816
Lilly Joseph	JOSH LILLY	1816
Turley S.	S·TURLEY	1816
Cope C. G.	COPE	1817
Pemberton & Mitchell	PEM BER TON	1817
Shephard J.	SHEP-HARD	1817
Markland W	W·MARKLAND	1818
Corn J. & J. Sheppard	CORN & Co	1819
Rogers J.	ROGERS	1819
Hall W.	HALL Whall	§ 1820
Moore F.	F·MOORE	1820
Turton J.	TUR TON. TUR TON	1820

Name of Firm.	Maker's Marks.	Date.
Blagden, Hodgson & Co.		1821
Holy D. & G.	HOLY, S & Co SHEFFIELD	1821
Needham C.	C NEEDHAM MAKER SHEFFIELD	1821
Sansom T. & Sons	SAN SOM	1821
Child T.	CHILD	1821
Smith I.	SMITH	1821
Worton S.	S WORTON	1821
Rodgers J. & Sons	JR J R G R ROD GERS	1822
Bradshaw J.	Brad shaw Brad shaw	1822
Briggs W.	B	1823
Harrison G.	GH GH F	1823
Smallwood J.		1823
Causer J. F.	CAUSER	1824
Jones	JONES	1824
Tonks & Co.	TONKS	1824
Roberts, Smith & Co.		1828
Smith J. & Son	SMI TH	1828
Askew	ASKEW MAKER NOTTINGHAM.	1828
Hall Henry		1829
Hobday J.	Hob day Hob day	1829
Watson J. & Son		1830

Name of Firm.	Maker's Marks.	Date.
Bishop Thomas... ...	Bis hop Bis hop	1830
Hutton W.	Hutton WH Sheffield WH	1831
Atkin Henry	H A S	1833
Waterhouse I. & I. & Co.	I & I W & Co	1833
Watson W.	W WATSON MAKER SHEFFIELD	1833
Dixon J. & Sons	D S D S Dixon J G R DIXON'S IMPERIAL DIXON SHEFFIELD	1835
Smith J.	JOSEPHUS SMITH	1836
Waterhouse, Hatfield & Co.		1836
Wilkinson H. & Co. ...		1836
Hutton W.	Hutton Hutton	1837
Hutton W.	H & S WH	1839
Prime J.	Prime PS Prime S Prime Prime	1839
Walker, Knowles & Co.		1840
Waterhouse George & Co.	W & Co S	1842
Smith, Sissons & Co. ...		1848
Padley, Parkin & Co. ...		1849

Name of Firm.	Maker's Marks.	Date.
Hutton W.	W H & S WH	1849
Mappin Bros.	MAP PIN BROT HERS	1850
Oldham T.	T. OLDHAM MAKER NOTTINGHAM	1860
Roberts & Briggs ...	R & B	1860

MISCELLANEOUS MARKS WHICH HAVE NOT BEEN TRACED.

Maker's Marks.	Approximate date of manufacture.
IK	1780-1790
BEST PLATE	1790
DEVER	1790
ALWH GA IH EE	1790-1800
Do.	1790-1800
R^D JEWESSON MIDLETON & Co *	1800-1810
W.B. PINE 352 STRAND	1815-1825
	1815 1825
WILSON	1815-1825
GILBERT LONDON	1840
REGISTERED BY MAPPLABECK & LOWE JANY 27 1840 No 223	1840
RW&W	1840
PAT ENT PAT ENT	1840
	1850
SALT	1850
	1850
GRC	1850

AMERICAN SILVERSMITHS' MARKS

One date indicates the period, two dates the birth and death.

A

Name	Place	Date	Marks
AARON, JOSEPH	Philadelphia, Pa.	1798	
ABBOTT, JOHN W.	Portsmouth, N.H.	1839	JABBOTT
ACKERMAN, DAVID	New York, N.Y.	1818	
ACKLEY, FRANCIS M.	New York, N.Y.	1797	F.ACKLEY
ACTON, GEORGE	New York, N.Y.	1795	
ADAM, I.	Alexandria, Va.	1800	IA · IA · I.Adam · I.ADAM
ADAM, JOHN B.	New Orleans, La.	1822	
ADAM, JOHN	Alexandria, Va.	1829	
ADAMS, JONATHAN	Philadelphia, Pa.	1785	I.ADAM
ADAMS, PYGAN	New London, Conn.	1712-1776	P·A · RA · PA
ADAMS, WM. L.	New York, N.Y.	1842	W.ADAMS · NEW YORK
ADDISON, GEORGE M.	Baltimore, Md.	1804	
ADGATE, WM.	Norwich, Conn.	1767	
ADRIANCE, E.	St. Louis, Mo.	1820	E.ADRIANCE · ST.LOUIS
AIKEN, GEORGE	Baltimore, Md.	1765-1832	G·A · G.Aiken · G.Aiken · G.AiKen · AIKEN · GAIKEN
AINSWORTH, MICHAEL	Fredricksburg Co., Va.	1755	
AITKEN, JOHN	Philadelphia, Pa.	1785	I.Aitken · IAITKEN
AITKINS, W.	Baltimore, Md.	1802	
AKIN, JOHN B.	Danville, Ky.	1850	JOHN B.AKIN DANVILLE KY
ALDIS, CHARLES	New York, N.Y.	1814	C.ALDIS
ALEXANDER, A.	Philadelphia, Pa.	1802	
ALEXANDER, S. & SIMMONS, A.	Philadelphia, Pa.	1800	
ALEXANDER, SAMUEL	Philadelphia, Pa.	1808	S·ALEXANDER
ALFORD, SAMUEL	Philadelphia, Pa.	1840	
ALFORD, THOMAS	Philadelphia, Pa.	1762	
ALLCOCK & ALLEN	New York, N.Y.	1820	ALLCOCK & ALLEN
ALLEN, CHARLES	Boston, Mass.	1760	C·ALLEN
ALLEN & EDWARDS	Boston, Mass.	1700	IA · IE
ALLEN, JAMES	Philadelphia, Pa.	1720	
ALLEN, JOEL	Middletown, Conn.	1787	
ALLEN, JOHN	Philadelphia, Pa.	1814	IA · IA · IA
ALLEN, JOHN	Boston, Mass.	1691-1760	
ALLEN, RICHARD	Philadelphia, Pa.	1816	
ALLEN, ROBERT	Philadelphia, Pa.	1776	
ALLEN, THOMAS	Boston, Mass.	1758	
ALLISON, PETER	New York, N.Y.	1791	
ALSTYNE, JEROMIMUS	New York, N.Y.	1787	I.Alstyne · IA · IA
ANDERSON, WM.	New York, N.Y.	1746	WA · WA
ANDRAS & CO.	New York, N.Y.	1800	ANDRAS & CO
ANDRAS & RICHARD	New York, N.Y.	1797	A&R
ANDRAS, WM.	New York, N.Y.	1795	ANDRAS
ANDREAS, ABRAHAM	Bethlehem, Pa.	1780	
ANDREW, JOHN	Salem, Mass.	1747-1791	I.ANDREW
ANDREWS, ABRAHAM	Philadelphia, Pa.	1795	
ANDREWS, H.	Boston, Mass.	1830	
ANDREWS, HENRY	Philadelphia, Pa.	1795	HA
ANDREWS, JEREMIAH	Philadelphia, Pa.	1776	J·ANDREWS · I.ANDREWS · NORFOLK · I.Andrews
ANDREWS, JOSEPH	Norfolk, Va.	1800	
ANDREWS, JR.	Philadelphia, Pa.	1746	
ANTHONY, ISAAC	Newport, R. I. Swansea, Mass.	1690-1773	IA
ANTHONY, J.	Philadelphia, Pa.	1770	
ANTHONY, JOSEPH	Philadelphia, Pa.	1783	J.A · J·A

ANTHONY, JOSEPH, JR.
Philadelphia, Pa. 1783-1814

JA JA JAnthony
J.Anthony
JAnthony

ANTHONY, JOSEPH & SONS
Philadelphia, Pa. 1810

J.A & I.A

ANTHONY, L. D.
Providence, R. I. 1805

ANTHONY, M. H. & T.
Philadelphia, Pa. 1814

ANTHONY, MICHAEL H.
Philadelphia, Pa. 1810

ANTHONY, THOMAS
Philadelphia, Pa. 1810

ANTHONY, WM.
New York, N.Y. 1800

ANWYL, KENRICK
Baltimore, Md. 1780

APPLETON, GEORGE B.
New York, N.Y. 1820

APPLETON

ARCHIE, JOHN
New York, N.Y. 1759

ARMS, T. N.
Albany, New York 1849

ARMSTRONG, ALLEN
Philadelphia, Pa. 1806

A.Armstrong
Philadelphia
A.Armstrong Phia.

ARMSTRONG, JOHN
Philadelphia, Pa. 1810

ARMSTRONG, WM.
Philadelphia, Pa. 1750

ARNOLD, THOMAS
Newport, R. I. 1739-1828

TA TA ARNOLD
TARNOLD TA TA
T.ARNOLD TA
ARNOLD TA
TARNOLD TA

ARNOLD, THOMAS
Philadelphia, Pa. 1760

ASHMEAD, WM.
Philadelphia, Pa. 1797

ATHERTON, NATHAN
Philadelphia, Pa. 1825

ATKINSON, ISAAC
Philadelphia, Pa. 1825

ATLEE, CHARLES
Philadelphia, Pa. 1837

ATTERBURY, J.
New Haven, Conn. 1799

AUSTEN, DAVID
Philadelphia, Pa. 1837

AUSTIN, BENJAMIN
Portsmouth, N. H. 1775

AUSTIN & BOYER
Boston, Mass. 1770

I.Austin Boyer

AUSTIN, EBENEZER
Hartford, Conn. 1782

Austin E·A
Austin

AUSTIN, EBENEZER J.
Boston, Mass. 1790

E.J.AUSTIN

AUSTIN, JAMES
Charlestown, Mass. 1780

AUSTIN, JOHN
Philadelphia, Pa. 1802

AUSTIN, JOSEPH
Hartford, Conn. 1740

AUSTIN, JOSIAH
Charlestown, Mass. ...1718-1780

I·AUSTIN I·A I·A
I·Austin J·AUSTIN

AUSTIN, NATHANIEL
Boston, Mass. 1734-1818

Austin N·A
AUSTIN

AVERY, JOHN
Preston, Conn. 1732-1794

IAVERY IA

AVERY, JOHN, JR.
Preston, Conn. 1776

AVERY, ROBERT STAUNTON..
Preston, Conn. 1792

AVERY, SAMUEL
Preston, Conn. 1760-1836

SA SA

AVERY, WM.
Preston, Conn. 1786

AVERY, WILLIS & BILLIS
Salisbury, N.Y. 1820

AYRES, S.
Lexington, Ky. 1805

S.AYRES·LEX.K.

AYRES, T.
Unknown 1800

T.AYRES.

B

BABCOCK, SAMUEL
Middletown, Conn. 1788-1857

Babcock

BACALL, THOMAS
Boston, Mass. 1836

BACHMAN, A.
New York, N.Y. 1848

BACHMAN

BACKUS, DELUCINE
New York, N.Y. 1792

D Backus D BACKUS
D Backus

BAIELLE, LEWIS
Baltimore, Md. 1799

BAILEY, BENJAMIN
Boston, Mass. 1820

BAILEY, B. M.
Ludlow, Vt. 1824-1913

B.M.BAILEY LUDLOW

BAILEY & CO.
Philadelphia, Pa. 1850

BAILEY & CO.

BAILEY, EDWARD
Baltimore, Md. 1779

BAILEY, E. E. & S. C.
Portland, Me. 1825

EE&SC BAILEY

BAILEY, HENRY
Boston, Mass. 1780

HB S M

BAILEY, JOHN
New York, N.Y. 1762

J·Bailey

BAILEY & KITCHEN
Philadelphia, Pa. 1853

BAILEY&KITCHEN

Name	Place	Date
BAILEY, LORING	Hingham, Mass.	1780
BAILEY, ROBERT H.	Woodstock, Vt.	1825
BAILEY, SIMEON A.	New York, N.Y.	1789
BAILEY, JOHN	Philadelphia, Pa.	1762
BAILY, WM.	New York, N.Y.	1820
BAKER	Boston, Mass.	1765
BAKER, ANSON	New York, N.Y.	1821
BAKER, E.	New York, N.Y.	1740-1790
BAKER, GEORGE	Providence, R. I.	1825
BAKER, S.	New York, N.Y.	1787-1858
BALCH, EBENEZER	Hartford, Conn.	1744
BALCH & FRYER	Albany, N.Y.	1784
BALDWIN & BAKER	Providence, R. I.	1817
BALDWIN & CO.	Newark, N.J.	1830
BALDWIN, EBENEZER	Hartford, Conn.	1723-1808
BALDWIN, JABEZ	Boston, Mass.	1808
BALDWIN, J. C.	Boston, Mass.	1815
BALDWIN, JEDEDIAH	Portsmouth, N. H.	1793
BALDWIN & JONES	Boston, Mass.	1813
BALDWIN, STANLEY S	New York, N.Y.	1820
BALL, BLACK & CO.	New York, N.Y.	1850
BALL & HEALD	Baltimore, Md.	1810
BALL, HENRY	New York, N.Y.	1833
BALL, JOHN	Boston, Mass.	1765
BALL, S. S.	Boston, Mass.	1838
BALL, THOMPKINS & BLACK	New York, N.Y.	1839
BALL, TRUE M.	Boston, Mass.	1815-1890
BALL, W.	Baltimore, Md.	1802
BALL, WM.	Philadelphia, Pa.	1752
BANCKER, ADRIEN	New York, N.Y.	1703-1772
BANGS, JOHN	Cincinnati, O.	1825
BARBERET, THEON	New Orleans, La.	1822
BARBIER, PETER	Philadelphia, Pa.	1823
BARD, CONRAD	Philadelphia, Pa.	1825
BARD, C. & SON	Philadelphia, Pa.	1850
BARD & HOFFMAN	Philadelphia, Pa.	1837
BARD, J.	Philadelphia, Pa.	1800
BARD & LAMONT	Philadelphia, Pa.	1841
BARDEER, CONNARD	Philadelphia, Pa.	1831
BARDICK, GEORGE	Philadelphia, Pa.	1790
BARDICK, JOHN	Philadelphia, Pa.	1805
BARDON, STEPHEN	Philadelphia, Pa.	1785
BARIA, WM.	New York, N.Y.	1805
BARNES, ABRAHAM	Boston, Mass.	1716
BARRET, JAMES	Norwich, Conn.	1717
BARRETT, JAMES	New York, N.Y.	1805
BARRETT, S.	Nantucket, Mass.	1800
BARRIER, DAVID	Baltimore, Md.	1810
BARRINGTON & DAVENPORT	Philadelphia, Pa.	1806
BARROWS, JAMES MADISON	Tolland, Conn.	1809
BARRY, STANDISH	Baltimore, Md.	1763-1844
BARTHOLOMEW, JOSEPH	Philadelphia, Pa.	1833

BARTHOLOMEW, LE ROUX	New York, N. Y.	1688-1713	BR BR
BARTHOLOMEW, ROSWELL	Hartford, Conn.	1781-1830	RB
BARTLETT, EDWARD	Philadelphia, Pa.	1833	
BARTLETT, NATHANIEL	Concord, Mass.	1760	N·BARTLETT
BARTLETT, SAMUEL	Boston, Mass.	1750-1821	S.B S·BARTLETT
BARTON, ERASTUS	New York, N. Y.	1810	
BARTON, ERASTUS & CO.	New York, N. Y.	1821	E.B&CO
BARTRAM, WM.	Philadelphia, Pa.	1769	
BASSET, FRANCIS	New York, N. Y.	1774	BASSETT
BATCHELLOR, N.	New York, N. Y.	1825	
BATTELS, A. T.	Utica, N. Y.	1847	A.T.BATTELS UTICA
BAY, A. S.	New York, N. Y.	1786	
BAYLEY, ALEXANDER	New York, N. Y.	1790	
BAYLEY & DOUGLAS	New York, N. Y.	1789	DB&AD
BAYLEY, S. & A.	New York, N. Y.	1790	
BAYLEY, S. H.	New York, N. Y.	1790	
BAYLEY, SIMON A.	New York, N. Y.	1789	BAYLEY BAYLEY
BAYLY, JOHN	Philadelphia, Pa.	1755	
BAYSSET, JOSEPH	New Orleans, La.	1822	
BEACH, A.	Hartford, Conn.	1823	A.BEACH
BEACH, ISAAC	New Milford, Conn.	1788	
BEACH, IVES & CO.	New York, N. Y.	1820	
BEACH, MILES	Litchfield, Conn.	1743-1828	MB M·B BEACH
BEACH & SANFORD	Hartford, Conn.	1785-1788	B&S B&S
BEACH & WARD	Hartford, Conn.	1789-1795	B&W
BEAL, CALEB	Boston, Mass.	1796	BEAL
BEAM, JACOB C.	Philadelphia, Pa.	1818	
BEAUVAIS, RENO	St. Louis, Mo.	1850	R.BEAUVAIS ST.LOUIS
BECHAM	Unknown	c 1740	BECHAM
BECK, THOMAS	Philadelphia, Pa.	1773	
BECKER, FREDERICK	New York, N. Y.	1736	
BECKER, PHILIP	Lancaster, Pa.	1764	
BEDFORD, JOHN	Fishkill, N. Y.	1781	I Bedford I Bedford
BEEBE, J. W. & CO.	New York, N. Y.	1844	J.W.BEEBE J.W.BEEBE&C
BEEBE, JAMES W.	New York, N.Y.	1835	
BEEBE, STANTON	Providence, R. I.	1824	
BEEBE, WILLIAM	New York, N. Y.	1850	BEEBE
BEECHER, CLEMENT	Berlin, Conn.	1778-1869	CB CB
BEECHER, C. & CO.	Meriden, Conn.	1820	
BELIN, LEWIS	Philadelphia, Pa.	1818	
BELKNAP, SAMUEL	Boston, Mass.	1789	
BELLIARD, FRANCOIS	New Orleans, La.	1822	
BELLONI, LOUIS J.	New York, N. Y.	1835	
BELLONI, & DURANDEAU	New York, N. Y.	1835	
BENEDICT, A. C.	New York, N. Y.	1840	A.C.BENEDICT.
BENEDICT, J.	New York, N. Y.	1830	
BENEDICT & SON	New York, N. Y.	1840	
BENEDICT & SQUIRE	New York, N. Y.	1825	BENEDICT & SQUIRE
BENJAMIN, BARZILLAI	New Hoven, Conn.	1799	BB B.BENJAMIN
BENJAMIN, BENJAMIN	New York, N. Y.	1825	B.B B.BENJAMIN
BENJAMIN, EVERERD	New Hoven, Conn.	1807-1874	E·BENJAMIN
BENJAMIN, JOHN	Stratford, Conn.	1731-1796	I·B I·B

Name	Place	Date	Marks
BENJAMIN, SAMUEL C.	New Haven, Conn.	1819	
BENJAMIN, SOLOMON	Baltimore, Md.	1817	
BENNET, JAMES	New York, N. Y.	1773	
BENNETT, JACOB	Philadelphia, Pa.	1839	
BENTLEY, THOMAS	Boston, Mass.	1762-1800	TB BENTLEY
BENTSON, PETER	Philadelphia, Pa.	1718	
BERARD, ANDREW	Philadelphia, Pa.	1797	
BERARD, E.	Philadelphia, Pa.	1800	E BERARD
BERKENBUSH, CHAS. H.	New York, N. Y.	1825	
BERRY, WM.	New York, N. Y.	1805	
BESLEY, THAUVET	New York, N. Y.	1727	B
BESSELIEVRE, THOMAS	Philadelphia, Pa.	1831	
BEST, JOSEPH	Philadelphia, Pa.	1723	
BEVAN, RICHARD	Baltimore, Md.	1804	
BIERSHING, HENRY	Hagerstown, Md.	1815	H·B
BIGELOW & BROS.	Boston, Mass.	1840	BIGELOW & BROTHERS
BIGELOW BROS. & KENNARD	Boston, Mass.	1845	BIGELOW BROS & KENNARD
BIGELOW, JOHN	Boston, Mass.	1830	JOHN BIGELOW
BIGGS, JOSEPH	New York, N. Y.	1830	
BIGOTUT, S.	New York, N. Y.	1800	
BIJOTAL, SILVIAN A.	New York, N. Y.	1795	
BILLING, A.	Troy, N. Y.	1780	A BILLING AB
BILLINGS, A.	Preston, Conn.	1780	A·B A·BILLINGS
BILLINGS, DANIEL	Preston, Conn.	1795	D. Billings
BILLON, CHARLES	St. Louis, Mo.	1821	C BILLON
BINGHAM, JOHN	Newark, N. J.	1664	
BINNEAU, THEODORE	Philadelphia, Pa.	1820	
BIRD, CONARD	Philadelphia, Pa.	1831	
BISSBROWN, THOMAS	Albany, N. Y.	1790	
BLACK, JAMES	Philadelphia, Pa.	1795	J.B
BLACK, JAMES	Philadelphia, Pa.	1811	JB JB
BLACK, JOHN	Philadelphia, Pa.	1819	
BLACK, WM.	New York, N. Y.	1833	
BLACKMAN, FRED'S. S. & CO.	Danbury, Conn.	1811-1898	
BLACKMAN, FRED'K STARR	Danbury, Conn.	1811-1898	F.S.BLACKMAN. F.S.B.&Co
BLACKMAN, JOHN C.	Danbury, Conn.	1829	
BLACKMAN, JOHN STARR	Danbury, Conn.	1777-1851	J.S.B
BLAKSLEE, WM.	Newtown, Conn.	1820	
BLAKSLEE, ZIBA	Newtown, Conn.	1790	A.BLANCHARD A.BLANCHARD
BLANCHARD, ASA	Lexington, Ky.	1810	
BLAUVELT, JOHN W.	New York, N. Y.	1835	
BLEASOM & REED	Portsmouth, N. H.	1830	BLEASOM & REED NASSAU
BLISS, JONATHAN	Middletown, Conn.	1800	
BLONDELL, ANTHONY	Philadelphia, Pa.	1797	
BLONDELL & DESCURET	Philadelphia, Pa.	1798	
BLOWERS, JOHN	Boston, Mass.	1710-1748	Blowers BLOWERS
BOEHLER, ANDREAS W.	New York, N. Y.	1784	
BOEHME, CHARLES L.	Baltimore, Md.	1774-1868	C·L·B C L B C.L.Boehme C.Boehme C.L.BOEHME
BOELEN, HENRICUS	New York, N. Y.	1684-1755	HB HB HB HB
BOELEN, JACOB	New York, N. Y.	1773	IB IB IB IB IB IB
BOELEN, JAMES	New York, N. Y.	1659-1729	IB
BOEMPER, ABRAHAM	Bethlehem, Pa.	1780	
BOGARDUS, EVERARDUS	New York, N. Y.	1698	EB

Name	Location	Date	Marks
BOGERT, ALBERT	New York, N. Y.	1815	
BOGERT, NICHOLAS J.	New York, N. Y.	1801	N·BOGERT N.J.BOGERT
BOLTON, JAMES	New York, N. Y.	1789	
BOND, W.	Unknown	C 1765	W.Bond
BONJEAN, VICTOR	New Orleans, La.	1822	
BONTECOU, TIMOTHY	New Haven, Conn.	1693-1784	T.B. TB.
BONTECOU, TIMOTHY, JR.	New Haven, Conn.	1723-1789	TB
BOONE, JEREMIAH	Philadelphia, Pa.	1791	I.BOONE
BORDEAUX, AUGUSTINE	Philadelphia, Pa.	1798	
BORHEK, E.	Philadelphia, Pa.	1835	E.BORHEK STANDARD
BOSS & KINDELL	New York, N. Y.	1794	
BOSTWICK, ZALMON	New York, N. Y.	1846	Z·BOSTWICK
BOSWORTH, SAMUEL	Buffalo, N. Y.	1835	BOSWORTH
BOTSFORD, GIDEON B.	Woodbury, Conn.	1776-1866	G.B.BOTSFORD
BOUDAR, JOSEPH	New York, N. Y.	1800	
BOUDINOT, ELIAS	Philadelphia, Pa.	1706-1770	EB BOUDINOT BOUDINOT
BOUDO, LOUIS	Charleston, S. C.	1825	L$BOUDO
BOULLIEN, MOUSIER	Philadelphia, Pa.	1811	
BOURDETT, STEPHAN	New York, N. Y.	1730	SB
BOUTIER, JOHN	New York, N. Y.	1805	J.BOUTIER
BOUTELLE, JAMES	Worcester, Mass.	1787	
BOUVAR, JOSEPH	Philadelphia, Pa.	1797	
BOWER, C.	Philadelphia, Pa.	1831	
BOWNE, SAMUEL	New York, N. Y.	1778	S:BOWNE SBOWNE
BOYCE, GERADUS	New York, N. Y.	1814	G.B G:BOYCE G.BOYCE
BOYCE & JONES	New York, N. Y.	1825	B&J. BOYCE&JONES
BOYCE, JARED	New York, N. Y.	1820	
BOYCE, JOHN	New York, N. Y.	1801	J.B
BOYD & HOYT	Albany, New York	1830	
BOYD, JOSEPH W.	New York, N. Y.	1820	J.W.B
BOYD & MULFORD	Albany, N. Y.	1840	BOYD&MULFORD
BOYD, WM.	Albany, N. Y.	1800	
BOYER, DANIEL	Boston, Mass.	1726-1779	DB DB BOYER Boyer BOYER
BOYER, JAMES	Boston, Mass.	1700-1741	
BOYLSTON E.	Stockbridge, Mass.	1789	
BRABANT, ISAAC	Savannah, Ga.	1750	
BRACKETT, JEFFREY R.	Boston, Mass.	1840	JEFFREY R BRACKETT
BRADBURY, THEOPHILUS	Newburyport, Mass.	1815	BRADBURY Bradbury
BRADBURY & BROTHER	Newburyport, Mass.	1810	
BRADFORD, CHARLES H.	Westerly, R. I.	Unknown	
BRADLEY, ABNER	New Haven, Conn.	1753-1824	A.BRADLEY
BRADLEY & BUNCE	Hartford, Conn.	1830	
BRADLEY, LUTHER	New Haven, Conn.	1772-1830	LB
BRADLEY & MERRIMAN	New Haven, Conn.	1826	B&M
BRADLEY, PHINEAS	New Haven, Conn.	1745-1797	PB PB
BRADLEY, RICHARD	Hartford, Conn.	1825	
BRADLEY, ZEBUL	New Haven, Conn.	1780-1859	Z.BRADLEY
BRADY, E.	New York, N. Y.	1825	BRADY E:BRADY
BRADY, WM. V.	New York, N. Y.	1835	
BRAINERD, CHARLES	Hartford, Conn.	1809	
BRAMHALL, S.	Plymouth, Mass.	1800	S.BRAMHALL
BRANDT, A. & C.	Philadelphia, Pa.	1800	A&C BRANDT
BRASHER, A.	New York, N. Y.	1790	ABRASHER

Name	Place	Date	Marks
BRASHER & ALEXANDER	New York, N.Y.	1800	
BRASHER, E. & CO.	New York, N.Y.	1790	
BRASHER, EPHRIAM	New York, N.Y.	1766	EB · EB · E·BRASHER · BRASHER · E·B&Co
BRASIER, A.	Unknown	Unknown	A·BRASIER
BRAY, HENRY	Philadelphia, Pa.	1799	
BREED, JOHN	Colchester, Conn.	1773	
BREED, WM.	Boston, Mass.	1750	WB · WB · WBreed
BRENTON, BENJAMIN	New York, N.Y.	1825	BB · BB · BB
BREVOORT, JOHN	New York, N.Y.	1715-1775	IBV · IBV · IBV · IBV
BREWER, CHARLES	Middletown, Conn.	1778-1860	CBrewer · C.BREWER · CBrewer · C.BREWER
REWER & CO.	Middletown, Conn.	1810	
BREWER & MANN	Middletown, Conn.	1803	
REWSTER, ABEL	Norwalk, Conn.	1797	BREWSTER
RIDGE, JOHN	Boston, Mass.	1723	BRIDGE · IBRIDGE
RIDGE, JOHN	Boston, Mass.	1751	BRIDGE · I BRIDGE · J·BRIDGE
RIGDEN, C.	Boston, Mass.	1770	C·B · C.B · Brigden
RIGDEN, TIMOTHY	Albany, N.Y.	1813	TB
BRIGDEN, ZACHARIAH	Boston, Mass.	1734-1787	Z·B · Z·B · Z B · Z.Brigden
RIGHT, ANTHONY	Philadelphia, Pa.	1739	
BRINKLEY, WM.	New York, N.Y.	1802	
BRINTON, GORDON & QUIRK	Boston, Mass.	1780	
BRITTON, ISAAC	Philadelphia, Pa.	1811	
BRITTON, JACOB	Philadelphia, Pa.	1807	
BROADHURST, SAMUEL	New York, N.Y.	1724	
BROCK, JOHN	New York, N.Y.	1833	I.BROCK
BOCK, L.	New York, N.Y.	1830	L.BROCK

Name	Place	Date	Marks
BROOKHOUSE, ROBERT	Salem, Mass.	1750	RB
BROOKS, SAMUEL	Philadelphia, Pa.	1793	BROOKS
BROTHEARS, MICHAEL	Philadelphia, Pa.	1772	
BROWER & RUSHER	New York, N.Y.	1834	B&R
BROWER, S. & B.	Albany, N.Y.	1810	S&B.BROWER
BROWN, S. D.	Albany, N.Y.	1834	
BROWER, WALTER S.	Albany, N.Y.	1850	
BROWN, ALEXANDER	Philadelphia, Pa.	1840	
BROWN, D.	Philadelphia, Pa.	1811	D.BROWN
BROWN, ELNATHAN C.	Westerly, R. I.	Unknown	
BROWN, EBENEZER	Boston, Mass.	1793	
BROWN, HENRY	Philadelphia, Pa.	1777	
BROWN & HOULTON	Baltimore, Md.	1799	
BROWN, JAMES	Philadelphia, Pa.	1785	
BROWN, JESSE	Philadelphia, Pa.	1813	
BROWN, JOHN	Philadelphia, Pa.	1785	J.B
BROWN, LIBERTY	Philadelphia, Pa.	1801	
BROWN, ROBERT	Baltimore, Md.	1830	RBROWN · R.BROWN · R.BROWN · R.BROWN&SON
BROWN, SAMUEL C.	New York, N.Y.	1850	S.BROWN · S.BROWN
BROWN, WM.	Albany, N.Y.	1849	
BROWN & SON, R.	Baltimore, Md.	1830	R.BROWN&SON
BROWNE & KIRBY	Philadelphia, Pa.	1825	BROWN&KIRBY
BROWNE & SEAL	Philadelphia, Pa.	1810	BROWNE&SEAL
BRUFF, CHARLES OLIVER	New York, N.Y.	1763	C.O.B
BRUFF, JOSEPH	Easton, Maryland	1790	IB
BRUFF, JOSEPH	Easton, Maryland	1730-1785	I·BRUFF

BRUFF, THOMAS
Easton, Maryland 1790

BRUSH, EDWARD
New York, N. Y, ...1774

BRYAN, PHILLIP
Philadelphia, Pa. 1802

BUCHE, PETER
New York, N. Y. 1795

BUCHOZ, I. R.
New York, N. Y. 1835

BUCKLEY & ANDERSON
Philadelphia, Pa. 1804

BUCKLEY, J. B.
Philadelphia, Pa. 1807

BUDDY, DANIEL
Philadelphia, Pa. 1769

BUEL, ABEL
New Haven, Conn. 1742-1825

BUEL, ADRIEN
New Haven, Conn. 1742-1825

BUEL, D. H.
Hartford, Conn. 1825

BUEL & GREENLEAF
New Haven, Conn. 1798

BUEL, JOHN
New Haven, Conn. 1789

BUEL & MIX
New Haven, Conn. 1783

BUEL, SAMUEL
Middletown, Conn. 1742-1819

BUICHLE, LEWIS
Baltimore, Md. 1798

BULL, CALEB
Hartford, Conn. 1840

BULL, EPAPHRAS
Boston, Mass. 1813

BULL, G. W.
East Hartford, Conn. 1840

BULL, MARTIN
Farmington, Conn. 1775

BULL & MORRISON
Hartford, Conn. 1780

BUMM, PETER
Philadelphia, Pa. 1814

BUMM & SHIPPER
Philadelphia, Pa. 1819

BUNKER, BENJAMIN
Providence, R. I. 1810

BURDICK, WILLIAM S.
New Haven, Conn. 1810

BURDOCK, GEORGE
Philadelphia, Pa. 1791

BURDOCK, NICHOLAS
Philadelphia, Pa. 1797

BURGALIE, J. P.
New York, N. Y. 1799

BURGER, DAVID I.
New York, New York ...1805

BURGER, JOHN
New York, New York ...1786

BURGER, JOHN
New York, New York 1767

BURGER, THOMAS
New York. New York 1805
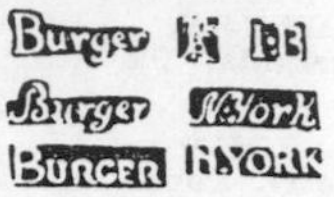

BURNAP, DANIEL
East Windsor, Conn. 1791

BURNETT, CHARLES A.
Alexandria, Va. 1793

BURNETT & RYDER
Philadelphia, Pa. 1795
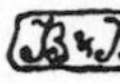

BURNHAM, ROBERT
New York, New York 1790

BURKLOE, SAMUEL
Philadelphia, Pa. 1795

BURNET, SAMUEL
Newark, N. J. 1796

BURNET & RYDER
Philadelphia, Pa. 1795

BURNETT, CHARLES A.
Alexandria, Va. 1793

BURNS, ANTHONY
Philadelphia, Pa. 1785

BURNS, JAMES
Philadelphia, Pa. 1810

BURNS, JOHN H.
New York, New York 1835

BUROT, ANDREW
Baltimore, Md. 1819

BURR, A. C.
Providence, R. I. 1815

BURR, CHRISTIAN A.
Providence, R. I. 1810

BURR, C. A. & CO.
Providence, R. I. 1820

BURR, E. & W.
Providence, R. I. 1793

BURR, EZEKIEL
Providence, R. I. 1764-1846
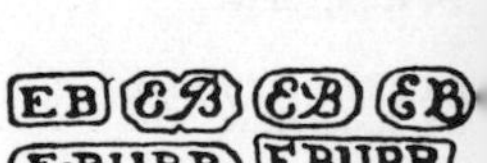

BURR & LEE
Providence, R.I. 1815

BURR, NATHANIEL
Fairfield, Conn. 1698-1784

BURR, WILLIAM
Providence, R. I. 1793

BURRILL, JOSEPH
Boston, Mass. 1823

BURRILL, SAMUEL
Boston, Mass. 1733

BURRILL, SAMUEL, JR.
Boston, Mass. 1829

BURRILL, THEOPHILUS
New London, Conn. 1736

BURROWS, WILLIAM
Philadelphia, Pa. 1831

BURT, BENJAMIN
Boston, Mass. 1691-1745

BURT, BENJAMIN
Boston, Mass. 1729-1803

BURT, JOHN
Boston, Mass. 1691-1745

BUSHNELL, PHINEAS
Guilford, Conn. 1762

BURT, WILLIAM
Boston, Mass. 1726-1752

BURTON, JACOB
Philadelphia, Pa. 1839

BURT, SAMUEL
Boston, Mass. 1724-1754

BUSSEY, BENJAMIN
Dedham, Mass. 1757-1842

BUSSEY, THOMAS
Baltimore, Maryland 1799

BUSWELL, JASON
Portsmouth, N. H. 1839

BUTLER, HENRY W.
Philadelphia, Pa. 1833

BUTLER, JAMES
Boston, Mass. 1713-1776

BUTLER, JOHN
Portland, Me. 1765

BUTLER, N.
Utica, New York 1800

BUTLER, N. H.
Philadelphia, Pa. 1837

BUTLER & LITTLE
Portland, Me. 1759

BUTLER & McCARTHY
Philadelphia, Pa. 1850

BUTLER WISE AND CO.
Philadelphia, Pa. 1845

BUZELL, J. L.
Unknown ....C 1750

BRYNE, JAMES
New York, New York 1789

BYRNE, JAMES
Philadelphia, Pa. 1784

C

CADY, SAMUEL
New York, New York 1792

CADY AND BACKUS
New York, New York 1792

CALDER AND COMPANY
Albany, New York 1830

CALDWELL, E.
New York, New York 1800

CAMERON, ALEXANDER
Albany, New York 1813

CAMMAN, ALEXANDER
Albany, New York 1813

CAMOIN
Philadelphia, Pa. 1797

CAMP, ELIAS
Bridgeport, Conn. 1825

CAMPBELL, CHRISTOPHER
New York, N.Y. 1808

CAMPBELL, JOHN W.
New York, New York 1814

CAMPBELL, R.
Baltimore, Md. 1824

CAMPBELL, R. & A.
Baltimore, Md. 1835

CAMPBELL, ROBERT
Baltimore, Md. 1819

CAMPBELL, R.
Baltimore, Md. 1824

CAMPBELL, THOMAS
New York, New York 1770

CAMPBELL, W.
Philadelphia, Pa. 1765

CANAVILLO, ANTONIO
New York, New York 1825

CANAVILLO, S.
New York, New York 1825

CANDEE & COMPANY, L. B.
Woodbury, Conn. 1830

CANDEE, LEWIS B.
Woodbury, Conn. 1825

CANDELL, CHARLES
New York, New York ... .1795

CANFIELD AND BROTHER
Baltimore, Md. 1830

CANFIELD AND FOOT
Middletown, Conn. 1798

CANFIELD AND HALL
New York, New York 1805

CANFIELD, SAMUEL
Middletown, Conn. 1780-1800

CANFIELD, SAMUEL
Lansingburg, N. Y. 1801

CANFIELD BROTHERS & CO.
Baltimore, Md. 1850

CANN, JOHN
New York, New York . 1835

CANON, GEORGE
Warwick, R. I. . . 1800

CANT, GODFREY
New York, N.Y. 1796

CAPELLE, J.
Stt. Louis, Mo. . . . 1850

CARALIN, PIERCE
New York, N.Y. 1804

CARBIN, THEODORE
Philadelphia, Pa. . . . 1758

CARGILL (Noted)

CARIO, MICHAEL
New York, N.Y. . . . 1728

CARIO, WILLIAM
New York, N.Y. 1721

CARIOLLE
New Orleans, La. 1822

CARLETON, GEORGE
New York, N.Y. 1810

CARLISLE, ABRAHAM
Philadelphia, Pa. 1791
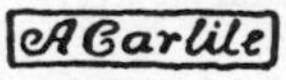

CARMAN, JOHN
Philadelphia, Pa. 1771

CARMAN, JOHN
New York, N.Y. 1800

CARMAN, SAMUEL
New York, N.Y. 1807

CARPENTER, CHARLES
Boston, Mass. 1807

CARPENTER, JOSEPH
Norwich, Conn. 1747-1804

CARREL, DANIEL
Philadelphia, Pa. 1806

CARRELL, JOHN & DANIEL
Philadelphia, Pa. 1785

CARRIBEC, PETER
Philadelphia, Pa. 1795

CARROL, JAMES
Albany, N.Y. 1834

CARROLL, JAMES
New York, N.Y. 1825

CARSON, DAVID
Albany, N.Y. 1849

CARSON, THOMAS
Albany, N.Y. 1815

CARSON & HALL
Albany, N.Y. 1813

CARY, LEWIS
Boston, Mass. 1820

CASE, GEORGE
East Hartford, Conn. 1779

CASEY, GIDEON
South Kingston, R.I. 1753

CASEY, GIDEON
Providence, R.I. 1726-1786

CASEY, SAMUEL
South Kingston, R.I. 1724-1773

CASHELL, RANDALL, H.
Philadelphia, Pa. . . . 1807

CASSEDY, ANDREW
Philadelphia, Pa. . . . 1840

CASTON, FRANCOISE
New York, N.Y. . . . 1804

CERNEAU, JOHN
New York, N.Y. . . . 1823

CERNEAU, JOSEPH
New York, N.Y. 1807

CERNEAU & CO.
New York, N.Y. . . . 1811

CHADWICK, THOMAS
Philadelphia, Pa. . . . 1809

CHALMERS, JAMES, Sr.
Annapolis, Md. 1749

CHALMERS, JOHN
Annapolis, Md. 1770

CHAMBERLAIN, WILSON
Portsmouth, N.H. 1839

CHAMPLIN, JOHN
New London, Conn. ..1745-1800

CHANDLER, STEPHEN
New York, N.Y. 1812

CHANDLESS, WILLIAM
New York, N.Y. 1846

CHAPIN, AARON
Hartford, Conn. 1790

CHAPIN, ALEXANDER
Hartford, Conn. 1838

CHARTERS, JAMES
New York, N.Y. 1844

CHARTERS, CANN & DUNN
New York,, N.Y. 1850

CHASE, J. D.
New York, N.Y. 1820

CHASE & EASTON
Brooklyn, N.Y. 1837

CHASLEY
Boston, Mass. 1764

CHAT, EASTON
Philadelphia, Pa. 1793

CHAT, LE SIEUR
New York, N.Y. 1790

CHAUDRONS & RASCH
Philadelphia, Pa. 1812

CHAUDRONS, SIMON
Philadelphia, Pa. 1798

Name	Location	Date	Marks
CHAUDRONS, SIMON & CO.	Philadelphia, Pa.	1807	SC&Co
CHENE, DANIEL	New York, N.Y.	1786	
CHERRY, JAMES	Philadelphia, Pa.	1824	
CHEVALIER, CLEMENT E.	Philadelphia, Pa.	1816	
CHEVALIER & TANGUAY	Philadelphia, Pa.	1816	
CHILDS, GEORGE H.	Philadelphia, Pa.	1828	
CHILDS, GEORGE K.	Philadelphia, Pa.	1837	
CHITRY, PETER	New York, N.Y.	1814	P.Chitry · P.Chitry
CHITTEN, EBENEZER	New Haven, Conn.	1747	EC · EC · E.CHITTENDEN
CHITTENDEN, BERIAH	New Haven, Conn.	1787	
CHITTENDEN, EBENEZER	New Haven, Conn.	1726-1812	
CHURCH, JOSEPH	New Haven, Conn.	1818	
CHURCH, JOSEPH	Hartford, Conn.	1794-1876	
CHURCH, RALPH	Buffalo, N.Y.	1832	
CHURCH & ROGERS	Hartford, Conn.	1825	CHURCH & ROGERS
CHURCHILL, JESSE	Boston, Mass.	1773-1819	I·CHURCHILL · CHURCHILL
CHURCHILL & TREADWELL	Boston, Mass.	1805	CHUrCHILL & Treadwell
CHURCHWELL, CHARLES	Philadelphia, Pa.	1781	
CLAPP, A. L.	New York, N.Y.	1802	A.L.CLAPP
CLAPP, PHILIP	New York, N.Y.	1802	
CLAPP & RIKER	New York, N.Y.	1802	
CLARK & ANTHONY	New York, N.Y.	1790	CLARK & ANTHONY
CLARK, ANDREW	New York, N.Y.	1744	
CLARK & BRO.	Norwalk, Conn.	1825	CLARK & BRO. NORWALK.
CLARK, C. & G.	Boston, Mass.	1833	
CLARK, CHARLES	Boston, Mass.	1798	
CLARK & COIT	Norwich, Conn.	1820	
CLARK, CURTIS	New York, N.Y.	1823	
CLARK, GABRIEL D.	Providence, R.I.	1824	G.D.CLARK
CLARK, GEORGE, C.	Providence, R.I.	1824	G.C.CLARK
CLARK, GEORGE D.	Baltimore, Md.	1826	G.D.CLARK
CLARK, HENRY	Philadelphia, Pa.	1813	
CLARK, I.	Boston, Mass.	1754	I·C · I CLARK · I.CLARK · I.CLARK · CLARK
CLARK, I. & H.	New York, N.Y.	1812	I&H·CLARK
CLARK, J. H.	New York, N.Y.	1812	J.H.CLARK
CLARK, JOSEPH	Danbury, Conn.	1791	JC · J:CLARK
CLARK, LEVI	Norwalk, Conn.	1801-1875	CLARK · NORWALK
CLARK, METCALF B.	Boston, Mass.	1835	
CLARK, PETER G.	New Haven, Conn.	1810	
CLARK, RICHARD	New York, N.Y.	1795	
CLARK, SAMUEL	Boston, Mass.	1681	
CLARK, THOMAS	Boston, Mass.	1783	T.Clark · T.Clark
CLARK, WILLIAM	New Milford, Conn.	1774	WC · WC
CLARKE, JAMES	Newport, R.I.	1734	
CLARKE, JONATHAN	Newport, R.I.	1734	IC · IC · J.Clarke · J:CLARKE · I·CLARKE
CLEVELAND, AARON	Norwich, Conn.	1820	AC · A·CLEVELAND
CLEVELAND, BENJAMIN	Norwich, Conn.	1760	B·CLEVELAND
CLEVELAND & POST	Norwich, Conn.	1815	C&P · C&P
CLEVELAND, WILLIAM	Norwich, Conn.	1770-1837	WC · Cleveland
CLEVELAND, WILLIAM	New London, Conn.	1770-1837	WC · WC
CLINE, CHARLES	Philadelphia, Pa.	1829	
CLUSTER, ISAAC D.	St. Louis, Mo.	1850	I.D.CLUSTER · ST.LOUIS.M
COAN, DANIEL B.	New York, N.Y.	1789	D·C

COBB, EPHRAIM
Boston, Mass. 1708-1777

COBURN, JOHN
Boston, Mass. 1765

COBURN, JOHN
Boston, Mass. 1725-1803

CODDINGTON, JOHN
Newport, R.I. 1690-1743

CODMAN, WILLARD
Boston, Mass. 1839

CODNER, JOHN
Boston, Mass. 1754-1782

COE & UPTON
New York, N.Y. 1840

COEN, DANIEL BLOOM
New York, N.Y. 1787

COFFMAN, WILLIAM
Philadelphia, Pa. 1839

COGSWELL, H.
Boston, Mass. 1760

COHEN, BARROW A.
New York, N.Y. 1825

COHEN, WILLIAM
Alexandria, Va., D.C. 1833

COIGNARD, LOUIS
New York, N.Y. 1805

COIT, E.
Norwich, Conn. 1839

COIT & MANSFIELD
Norwich, Conn. 1816
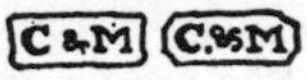

COIT, THOMAS CHESTER
Norwich, Conn. 1812

COLE, ALBERT
New York, N.Y. 1844

COLE, EBENEZER
New York, N.Y. 1818

COLE, JACOB
Philadelphia, Pa. 1785

COLE, JOHN
Boston, Mass. 1686

COLEMAN, B.
Burlington, N.J. 1785

COLEMAN, C. C.
Burlington, N.J. 1835

COLEMAN, JOHN
New York, N.Y. 1814

COLEMAN, NATHANIEL
Burlington, N.J. 1776

COLEMAN, S.
Burlington, N.J. 1805

COLES, JOHN A.
New York, N.Y. 1830

COLEY, SIMEON
New York, N.Y. 1767

COLEY, WILLIAM
New York, N.Y. 1801
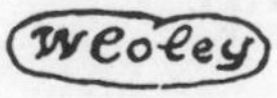

COLLET, J. B.
New York, N.Y. 1805

COLLETTE, LAMBERT
Buffalo, N.Y. 1835

COLLINS, ARNOLD
Newport, R.I. 1690

COLLINS & J. W. FORBES
New York, N.Y. 1825

COLLINS, S.
Utica, N.Y. 1840

COLLINS, W. & L.
New York, N.Y. 1830

COLNER, JOHN
New York, N.Y. 1818

COLONEL, JOHN
Philadelphia, Pa. 1804

COLTON & BALDWIN
New York, N.Y. 1819

COLTON & COLLINS
New York, N.Y. 1832

COLTON, LEVI
New York, N.Y. 1825

COLTON, OREN
New York, N.Y. 1818

COLWELL & LAWRENCE
Albany, N.Y. 1850

CONEY, JOHN
Boston, Mass. 1655-1722

CONNELL, M.
Philadelphia, Pa. 1800

CONNING, J.
New York, N.Y. 1840

CONNOR, JOHN H.
New York, N.Y. 1812

CONNOR, JOHN W.
Norwalk, Conn. 1836

CONYERS, JOSEPH
Boston, Mass. 1708

CONYERS, RICHARD
Boston, Mass. 1688

COOK, JOHN
New York, N.Y. 1795

COOK, JOHN
New York, N.Y. 1797-1805

COOK & COMPANY
New York, N.Y. 1797

COOKE, JOSEPH
Philadelphia, Pa. 1785

COOKE & COMPANY
Philadelphia, Pa. 1785

Name	Place	Date	Marks
OOLIDGE, JOSEPH, Jr.	Boston, Mass.	1770	Coolidge · Coolidge
OOPER	Philadelphia, Pa.	1816	
OOPER, B.	New York, N.Y.	1814	
OOPER, B. & J.	New York, N.Y.	1810	
OOPER, FRANCIS W.	New York, N.Y.	1846	F.W.C. N.Y · F.W.COOPER.
OOPER, JOHN	New York, N.Y.	1814	
OOPER, JOSEPH	New York, N.Y.	1770	
OPP, JOSEPH	New London, Conn.	1757	J·COPP
OPP, NATHANIEL P.	Albany, N.Y.	1834	
ORLEY, WILLIAM	New York, N.Y.	1811	
ORNELISON, CORNELIUS	New York, N.Y.	1711	
ORNELIUS, CHRISTIAN	Philadelphia, Pa.	1810	C CORNELIUS
ORNWELL, N.	Danbury, Conn.	1776-1837	N.CORWELL
ORNELL, WALTER	Providence, R.I.	1780	CORNELL
ORRIN, JOSIAH	Philadelphia, Pa.	1823	
OURCELLE, HILAIRE	New Orleans, La.	1822	
OUVERTIE, LOUIS	New Orleans, La.	1822	L'COUVERTIE
OVERLY, THOMAS	Newport, R.I.	1765	T.COVERLY
OVERLY, THOMAS	Newburyport, Mass.	1730-1800	T·COVERLY
OWAN, WILLIAM D.	Philadelphia, Pa.	1808	W.COWAN
OWELL, WM.	Boston, Mass.	1682-1736	WC · WC · WC · W.C · W:Cowell (marks shared with the next entry)
OWELL, WILLIAM J.	Boston, Mass.	1736	
OWELL, WILLIAM, Jr.	Boston, Mass.	1713-1761	W:Cowell · W.Cowell
OWLES, RALPH	Cleveland, Ohio	1850	COWLES
OX, J. & I.	New York, N.Y.	1844	J&I COX · J&I COX
OX, JOHN	Philadelphia, Pa.	1818	
CRAFT, STEPHEN	New York, N.Y.	1811	
CRAIG, JAMES	Williamsburg, Va.	1750	
CRANDALL, BENJAMIN	Providence, R.I.	1824	
CRANDALL, BENJAMIN	Portsmouth, N.H.	1839	
CRANE, STEPHEN M.	New York, N.Y.	1813	
CRANSTON, SAMUEL	Newport, R.I.	1684	
CRAWFORD, JOHN	New York, N.Y.	1820	J.CRAWFORD
CRAWFORD, JOHN	New York, N.Y.	1815	J.CRAWFORD · J.Crawford · J.Crawford
CREW, J. T.	Albany, N.Y.	1849	
CRITTENDEN, NEWTON E.	Cleveland, Ohio	1839	
CRONE, HENRY	Cleveland, Ohio	1780	
CROSBY, JONATHAN	Boston, Mass.	1743-1769	JC
CROSBY, SAMUEL T.	Boston, Mass.	1850	
CROSS, WILLIAM	Boston, Mass.	1712	WC
CROUCKESHANKS, ALEX.	Boston, Mass.	1768	
CUMMINGS, DAVID B.	Philadelphia, Pa.	1811	
CURRIER & TROTT	Boston, Mass.	1836	Currier&Trott
CURRIN, JOSEPH	Philadelphia, Pa.	1829	
CURRY, JOHN	Philadelphia, Pa.	1831	J.CURRY
CURRY & PRESTON	Philadelphia, Pa.	1831	C&P · CURRY&PRESTON
CURTIS, CANDEE & STILES	Woodbury, Conn.	1831	C.C.&S · CURTISS·CANDEE & STILES
CURTIS, DANIEL	Woodbury, Conn.	1831	
CURTIS, JOEL	Wolcott, Conn.	1810	
CURTIS, LEWIS	Farmington, Conn.	1797	L·CURTIS
CURTIS, THOMAS	New York, N.Y.	1835	
CURTIS & CANDEE	Woodbury, Conn.	1826	

Name	Location	Date	Marks
CURTISS, CANDEE & STILES	Woodbury, Conn.	1825	
CURTISS & DUNING	Woodbury, Conn.	1828	CURTISS & DUNING
CURTISS & STILES	Woodbury, Conn.	1835	
CUSHMAN, ISAAC	Boston, Mass.	1823	
CUTLER, A.	Boston, Mass.	1820	A.CUTLER · BOSTON
CUTLER, E.	New Haven, Conn.	1820	E CUTLER
CUTLER, J. N.	Albany, N.Y.	1849	
CUTLER, RICHARD	New Haven, Conn.	1760	
CUTLER, RICHARD, Jr.	New Haven, Conn.	1800	
CUTLER, RICHARD & SONS	New Haven, Conn.	1800	
CUTLER, SILLIMAN, WARD	New Haven, Conn.	1767	
CUTLER, WILLIAM	New Haven, Conn.	1806	
CUTTER WILLIAM	Portland, Me.	1823	

D

Name	Location	Date	Marks
DAGGETT, HENRY	New Haven, Conn.	1763	
DALLON, JOHN	Philadelphia, Pa.	1791	
DALLY, PHILLIP	New York, N.Y.	1779	PD · PD
DALLY & HALSEY	New York, N.Y.	1787	
DANE, THOMAS	Boston, Mass.	1723-1796	T.DANE · T DANE
DANIEL, PERRY O.	Unknown	1830	PERRY O.DANIEL
DANIELS, CHARLES W.	Troy, N.Y.	1836	
DARGEE, JOHN	New York, N.Y.	1810	
DARROW, DAVID	New York, N.Y.	1825	
DAUBAYSON, VICTOIRE	Philadelphia, Pa.	1820	
DAUCE, SIMON	Philadelphia, Pa.	1798	
DAVENPORT, JONATHAN	Baltimore, Md.	1789-1801	I·D
DAVENPORT, ROBERT	Philadelphia, Pa.	1808	
DAVENPORT, SAMUEL	Milton, Mass.	1741	
DAVERNE, JOHN	Baltimore, Md.	1799	
DAVID & DUPUY	Philadelphia, Pa.	1792	
DAVID, JOHN	Philadelphia, Pa.	1736-1794	J.D · ID · ID · I·DAVID · I.DAVID · I DAVID
DAVID, JOHN, Jr.	Philadelphia, Pa.	1792	JD · JD · JD
DAVID, LEWIS A.	Philadelphia, Pa.	1825	
DAVID, PETER	Philadelphia, Pa.	1707-1755	PD · PD
DAVIS & BABBITT	Providence, R.I.	1820	
DAVIS & BROWN	Boston, Mass.	1802	DAVIS & BROWN
DAVIS, E.	Newburyport, Mass.	1775	ED · EDavis · EDAVIS · EDavis
DAVIS, JOSHUA, G.	Boston, Mass.	1796	I DAVIS
DAVIS, PALMER & CO.	Boston, Mass.	1841	Davis Palmer & Co · Davis, Palmer & Co.
DAVIS, SAMUEL	Providence, R.I.	1801	S.DAVIS
DAVIS, SAMUEL	Boston, Mass.	1813	DAVIS
DAVIS, T. A.	Boston, Mass.	1824	T·A·DAVIS · T.A.DAVIS
DAVIS & WATSON	Boston, Mass.	1815	D&W · DAVIS WATSON & CO
DAVIS, WILLIAM	Boston, Mass.	1823	
DAVISON, BRAZILLIA	Norwich, Conn.	1765	
DAVISON, CHARLES	Norwich, Conn.	1805	C DAVISON · C.DAVISON
DAVY, ADAM	Philadelphia, Pa.	1795	
DAWES, WILLIAM	Boston, Mass.	1766	
DAWS, R.	Unknown	1800	R·DAWS
DAWSON, JOHN	New York, N.Y.	1769	
DAWSON, WILLIAM	Philadelphia, Pa.	1763	
DEANE, JAMES	New York, N.Y.	1760	
DEAS, DAVID	Philadelphia, Pa.	1831	

DECKER, J.
New York, N.Y. 1830

DELAGROW, ANDREW
Philadelphia, Pa. 1795

DELANO, JABEZ
New Bedford, Mass. 1784

DE LAROUX, JOHN
New Orleans, La. 1822

DELAUNEY, JEAN
New York, N.Y. 1805

DEMILT, ANDREW
New York, N.Y. 1805

DEMMOCK, JOHN
Boston, Mass. 1798

DEMORSY, JEAN
New Orleans, La. 1822

DEMORT, JOHN
New York, N.Y. 1810

DEMORT, LUCIEN
New York, N.Y. 1810

DENISE, JOHN
New York, N.Y. 1798

DENISE, JOHN
Philadelphia, Pa. 1698

DENISE, JOHN & TUNIS
South Kingtson, R.I. 1770

DENISON, T.
Uknown 1790
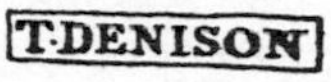

DENNIS, EBENEZER
Hartford, Conn. 1782

DENNIS & FITCH
Troy, N.Y. 1836

DENNIS, GEORGE, Jr.
Norwich, Conn. 1770

DE PARISIEN, OTTO PAUL
New York, N.Y. 1763
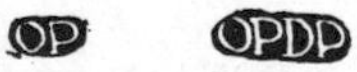

DE PERRIZANG, OTTO
New York, N.Y. 1786

DE PEYSTER, WILLIAM
New York, N.Y. 1732

DE RIEMER, CORNELIUS B.
Ithaca, N.Y. 1804

DE RIEMER, JACOB R.
New York, N.Y. 1830

DE RIEMER & MEAD
Ithaca, N.Y. 1831

DE RIEMER, PETER
New York, N.Y. 1738-1814

DESHON, DANIEL
New London, Conn. ..1697-1781

DE SPIEGEL, JACOBUS VAN
New York, N.Y. 1668-1708

DESQUET & TANGUY
Philadelphia, Pa. 1805

DESURET, LEWIS
Philadelphia, Pa. 1799

DEVERELL, JOHN
Boston, Mass. 1764-1813
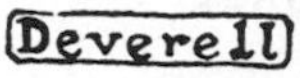

DEVERELL, JOHN
Boston, Mass. 1785

DEXTER, JOHN
Marboro, Mass. 1756

DE YOUNG, MICHAEL
Baltimore, Md. 1816

DICKERSON, H. & CO.
Philadelphia, Pa. 1815

DICKERSON, JOHN
Morristown, Mass. 1778

DICKINSON, JONATHAN
Philadelphia, Pa. 1794

DICKINSON & ROBINSON
Philadelphia, Pa. 1796

DIMMOCK, JOHN
New York, N.Y. 1801

DIMOND, ISAAC M.
New York, N.Y. 1830

DISBROW, G. E.
New York, N.Y. 1825

DIXWELL, BASIL
Boston, Mass. 1732

DIXWELL, JOHN
Boston, Mass. 1680-1725

DOANE, JOSHUA
Providence, R. I. 1753

DOBBS
New York, N.Y. 1788

DOBLEMAN, FREDERICK
Philadelphia, Pa. 1813

DOBLEMAN, F. F. G.
Philadelphia, Pa. 1810

DODGE, BENJAMIN
Boston, Mass. 1836

DODGE, EZEKIEL
New York, N.Y. 1792

DODGE, EZRA
New London, Conn. 1787

DODGE, JOHN
New York, N.Y. 1790

DODGE, NEHEMIAH
Providence, R.I. 1795

DODGE, SERIL
Providence, R.I. 1765-1803

DOLE, D. N.
Portsmouth, N.H. 1805
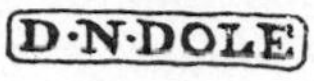

Name	Place	Date	Marks
DOLE, E. G.	Portsmouth, N.H.	1820	EGDole
DOLER, DANIEL	Boston, Mass.	1765	
DONALON, JOHN W.	Boston, Mass.	1823	
DONOVAN, WILLIAM	Philadelphia, Pa.	1784	W.DONOVAN
DONTREMEI, C.	Philadelphia, Pa.	1805	
DOOLITTLE, AMOS	New Haven, Conn.	1754-1832	AD AD
DOOLITTLE, ENOS	Hartford, Conn.	1781	
DORAN, JOHN	Cincinnati, Ohio	1826	
DORGY, PETER	Philadelphia, Pa.	1816	
DORSEY, JOSHUA	Philadelphia, Pa.	1796	I·DORSEY
DORSEY, SAMUEL	Philadelphia, Pa.	1804	
DORSEY, SIMON	Philadelphia, Pa.	1820	
DORSON, JOSHUA	Philadelphia, Pa.	1802	
DOSTER, MICHAEL	Philadelphia, Pa.	1831	
DOUGLAS, ALEXANDER	New York, N.Y.	1792	
DOUGLAS, CANTWELL	Baltimore, Md.	1799	
DOUGLAS, JAMES, W.	Philadelphia, Pa.	1791	
DOUGLAS, ROBERT	New London, Conn.	1776	RD RD R·D
DOUGLASS & HECKMAN	Philadelphia, Pa.	1837	
DOUGLASS, JAMES	New York, N.Y.	1800	JDougles
DOUGLASS, JEREMOTT W.	Philadelphia, Pa.	1790	Douglass
DOUGLASS, JOHN	Philadelphia, Pa.	1840	
DOUTIEMER, CULE	Philadelphia, Pa.	1791	
DOWIG, CHRISTOPHER	Philadelphia, Pa.	1765	
DOWIG, GEORGE	Baltimore, Md.	1724-1807	G·D
DOWIG, GEORGE	Philadelphia, Pa.	1770	GD GD GD
DOWNES, J.	Philadelphia, Pa.	1770	J.Downes JDOWNES J.Downes
DOWNING, G. R.	New York, N.Y.	1810	GRD N·YORK
DOWNING & PHELPS	New York, N.Y.	1810	D&P DOWNING&PHELPS
DRAPER, J.	Wilmington, Del.	1816	J.DRAPER
DREWRY, GEORGE	Philadelphia, Pa.	1763	GD
DRINKER, JOHN	New York, N.Y.	1835	
DROWN, T. P.	Boston, Mass.	1790	T.P.DROWN T P DROWN
DROWNE, BENJAMIN	Portsmouth, N.H.	1800	
DROWNE, SAMUEL	Portsmouth, N.H.	1749-1815	S·D S·Drowne
DROWNE, SHEM	Boston, Mass.	1749	SD
DRUMONT, ANTOINE	New York, N.Y.	1808	
DUBOIS, ABRAHAM	Philadelphia, Pa.	1777	AD A.DUBOIS A·DUBOIS
DUBOIS, A., Sr. & Jr.	New York, N.Y.	1803	
DUBOIS, JOSEPH	New York, N.Y.	1790	J·DUBOIS I·DUBOIS
DUBOIS, TUNIS, D.	New York, N.Y.	1799	T·D·D T·D·DUBOIS
DUBOIS & CO.	New York, N.Y.	1803	
DUCHE, RENE	New York, N.Y.	1795	
DUCHE & DONARD	Philadelphia, Pa.	1820	
DUDLEY, BENJAMIN	Birmingham, Ga.	1768	
DUFFEL, JAMES	New York, N.Y.	1801	I·DUFFEL
DUHME & CO.	St. Louis, Mo.	1850	DUHME
DUMMER, JEREMIAH	Boston, Mass.	1645-1718	ID ID
DU MORTE, JOHN	Philadelphia, Pa.	1796	
DUMOURIER, JOSEPH	Philadelphia, Pa.	1816	
DUMOUTET, JOHN BAPTISTE	Philadelphia, Pa.	1793	DUMOUTET DUMOUTET
DUNDAS, PRATT	Philadelphia, Pa.	1837	

DUNKERLY, JOSEPH
Boston, Mass. 1787

DUNLEVY, ROBERT
Philadelphia, Pa. 1831

DUNN, CARY
New York, N.Y. 1764

DUNN, DAVID
New York, N.Y. 1835

DUNN & SON
New York, N.Y. 1787

DUNSCOMB, DENNIS
New York, N.Y. 1765

DUON, H.
Baltimore, Md. 1819

DUPUY, DANIEL
Philadelphia, Pa. 1719-1807

DUPUY, DANIEL, Jr.
Philadelphia, Pa. 1782

DUPUY, JOHN
Philadelphia, Pa. 1770

DUPUY, JOHN & DANIEL, Jr.
Philadelphia, Pa. 1783

DUPUY & SONS
Philadelphia, Pa. 1784

DURAND, JOHN
New York, N.Y. 1835

DURANDEAU, JOHN
New York, N.Y. 1835

DURGIN, WILLIAM B.
Concord, N.H. 1850

DUSENBERRY, W. C.
New York, N.Y. 1830

DUTEUS, CHARLES J.
Philadelphia, Pa. 1751

DUTEUS & HARPER
Philadelphia, Pa. 1755

DUVALIER
Unknown ....c. 1800

DUYCKINCK, DANIEL
New York, N.Y. 1798

DWIGHT, TIMOTHY
Boston, Mass. 1645-1691

E

EAGLES & MORRIS
New York, N.Y. 1799

EAMES, JOSHUA
Boston, Mass. 1828

EASTON, J.
Nantucket, Mass. 1828

EASTON, NATHANIEL
Nantucket, Mass. 1780

EASTON & SANFORD
Nantucket, Mass. 1830

EASTWICK, THOMAS
Boston, Mass. 1743

EATON, TIMOTHY
Philadelphia, Pa. 1793

EAYRES, THOMAS S.
Boston, Mass. 1760-1803

EDGAR, JOHN
New York, N.Y. 1807

EDMECHAT, CLAUDE
New York, N.Y. 1790

EDWARDS, ABRAHAM
Ashby, Mass. 1763

EDWARDS, ANDREW
Boston, Mass. 1796

EDWARDS, CALVIN
Ashby, Mass. 1710

EDWARDS, JOHN
Boston, Mass. 1700

EDWARDS, JOSEPH, Jr.
Boston, Mass. 1707-1777

EDWARDS, SAMUEL
Boston, Mass. 1705-1762

EDWARDS, SAMUEL
Natick, Mass. 1726-1783

EDWARDS, THOMAS
Boston, Mass. 1701-1755

EDWARDS, THOMAS
New York, N.Y. 1731

EMBREE
Unknown ....c. 1790

ELDERKIN, ALFRED
Killingsworth, Conn. 1792

ELDERKIN, ELISHA
New Haven, Conn. 1777

ELDERKIN & STANIFORD
Windom, Conn. 1790

ELLIOTT, JOHN A.
Sharon, Conn. 1815

ELLIOTT, JOSEPH
New Castle, Delaware 1768

ELLIS, LEWIS W.
Philadelphia, Pa. 1837

ELLISON, PETER
New York, N.Y. 1792

ELLSWORTH, DAVID
Windsor, Conn. 1772

ELTONHEAD, THOMAS
Baltimore, Md. 1835

EMERY, STEPHEN
Boston, Mass. 1746-1789

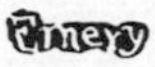

EMERY, STEPHEN
Boston, Mass. 1725-1801

Name	Location	Date	Marks
EMERY, THOMAS KNOX	Boston, Mass.	1781-1815	T·Emery · T·K·E · T·K·EMERY · T·Emery
EMERY & COMPANY	New York, N.Y.	1798	
ENGLAND, GEORGE	New York, N.Y.	1800	
ENGLAND, WILLIAM	Philadelphia, Pa.	1717	
ENSIGN	Unknown	c. 1800	ENSIGN
EOFF & CONNOR	New York, N.Y.	1833	J.H.CONNOR & G.EOFF
EOFF, EDGAR W.	New York, N.Y.	1785-1858	EME
EOFF, GARRET	New York, N.Y.	1785-1858	G.EOFF · G.Eoff
EOFF & HOWELL	New York, N.Y.	1805	EOFF & HOWELL
EOFF & MOORE	New York, N.Y.	1835	G.EOFF · J.C.MOORE
EOFF & PHYFE	New York, N.Y.	1844	E&P
EOFF & SHEPARD	New York, N.Y.	1825	E&S
EOLLES & DAY	Hartford, Conn.	1825	EOLLES & DAY HARTFORD
EPPS, ELLERY	Boston, Mass.	1808	
EQUER & AQUIMAC	New York, N.Y.	1816	
ERWIN, ANDREW	Philadelphia, Pa.	1837	
ERWIN, HENRY	Philadelphia, Pa.	1817	H.ERWIN · H.ERWIN
ERWIN, JOHN	New York, N.Y.	1815	J.ERWIN
ESTEVA, HAYACINTH	New York, N.Y.	1804	
ETTER, B.	Unknown	c. 1780	B·ETTER
ETTING, BENJAMIN	New York, N.Y.	1769	
EVANS, HENRY	New York, N.Y.	1820	HENRY EVANS
EVANS, JOHN	New York, N.Y.	1830	EVANS
EVANS, ROBERT	Boston, Mass.	1768-1812	RE · R·E · R.EVANS · EVANS · EVANS
EVERITT, JESSE	New York, N.Y.	1811	
EVERSTEN, JOHN	Albany, N.Y.	1813	
EWAN, JOHN	Charleston, S.C.	1800	J.EWAN

F

Name	Location	Date	Marks
FABER, WILLIAM	Philadelphia, Pa.	1837	
FABER & HOOVER	Philadelphia, Pa.	1837	
FAGALER, GEORGE M.	Philadelphia, Pa.	1808	
FAIRCHILD, JAMES L.	New York, N.Y.	1830	
FAIRCHILD, JOSEPH	New Haven, Conn.	1824	
FAIRCHILD, ROBERT	Durham, Conn.	1703-1794	R·F · R.FAIRCHILD · RF · RF · R·FAIRCHILD
FARIS, CHARLES	Boston, Mass.	1790	Cs Faris · Chas Faris · Chas Faris · Cs Faris
FARIS, WILLIAM	Annapolis, Md.	1728-1804	W·F · W·F · W.F.
FARLEY, CHARLES	Portland, Me.	1812	C.FARLEY · FARLEY
FARNAM, HENRY	Boston, Mass.	1799	H·FARNAM
FARNAM, R. & H.	Boston, Mass.	1807	R&H·FARNAM
FARNAM, RUFUS	Boston, Mass.	1796	R.FARNAM
FARNAM, THOMAS	Boston, Mass.	1836	Th: Farnam
FARNUM & WARD	Boston, Mass.	1810	FARNAM & WARD
FARNHAM & OWEN	Unknown	1810	
FARR, JOHN C.	Boston, Mass.	1812	J.C:FARR · JOHN C FARR
FARRINGTON & HUNNEWELL	Boston, Mass.	1830	F&H · FARRINGTON & HUNNEWELL
FARRINGTON, JOHN	Boston, Mass.	1826	
FAULKNER, J. W.	New York, N.Y.	1835	J.W.F · J.W.FAULKNER · 37 P[illegible]
FELLOWS, ABRAHAM	Newport, R.I.	1826	FELLOWS
FELLOWS & GREEN	Maine	1825	FELLOWS & GREEN
FELLOWS, JOHN F.	Portsmouth, N.H.	1824	
FELLOWS & STORM	Albany, N.Y.	1839	FELLOWS & STORM
FENNO, J.	Unknown	1825	J.Fenno
FERGUSON, JOHN	Philadelphia, Pa.	1802	

Name	Place	Date	Marks
FERRIER, JOHN	New Orleans, La.	1802	
FERRIS, BENJAMIN	New York, N.Y.	1816	
FESSENDEN	Newport, R.I.	1845	FESSENDEN PURE SILVER
FEURT, JETER	New York, N.Y.	1731	PF
FIELDING, GEORGE	New York, N.Y.	1731	GF
FIELDS, SAMUEL	Philadelphia, Pa.	1816	
FIFIELD, JOHN S.	Westerly, R.I.		
FINCH, HIRAM	Albany, N.Y.	1840	
FINEWELL, SAMUEL	New York, N.Y.	1835	
FIRENG, J. P.	Burlington, N.J.	1810	J.P.FIRENG BURLINGTON NJ
FISHER, JAMES	New York, N.Y.	1821	
FISHER, THOMAS	Philadelphia, Pa.	1797	T.Fisher T.FISHER TFisher
FITCH, ALLEN	New Haven, Conn.	1808	
FITCH, D. M.	New Haven, Conn.	1840	D.M.FITCH
FITCH & HOBART	New Haven, Conn.	1811	
FITCH, JOHN	Trenton, N.J.	1769-1875	J.FITCH
FITE, JOHN	Baltimore, Md.	1810	I·FITE
FLAGG, JOSIAH	Boston, Mass.	1765	
FLAGG, JOSIAH, Jr.	Boston, Mass.	1810	
FLETCHER & BENNETT	Philadelphia, Pa.	1837	
FLETCHER, CHARLES	Philadelphia, Pa.	1817	
FLETCHER & BARDINER	Philadelphia, Pa.	1812	F&G. F&G.
FLETCHER, THOMAS	Philadelphia, Pa.	1813	T.FLETCHER PHILAD·
FLING, GEORGE	Philadelphia, Pa.	1749	
FLOTT, LEWIS	Baltimore, Md.	1817	
FOLLOPPE, A. A.	Boston, Mass.	1808	
FOLSOM, JOHN	Albany, N.Y.	1781	
FOOTE, WILLIAM	Middletown, Conn.; East Haddam, Conn.	1796	
FORBES, ABRAHAM G.	New York, N.Y.	1769	AGF AF N.YORK
FORBES, BENJAMIN G.	New York, N.Y.	1817	
FORBES, COLLINS V. G.	New York, N.Y.	1816	CVGF
FORBES, C. V. G. & SON	New York, N.Y.	1835	FORBES&SON
FORBES, G.	New York, N.Y.	1816	
FORBES, G. & J. W.	New York, N.Y.	1810	
FORBES, GARRET	New York, N.Y.	1808	G.FORBES
FORBES, I. W.	New York, N.Y.	1805	
FORBES, JOHN W.	New York, N.Y.	1805	IWF NY IWF NY I.W.FORBES I.W.FORBES
FORBES & SON, C. V. G.	New York, N.Y.	1835	WF NEW YORK
FORBES, WILLIAM	New York, N.Y.	1830	W.FORBES NY N.YORK
FORBES, WILLIAM G.	New York, N.Y.	1773	W.FORBES W.G.Forbes WGForbes WGForbes W.G.FORBES N·YORK
FORCE, JABEZ W.	New York, N.Y.	1819	J.W.FORCE
FORD, SAMUEL	Philadelphia, Pa.	1797	SF
FOREST, ALEXANDER	Balitmore, Md.	1802	
FORMAN, BENONI B.	Albany, N.Y.	1813	
FORREST, ALEXANDER	Baltimore, Md.	1802	
FORTUNE, ANTHONY	Philadelphia, Pa.	1767	
FOSTER, ABRAHAM	Philadelphia, Pa.	1816	
FOSTER, G.	Salem, Mass.	1838	
FOSTER, I.	Unknown	1761	
FOSTER, JOHN	New York, N.Y.	1811	J.FOSTER
FOSTER, JOSEPH	Boston, Mass.	1760-1839	FOSTER I·FOSTER
FOSTER, N. & J.	Newburyport, R.I.	1823	

Name	Location	Date	Marks
FOSTER & RICHARDS	New York, N. Y.	1815	J·F T.RICHARDS
FOSTER, SAMUEL	Boston, Mass.	1676-1702	
FOSTER, THOMAS	Newburyport, Mass.	1823	T.FOSTER T.FOSTER
FOURNIQUET, LOUIS	New York, N. Y.	1795	Fourniquet Fourniquet
FOURNIQUET & WHEATLEY	New York, N. Y.	1817	
FOWLER, GILBERT	New York, N. Y.	1825	
FRADGLEY, THOMAS	New York, N. Y.	1797	
FRANCIS, JULIUS C.	Middletown, Conn.	1807	
FRANCIS, NATHANIEL	New York, N. Y.	1804	N FRANCIS FRANCIS
FRANCIS, NATHANIEL	New York, N. Y.	1819	NFRANCIS
FRANCISCUS, GEORGE	Baltimore, Md.	1776	GFRANCISCUS
FRANK, JACOB	Philadelphia, Pa.	1793	J·FRANK
FRANKS, WILLIAM	Philadelphia, Pa.	1839	
FRASER, WILLIAM	Philadelphia, Pa.	1735	
FREEBORN, N.	Unknown	C 1800	N·FREEBORN
FREEMAN, WILLIAM	Philadelphia, Pa.	1839	
FREEMANS, J. M. & CO.	Unknown	C 1800	J.M.FREEMANS & Co
FRINTH, JAMES	Philadelphia, Pa.	1840	
FROBISHER, BENJAMIN C.	Boston, Mass.	1836	B.C.Frobisher. FROBISHER
FROST & MUMFORD	Providence, R. I.	1810	F.&M.
FROTHERINGHAM, EBENEZER	Boston, Mass.	1756-1814	
FRYER, JOHN W.	Albany, N. Y.	1784	
FUETER, DANIEL C.	New York, N. Y.	1756	DCF N YORK
FUETER, DAVID	New York, N. Y.	1789	
FUETER, LEWIS	New York, N. Y.	1775	L.FUETER N. YORK
FULLER, ALEXANDER	New York, N. Y.	1811	
FURIS, LEWIS	New York, N. Y.	1810	Furis

G

Name	Location	Date	Marks
GADLEY & JOHNSON	Albany, N. Y.	1849	
GAFKINS, J.	Providence, R. I.	1832	
GAITHER, GREENBERG	District of Columbia	1834	
GALE & HAYDEN	New York, N. Y.	1846	G&H
GALE, JOHN	New York, N. Y.	1816	J.GALE
GALE, JOHN	New York, N. Y.	1819	J.L.G. J.L.GALE
GALE, JOHN S.	New York, N. Y.	1820	J.GALE
GALE & MOSELY	New York, N. Y.	1830	G&M
GALE & STICKLER	New York, N. Y.	1823	G&S
GALE, WILLIAM	New York, N. Y.	1816	W.G
GALE, WILLIAM, JR.	New York, N. Y.	1823	WM.GALE JR
GALE & SON, WM.	New York, N. Y.	1823	W.G&S
GALE & WILLIS	New York, N. Y.	1840	GALE&WILLIS
GALE, WOOD & HUGHES	New York, N. Y.	1835	G.W&H
GALLOP, CHRISTOPHER	Ledyard, Conn.	1790	
GALT, SAMUEL	Williamsburg, Va.	1749	
GARDINER, B.	New York, N. Y.	1829	
GARDINER, BALDWIN	Philadelphia, Pa.	1814	B·G B.GARDINER B·G&CO
GARDINER & CO.	New York, N. Y.	1836	B.GARDINER&CO. B.G.&CO
GARDINER, JOHN	New London, Conn.	1734-1776	JG IG J:GARDNER
GARDINER, SIDNEY	Philadelphia, Pa.	1810	
GARDINER, JOHN J.	Boston, Mass.	1730-1776	
GARLLOW, SHAVELIER	Philadelphia, Pa.	1813	
GARNER, JOHN	Cincinnati, Ohio	1825	
GARRE, S.	New York, N. Y.	1825	SG SGARRE

Silversmith	Location	Date	Marks
GERREN, ANTHONY	Philadelphia, Pa.	1813	
GARRETT, P.	Philadelphia, Pa.	1811	P.GARRETT
GARRETT, T. C.	Philadelphia, Pa.	1815	
GARRETT, T. C. & CO.	Philadelphia, Pa.	1815	T.C.GARRETT & CO
GARRISON, JOHN	New York, N.Y.	1825	
GARROW & DORSEY	Baltimore, Md.	1800	
GASKINS, J.	Unknown	1760	
GASKINS, W. W.	Providence, R. I.	1830	WWG
GATHAM, WILLIAM	Philadelphia, Pa.	1802	
GAY, CHARLES	Baltimore, Md.	1779	
GAY, NATHANIEL	Boston, Mass.	1664	
GEE, JOSEPH	Philadelphia, Pa.	1785	
GEFFROY, NICHOLAS	Newport, R.I.	1761-1839	N GEFFROY · GEFFROY · N.GEFFROY
GELEY, PETER	Philadelphia, Pa.	1793	
GELSTON & CO.	New York, N.Y.	1837	GELSTON&CO
GELSTON, GEORGE S.	New York, N. Y.	1833	G.S.GELSTON
GELSTON & GOULD	Baltimore, Md.	1819	
GELSTON, HUGH	Baltimore, Md.	1794-1873	HU.GELSTON · GELSTON
GELSTON, LADD & CO.	New York, N. Y.	1836	GELSTON LADD & CO
GELSTON & TREADWELL	New York, N. Y.	1836	
GEORGEON, BERNARD	Philadelphia, Pa.	1797	
GERMON, J. D.	Philadelphia, Pa.	1819	
GERMON, JOHN D.	Philadelphia, Pa.	1782	I.G
GERRISH & PEARSON	New York, N.Y.	1800	Gerrish&Pearson
GERRISH, TIMOTHY	Portsmouth, N. H.	1753-1813	TG · T.Gerrish · GERRISH · TGerrish
GETHEN, JOHN	Philadelphia, Pa.	1811	
GETHEN, WILLIAM	Philadelphia, Pa.	1797	W.GETHEN
GETTY, JAMES	Williamsburg, Va	1772	
GETZ, PETER	Lancaster, Pa.	1792	P.Getz
GHISELIN, CESAR	Philadelphia, Pa.	1695	CG · CG · CG
GHISELIN, WILLIAM	Philadelphia, Pa.	1751	WG · GHISELIN
GIBBS, DANIEL	Boston, Mass.	1716	
GIBBS, JOHN	Providence, R.I.	1798	J GIBBS
GIBBS, JOHN F.	Providence, R. I.	1803	
GIBSON, WILLIAM	Philadelphia, Pa.	1845	GIBSON
GIFFING, CHRISTOPHER	New York, N. Y.	1816	C.Gifing.N.Y.
GILBERT, SAMUEL	Hebron, Conn.	1798	SG · SG
GILBERT, WILLIAM W.	New York, N. Y.	1767	WG · N.YORK · GILBERT · W.Gilbert · Gilbert · N.York
GILBERT & CUNNINGHAM	New York, N. Y.	1839	
GILL, CALEB	Boston, Mass.	1774-1855	GILL
GILL, LEAVITT	Hingham, Mass.	1810	
GILLEY, PETER	Philadelphia, Pa.	1797	
GILMAN, BENJAMIN CLARK	Exeter, N. H.	1763-1835	BCG
GILMAN, JOHN WARD	New York, N. Y.	1792	I·W·G
GIQUEL, JOHN B. F.	New Orleans, La.	1822	
GIRARD, FRANCIS	Philadelphia, Pa.	1817	
GIRAUD, HENRY	New York, N. Y.	1805	
GIRRAD, HENRY	New York, N. Y.	1805	
GIRREAUN, STEPHEN	Philadelphia, Pa.	1785	
GIVEN, A.	Albany, N. Y.	1849	
GLIDDEN, JOSEPH	Boston, Mass.	1607-1780	
GODDARD D. & SON	Worcester, Mass.	1845	D.GODDARD & SON

Name	Location	Date	Marks
GOELET, PHILIP	New York, N. Y.	1731	PG PG PG
GOFORTH, JEREMIAH	Philadelphia, Pa	1700	
GOLDTHWAITE, JOSEPH	Boston, Mass.	1706-1780	I·G I·G IG
GOMBACH, JOHN	Philadelphia, Pa.	1802	
GOODHUE, D. T.	Boston, Mass.	1840	DTG DTGOODHUE
GOODHUE, JOHN	Salem, Mass.	1840	J.GOODHUE
GOODING, HENRY	Boston, Mass.	1833	GOODING GOODING
GOODING, JOSEPH	Boston, Mass.	1815	
GOODING, JOSIAH	Unknown	1810	Josiah Gooding / Joys Building
GOODWIN, ALLYN	Hartford, Conn.	1811	
GOODWIN, BENJAMIN	Boston, Mass.	1756	B:Goodwin
GOODWIN & DODD	Hartford, Conn.	1812	G&D
GOODWIN, H. & A.	Hartford, Conn.	1811	
GOODWIN, HORACE	Hartford, Conn.	1811	
GOODWIN, HORACE & ALLYN	Hartford, Conn.	1811	GOODWIN
GOODWIN, RALPH	Hartford, Conn.	1828	
GORDON, A. & J.	New York, N. Y.	1798	
GORDON, ALEXANDER S.	New York, N. Y.	1795	GORDON
GORDON, ANDREW	New York, N. Y.	1796	
GORDON & COMPANY	Boston, Mass.	1849	
GORDON, G.	New York, N. Y.	1800	G.Gordon
GORDON, JAMES	New York, N. Y.	1795	
GORDON, JAMES S.	Philadelphia, Pa.	1769	
GORHAM, JABEZ	Providence, R. I.	1792	J.GORHAM
GORHAM, JABEZ & SON	Providence, R. I.	1842	J.GORHAM&SON
GORHAM, JOHN	New Haven, Conn.	1814	
GORHAM, MILES	New Haven, Conn.	1757-1847	M.G M.GORHAM
GORHAM, RICHARD	New Haven, Conn.	1799	
GORHAM & THURBER	Providence, R. I.	1850	Gorham&Thurber
GORHAM & WEBSTER	New York, N. Y.	1831	Gorham & Webster
GOUGH, JAMES	New York, N. Y.	1769	IG
GOULD, J.	Balimore, Md.	1795-1874	
GOULD, JAMES	Baltimore, Md.	1816-1868	J·GOULD J.GOULD 10-15
GOULD, JOHN	Philadelphia, Pa.	1840	
GOULD, STOWELL & WARD	Baltimore, Md.	1840	
GOULD & WARD	Baltimore, Md.	1850	GOULD & WARD
GOVERT, JAMES	Philadelphia, Pa.	1802	
GOWEN, WILLIAM	Medford, Mass.	1772	WG W·GOWEN
GRAHAM, DANIEL	West Suffield, Conn.	1789	
GRANT, THOMAS	Marblehead, Mass.	1754	T·GRANT
GRANT, WILLIAM, JR.	Philadelphia, Pa.	1785	
GRAVELLE, RENE S.	Philadelphia, Pa.	1813	
GRAVES, THOMAS	Cincinatti, Ohio	1828	
GRAVIER, NICHOLAS	New Orleans, La.	1822	
GRAY, G.	Portsmouth, N. H.	1839	G.GRAY
GRAY, JOHN	New London, Conn.	1692-1720	I.G IG
GRAY, ROBERT	Portsmouth, N. H.	1850	ROBT GRAY R·Gray ROBT GRAY
GRAY, SAMUEL	New London, Conn.	1684-1713	S:GRAY GRAY
GRAY, SAMUEL	Boston, Mass.	1732	S:GRAY
GREEN, BENJAMIN	Boston, Mass.	1712-1748	B:GREEN
GREEN, JAMES	New York, N. Y.	1805	
GREGG, HAYDEN & CO.	New York, N. Y.	1850	GREGG HAYDEN & CO

GREENE, RUFUS
Boston, Mass. 1707-1777

GREENE, WM. & CO.
Providence, R. I. 1815

GREENLEAF, DAVID
Norwich, Conn. 1737-1800

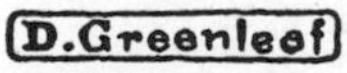

GREENLEAF, DAVID, Jr.
Hartford, Conn. 1766

GREENLEAF, JOSEPH
New London, Conn. ...1779-1798

GREFFIN, PETER
Philadelphia, Pa. 1801

GRIFFEN & HOYT
Albany, N. Y. 1830

GRIFFEN, P.
Albany, N. Y. 1825

GRIFFING, CHRISTOPHER
New York, N. Y. 1816

GRIFITH, DAVID
Boston, Mass. 1789

GRIGG, WM.
New York, N. Y. 1765

GRIGNON, BENJAMIN
Boston, Mass. 1685

GRIGNON, RENE
Norwich, Conn. 1715

GRIMKE, JOHN P.
Charleston, S. C. 1744

GRISCOM, GEORGE
Philadelphia, Pa. 1791

GRISELM, CAESAR
Philadelphia, Pa. 1700

GRISWOLD, GILBERT
Middletown, Conn. 1825

GRISWOLD, WILLIAM
Middletown, Conn. 1820

GROEN, JACOB MARIUS
(Morrisgreen)
New York, N. Y. 1701

GUERCY, DOMINICK
New York, N. Y. 1795

GUERIN, ANTHONY
Philadelphia, Pa. 1791

GUILLE, NOAH
Boston, Mass. 1701

GUIRNA, ANTHONY
Philadelphia, Pa. 1796

GUNN, ENOS
Waterbury, Conn. 1792

GURLEY, WILLIAM
Norwich, Conn. 1804

GURNEE, BENJAMIN
New York, N. Y. 1820

GURNEE, B. & S.
New York, N. Y. 1833

GURNEE & COMPANY
New York, N. Y. 1820

H

HACKLE, WILLIAM
Baltimore, Md. 1776

HADDOCK & ANDREWS
Boston, Mass. 1838

HADDOCK, HENRY
Boston, Mass. 1836

HADWEN, WILLIAM
Nantucket, Mass. 1816

HAGGENMACHER, J. H. & CO.
Philadelphia, Pa. 1836

HAINES, ABRAHAM
New York, N. Y. 1801

HALL, ABIJAH
Albany, N. Y. 1813

HALL & BROWER
Albany, N. Y. 1830

HALL, BROWER & CO.
Albany, N. Y. 1836

HALL, CHARLES
Lancaster, Pa. 1755

HALL, DAVID
Philadelphia, Pa. 1760-1779

HALL, DREW
New York, N. Y. 1789

HALL, GREEN
Albany, N. Y. 1813

HALL & HEWSON
Albany, N. Y. 1819

HALL, HEWSON & MERRIFIELD
Albany, N. Y. 1814

HALL, IVORY
Concord, N. H. 1781

HALL & MERRIMAN
New Haven, Conn. 1825

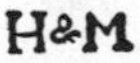

HALL & MERRIMAN
Albany, N. Y. 1825

HALLAM, JOHN
New London, Conn. 1773

HALSEY, JABEZ
New York, N. Y. 1762-1820

HALSTED, BENJAMIN
New York, N. Y. 1764

HALSTED & SON
New York, N. Y. 1799

HALSTRICK, J.
Boston, Mass. 1846

HAM, GEORGE
Portsmouth, N. H. 1810

HAMILL & COMPANY
New York, N. Y. 1817

HAMILL, JAMES
New York, N. Y. ....1816 — J·HAMILL.N.Y.

HAMILTON, JAMES
Annapolis, Md. 1766

HAMILTON, JOHN
New York, N. Y. 1798

HAMLIN, CYRUS
Portland, Me. 1831

HAMLIN, WILLIAM
Middletown, Conn. ....1761 — W.H — WH — HAMLIN

HAMMERSLEY, THOMAS
New York, N. Y. ....1727-1781 — TH — T·H — TH

HANCOCK, JOHN
Boston, Mass. ....1732-1772 — J·HANCOCK — J.HANCOCK — J·HANCOCK

HANDLE, JOHN
Philadelphia, Pa. 1830

HANKS, BENJAMIN
Wyndham, Conn. 1777

HANNAH, W. W.
New York, N. Y. ....1840 — W.W.HANNAH

HANNERS, GEORGE
Boston, Mass. ....1697-1740 — GH — G·HANNERS

HANNERS, GEORGE, JR.
Boston, Mass. ....1721-1760 — GH — G.H

HANSELL, ROBERT
Boston, Mass. 1823

HARACHE, PIERRE
Williamsburg, Va. 1691

HARDING, N. & C.
New York, N. Y. 1830

HARDING & CO. N.
Boston, Mass. ....1830 — NH&CO

HARDING, NEWELL
Boston, Mass. ....1822 — N.Harding — NHarding — N.HARDING — N.H&CO — N.Harding&Co

HARDWOOD, JOHN
Philadelphia, Pa. 1816

HARDY, STEPHEN
Portsmouth, N. H. ....1781-1843 — HARDY — HARDY

HARLAND, THOMAS
Norwich, Conn. ....1735-1807 — HARLAND

HARLAND, THOMAS, JR.
Norwich, Conn. 1777

HARPEL, THOMAS W.
Philadelphia, Pa. 1813

HARPER, ALEXANDER
Philadelphia, Pa. ....

HARPER, DAVID
Philadelphia, Pa ....

HARPER, THOMAS W.
Philadelphia, Pa. 1813

HARRIS, GEORGE
New York, N. Y. 1802

HARRIS, H.
Albany, N. Y. 1820

HARRIS & STANWOOD
Boston, Mass. ....1835 — HARRIS & STANWOOD

HARRIS & WILCOX
Albany, N. Y. ....1844 — HARRIS & WILCOX

HART & BLISS
Middletown, Conn. 1803

HART & BREWER
Middletown, Conn. ....1800-1803 — H&B

HART, ELIPHAZ
Norwich, Conn. ......1789-1866 — EH — E.HART

HART, JOHN
Philadelphia, Pa. 1776

HART, JOHN J.
New York, N. Y. 1820

HART, JUDAH
Middletown, Conn. ....1777-1824 — J.HART — J.Hart — JHART

HART & SMITH
Baltimore, Md. ....1816 — H&S

HART & WILCOX
Norwich, Conn. ....1805-1807 — H&W

HART, WILLIAM
Philadelphia, Pa. ....1818 — W.HART.

HARTFORD, GEORGE
Philadelphia, Pa. 1794

HARTIN & BARGI
Bound Brook, N. J. 1766

HARTLEY, SAMUEL
Philadelphia, Pa. 1818

HARTMAN, PHILIP
Philadelphia, Pa. 1813

HARVEY, LEWIS
Philadelphia, Pa. ....1811 — HARVEY.LEWIS

HASCY, ALEXANDER
Albany, N. Y. 1849

HASCY, NELSON
Albany, N. Y. 1849

HASKELL, BARNABUS
Boston, Mass. 1833

HASTIER, JOHN
New York, N. Y. ....1726 — IH — IH — IH — IH — J·H

HASTIER, MARQUERIETTE
New York, N. Y. ....1771 — MH

HASTINGS, B. B.
Cleveland, Ohio ....1835 — HASTINGS

HASTINGS, H.
New York, N. Y. ....1815 — H·HASTINGS

HAUGH, SAMUEL
Boston, Mass. 1675-1717

HAVERSTICK, WILLIAM
Philadelphia, Pa. 1781

HAWLEY, NOAH
New York, N. Y. 1816

HAWS, JOHN
Philadelphia, Pa. 1837

HAYDEN & GREGG
New York, N. Y. 1840

HAYES & COLTON
Newark, N. J. 1831

HAYES, W.
Connecticut 1780

HAYS, ANDREW
Newark, N. J. 1769

HAYS & MYERS
New York, N. Y. 1770

HEAD, JOSEPH
Philadelphia, Pa. 1798

HEALD, J. S.
Baltimore, Md. 1810

HEALY
Boston, Mass. 1773

HEATH, JOHN
New York, N. Y. 1761

HEBBERD
New York, N. Y. 1847

HECK, LUDWIG
Lancaster, Pa. 1760

HEDGES, DANIEL
Unknown ....C 1830

HEDGES, DANIEL, JR.
East Hampton, N. Y. ..1779-1856

HEGUENBURG, CHARLES, JR.
New Haven, Conn. 1809

HELME, NATHANIEL
South Kingston, R.I. .1761-1789

HEMPSTED & CHADLER
New York, N.Y. 1811

HENCHMAN, DANIEL
Boston, Mass. 1730-1775

HENDERSON, A. A.
Philadelphia, Pa. 1837

HENDRICKS, AHASUERUS
New York, N. Y. 1676

HENRY, FELIX
New York, N. Y. 1815

HEQUENBOURG, CHARLES, Jr.
New Haven, Conn. ... 1760-1851

HERBERT, TIMOTHY B.
New York, N. Y. 1816

HERILS, FRANÇIS
Philadelphia, Pa. 1804

HERON, ISAAC
New York, N. Y. 1768

HEURTIN, WILLIAM
New York, N. Y. 1731

HEWS, ABRAHAM, JR.
Boston, Mass. 1823

HEWSON, JOHN D.
Albany, N. Y. 1815

HEYDORN & IMLAY
Hartford, Conn. 1810

HEYER & CALE
New York, N. Y. 1807

HEYER, WILLIAM B.
New York, N. Y. 1798

HIGBIE & CROSBY
Boston, Mass. 1820

HILDEBUR
Philadelphia, Pa. 1790

HILL, JAMES
Boston, Mass. 1770

HILL & WADDILL
Petersburgh, Va. 1780

HILLDRUP, THOMAS
Hartford, Conn. 1774

HILLER, BENJAMIN
Boston, Mass. 1687

HILLER, JOSEPH
Boston, Mass. 1745

HILLDRAUP, THOMAS
Hartford, Conn. 1772

HILTON, WM.
Philadelphia, Pa. 1814

HIND, JOHN
Philadelphia, Pa. 1760

HINSDALE & ATKIN
New York, N. Y. 1830

HINSDALE, EPAPHRAS
New York, N. Y. 1797

HINSDALE, H.
New York, N. Y. 1831

HITCHBORN, DANIEL
Boston, Mass. 1773

HITCHBORN, SAMUEL
Boston, Mass. 1752

HITCHCOCK, ELIAKIM
Boston, Mass. 1752

HOBARTH, JOSHUA
New Haven, Conn. 1811

HOBBS, NATHAN
Boston, Mass. 1792-1868

Name	Location	Date	Marks
HODGE, JOHN	Hadley, Mass.	1775	J.HODGE · HADLEY
HOFFMAN, FREDERICK	Philadelphia, Pa.	1819	
HOFFMAN, JAMES M.	Philadelphia, Pa.	1820	J.M.HOFFMAN
HOLLAND, LITTLETON	Baltimore, Md.	1804	LH · L.Holland · L·HOLLAND · HOLLAND · HOLLAND
HOLLINGSHEAD, JOHN	Philadelphia, Pa.	1768	
HOLLINGSHEAD, WILLIAM	Philadelphia, Pa.	1770	WH · WH
HOLMES, ADRIAN B.	New York, N. Y.	1801	A.HOLMES
HOLMES, ISRAEL	Waterbury, Conn.	1793	
HOLMES, J.	New York, N. Y.	1816	
HOLMES, WILLIAM	New York, N. Y.	1801	
HOLSEY, E.	Philadelphia, Pa.	1820	E.HOLSEY
HOLTON, DAVID	Baltimore, Md.	1804	
HOLTON, JOHN	Philadelphia, Pa.	1794	
HOLYOKE, EDWARD	Boston, Mass.	1817	HOLYOKE
HOMES, WILLIAM	Boston, Mass.	1717-1783	W·H · WH · HOMES · W·HOmes
HOMES, WILLIAM, JR.	New York, N. Y.	1742-1825	WH · W·H · HOMES
HOOD & TOBY	Albany, N. Y.	1849	HOOD & TOBEY
HOOKEY, WILLIAM	Newport, R. I.	1750	
HOOVER, HENRY	Philadelphia, Pa.	1816	
HOOVER, JOSEPH E.	Philadelphia, Pa.	1837	
HOPKINS, JESSE	Waterbury, Conn.	1787	
HOPKINS, JOSEPH	Waterbury, Conn.	1730-1801	HOPKINS
HOPKINS, STEPHEN	Waterbury, Conn.	1721-1796	SH
HOPPER, SAMUEL	Philadelphia, Pa.	1835	
HORN, E. B.	Boston, Mass.	1847	
HOSFORD, HARLEY	New York, N. Y.	1820	HOSFORD
HOTCHKISS, HEZEKIAH	New Haven, Conn.	1754	
HOUGH, SAMUEL	Boston, Mass.	1675-1717	SH
HOULTON, JOHN	Philadelphia, Pa.	1797	HOULTON
HOUTZELL, JACOB	Philadelphia, Pa.	1801	
HOW, DAVID	Boston, Mass.	1790	
HOWARD, ABRAHAM	Salem, Mass.	1810	
HOWARD, JOHN	Philadelphia, Pa.	1819	
HOWARD, THOMAS	Philadelphia, Pa.	1620	
HOWARD, WILLIAM	Boston, Mass.	1800	
HOWE, GEORGE C.	New York, N. Y.	1810	GEORGE C.HOWE
HOWE, OTIS	Boston, Mass.	1788	
HOWELL & ARNOLD	Albany, N.Y.	1797	
HOWELL, G. W.	Unknown	1790	G W Howell
HOWELL, JAMES	Philadelphia, Pa.	1802	J.Howell · Howell · J.Howell
HOWELL, PAUL	New York, N. Y.	1812	P.HOWELL
HOWELL, SILAS W.	Albany, N. Y.	1798	S.W.Howell · S.W.Howell
HOYT, GEORGE B.	Albany, N. Y.	1827	GEO.B.HOYT
HOYT, HENRY E.	New York, N. Y.	1820	HENRY HOYT
HOYT, S.	New York, N. Y.	1840	S·HOYT
HUBBAL	Washington, D. C.	1834	
HUERTIN, WILLIAM	New York, N. Y.	1731-1771	WH · WH · WH
HUGHES & BLISS	Middletown, Conn.	1806	
HUGHES, CHRISTOPHER	Baltimore, Md.	1744-1824	CH · CH
HUGHES & FRANCIS	Middletown, Conn.	1807	
HUGHES, HENRY	Baltimore, Md.	1781	
HUGHES, J.	Middletown, Conn.	1798	J.HUGHES · STERLING

HUGHES, JEREMIAH
Annapolis, Md. 1805

HUGHES, WILLIAM
Baltimore, Md. 1785-1791

HULBEART, PHILIP
Philadelphia, Pa. 1761

HULL, JOHN
Boston, Mass. 1624-1683

HULL & SANDERSON
Boston, Mass. 1652

HUMBERT, AUGUSTUS
New York, N. Y. 1818

HUMPHREYS, RICHARD
Philadelphia, Pa. 1772

HUMPHREYS, THOMAS
Philadelphia, Pa. 1814

HUNLOCK, BOUMAN
Philadelphia, Pa. 1752

HUNNEWELL, GEORGE W.
Boston, Mass. 1836

HUNT, EDWARD
Boston, Mass. 1717

HUNT, WILLIAM
Boston, Mass. 1819

HUNTINGTON, PHILIP
Norwich, Conn. 1770-1825

HUNTINGTON, ROSWELL
Norwich, Conn. 1763

HUNTINGTON, S.
Maine 1850

HURD, BENJAMIN
Boston, Mass. 1739-1781

HURD, ISAAC
Roxbury, Mass. 1754

HURD, JACOB
Boston, Mass. 1702-1758

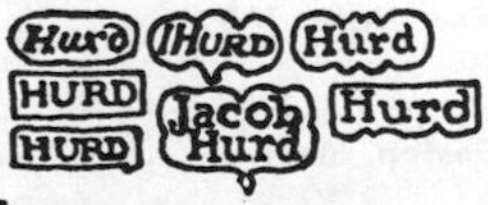

HURD, NATHANIEL
Boston, Mass. 1730-1777

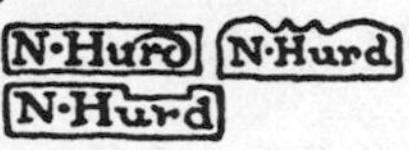

HURLBEART, PHILLIP
Philadelphia, Pa. 1761

HURST, HENRY
Boson, Mass 1665-1717

HURTIN & BURGI
Bound Brook, N.J. 1766

HUSBAND, JOHN
Philadelphia, Pa. 1796

HUSSEY, STEPHEN
Maryland 1818

HUSTON, JAMES
Baltimore, Md. 1799

HUTCHINS, JACOB
New York, N. Y. 1774

HUTCHINS, NICHOLAS
Baltimore, Md. 1777-1845

HUTTON, GEORGE
Albany, N. Y. 1799

HUTTON, I & G.
Albany, N. Y. 1799

HUTTON, ISAAC
Albany, N. Y. 1767-1855

HUTTON, JOHN
New York, N. Y. 1720

HUTTON, JOHN S.
New York, N. Y. ... 1684

HYDE
Newport, R. I. 1730

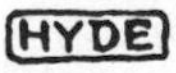

HYDE & GOODRICH
New Orleans, N. Y. .. 1810

HYDE & NEVINS
New York, N. Y. 1798

I

IAGO, HENRY
New York, N. Y. 1745

INCH, JOHN
Annapolis, Md. 1720-1763

INGRAHAM, JOSEPH
Portland, Me. 1785

INMAN, BENJAMIN
Philadelphia, Pa. 1816

ISAACKS, MICHAEL
New York, N. Y. 1765

IVERS, B.
Unknown ....C 1800

J

JACCARD & COMPANY
St. Louis, Mo. 1850

JACKS, JAMES
Charleston, S. C. 1795

JACKS, WILLIAM
Philadelphia, Pa. 1798

JACKSON, DANIEL
New York, N. Y. 1782

JACKSON, JAMES
Baltimore, Md. 1775

JACKSON, JOHN
New York, N. Y. 1731

JACKSON, JOSEPH
Baltimore, Md. 1803

JACOB, GEORGE
Baltimore, Md. 1802

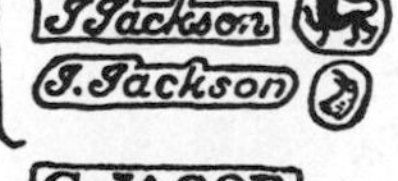

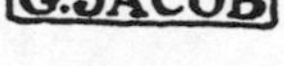

JACOB, MOSES
Philadelphia, Pa. 1775

JAÇOBS, ABEL
Philadelphia, Pa. 1816

Name	Location	Date	Mark
JACOBS & CO. A.	Philadelphia, Pa.	1820	A.J.& Co
JANVIER, LOUIS	Charleston, S. C.	1744	
JARVIS, MUNSON	Stamford, Conn.	1742-1824	MJ MJ
JENCKES, JOHN C.	Providence, R.I.	1798	J JENCKES / JCJENCKES
JENCKES & COMPANY	Providence, R. I.	1798	
JENKINS, JOHN	Philadelphia, Pa.	1777	IJ
JENNINGS, JACOB	Norwalk, Conn.	1739-1817	I·I
JENNINGS, JACOB, JR.	New London, Conn.	1800	
JESSE, DAVID	Boston, Mass.	1670-1705	DI D·I
JOHANNES, JOHN M.	Baltimore, Md.	1835	
JOHN	Unknown	C 1760	
JOHNSON & BALL	Baltimore, Md.	1785	J&B
JOHNSON, C.	Albany, N. Y.	1828	
JOHNSON & GODLEY	Albany, N. Y.	1847	
JOHNSON, JOHN	Pittsburg, Pa.	1815	
JOHNSON, MAYCOCK W.	Albany, N. Y.	1815	M.W.JOHNSON
JOHNSON & REAT	Baltimore, Md.	1786	JOHNSON & REAT / JOHNSON&REAT
JOHNSON & RILEY	Baltimore, Md.	1786	J&R
JOHNSON, SAMUEL	New York, N. Y.	1780	SJ S.J
JOHNSON, SAMUEL	New York, N. Y.	1796	JOHNSON
JOHNSTON, A.	Philadelphia, Pa.	1830	A.JOHNSTON STER
JOHONNOT, WILLIAM B.	Middletown, Conn.	1766-1849	WJ
JONES, BALL & POOR	Boston, Mass.	1840	JONES.BALL&POOR
JONES, E.	Baltimore, Md.	1820	
JONES, GEORGE B.	Boston, Mass.	1839	
JONES, JAMES	Philadelphia, Pa.	1815	
JONES, JOHN	Boston, Mass.	1810	J.JONES
JONES, JOHN B.	Boston, Mass.	1782-1854	J.B.Jones
JONES, JOHN B. & COL.	Boston, Mass.	1813	J.B.JONES&CO
JONES, LOWS & BALL	Boston, Mass.	1850	
JONES & WARD	Boston, Mass.	1815	JONES&WARD
JONES, WILLIAM	Marblehead, Mass.	1694-1730	W·I
JONES, WILLIAM	New York, N. Y.	1820	
JORDAN, PETER	Philadelphia, Pa.	1823	
JOUBERT, P.	Philadelphia, Pa.	1807	
JUDAH	New York, N. Y.	1774	
KAY, AMOS	Boston, Mass.	1725	AK
KEDZIE, J.	Philadelphia, Pa.	1830	J.KEDZIE
KEELER, A.	Norwalk, Conn.	1800-	KEELER
KEELER, JOSEPH	Norwalk, Conn.	1786-1824	IK IK KEELER
KEELER, THADDEUS	New York, N.Y.	1805	T.KEELER
KEIFF, JOSEPH	Philadelphia, Pa.	1831	
KEITH, T. & W.	New York, N.Y.	1805	T.&W.KEITH
KELEY, GRAEL	Boston, Mass.	1823	
KELLEY, ALLEN	Providence, R.I.	1810	
KELLEY, E. G. & J. H.	Providence, R.I.	1820	
KENDLE, CHARLES	New York, N.Y.	1807	
KENDRICK, WILLIAM	Louisville, Ky.	1840	W.KENDRICK.LOUISVILLE
KENNEDY, MATHEW	Philadelphia, Pa.	1825	
KENRICK, ANWYL	Maryland	1775	
KEPLINGER, SAMUEL	Baltimore, Md.	1770-1849	SKEPLINGER
KETCHAM, JAMES	New York, N.Y.	1814	I.KETCHAM

Name	Location	Date	Marks
KETTELL, THOMAS	Charlestown, Mass.	1781	T.K
KEYWORTH, ROBERT	Washington, D.C.	1831	R.KEYWORTH
KIDNEY, CANN & JOHNSON	New York, N.Y.	1850	K.C.&J.
KIDNEY & DUNN	New York, N.Y.	1844	K&D K&D
KIERSTEADE, CORNELIUS	New York, N.Y.	1753	CK CK
KIERSTEADE, CORNELIUS	New Haven, Conn.	1722	(same marks as above)
KIMBERLY, WILLIAM	New York, N.Y.	1792	WK Kimberly
KING, JOSEPH	Middletown, Conn.	1770	
KING, THOMAS R.	Baltimore, Md.	1819	TRKING
KINGSTON, JOHN	New York, N.Y.	1775	
KINNEY, THOMAS	Norwich, Conn.	1786-1824	TK T.K
KINSEY, DAVID	Cincinatti, Ohio	1850	DKINSEY
KINSEY, E. & D.	Cincinnati, Ohio	1845	E.&D.KINSEY
KIP, BENJAMIN	New York, N.Y.	1702	
KIPPEN, GEORGE	Bridgeport, Conn.	1820	G.KIPPEN
KIRBY, WILLIAM	New York, N.Y.	1783	
KIRK, SAMUEL	Baltimore, Md.	1792-1872	S.K S.Kirk Kirk S.KIRK KIRK S.KIRK SAM!.KIRK
KIRK & SMITH	Baltimore, Md.	1815	(same marks as above); KIRK&SMITH
KIRKWOOD, PETER	Annapolis, Md.	1799	PK
KIRKWOOD, PETER	Chestertown, Md.	1790	(same mark as above)
KIRTLAND, JOSEPH P.	Middletown, Conn.	1796	
KITCHEN, ANDREW	Philadelphia, Pa.	1835	
KLINE, BARTHOLOMEW	Philadelphia, Pa.	1837	
KLINE, B. & CO.	Philadelphia, Pa.	1837	
KNEELAND, JOSEPH	Boston, Mass.	1698-1760	I.Kneeland
KRAUSE, JOHN S.	Bethlehem, Pa.	1805	
KRIDER & BIDDLE	Philadelphia, Pa.	1830	K B
KRIDER, PETER L.	Philadelphia, Pa.	1850	P.L.K
KUCHER, JACOB	Philadelphia, Pa.	1813	I.KUCHER
KUMBEL, WILLIAM	New York, N.Y.	1780	

L

Name	Location	Date	Marks
LACHAISE, PETER	New York, N.Y.	1794	
LADD, WILLIAM F.	New York, N.Y.	1830	WM.F.LADD NEW-YORK
LAFORME, ANTOINE	Boston, Mass.	1836	
LAFORME, BERNARD	Boston, Mass.	1836	
LAFORME, F. J.	Boston, Mass.	1835	
LAFORME, VINCENT	Boston, Mass.	1850	V.LAFORME
LAINECOURT, STEPHEN	New York, N.Y.	1800	
LAKEMAN, E. K.	New York, N.Y.	1800	E.K.LAKEMAN
LAMAR, BENJAMIN	Philadelphia, Pa.	1785	BL LAMAR
LAMAR, MATHIAS	Philadelphia, Pa.	1796	ML
LAMESIERE, PETER	Philadelphia, Pa.	1811	
LAMOTHE, JOHN	New Orleans, La.	1822	
LAMOTHE, PIERRE	New Orleans, La.	1822	Lamothe Lamothe
LAMPE, JOHN	Baltimore, Md.	1787	
LAMSON, J.	Unknown	1790	J.LAMSON J.L
LANE, AARON	Elizabeth, N.J.	1780	AL
LANG, EDWARD	Salem, Mass.	1742-1830	EL LANG
LANG, JEFFERY	Salem, Mass.	1708-1758	I.LANG LANG I.LANG
LANG, RICHARD	Salem, Mass.	1733-1810	R.LANG
LANGE, WILLIAM	New York, N.Y.	1844	.LANGE.
LANGER, JOSEPH	Philadelphia, Pa.	1811	
LANSING, JACOB G.	Albany, N.Y.	1736	IGL

LAPEROUSE, JOHN B.
New Orleans, La. 1832

LAROUSSEBIERRE, PETER
New York, N.Y. 1797

LASHING, PETER
New York, N.Y. 1805

LATHROP, RUFUS
Norwich, Conn. 1755

LATRUIT, JOHN P.
Washington, D.C. 1833

LAWRENCE, JOSIAH H.
Philadelphia, Pa. 1817

LAWRIE, ROBERT O.
Philadelphia, Pa. 1840

LEA, SAMUEL J
Baltimore, Md. 1814

LEACH, CHARLES
Boston, Mass. 1765-1814

LEACH, JOHN
Boston, Mass. 1780

LEACH, NATHANIEL
Boston, Mass. 1789

LEACH, SAMUEL
Philadelphia, Pa. 1741

LEACH & BRADLEY
Philadelphia, Pa. 1832

LEACOCK, JOHN
Philadelphia, Pa. 1751

LAYCOCK, PETER
Philadelphia, Pa. 1750

LE BLANC, LEWIS
Philadelphia, Pa. 1815

LEDELL, JOSEPH
Philadelphia, Pa. 1797

LE DORC
Philadelphia, Pa. 1797

LEE, SAMUEL J.
Baltimore, Md. 1815

LEE, S. W.
Providence, R.I. 1815

LEFEVRE, F.
Philadelphia, Pa. 1818

LEFEVRE & GRAVELLE
Philadelphia, Pa. 1811

LEFEVRE, JOHN F.
Philadelphia, Pa. 1806

LEGARE, DANIEL
Boston, Mass. 1688-1724

LEGARE, FRANCIS
Boston, Mass. 1657

LEMAIRE, BAPTISTE
Philadelphia, Pa. 1804

LEMAIRE, MATHIAS
Philadelphia, Pa. 1781

LENCH, PETER
New York, N.Y. 1805

LENDIGREE, M.
New York, N.Y. 1814

LENT, JOHN
New York, N.Y. 1787

LEONARD, S.
New York, N.Y. 1830

LEONARD, SAMUEL
Baltimore, Md. 1786-1848

LEONARD & WILSON
Philadelphia, Pa. 1847

LERET, PETER
Baltimore, Md. 1787

LE ROUX, BARTHOLOMEW
New York, N.Y. 1700

LE ROUX, CHARLES
New York, N.Y. 1689-1745

LE ROUX, JOHN
New York, N.Y. 1723

LESCURE, EDWARD
Philadelphia, Pa. 1822

LE TELIER, JOHN
Philadelphia, Pa. 1770

LETOURNEAUX
New York, N.Y. 1797

LEVELY
Baltimore, Md. 1788

LEVERETT, KNIGHT
Boston, Mass. 1736

LEWYN, GABRIEL
Baltimore, Md. 1771

LEWIS, WILLIAM
Philadelphia, Pa. 1810

LEWIS, HARVEY
Philadelphia, Pa. 1811

LEWIS, ISAAC
Huntington, Conn. 1796

LEWIS & SMITH
Philadelphia, Pa. 1805

LEWIS, TUNIS
New York, N.Y. 1805

LIBBY, J. G. L.
Boston, Mass. 1830

LIDDEN, JOHN
St. Louis, Mo. 1850

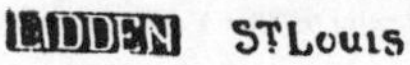

LIGHTFOOT, JAMES
New York, N.Y. 1749

LINCH, PETER
New York, N.Y. 1805

Name	Location	Date	Mark
LINCOLN, A. L.	St. Louis, Mo.	1850	A.L.Lincoln
LINCOLN, ELIJAH	Boston, Mass.	1794-1861	E.LINCOLN
LINCOLN & FOSS	Boston, Mass.	1829	LINCOLN & FOSS
LINCOLN & GREEN	Boston, Mass.	1810	L&G
LINCOLN & READ	Boston, Mass.	1835	LINCOLN & READ
LINDNER, GEORGE	Philadelphia, Pa.	1837	
LINGLEY, HENRY	New York, N. Y.	1810	
LINK, PETER	Philadelphia, Pa.	1811	
LINTOT	New York, N. Y.	1762	
LITTLE, PAUL	Portland, Me.	1760	
LITTLE, WILLIAM	Newburyport, Mass.	1775	W·L WL
LOCKWOOD, A.	New York, N. Y.	1810	A·LOCKWOOD
LOCKWOOD, F.	New York, N. Y.	1845	F.LOCKWOOD
LOCKWOOD, JAMES	New York, N. Y.	1799	J.LOCKWOOD
LOFLAND, PURNEL	Philadelphia, Pa.	1810	
LOGAN, ADAM	New York, N. Y.	1803	A·LOGAN
LOGAN, JAMES	Philadelphia, Pa.	1810	
LONG, ANDREW	Philadelphia, Pa.	1837	
LONG, WILLIAM	Philadelphia, Pa.	1807	
LONGLEY, HENRY	New York, N. Y.	1810	H·Longley Longley
LOOMIS, G. & CO.	Erie, Pa.	1850	G.LOOMIS&CO ERIE
LORD, BENJAMIN	Pittsfield, Mass.	1786	
LORD, JABEZ C.	New York, N. Y.	1835	J.LORD
LORD, JOSEPH	Philadelphia, Pa.	1815	
LORD & SMITH	New York, N. Y.	1823	
LORING, ELIJAH	Barnstable, Mass.	1744-1782	E.Loring. E.Loring
LORING, HENRY	Boston, Mass.	1773-1818	HL
LORING, JOSEPH	Boston, Mass.	1743-1815	J·L J·Loring J·Loring J.Loring J·Loring I·Loring
LOUS, ASA	Hartford, Conn.	1792	
LOW, BALL & COMPANY	Boston, Mass.	1840	
LOW, FRANCIS	Boston, Mass.	1827	
LOW, JOHN J. & COMPANY	Boston, Mass.	1828	J.J.LOW & CO
LOW, JOHN S.	Salem, Mass.	1821	
LOWER, JOSEPH	Philadelphia, Pa.	1803	LOWER
LOWNER, JACOB	Philadelphia, Pa.	1833	
LOWNER, WILLIAM	Philadelphia, Pa.	1833	
LOWNES, EDWARD	Philadelphia, Pa.	1817	E.LOWNES E.LOWNES
LOWNES & ERWIN	Philadelphia, Pa.	1816	
LOWNES, J. & J. H.	Philadelphia, Pa.	1816	
LOWNES, JOSEPH	Philadelphia, Pa.	1780	JL J.Lownes
LOWNES, JOSIAH H.	Philadelphia, Pa.	1822	IHL JHL
LOYER, ADRIAN	Savannah, Ga.	1860	
LUCET, JAMES	New York, N. Y.	1802	
LULIS, LAMBERT	New York, N. Y.	1804	
LUPP, HENRY	New Brunswick, N. J.	1783	H.Lupp
LUPP, PETER	New Brunswick, N.J.	1797-1827	PL
LUPP, S. V.	New Brunswick, N. J.	1815	S.V.LUPP
LUSADA, BENJAMIN	New York, N. Y.	1797	
LUSCOMB, JOHN G.	Boston, Mass.	1823	
LUSSAUR, JOHN	New York, N. Y.	1791	
LUZERDER, BENJAMIN	New York, N. Y.	1796	
LYELL, DAVID	New York, N. Y.	1699	

LYNCH, JOHN
Baltimore, Md. 1761-1848

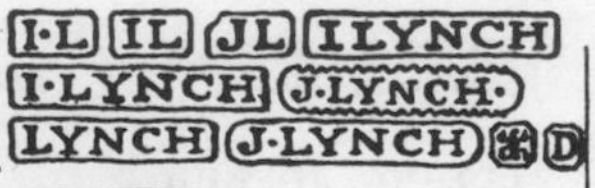

LYNDE, THOMAS
Worcester, Mass. 1748-1812

LYNG, JOHN
Philadelphia, Pa. 1734

LYNG, JOHN BURT
New York, N. Y. 1759

LYNN, ADAM
District of Columbia 1796

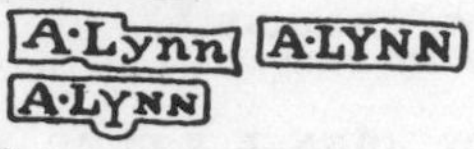

LYTLE, R. A.
Baltimore, Md. 1825

M

MABRID & COMPANY
New York, N. Y. 1787

MACHON, AUSTIN
Philadelphia, Pa. 1759

MAIN, DAVID
Stonington, Conn. 1773

MAINWARING, THOS.
West New Jersey 1664

MARIOT, JEAN C.
New Orleans, La. 1822

MANN, ALEXANDER
Middletown, Conn. 1804

MANNERBACK, W.
Reading, Pa. 1825

MANNING, DANIEL
Boston, Mass. 1823

MANNING, JOSEPH
New York, N. Y. 1823

MANNING, SAMUEL
Boston, Mass. 1823

MANSFIELD, ELISHA H.
Norwich, Conn. 1816

MANSFIELD, JOHN
Charlestown, Mass. 1634

MANSFIELD, THOMAS
Philadelphia, Pa. 1804

MARBLE, SIMEON
New Haven, Conn. 1777-1856

MARCHAND, EVARISTE
New Orleans, La. 1822

MARQUAND & BROTHER
New York, N. Y. 1825

MARQUAND & COMPANY
New York, N. Y. 1810

MARQUAND, FREDERICK
New York, N.Y. 1823

MARQUARD, ISAAC
New York, N. Y. 1810

MARS, S.
Unknown ....C 1770

MARSH, T. K.
Paris, Kentucky 1830

MARSHALL, JOSEPH
Philadelphia, Pa. 1818

MARSHALL & TEMPEST
Philadelphia, Pa. 1813

MARSHALL, THOMAS
Troy, N.Y. 1839

MARTIN, ABRAHAM W.
New York, N. Y. 1835

MARTIN, PETER
New York, N. Y. 1756

MARTIN, V.
Boston, Mass. 1859

MASI, SERAPHIM
Washington, D. C. 1832

MASON, J. D.
Philadelphia, Pa. 1830

MATHER & NORTH
New Britain, Conn. 1827

MATLACK, WILLIAM
Philadelphia, Pa. 1828

MAVERICK, D.
New York, N. Y. 1828

MAVERICK, PETER R.
New York, N. Y. 1780

MAYSENHOEDER, C.
Philadelphia, Pa. 1824

MEAD & ADRIANCE
St. Louis, Mo. 1835

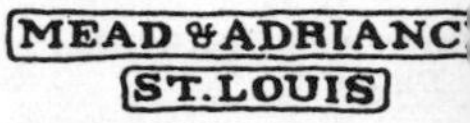

MEAD, EDMUND
St. Louis, Mo. 1850

MEADOWS & CO.
Philadelphia, Pa. 1831

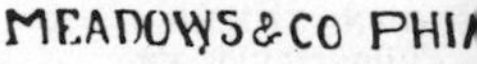

MECOM, JOHN
New York, N. Y. 1770

MECOM, GEORGE
Boston, Mass. 1836

MERCHANT, J.
New York, N. Y. 1795

MEREDITH, JOSEPH P.
Baltimore, Md. 1824

MERKLER, JOHN H.
New York, N. Y. 1780

MERRIFIELD, THOMAS V. Z.
Albany, N. Y. 1840

MERRIMAN & BRADLEY
New Haven, Conn. 1817

MERRIMAN, C.
New York, N. Y. 1825

MERRIMAN, MARCUS
New Haven, Conn. 1762-1850

Name	Location	Date	Marks
MERRIMAN, MARCUS & CO.	New Haven, Conn.	1817	M·M·&Co
MERRIMAN, REUBEN	Litchfield, Conn.	1783-1866	R.MERRIMAN, Pure Coin, R·M
MERRIMAN, SAMUEL	New Haven, Conn.	1769-1805	S.Merriman
MERRIMAN, SILAS	New Haven, Conn.	1760	
MERRIMAN & TUTTLE	New Haven, Conn.	1802	
MERROW, NATHAN	East Hartford, Conn.	1783	
MICHAELS, JAMES	New York, N. Y.	1820	
MIKSCH, JOHN MATHEW	Bethlehem, Pa.	1775	I·M·MIKSCH
MILES, JOHN	Philadelphia, Pa.	1785	
MILHE, STEPHEN	Philadelphia, Pa.	1780	
MILLAR, JAMES	Boston, Mass.	1832	
MILLARD, GEORGE	Philadelphia, Pa.	1816	
MILLER, D. B.	Boston, Mass.	1850	D.B.MILLER
MILLER, I. R.	Philadelphia, Pa.	1810	I.R.MILLER
MILLER, P.	Philadelphia, Pa.	1810	P.MILLER, P.MILLER
MILLER, WILLIAM	Philadelphia, Pa.	1814	MILLER, Miller
MILLER & SON	Philadelphia, Pa.	1833	
MILLNER, THOMAS	Boston, Mass.	1690-1745	TM, TM
MILNE, EDMUND	Philadelphia, Pa.	1757	EM, EM, E·MILNE
MILNE, F.	New York, N. Y.	1800	
MILNE, THOMAS	New York, N. Y.	1795	
MILLON, PETER	New York, N. Y.	1820	
MILLOUDON, PHILLIPPE	Philadelphia, Pa.	1811	
MILLS, EDMUND	Philadelphia, Pa.	1785	
MILLS, EDWARD	Philadelphia, Pa.	1794	
MILLS, JOHN	Philadelphia, Pa.	1793	
MINOTT & AUSTIN	Boston, Mass.	1765-1769	Minott, Minott, I·A, I·Austin
MINOTT, SAMUEL	Boston, Mass.	1732-1803	M, S·M, M, S·M, Minott, Minott, Minott
MINOTT & SIMPKINS	Boston, Mass.	1769	WS, Minott
MINSHALL, WILLIAM	Philadelphia, Pa.	1773	
MITCHELL, HARRY	Philadelphia, Pa.	1844	MITCHELL
MITCHELL, PHINEAS	Boston, Mass.	1812	
MITCHELL, WILLIAM	Boston, Mass.	1820	W.MITCHELL
MIX, JAMES	Albany, N.Y.	1817	
MIX, VISSCHER	Albany, N. Y.	1849	
MOBBS, WILLIAM	Buffalo, N. Y.	1835	
MOFFAT, CHARLES H.	New York, N. Y.	1830	
MOFFAT, J. L.	New York, N. Y.	1815	J.L.MOFFAT
MOHLER, JACOB	Baltimore, Md.	1744-1773	I·M
MUNROE, JAMES	Barnstable, Mass.	1806	
MONTIETH, J. & R.	Baltimore, Md.	1814	MONTEITH
MONTIETH, ROBERT	Baltimore, Md.	1814	RM
MOOD, J. & P.	Charleston, S. C.	1806	J.&P.MOOD
MOOD, JOSEPH	Charleston, S. C.	1806	I, MOOD, IMOOD, JMOOD, J.&P.MOOD
MOOD, P.	Charleston, S. C.	1806	PM
MOORE & BREWER	New York, N. Y.	1835	
MOORE & BROWN	New York, N. Y.	1833	
MOORE, CHARLES	Philadelphia, Pa.	1804	
MOORE, & FERGUSON	Philadelphia, Pa.	1804	MOORE & FERGUSON
MOORE, JOHN C.	New York, N. Y.	1844	J.C.M.
MOORE, JOHN L.	New York, N. Y.	1835	J.L.MOORE
MOORE, ROBERT	Maryland	1778	

Name	Location	Date	Marks
MOORE, THOMAS	Philadelphia, Pa.	1805	
MORGAN, E.	Poughkeepsie, N. Y.	1810	E.MORGAN POUGHKEEPSIE
MORGAN, JOHN	Philadelphia, Pa.	1813	
MORMAGEA, MICHAEL	Philadelphia, Pa.	1816	
MORRIS, JOHN	New York, N. Y.	1796	
MORRIS, SYLVESTER	New York, N. Y.	1709-1783	SM
MORRIS, WILLIAM H.	New York, N. Y.	1759	
MORRISON, ISRAEL	Philadelphia, Pa.	1823	
MORSE, DAVID	Boston, Mass.	1798	
MORSE, HAZEN	Boston, Mass.	1815	
MORSE, J. H.	Boston, Mass.	1792	J.H.MORSE
MORSE, MOSES	Boston, Mass.	1816	M.MORSE
MORSE, NATHANIEL	Boston, Mass.	1709	NM; N·M; NM
MORSE, STEPHEN	Boston, Mass.	1764	MORSE
MOSELEY, DAVID	Boston, Mass.	1753-1812	DM; DMoseley; D.Moseley
MOSELEY, JOSEPH	New York, N. Y.	1830	
MOSES, JACOB	Birmingham, Ala.	1768	MOSES
MOSES, M.	Boston, Mass.	1830	
MOSES, ISAAC N.	Derby, Conn.	1781	
MOTT, J. S.	New York, N. Y.	1790	J.MOTT; JMOTT; J.S.MOTT
MOTT, JOHN & WILLIAM	New York, N. Y.	1789	
MOTT, W. & J.	New York, N. Y.	1789	MOTT'S
MOULINAR, JOHN	New York, N.Y.	1744	I.M; IM
MOULTON, ABEL	Newburyport, Mass.	1815	A·MOULTON
MOULTON & BRADBURY	Newburyport, Mass.	1796	MOULTON; B
MOULTON & DAVIS	Newburyport, Mass.	1824	
MOULTON, EBENEZER S.	Boston, Mass.	1796	E.S.MOULTON; E.S.Moulton
MOULTON, ENOCH	Portland, Me.	1801	E.MOULTON
MOULTON, JOSEPH, I	Newburyport, Mass.	1680	J·M
MOULTON, JOSEPH, II	Newburyport, Mass.	1757	I·M; I·M; IM; I·MOULTON
MOULTON, JOSEPH, III	Newburyport, Mass.	1814	J.MOULTON.; J.MOULTON
MOULTON, WILLIAM, I	Newburyport, Mass.	1710	
MOULTON, WILLIAM, II	Newburyport, Mass.	1720	
MOULTON, WILLIAM, III	Newburyport, Mass.	1772	W·M; W.MOULTON; MOULTON; MOULTON
MULFORD, JOHN H.	Albany, N. Y.	1835	
MULFORD & WENDELL	Albany, N. Y.	1842	MULFORD WENDELL
MULLIGAN, H.	Philadelphia, Pa.	1840	H.MULLIGAN ... 2d ST PHILA
MUMFORD, H. G.	Providence, R. I.	1813	
MUNROE, JAMES	Barnstable, Mass.	1784-1879	JamesMunroe; PureCoin; I·MUNROE; I·MUNROE; JamesMunroe
MUNROE, NATHANIEL	Baltimore, Md.	1777-1861	N.MUNROE; N.MUNROE
MUNSON, AMOS	New Haven, Conn.	1776	
MUNSON, CORNELIUS	Wallingford, Conn.	1742	
MURDOCK, JAMES	Philadelphia, Pa.	1779	I.M.; J.Murdock
MURPHY, JAMES	Philadelphia, Pa.	1823	J.MURPHY
MUSGRAVE, JAMES	Philadelphia, Pa.	1795	Musgrave
MYER, H. B.	New York, N. Y.	1810	HBMyer
MYERS, ALBERT	Philadelphia, Pa.	1837	
MYERS & JACOB	Philadelphia, Pa.	1839	
MYERS, JOHN	Philadelphia, Pa.	1773	I·MYERS; J.Myers
MYERS, MYER	New York, N.Y.	1723-1795	MM; M·M; Myers; Myers
MYGATT, COMFORT	Danbury, Conn.	1763-1823	
MYGATT, DAVID	Danbury, Conn.	1777-1822	DM; D.MYGATT; D·MYGATT

MYGATT, ELY
Danbury, Conn. 1742-1807

MYSENDHENDER
Philadelphia, Pa. 1813

Mc

McCLYMON, JOHN C.
New York, N.Y. 1805
I.McClymon | I.McClymon

McCONNEL, HUGH
Philadelphia, Pa. 1813
McCONNEL

McCONNELLY, H.
Philadelphia, Pa. 1811

McCORMICK, JOHN
Philadelphia, Pa. 1837

McCREA, ROBERT
Philadelphia, Pa. 1785

McDANIEL, PETER
New York, N.Y. 1743

McDONALD, DANIEL
Philadelphia, Pa. 1828

McDONNOUGH, PATRICK
Philadelphia, Pa. 1811

McDONNOUGH, JOHN
Philadelphia, Pa. 1775

M'FADDEN, J. B.
Pittsburgh, Pa. 1840
J.B.M'FADDEN

McFARLANE, JOHN
Boston, Mass. 1796
J.McF | J.McFARLANE

McFEE, JOHN
Philadelphia, Pa. 1793

McFEE, M.
Philadelphia, Pa. 1769

McFEE & REEDER
Philadelphia, Pa. 1796
M&R

McGRAW, DANIEL
Chester, Pa. 1772

McHARG, ALEXANDER
Albany, N.Y. 1849

McINTIRE, JAMES
Philadelphia, Pa. 1840

McINTOSH, JOHN
Ft. Stanwix, Pa. 1761

McKEEN, HENRY
Philadelphia, Pa. 1823
H.McKEEN

McKLIMENT, JOHN
New York, N.Y. 1804

McLAWRENCE, JOHN
New York, N.Y. 1818

McMAHON, JOHN
Philadelphia, Pa. 1804

McMASTER, HUGH A.
Philadelphia, Pa. 1839
H.A.McMASTER

McMULLEN, JAMES
Philadelphia, Pa. 1814
I.M | I.McMullin | IMcMullin | I.M.MULLIN

McMULLEN, WILLIAM
Philadelphia, Pa. 1791

McMULLIN & BLACK
Philadelphia, Pa. 1813
McMuLLin & BLack

McMULLIN, JOHN
Philadelphia, Pa. 1765-1843

McPARLIN, WILLIAM
Maryland 1780-1850
W.McP

McPHERSON, ROBERT
Philadelphia, Pa. 1831

N

NAGLES, JOHN
Philadelphia, Pa. 1748

NEEDELS, WILLIAM
Easton, Md. 1798
W.NEEDELS

NEVILL, RICHARD
Boston, Mass. 1674

NEUSS, JAN
Philadelphia, Pa. 1698

NEVILL R,ICHARD
Boston, Mass. 1764

NEWBERRY, EDWIN C.
Mansfield, Conn. 1828

NEWHALL, DUDLEY
Salem, Mass. 1730

NEWKIRKE, JOHN VAN
New York, N.Y. 1716
I.N | I.N

NEWMAN, TIMOTHY H.
New York, N.Y. 1799
Newman | Newman

NICHOLAS, WILLIAM S.
Newport, R.I. 1785-1871
W.S.N | NICHOLS

NICHOLS, BASSET
Providence, R.I. 1815
NICHOLS

NICHOLS, WILLIAM S.
Newport, R.I. 1808

NICHERSON, BATY
Harwich, Mass. 1825

NIXON, RICHARD
Philadelphia, Pa. 1820

NOBLE, JOSEPH
Portland, Maine 1823

NORCROSS, NEHEMIAH
Boston, Mass. 1796
NN

NORRIS, GEORGE
Philadelphia, Pa. 1779

NORTH, W. B. & CO.
New York, N.Y. 1823
W.B.NORTH & CO

NORTH, WILLIAM B.
New York, N.Y. 1787-1838
W.B.N

NORTHEE, DAVID I.
Salem, Mass. 1788
DN | D.I.NORTHEE

NORTHEY, ABIJAH
Salem, Mass. 1775
AN

Name	Place	Date	Marks
NORTON, ANDREW	Goshen, Conn.	1787	
NORTON, BENJAMIN	Boston, Mass.	1810	
NORTON, C. C.	Hartford, Conn.	1820	C.C.NORTON
NORTON, SAMUEL	Hingham, Mass.	1795	
NORTON, THOMAS	Farmington, Conn.	1796-1806	TN TN
NORTON & PITKIN	Hartford, Conn.	1825	C.C.NORTON & W.PITKIN
NORWOOD, RICHARD	New York, N.Y.	1774	
NOXON	Unknown	c 1800	NOXON
NOYES, JOHN	Boston, Mass.	1695	IN IN IN
NOYES, JOSEPH	Philadelphia, Pa.	1719	IN IN
NOYES, SAMUEL	Norwich, Conn.	1770	
NUSZ, FREDERICK	Frederick, Md.	1819	F.NUSZ.
NUTTALL, JOSEPH	Maryland	1778	
NYS, JOHANNIS	Philadelphia, Pa.	1695	IN IN IN

O

Name	Place	Date	Marks
OAKES, FREDERICK	Hartford, Conn.	1825	OAKES OAKES
OAKES & SOENCER	Hartford, Conn.	1814	O&S
OBRIHIM, JOSEPH	Annapolis, Md.	1784	
ODELL, LAWRENCE	New York, N.Y.	1830	
OERTELT, CHARLES E.	Philadelphia, Pa.	1831	
OGIER, JOHN	New York, N.Y.	1791	
OGILVIE, GABRIEL	New York, N.Y.	1791	
OLIVER, ANDREW	Boston, Mass.	1722	A·OLIVER
OLIVER, DANIEL	Philadelphia, Pa.	1805	D.OLIVER
OLIVER, PETER	Boston, Mass.	1709	PO PO
OLIVIER, PETER	Philadelphia, Pa.	1797	P.O
OLMSTED, NATHANIEL	Farmington, Conn.	1808	N.OLMSTED P
OLMSTED, N. & SON	Farmington, Conn.	1847	N.OLMSTED & SON P
ONCLEBAGH, GARRETT	New York, N.Y.	1698	B GO
OSGOOD, J.	Salem, Mass.	1817	J:OSGOOD
OSTHOFF, ANDREW	Baltimore, Md.	1810	A·OSTHOFF
OTIS, JOHN	Barnstable, Mass.	1703	
OTIS, JONATHAN	Newport, R.I.	1723-1791	I·O J.Otis Otis J.Otis OTIS J·OTIS
OTT, DANIEL	New York, N.Y.	1792	
OTT, GEORGE	Norfolk, Va.	1806	J.Ott Ott.
OVERIN, RICHARD	New York, N.Y.	1702	
OWEN, JESSE	Philadelphia, Pa.	1794	OWEN J^SE OWEN
OWEN, JOHN	Philadelphia, Pa.	1802	I·OWEN
	Philadelphia, Pa.	1804	

P

Name	Place	Date	Marks
PADDY, SAMUEL	Boston, Mass.	1659	
PAINTER, JOHN	Philadelphia, Pa.	1735	
PALMER & BACHLADER	Boston, Mass.	1815	PALMER & BACHLADER
PALMER & CLAPP	New York, N.Y.	1823	
PALMER & HINSDALE	New York, N.Y.	1815	
PALMER, JAMES	New York, N.Y.	1815	
PANCOAST, SAMUEL	Philadelphia, Pa.	1785	
PANGBORN & BRINSMAID	Burlington, Vermont	1833	
PARADICE, WILLIAM A.	Philadelphia, Pa.	1799	
PARASET, WILLIAM	Philadelphia, Pa.	1811	
PARHAM, WILLIAM	Philadelphia, Pa.	1785	
PARIE, JOSEPH	Philadelphia, Pa.	1811	
PARISEN, OTTO	New York, N.Y.	1763	PARISIEN
PARISIEN, O & SON	New York, N.Y.	1789	OPDP

Name	Location	Date	Marks
PARISIEN, OTTO W.	New York, N.Y.	1791	
PARKER, DANIEL	Boston, Mass.	1726-1785	D:P D:PARKER D.PARKER
PARKER, GEORGE	Baltimore, Md.	1804	G.PARKER
PARKER, ISAAC	Deerfield, Mass.	1780	I·PARKER
PARKER, RICHARD	Philadelphia, Pa.	1785	
PARKER, WILLIAM H.	New York, N.Y.	1835	
PARKMAN, C.	Boston, Mass.	1790	C.PARKMAN
PARKMAN, JOHN	Boston, Mass.	1738	PARKMAN
PARKMAN, THOMAS	Boston, Mass.	1793	T·PARKMAN
PARKS, JOHN	New York, N.Y.	1791	
PARMELE, JAMES	Durham, Conn.	1763-1828	
PARMELEE, SAMUEL	Guilford, Conn.	1737-1803	SP SP S·Parmele S·P S·Parmele
PARROTT, T.	Unknown	1760	T.PARROTT
PARSONS	Unknown	1750	PARSONS
PARRY, MARTIN	Portsmouth, N.H.	1737-1807	PARRY
PARRY & MUSGRAVE	Philadelphia, Pa.	1793	P&M
PARRY, ROWLAND	Philadelphia, Pa.	1819	R.PARRY
PARSONS, JOHN	Boston, Mass.	1780	I·PARSONS
PASCAL, WILLIAM	Philadelphia, Pa.	1765	
PATTERSON, GEORGE	New York, N.Y.	1835	
PATON, A.	Boston, Mass.	1850	
PATTERSON, JOHN	Annapolis, Md.	1751	I·P
PATTIT, THOMAS	New York, N.Y.	1796	
PATTON, THOMAS	Philadelphia, Pa.	1824	
PAULGREEN, OUOM	Philadelphia, Pa.	1798	
PAXSON, JOHN A.	Philadelphia, Pa.	1810	
PEABODY, JOHN	Enfield, Conn.	1799	J.PEABODY
PEALE, CHARLES W.	Philadelphia, Pa.	1765	
PEAR, EDWARD	Boston, Mass.	1836	EP E.P.
PEAR & BACALL	Boston, Mass.	1850	
PEARCE, WILLIAM	Norfolk, Va.	1820	W.PEARCE VA. NORFOLK W.PEARCE VA NORFOLK
PEARSE, SAMUEL	New York, N.Y.	1783	
PEARSON, JOHN	New York, N.Y.	1791	IP J.Pearson J.Pearson
PECK, B.	Connecticut	1820	B·PECK
PECK, LAWRENCE M.	Philadelphia, Pa.	1837	
PECK, TIMOTHY	Middletown, Conn.	1786	
PEDASY, S.	Philadelphia, Pa.	1810	
PEIRCE, JOHN	Boston, Mass.	1810	PEIRCE
PEIRI, JOSEPH	Philadelphia, Pa.	1811	
PELLETREAU, ELIAS	Southampton, N.Y.	1726-1810	EP
PELLETREAU, JOHN	Southampton, L.I.	1785	
PELLETREAU, MALTBY	New York, N.Y.	1813	
PELLETREAU & RICHARDS	New York, N.Y.	1825	W.S.P TR
PELLETREAU & UPSON	New York, N.Y.	1818	P&U
PELLETREAU & VAN WYCK	New York, N.Y.	1815	W.S.PELLETREAU S.VAN WYCK
PELLETREAU, W. SMITH	Southampton, N.Y.	1786-1842	
PEPPER, HENRY I.	Philadelphia, Pa.	1766	H.I.PEPPER HIPEPPER H.J.PEPPER
PERKINS, HAUGHTON	Boston, Mass.	1762	
PERKINS, ISAAC	Charlestown, Mass.	1707	IP
PERKINS, JACOB	Newburyport, Mass.	1766-1849	IP J.PERKINS
PERKINS, JOSEPH	Little Rest, R.I.	1770	J:PERKINS
PERKINS, T.	Boston, Mass.	1810	T.PERKINS

Name	Place	Date	Mark
PERPIGNAN, PETER	Philadelphia, Pa.	1809	
PERPIGNAN & VARNIER	Philadelphia, Pa.	1800	
PERRET & SANDOR	New York, N.Y.	1810	
PERREAUX, PETER	Philadelphia, Pa.	1797	P·P; PP
PERRET, AUGUSTA	New York, N.Y.	1801	
PERRY, THOMAS	Westerly, R.I.		
PETERS, JAMES	Philadelphia, Pa.	1821	
PETERS, R.	Philadelphia, Pa.	1807	
PETIT, MATTHEW	New York, N.Y.	1811	M·P
PETTIT, THOMAS	New York, N.Y.	1791	
PHELPS, CHARLES H.	Bainbridge, N.Y.	1825	CH.PHELPS
PHELPS, JEDEDIAH	Great Barrington, Vt.	1781	
PHILIP & YVER	Philadelphia, Pa.	1796	
PHILIPS, JASPER D.	Cincinatti, Ohio	1820	JAS D.PHILIPS
PHILLIPE, JOSEPH	Baltimore, Md.	1796	J.P
PHILLIPS, JAMES D.	Cleveland, Ohio	1829	
PHILLIPS, SAMUEL	Salem, Mass.	1680	SP
PHINNEY & MEAD	Unknown	1825	P&M
PHYFE, WILLIAM	Boston, Mass.	1830	
PICKERING, CHARLES	Philadelphia, Pa.	1683	
PIERCE, HART	New York, N.Y.	1835	
PIERCE, JOHN	Boston, Mass.	1810	PEIRCE
PIERCE, O.	Boston, Mass.	1824	O.PIERCE
PIERPONT, BENJAMIN H.	Boston, Mass.	1730-1797	B·P; BP; B.P; B·PIERPONT; PIERPONT; PIERPONT; B·PIERPONT
PIERSON, PHILLIP	New York, N.Y.	1798	
PINCHIN, WILLIAM	Philadelphia, Pa.	1779	
PINTO, JOSEPH	New York, N.Y.	1758	
PITKIN, HENRY	East Hartford, Conn.	1834	HP
PITKIN, HORACE E.	Hartford, Conn.	1832	
PITKIN, JAMES F.	East Hartford, Conn.	1834	
PITKIN, JOHN O.	East Hartford, Conn.	1803-1891	PITKIN
PITKIN, J. O. & W.	East Hartford, Conn.	1826	J.O&W.PITKIN
PITKIN & NORTON	Hartford, Conn.	1825	W.PITKIN; C.C.NORTO
PITKIN, WALTER	East Hartford, Conn.	1808-1885	W.PITKIN
PITKIN, WILLIAM J.	East Hartford, Conn.	1820	WM.J.PITKIN
PITKIN, WILLIAM L.	East Hartford, Conn.	1825	WM L PITKIN
PITKINS, JAMES	Hartford, Conn.	1812	
PITMAN, BENJAMIN	Providence, R.I.	1810	B.PITMAN
PITMAN & DORRANCE	Providence, R.I.	1795	
PITMAN & DODGE	Providence, R.I.	1790	
PITMAN, JOHN K.	Providence, R.I.	1805	
PITMAN, SANDERS	Providence, R.I.	1760	
PITMAN, WILLIAM R.	New Bedford, Mass.	1835	Pitman; PITMAN
PITT, RICHARD	Philadelphia, Pa.	1741	
PITTMAN, I.	Unknown	1785	I.Pittman
PITTS, A.	Philadelphia, Pa.	1790	
PITTS, RICHARD	Philadelphia, Pa.	1741	Pitts
PLAIN, EDWARD	New York, N.Y.	1835	
PLANQUET, GREGORY	New York, N.Y.	1797	
PLATT & BROTHER	New York, N.Y.	1820	PLATT & BRO; PLATT & BROTHER
PLATT, GEORGE W.	New York, N.Y.	1820	
PLATT, G. W. & N. C.	New York, N.Y.	1820	G.W.& N.C.PLATT; PLATT & BROTHER

PLATT, JAMES
New York, N.Y. 1835

PLATT, M. C.
New York, N.Y. 1820

POINCIGNON, FRANCIS
Philadelphia, Pa. 1796

POINCY, PETER
Philadelphia, Pa. 1813

POINTE, JAMES
Philadelphia, Pa. 1813

POINTE & TANGUY
Philadelphia, Pa. 1818

POISSENOT, N. J.
Philadelphia, Pa. 1806

POISSONIER, FRANCIS
Philadelphia, Pa. 1795

POLAND, P.
Philadelphia, Pa. 1837

POLGRAIN, QUOM
Philadelphia, Pa. 1797

POLHAMUS, J.
New York, N.Y. 1802

POLLARD, WILLIAM
Boston, Mass. 1711

PONCET, LEWIS
Baltimore, Md. 1800

PONS, THOMAS
Boston, Mass. 1789

POOR, NATHANIEL
Boston, Mass. 1829

PORTER, F. W.
New York, N.Y. 1820

PORTER, HENRY C.
New York, N.Y. 1820

PORTER & CO., HENRY C.
New York, N.Y. 1830

PORTER, I. S.
New York, N.Y. 1850

PORTRAM, ABRAHAM
New York, N.Y. 1727

POSEY, FREDERICK J.
Hagerstown, Md. 1820-1850

POST, SAMUEL
New London, Conn. 1783

POTTER, NILES
Westerly, R.I.

POTTER, J. O. & J. R.
Providence, R.I. 1824

POTWINE, JOHN
Boston, Mass. 1737

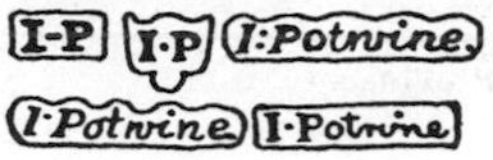

POTWINE & WHITING
Hartford, Conn. 1761

POUPARD, JAMES
Boston, Mass. 1751

POUTREAU, ABRAHAM
New York, N.Y. 1726

POWELL, C. F.
Boston, Mass. 1746

POWELSON, CHARLES
Albany, N.Y. 1840

PRATT, HENRY
Philadelphia, Pa. 1730

PRATT, NATHAN
Essex, Conn. 1792

PRATT, PHINEAS
Lyme, Conn. 1747-1813

PRATT, SETH
Lyme, Conn. 1754

PRESTON, S. L.
Philadelphia, Pa. 1830

PRICE, BENJAMIN
Boston, Mass. 1767

PRICE, HENRY P.
Philadelphia, Pa. 1810

PRICE, JOHN
Lancaster, Pa. 1764

PRIE, P.
Unknown 1780

PRINCE, JOB
Milford, Conn. .. 1680-1704

PURSELL, HENRY
New York, N.Y. 1775

PUTNAM, EDWARD
Salem, Mass. 1710

PUTNAM & LOW
Boston, Mass. 1822

PUTNAM, RUFUS
Albany, N.Y. 1814

Q

QUARITUS, FREDERICK
New York, N.Y. 1835

QUINCY, DANIEL
Braintree, Mass. 1651

QUINTARD, PETER
New York, N.Y. 1731
Norwalk, Conn. 1737

R

RABETH, JAMES
New York, N.Y. 1835

RAIT, DAVID
New York, N.Y. 1835

RAIT, ROBERT
New York, N.Y. 1830

RASCH, ANTHONY
Philadelphia, Pa. 1807

RASCH, ANTHONY & CO.
Philadelphia, Pa. 1820

RASCH, W. A.
New Orleans, La. 1830

RASCH & WILLIG
Philadelphia, Pa. 1819

RAVEE, XAVIER
Philadelphia, Pa. 1796

RAYMOND, JOHN
Boston, Mass. 1775

REED, A. G. & CO.
Nassau, N.H. 1835

REED, ISAAC
Stamford, Conn. 1776

REED, ISAAC & SON
Stamford, Conn. 1810

REED, JONATHAN
Boston, Mass. 1725-1740

REED, LEWIS
New York, N.Y. 1810

REED, O. & CO.
Philadelphia, Pa. 1841

REED, OSMAN
Philadelphia, Pa. 1840

REED, STEPHEN
Philadelphia, Pa. 1846

REEDER, ABNER
Philadelphia, Pa. 1797

REEDER, JOHN
Philadelphia, Pa. 1835

REEVE, G.
Unknown 1825

REEVE, I.
New York, N.Y. 1790

REEVES, ENOS
Charleston, S.C. 1746-1807

REEVES, STEPHEN
Burlington, N.J. 1767
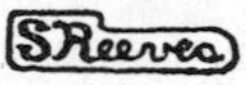

REVERE, EDWARD
Boston, Mass. 1796

REVERE, J. W.
Boston, Mass. 1798

REVERE, PAUL
Boston, Mass. 1735-1818

REVERE, PAUL, Sr.
Boston, Mass. 1702-1754

REVERE, PAUL, III
Boston, Mass. 1795

REVERE & SON
Boston, Mass. 1796

REVERE, THOMAS
Boston, Mass. 1789

REYNOLDS, JOHN
Hagerstown, Md. 1790-1832
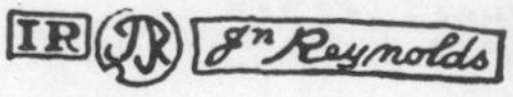

REYNOLDS, THEODORE J.
Philadelphia, Pa. 1835

RICE
Unknown ....c. 1780

RICE, HENRY P.
Albany, N.Y. 1815

RICE, JOSEPH
Baltimore, Md. 1784

RICE, JOSEPH T.
Baltimore, Md. 1785

RICE, JOSEPH T.
Albany, N.Y. 1835

RICH, OBADIAH
Boston, Mass. 1836

RICHARD, AUGUSTA
Philadelphia, Pa. 1818

RICHARD, STEPHEN
New York, N.Y. 1828
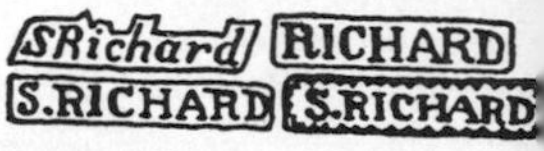

RICHARDS, SAMUEL
New York, N.Y. 1828

RICHARDS, SAMUEL
Philadelphia, Pa. 1770

RICHARDS, SAMUEL R., Jr.
Philadelphia, Pa. 1793

RICHARDS, STEPHEN
Cohansey Bridge, N.J. 1767

RICHARDS, T.
Unknown ....c. 1800

RICHARDS, THOMAS
New York, N.Y. 1815

RICHARDS, W.
Philadelphia, Pa. 1813

RICHARDS, W. & S. R.
Philadelphia, Pa. 1818

RICHARDS, & WILLIAMSON
Philadelphia, Pa. 1797

RICHARDSON, FRANCIS
Philadelphia, Pa. 1718

RICHARDSON, JOSEPH
Philadelphia, Pa. ... 1711-1784

RICHARDSON, JOSEPH, Jr.
Philadelphia, Pa. 1777

RICHARDSON, JOSEPH & NATHANIEL
Philadelphia, Pa. 1785

RICHARDSON, RICHARD
Philadelphia, Pa. 1793

RICHMOND, FRANKLIN
Providence, R.I. 1815

RICHMOND, G. & A.
Providence, R.I. 1815

Name	Place	Date	Marks
IDGEWAY, JAMES	Boston, Mass.	1789	
IDGEWAY, JOHN	Boston, Mass.	1813	J:RIDGWAY
IDOUT, GEORGE	New York, N.Y.	1745	GR
IED, JOHAN	Philadelphia, Pa.	1810	
IELLY, BERNARD	New York, N.Y.	1835	
IGGS, GEORGE W.	Georgetown, D.C.	1805-1810	GR · Riggs · RIGGS · RIGGS
	Baltimore, Md.	1810-1840	
IGGS AND GRIFFITH	Baltimore, Md.	1816	R&G
IGGS, RICHARD	Philadelphia, Pa.	1819	RR · Riggs
IKER, PETER	New York, N.Y.	1802	P.RIKER
IKER & ALEXANDER	New York, N.Y.	1800	
ITTER, MICHAEL	New York, N.Y.	1786	
OATH, ROSWELL W.	Norwich, Conn.	1826	
OBBINS, ELISHA	Philadelphia, Pa.	1831	
OBBS	New York, N.Y.	1788	
OBERT, CHRISTOPHER	New York, N.Y.	1708-1783	CR
OBERTS, FREDERICK	Boston, Mass.	1770	
OBERTS & LEE	Boston, Mass.	1775	R&L
OBERTS, MICHAEL	New York, N.Y.	1786	
OBERTSON, ALEXANDER	Philadelphia, Pa.	1740	
OBERTSON, ANTHONY W.	Philadelphia, Pa.	1798	
OBERTSON, ROBERT	Philadelphia, Pa.	1777	
OBINSON, ANTHONY W.	Philadelphia, Pa.	1798	A·ROBINSON
ROBINSON, BENJAMIN	Philadelphia, Pa.	1818	
ROBINSON, E.	Unknown	1820	E.ROBINSON
ROBINSON, ISBEAL	Philadelphia, Pa.	1840	
ROBINSON, & HARWOOD	Philadelphia, Pa.	1814	
ROBINSON, O.	New Haven, Conn.	1800	O·ROBINSON
ROCKWELL, EDWARD	New York, N.Y.	1825	ROCKWELL · ROCKWELL
ROCKWELL, S. D.	New York, N.Y.	1830	S.D.ROCKWELL · NEW YORK
ROCKWELL, THOMAS	New London, Conn.	1795	Rockwell
RODIER, PETER G.	New York, N.Y.	1825	
ROE, WILLIAM	Kingston, N.Y.	1805	W·ROE · W·ROE
ROE, W. & STOLLENWERCK	New York, N.Y.	1800	W.ROE & STOLLENWERCK
ROFF	New York, N.Y.	1813	
ROGERS, AUGUSTUS	Boston, Mass.	1818	
ROGERS, DANIEL	Newport, R.I.	1792	D·R · DR · D.R · D·ROGERS
ROGERS, DANIEL	New York, N.Y.	1835	
ROGERS, JOSEPH	Hartford, Conn.	1808	IR · JR · I·R · I·R
ROGERS & WENDT	Boston, Mass.	1850	
ROGERS, WILLIAM	Hartford, Conn.	1801-1873	WROGERS · WM ROGERS · HARTFORD
ROGERS, WILLIAM & SON	Hartford, Conn.	1850	WM.ROGERS&S
ROHR, JOHN A.	Philadelphia, Pa.	1807	I.ROHR
ROLLINGSON, WILLIAM	New York, N.Y.	1783	
ROMNEY, JOHN	New York, N.Y.	1770	
ROOSEVELT, NICHOLAS	New York, N.Y.	1745-1769	N·R · NR
ROOT, W. N. & BRO.	New Haven, Conn.	1850	W.N.ROOT & BROTHER
ROSE, ANTHONY	New York, N.Y.	1755	
ROSHORE, JOHN	New York, N.Y.	1792	
ROSHORE, & PRIME,	New York, N.Y.	1825	
ROSS, JOHN	Baltimore, Md.	1756-1798	IR · I·R
ROSS, ROBERT	Frederika, Delaware	1789	
ROUND, JOHN	Portsmouth, N.H.	1634	

ROUSE, ANTHONY
Philadelphia, Pa. 1807

ROUSE, MICHAEL
Boston, Mass. 1711

ROUSE, WILLIAM
Boston, Mass. 1639-1705

ROYALSTON, JOHN
Boston, Mass. 1770

RULE
Massachusetts 1780

RUSSEL, DANIEL
Newport, R.I. 1792

RUSSEL, JONATHAN
Ashford, Conn. 1770-1804

RUSSELL, GEORGE
Philadelphia, Pa. 1831

RUSSELL, JOHN H.
New York, N.Y. 1794-1798

RUSSEL, MOODY
Barnstable, Mass. 1694

RUSSELIER, PETER
New York, N.Y. 1794

RUTTER, RICHARD
Baltimore, Maryland 1790

RYERSON, LOW
York, Pa. 1760

S

SACHEVERELL, JOHN
Philadelphia, Pa. 1732

SACKETT & WILLARD
Providence, R.I. 1815

SADD, HARVEY
New Hartford, Conn. .1776-1840
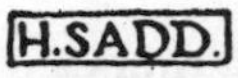

SADTLER, P. B. & SON
Baltimore, Md. 1850

SADTLER, PHILIP B.
Baltimore, Md. 1771-1860

SADTLER, PHILLIP P.
Baltimore, Md. 1819
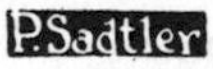

SAINT MARTIN, ANTHONY
Philadelphia, Pa. 1796

SANBORN, A.
Lowell, Mass. 1850

SANDELL, EDWARD
Baltimore, Md. 1816

SANDERSON, BENJAMIN
Boston, Mass. 1649-1678

SANDERSON, ROBERT
Boston, Mass. 1693

SANDERSON, ROBERT, Jr.
Boston, Mass. 1638

SANDERSON, WILLIAM
New York, N.Y. 1799

SANDFORD, ISAAC
Hartford, Conn. 1793

SANFORD, F. S.
Nantucket, Mass. 1828
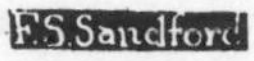

SANFORD, WILLIAM
Nantucket, Mass. 1817

SANDOZ & BROTHER
New York, N.Y. 1811

SANDOZ, PHILIP A.
Philadelphia, Pa. 1814

SANDS, STEPHEN
New York, N.Y. 1774

SANFORD, ISAAC
Hartford, Conn. 1785

SARDO, MICHAEL
Baltimore, Md. 1817

SARGANT, ENSIGN
Boston, Mass. 1820

SARGEANT, JACOB
Hartford, Conn. 1761-1843

SAVAGE, EDWARD
Philadelphia, Pa. 1794

SAVAGE, THOMAS
Boston, Mass. 1689

SAVAGE, THOMAS, Jr.
Boston, Mass. 1719

SAWIN, SILAS
Boston, Mass. 1823

SAWIN, SILAS W.
New York, N.Y. 1835

SAWYER, H. L.
New York, N.Y. 1840
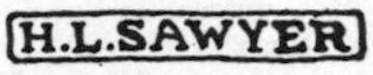

SAYRE, JOEL
New York, N.Y. 1778-1818

SAYRE, JOHN
New York, N.Y. 1771-1852

SAYRE & RICHARDS
New York, N.Y. 1802

SCARRET, JOSEPH
Philadelphia, Pa. 1797

SCHAATS, BARTHOLOMEW
New York, N.Y. 1683-1758

SCHAFFIELD, JEREMIAH
Philadelphia, Pa. 1785

SCHANK, GARRET
New York, N.Y. 1791

SCHANK, JOHN A.
New York, N.Y. 1792

SCHOFIELD, SOLOMON
Albany, New York 1815

SCOT, I.
Albany, N.Y. 1750

SCOTT, J. B.
New York, N.Y. 1820

SCOVIL & KINSEY
Cincinatti, Ohio 1830

SCRYMAGEOUR, JAMES
New York, N.Y. 1835

SCWIND, JOHN
New York, N.Y. 1790

SEAL, WILLIAM
Philadelphia, Pa. 1817

SEARS, MATTHEW
New York, N.Y. 1835

SEBASTIEN, JEANNE L.
New York, N.Y. 1814

SEGN, GEORGE
Philadelphia, Pa. 1820

SELKIRK, WILLIAM
New York, N.Y. 1817

SELL, J.
New York, N.Y. 1800

SENEMAND, JOHN B.
Philadelphia, Pa. 1798

SEVEIGNES, JACQUES
New Orleans, La. 1822

SEVRIN, LEWIS
Philadelphia, Pa. 1837

SEXNINE, SIMON
New York, N.Y. 1722

SEYMOUR & HOLLISTER
Hartford, Conn. 1845

SEYMOUR, JOSEPH
New York, N.Y. 1835

SEYMOUR, OLIVER D.
Hartford, Conn. 1843
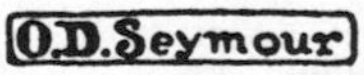

SHARP, W.
Philadelphia, Pa. 1835

SHARP, W. & G.
Philadelphia, Pa. 1848

SHAW, I. A.
Unknown 1800

SHARRARD, J. S.
Shelbyville, Ky. 1850

SHAW & DUNLEVY
Philadelphia, Pa. 1833

SHAW, EDWARD, G.
Philadelphia, Pa. 1825

SHAW, JOHN A.
Newport, R.I. 1819

SHEETS
Henrico, Va. 1697

SHEPHERD & BOYD
Albany, N.Y. 1810

SHEPHERD, ROBERT
Albany, N.Y. 1805

SHEPPER, JOHN D.
Philadelphia, Pa. 1818

SHETHAR, SAMUEL
Litchfield, Conn. 1801

SHETHAR & GORHAM
New Haven, Conn. 1806

SHETHAR & THOMPSON
Litchfield, Conn. 1801

SHEILDS, CALEB
Baltimore, Md. 1773

SHIELDS, THOMAS
Philadelphia, Pa. 1771

SHIPMAN, NATHANIEL
Norwich, Conn. 1764-1853
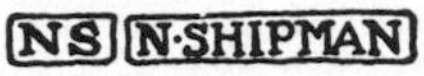

SHIVING, GODFREY
Philadelphia, Pa. 1779

SHOEMAKER, CHARLES
New York, N.Y. 1825

SHOEMAKER, JOSEPH
Philadelphia, Pa. 1798

SHONNARD, GEORGE
New York, N.Y. 1797

SHOPSHIRE, ROBERT
Baltimore, Md. 1778

SHREVE, BENJAMIN
Boston, Mass. 1834

SIBLEY, CLARK
New Haven, Conn. ...1778-1808

SIBLEY, JOHN
New Haven, Conn. 1810

SIBLEY & MARBLE
New Haven, Conn. ...1801-1806

SILLIMAN, HEZEKIAH
New Haven, Conn. ...1739-1804

SIME & MOSES
Birmingham, Ga. 1768

SIME, WILLIAM
Birmingham, Ga. 1768

SIMES, WILLIAM
Portsmouth, N.H. 1773-1824

SIMMONS & ALEXANDER
Philadelphia, Pa. 1798

SIMMONS, ANDREW
Philadelphia, Pa. 1796

SIMMONS, ANTHONY
Philadelphia, Pa. 1797

SIMMONS, J.
Philadelphia, Pa. 1810
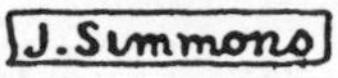

SIMMONS, J. & A.
New York, N.Y. 1805

SIMMONS, JAMES
New York, N.Y. 1815

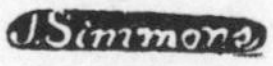

SIMMONS, JOSEPH
Philadelphia, Pa. 1828

SIMMONS, PETER
New York, N.Y. 1816

SIMMONS, S.
Philadelphia, Pa. 1797

SIMPKINS, THOS. BARTON
Boston, Mass. 1728-1804

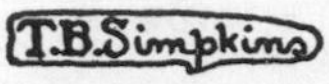

SIMPKINS, WILLIAM
Boston, Mass. 1704-1780

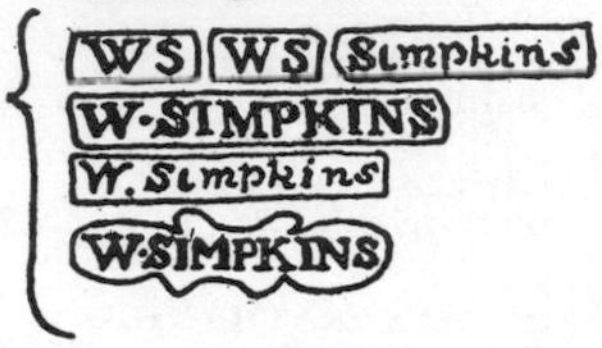

SIMPSON & BECKEL
Albany, N.Y. 1849

SINGLETON & YOUNG
New York, N.Y. 1800

SIXTE, JOSEPH A.
Philadelphia, Pa. 1837

SIXTE, VINCENT B.
Philadelphia, Pa. 1837

SKATTS, BARTHOLOMEW
Freeman, N.Y. 1784

SKERRET, JOSEPH
Philadelphia, Pa. 1797

SKERRY, GEORGE W.
Boston, Mass. 1837

SKINNER, ABRAHAM
New York, N.Y. 1756

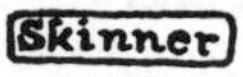

SKINNER, ELIZER
Hartford, Conn.

SKINNER, MATT
Philadelphia, Pa. 1752

SKINNER, THOMAS
New York, N.Y. 1712-1761

SLIDELL, JOSHUA
New York, N.Y. 1765

SLOAN, WILLIAM
Hartford, Conn.. 1794

SMITH, DAVID
Philadelphia, Pa. 1778

SMITH, CHRISTIAN
Philadelphia, Pa. 1820

SMITH, EBENEZER
Brookfield, Conn. 1775

SMITH, GEORGE
Philadelphia, Pa. 1831

SMITH, GEORGE O.
New York, N.Y. 1825

SMITH, I.
Boston, Mass. 1742-1789

SMITH & GRANT
St. Louis, Mo. 1850

SMITH, JACOB
Philadelphia, Pa. 1809

SMITH, JAMES
New York, N.Y. 1794

SMITH, JAMES
Philadelphia, Pa. 1807

SMITH, JOHN
Philadelphia, Pa. 1819

SMITH, JOHN & THOMAS
Baltimore, Md. 1817

SMITH, JOSEPH
Boston, Mass. 1742-1789

SMITH, JOSEPH
Philadelphia, Pa. 1804

SMITH, J. & T.
Baltimore, Md. 1817

SMITH, LEVIN H.
Philadelphia, Pa. 1837

SMITH, ROBERT E.
Philadelphia, Pa. 1820

SMITH, SAMUEL
Philadelphia, Pa. 1785

SMITH, WILLIAM
New York, N.Y. 1770

SMITH, ZEBULON
Maine 1786-1865

SOMERBY, ROBERT
Mass. 1794-1821

SNOW, J.
Unknown 1750

SNYDER, GEORGE
Philadelphia, Pa. 1816

SOLOMON, SAMUEL
Philadelphia, Pa. 1811

SONNIER, JOSEPH
Philadelphia, Pa. 1811

SOUMAIEN, SAMUEL
Philadelphia, Pa. 1754

SOUMAIN, SIMEON
New York, N.Y. 1685-1750

SOQUE, MICHAEL
New York, N.Y. 1794

SOWERLT, ANTHONY
Philadelphia, Pa. 1823

SPARROW, HENRY
Philadelphia, Pa. 1811

SPARROW, THOMAS
Annapolis, Md. 1764-1784

SPEAR, ISAAC
Boston, Mass. 1836

Name	Location	Date	Mark
SPENCER, GEORGE	Essex, Conn.	1810	
SPENCER, JAMES	Hartford, Conn.	1793	
SQUIRE & BROTHER	New York, N.Y.	1846	SQUIRE&BROTHER OF COIN
SQUIRE & LANDER	New York, N.Y.	1840	SQUIRE&LANDER
SQUIRE, S. P.	New York, N.Y.	1835	S.P.SQUIRE
STACY, P.	Boston, Mass.	1819	P.STACY
STALL, JOSEPH	Baltimore, Md.	1804	
STANIFORD, JOHN	Windham, Conn.	1737-1811	JS Stanford
STANTON, DANIEL	Stonington, Conn.	1755-1781	D.Stanton
STANTON, ENOC	Stonington, Conn.	1745	
STANTON, ZEBULON	Stonington, Conn.	1753-1828	ZS STANTON
STANWOOD & HALSTRICK	Boston, Mass.	1850	
STANWOOD, HENRY B.	Boston, Mass.	1818-1869	HenryB.Stanwood
STANWOOD, J. E.	Philadelphia, Pa.	1850	J.E.STANWOOD
STANWOOD, JAMES D.	Boston, Mass.	1846	
STAPLES, JOHN J.	New York, N.Y.	1788	IIS J.J.S.
STAPLES, JOHN J., Jr.	New York, N.Y.	1788	
ST. CYR., S. L.	New Orleans, La.	1822	
STARR, R.	Unknown	1800	R·STARR
STARR, RICHARD	Philadelphia, Pa.	1813	R.STARR
STEBBINS & CO. E.	New York, N.Y.	1810	E.STEBBINS&CO
STEBBINS & HOWE	New York, N.Y.	1815	STEBBINS&HOWE
STEBBINS, T. E.	New York, N.Y.	1810	STEBBINS T.STEBBINS
STEDMAN, ALEXANDER	Philadelphia, Pa.	1793	
STEELE, JOHN	Annapolis, Md.	1710	
STEELE, T. & CO.	Hartford, Conn.	1805	T.Steele&Co
STEELE, T. S.	Hartford, Conn.	1790	T.Steele
STEPHANIS, GOTHELF	New York, N.Y.	1791	
STEPHEN, THOMAS H.	Philadelphia, Pa.	1839	
STEPHENS, GEORGE	New York, N.Y.	1790	G.S
STEPHENSON, THOMAS	Buffalo, N.Y.	1840	STEPHENSON
STEVEN, GEORGE	New York, N.Y.	1719	
STEVENS & LAKEMAN	Salem, Mass.	1825	STEVENS&LAKEMAN
STEWART C. W.	Lexington, Ky.	1850	C.W.STEWART LEX.KT.
STEWART, JOHN	New York, N.Y.	1791	
STICKLER, JOHN	New York, N.Y.	1823	
STICKNEY, JONATHAN, Jr.	Newburyport, Mass.	1798	I·STICKNEY
STICKNEY, M. P.	Newburyport, Mass.	1820	M.P.STICKNEY
STILES, BENJAMIN	Woodbury, Conn.	1831	
STILLMAN, ALEXANDER	Philadelphia, Pa.	1806	
STILLMAN, BARTON	Westerly, R.I.		
STILLMAN, E.	Stonington, Conn.	1825	E.Stillman E.Stillman
STILLMAN, PAUL	Westerly, R.I.		
STILLMAN, RICHARD	Philadelphia, Pa.	1805	R.STILLMAN
STILMAN, WILLIAM	Hopkington, R.I.	1788	
STINSON, WILLIAM	New York, N.Y.	1813	
STOCKMAN & PEPPER	Philadelphia, Pa.	1840	STOCKERMAN&PEPPER
STOCKMAN, JACOB	Philadelphia, Pa.	1828	
STODDER & FROBISHER	Boston, Mass.	1817	STODDER&FROBISHER
STOLLENWRECK	New York, N.Y.	1800	Stollenwerck
STOLLENWERCK & BROS.	New York, N.Y.	1805	Stollenwerck&Bros
STOLLENWERCK & CO.	New York, N.Y.	1800	

STONE, ADAM
Baltimore, Md.

STONE & OSBORN
New York, N.Y. 1796

STORM, A. G.
Albany, N.Y. 1830

STORM, A. G. & SON
Albany, N.Y. 1835

STORRS & COOLEY
New York, N.Y. 1832

STORRS, N.
New York, N.Y. 1825

STOUT, J. D.
New York, N.Y. 1850

STOUT, SAMUEL
Princeton, N.J. 1779

STOW, JOHN
Wilmington, Del. 1772

STOUTENBURGH, TOBIAS
New York, N.Y. 1700-1759

STOWELL, A., Jr.
Baltimore, Md. 1855

STRONG, JOHN
Maryland 1778

STRONG, WILLIAM
Philadelphia, Pa. 1807

STUART, H.
New York, N.Y. 1808

STUART, JOHN
Providence, R.I. 1737

STUCKERT, ISAAC
Philadelphia, Pa. 1809

STUDLEY, D. F.
Unknown 1830

SULLIVAN, C. D.
St. Louis, Mo. 1850

SULLIVAN, D. & CO.
New York, N.Y. 1820

SUPPLEE, JACOB
Philadelphia, Pa. 1791

SUTHERLAND, GEORGE
Boston, Mass. 1810

SUTTON, ROBERT
Boston, Mass. 1820

SWAN, B.
Unknown 1825

SWAN, CALEB
Boston, Mass. 1775

SWAN, ROBERT
Philadelphia, Pa. 1824

SWAN, ROBERT
Philadelphia, Pa. 1799

SWAN, WILLIAM
Worcester, Mass. 1715-1774

SWEETER, HENRY P.
Worcester, Mass. 1768

SYMMES, JOHN
Boston, Mass. 1766

SYNG, DANIEL
Lancaster, Pa.

SYNG, PHILIP
Philadelphia, Pa. 1703-1789

SYNG, PHILIP, Jr.
Philadelphia, Pa. 1676-1739

T

TABER, WILLIAM
Philadelphia, Pa. 1835

TANGUY, J. & P.
Philadelphia, Pa. 1808

TANGUY, JOHN
Philadelphia, Pa. 1818

TANGUY, PETER
Philadelphia, Pa. 1810

TANGUY, REPITON
Philadelphia, Pa. 1806

TANNER, JOHN
Newport, R.I. 1740

TANNER, P. G.
Newport, R.I. 1800

TARBELL, E.
Unknown ....c. 1830

TARGEE, JOHN
New York, N.Y. 1799

TARGEE, JOHN & PETER
New York, N.Y. 1811

TARGEE, PETER
New York, N.Y. 1811

TARGEE, WILLIAM
New York, N.Y. 1807

TAYLOR, GEORGE W.
Philadelphia, Pa. 1824

TAYLOR & HINSDALE
New York, N.Y. 1801

TAYLOR, JOHN
New York, N.Y. 1801

TAYLOR & LAWRIE
Philadelphia, Pa. 1841

TAYLOR, NAJAH
New York, N.Y. 1793

TAYLOR, N. & CO.
New York, N.Y. 1825

TAYLOR, THOMAS
Providence, R.I. 1727

TAYLOR, WILLIAM
Philadelphia, Pa. 1772

TAYLOR & LAWRIE
Philadelphia, Pa. 1837

TEMPEST, ROBERT
Philadelphia, Pa. 1814

TEN EYCK, JACOB
Albany, N.Y. 1704-1793

TEN EYCK, KOENRAET
New York, N.Y. 1678-1753

TENNEY, WILLIAM I.
New York, N.Y. 1840
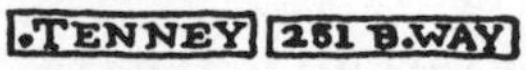

TERRY, GEER
Enfield, Conn. 1775-1858

TERRY, JOHN
New York, N.Y. 1820

TERRY, L. B.
Enfield, Conn. 1810

TERRY, WILBERT
Enfield, Conn. 1810

TERRY, WILLIAM
Enfield, Conn. 1785

THAXTER, JOSEPH B.
Highham, Mass. 1815

THEOFILE, WILLIAM
New Orleans, La. 1822

THIBAULT & BROS.
Philadelphia, Pa. 1810

THIBAULT & COMPANY
Philadelphia, Pa. 1797

THIBAULT, FELIX
Philadelphia, Pa. 1814

THIBAULT, FRANCIS
Philadelphia, Pa. 1800

THIBAULT, FRANCIS & FELIX
Philadelphia, Pa. 1807

THIBAULT, FREDERICK
Philadelphia, Pa. 1818

THIBAULT, FREDERICK & FELIX
Philadelphia, Pa. 1813

THOMAS, CARSON & HALL
Albany, N.Y. 1818

THOMAS, THOMAS
New York, N.Y. 1784

THOMAS, WALTER
New York, N.Y. 1769

THOMAS, WILLIAM
Trenton, N.J. 1775

THOMISON, PETER
Boston, Mass. 1817

THOMPSON, D. B.
Litchfield, Conn. 1825
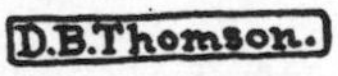

THOMPSON, WILLIAM
Maryland 1762-1774

THOMSON, ISAAC
Litchfield, Conn. 1801

THOMSON, JAMES
New York, N.Y. 1834

THOMSON, PETER
Philadelphia, Pa. 1835

THOMSON, JAMES
New York, N.Y. 1834

THOMSON, WILLIAM
New York, N.Y. 1810

THORNTON HENRY
Providence, R.I. 1824

TILEY, JAMES
Hartford, Conn. 1740-1792

TINGLEY, SAMUEL
New York, N.Y. 1767

TISDALE, B. H.
Providence, R.I. 1824

TITCOMB, FRANCIS
Newburyport, Mass. 1813

TOMPKINS, EDMUND
Waterbury, Conn. 1779

TOUZELL, JOHN
Salem, Mass. 1756

TOWNSHENDT, THOMAS
Boston, Mass. 1727

TOWNSEND, S.
Unknown 1775

TOWSON, OBADIAH W.
Philadelphia, Pa. 1819

TOWZELL, JOHN
Salem, Mass. 1726-1785

TOY, ISAAC NICHOLAS
Maryland 1771-1834

TOY, JOSEPH
Abingdon, Md. 1748-1826

TRACY, ERASTUS
Norwich, Conn. 1791

TRACY, GORDON
Norwich, Conn. 1767-1792

TRAUX, HENRY R.
Albany, N.Y. 1815

TRIPLER, CHRISTIAN
New York, N.Y. 1794

TROLL, WILLIAM
Philadelphia, Pa. 1810

TROTH, JAMES
Pittsburgh, Pa. 1800

TROTT & BROOKS
New London, Conn. 1798
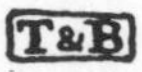

TROTT & CLEVELAND
New London, Conn. ..1792-1794
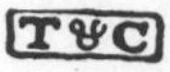

TROTT, GEORGE
Boston, Mass. 1765

TROTT, J. P.
New London, Conn. 1769

TROTT, J. P. & SON
New London, Conn. 1820

TROTT, J. PROCTOR
New London, Conn. 1799

TROTT, JOHN PROCTOR
New London, Conn. 1792

TROTT, JONATHAN
Boston, Mass. 1771

TROTT, JONATHAN, Jr.
New London, Conn. 1800

TROTT & SON, JOHN P.
New London, Conn. 1820

TROTT, THOMAS
Boston, Mass. 1701-1777

TRUAX, HENRY, R.
Albany, N.Y. 1815

TRUMBUL, RICHARD
Boston, Mass. 1767

TUCKER, DANIEL
Portland, Me. 1781

TUCKER, J. W.
New York, N.Y. 1803

TURNER, JAMES
Boston, Mass. 1759

TUTHILL, CHRISTOPHER
Philadelphia, Pa. 1731

TUTTLE, BETHUEL
New Haven, Conn. 1802

TUTTLE, WILLIAM
New Haven, Conn. 1821

TYLER, ANDREW
Boston, Mass. 1692-1741

TYLER & CO., JOHN H.
Boston, Mass. 1840

TYLER, DAVID
Boston, Mass. 1760-1804

TYLER, D. M.
Boston, Mass. 1810

TYLER, GEORGE
Boston, Mass. 1740-1785

U

UBELIN, FREDERICK
Philadelphia, Pa. 1773

UFFORD, & BURDICK
New Haven, Conn 1814

UNDERHILL, ANDREW
New York, N.Y. 1780

UNDERHILL, THOMAS
New York, N.Y. 1779

UNDERHILL & VERNON
New York, N.Y. 1787

UNDERWOOD, JOHN
Philadelphia, Pa. 1797

V

VAIL, ELIJAH
Troy, N.Y. 1836

VAISSIERE, VICTOR
New York, N.Y. 1816

VALET, PETER
New York, N.Y. 1787

VALLEE, ANTOINE
New Orleans, La. 1822

VAN BERGEN, JOHN
Albany, N.Y. 1813

VAN BEUREN, PETER
New York, N.Y. 1798

VAN BEUREN, WILLIAM
New York, N.Y. 1790

VANDERBURGH, CORNELIUS
New York, N.Y. 1677

VANDERHAN, J.
Philadelphia, Pa. 1740

VANDERHAUL
Philadelphia, Pa. 1740

VANDERSPIEGEL
New York, N.Y. 1701

VANDERSPIEGEL, JACOBUS
New York, N.Y. 1702

VANDERSPIEGEL, JOHANNIS
New York, N.Y. 1687

VAN DYKE, PETER
New York, N.Y. 1684-1750

AN DYKE, RICHARD
New York, N.Y. 1717-1770

AN HORN, DAVID
Philadelphia, Pa. 1801

AN INBURGH, PETER
New York, N.Y. 1689-1740

AN NESS, & WATERMAN
New York, N.Y. 1835

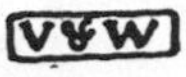

AN RIPER, TUNIS
New York, N.Y. 1813

AN SCHAICK, G.
Unknown 1840

AN VEGHTEN, HENRY
Abany, N.Y. 1760

AN VLEIT, B.V.
Poughkeepsie, N.Y. 1840

AN VOORHIS, DANIEL
New York, N.Y. 1779

AN VOORHIS & COOLEY
New York, N.Y. 1786

AN VOORHIS & SCHANCK
New York, N.Y. 1791

AN VOORHIS & SON
New York, N.Y. 1798

AN WYCK & PELLETREAU
New York, N.Y. 1815

AN WYCK, S.
New York, N.Y. 1810

ARNEY, JOHN
Philadelphia, Pa. 1795

EAZIE, JOSEPH
Providence, R.I. 1815

ERGEREAU, PETER
New York, N.Y. 1700-1755

ERNON, J. & CO.
New York, N.Y. 1798

ERNON, JOHN
New York, N.Y. 1793

ERNON, N. & CO.
Charleston S.C. 1800

ERNON, NATHANIEL
Charleston, S.C. 1777-1843

ERNON, SAMUEL
Newport, R.I. 1683-1735

ERNON & PARK
Pittsburg, Pa. 1815

ILANT, WILLIAM
Philadelphia. Pa. 1725

VILLARD, R. H. L.
Georgetown, D.C. 1833

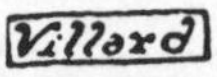

VINCENT, RICHARD
Baltimore, Md. 1799

VINTON, DAVID
Providence, R.I. 1790

VIRGIN, W. M.
Unknown 1830

VOORHIS, DANIEL VAN
New York, N.Y. 1769

W

WACHNER, F. W.
New York, N.Y. 1819

WADDILL, NOEL
Petersburg, Va. 1778

WAGLIN, THOMAS
Philadelphia, Pa. 1837

WAGSTAFF, THOMAS
New York, N.Y. 1791

WAGSTER, ISAIAH
Baltimore, Md. 1776-1793

WAIT & WRIGHT
Philadelphia, Pa. 1837

WAITE, JOHN
Kingstown, R.I. 1770

WAITE, JOHN
New York, N.Y. 1798

WAITE, W.
Unknown 1770

WAITE, WILLIAM
Kingstown, R.I. 1760

WALDRON, D.
New York, N.Y. 1789

WALKER, GEORGE
Philadelphia, Pa. 1797

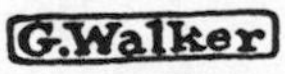

WALKER, HANNAH
Philadelphia, Pa. 1816

WALKER, JOHN, Jr.
Philadelphia, Pa. 1798

WALKER, L.
Boston, Mass. 1825

WALKER, WILLIAM
Philadelphia, Pa. 1793

WALKER, W. & S.
Phialdelphia, Pa. 1795

WALLACE, WILLIAM F.
Westerly, R.I.

WALLER, JOHN
Philadelphia, Pa. 1804

Name	Place	Date	Marks
WALLIS, THOMAS	Philadelphia, Pa.	1804	
WALRAVEN, JOHN	Baltimore, Md.	1771-1814	I.Walraven
WALTER, JACOB	Baltimore, Md.	1782-1865	J.WALTER
WALTON, DANIEL	Philadelphia, Pa.	1808	
WALWORTH, DANIEL	Middletown, Conn.	1785	
WARD, AMBROSE	New Haven, Conn.	1767	
WARD & BARTHOLOMEW	Hartford, Conn.	1804	W&B W&B; WARD & BARTHOLOMEW.HARTFORD; WARD& BARTHOLOMEW HARTFORD
WARD, BARTHOLOMEW & BRAINARD	Hartford, Conn.	1809	
WARD, BILLIOUS	Guilford, Conn.	1729-1777	BW BW BW B·W
WARD & COX	Hartford, Conn.	1811	
WARD & GAVETT	Hartford, Conn.	1813	
WARD & HUGHES	Middletown, Conn.	1805	
WARD, JAMES	Hartford, Conn.	1768-1856	JW WARD HARTFORD
WARD, JOHN	Philadelphia, Pa.	1808	WARD, 67 MARKET ST.
WARD, JOHN	Middletown, Conn.	1805	WARD.67MARKET ST
WARD & MILLER	Philadelphia, Pa.	1822	
WARD & RICH	Boston, Mass.	1830	
WARD, RICHARD	Boston, Mass.	1815	
WARD, SAMUEL L.	Boston, Mass.	1830	
WARD, TIMOTHY	Middletown, Conn.	1776	
WARD, WILLIAM, Jr.	Guilford, Conn.	1705-1761	W.W. W.W. W.WARD W.Ward W.Ward
WARD, WILLIAM	Litchfield, Conn.	1742-1828	
WARDIN, DANIEL	Bridgeport, Conn.	1811	
WARNER, A. E. & T. H.	Baltimore, Md.	1805	
WARNER, ANDREW E.	Baltimore, Md.	1786-1870	A·E·W AEW A·E·W A·E·W A·E·WARNER ANDW E.WARNER A.E.WARNER
WARNER, ANDREW E., Jr.	Baltimore, Md.	1805	
WARNER, CALEB	Portsmouth, N.H.	1784-1861	C.Warner C.Warner C.WARNER
WARNER, C. & J.	Baltimore, Md.	1825	C.&J.WARNER
WARNER, D.	Ipswich, Mass.	1810	D.WARNER
WARNER & FELLOWS	Portsmouth, N.H.	1824	
WARNER, JOSEPH	Philadelphia, Pa.	1811	J.Warner
WARNER, JOSEPH	Wilmington, Del.	1768	J.Warner
WARNER, JOSEPH P.	Baltimore, Md.	1811-1862	J.P.W
WARNER, SAMUEL	Philadelphia, Pa.	1797	SW WARNER
WARNER, THOMAS & A. E.	Baltimore, Md.	1805	T.&A.E.WARNER
WARNER, THOMAS H.	Baltimore, Md.	1780-1828	T.W T.WARNER
WARREN, BENJAMIN	Philadelphia, Pa.	1809	
WATERMAN, GEORGE,	Albany, N.Y.	1849	
WATERS, SAMUEL	Philadelphia, Pa.	1790	S·W SW S.WATERS
WATKINS, JAMES	New York, N.Y.	1819	
WATLING, JAMES	Philadelphia, Pa.	1837	
WATSON & BROWN	Philadelphia, Pa.	1830	WATSON & BROWN
WATSON, EDWARD	Boston, Mass.	1821	E.WATSON E.Watson
WATSON, JAMES	Philadelphia, Pa.	1830	J.WATSON
WATTS, J. & W.	Philadelphia, Pa.	1829	
WATTS, JAMES	Philadelphia, Pa.	1835	
WATTS, JOHN W.	New York, N.Y.	1794	
WAYNES, RICHARD	Philadelphia, Pa.	1750	RW

Silversmith	Place	Date	Marks
WEATHERS, MICHAEL	New York, N.Y.	1794	
WEAVER, EMMOR T.	Philadelphia, Pa.	1808	Weaver
WEAVER, JOSHUA	Westchester, Pa.	1815	IW
WEBB, BARNEBUS	Boston, Bass.	1762	BW
WEBB & BOON	Philadelphia, Pa.	1785	
WEBB, CHARLES	Philadelphia, Pa.	1738	
WEBB, EDWARD	Boston, Mass.	1718	WEBB
WEBB, GEORGE W.	Baltimore, Md.	1812-1890	GEO.W.WEBB
WEBB, JAMES	Baltimore, Md.	1788-1844	J.WEBB (circular mark)
WEBB, ROBERT	Philadelphia, Pa.	1798	
WEBSTER, HENRY L.	Providence, R.I.	1831	H.L.WEBSTER
WEBSTER, HENRY L. & CO.	Providence, R.I.	1842	H.L.W.&CO Providence R.I.
WEDGE, S.	Baltimore, Md.	1804	
WEDGE, SIMON, Sr.	Baltimore, Md.	1774-1823	S.W (oval mark) SW S.Wedge S.WEDGE
WEEDER, PELEG	North Kingstown, R.I.		
WELCH, JOHN	Boston, Mass.		
WELLES, A. & G.	Boston, Mass.	1830	A&G.WELLES
WELLES, ANDREW	Hebron, Conn.	1804	
WELLES & CO.	Boston, Mass.	1810	WELLES&CO
WELLES & GELSTON	New York, N.Y.	1840	WELLES&GELSTON
WELLES, GEORGE	Hebron, Conn. Boston, Mass.	1784 1827	WELLES WELLES WELLES&CO BOSTON
WELLES, GEORGE I.	Boston, Mass.	1784-1823	WELLES BOSTON
WELLES, JAMES M.	New York, N.Y.	1835	
WELLS, L. & C.	New York, N.Y.	1798	
WELLS, L. & H.	New York, N.Y.	1794	
WELLS, LEMUEL	New York, N.Y.	1791	LW
WELLS, LEMUEL & CO.	New York, N.Y.	1794	L.W.&Co
WELLS, WILLIAM	Hartford, Conn.	1828	
WENDOVER, JOHN	New York, N.Y.	1694	J.W IW JW
WENNAM, BARNARD	New York, N.Y.	1789	BW N.YORK B.WENMAN BWENMAN
WENTWORTH & CO.	New York, N.Y.	1850	WENTWORTH&CO
WEST, BENJAMIN	Boston, Mass.	1770	B.WEST
WEST, CHARLES	Boston, Mass.	1830	
WEST, JOSEPH	Philadelphia, Pa.	1797	
WESTERVELL, JOHN L.	Newburgh, N.Y.	1845	J.L.W
WESTON, BENJAMIN	Philadelphia, Pa.	1797	
WESTPAHL, CHARLES W.	Philadelphia, Pa.	1802	C.WESTPHAL C.WESTPHAL
WHARTENBY & BUNN	Philadelphia, Pa.	1816	
WHARTENBY, JOHN	Philadelphia, Pa.	1829	
WHARTENBY, THOMAS	Philadelphia, Pa.	1811	T.W WHARTENBY
WHARTENBY, THOMAS & CO.	Philadelphia, Pa.	1850	
WHEATLEY, FREDERICK G.	New York, N.Y.	1805	
WHEATON, CALEB	Providence, R.I.	1784-1827	
WHEATON, CALVIN	Providence, R.I.	1791	C.WHEATON C.WHEATON
WHETCROFT, WILLIAM	Baltimore, Md.	1735-1799	WW

Name	Place	Date	Mark
WHITAKER & GREENE	Providence, R.I.	1825	
WHIPPLE, ARNOLD	Providence, R.I.	1825	
WHITE, ALFRED	Boston, Mass.	1807	
WHITE, AMOS	East Haddam, Conn.	1745-1825	A.WHITE / WHITE
WHITE, EDWARD	Ulster County, N.Y.	1757	E:WHITE
WHITE, GEORGE L.	Cincinnati, Ohio	1829	
WHITE, PEREGINE	Woodstock, Conn.	1774	P.WHITE
WHITE, PETER	Norwalk, Conn.	1738	
WHITE, SAMUEL	New York, N.Y.	1805	
WHITE, SILAS	New York, N.Y.	1792	S.WHITE
WHITE, STEPHEN	New York, N.Y.	1805	
WHITE, WILLIAM	Philadelphia, Pa.	1805	W.W.WHITE
WHITE, WILLIAM J.	New York, N.Y.	1835	
WHITE, WILLIAM W.	New York, N.Y.	1835	Wm W.WHITE
WHITEMAN, IRA	New York, N.Y.	1761	
WHITING, B.	Norwich, Conn.	1755	B:WHITING
WHITING, CHARLES	Norwich, Conn.	1725-1765	CW / WHITING
WHITING, S.	New York, N.Y.	1700	
WHITLOCK, THOMAS	New York, N.Y.	1796	
WHITLOCK, THOMAS B.	New York, N.Y.	1805	Whitlock
WHITLOCK, WILLIAM H.	New York, N.Y.	1805	Wm H.WHITLOCK
WHITON, EBED	Boston, Mass.	1826	E.WHITNEY. / Whitney
WHITTEMORE	Unknown	1736	
WHITNEY, AMOS	New York, N.Y.	1800	A.WHITNEY
WHITNEY, E.	New York, N.Y.	1805	
WHITNEY, M.	Unknown	1823	M.WHITNEY
WHITNEY & HOYT	New York, N.Y.	1808	WHITNEY & HOYT
WHITON, EBED	Boston, Mass.	1813-1879	E.Whiton. / E.Whiton
WHITTAKER & GREEN	Providence, R.I.	1825	
WHITTEMORE, WILLIAM	Portsmouth, N.H.	1710-1770	Whittemore / Whittmore
WICKHAM, DANIEL H.	New York, N.Y.	1835	
WILCOX, MICHAEL	Maryland	1772-1799	XXXX
WILLARD, A.	Utica, N.Y.	1810	A.WILLARD / Utica
WILLARD, JAMES	East Windsor, Conn.	1815	WILLARD
WILLCOX, ALVAN	New Haven, Conn.	1805	
WILLCOX, CYPRIAN	New Haven, Conn.	1827	
WILLEY, B.	Unknown	1790	B.WILLEY
WILLIAMS, A. WILLIAM	Washington, D.C.	1829	W.A.WILLIAMS
WILLIAMS, ALEXANDER	Philadelphia, Pa.	1807	
WILLIAMS, CHARLES M.	New York, N.Y.	1825	
WILLIAMS, DEODAT	Hartford, Conn.	1776	
WILLIAMS, JOHN	Philadelphia, Pa.	1793	
WILLIAMS, STEPHEN	Providence, R.I.	1799	
WILLIAMS, W. A.	Washington, D.C.	1829	
WILLIAMS, W. W.	Washington, D.C.	1829	

WILLIAMSON, SAMUEL
Philadelphia, Pa. 1794

WILLIG, GEORGE
Philadelphia, Pa. 1819

WILIS, J.
Boston, Mass. 1820

WILLIS, STILLMAN
Boston, Mass. 1823

WILLIS, WILLIAM S.
Boston, Mass. 1825

WILLS, HENRY
New York, N.Y. 1774

WILMOT, SAMUEL
New Haven, Conn. 1777-1846

WILMOT, SAMUEL, Jr.
New Haven, Conn. ...1808-1846

WILMOT & STILLMAN
New Haven, Conn. 1800

WILMOT, T. T.
New Haven, Conn. 1810

WILSON, ALBERT
Troy, N.Y. 1834

WILSON, GEORGE
Philadelphia, Pa. 1850

WILSON, H. & CO.
Philadelphia, Pa. 1815

WILSON, HOSEA
Philadelphia, Pa. 1812

WILSON, HOSEA & CO.
Baltimore, Md. 1814-1816

WILSON, JAMES
Trenton, N.J. 1769

WILSON, JOHN
Philadelphia, Pa. 1770

WILSON, R. & W.
Philadelphia, Pa. 1825

WILSON, ROBERT
New York, N.Y. 1816

WILSON, S.
Philadelphia, Pa. 1805

WILSON, S. & S.
Philadelphia, Pa. 1797

WILSON, THOMAS
Philadelphia, Pa. 1837

WILSON, WILLIAM
Philadelphia, Pa. 1829

WILTBERGER & ALEXANDER
Philadelphia, Pa. 1797

WILTBERGER, CHRISTIAN
Philadelphia, Pa. 1770-1851

WINDOVER, JOHN
New York, N.Y. 1694

WINSLOW, EDWARD
Boston, Mass. 1669-1753

WINSOR, WILLIAM
Boston, Mass. 1759

WISHART, ALEXANDER
New York, N.Y. 1808

WISHART, DANIEL
New York, N.Y. 1825

WISHART, HUGH
New York, N.Y. 1784

WISHART, WILLIAM
New York, N.Y. 1800

WOLCOTT & GELSTON
Boston, Mass. 1824

WOLF, JAMES G.
Philadelphia, Pa. 1831

WOLFE, FRANCIS H.
Philadelphia, Pa. 1829

WOLFE & WRIGGINS
Philadelphia, Pa. 1837

WOOD, A. & W.
New York, N.Y. 1850

WOOD, ALFRED
Unknown 1800

WOOD, BENJAMIN B.
New York, N.Y. 1805

WOOD & HUGHES
New York, N.Y. 1846

WOOD, J. E.
New York, N.Y. 1845

WOODCOCK, BANCROFT
Wilmington, Del. 1754

WOODRUFF, ENOS
Cincinnati, Ohio 1820

WOODRUFF & WHITE
Cincinnati, Ohio 1829

WOODS, FREEMAN
New York, N.Y. 1791

WOODWARD, ANTIPAS
Middletown, Conn. 1791

WOODWARD, CHARLES
New York, N.Y. 1825

WOODWARD, ELI
Boston, Mass. 1812

WOODWARD & GROSJEAN
Boston, Mass. 1847

WOODWORTH, E.
Unknown 1800

WOOL, JEREMIAH W.
New York, N.Y. 1791

WRIGGIN & CO.
Philadelphia, Pa. 1831

WRIGGINS, THOMAS
Philadelphia, Pa. 1837

WRIGHT, ALEXANDER
Maryland 1776

WRIGHT, JOHN F.
Philadelphia, Pa. 1831

WRIGHT, W.
Unknown 1800

WYATT, JOSEPH
Philadelphia, Pa. 1797

WYER, ELEAZER
Portland, Me. 1768-1848

WYER, ELEAZER, Jr.
Boston, Mass. 1773

WYER & FARLEY
Portland, Me. 1828-1832
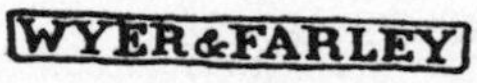

WYER & NOBLE
Portland, Me. 1823

WYNKOOP, BENJAMIN
New York, N.Y. 1675-1751

WYNKOOP, CORNELIUS
New York, N.Y. 1724

WYNKOOP, JACOBUS
New York, N.Y. 1765

WYNN, CHRISTOPHER
Baltimore, Md. 1795-1883

Y

YATES, S.
Albany, N.Y. 1810

YATES, S.
Unknown ... .c. 1825

YEOMANS, ELIJAH
Hadley, Mass. 1771

YETTONS, RANDELL
Philadelphia, Pa. 1739

YOU, DANIEL
Charleston, S.C. 1744

YOU, THOMAS
Charleston, S.C. 1756

YOUNG, ALEXANDER
Camden, S.C. 1800

YOUNG, EBENEZER
Hebron, Conn. 1778

YOUNG, LEVI
Bridgeport, Conn. 1827

YOUNG, S. E.
Laconia, N.H. 1840

YOUNG, WILLIAM
Philadelphia, Pa. 1761

Z

ZAHM, G. M.
Lancaster, Pa. 1840

ZAHM & JACKSON
New York, N.Y. 1830

FRENCH HALLMARKS

NOTE: Most town marks have variable date letters. A mark identical to one shown except for the letter will represent the same town, but a different year.

A

Aix; charge mark; 1781-Revolution.

Paris; charge mark; 1789.

Paris; charge mark; 1681-1684.

Paris; charge mark; 1677-1680.

Paris; charge mark; 1687-1691.

Paris; charge mark; 1684-1687.

Paris; charge mark; 1684-1687.

Paris; charge mark; 1691-1698.

Paris; charge mark; 1672-1677.

Paris; charge mark; 1698-1703.

Paris; charge mark; 1703-1708.

Paris; charge mark; 1708-1715.

Paris; charge mark; 1726-1732.

Arras; town mark.

Paris; charge mark; 1744-1750.

Paris; charge mark; 1715-1717.

Paris; charge mark; 1732-1738.

Paris; charge mark; 1756-1762.

Vicinity of Paris; charge mark; 1781.

Paris; charge mark; 1768-1774.

Paris; charge mark; 1762-1768.

Paris; charge mark; 1738-1744.

Paris; charge mark; 1717-1722.

Vicinity of Paris; charge mark; 1672-1768.

Paris; charge mark; 1750-1756.

Paris; charge mark; 1774-1780.

Paris; charge mark; 1780-1782.

Paris; charge mark; 1782-1789.

Apt; town mark.

Paris; discharge mark; 1687-1691.

Metz; charge mark; 1775-1781.

Metz; charge mark; 1781-Revolution.

AB **Bayonne; town mark.**

Paris; Bailly, Antoine; 1748-1756.

Paris; Bertin, Antoine; 1700.

Paris; Boullier, Antoine; 1775.

Paris; Bourgeois, Antoine; 1708.

Paris; Brigal, Antoine; 1746.

Abbeville; town mark.

Makers mark; after 1797.

Paris; Dutry, Antoine; 1767.

Paris; Deroussy, Alexandre; 1758.

Paris; Fillassier, Antoine; 1704.

Paris; Fillassier, Antoine-Philippe; 1720-1739.

Paris; Loret, Antoine-Gaspard; 1769.

Paris; Haudry, Antoine; 1718.

Paris; Joubert, Aimé; 1703.

Aix; town mark.

Paris; Masse, Ange-Jacques; 1780.

Paris; Jan de Villeclair, Antoine; 1750.

Paris; Loir, Alexis; 1733.

Paris; Lucas, Antoine; 1770.

Paris; Cassé, André-Louis; 1763.

Paris; charge mark; 1722-1726.

Strasbourg; makers mark.

Alais; town mark.

Amiens; town mark.

Amiens; charge mark; 1775-1781.

Paris; Maillet, Claude-Antoine; 1781.

Paris; Marsillac, Antoine; 1777.

Paris; Micallef, Alexis; 1756.

Paris; Raveché, Antoine-Martin; 1772.

Paris; Cousinet, Ambroise-Nicolas; 1745.

Angers; town mark; 18th century.

Angers; town mark; after 1750.

Arles; town mark.

Amiens; charge mark; 1781-Revolution.

Paris; Durand, Antoine-Sébastien; 1740.

Paris; Saint-Nicolas, Antoine; 1714.

Temporary admission mark; 1911.

Paris; Vachette, André-Maximilien; 1779.

Bayonne; town mark?

Aix; charge mark; 1775-1781.

B

Bourges; charge mark; 1781-Revolution.

Bordeaux; charge mark; 1781 Revolution.

Besancon; town mark; 18th cent

Troyes; town mark.

Saint-Germain-en-Laye; town mark.

Paris; town marks; 1765.

Besancon; town mark; 18th cent.

Paris; town mark, 1695.

Rouen; charge mark; 1768-1775.

Rouen; charge mark; 1775-1781.

Rouen; charge mark; 1781-Revolution.

Versailles; charge mark; 1780.

Bagnols; town mark.

Bayonne; town mark.

Paris; Charlié, Brice; 1704.

Beaucaire; town mark.

Bordeaux; charge mark; 1775-1781.

Béziers; town mark.

Bourges; charge mark; 1775-1781.

Bordeaux; town mark.

Bordeaux; town mark.

Bayonne; charge mark; 1775-1781.

Bordeaux; town mark.

Bordeaux; town mark.

Bordeaux; town mark.

Béziers; town mark.

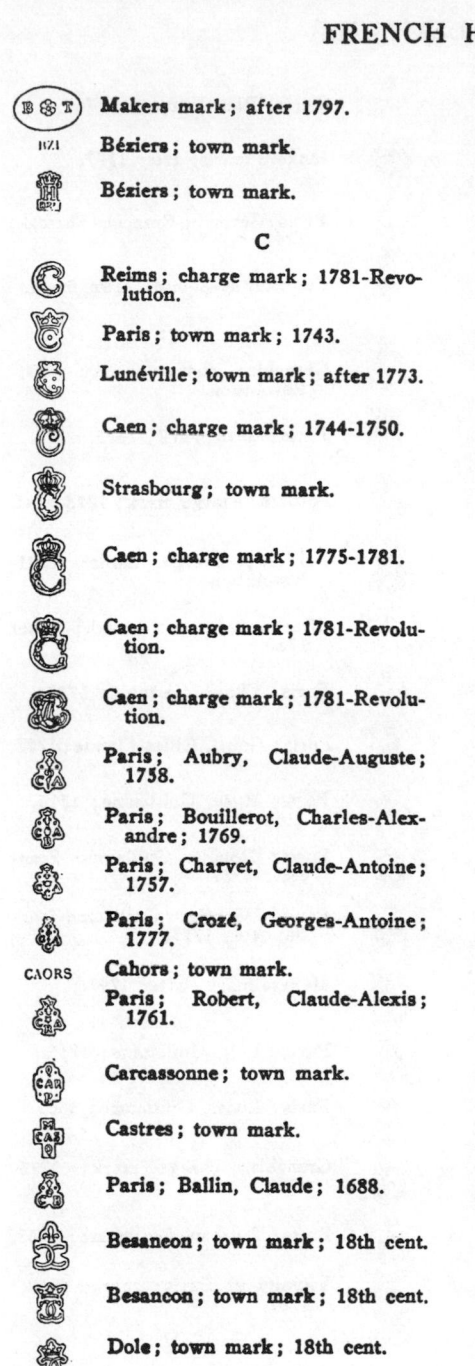

Makers mark; after 1797.

BZI **Béziers; town mark.**

Béziers; town mark.

C

Reims; charge mark; 1781-Revolution.

Paris; town mark; 1743.

Lunéville; town mark; after 1773.

Caen; charge mark; 1744-1750.

Strasbourg; town mark.

Caen; charge mark; 1775-1781.

Caen; charge mark; 1781-Revolution.

Caen; charge mark; 1781-Revolution.

Paris; Aubry, Claude-Auguste; 1758.

Paris; Bouillerot, Charles-Alexandre; 1769.

Paris; Charvet, Claude-Antoine; 1757.

Paris; Crozé, Georges-Antoine; 1777.

CAORS **Cahors; town mark.**

Paris; Robert, Claude-Alexis; 1761.

Carcassonne; town mark.

Castres; town mark.

Paris; Ballin, Claude; 1688.

Besaneon; town mark; 18th cent.

Besancon; town mark; 18th cent.

Dole; town mark; 18th cent.

Paris; Charvet, Claude; 1728.

Paris; Crozé, Charles-Francois; 1712.

Makers mark; after 1797.

Paris; Haudry, Charles-César; 1732.

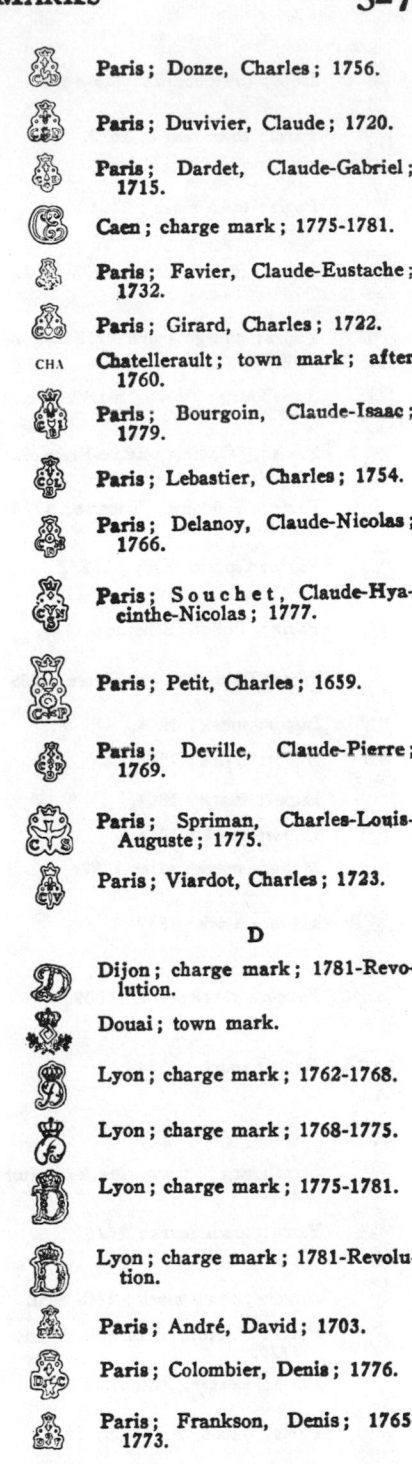

Paris; Donze, Charles; 1756.

Paris; Duvivier, Claude; 1720.

Paris; Dardet, Claude-Gabriel; 1715.

Caen; charge mark; 1775-1781.

Paris; Favier, Claude-Eustache; 1732.

Paris; Girard, Charles; 1722.

CHA **Chatellerault; town mark; after 1760.**

Paris; Bourgoin, Claude-Isaac; 1779.

Paris; Lebastier, Charles; 1754.

Paris; Delanoy, Claude-Nicolas; 1766.

Paris; Souchet, Claude-Hyacinthe-Nicolas; 1777.

Paris; Petit, Charles; 1659.

Paris; Deville, Claude-Pierre; 1769.

Paris; Spriman, Charles-Louis-Auguste; 1775.

Paris; Viardot, Charles; 1723.

D

Dijon; charge mark; 1781-Revolution.

Douai; town mark.

Lyon; charge mark; 1762-1768.

Lyon; charge mark; 1768-1775.

Lyon; charge mark; 1775-1781.

Lyon; charge mark; 1781-Revolution.

Paris; André, David; 1703.

Paris; Colombier, Denis; 1776.

Paris; Frankson, Denis; 1765-1773.

Dijon; charge mark; 1775-1781.

E

Dole; town mark; 18th cent.

Paris; town mark; 1673.

Paris; town mark; 1721.

Tours; charge mark; 1775-1781.

Tours; charge mark; 1781-Revolution.

Strasbourg; town mark; after 1752.

Paris; Godin, Edme-Francois; 1747.

Paris; Gondouin, Etienne; 1778-1786.

Paris; Guérin, Eloy; 1727.

Paris; Pollet, Etienne; 1747.

Paris; Balzac, Edme-Pierre; 1739.

Import mark; 1864.

Import mark; 1864.

Import mark; 1864.

Import mark; 1864.

Makers mark; after 1797.

Makers mark; 1819.

Foreign mark; 1797/1809.

Export mark; 1884.

F

Strasbourg; town mark; after 1752.

Paris; town mark; 1674.

Angers; town mark; 18th cent.

Paris; Caron, Francois-Alexis; 1777.

Paris; Corbie, Francois; 1777.

Paris; Jacob, Francois; 1637.

Paris; Aubert, Francois-Joachim; 1747.

Paris; Joubert, Francois; 1749.

Paris; Riel, Francois; 1769.

Makers mark; after 1797.

Paris; Germain, Francois-Thomas; 1748.

Fontenay-le-Comte; town mark.

G

Grenoble; charge mark; 1781-Revolution.

Paris; town mark; 1675.

Poitiers; charge mark; 1775-1781.

Poitiers; charge mark; 1781-Revolution.

Strasbourg; town mark; after 1752.

Paris; Chayé, Germain; 1755.

Paris; Gouel, Gilles-Claude; 1727.

Paris; Egée, Guillaume; 1716.

Paris; Roland, Guillaume Francois; 1777.

Paris; Gouffé, Guillaume-Jean-Baptiste; 1775.

Makers mark; after 1797.

Paris; Loir, Guillaume; 1716.

Paris; Lucas, Guillaume; 1665.

Grenoble; charge mark; 1775-1781.

Paris; Pigeron, Guillaume; 1762.

Vicinity of Paris; charge mark; 1781.

H

Salins; town mark.

Paris; town mark; 1771.

La Rochelle; charge mark; 1775-1781.

La Rochelle; charge mark; 1781-Revolution.

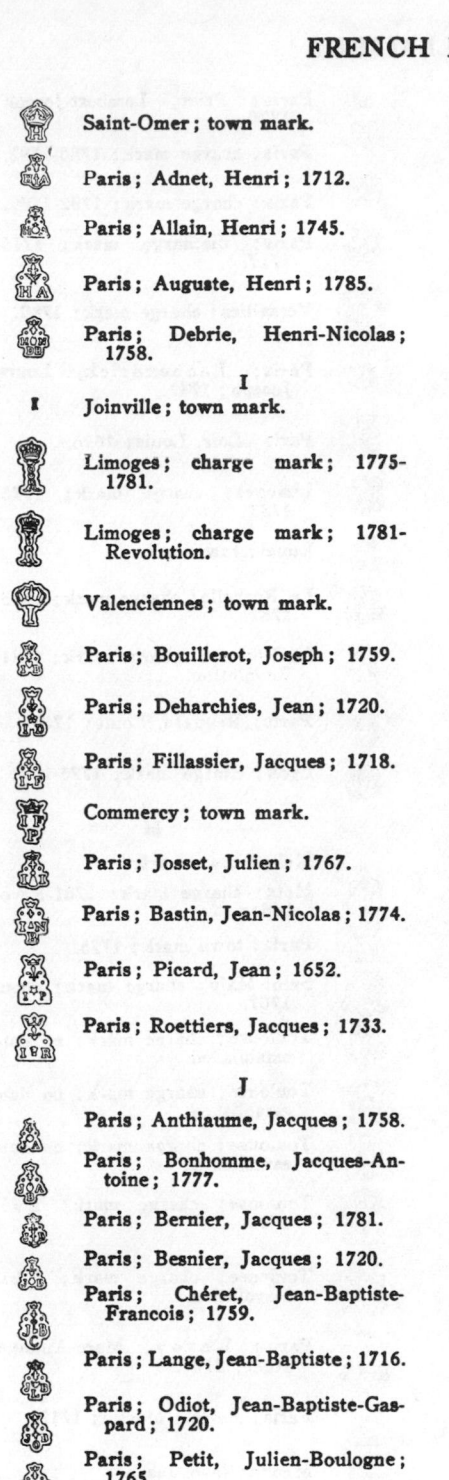

Saint-Omer; town mark.

Paris; Adnet, Henri; 1712.

Paris; Allain, Henri; 1745.

Paris; Auguste, Henri; 1785.

Paris; Debrie, Henri-Nicolas; 1758.

I

Joinville; town mark.

Limoges; charge mark; 1775-1781.

Limoges; charge mark; 1781-Revolution.

Valenciennes; town mark.

Paris; Bouillerot, Joseph; 1759.

Paris; Deharchies, Jean; 1720.

Paris; Fillassier, Jacques; 1718.

Commercy; town mark.

Paris; Josset, Julien; 1767.

Paris; Bastin, Jean-Nicolas; 1774.

Paris; Picard, Jean; 1652.

Paris; Roettiers, Jacques; 1733.

J

Paris; Anthiaume, Jacques; 1758.

Paris; Bonhomme, Jacques-Antoine; 1777.

Paris; Bernier, Jacques; 1781.

Paris; Besnier, Jacques; 1720.

Paris; Chéret, Jean-Baptiste-Francois; 1759.

Paris; Lange, Jean-Baptiste; 1716.

Paris; Odiot, Jean-Baptiste-Gaspard; 1720.

Paris; Petit, Julien-Boulogne; 1765.

Paris; Saurin, Jean-Baptiste; 1774.

Paris; Boudou, Jean-Charles-Marie; 1783.

Paris; Ducrollay, Jean-Charles; 1755.

Paris; Morée, Jacques-Charles; 1754.

Paris; Roquillé-Desnoyers, Jean-Charles; 1772.

Paris; Ducrollay, Jean; 1734.

Paris; Debrie, Jacques; 1777.

Paris; Dubois, Jacques; 1779.

Paris; Ecosse, Jean; 1705.

Paris; Famechon, Jacques; 1770.

Paris; Formey, Jean; 1754.

Paris; Balzac, Jean-Francois; 1749.

Paris; Balzac, Jean-Francois, 1755.

Makers mark; after 1797.

Paris; Caron, Jean-Francois-Nicolas; 1775.

Paris; Genu, Jean-Francois; 1754.

Paris; Garand, Jean-Francois; 1748.

Paris; Georges, Jean; 1752.

Paris; Gouel, Jean; 1728.

Paris; Barriere, Jean-Joseph; 1763.

Paris; Baudet, Jean-Joseph; 1782.

Paris; Moillet, Jacques-Joseph; 1742.

Paris; Outrebon, Jean-Louis-Dieudonné; 1772.

Paris; Mauzié, Jean; 1723.

Paris; Quin, Jean-Malquis le; 1735.

Paris; Roettiers, Jacques-Nicolas; 1765.

Paris; Pigeon, Jerome; 1705.

Paris; Charpenat, Jean-Pierre; 1782.

Saumur; town mark.

Paris; Pontaneau, Jean-Simon; 1776.

Paris; Van Conwenberghe, Joseph-Théodore; 1770.

Paris; Valot, Jean; 1742.

Paris; Huguet, Jean-Vincent; 1745.

K

Paris; town mark; 1726.

Bordeaux; town mark.

Bordeaux; town mark.

Bordeaux; town mark.

Bordeaux; town mark.

Bordeaux; town mark.

Bordeaux; town mark.

Bordeaux; charge mark; 1775-1781.

Bordeaux; charge mark; 1781-Revolution.

Lille; town mark.

Strasbourg; makers mark.

L

Lyon; charge mark; 1781-Revolution.

Vesoul; town mark.

Paris; town mark; 1752.

Bayonne; charge mark; 1775-1781.

Paris; Antoine, Léopold; 1706.

Paris; Taillepied, Louis-Antoine; 1760.

Paris; Charonnat, Louis; 1748.

Lucon; town mark.

Paris; Gabriel, Louis-Emmanuel; 1773.

Limoges; charge mark; 1781-Revolution.

Paris; Anthiaume, Louis-Julien; 1779.

Paris; Gresset, Louis-Joseph; 1781.

Paris; Prion, Lambert-Joseph; 1770.

Paris; charge mark; 1780-1782.

Paris; charge mark; 1782-1789.

Paris; discharge mark; 1715-1717.

Versailles; charge mark; 1780.

Paris; Lenhendrick, Louis-Joseph; 1747.

Paris; Loir, Louis; 1696.

Limoges; charge mark; 1775-1781.

Lunel; town mark.

La Rochelle; charge mark; 1775-1781.

La Rochelle; charge mark; 1781-Revolution.

Paris; Regnard, Louis; 1733.

Lyon; charge mark; 1775-1781.

M

Melle; town mark.

Metz; charge mark; 1781-Revolution.

Paris; town mark; 1775.

Saint-Malo; charge mark; about 1707.

Toulouse; charge mark; no date established.

Toulouse; charge mark; no date established.

Toulouse; charge mark; no date established.

Toulouse; charge mark; 1775-1781.

Toulouse; charge mark; 1781-Revolution.

Paris; Leroy, Marc-Antoine, Noel; 1769.

Paris; Berthe, Martin; 1712.

Mende; town mark.

Paris; Janety, Marc-Etienne; 1777.

Paris; Georges, Marie-Gabriel; 1745.

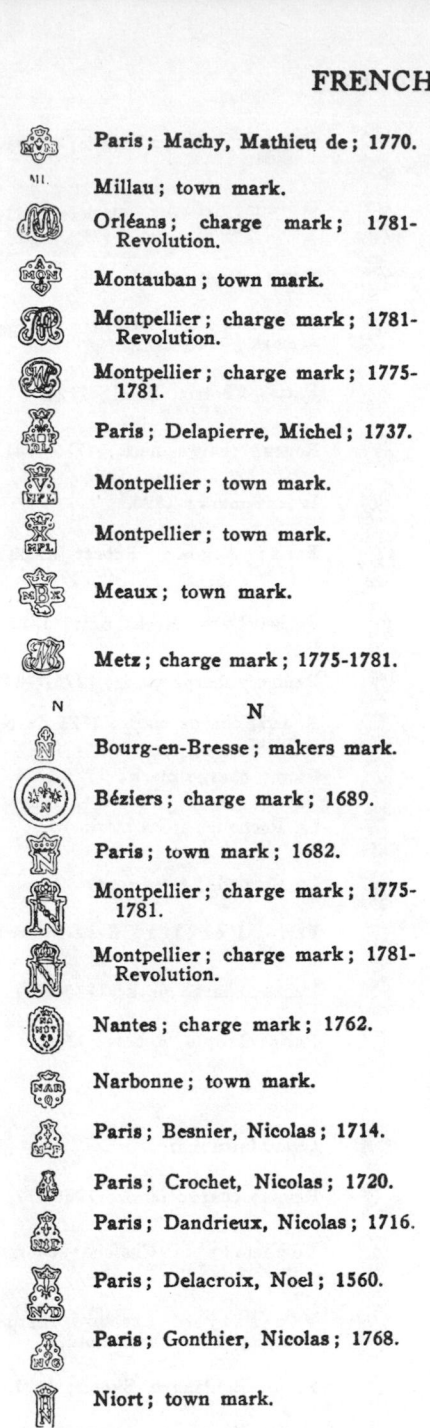

Paris; Machy, Mathieu de; 1770.

ML. Millau; town mark.

Orléans; charge mark; 1781-Revolution.

Montauban; town mark.

Montpellier; charge mark; 1781-Revolution.

Montpellier; charge mark; 1775-1781.

Paris; Delapierre, Michel; 1737.

Montpellier; town mark.

Montpellier; town mark.

Meaux; town mark.

Metz; charge mark; 1775-1781.

N

N Bourg-en-Bresse; makers mark.

Béziers; charge mark; 1689.

Paris; town mark; 1682.

Montpellier; charge mark; 1775-1781.

Montpellier; charge mark; 1781-Revolution.

Nantes; charge mark; 1762.

Narbonne; town mark.

Paris; Besnier, Nicolas; 1714.

Paris; Crochet, Nicolas; 1720.

Paris; Dandrieux, Nicolas; 1716.

Paris; Delacroix, Noel; 1560.

Paris; Gonthier, Nicolas; 1768.

Niort; town mark.

Paris; Lefevre, Nicolas; 1759.

Paris; Langlois, Nicolas-Martin; 1750.

Paris; Outrebon, Nicolas; 1735.

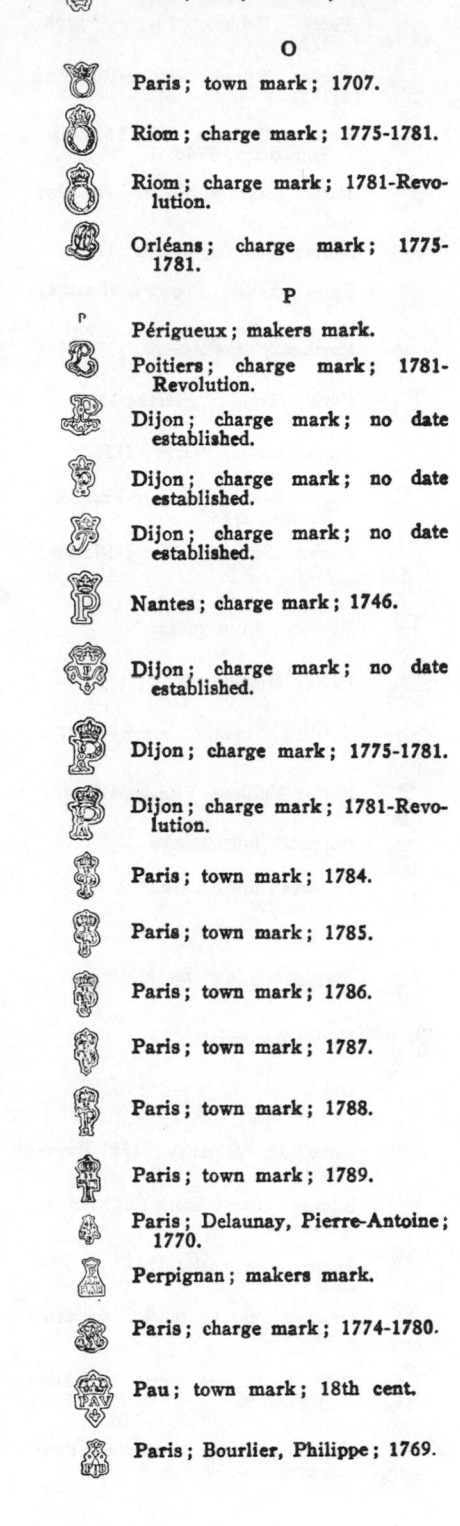

Paris; Vial, Nicolas; 1781.

O

Paris; town mark; 1707.

Riom; charge mark; 1775-1781.

Riom; charge mark; 1781-Revolution.

Orléans; charge mark; 1775-1781.

P

P Périgueux; makers mark.

Poitiers; charge mark; 1781-Revolution.

Dijon; charge mark; no date established.

Dijon; charge mark; no date established.

Dijon; charge mark; no date established.

Nantes; charge mark; 1746.

Dijon; charge mark; no date established.

Dijon; charge mark; 1775-1781.

Dijon; charge mark; 1781-Revolution.

Paris; town mark; 1784.

Paris; town mark; 1785.

Paris; town mark; 1786.

Paris; town mark; 1787.

Paris; town mark; 1788.

Paris; town mark; 1789.

Paris; Delaunay, Pierre-Antoine; 1770.

Perpignan; makers mark.

Paris; charge mark; 1774-1780.

Pau; town mark; 18th cent.

Paris; Bourlier, Philippe; 1769.

Paris; Clément, Pierre; 1694.

Paris; Delions, Pierre; 1720-1722.

Paris; Buron, Pierre-Etienne; 1735.

Paris; Garbe, Philippe-Emmanuel; 1748.

Paris; Goguely, Pierre-Francois; 1768.

Paris; Germain, Pierre; 1744.

Paris; Sallot, Pierre-Guillaume; 1750.

Parthenay; town mark.

Paris; Hannier, Pierre; 1716.

Paris; Jarrin, Pierre; 1712.

Paris; Beaulieu, Pierre-Francois-Mathis; 1768.

Paris; Sommé, Pierre-Nicolas; 1768.

Poitiers; town mark.

Paris; Soulaine, Paul; 1720.

Poitiers; charge mark; 1775-1781.

Paris; Valliere, Pierre; 1776.

Pézenas; town mark.

PZS **Pézenas**; town mark.

Q

Perpignan; town mark.

Paris; town mark; 1709.

R

Riom; charge mark; 1781-Revolution.

Rennes; charge mark; 1781-Revolution.

Paris; town mark; 1733.

Orléans; charge mark; no date established.

Orléans; charge mark; no date established.

Orléans; charge mark; no date established.

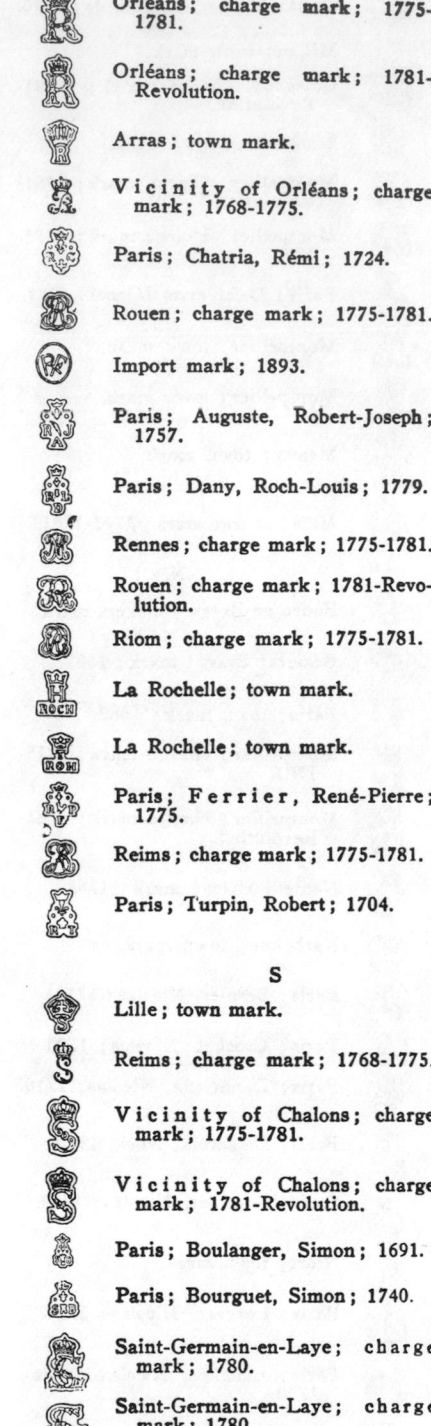

Orléans; charge mark; 1775-1781.

Orléans; charge mark; 1781-Revolution.

Arras; town mark.

Vicinity of Orléans; charge mark; 1768-1775.

Paris; Chatria, Rémi; 1724.

Rouen; charge mark; 1775-1781.

Import mark; 1893.

Paris; Auguste, Robert-Joseph; 1757.

Paris; Dany, Roch-Louis; 1779.

Rennes; charge mark; 1775-1781.

Rouen; charge mark; 1781-Revolution.

Riom; charge mark; 1775-1781.

La Rochelle; town mark.

La Rochelle; town mark.

Paris; Ferrier, René-Pierre; 1775.

Reims; charge mark; 1775-1781.

Paris; Turpin, Robert; 1704.

S

Lille; town mark.

Reims; charge mark; 1768-1775.

Vicinity of Chalons; charge mark; 1775-1781.

Vicinity of Chalons; charge mark; 1781-Revolution.

Paris; Boulanger, Simon; 1691.

Paris; Bourguet, Simon; 1740.

Saint-Germain-en-Laye; charge mark; 1780.

Saint-Germain-en-Laye; charge mark; 1780.

Paris; Leblond, Sébastien; 1675.

Saint-Omer; town mark.

Saint-Omer; town mark.

Paris; Parisy, Séverin; 1771.

Soissons; town mark.

T

Toul; town mark.

Thouars; town mark.

Tours; charge mark; 1781-Revolution.

Dinan; charge mark; 1759.

Nantes; charge mark; 1744.

Dunkerque; town mark.

Tarascon; town mark.

Paris; Germain, Thomas; 1720.

Toulouse; charge mark; 1775-1781.

Toulouse; charge mark; 1781-Revolution.

Toulouse; town mark; 17th cent.

Toulouse; town mark; 17th cent.

Toulouse; town mark: 18th cent.

Paris; Breton, Thomas-Pierre; 1739.

Tours; charge mark; 1775-1781.

U

Paris; town mark; 1783.

V

Verdun; town mark.

Nantes; charge mark; no date established.

Troyes; charge mark; 1768-1774.

Uzes; town mark.

Paris; Bréant, Vincent; 1754.

Le Vigan; town mark.

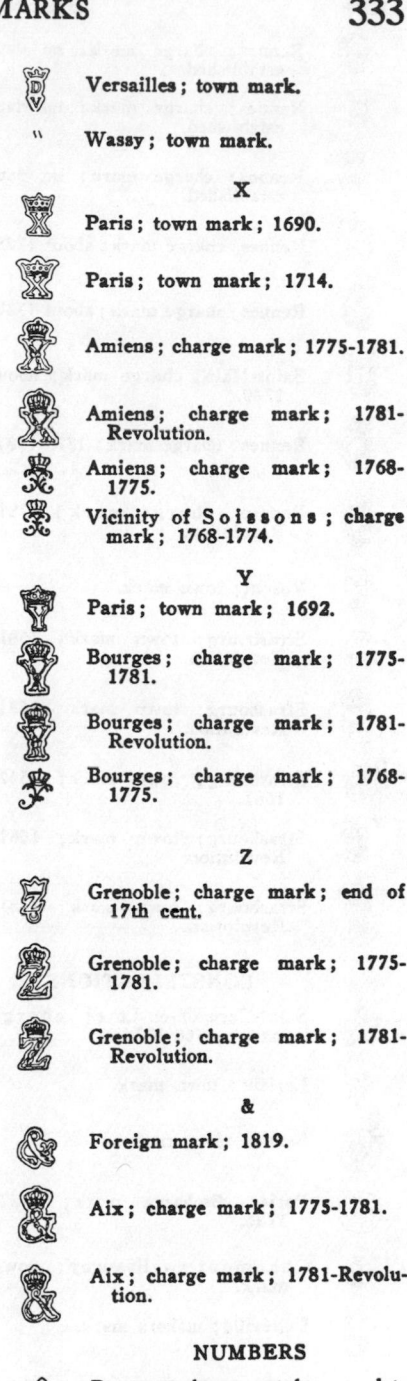

Versailles; town mark.

Wassy; town mark.

X

Paris; town mark; 1690.

Paris; town mark; 1714.

Amiens; charge mark; 1775-1781.

Amiens; charge mark; 1781-Revolution.

Amiens; charge mark; 1768-1775.

Vicinity of Soissons; charge mark; 1768-1774.

Y

Paris; town mark; 1692.

Bourges; charge mark; 1775-1781.

Bourges; charge mark; 1781-Revolution.

Bourges; charge mark; 1768-1775.

Z

Grenoble; charge mark; end of 17th cent.

Grenoble; charge mark; 1775-1781.

Grenoble; charge mark; 1781-Revolution.

&

Foreign mark; 1819.

Aix; charge mark; 1775-1781.

Aix; charge mark; 1781-Revolution.

NUMBERS

Rennes; charge mark; no date established.

Rennes; charge mark; about 1680.

Rennes; charge mark; no date established.

Rennes; charge mark; no date established.

Rennes; charge mark; no date established.

Rennes; charge mark; no date established.

Rennes; charge mark; about 1725.

Rennes; charge mark; about 1730.

Saint-Malo; charge mark; about 1740.

Rennes; charge mark; 1775-1781.

Rennes; charge mark; 1781-Revolution.

Vesoul; town mark.

Strasbourg; town mark; 1681-Revolution.

Strasbourg; town mark; 1681-Revolution.

Strasbourg; town mark; 1567-1681.

Strasbourg; town mark; 1681-Revolution.

Strasbourg; town mark; 1681-Revolution.

CONSTELLATIONS

Saint-Germain-en-Laye; charge mark; 1768-1774.

Lorient; town mark.

Senlis; town mark.

Paris; discharge mark; 1722-1726.

Chaumont-en-Bassigny; town mark.

Lunéville; makers mark.

HUMAN FACES AND PARTS OF THE HUMAN BODY

Beaune; makers mark.

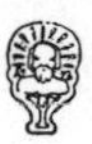
Saint-Quentin; town mark.

Vicinity of Orléans; discharge mark; 1781-Revolution.

Orléans; town mark; after 1784.

Toul; town mark; after 1784.

Rouen; discharge mark; 1781-Revolution.

Departments; recense mark; 1819.

Export mark; 1840.

Export mark; 1840.

Export mark; 1879.

Export mark; 1879.

Export mark; 1879

Export mark; 1879.

Export mark; 1879.

Export mark; 1879.

Export mark; 1879.

Departments; standard mark; 1819-1838.

Metz; discharge mark; 1775-1781.

Paris; discharge mark; 1780-1782.

Paris; standard mark; 1819.

1st standard mark; 1838.

2nd standard mark; 1838.

Paris; recense mark; 1819.

Paris; standard mark; 1819-1838.

Paris; standard mark gold; 1819-1838.

Paris; discharge mark; 1780-1782.

Vicinity of Chalons; discharge mark; 1781-Revolution.

Paris; recense mark; 1798-1809.

Departments; recense mark; 1798-1809.

Paris; recense mark; 1798-1809.

Departments; recense mark; 1798-1809.

Caen; discharge mark; 1775-1781.

Departments; 2nd standard mark; 1819-1838.

Paris; 1st standard mark; 1819-1838.

Paris; 2nd standard mark; 1819-1838.

Vannes; town mark; after 1784.

Sens; discharge mark; 1768-1774.

Dijon; discharge mark; 1781-Revolution.

Orléans; discharge mark; 1768-1775.

Blois; discharge mark; 1768-1775.

Lyon; discharge mark; 1762-1768.

Amiens; discharge mark; 1775-1781.

Paris; garantie mark; 1798-1809.

Departments; garantie mark; 1798-1809.

Paris; garantie mark; 1798-1809.

Departments; garantie mark; 1798-1809.

Departments; garantie mark; 1819.

Meaux; discharge mark; 1672-1768.

Reims; discharge mark; 1768-1774.

Export mark; 1912.

Paris; discharge mark; 1756-1762.

Paris; discharge mark; 1768-1774.

Paris; discharge mark; 1782-1786.

Departments; 1st standard mark; 1819-1838.

Paris; discharge mark; 1768-1774.

Vicinity of Orléans; discharge mark; 1781-Revolution.

Paris; garantie mark; 1819.

Departments; garantie mark; 1819.

Uzes; town mark; after 1784.

Paris, foreign mark; 1819-1838.

Export mark; 1884.

Export mark; 1884.

1st standard mark gold; 1838.

2nd standard mark gold; 1838.

3rd standard mark gold; 1838.

Toulon; town mark; after 1784.

Paris; foreign mark; 1819-1838.

Poitiers; discharge mark; 1781-Revolution.

Bordeaux; discharge mark; 1775-1781.

Paris; garantie mark; 1819-1838.

Departments; garantie mark gold; 1819-1838.

Import mark; 1912.

Import mark; 1926.

Maubeuge; town mark; after 1784.

Departments; recense mark; 1819.

Paris; discharge mark; 1789.

Lyon; discharge mark; 1775-1781.

Tours; discharge mark; 1781-Revolution.

Melle; town mark; after 1784.

Paris; recense mark; 1819.

Saint-Lo; town mark; after 1784.

Senlis; charge mark; 1768-1774.

Versailles; charge mark; 1768-1774.

Saint-Germain-en-Laye; charge mark; 1768-1774.

Montpellier; charge mark; no date established.

Macon; town mark; after 1784.

Departments; garantie mark gold; 1819.

Besancon; makers mark; 15th cent.

Paris; recense mark; 1819.

Vicinity of Orléans; discharge mark; 1775-1781.

Bourges; discharge mark; 1775-1781.

Paris; charge mark; 1744-1750.

Paris; charge mark; 1738-1744.

Riom; discharge mark; 1775-1781.

Tours; discharge mark; 1775-1781.

Bayonne; discharge mark; 1775-1781.

MAMMALS

Paris; discharge mark; 1738-1744.

Paris; discharge mark; 1774-1780.

Avallon; town mark; after 1784.

Rennes; discharge mark; 1781-Revolution.

La Rochelle; discharge mark; 1775-1781.

Gold watch mark; 1819-1838.

Paris; 3rd gold standard mark; 1819-1838.

Pau; town mark; after 1784.

Caen; discharge mark; 1781-Revolution.

Bourges; town mark; after 1784.

Paris; garantie mark; 1819-1838.

Les Sables; town mark; after 1784.

Amiens; discharge mark; 1781-Revolution.

Bourges; discharge mark; 1775-1781.

Rouen; makers mark; 15th and 16th centuries.

Rouen; makers mark; 17th and 18th centuries.

Poitiers; discharge mark; 1775-1781.

Compiegne; town mark; after 1784.

Nantes; discharge mark; 1746.

Metz; discharge mark; 1775-1781.

Recense mark; 1838.

Paris; discharge mark; 1732-1738.

Caen; discharge mark; 1781-Revolution.

Lyon; discharge mark; 1775-1781.

Limoges; discharge mark; 1781-Revolution.

Cambrai; town mark; after 1784.

Gold garantie mark; 1838.

Angouleme; town mark; after 1784.

Riom; discharge mark; 1781-Revolution.

Sedan; town mark; after 1784.

Sedan; makers mark.

Paris; discharge mark; 1750-1756.

Toulouse; discharge mark; 1781-Revolution.

Paris; garantie mark; 1838.

Paris; gold chain mark; 1838.

Departments; gold chain mark; 1838.

Paris; gold mark; 1847.

Alloy mark; 1905.

Departments; 2nd gold standard marks; 1819-1838.

Angers; charge mark; 18th cent.

Valenciennes; town mark.

Caen; discharge mark; 1744-1750.

Lyon; town mark.

Lyon; discharge mark; 1762-1768.

Lyon; discharge mark; 1781-Revolution.

Paris; gold garantie mark; 1819.

Lyon; town mark; after 1784.

Grenoble; discharge mark; 1775-1781.

Montpellier; charge mark; no established date.

Caen; makers mark.

Laval; makers mark.

Poitiers; discharge mark; 1775-1781.

Meaux; town mark; after 1784.

Cahors; town mark; after 1784.

Montargis; discharge mark; 1768-1775.

Paris; discharge mark; 1732-1738.

Paris; discharge mark; 1762-1768.

Paris; discharge mark; 1782-1789.

Saint-Germain-en-Laye; discharge mark; 1780.

Platinum mark; 1912.

Recense mark; 1838.

Salins; town mark; after 1784.

Paris; discharge mark; 1744-1750.

Paris; 1st gold standard mark; 1819-1838.

Departments; recense mark; 1819-1838.

Departments; 1st gold standard mark; 1819-1838.

Lyon; discharge mark; 1768-1775.

Limoges; discharge mark; 1781-Revolution.

Amiens; discharge mark; 1775-1781.

Vesoul; town mark; after 1784.

Paris; discharge mark; 1738-1744.

Nantes; charge mark; no date established.

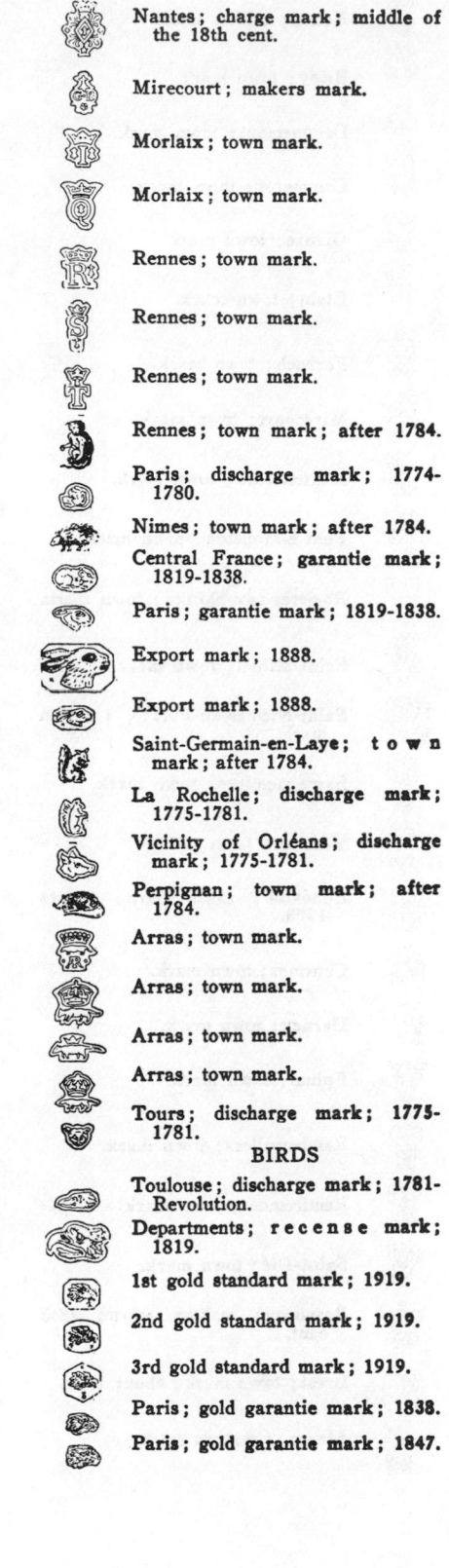

Nantes; charge mark; middle of the 18th cent.

Mirecourt; makers mark.

Morlaix; town mark.

Morlaix; town mark.

Rennes; town mark.

Rennes; town mark.

Rennes; town mark.

Rennes; town mark; after 1784.

Paris; discharge mark; 1774-1780.

Nimes; town mark; after 1784.

Central France; garantie mark; 1819-1838.

Paris; garantie mark; 1819-1838.

Export mark; 1888.

Export mark; 1888.

Saint-Germain-en-Laye; town mark; after 1784.

La Rochelle; discharge mark; 1775-1781.

Vicinity of Orléans; discharge mark; 1775-1781.

Perpignan; town mark; after 1784.

Arras; town mark.

Arras; town mark.

Arras; town mark.

Arras; town mark.

Tours; discharge mark; 1775-1781.

BIRDS

Toulouse; discharge mark; 1781-Revolution.

Departments; recense mark; 1819.

1st gold standard mark; 1919.

2nd gold standard mark; 1919.

3rd gold standard mark; 1919.

Paris; gold garantie mark; 1838.

Paris; gold garantie mark; 1847.

Nancy; makers mark.

Briey; town mark.

Bouquemont; town mark.

Commercy; town mark.

Dieuze; town mark.

Etain; town mark.

Forbach; town mark.

Mirecourt; town mark.

Neufchateau; town mark.

Pont-a-Mousson; town mark.

Rosieres-aux-Salines; town mark.

Saint-Mihiel; town mark.

Saint-Nicolas-du-Port; town mark.

Sarreguemines; town mark.

Vézelise; town mark.

Lunéville; town mark; before 1773.

Charmes; town mark.

Darney; town mark.

Epinal; town mark.

Rambervillers; town mark.

Remiremont; town mark.

Saint-Dié; town mark.

Besancon; makers mark; 18th cent.

Brest; town mark; about 1770.

Alencon; makers mark.

Import mark; 1893.

Chateau-Thierry; town mark; after 1784.

Paris; discharge mark; 1708-1715.

Soissons; discharge mark; 1768-1774.

Beauvais; discharge mark; 1768-1774.

Montpellier; charge mark; no date established.

Paris; 1st gold standard mark; 1798-1809.

Paris; 2nd gold standard mark; 1798-1809.

Paris; 3rd gold standard mark; 1798-1809.

Departments; 1st gold standard mark; 1798-1809.

Departments; 2nd gold standard mark; 1798-1809.

Departments; 3rd gold standard mark; 1798-1809.

Paris; 1st standard mark; 1798-1809.

Paris; 2nd standard mark; 1798-1809.

Departments; 1st standard mark; 1798-1809.

Departments; 2nd standard mark; 1798-1809.

Paris; 1st gold standard mark; 1819.

Paris; 2nd gold standard mark; 1819.

Paris; 3rd gold standard mark; 1819.

Departments; 1st gold standard mark; 1819.

Departments; 2nd gold standard mark; 1819.

Departments; 3rd gold standard mark; 1819.

Paris; 1st standard mark; 1819.

Paris; 2nd standard mark; 1819.

Departments; 1st standard mark; 1819.

Departments; 2nd standard mark; 1819.

Paris; discharge mark; 1750-1756.

Vicinity of Paris; discharge mark; 1781.

Paris; gold garantie mark; 1798-1809.

Departments: gold garantie mark; 1798-1809.

Paris; gold garantie mark; 1819.

Paris; gold garantie mark; 1819.

Departments; gold garantie mark; 1819.

Departments; gold garantie mark; 1819.

Metz; town mark; after 1784.

Vicinity of Paris; discharge mark; 1781.

Versailles; discharge mark; 1768-1774.

Import mark; 1893.

Montpellier; charge mark; no date established.

Morlaix; town mark; about 1740.

Chartres; town mark; after 1784.

Toulouse; discharge mark; 1775-1781.

Lille; town mark; after 1784.

Trévoux; town mark; after 1784.

Beaumont-sur-Oise; discharge mark; 1768-1774.

Paris; discharge mark; 1786-1789.

Import mark; 1893.

Aix; discharge mark; 1775-1781.

Saint-Martin-de-Ré; town mark; after 1784.

Saint-Esprit; town mark; after 1784.

Paris; discharge mark; 1726-1732.

Laon; makers mark.

Angers; charge mark; 18th. cent.

Aix; town mark; after 1784.

Laon; discharge mark; 1768-1774.

Pontoise; discharge mark; 1672-1768.

FISH

Bar-le-Duc; town mark; after 1784.

Beauvais; town mark; after 1784.

Dieppe; town mark; after 1784.

Southern France; 800 mark; 1819-1838.

Parthenay; town mark; after 1784.

Northwest France; 800 mark; 1819-1838.

Melun; town mark; after 1784.

Grenoble; town mark; after 1784.

Paris; discharge mark; 1744-1750.

Bray-sur-Seine; discharge mark; 1768-1774.

La Rochelle; discharge mark; 1781-Revolution.

Dunkerque; town mark.

Grenoble; town mark.

Grenoble; town mark.

Grenoble; town mark.

Gisors; town mark; after 1784.

AMPHIBIANS AND REPTILES

Laval; town mark; after 1784.

Southwest France; 800 mark; 1819-1838.

Le Havre; makers mark.

Vitry-le-Francois; town mark.

Nimes; town mark.

Nimes; town mark.

INVERTEBRATES

Abbeville; town mark; after 1784.

Rennes; discharge mark; about 1730.

Sainte-Ménehould; town mark; after 1784.

Compiegne; discharge mark; 1768-1774.

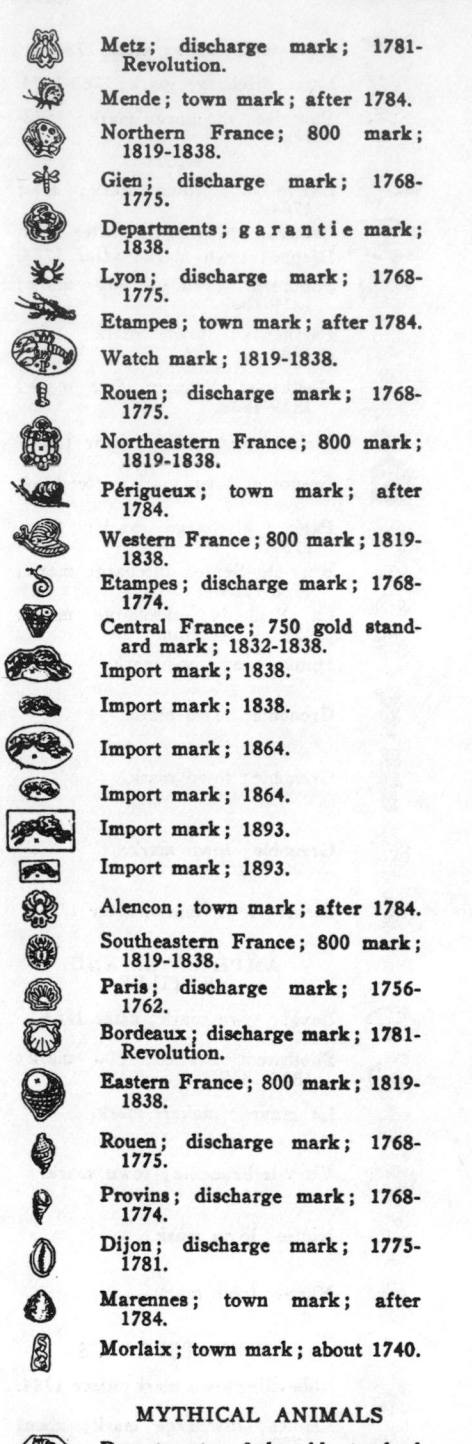

Metz; discharge mark; 1781-Revolution.

Mende; town mark; after 1784.

Northern France; 800 mark; 1819-1838.

Gien; discharge mark; 1768-1775.

Departments; garantie mark; 1838.

Lyon; discharge mark; 1768-1775.

Etampes; town mark; after 1784.

Watch mark; 1819-1838.

Rouen; discharge mark; 1768-1775.

Northeastern France; 800 mark; 1819-1838.

Périgueux; town mark; after 1784.

Western France; 800 mark; 1819-1838.

Etampes; discharge mark; 1768-1774.

Central France; 750 gold standard mark; 1832-1838.

Import mark; 1838.

Import mark; 1838.

Import mark; 1864.

Import mark; 1864.

Import mark; 1893.

Import mark; 1893.

Alencon; town mark; after 1784.

Southeastern France; 800 mark; 1819-1838.

Paris; discharge mark; 1756-1762.

Bordeaux; discharge mark; 1781-Revolution.

Eastern France; 800 mark; 1819-1838.

Rouen; discharge mark; 1768-1775.

Provins; discharge mark; 1768-1774.

Dijon; discharge mark; 1775-1781.

Marennes; town mark; after 1784.

Morlaix; town mark; about 1740.

MYTHICAL ANIMALS

Departments; 3rd gold standard mark; 1819-1838.

Paris; 2nd gold standard mark; 1819-1838.

Bordeaux; town mark; after 1784.

Import mark; 1838.

Import mark; 1838.

La Rochelle; town mark; after 1784.

Liesse; discharge mark; 1768-1774.

Paris; charge mark; 1732-1738.

PLANTS

Clermont-Ferrand; town mark; after 1784.

Amiens; discharge mark; 1781-Revolution.

Alais; town mark; after 1784.

Draguignan; town mark; after 1784.

Vicinity of Chalons; discharge mark; 1775-1781.

Valognes; makers mark.

Payrat; town mark; after 1784.

Riom; discharge mark; 1781-Revolution.

Thiers; town mark; after 1784.

Rouen; town mark; after 1784.

Rouen; discharge mark; 1781-Revolution.

Rouen; discharge mark; 1775-1781.

Verdun; town mark; after 1784.

Grenoble; discharge mark; 1781-Revolution.

Montpellier; charge mark; no date established.

Paris; discharge mark; 1726-1732.

Reims; town mark; after 1784.

Dijon; discharge mark; 1781-Revolution.

Troyes; town mark; after 1784.

Vicinity of Chalons; discharge mark; 1781-Revolution.

Toulouse; discharge mark; 1775-1781.

Paris; discharge mark; 1789.

Laon; town mark; after 1784.

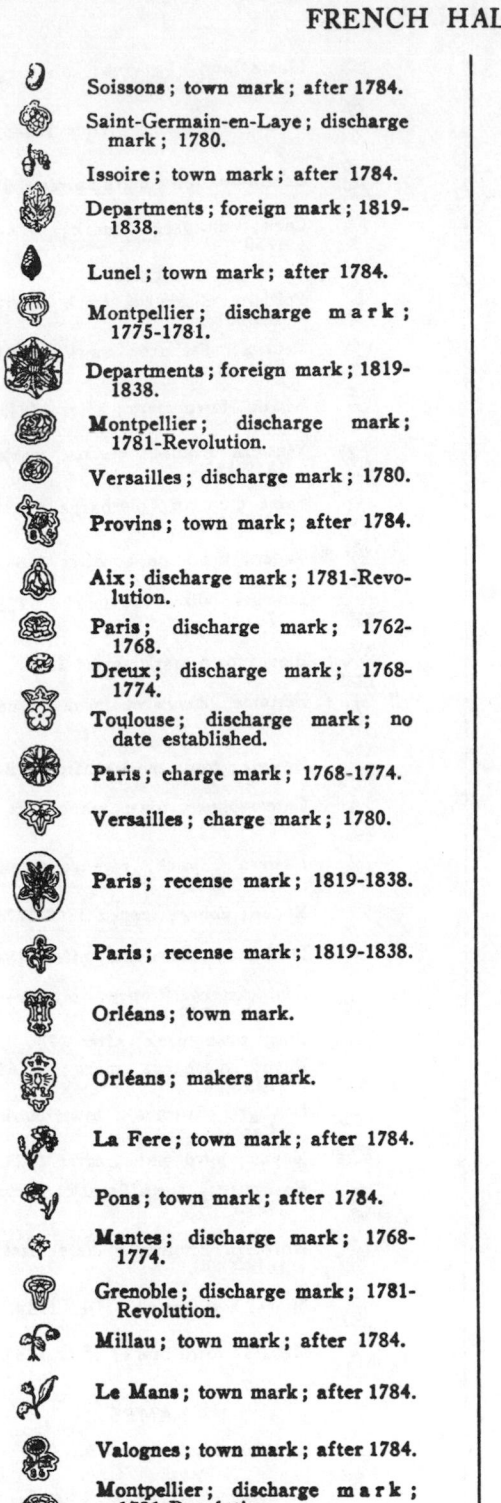

Soissons; town mark; after 1784.

Saint-Germain-en-Laye; discharge mark; 1780.

Issoire; town mark; after 1784.

Departments; foreign mark; 1819-1838.

Lunel; town mark; after 1784.

Montpellier; discharge mark; 1775-1781.

Departments; foreign mark; 1819-1838.

Montpellier; discharge mark; 1781-Revolution.

Versailles; discharge mark; 1780.

Provins; town mark; after 1784.

Aix; discharge mark; 1781-Revolution.

Paris; discharge mark; 1762-1768.

Dreux; discharge mark; 1768-1774.

Toulouse; discharge mark; no date established.

Paris; charge mark; 1768-1774.

Versailles; charge mark; 1780.

Paris; recense mark; 1819-1838.

Paris; recense mark; 1819-1838.

Orléans; town mark.

Orléans; makers mark.

La Fere; town mark; after 1784.

Pons; town mark; after 1784.

Mantes; discharge mark; 1768-1774.

Grenoble; discharge mark; 1781-Revolution.

Millau; town mark; after 1784.

Le Mans; town mark; after 1784.

Valognes; town mark; after 1784.

Montpellier; discharge mark; 1781-Revolution.

Liesse; discharge mark; 1768-1774.

Clermont; discharge mark; 1768-1774.

Melun; discharge mark; 1768-1774.

Crépy; discharge mark; 1768-1774.

Nancy; town mark.

Nancy; town mark.

Paris; charge mark; 1762-1768.

Montpellier; discharge mark; 1775-1781.

Versailles; discharge mark; 1768-1774.

Rennes; discharge mark; 1775-1781.

Dunkerque; town mark; after 1784.

ARTICLES OF CLOTHING

Eastern France; gold 750 mark; 1819-1838.

Bordeaux; discharge mark; 1775-1781.

Limoges; discharge mark; 1775-1781.

Senlis; discharge mark; 1768-1774.

Arles; town mark; after 1784.

Dijon; discharge mark; 1775-1781.

Boulogne-sur-Mer; discharge mark; after 1784.

Bourges; discharge mark; 1781-Revolution.

Poitiers; town mark; after 1784.

Riom; discharge mark; 1775-1781.

Tarascon; town mark; after 1784.

La Rochelle; discharge mark; 1781-Revolution.

Western France; gold 750 mark; 1819-1838.

Strasbourg; town mark; after 1784.

Grenoble; discharge mark; 1775-1781.

Aix; discharge mark; 1781-Revolution.

Southern France; gold 750 mark; 1819-1838.

Vitry-le-Francois; town mark; after 1784.

Marseille; town mark; after 1784.

Rennes; discharge mark; 1775-1781.

Lyon; discharge mark; 1781-Revolution.

Saintes; town mark; after 1784.

Bayonne; discharge mark; 1775-1781.

Bourg-en-Bresse; town mark; after 1784.

Colmar; town mark; after 1784.

Aurillac; town mark; after 1784.

Abbeville; discharge mark; 1768-1775.

Autun; town mark; after 1784.

Metz; discharge mark; 1781-Revolution.

Calais; town mark; after 1784.

ARMS

Saint-Germain-en-Laye; discharge mark; 1768-1774.

Saumur; town mark; after 1784.

Northeastern France; gold 750 mark; 1819-1838.

Gien; town mark; after 1784.

Lyon; town mark.

Angers; makers mark.

Amiens; town mark; 1748.

Rethel; town mark; after 1784.

Cognac; town mark; after 1784.

Nantes; town mark; after 1784.

Hasard mark; 1798-1809.

Liesse; town mark; after 1784.

Paris; garantie mark; 1798-1809.

Departments; garantie mark; 1798-1809.

Paris; garantie mark; 1819.

Departments; garantie mark; 1819.

Vicinity of Chalons; discharge mark; 1775-1781.

Mézieres; town mark; after 1784.

Marle and Vervins; discharge mark; 1768-1774.

Guise; town mark; after 1784.

Le Havre; town mark; after 1784.

Caen; discharge mark; 1744-1750.

VASES

Poitiers; discharge mark; 1781-Revolution.

Rennes; discharge mark; 1781-Revolution.

Semur; town mark; after 1784.

Western France; recense mark; 1819-1838.

Saint Quentin; discharge mark; 1768-1775.

Rodez; town mark; after 1784.

Limoges; discharge mark; 1775-1781.

Blois; town mark; after 1784.

Péronne; discharge mark; 1768-1775.

Beaune; town mark; after 1784.

Carcassonne; town mark; after 1784.

Eastern France; recense mark; 1819-1838.

Rouen; charge mark; 1768-1775.

Issoudun; town mark; after 1784.

Southeastern France; makers mark; 1819-1838.

Riez; town mark; after 1784.

Roye; discharge mark; 1768-1775.

D'Aligre (Marans); town mark; after 1784.

Noyon; town mark; after 1784.

Beaucaire; town mark; after 1784.

Northern France; makers mark; 1819-1838.

Niort; town mark; after 1784.

Nevers; town mark; after 1784.

LAMPS

Le Mans; makers mark.

Auxerre; town mark; after 1784.

Lons-le-Saunier; town mark; after 1784.

La Fere; discharge mark; 1768-1774.

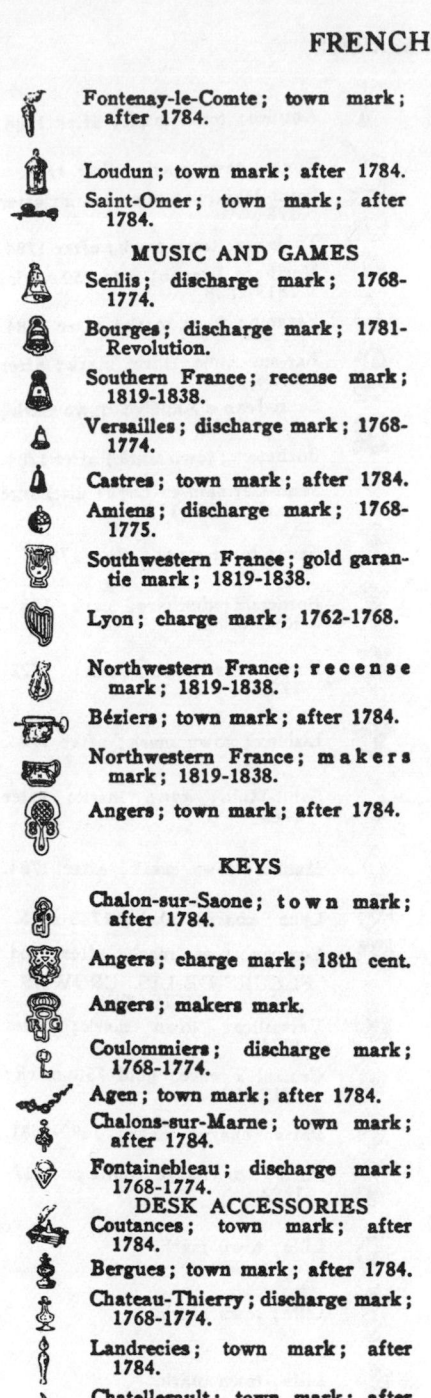

Fontenay-le-Comte; town mark; after 1784.

Loudun; town mark; after 1784.

Saint-Omer; town mark; after 1784.

MUSIC AND GAMES

Senlis; discharge mark; 1768-1774.

Bourges; discharge mark; 1781-Revolution.

Southern France; recense mark; 1819-1838.

Versailles; discharge mark; 1768-1774.

Castres; town mark; after 1784.

Amiens; discharge mark; 1768-1775.

Southwestern France; gold garantie mark; 1819-1838.

Lyon; charge mark; 1762-1768.

Northwestern France; recense mark; 1819-1838.

Béziers; town mark; after 1784.

Northwestern France; makers mark; 1819-1838.

Angers; town mark; after 1784.

KEYS

Chalon-sur-Saone; town mark; after 1784.

Angers; charge mark; 18th cent.

Angers; makers mark.

Coulommiers; discharge mark; 1768-1774.

Agen; town mark; after 1784.

Chalons-sur-Marne; town mark; after 1784.

Fontainebleau; discharge mark; 1768-1774.

DESK ACCESSORIES

Coutances; town mark; after 1784.

Bergues; town mark; after 1784.

Chateau-Thierry; discharge mark; 1768-1774.

Landrecies; town mark; after 1784.

Chatellerault; town mark; after 1784.

Chateau-Gontier; town mark; after 1784.

Departments; makers mark; 1798-1809.

Manosque; town mark; after 1784.

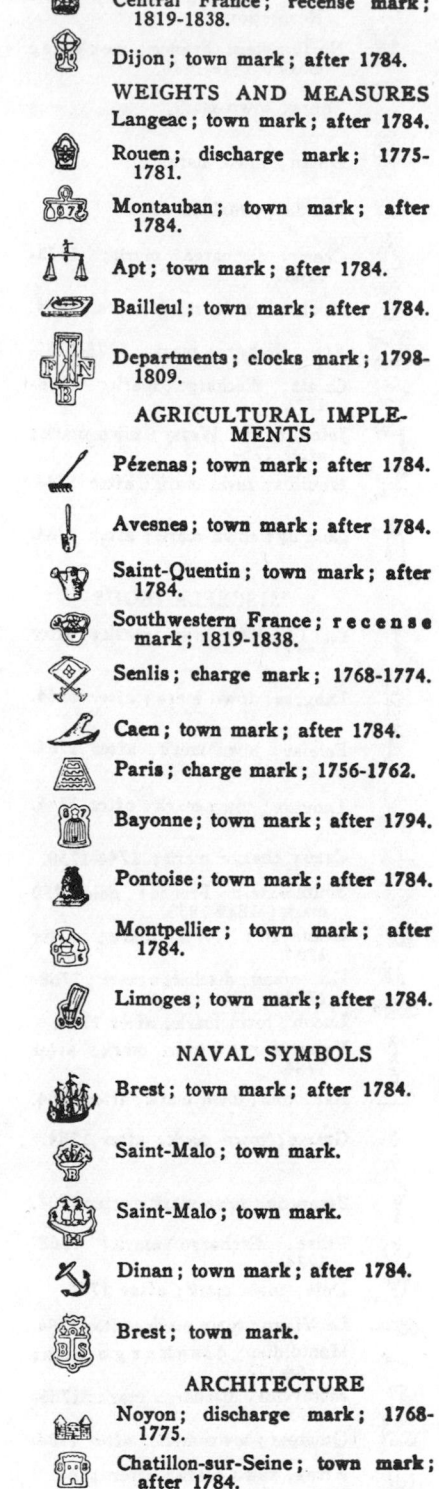

Central France; recense mark; 1819-1838.

Dijon; town mark; after 1784.

WEIGHTS AND MEASURES

Langeac; town mark; after 1784.

Rouen; discharge mark; 1775-1781.

Montauban; town mark; after 1784.

Apt; town mark; after 1784.

Bailleul; town mark; after 1784.

Departments; clocks mark; 1798-1809.

AGRICULTURAL IMPLEMENTS

Pézenas; town mark; after 1784.

Avesnes; town mark; after 1784.

Saint-Quentin; town mark; after 1784.

Southwestern France; recense mark; 1819-1838.

Senlis; charge mark; 1768-1774.

Caen; town mark; after 1784.

Paris; charge mark; 1756-1762.

Bayonne; town mark; after 1794.

Pontoise; town mark; after 1784.

Montpellier; town mark; after 1784.

Limoges; town mark; after 1784.

NAVAL SYMBOLS

Brest; town mark; after 1784.

Saint-Malo; town mark.

Saint-Malo; town mark.

Dinan; town mark; after 1784.

Brest; town mark.

ARCHITECTURE

Noyon; discharge mark; 1768-1775.

Chatillon-sur-Seine; town mark; after 1784.

Tours; discharge mark; 1781-Revolution.

Northeastern France; recense mark; 1819-1838.

Tours; town mark.

Dinan; town mark.

Honfleur; makers mark.

Caen; discharge mark; 1775-1781.

Morlaix; town mark; after 1784.

Aix; discharge mark; 1775-1781.

Calais; discharge mark; 1768-1775.

Joinville and Wassy; town mark; after 1784.

Moulins; town mark; after 1784.

Le Puy; town mark; after 1784.

MISCELLANEOUS

La Charité; town mark; after 1784.

Langres; town mark; after 1784.

Falaise; town mark; after 1784.

Thouars; town mark; after 1784.

Caen; charge mark; 1744-1750.

Southeastern France; gold 750 mark; 1819-1838.

Montargis; town mark; after 1784.

Montereau; discharge mark; 1768-1774.

Luçon; town mark; after 1784.

Valenciennes; town mark; after 1784.

Narbonne; town mark; after 1784.

Grasse; town mark; after 1784.

Besancon; town mark; after 1784.

Guise; discharge mark; 1768-1774.

Dole; town mark; after 1784.

Le Vigan; town mark; after 1784.

Montdidier; discharge mark; 1768-1775.

Montreuil; discharge mark; 1768-1775.

Quimper; town mark; after 1784.

Arras; town mark; after 1784.

Antibes; town mark; after 1784.

Tours; town mark; after 1784.

Saint-Maixent; town mark; after 1784.

Toulouse; town mark; after 1784.

Northern France; gold 750 mark; 1819-1838.

Fécamp; town mark; after 1784.

Bar-sur-Aube; town mark; after 1784.

Saint-Jean-d'Angély; town mark; after 1784.

Rochefort; town mark; after 1784.

Saint-Germain-en-Laye; discharge mark; 1768-1774.

Sens; town mark; after 1784.

Bordeaux; discharge mark; 1781-Revolution.

Paris; discharge mark; 1722-1726.

Lisieux; town mark; after 1784.

Saint-Malo; town mark; after 1784.

Mantes; town mark; after 1784.

Lyon; charge mark; 1768-1775.

Longwy; town mark; after 1784.

FLEURS-DE-LIS. CROWNS. CRUCIFIXES

Versailles; town mark; after 1784.

Central France; gold 750 mark; 1819-1832.

Paris; charge mark; 1680-1681.

Paris; discharge mark; 1717-1722.

Lille; town mark.

Lille; town mark.

Lille; town mark.

Montpellier; charge mark; no date established.

Calais; town mark.

Bolbec; makers mark.

Languedoc; charge mark; 1700.

Paris; discharge mark; 1717-1722.

Paris; discharge mark; 1717-1722.

Morlaix; town mark; about 1725.

Paris; discharge mark; 1691-1698.

Paris; discharge mark; 1687-1691.

Paris; discharge mark; 1703-1708.

Paris; discharge mark; 1681-1684.

Paris; discharge mark; 1681-1684.

Paris; discharge mark; 1684-1687.

Paris; discharge mark; 1684-1687.

Paris; discharge mark; 1698-1703.

Brest; town mark; about 1720.

Morlaix; town mark; about 1725.

Riom; town mark; after 1784.

Boulogne; discharge mark; 1768-1775.

Neufchateau; town mark.

Pont-a-Mousson; town mark.

Rosieres-aux-Salines; town mark.

Saint-Mihiel; town mark.

Saint-Nicholas-du-Port; town mark.

Sarreguemines; town mark.

Vézelise; town mark.

Lunéville; town mark; before 1773.

Lunéville; town mark; after 1773.

Charmes; town mark.

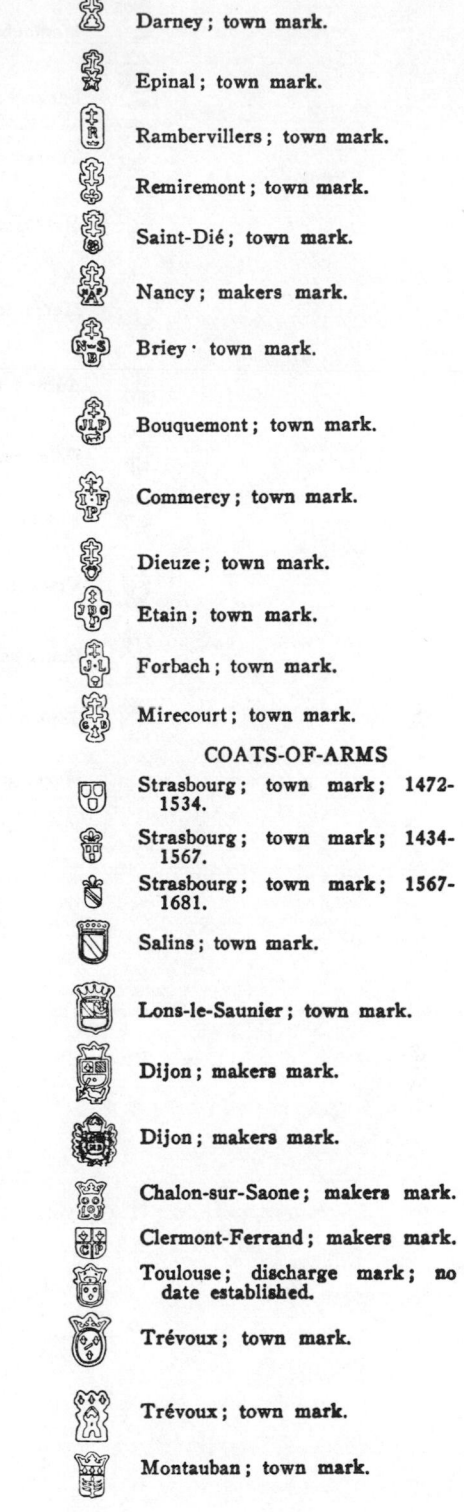

Darney; town mark.

Epinal; town mark.

Rambervillers; town mark.

Remiremont; town mark.

Saint-Dié; town mark.

Nancy; makers mark.

Briey· town mark.

Bouquemont; town mark.

Commercy; town mark.

Dieuze; town mark.

Etain; town mark.

Forbach; town mark.

Mirecourt; town mark.

COATS-OF-ARMS

Strasbourg; town mark; 1472-1534.

Strasbourg; town mark; 1434-1567.

Strasbourg; town mark; 1567-1681.

Salins; town mark.

Lons-le-Saunier; town mark.

Dijon; makers mark.

Dijon; makers mark.

Chalon-sur-Saone; makers mark.

Clermont-Ferrand; makers mark.

Toulouse; discharge mark; no date established.

Trévoux; town mark.

Trévoux; town mark.

Montauban; town mark.

Montauban; town mark.

Langres; makers mark

Tours; makers mark.

Metz; town mark.

Metz; town mark.

Autun; makers mark.

Dole; makers mark.

Vesoul; town mark.

Vesoul; makers mark.

Bourg-en-Bresse; makers mark

Toulon; town mark.

Marseille; town mark

A

27 „A“
89 „A“
1293 „A“
110 A
1166 A
1377 A
1154 A
306 A
185
278 A
238
108 A 13
65 12 A
66 12 A
67 12 A
73 A
110 A
1065 A
1064 A
62 „AB“
579 AB
443 AB
1146 AB
580 AB
1001 „A BM“
20 „ACH“
21 „ACH“
982 ACH
18 ACH
1012 „AC W“
936 AD
597 AD
550 AE
948 „A FS“
947 A FS
989 AG
643 AG
1005 AG
508 AH
1400 AH
1312 AH
55 „AK“
1334 AK
642 AL
492 AL
51 „AM“
90 „AM“
675 AM
522 AM
452 AN
840 „AP“
1447 AP
380 AP
1040 A PG
1325 „AR“
501 AR
381 AR
54 „AS“
970 AS
661 AS
448 AS
362 AS
1324 AS
516 AW
1389 AW
1388 AW
433 AW
1436 A VN
805 A W
920 AW
540 AW
781 AW
1313 AW
520 AW
641 A W

B

307 „B“
1294 „B“
1355 „B“
1459 „B“
1085 B
1106 B
1088 B
1090 B
1089 B
693 B
1091 B
1095 B
1356 B
1473 „B“
1379 B
1230 B
1092 B
1460 B
1461 B
1378 B
1084 b
1086 B
1098 B 13
1096 B 13
1103 B 13
1097 B 13
1235 B
1238 B
239 B
279 B
280 B
1474 „B“
375 B
1309 BB
566 BB
1317 B
587 B
378 B
84 B DO
484 BE
707 BE
1448 BH
903 BH
1039 BL
1320 „B IB“
1315 BK
432 BK
377 BL
474 BL
1180 BQ
679 BS
891 BS
386 BV
538 „B W“
537 B W

C

1295 „C“
1380
1155
240 C
281 C
308 C
76 C
109 CB
453 CB
944 CB
1404 CB
445 „CCC“
1417 „CD“
987 CD
885 CD
366 CE
398 CE
38 „CF“
649 CF
70 CF H
68 CF S
1030 CFT
1037 CG S
602 CH
1438 CH
1126 CH
429 CH
623 CI
933 „C IS“
58 „CK“
682 „CK“
1451 CK
949 CKM
974 CL
839 CL
585 CL
932 CL
584 CL
412 C
1202 CLP
1425 CM
827 C M
1433 CM
1332 „C NH“
1467 „CO W“
731 CP
1466 CP
59 CP
1411 CP
454 CP
1446 CP T
633 CR
1131 CR
1127 CS
768 CS
1004 CSB
1445 C SG
1220 CV
1434 CW
763 CW
1139 CW
1440 CW H
1016 CXS

D

1296 „D“
1381 D
282 D
309 D
241 D
242 D
243 D
370 „DA“
370 DA
370 „D·A·F“
753 „DB“
1470 „DF“
485 DF
1353 DB
1171 DM
467 DM
468 DM
1409 DM
802 DN
628 DF
1415 DP
34 DB
1077 „DS“
788 DS
801 DS
360 DS
640 DW
439 DW
1464 DW
496 DZ

E

310 „E“
1297 „E“
86 „E“
31 E
1142 E
1157 E
283 E
246 E
245 E
244 E
75 E
809 EA
810 EA
811 EB
663 EB
1217 „ECH“
1453 „E CS“
835 ED
938 ED
507 E
506 E
1432 EG
1147 EGB
1221 EGE
1011 EGM
608 „EH“
502 „EL“
1398 E
1178 „ERF“
1393 „ES“
803 ES
1119 ES
764 EW
626 „E W“

F

1298 „F“
421 F
705 F
777 F
1167 F
1382 F
1156 F
1158 F
284 F
311 F
249 F
248 F
247 F
498 F
940 „FAB“
858 FAB
999 FAG
981 „FA L“
81 FA L
83 F AL
847 „FB“
1314 „FB“
899 FCM
928 FC M
1047 FD
1452 FG
100 FG
1429 F GH
751 FI
1007 „FI M“
878 „F IS“
1051 „FK“
1414 FN
917 „FR L“
1482 „FS“
646 FS
853 „FS“
1135 FS
1248 „FT I“
869 FT
1416 FV
594 „F W“
1179 FW

G

28 „G“
1384 G
1383 G
285 G
251 G
312 G
250 G
78 G
22 G ACH
829 G AS
1125 G W
729 GB
909 GB
1144 GB
931 GCD
1054 GCN
683 GE
527 GE
1321
1322
1323
988 G EŒ
736 „GF“
737 GF
1022 GFG
1021 GFG
1335 „GG B“
1426 GH
1408 GH

359 GH
687 GG
1435 GI
1330 GIB
975 GIB
995 „GIK“
1430 GK
1449 GK
1443 GK
543 GL
524
541
441 G
837 GLG
812 „GM“
836 GM
1117 GM

1418 GN
394
620 GR
1170 GR
968 GS
371 GS
494 GST
983 „G W“
684 GW

H

1299 „H“
1265 „H?“
437 „H“
87 „H“
1385 H
1392 H

1159 H
252 H
286 H
313 H
390 H
879 HAO
404 HB
536 HB
658 HB
1419 HB
770 HB
376 HB
555 HB
616 HBS
910 HBW
790 HCI

791 HCI
459 HD
632 H
542 HF
635 HFS
1026 HGM
1327 HGM
1129 HH
636 HH
353
396 HP
972 „HI“
1421 HI
793 „HI“
473 HI
1175 HD
656 HIE

441
441 1621
531 HL
615 HIM
749 HP
504 HP
464 HP
654 HIS
1333
695 HW
368 „HK“
417 „HK“
517 HK
653 HL
486 HL
407 HL
774 HLS
40 „HM“
1017 „HM“

609 „I CH“
63 „ICHS“
1190 ICL
816 ICL
61 „ICM“
918 „IC M“
696 ICM
1019 ICN
782 ICP
924 ICP
710 ICR
967 ICR
1075 ICS
1337 „ICS“
776 ICS
906 ICS

914 ICS
908 ICS
907 ICS
922 ICS
1255 ICS
1003 ICT
704 ICT
919 ICT
1444 ICV
939 „ID“
551 ID
676 ID
715
1025 IDM
798 „I DO“
748 IDS
760 IDS

799 IDS
462
814 IE
1130 IEP
862
1032 IEN
373 IF
513 IF
514 IF
732 IF
871 IF
69 IB
828 FIB
874 IFB
817 IFB
104 IFD
1036 „I FF“

868 „I FH“
792 IFH
1053 IFN
926 „I FS“
780 IFW
47 „IG“
888 „IG“
521 IG
1048 „IG“
1176 IG
1049
1203 „IG H“
950 IGI
72 „IGK“
951 IGK
1247 IGN
1177 „IGP“
1008 „I GS“

972 „IH“
793 „IH“
1402 IH
472 IH
775 „IH“
36 IH
941 IH
896 IH
102
1308
598 HW
886 IHM
1423 IHP
1002 „IHS“
1243 IHS
716 II
821 II

611 HM
769 „HM“
1469 HM
915 HM
364 HM
1462 M
451 HM
500
773 HM
511
545
426
699 „HO“
586 HO
629 HO
528 HP
1422 HP

458 „HP“
1121 HP
1143 HP
787 HP
401
401'
612 HPC
634 „HP S“
603 HR
53 HS
510
350
1399 HS
461
625 HSP
56 „H.S.Z.“
969 HT

1413
489 HZ
408 HW

I

314 „I“
1160
253
287
1361
509 I
631 „IA“
1145 AB
1033 IAD
1257 „I AF“
1223 IAG
893 IAM

1010 „IAO“
943 „IA R“
1018 IAS
980 „IA W“
1245 IB
664 IB
525 IB
965 IB
718 IB
1076 „I:B“
785 B
103 B
582 IB
758 IB
934
655 IBE

824 „I BE“
957 „IBH“
576 B
1210 IBM
1336 IBM
1014 „IBS“
1015 „IBS“
971 ICB
900 „ICB“
990 „IC B“
991 ICB
973 „I CB“
1028
867 ICD
960 „ICD“
927 ICE
925 „ICG“
898 „ICH“

750 II
766 II
771 II
621
622
60 „IIA“
956 IIA
844 IIB
986 „I IB“
901 IIB
583 IIB
650 IH
786 IIK
1000 „IIM“
820 IIS
895 IIS

894 IIS
795
1006 IIW
730 „IK“
674 IK
1034 IK
414 „JK.F“
415 „JKF“
890 IKH
759 IL
845 IL
565 IL
911 ILA
574 ILB
573 ILB
1339 „IL M“

1200 ILM
779 ILS
850 „L̇S“
806 LS
592 IM
469 IM
1024 IM
403 IM
1059 IM
953 IM
665 IM
666 IM
667 IM
823 IM
82 IM
954 IML
1128 IMM

866
735 IMR
784 IMR
942 IMS
992 „I MS“
1450 IMS
887 „IMZ“
1044 INS
937 INS
1045 „I NS“
993 „IO G“
833 „IO M“
599 IP
881 IP
30
872 IPD

1138 „IPH“
955 IPH
998 „I PH“
897 IPM
852 IPN
813 IPR
1123
875 „I PS“
734 PS
562 IP
996 „IR“
563 „IR“
560 R
561 R
1050 IRH
119 „IS“
610 IS
686 IS

873
685
1046
1052
719 „ISP“
1174
880 „IT“
994
1485
977 „IVG“
830
689
385
1319 „IW“
688
860
958
959

963 „IWG“
964 „IW G“
1023
447 „IZ“
756

K

1300
598
457
1161
288
254
255
315
423
32
717

80 K.M.

L

547
1168
316
289
256
290
570 „LB“
930
843
577
569
568
85 „LE“
1483 „LF“
402
593
549

815 „LK“
415 „LKI“
1405
495
772
1029
727
877 „LS“
424
1326
702

M

26 „M“
317 „M“
672
870 „M“
700
1316
257

291
345
422
822
723
711
383
384
553
505
794 „MDW“
1352
668
478
1329 „M GE“
692 „M:H“
601
590

37 „PIS“
652
671 „PLD“
1401
800
765
1211
648 „PS“
670
778
834
861 „PV“
613
1136

Q

321 „Q“
1302 „Q“
677
295

264
265
266
77

R

296 „R“
322 „R“
1303 „R“
1116 „R“
681
267
1340 „RGS“
1132

S

323 „S“
1304 „S“
1386
1133

706 „S“
946 „S“
1134
849
297
268
460 „SA“
1246 „SA b“
997 „SB“
1311
1035 „SC“
1124
1407
912
673
1410
1189
783

52 „SH“
106
1027
471
530
1241
405
1242
419
1120
1182
714
724
929
382
660
761

754
865

T

298 „T“
1305 „T“
1387
270
269
218
324
725 „TB“
708
709
1442
497
832
1060 „T DI“

721
730
1465
789
1412
698
826 „MK“
1057 „ML“
591
105
882 „MM“
690
691
639
924 „MM“
488 „MN“
35 „MO“

662 „MP“
1437 „MP B“
369
529
491
1056 „MU“
1441
726

N

318 „N“
1162
292
258
259
564
863
477

1463
430
431
519
738
372

O

319 „O“
293
261
260
230
96
99
95
97

98
33
1396
1185
41
1391

P

320 „P“
1301 „P“
512
392
393
1164
294
263

262
74
1041 „PAG“
945 „PCS“
857
819
703
902 „PH“
1328
410
595
552
647
1115
713
637
722

923
1427
1428
515
481
984 „T- M“
1431
1193
1187
1439
916 „TV G“
373

U

325 „U“
299
300

V

301 „V“
326 „V“
25
271
272
694 „VB“
436
374
113
808 „V·I“
1406
1390
1420 VM
440
556 „VS“
859 „VSI“

W

302 „W“
327 „W“
627 „W“
1371 „W“
1368
1366
1365
1367
1370
1369
463
1169 W
767
274
273
892 „W“

1222 „WB“
966 „WD“
490
1331 „WG“
411
39 „WH“
638
518
1354
728 „WS“

X

328 „X“
275
303

Y

304 „Y“
329
276
119 „YS 1549“

Z

330 „Z“
848 „Z“
913
277
305
1318 „ZB“
420
413 Z L
413 „Z.L.F.“
332
1338 „ZU Z“

Heavenly Bodies

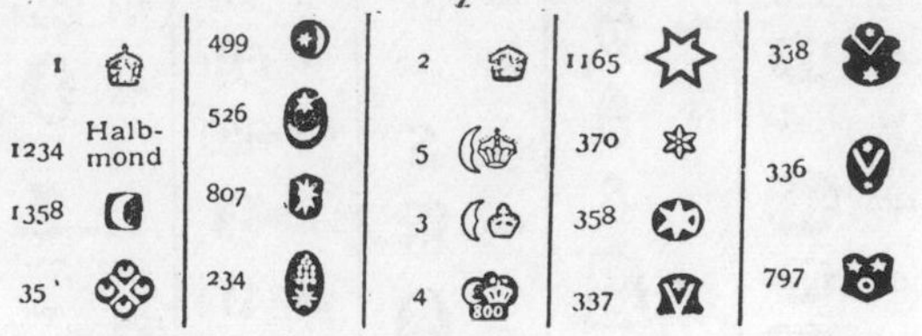

Man

Lions

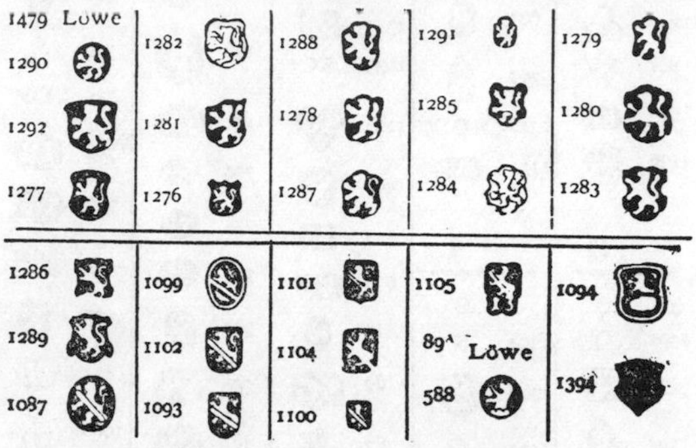

Miscellaneous Mammals

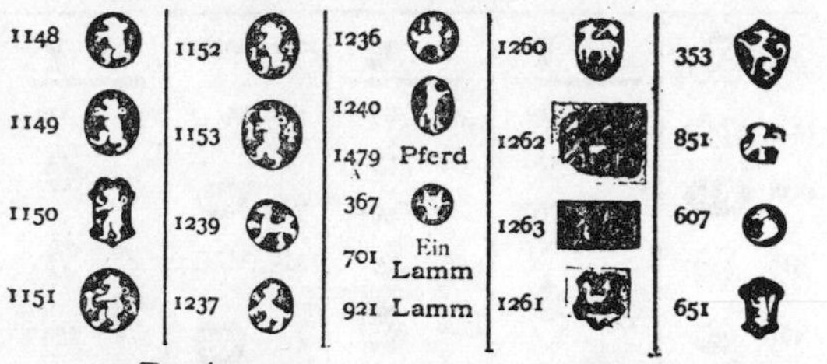

Eagles and Miscellaneous Birds

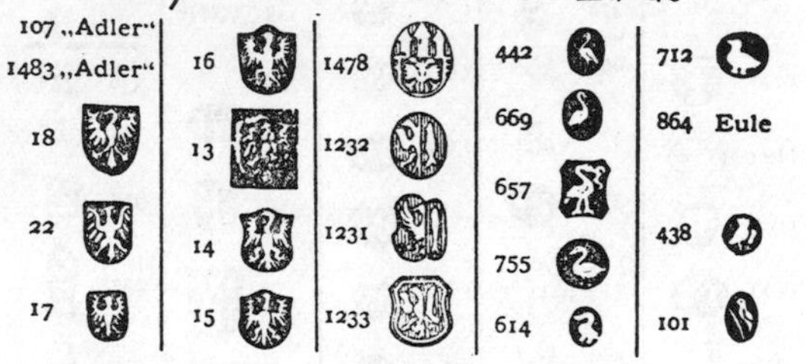

Water

Plants

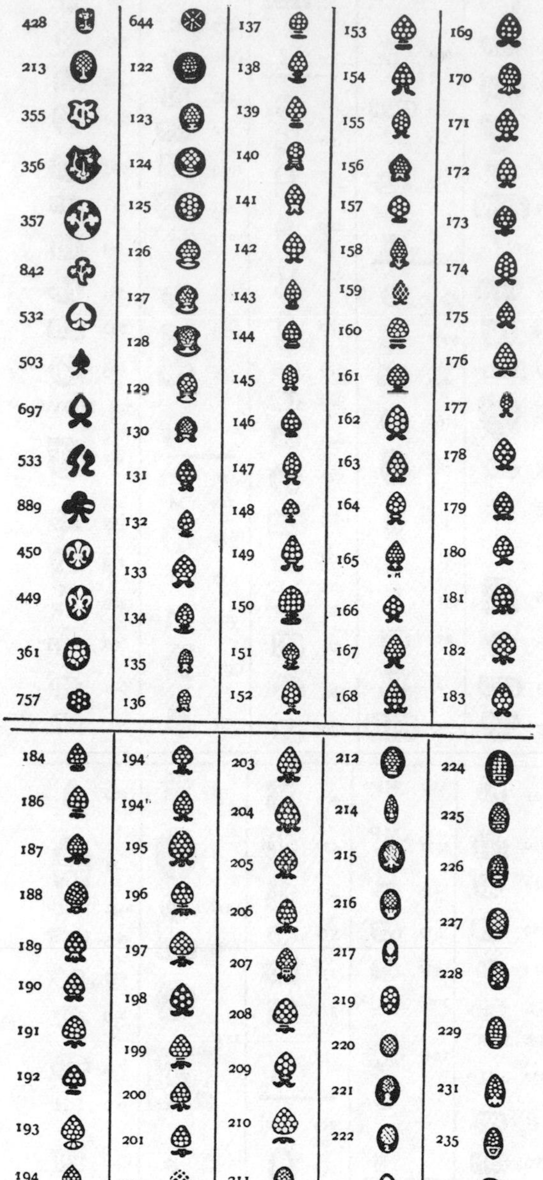

Scepters and Arms

Utensils

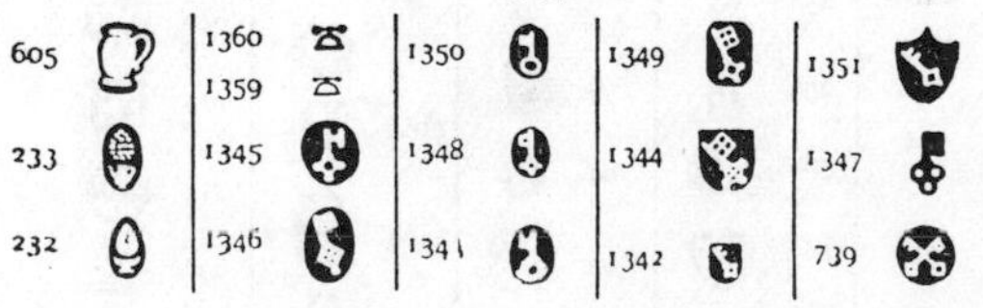

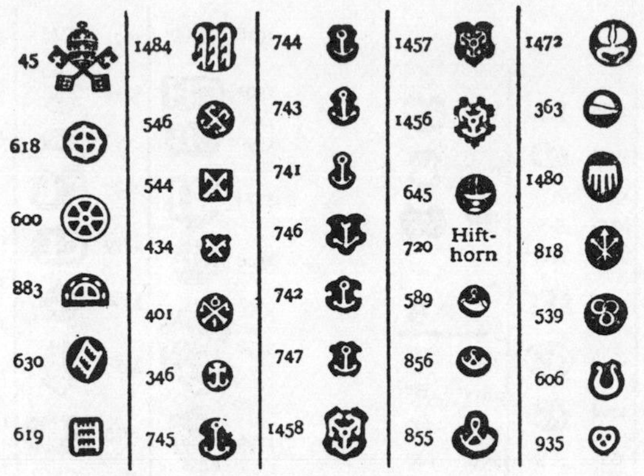

Architecture

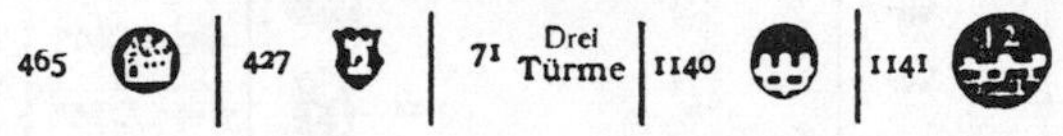

Crosses

Trade Marks

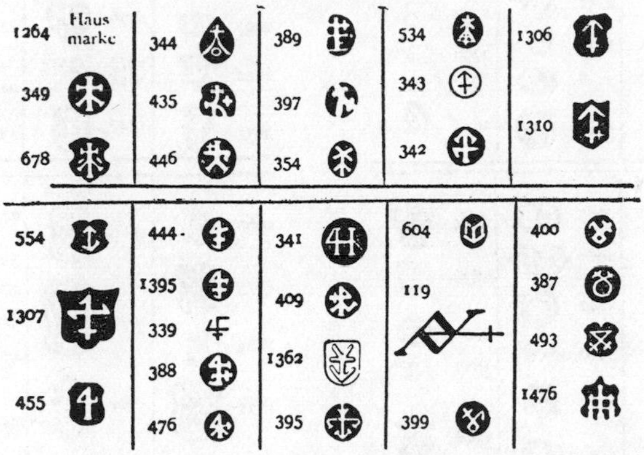

Shields

Numbers

A

- 1687 „A"–„Z"
- 1851 „A" „Z"
- 1934 „A" „Z"
- 3362 „A" „Z"
- 1696 „A"
- 2834 A
- 2835 A
- 3017 A
- 1687 A
- 3013 A
- 2513 A
- 1706 A
- 2822 a
- 2697
- 2357 A
- 2146 AA
- 2148 AA
- 3062 AA
- 3523 „AB"
- 2392 „AB"
- 1966 AR
- 3531 AD
- 2090 AF
- 1828 AF
- 1967 AF
- 1827 AF
- 2450 AFL
- 3559 „A FS"
- 1970 AF S
- 1986 AG
- 2462 2464 „AH"
- 2324 AH
- 1578 AH
- 1898 AI
- 2877 AI
- 2878 AI
- 3052 „AIR"
- 3117 AK
- 3038 AK
- 1786 „AK D"
- 2759 AL
- 1588 AL
- 2326 AL
- 2102 AM
- 1862 ANK
- 3225 „AN L"
- 3513 AP
- 3515 „AP"
- 3514 „AP"
- 2746 AR
- 2099 AR
- 3043 AR
- 1743 „AS"
- 2779 „AS"
- 3558 „AS"
- 3084 AS
- 1636 AS
- 2494 AS
- 3557 „AS"
- 3489 A
- 1646 ASI
- 3268 AW
- 2477 AX
- 2322 AR
- 2241 „AW"
- 1649 AW
- 2238 AW
- 2239 AW
- 2240 AW
- 1612 AW
- 2247 AAB

B

- 2505 „B"
- 2617 „B"
- 2766 „B"
- 2539 „B"
- 1526 B
- 1899 B
- 2833 B
- 1852 B
- 2514 B
- 1527 B
- 2206 „B"
- 2823 B
- 2698
- 2923 BX
- 2455 „Bad"
- 1504 BB
- 1569 BC
- 2124 „BF"
- 2129 BF
- 1565 BG
- 1897 „BH"
- 2499 BH
- 2932 BF
- 2963 „BK"
- 2867 BK 07
- 2866 BK 86
- 3057 „BL" „1670"
- 3058 BL
- 3585 „BM"
- 2402 NBR
- 3306 BNB
- 3496 BP
- 1615 „BR"
- 2566 BS
- 3064 BV
- 2756 „B W"
- 2754 BW
- 2755 BW
- 2045 BW

C

- 2683 „C"
- 3255 „C"
- 1882 C
- 2498 C
- 2955 „C"
- 2950 C
- 2956 C
- 2951 C
- 3255 C
- 2308 C
- 1697 C
- 2824 c
- 2683 „C"
- 3014 C
- 1721 t
- 2699
- 2358 C
- 2370
- 3615 „CB"
- 2038 CB
- 3051 CB
- 2101 CB
- 2985 CB
- 2063 CB
- 2842 CB
- 3410 „CB"
- 3059 CB
- 3183 CB
- 1566 CBH
- 1660 CBS
- 2873 CB VR
- 2727 G
- 1805 CDS
- 1806 CDS
- 1808 C.D. SCHRODEL
- 1807 C.D. Schrodel
- 1638 CEA
- 2274 CF M
- 2876 CE S
- 2790 CF
- 2927 „CF"
- 2868 CF 88
- 2882 CFH
- 1792 CF H
- 2057 „CFI"
- 2988 „CFR"
- 1787 CT
- 1790 CGI
- 1800 C.G INGERMANN
- 1793 CG M
- 1865 CH
- 2980 CH
- 1864 CH
- 1916 „CH"
- 1502 CH
- 1590 CH
- 3274 CH
- 2508 CH
- 1798 CH
- 1799
- 1568 CH IOD
- 3104 CH L
- 2064 „CH M"
- 1822 CHR
- 1981 CH W
- 2497 CI
- 1542 CI
- 3027 C B
- 1971 „CK"
- 2316 CK
- 3097 CK
- 2880 CL
- 2879 CL
- 3398 CL
- 3278 CL
- 2075 CLK
- 3055 „CM"
- 3087 „CM"
- 2409 „CM"
- 3119 „CM"
- 2381 CM
- 3056 CM
- 1992 CM
- 2776 CM N
- 1973 3614 „CP"
- 1549 CP
- 3184 „CR"
- 2041 CR
- 2296 CR
- 2192
- 2670 „CS"
- 3209 „CS"
- 3288 „CS"
- 2175 CS
- 1556 CS
- 2780 „C.S"
- 3122 CS
- 1913
- 3525 „CST"
- 1532 CS
- 1510 CT
- 2391
- 2418
- 1755 „CW"
- 2204 „CW"
- 3026 CW
- 2315 „CW"
- 1797 CW K
- 2787

D

- 1659 „D"
- 3299 „D"
- 1896 D
- 1658 D
- 1659 D
- 1622 D
- 1650 „D"
- 1651 „D"
- 1621 D
- 1623 D
- 2825 D
- 1853 D
- 1625 D
- 1624 D
- 1626 D
- 2263 D
- 2309 D
- 3022 D
- 1722 D
- 1620 „D"
- 2504 D
- 2700
- 1663
- 1661
- 1664
- 1681
- 1673
- 1678
- 1674
- 1660
- 1675
- 1683
- 1672
- 1662
- 1667
- 1680
- 1677
- 1676
- 1668
- 1679
- 1684
- 1685
- 1669
- 1671
- 1682
- 2359 D
- 3289 „D CW"
- 2860 DD
- 2503 DD
- 2861 DD
- 3216 „D GM"
- 1908 DH
- 1909 DH
- 2388 DHK
- 1991 DP
- 1915 „DH S"
- 2473 DI
- 3356 „DIW"
- 1747 „DK"
- 1748 „DK"
- 1748 „DK" „1629"
- 1744 K
- 3203 B
- 1745 „1613" DK
- 1746 „DKF" „1617"
- 2517 D
- 1583 „DM"
- 2404 DM
- 3342 DP
- 2893 „DS"
- 3221 „D S"
- 1912 DS
- 1910 DS
- 1911 DS
- 2851 D
- 2044 DT
- 2074 DT
- 2657 DH
- 1937 D
- 2765 „DW"
- 2093 DW

E

- 3113 „E"
- 1925 E
- 1926 E
- 1933 E
- 1948 E
- 1956 E
- 1525 E
- 2532 E
- 3256 E
- 1955 E
- 1954 E
- 1949 E
- 1950 E
- 1952 E
- 1951 E
- 1953 E
- 1518 E
- 1519 E
- 3005 E
- 2813 E
- 2830 E
- 2618 E
- 1874 E
- 1930
- 1941
- 1942

- 2761 „EA"
- 3213 „E AM"
- 1928
- 2125
- 1524
- 2668
- 3363
- 1757
- 3082 „EH"
- 2401
- 3573 „EI"
- 1555
- 1554
- 1929
- 3035
- 3060
- 2070 „E.S.&Co."
- 1962
- 1961

F

- „F"
- 2118 Kreuz?
- 2310 „F"
- 3114 „F"
- 2080
- 2078
- 2079
- 2082
- 2081
- 1982 „F"
- 2083
- 2106
- 3257
- 2197
- 1983 „F"
- 1528
- 2284
- 1523
- 2826
- 2814
- 1698
- 3006
- 1723
- 2152
- 2010
- 2013
- 2619
- 2084
- 2086
- 2085
- 2360
- 2015
- 2373
- 3018 „FAO"
- 3284 „FAR"
- 2941
- 2294
- 2777
- 3528 „FC"
- 1492 „FCM"
- 1491
- 3078
- 2751
- 2741 „FE"
- 2774
- 2384 „FF"
- 2395
- 3046
- 1990 „FG"
- 3592 „FG"
- 2390
- 3086
- 2131 „FH"
- 2530
- 2478 „FHV"
- 2940
- 2269 „FI M"
- 3336 „FK"
- 3507
- 3508
- 1753
- 3553 „FL"
- 1647
- 2527
- 2297
- 2472
- 3504
- 3568 „FP"
- 3526

H

- 1522 „H"
- 1508
- 3212 „H"
- 3174
- 3597
- 1531
- 1707
- 2815
- 2264
- 2311
- 1725
- 3276
- 3173 „H"
- 2363
- 2368
- 2230
- 2564
- 2049
- 3218 „HAS" Totenschädel
- 2394 „HB"
- 3414 „HB"
- 2534
- 3067
- 3598 „HB"
- 3598
- 2445 Hammer „HB"
- 1546 „H C"
- 3068
- 2669 „HCH"
- 2068 „H. & Co."
- 3364
- 2981 „HD(?)"
- 3608 „HD"
- 1900 „HD"
- 1901
- 3199
- 1732
- 2139 „HE"
- 2138
- 1548
- 2407 „HE"
- 2922
- 2140 „HF"
- 2389 „HF"
- 2476 „HF"
- 1917
- 3307
- 3493 „HG"
- 2638
- 3287
- 3206 „HH"
- 3049
- 3047
- 3048
- 2538 „HH"
- 1875 „HH"
- 3505 „HH"
- 2926
- 3617 „HH O"
- 1979 „HI"
- 2730
- 1903
- 3269 „HI"
- 3223 „HI B"
- 2939
- 2127 „HIH"
- 3175 „H"
- 1936
- 2040
- 2662 „I-K"
- 3102 „HK"
- 1733 (Ao: 1585)
- 3103
- 2742 „HL"
- 3188 „HL"
- 2378 „HL"
- 2953
- 1964
- 2410
- 2417
- 2397 „HL"
- 2565
- 2422
- 2423
- 1969

- 1813
- 2930
- 3407
- 2203
- 2161 „F SH"
- 2760
- 2438
- 2529
- 2143
- 3495

G

- 1688 „G"
- 2249 „G"
- 2252 „G"
- 3115 „G"
- 3259
- 2174
- 2236
- 2235
- 3484
- 3300
- 3018
- 3007
- 3469
- 1724
- 2170
- 2620
- 2234
- 2162
- 2233
- 2216
- 2215
- 2361
- 2218
- 2217
- 2321 „GA W"
- 1834 „GB"
- 2935
- 1957
- 2518
- 2525 „GD"
- 2749
- 2285
- 2674
- 1815
- 2954
- 3349 „GG"
- 1593 „GG"
- 3080
- 3292
- 2625 „G H"
- 1545 „GH"
- 2626
- 2029
- 3032
- 2286 „GK"
- 2223
- 3405
- 2396
- 3497
- 2098 „GL K"
- 1740
- 1739
- 1818
- 1817
- 3305
- 3377 „GP" „1692"
- 1836 „GR"
- 3500 „GR"
- 3090 „GS"
- 3053
- 3063
- 3551
- 2627
- 2849
- 3525 „GST"
- 3587 „GST"
- 1592
- 2555 „GW"
- 1594
- 2938
- 2541 „GWR"
- 2059
- 3576 „GZ"
- 3479
- 2426 „H·L·P"
- 1795
- 2453
- 2433 „HM"
- 2856
- 2857
- 2850
- 2888
- 2042
- 2199
- 2036
- 2039
- 1557
- 2412
- 3194 Turm „HO"
- 1582
- 2033
- 2250 „HP"
- 3600 „HP"
- 2533
- 2435
- 3603
- 2862
- 3030
- 3031
- 3482
- 3483 „HR"
- 3030
- 3270
- 1641
- 2493
- 2733
- 3477 (I·5·H·R·F·63)
- 3477 (I·5·H·R·F·75)
- 2557 „HS"
- 3211 „HS"
- 2507
- 1904 „HS"
- 3418
- 2768
- 3499
- 3045
- 2771
- 2495
- 1965
- 1741
- 3399
- 1635
- 3081
- 2406
- 3304
- 2200

I

- 3185 „I"
- 2836
- 3011
- 2799
- 2346
- 2663
- 2198
- 2054
- 2231
- 3400 „I ? M"
- 3406 „IAR"
- 2943
- 3121 „IB"
- 3286 „IB"
- 2221
- 3041
- 2630
- 3079
- 1863
- 2429
- 2624
- 2871

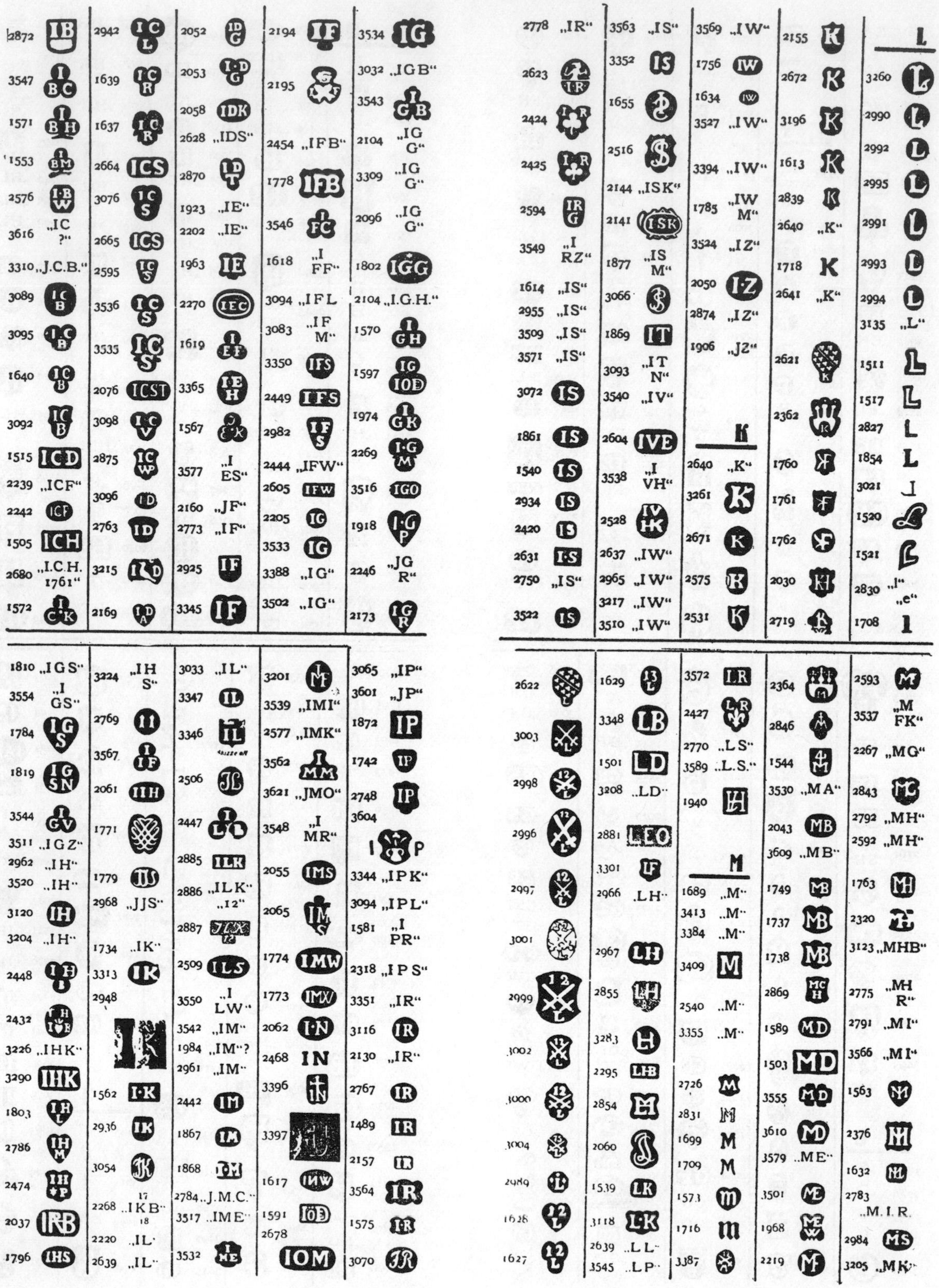

2872
3547
1571
1553
2576
3616 „IC ?"
3310 „J.C.B."
3089
3095
1640
3092
1515
2239 „ICF"
2242
1505
2680 „I.C.H. 1761"
1572

2942
1639
1637
2664
3076
2665
2595
3536
3535
2076
3098
2875
3096
2763
3215
2169

2052
2053
2058
2628 „IDS"
2870
1923 „IE"
2202 „IE"
1963
2270
1619
3365
1567
3577 „I ES"
2160 „JF"
2773 „IF"
2925
3345

2194
2195
2454 „IFB"
1778
3546
1618 „I FF"
3094 „IFL"
3083 „IF M"
3350
2449
2982
2444 „IFW"
2605
2205
3533
3388 „IG"
3502 „IG"

3534
3032 „IGB"
3543
2104 „IG G"
3309 „IG G"
2096 „IG G"
1802
2104 „I.G.H."
1570
1597
1974
2269
3516
1918
2246 „JG R"
2173

2778 „IR"
2623
2424
2425
2594
3549 „I RZ"
1614 „IS"
2955 „IS"
3509 „IS"
3571 „IS"
3072
1861
1540
2934
2420
2631
2750 „IS"
3522

3563 „IS"
3352
1655
2516
2144 „ISK"
2141
1877 „IS M"
3066
1869
3093 „IT N"
3540 „IV"
2604
3538 „I VH"
2528
2637 „IW"
2965 „IW"
3217 „IW"
3510 „IW"

3569 „IW"
1756
1634
3527 „IW"
3394 „IW"
1785 „IW M"
3524 „IZ"
2050
2874 „IZ"
1906 „JZ"

K

2640 „K"
3261
2671
2575
2531

2155
2672
3196
1613
2839
2640 „K"
1718
2641 „K"
2621
2362
1760
1761
1762
2030
2719

L

3260
2990
2992
2995
2991
2993
2994
3135 „L"
1511
1517
2827
1854
3021
1520
1521
2830 „I" „e"
1708

1810 „IGS"
3554 „I GS"
1784
1819
3544
3511 „IGZ"
2962 „IH"
3520 „IH"
3120
3204 „IH"
2448
2432
3226 „IHK"
3290
1803
2786
2474
2037
1796

3224 „IH S"
2769
3567
2061
1771
1779
2968 „JJS"
1734 „IK"
3313
2948
1562
2936
3054
2268 „IKB" 17 18
2220 „IL"
2639 „IL"

3033 „IL"
3347
3346
2506
2447
2885
2886 „ILK" „I2"
2887
2509
3550 „I LW"
3542 „IM"
1984 „IM"?
2961 „IM"
2442
1867
1868
2784 „J.M.C."
3517 „IME"
3532

3201
3539 „IMI"
2577 „IMK"
3562
3621 „JMO"
3548 „I MR"
2055
2065
1774
1773
2062
2468
3396
3397
1617
1591
2678

3065 „IP"
3601 „JP"
1872
1742
2748
3604
3344 „IPK"
3094 „IPL"
1581 „I PR"
2318 „IPS"
3351 „IR"
3116
2130 „IR"
2767
1489
2157
3564
1575
3070

2622
3003
2998
2996
2997
3001
2999
3002
3000
3004
2989
1628
1627

1629
3348
1501
3208 „LD"
2881
3301
2966 „LH"
2967
2855
3283
2295
2854
2060
1539
3118
2639 „LL"
3545 „LP"

3572
2427
2770 „LS"
3589 „L.S."
1940

M

1689 „M"
3413 „M"
3384 „M"
3409
2540 „M"
3355 „M"
2726
2831
1699
1709
1573
1716
3387

2364
2846
1544
3530 „MA"
2043
3609 „MB"
1749
1737
1738
2869
1589
1503
3555
3610
3579 „ME"
3501
1968
2219

2593
3537 „M FK"
2267 „MG"
2843
2792 „MH"
2592 „MH"
1763
2320
3123 „MHB"
2775 „MH R"
2791 „MI"
3566 „MI"
1563
2376
1632
2783 „M.I.R."
2984
3205 „MK"

2673 MK
2526 MK H
3039 ML
2377
1766 „MR"
2323 „MS"
3512 „MS"
2196 MS
2983 MS
1780 „MS"
3516 „MV"
3518 „MV"
3200 „MvB"
3472 „MZ"

N

1690 N
1700 N
3015 N
2369

1768 NB
2658 NC
2399 „NF"
2403 NG
2772 „NH"
2463 „NH"
1902 NH
2666 „NIT"
2782 „NK I"
1947 NM
1769 „NM"
3282 NM
2056 NN
1576 NP
1577 NP
1561 NP
1559 „NPI"
1585 NS

1586 NS
1584 NS
2682 „NW"
1616 NW

O

1701 O
2072 O
2721
3167 OO
2864 OS 86
2865 OST4

P

1894 P
3599 P
2071 „P"
2816 P

3012 P
3008 P
1642 PA
2681 PB
2629 PB
2548 P.B.&C
3222 „PB VA"
1574 P CG
2788 PE
2847 PE
2848 PE
3088 PG
3085 PGH
2838 „PH"
2661 PH
2379 PI
2863 PI

3220 „P HK"
1558 P HL
3285 „PHM"
2046 PHS
2047 13 PHS
3069 PI
2659 PI
1781 PI
2325 P IF
2568 „PI S"
2567 PI S
2667 „P·I W"
2789 PK
2451 ? „P·K."
1727

2762 SS
3073 S
1533 St
1536 St
2553 „SV"
1794 „SW"
3506 SW
3521 S·W
2537 „SZ"
2944 S·Z
„ZS"
2945 SZ
„ZS"

T

1692 „T"
3202 T
2312 T
2820 T

3016 T
1711 T
3096 „TB"
2023 „TB.fe"
1514 T
2405 DM
2764 TS
2222 TK
1941 T
1767 „TL"
1552 T
2757 „TN"
3182 TN
2758 T
2158 „TS"
1655 T
2747 TS
1914 TS

2266 T·T 1700
3498 T
2722 TH
2723 TI
3124 „TW"

U

1717 U
2366 U
2371 U

Lit. V

3470 V
1719 V
2372 V
1516 V CH
2937 „VE"
3312 „VG"

1731 VG
2443 VH
2440 VH
2929 V
3480 VM
2978 VS
3413 „VS"
3519 V·S
1726 VS
2094 VS
3471 VT
2201 VV

W

1693 „W"
2128 „W"
2165 W
1656 „W"

1506 W
1537 W
2844 W
3552 „W"
2408 W
1535 W
2726 W
2088 W
2821 W
3611 „W"
3187 Hausmarke „W"
3181 „W"
3277
3170
1804 „WB"
3207 „WB"
2134 WF
3091 „WH"

2025 P
2858 PS
2027 R
3303 PSO
2156 „PP"
2319 PR
1560 PR
1580 PR
2237 „P.S."
3077 PS
3074 PS
3071 PS
2859 PSM
3575 „P ST"
3061 „PT"
3541 „PV"
3341 PV

1550 RR
3042 PR
1755 „PZ"
2496 PZ

Q

1691 „Q"
1507 Q
2817 Q
1702 Q
3019 Q
3343 QR

R

3195 „R"
1547 R
3075 R
1534 R

1509 R
1550 „R"
2166 „R"
2818 R
3020 Я
2798 „R"
2028 R
1905 RE
2437 „RG"
1633 R
2920 RI
2732 RM
3386 „RT"
2717

S

1538 „S"
1821 „S"
2819 „S"
2428 S

3272 S
2105 S
1512 S
1513 S
3611 S
2828 S
1530 S
1710 S
1769 S
3529 „S"
2924 S
2051 SB
2126 SB
1811 „S.BS."
1788 SG
2852 S
2853 S

1750 S
1551 SDR
3214 „SFS"
2103 SH
3219 Anker „SH"
1770 SB
2069 S.H.&Co.
3180 „SI"
2745 S
2097 SK
3029 SK
3044 S
2095 SL
2928 „SL"
1587 SO
2554 „S OW"
1490 SR

1938 Wh
2434 I W H
1564 W 10D
3308 WL
3620 „WO"
3503 „WR"
2785 WS
3280 WS

1978 „WV"
3040 „WZ"

X

1703 „X"
2832 X
3009 X
1712 X
1855 X
1694 X

3578 „XB"
1924 „XE"
3561 XL
3560 X·L

Y

1704 Y
1705 Y
1713 Y
2367

Z

1695 „Z"
3357 Z
2829 Z
1715 Z
1720 Z
3010 Z
1714 Z

1758 ZB „ZR"
1907 Z
1758 „ZR" „ZB"
2944 „ZS"
2945 „ZS"
1751 ZS
1752 ZS
1764 Z

Heavenly Bodies

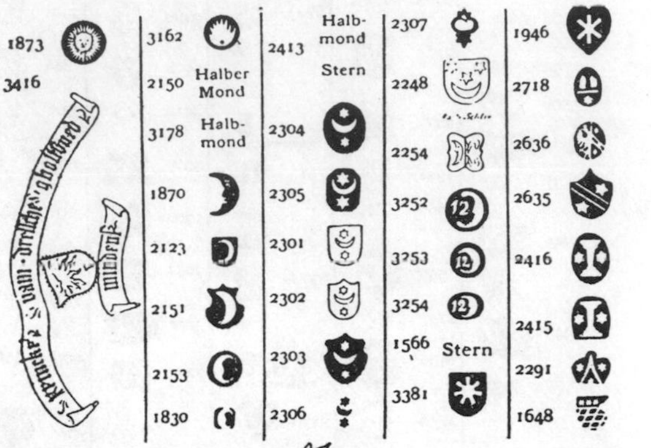

Man

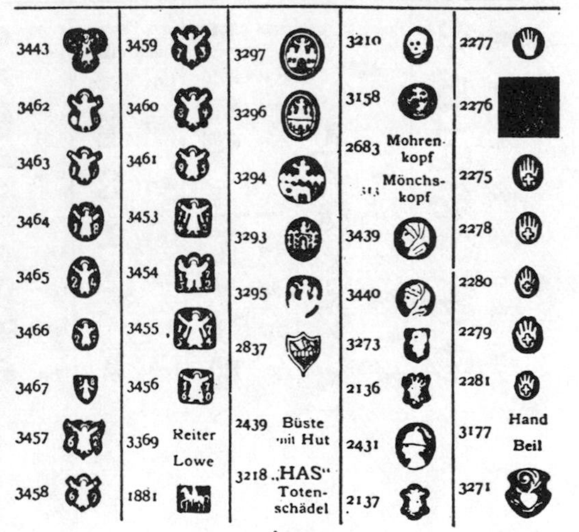

Lions

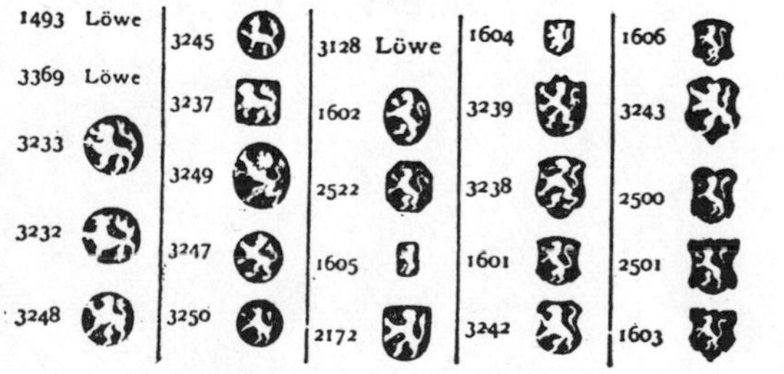

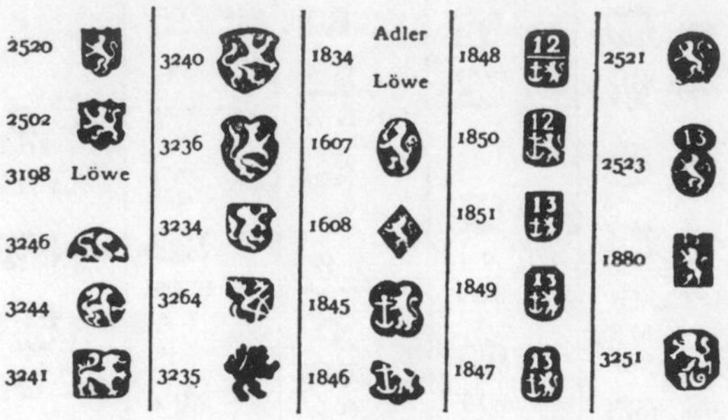

Misc. Mammals

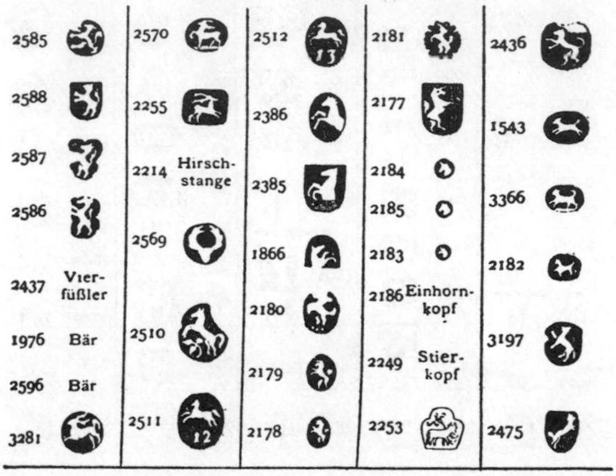

Griffins, Eagles, Misc. Birds

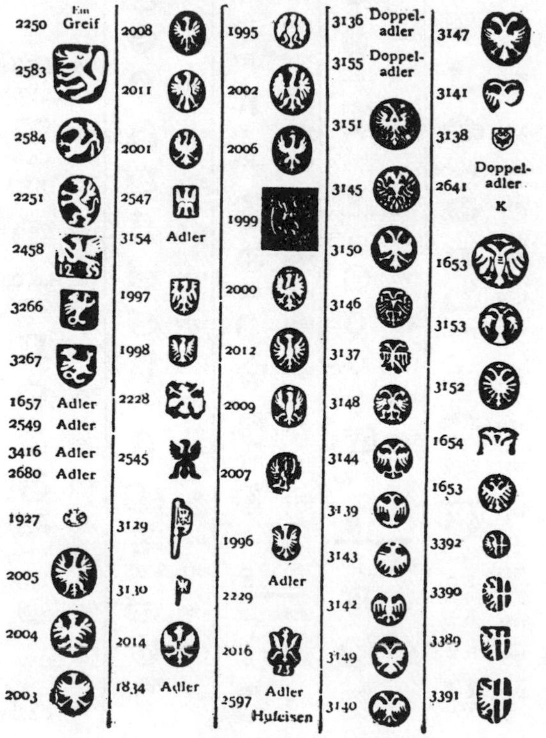

2560
2559
2948
2562 Adler 49
2561 Adler 16 45

2563
2891 Ein Schwan
2841
2383
2393
2382
2441

2573
2574
2073
3186
1541
2471
2352

3298
1876 Flug „10"
1878 Flug „12"
2111 Rabenkopf
2118 Rabenkopf
2107
2109

2108
2117
2110
2114
2115
2116
2113
2112

Marine Life and Water

2397 Schlange „PO"
2167 Salm
1529
2947 Krebs
2283
2375

Plants

1860 Baum
3192 Baumstrunk
2606
2290
2653

2643
2647
2649
2654

2648
2644
2646
2645
2652

2651
2650
2481
2481
2289

3179
2800 Kleeblatt
2419 Kleeblatt
2958 Dreiblatt 8
2489

2491
2490
2492
2483
2484
2485
2486
2487

2488
3279
2612
2613
2615
2614
2616

3487
2515
1644
1645
1643
2213
1858

2374
3172
2430
2744
3166 Rosette
2164
3193
2163
3275

3165
2288
2293
2292
2168 Frucht
2031
1859

Crowns, Scepters, and Arms

2713 Krone
1782
2677
2676
2675
2313

2314
2713 Krone 13
2691
2693
2692
2694
2695

2380
2696
2705
2704
2711
2701
2708

2712
3416 Szepter
3263
3265
2970 Ritterhelm
2975

2974
2971
2976
2972
2973
2969 3 Helme

1977
1666
1670
1665
3037

Implements

2398 Becher (?)
3159
2552 „Gekreuzte Abtstäbe"
2986 Gekreuzte Schlüssel
3111 Gekreuzte Schlüssel
3107
3108
3109
3110
3112 Gekreuzte Schlüssel 12
3337
3169
3339

3163
3330
3325
3324
3326
3327
3335
3331
3328
3332
3168
3359
3358
2256

2261
2258
2259
2260
2262
3360
3361
2257
2892 Kesselhaken
3164 Anker
1840
1839

1841
1838
1837
1844
1843
1842
Anker „CL"
3398
3219 Anker „SH"
2414
1486
1488
1487
3157 Faß

2457
3417
2482 Sichel
2445 Hammer „HB"
2193
3340 Schere
3189 Hifthorn
3191 Hifthorn
3190 Posthorn
2680 Hufeisen
3034 Hufeisen,
1920
3380
1921
3160

Architecture

1975 Architekturmarke
3194 Turm „HO"
2987 Torturm
3099
3100
3101
2600 Tor
1985

2335
2334
2344
3373
2327
3376
2347
2330

2331
2336
2329
2343
2342
2348
2349
2338

2328
2341
2519
2339
2350
2351
3375
3374

2345
2356
2340
2365
2355
2353
2354

Crosses

2118 „F" Kreuz?
1943 Andreaskreuz?
3402
3404
1980
3403 Kreuz

2139
2905
2911
2908
2914
2904

2906
3230
3229
2960
2191

2145
2147
2459 Kreuz
2800 Krone
2810

2800
2801
2804
2802
2807

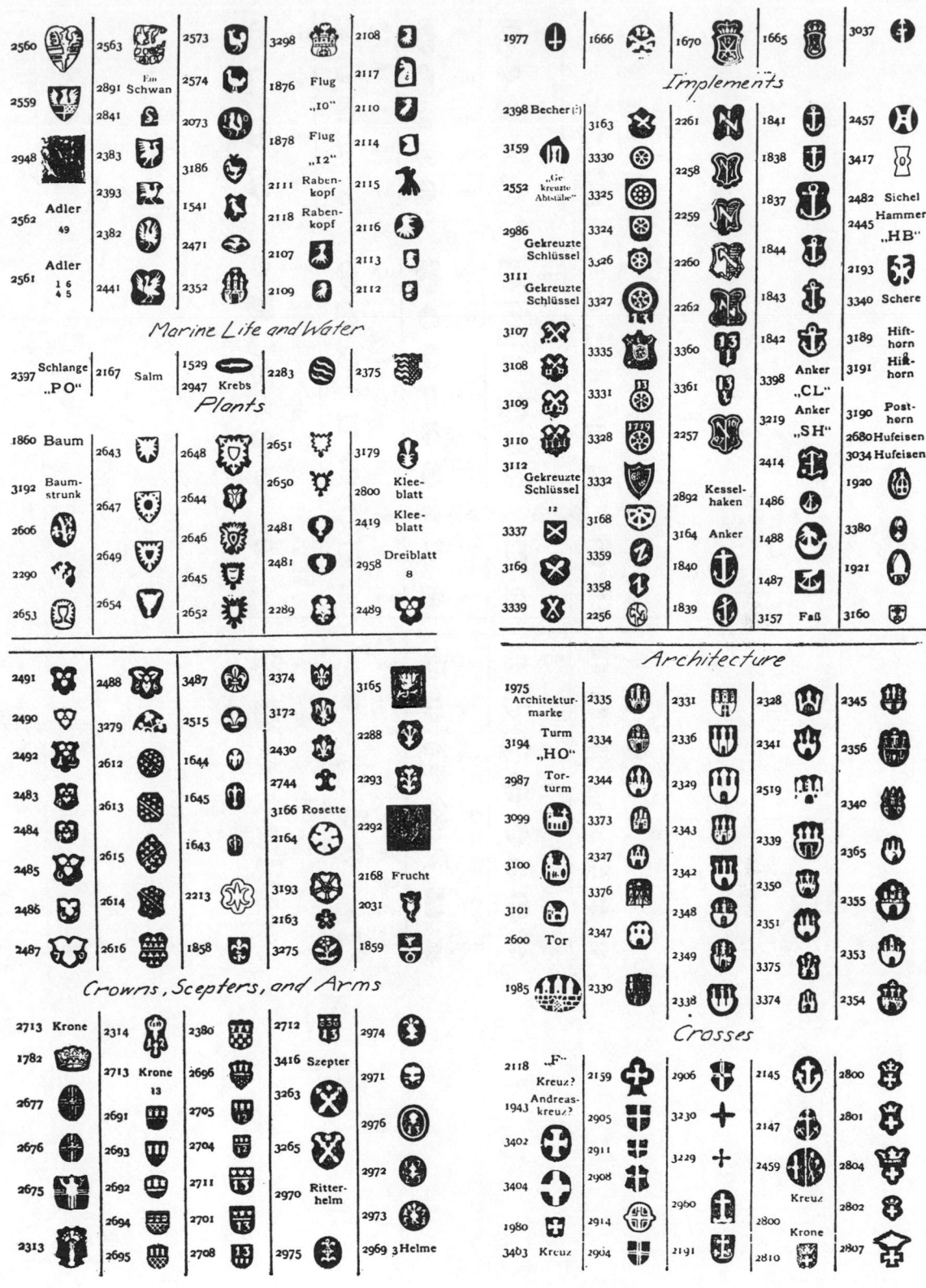

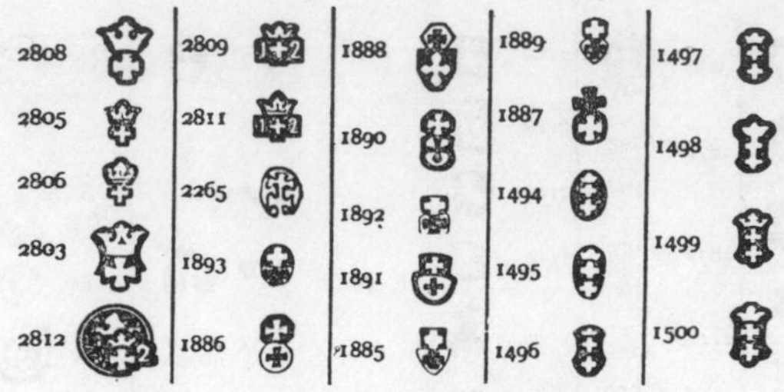

Trade Marks

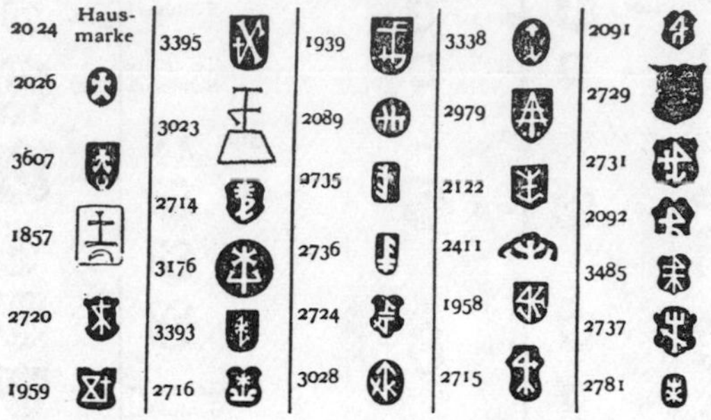

Shields and Geometrical Forms

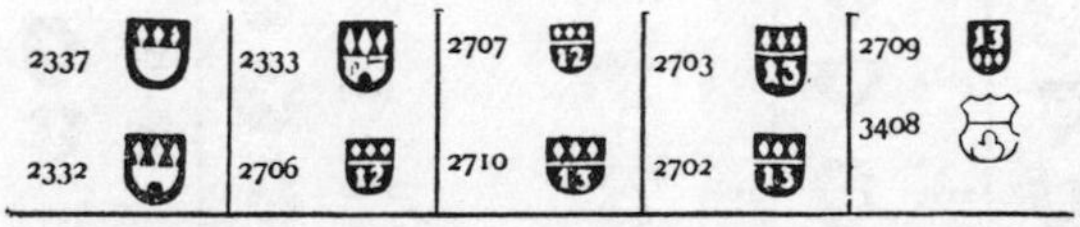

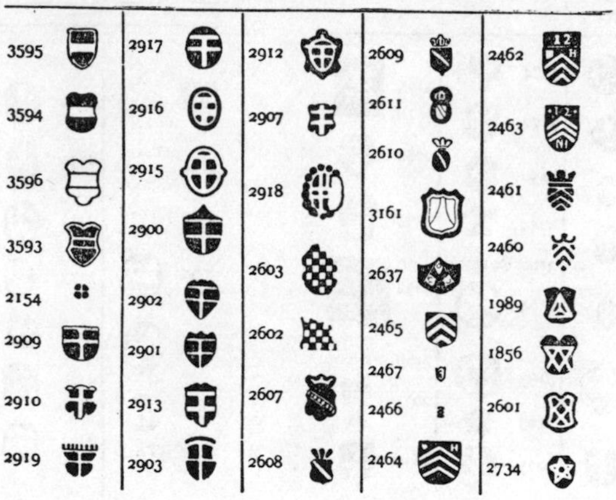

A

3638 „A"
4410 A
3772 A
3631 „A"
3637 „a"
4540
4438
4187 „AA"
4535 ABE
4228 ABM
4229 ABM
3644 „AD"
4697 „AG"
4531 AH
3838 AI

4675 AK
4677 AL
4149 AL
4150 AL
4660 „AM"
4165 AM
4062 AP
4448 AP
3944 AR
3924 AR
4065 AR
3925 „AR"
4903 „AR"
4480 AR
4778 AR
4212 AR
4099 AR

4100 AR
3978 AS
4189 ASZ
4456 AS
3656 „ASZ"
4050 AT
4051 AT
4164 AX
3907 AZ
3982 AV
4487 „AV"
4637 AX
3920 AV

B

4582 „B"
4411 B
3773 B

4802 B
4884 B
3632 „B"
3980 B
3797 b
3756
3971 „BG"
3972 „BG"
4112 BI
4853 „BK"
4021 BK
4445 B
4792 BM
4339 BG
4226 BP
3653 BR
4770 BS
4951 „B W"

4952 „BW"
4391 BW
4950 „B W"
4450 BZ

C

3774 C
3633 „C"
4698 „?C"
3839 C
4147 C
4567 CB
4888 CB
4163 „CD"
4347
4471 „CDH"

4916 CDH
4168 CE
4804 „CE O"
4334 CFR
3646 CGB
4592 CGH
4412 CG KEL
3673 „CH"
4266 CHB
4117 HC
4267 CHC
4639 CE
4915
4324 CIK
4233 CK
4259 C-K

4699 C
4076 „CK"
4791 CK
3929 CK
4596 „CK"
4286 „CK"
4079 „CL"
4813 „CL W"
4532 CM
4788 CM
4796 CM
4330 CM
4192 CM
4928 CM
4201 CP
4646 CP
4386 CR

4066 „CS"
4961 CS
4067 CS
4600 „CV"
4361 CV
4595 „CV"
3861
4975 „CW"
4331 CW
4251 CW
3999 CW
4260 „CW"
4245 CW
4261 CWM
4648 CY
4982 „CZ"

D

3639 „D"
3775 D

4403
3634 „D"
3798 D
4588 DB
4700 DB
3997 DI
3998 DH
4490 DH
4468 „D MB"
4467 DMB
4598 DS
3984 „DS"
4270 „D W" Vogel

E

3776 E
4620 E

4542
4674 EB
4587 EB
4308 EP
4500 „EC P"
4679 EE
4074 „EH"
4033 EI
3994 EK
3910 „EL"
4678 EL
3951 EL
4767 EM
4183 EMD
4351 EP
4654 ES
4460 SS

F

3777 F
3799 F
4871 FH
4599 „FB"
4390 FDS
3947 F
4854 „F.H."
4244 FH
4017 FH
3980 FH
4458 FH
3660 FH
4175 FH
4287 FIW
4862 „FK"
4416 „FM"
4793
4248 P
4063 F
4064 F

4309 FS
4421 FW
4420 FW
4419 FW
4422 FW
4870 „FWL"

G

4913 „G"
4932 „G"
3778 G
4442
4443
4444
3922 „GB"
4200 „GB"
4202 GB
4346 „GB"
4931 „GC C"
4303 „G CG"

4284 „GDW"
4918 GE
3647 GFS
4314 GH
4313 GH
4872 GH
4166 „GHB"
4783 GB
3875
3662 „G IN"
4333 GK
4319 G
4808 GLA
4290 GIF
4945 GM
4249 GM
4721 GM
4293 GNB

3855 GP
4908 „GP"
4787 GP
4262 GR
4049 „GS"
4819 „GS"
4611 CS
4569 GS
4954 „GS D"
3879 G

H

4493 „H"
3779 H
4435 „H"
3835 H
4068 H
4056 H
4758 H

3889
4176 HA
4083 HADB
4085 HADB
4084 HADB
4929 „HB"
3876 HB
4089 HB
4090 HB
4091 HB
4092 HB
4917 HB
4096 HB
4093 HB
4095 HB
4094 HB
4774 HB
3853

3890 HB
4682 HB
4057 HB
3995 HBK
4108 „HC"
4225 HC
4717 HC
4282 HCI
4647 HK
4340 HP
3645 HR
4140 „HD"
4128 HD
3987 HE
4187 HE
4453 HF
4221 HF
4098 HG

4178 HG
4350
4268 HH
4359 HH
4047 HH
4934 „HIB"
4436 „HIK"
4491 HK
4454 HK
4780 HK
4185 HK
4256 HL
3859 HL HL
3657 HL
3981 HL
3905 HL

4132 HC
4781 HE
4782 HK
4645 „HM"
4019 HM
3811 „HM"
4644 „HM"
3862 HM „HM"
4643 HM
4534 HM
4694 HM
4927 HM
4145 HM
4762 HM
3942 HM
4511 MR
4461 HMS
4459 HMS

4289 HN
4371 HN
3655 HO
4852 „HP"
4608 HP
4638 HP
4354 HP
4861 PK
3932 HR
4126 HR
4137 „HR"
3955 HR
4133 HR
4156 „HR"
4134 HR
4136 HR
4720 HR

4919 „HS"
4111 „HS"
3685 „HS"
4447 HS
4642 HS
3969 HSI
4937 „HT"
4059 HT
4060 HT
4223 „HV"
4058 HV
4352 HV
3641 HW
3811 M
4655 Hul
4138 HW
4139 „HW"
4043 HW
4216 HWH

4041 HZ
4018 HZ
3931 H

I

4309 „I"
4672 „I"
3780 I
3836
4552
4302 I AH
4859 IAK
4723 IAS
4722 IAS
4695 „IB"
3967 IB
4789 IB
4795 IB
4597 „IB"
3968 IB

4272
4613 „IC"
4311
4205 IC
4300 „IC B"
4948 „IC P"
4947 IGP
4389
4650 ICS
4279 ICW
4122 ID
4962 ID
4949
4285 DE
4553 IDS
3991 IE
3992 IE

4905 „IE"
4211 „I·F"
4304
4725 IFH
4107 IFI
4306 IFK
4501 „I FL"
4364 IFSI
4193 IFT
4462 „IG"
3926 G
4935 Stern „IG"
4291 IGH
3659 „IG P"
4533 IGV
3960 IH
4360 „IH"
4238 IH

4288 IHM
4288 IHM
4680 IHS
4273 IHF
4301 IIR
4651. IIS
4181 „IK"
4120 IK
4946 „IK"
4182 IK
4585 „JKOR"
3958 IL
3959 „IL"
4800
4277
4785 IIK
4653 ILW
4469 „IM"
4464 IM

4519 IMF
4805 „IM W"
3672 „J NB"
4814 „INP"
4298 INW
4574 IOS
4143 IP
4641 IP
4640 I·P
4551 IP
3950 IP
4518 I·P
4257 IP
4265 IPH
3904 „IR"
4806 IR
4217 IR

4151 MM
3975 MM
3976 MM
4008 „MN"
4505 „MP"
4797 MR
3962 MR
4981 MR
4129 RI
3654 MR
4039 MS
3652 MTV
4612 MV
4610 MX
4973
4973 „MWA"
4280

N

3684 N
3686
3687
3756
3784 „N"
3736 N
3759
3763
3765 N
3761 N
3767 N
3766 N
3760 N
3762 N

3764 N
3758 N
3768 „N"
3757 N
3769 N
3770 N
4029 NE
4372 NH
4075 NI
3939
4106 NR
4759 NR
3822 NT
4014
4652 NTH

O

3785 „O"
4914 „O"
4355 O

4356 O
4357 O
4358 12 O
4318 OF
4214 OH
4860 OK
4327 OL
4363 OM
3756
4842 OIO

P

3786 „P"
4375 „P"
4393 „P"
3913
3912 P
4455 P
4451 „PA"

4208 PB
3952 PF
4110 PF
4790 PH
4862 „PK"?
4863 PK
3863 „PL"
4242 „PM"
3669 PN
4203 PR
4449 PR
4069 „PS"
4070 „PS"
4071 PS
4478 PS
3933
3934
3935
4877 „PTS"

4153 IR
4218 IR
4086 IR
3661 IR
4665
4154 IR
4307 IRK
4974 IS
3986 IS
3974 IS
4073 IS
3985
4976 „ISB"
4466 „I SG"
4465
4963 ISM
3643

4724 „ISS"
3917 IT
4798 ITN
4362 IV
4719
4609 IW
4799 IW
4353 IWV
4299 „I.W W"
3678 IZ

K

4673 „K"
3781 K
4666 K
4784 K
4004 K
3856 KB
3857 KB

3813 K
4271 A K
4271 B K
3909 K

L

3782 „L"
3810 L
4328 L
4329 L
4505 „12 L"
4310 LAL
4936 „LB"
4476 „LD"
4818
4028 LH
4885 LI
3668 LK
4909 L

4034 „LO"
4408 12 LO
4179 LR
4142 „LT"
4177 LT
3963 LT
4186 LV

M

3783 „M"
4659 „M"
3658 M
4841 M
4812 M
4760 M
4562 M
3846 „M"
4775
3845

3849
4148 MB
3804 ·M·B·
3806 MB
3993 MB
4097 MD
3744 „ME"
3979 ME
3979 „ME"
3949 MF
3949 „MF"
4463 MF
4489 MF
4109 MH
4488 MH
4452
4037

4061
4119

Q

3787 „Q"
4580 Q
4629

R

4483 R
4484 R
4482 R
4485 R
3788 „R"
4020 „R"
4702 R
4232 RR

3814
4387 „RZ"

S

3789 „S"
4536 „S"
4537 „S"
4538 „S"
4509 „S"
4527 S
4803 S
4622
4617
4526 S 12
4525 S 12
4498 „SA"
4236 „SB"
4904 „SB"
4227 SBF

4275
3928
4118 SG
4938 „SI"
4104
3870
4199
4105
4470 „SI A"
3943 SK
4222
4676
3756
4446 SP
3936
3961

3989 SR
4657
4930

T

3790 „T"
4082 T
4670 T
4671 T
3918 T
4180 TD
4417 „TE"
3756
4174 „TH"
4209 H
4933 „T HD"
4082 „TL"
4246 „TR"
4081
4207

4171 „TW"
4121

U

3791 „U"

V

3792 „V"
4481 „V"
4794 V
4816
4432
4728
4731
4733
4732
4735
4487 VA

4372 „VH“
3906 „VK“
4953 „VPT“
4457

W

3793 „W“
4870 „W“
4878 „W“
4169 „W“
4332
4955
4855
4867
4868
4001

4851
4801
3635 „W“
4517
4253 „W“
3670
3832
4807
4188
3965
4584
3956

4881 „W 12“
4876 „13 W“
4943
4539 „WD“
3988
4312
4294 „W IW(?)“
3966
4428
3854
4305 „WS“
4388
4402 „WV“
4401

4044
4022 WZ
4024
4026 „WZ“

X

4206
3794 „X“

Y

3795 „Y“

Z

3796 „Z“
3636 „Z“
4959
4957

4960
4964
3800
4768
4769
4958
4965
4966
4255 „ZH“
4023 ZM
4195 „ZM“
4025
4027 „ZM“

Heavenly Bodies

4892 Halbmond
4508 Stern, Mond
Ringe
Rose
4509 Halbmond
4006

4696
4690
3841
4131
4130
3888

4197
4220
4718
4278
4250

3681
3680
3682
4040
3880
3881

3880
3884
3818
3882
3683 HICKEN

Man

4283
4667
3828

Lions

3665 Löwe?
4376
4337 Löwe
4499

4381
4382
4856 Löwe

4315
4821
4504

4869
4146
3834

3921
4968
3675 Tatze

Misc. Mammals

4437 Tier?
4727
4379 Wolf
4383
4384
4385
4590
4080
4243
3824
4321 Hirschstangen
4631

4630
3964
4701
4510
4625
4618
4615
4616
4623
4628
4621
4626

4627
4624
4911
4912
4619
4910
4880 Stierkopf
4902
4895

4901
4894
4900
4897
4899
4898
4219 Schaf
4002
4003

4269
4516
4515
4159
4969
4237
4087
4231
4323
4365
4263
4887

Griffins, Eagles, Misc Birds

4486 Greif
4475 Adler
4891 Adler
4320 Adler
4322 Adler
4838
4522
4839
4704
3677
4524

4714
4716
4715
4712
4523
4713
4711
4709

4710
4705
4708
4707
4706
4406
4407
4423

4424
4425
4336 Adler
4427
4882
4971
4972
4687 Schwanenhals
4295

4326 Hahn
3957
4196
4141
4247
4577
4579
4578
3871

Marine Life

4101
4591

4703

4492 Fische
4167

4687 Muschel
4160

3945
4005

Plants

4235
4135

4530
4757

3817
4756

3864
3865

3927

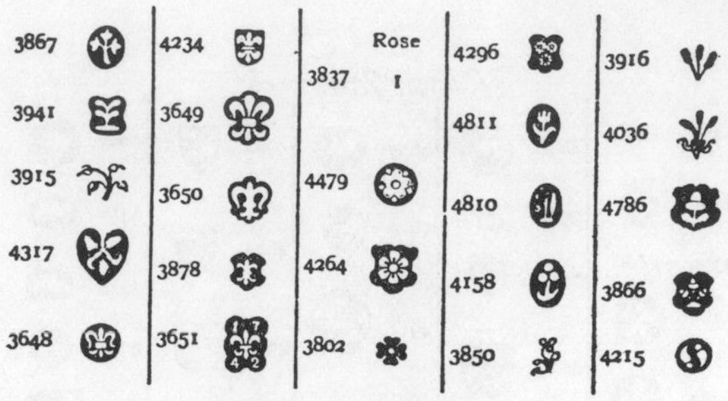

3867, 3941, 3915, 4317, 3648
4234, 3649, 3650, 3878, 3651
Rose 3837, 4479, 4264, 3802
4296, 4811, 4810, 4158, 3850
3916, 4036, 4786, 3866, 4215

Crowns, Scepters, and Arms

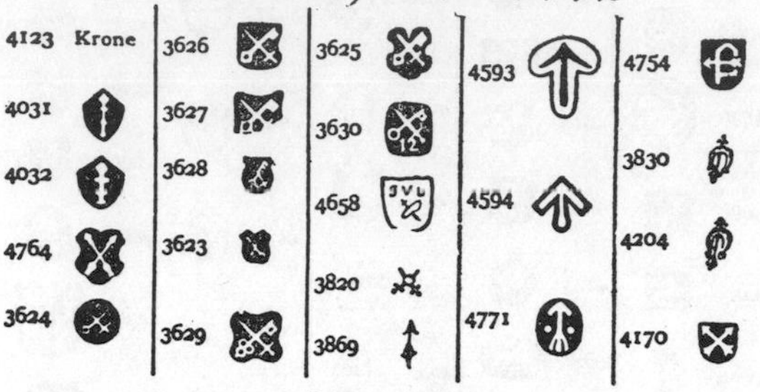

4123 Krone, 4031, 4032, 4764, 3624
3626, 3627, 3628, 3623, 3629
3625, 3630, 4658, 3820, 3869
4593, 4594, 4771
4754, 3830, 4204, 4170

Implements

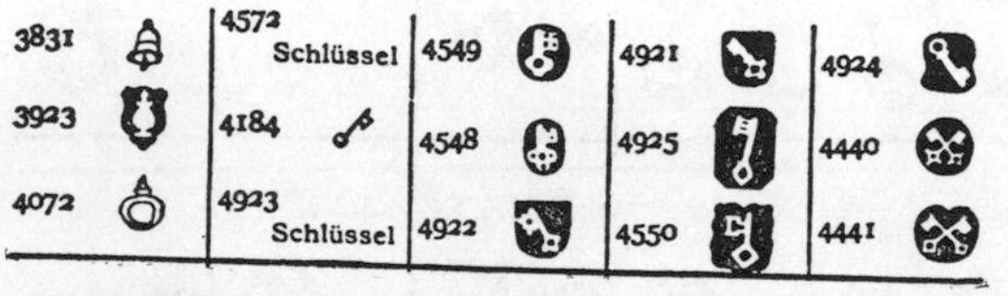

3831, 3923, 4072
4572 Schlüssel, 4184, 4923 Schlüssel
4549, 4548, 4922
4921, 4925, 4550
4924, 4440, 4441

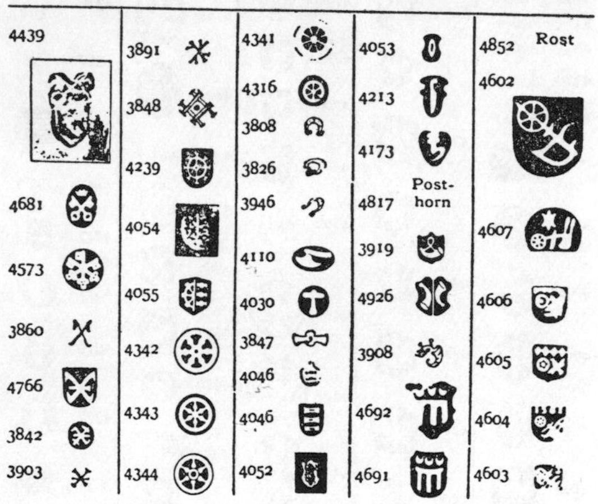

4439, 4681, 4573, 3860, 4766, 3842, 3903
3891, 3848, 4239, 4054, 4055, 4342, 4343, 4344
4341, 4316, 3808, 3826, 3946, 4110, 4030, 3847, 4046, 4046, 4052
4053, 4213, 4173, 4817 Posthorn, 3919, 4926, 3908, 4692, 4691
4852 Rost, 4602, 4607, 4606, 4605, 4604, 4603

Architecture

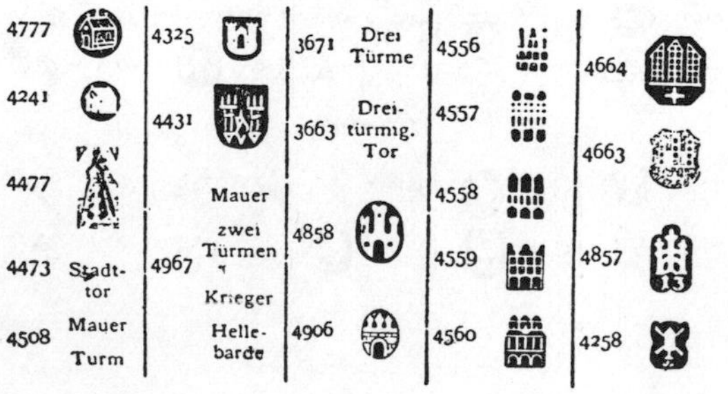

4777, 4241, 4477, 4473 Stadttor, 4508 Mauer Turm
4325, 4431, Mauer zwei Türmen, 4967 Krieger, Hellebarde
3671 Drei Türme, 3663 Dreitürmig. Tor, 4858, 4906
4556, 4557, 4558, 4559, 4560
4664, 4663, 4857, 4258

Crosses

4369, 4224, 4823, 4368, 4693, 4748, 4980

Trade Marks

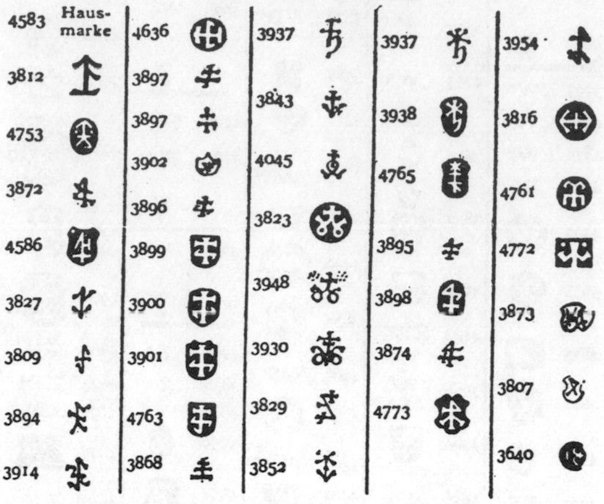

4583 Hausmarke, 3812, 4753, 3872, 4586, 3827, 3809, 3894, 3914
4636, 3897, 3897, 3902, 3896, 3899, 3900, 3901, 4763, 3868
3937, 3843, 4045, 3823, 3948, 3930, 3829, 3852
3937, 3938, 4765, 3895, 3898, 3874, 4773
3954, 3816, 4761, 4772, 3873, 3807, 3640

Shields and Geometrical Forms

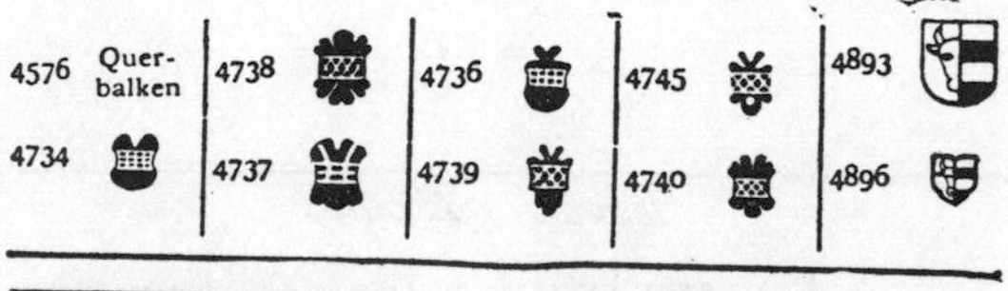

4576 Querbalken, 4734
4738, 4737
4736, 4739
4745, 4740
4893, 4896

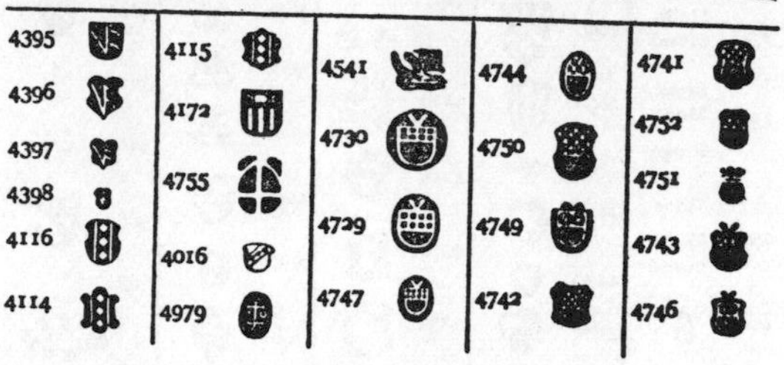

4395, 4396, 4397, 4398, 4116, 4114
4115, 4172, 4755, 4016, 4979
4541, 4730, 4729, 4747
4744, 4750, 4749, 4742
4741, 4752, 4751, 4743, 4746

Numbers

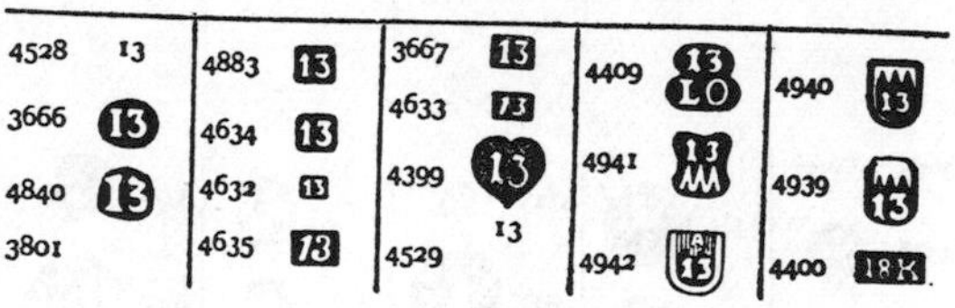

4528 13, 3666, 4840, 3801
4883, 4634, 4632, 4635
3667, 4633, 4399, 13, 4529
4409, 4941, 4942
4940, 4939, 4400

NATIONAL

AACHEN

ALLENSTEIN

ALTENBURG

ALTONA

ANSBACH

AUGSBURG

411. Hans Waidely, 1606 or H. Waidli, 1603
412. Christoph Lencker, 1583-1613
419. Heinrich Winterstein, 1585-1634
423. Cornelius Erb from Genova, 1586-1618
428. Mathaeus Wallbaum from Kiel, 1590-1632
433. Bartholme Lotter, 1590-1606
434. Jeremias Nathan (Nathen), 1623
441. Georg Lang the older, 1620
442. perhaps Balthasar Grill, 1617
456. Johannes Lencker, 1616-1637 ?
464. Hans Jacob Bair, 1604-1628
465. perhaps David Eckirch, 1604-1613
477. Nicolaus Kolb, 1582-1621
479. Philipp (Jacob) Benner, 1615-1634
481. Tobias Leuckhardt, 1615-1632
484. Benedikt Engelschalk, 1623 or Bernhart Elsesser, 1634
492. perhaps Abraham Lotter, 1626
493. perhaps Tobias Kramer, 1634
494. Gabriel Schmidt, 1643
495. Lucas Neisser, 1657
499. Hans Andreas Anthoni, 1630 ?
503. Melchior Gelb, 1617
524. Gregor Leider (Linderer), 1673
526. Hans Peters, 1672 ? or Hans Christoff Petters, 1677
548. Johannes Mair, 1687
566. Johann Baptist Biller, 1683
584. Christoph Leipziger, 1678
586. Hans Ott(o), 1678 ?
587. David Bessmann, 1677 ?
589. David Jäger, 1661 ?
592. Johannes Miller, 1624 ?
595. Paul Höschel, 1664
597. Abraham Drentwett, 1666 ?
599. Joh. Pepfenhauser, 1681 or Joh. Priester, 1694
603. Heinrich Rott (Roth), 1683 or Hans Ramminger, 1676
606. Hohleisen, late 17. cent.
610. Johannes Scheppich, 1701
611. Heinrich Mannlich, 1659-1698
613. Peter Winter, 1651-1703
620. Georg Reischli, 1700
621. Johann (Hans) Jäger, 1669 or Jacob Jäger, 1674
632. Heinrich Eichler, 1708 ?
633. Caspar Riss von Rissenfels, 1712 ?
636. Hans Heinrich Hering, 1696 ?
638. Wolfgang John, 1685
639. Moritz Mittnacht, 1690 ?
641. Abraham Waremberger, 1704 ?
643. Adolf Gaap, 1695 ?
644. Heckel ?
651. Christoph Drentwett, 1705 ?
652. Philipp Kuesel, 1700
654. Hans Jacob Schech, 1692
655. Joh. Babtist Ernst, 1697
656. Hans Jacob Ernst, 1703
660. Samuel Schneeweiss, 1697 ?
685. Joh. Sigmund Schuch, 1715
689. Johann Wagner, 1725 ?
690-691. Michael Mayr, 1714
695. Hans Jacob Wildt, 1733
704. Johann Christoph Treffler, 1722
722. Philipp Jacob Drentwett, 1712 ?
726. Mattheus or Markus Wolff, 1716 ?
727. Ludwig Schneider, 1729 ?
729. Gottlieb Bauer, 1735 or Gabriel Besmann, 1735
731. Cornelius Poppe, 1723
732. perhaps Johannes Fassnacht, 1726
734. Joh, Phil. Schuch, 1733
756. Johann Zeckel, 1728
761. Samuel Wolffgang, 1737 ?
765. Peter Rams, 1737
773. Johann Heinrich Mannlich, about 1700
778. Philipp Stenglin, 1744
779. Johann Lukas Sigel, 1745
781. Andreas Wickhardt, 1728
784. Johann Matthäus Rem, 1707
788. Dominikus Saler, 1718
795. Johann Jacob Vogelhund, 1745
799. Johann David Schoap, 1751
801. Daniel Schaeffler, 1727
809-810. Elias Adam, 1745
814. Johannes Engelgrecht, 1748
816. Johann Christoph Laminet, 1705-1753
817. Joh. Friedr. Bräuer, 1706-1753
836. Gottlieb Mentzel, 1709-1757
844. Joh. Jac. Bruglocher, 1710-1752
845. Jakob Lutz, 1747
860. Johann Wagenknecht, 1716-1752 ?
862. Joh. Erhard Heuglin 2nd, 1717-1757
867. Joh, Christoph Drentwett, 1749-1763
869. Franz Thaddaeus Lang, 1748-1773
872. Phil. Jakob Drentwett, 1718-1754
894. Joh. Ignaz Saler, 1727-1764
895. Johann Jabok Schoap, 1732-1766 ?
899. Franz Christoph Mäderl, 1747-1765
901. Joh. Jak. Baur, 1745-1774 ?
910. Bernhard Heinrich Weye, 1753-1782
911. Johann Leonhart Allmann, 1733-1775
912. Salomon Dreyer, 1761-1762
920. Abraham Winkler, 1736-1768
928. Friedr. Conrad Mittnacht, 1788
934-935. Johann Bartermann, 1741-1782 or Johann Busch, 1748-1794
936. Abraham Drentwett, 1741-1785 ?
941. Johannes Hübner, 1743-1776
950. Johann Georg Jaser, 1746-1760
955. Joh. Ph. Heckenauer, 1765-1794
956. Joh. Jacob Adam, 1762-1792
958-959. Johann Wilhelm Dammann, 1773-1784
965. probably Johann Becker, 1749-1761
967. Johann Christian Reinhardt, 1750-1772
968. Gottlieb Satzger, 1750-1783
971. Johann Karl Burger, 1750-1795
975-976. Georg Ignatius Bauer, 1764-1790
987. Christian Drentwett the younger, about 1800
994. Joseph Tobias He(r)zebik, 1788
1016. Caspar Xaver Stippeldey, 1766-1809
1018. Jos. Ant. Seethaler, 1788-1813 ?
1029. Lukas Römer, 1797-1819
1030. Karl Ferdinand Tautenhahn, 1781-1810 ?
1032. Johann Esaias Niggus, 1782-1818

AURICH

1064. 16. cent.
1065. 19. cent.

BADEN-BADEN

1068. 16. cent.
1069. 16.-17. cent.
1070. 17. cent.
1071. 10.-19. cent.
1072. 19. cent.

BAMBERG

1084. 16.-16. cent.
1085. about 1600

1908-1912. Daniel Herrmann, 1730-1740

ELLWANGEN

1920-1921. 18. cent.

EMDEN

1925. 1474 ?
1926. 16. cent.
1927. about 1601, seems to be a spread eagle
1928. in connection with annual letter "C," 1603
1929. 1612
1930. 1632
1931. 1634
1932. 1645
1933. 1820

ENGEN

1946. 17. cent.

ERFURT

1948. 16. cent.
1949-1950. 16.-17. cent.
1951-1952. first half of 17. cent.
1953. second half of 17. cent.
1954. 17.-18. cent.
1955. first half of 18. cent.
1956. second half of 18. cent.
1960-1962. Erasmus Wagner, 1606-1645

ESSENS (HANNOVER)

1976. inspection mark

ESSEN (RHINE)

1977. 17. cent.

EUTIN

1980. 1623

FLENSBURG

1982. 1673
1983. 18. cent.

FRANKENSTEIN

1987. beginning of 18. cent.

FRANKENTHAL

1989. 17. cent.

FRANKFURT A/MAIN

1995. about 1500
1996-1999. 16.-17. cent.
2000-2002. 17. cent.
2003-2004. 17.-18. cent.
2005-2007. early 18. cent.
2008-2015. middle of 18. cent.
2016. end of 18. cent.
2017-2018. 1850-1860
2029. Georg (Jörg) Haas, 1588-1605
2031. Paul Birckenholtz, 1559-1633

2038. Caspar Birckenholtz, 1661-1689 ?
2046-2047. Philipp Heinrich Schonling, 1696-1755
2052-2053. Joh. David Griebel, 1705-1744

FRANKFURT / ODER

2072. 17.-18. cent.
2073. 1772

FREIBERG (SILESIA)

2078. 1562
2079. end of 16. and beginning of 17. cent.
2080. 1654
2081. 1658
2082. 1660-1667
2083. 1668
2084. 18. cent.
2085. middle of 18. cent.
2086. 18.-19. cent.
2097. Samuel Klemm, 1644-1678

FREIBURG (BREISGAU)

2106. 1466
2107. about 1528
2108-2110. 16. cent.
2112. 1607
2113. 1609
2114. 17. cent.
2115-2116. 17.-18. cent.
2117. 18. cent.
2119. 19. cent.
2134. Wilhelm Feuerstein, 1883 with standardmark 13

FREISING

2136. end of 17. cent.
2137. 18. cent.

FRIEDEBERG near AUGSBURG

2145. 16. cent.
2147. 16. cent.

FUERTH

2151. 16. cent.
2152. 18. cent.
2153. 19. cent.
2154. control mark
2157. J. Rimonim, first half of 18. cent. ?

FULDA

2159. beginning of 18. cent.

GANDERSHEIM

2162. second half of 18. cent.

GEISLINGEN

2163. 17.-18. cent.
2164. middle of 18. cent.

GIENGEN

2170. 1745

GLATZ

2172. 18. cent

GLOGAU

2174. 17. cent.

SCHWAEBISCH-GMUEND

2177. 16.-early 18. cent.
2178-2179. about 1720-about 1788
2180. about 1740
2181. about 1762-1786.
2182. about 1791
2183-2186. beginning-middle of 19. cent.
2187-2190. 18.-19. cent.
2195. Joseph Fischer, 1699-1728

GNOIEN

2213. 18. cent.

GOERLITZ

2215. 16. cent.
2216. 17. cent.
2217-2218. 18. cent.

GOSLAR

2228. till 1782
2229. after 1782

GOTHA

2233. 17. cent.
2234. about 1688
2235. about 1689
2236. about 1701

GRABOW

2248. inspection mark

GREIFFENBERG

2251. 1794

GUESTROW

2252. end of 17. till middle of 18. cent.
2253. second half of 18. cent.

GUTTSTADT

2255. 18. cent.

HALBERSTADT

2256. middle of 17. cent.
2257. 1697
2258-2260. early 18. cent.
2261-2262. middle of 18. cent.
2263-2264. date letters late 17.-18. cent.
2266. master mark with changing annual letter
2267. master mark, 1697
2269. master mark
2273. master mark, 1709

SCHWAEBISCH HALL

2275. second half of 16. cent.
2276-2279. 17. cent.

2280-2281. 18. cent.
2282. early 19. cent.
2293. 17. cent.

HALLE / SAALE

2301. 16. cent.
2302-2303. 17. cent.
2304-2305. 17.-18. cent.
2306-2307. 18. cent.

ANNUAL LETTERS

2308. 1710
2309. 1711 ?
2310. 1713
2311. 1715
2312. 1 ? ? control mark
2313. 1728-1769 ?
2314. 1786-1808 ?
2319. Peter Rockenthin, 1645-1663
2324. early 18. cent.
2325. early 18. cent.
2326. 1749-1765

HAMBURG

2327. end of 16. cent.
2328. 16.-17. cent.
2330-2333. early 17. cent.
2334-2349. middle of 17. cent.
2350-2356. late 17. cent.
2357-2362. 17.-18. cent.
2363-2364. early 18. cent.
2365-2367. middle of 18. cent.
2368-2369. late 18. cent.
2370-2372. early 19. cent.
2373. "Hamburger" watchmaker
2382. 17. cent.
2383. master mark
2395. Frederich Frederichs, 1628-1767
2396. Gregorius Lambrecht, 1628-1672
2401. Heinrich Eickhoff, 1628-1708
2405. Dietrich Thor Moye, 1633-1652
2409. 1662
2415. 1648
2417. first half of 17. cent.
2422. Lambrecht, 17. cent.
2424. Juergen Richels, 1664-1711
2427. Leonhard Rothaer, 1671-1698 ?

HAMELN

2457. 17. and 18. cent.
2458. 18. cent.

HAMMELBURG

2459. early 18. cent.

HANAU

2460. about 1600
2461. 16.-17. cent.
2462. (Old-Hanau) 17.-18. cent.
2463. (New-Hanau) middle of 18. cent.
2464. (Old-Hanau) 18. cent.
2465. 18. cent.
2466-2467. 18.-19. cent.
2468. 19. cent.
2469. standard mark
2475. Johann Benedict Fuchs, 1724-1747

HANNOVER, CITY

Hannover-Altstadt

2483. 1640
2484. 1644
2485. 1663
2486. 1665
2487. 1670
2488. 1686
2489-2491. early 18. cent.
2492. middle of 18. cent.
2493. Hans Rhaders, 1627-1644
2494. Andreas Scheele (Scheilen), 1638-1675
2495. Hinrich Saedeler, 1665

Hannover-Neustadt

2500-2501. 17.-18. cent.
2502. 1726
2503-2504. about 1700
2505. 1726
2508. master mark

Hannover-(King's Court)

2510-2512. 18. cent.
2513-2514. 18. cent.
2515. gold stamp. 18. cent.
2516. Joachim Sander, 1680
2517. master mark
2518. master mark

HAYNAU (SILESIA)

2519. about 1708

HEIDELBERG

2520. 17.-18. cent.
2521-2522. 18. cent.
2523. 18.-19. cent.

HEILBRONN

2533. middle of 17. cent.
2534. early 18. cent.
2535-2536. 19. cent.
2542. Peter Bruckmann, 1805-1850

HILDBURGHAUSEN

2557. 17. cent.

HILDESHEIM

2559. 16. cent.
2560. 17. cent.
2561. 1645
2562. 1649
2563. 1705
2567-2568. P. J. Syring, 1726

HIRSCHBERG

2569. 18. cent.
2570. 18. cent.

ILMENAU (SACHSEN)

2573. 17. cent.
2574. about 1700

INGOLSTADT ?

2583. 15. cent.
2584. 15.-16. cent.
2585. 17. cent.
2586-2587. 17. cent.
2588. 18. cent.

INSTERBURG

2596. about 1677

JAUER (SILESIA)

2601. about 1693
2602-2603. early 18. cent.

JULIUSBURG (SILESIA)

2606. about 1707

KARLSRUHE (BADEN)

2607-2611. after 1806

KASSEL

2612. before 1658
2613-2614. 17. cent.
2615. 17.-18. cent.
2616. 18. cent.
2618-2622. 18. and 19. cent., connected with annual letters

KAUFBEUREN

2635. 16. cent.
2636. 18. cent.

KIEL

2643. 15. cent.
2644. 16.-17. cent.
2645-2649. 17. cent.
2650-2653. 18. cent.
2654-2655. 19. cent.
2661. 1695
2662. 1698
2665. 1714

KITZINGEN (BAVARIA)

2671. about 1595
2672. 18.-19. cent.

KOBLENZ (RHINE PROVINCE)

2675. 17. cent.
2676-2677. 18. cent.

KOELN

2691-2693. 16. cent.
2694-2697. 16.-17. cent.
2697-2700. second half of 17. cent.
2702-2706. first half of 18. cent.
2707-2708. middle of 18. cent.
2709-2712. end of 18. cent.
2767. Johann Ruetgers, 1700-1744 ?
2798. Ernst Riegel from Muenchen, 1907-1912

KOENIGSBERG (PRUSSIA)

2800. 1684-1703
2801. 1704-1716
2802. 1714 and later

2803. 1754-1761
2804. 1760-1772
2805. 1760-1770
2806. 1780-1790
2807. 1784-1786
2808. 1788-1800
2809. 1800-about 1830
2810. for more than 6 oz. silver, only 1815
2811. about 1830-1860
2812. 19. cent.

Annual letters

2813. 1693
2814. 1694
2815. 1696
2816. 1703
2817. 1704
2818. 1705
2819. 1706
2820. 1707
2821. 1709
2822. 1713
2823. 1714
2824. 1715
2825. 1740
2826. 1742
2827. 1747
2828. 1754
2829. 1761
2830. 1766 or 1772
2831. 1773
2832. 1784
2833. 1788
2834. 1818
2835. 1843
2846. Andreas Meyer from Nuremberg, 1608-1647
2847-2848. Paul Eckloff, 1612-1646
2854-2855. Lorenz Hoffmann from Nuremberg, 1659-about 1684
2856-2857. Johann (Hans) Meyer, 1662-1688
2858-2859. Peter Schoenermark, 1665-1703
2860-2861. David Doehring, 1670-1696
2862-2863. Peter Andreas Haendel (Hendel), 1671-1699
2863-2865. Otto Schwerdtfeger, 1685-1713
2868. Christian Friedrichs, 1688-1708
2869. Michael Christian Hetsch 1st, 1695-1721
2870. Johann Daniel Tamnau 1st, 1696-1732
2877-2878. Andreas Junge 1st, 1710-1757
2879-2881. Christian Leo, 1734-1771
2884. Christoph Philipp Hartung, about 1777-1800
2885-2888. Johann Leopold Kaewerstein, 1790-1812

KONSTANZ

2900. about 1557
2901-2905. 16.-17. cent.
2906-2909. early 17. cent.
2910-2911. middle of 17. cent.
2912-2913. end of 17. cent.
2914-2917. 18. cent.
2918-2919. 19. cent.

KULMBACH

2950-2951. 16.-17. cent.

LANDSBERG

2960. 17.-18. cent.

LANDESHUT

2966-2967. 18. cent.

LANDSHUT

2969. 15. cent.
2970. middle of 16. cent.
2971. 16. cent.
2973. 1723
2973. 1751
2974-2975. middle of 18. cent.
2976. end of 18. cent.
2982. Joseph Ferdinand Schmid (1), 1741-1790
2983-2984. Martin Spitzelberger, end of 18. cent.
2985. Caspar Bettinger (Pettinger), 1780-1794

LAUBAN

2986. inspection mark

LEER (EAST FRESLAND)

2989. end of 18. cent.

LEIPZIG

2990-2991. 16. cent.
2992. 16. perhaps 17. century too
2994-2996. 17. perhaps 18. century too
2997. 17.-18. cent.
2998-2999. early 18. cent.
3000-3003. 18. cent.
3004. end of 18. cent.

DATE LETTERS

3005. 1587-89
3006. 1588-90
3007. 1589-91
3008. 1597-99
3009. 1626-28
3010. 1627-29
3011. 1635-37
3012. 1641-43
3013. 1650-52
3014. 1656-58
3015. 1662-64
3016. 1668-71
3017. 1675-77
3018. 1682-84
3019. 1692-94
3020. 1693-95
3021. about 1711
3022. about 1725
3032. Elias Geier, 1589
3038. Andreas Kauxdorf, 1618-1669
3039. Melchior Lauch, 1622-1665
3042. perhaps Peter Richter, 1633
3043. Augustus Richter, 1633
3044. Sebald Krumbholz, 1634-1656
3045. Hans Scholler, 1642
3049. master mark, 1800
3053. Gottfried Schmidt, 1667-1681
3054. Joachim Krumbholz, 1669
3066. Johann Paul Schmidt, 1683-1703
3084. perhaps Andreas Schroeder, 1700
3085. Paul Gottfried Haussmann, 1732

LEUTKIRCH

3099. 16. cent.
3100-3101. 17. cent.

LIEGNITZ

3107. 16. and 17. cent.
3108. early 17. cent.
3109-3110. end of 17. cent.
3111. 17.-18. century (crossed keys in a square)
3112. about 1720 (crossed keys with 12)

ANNUAL LETTERS

3113. 1729 ?
3114. 1730
3115. 1731

LUDWIGSBURG

3129-3130. 19. cent.
3131. 19. cent.
3132. date letter

LUDWIGSLUST

3135. 19. cent.

LUEBECK

3137. 15. cent.
3139. 1501
3140. 1507
3141. early 16. cent.
3142. 1540
3143. middle of 16. cent.
3144. second half of 16. cent.
3145. 16.-17. cent.
3146. 1622
3147. 1631
3148-3151. middle of 17. cent.
3152-3153. 18. cent.
3154. 1828-1831
3155. 1831-1834

LUENEBURG

3232-3234. 15.-16. cent.
3235-3238. first half of 16. cent.
3239. middle of 16. cent.
3240. second half of 16. cent.
3241-3244. second half of 16. cent.
3245-3248. 16.-17. cent.
3249-3250. about 1650
3251. beginning of 17. cent.

STADTAMHOF
4573. 1767

STETTIN
4577. 16.-17. cent.
4578. 18. cent.
4579. gold 18. cent.
4580. 18. cent.

WERNIGERODE
and
STOLBERG
4590-4591. 18. cent. (stag for Stolberg, fish for W.)

STRALSUND
4593-4594. 17. cent.

STRAUBING (BAVARIA)
4602. tln (1614)
4603-4606. second half of 16. cent.
4607. middle of 18. cent.

STUTTGART
4615. end of 16. cent.
4616. middle of 17. cent.
4617. end of 17. cent.
4618-4619. about 1700
4620-4621. about 1700-1760
4623-4624. 18.-19. cent.
4625-4629. 19. cent.
4632-4635. 19. cent.

SUHL
4657-4658. 17.-18. cent.

TILSIT
4663. 18. cent.
4664. beginning of 19. cent.

TORGAU
4670. 16.-17. cent.
4671. 17. cent.
4672-4673. 17. cent.

TREBNITZ
4681. 17. cent.

TUEBINGEN (WUERTTEMBERG)
4690. 16.-17. cent.
4691. beginning of 17. cent.
4692. 17. cent.
4693. 18. cent.

TUTTLINGEN (WUERTTEMBERG)
4701. about 1660
4702. about 1660

UEBERLINGEN (BADEN)
Inspection marks
4704-4706. end of 16. cent.
4707-4709. 16.-17. cent.
4710-4713. 17. cent.
4714-4716. 18. cent.

ULM
Inspection marks
4728-4729. 16. cent.
4730. 16.-17. cent.
4731-4736. 17. cent.
4737-4744. 17.-18. cent.
4745-4752. 18. cent.
4784. Johann Adam Keinlin the older, 1651-1691 ?
4787. Georg Preg, 1658-1691

URACH
4816. about 1700
4817. 17.-18. cent.

VELBURG
4821. 18.-19. cent.

VERDEN
4823. 17. cent.

VILLINGEN
4838. 15. to 16. cent.
4839. 18. cent.
4840. 18. cent.

WAREN
4851. 18. cent.

WEILHEIM
4857. 17.-18. cent.
4858. 18. cent.

WEIMAR
4867-4868. 17. cent.
4869. end of 17. cent.

WERTHEIM
4882. about 1660
4883. 19. cent.

WESEL
4887. 16. and also 17. cent.

WISMAR
4893. end of 16. cent.
4894. beginning of 17. cent.

4895. 1694, probably since 1686
4869. end of 17. cent.
4897. beginning of 18. cent.
4898. about 1730-1748
4899. about 1736-1746
4900. middle of 18. cent.
4901. end of 18.-beginning of 19. cent.
4902. 19. cent.

WITTENBERG
4906. middle of 17. cent.

WOLFENBUETTEL
4910. 1668.
4911. 17. cent.
4912. 17.-18. cent.
4913. 1707
4914. 1714.

WORMS
4921-4922. 16.-17. cent.
4923. 17. cent.
4924-4925. 17. to 18. cent.

WUERZBURG
4939. early 18. cent.
4940-4942. 18. cent.
4943. early 18. cent.

WURZEN
4955. 18. cent.

ZERBST
4957. 1696
4958. about 1700
4959. 1723
4960. 1752

ZITTAU
4964. 1710
4965. 1731
4966. about 1750

ZWEIBRUECKEN
4968. 18. cent.

ZWICKAU
4971. 16.-17. cent.
4972. 17. cent.

FRAUSTADT
4979-4980. 17.-18. cent.

A

„A“
5257 „A“
8176
8181
8319 „A“
8321
8333
8340
9520
9115
5007
5006
5363
9597 „A“
7217
7877
7880
7863
5100
9500

5060
9534
8710
6016
5968
7501
8592
7111
7175
7187
7201
7219
7220
8763 „A“

6086 „A“
6128 „A“
6174 „A“
6791 „A“
6453
6455
7633
6290 „A“
6449
6459
6461
6463
9454
6027 „A“

6353 „A“
5805
8722
6357
6383
6396
5553
5961
6502
5160

6369
6544
6527
6538
6511
6521
6472
6470
6423
6490

6474
6495
6451
6515
6534
6506
6479
6499
5161 „A“
„A“
6292
7859

7860
7861
7862
6555
7963 „AI“
7962 „AI“
5004
5005
7873
9240 „A 6“
9241 „A 6“
9264 „A 7“
9265 „A 7“
9306 „A 8“
9307 „A 8“
9382 „A 10“

5960 „A“ 87
6084 „AA“
9154
6236
6232
7246
7892
6084 „AB“
8621 „AB“
9585
5733 „AB“
7770
7233
7420
6686
6026

6969
7084
9063
7085
9499
8883
7518
7075
6629 „AC“
9094
6096
5792 „ACB“
5788 „ACR“
7358 „A$_R$C“
7950

5498 „AD“
7959
5785 „AD“
5811 „AD“
7918
5417
5468 „AD“
7945 DOMANEK
6704
5642 „AE“
5440
8032 „A“ „Ev(O)RA“ „7“
7293
8808 „AF“
5415 „AF“
6781 „AF“

5531 „AF“
7930
9386 „AF K“
5451 „AG“
7351 „AH“
9507
„AH“
8824
7636
8366
5815 „AI“
7961 „AI“
7675
6666
9248 „AI A“
6628 a) „AIV“
6693

8798 „AK“
7818
9450
9331
8609
8671 „ÅKERMAN“
7768
7767
8397
6651
5679
7015 ALBERTI
6487
8659
9157

6278
8846
5768 „AM“
8623
5979
5974 „AM“
5169
9079 A:MANZ
5975 „AM“ „G“
8845 „A MOLL“
5720 „A N“
5080
9154
6687 „ANC“
5991 | 5992 | „AN-GERS“

8820 „Annoni“
8653 „AO“
5692 „AP“
8709
7405
9176
7336
7337
5958
5577
5682 „AR“ 84
5832 | 8876 | „ARGENT“
5684

7421
7236
5983
8718
6668
8672 „A. STAF-HELL“
8676 „ÅSTRÖM“
9528
7281
8710 „AT“
5646 „AT“
5472
7887
7082 „AΘENAI“

7889
7890
7891
7283
7711
7711
7721
9463
7893
7894
6759
6760
6458
7895
6760
8644
7819

8364
6277
5964

B

„B“
8182
8188
8341 „B“
6344
5548
7107
7194
5242
7167
7164

5362
5554
8343
7502
5366
6063
6076
7176
7161
5549
7215
7341 „B“
8748 „B“
8843 „B“
9327 „B“
9328 „B“
5295 „B“
7749 „B“
6041 „B“
8027 „B“

8026 „B“
9530
6397
6859
6855
6424
5174
5172
5176
6054 „B“
5194 „B?“
5202 „Bet...“
6770
6340

6042 „B“
8789
8790
8791
8783
8784
8785
8786
8787
8788
7481
9429
7569
9234
9323

9324
7836 „B 4"
5376 „BA"
9101
9100
9104
9102
9105
9103
9098
9096
9097 „BARK NONA"
7479
7470
7477 „BC"
6059

5535 „B D"
5654 „D B H" 1708
9135
8684 „BERGS"
7361 „BERS"
8654 „BFR"
6072
8838
8951 „BH"
9246
8606
5133
6084 „BI"
6768
5132 „BK"
6034 „BK"
5401 „BM"
8885 „BM"

9075
7841
6055
7478 „BP?"
7784
9538
7470
7771
9456
9123
9090
9371
7765

C

5637 „C"
8220, 8222, 8228, 8271, 8383, 8390 „C"
9325 „C"
7195
7573
5364
7739
5056
6972
6109
5550
5097
9440 „C"
7503

9403
5273
7205
7049 „C"
7070 „C"
7834 „C"
7837 „C"
8749 „C"
9326 „C"
6005
6291 „C"
7776 „C"
7777 „C"
8031 „C"
8227, 8393 „C"
8390
6384
6398
6094

6319
6698
9599
5607
5779 „CM"
7511
7470
5778 „CMF"
5776
5777
9577
9088 „CM K"
9575
6252
8074
7939

6757
7949
9196
9134
7362 „COZ"
5715 „C P"
7254 „CP"
7617
8726 „C·P·A"
7019 „CR"
9509
5331 „CR"
9571
9483
7280
5638
7729

6744
9523
9473
5105
5678 „C.WER"
9477

D

„D"
6678 „D"
5635 „D"
5272
7160
7170
9239 „D"
7600
6956
5551

8593
6139
7504
6223, 6268, 6850, 7986, 7989 „D"
8750 „D"
6939
6315 „D"
6356
5319
5507
6399
5071
5075
6206
6202

6938
6425
9263 „D 1"
9305 „D 2"
9381 „D 4"
7359 „DA"
5656 „D B" 1688
5663 „DB" 1708
6974
5410 „D B"
8082
5404 „DC"
8915 „DCC"
7958
„DD"
8909 „P"
5773 „DE"
8604
8349

6090
5200
8392
8393
5277
6293 „C"
9276
6804 „C 5"
6192 „C 6."
9252 „C 7"
9253 „C 7"
7775
7876 „CA"
9130
9187
6710

9131
9330 u. 7894
8895
8435
8939
7248
8358
7476
7289
6650
8610
8375
„CC"
6779

8221, 8385 „C C"
6045 „ƆC"
6044 „ƆC"
8384
6044
6152
5821 „C.C.T"
6674 „CD"
8922
9054
8944
7526
6092
9142

9133
9181
9180
8388 „CG"
6669
5734
9548
5681 „C H"
7527
7921
9050 „CH"
7288
9088
9072
7635
9522

7179
7743
8018
6628
6279 „CI M"
8984
5752 „CK"
9513
9550
8013
8014
7773
7581
9525
9588
9281

5402
9288
9497
7411
8350
6986
6987
8617
9073
6991
6992
6993
5676
5482 „DI"
6135
5197
7763
7937

7938
7285
5736 „DO"
8888 „DOUBLE"
5134 „DP"
5675 „DP" 1747
5659
5660 „DSK" 1720
5406 „DT"
5636
7522
6124
8836
6122
7845
9126 „DX"

E

„E"
5843, 6442 „E"

7810 „E"
8189 bis 8192, 8322, 8347, 8352 „E"
5844
7211
5002
5367
7976 „E"
7640
5052
7168
7505
5523
5845
5046
7216

7206
5505
7188
9404
5973, 6010, 6050, 6194, 6245, 6828, 7977, 7978 „E"
6947
8034 „E"
5072
5552
6400
6947
7055

7051
6946
6412
6426
7567
7811
7971
7344 „E 1"
7789 „E 3"
9581
9446
7383
7387
5771 „EG"
7290
8953 „E?GO"

5324 „E H“
6120 EH
8351 EH
8840 E I
8841 „EK“
8812 „EL“
5384 „EM“
8998 EMG
9195 EN 3150
6019 EP
6015 EP
6684 E P B
6117 „ES“
8625 „ES“
9256 „ES“
7330
9095 ESTOR GA

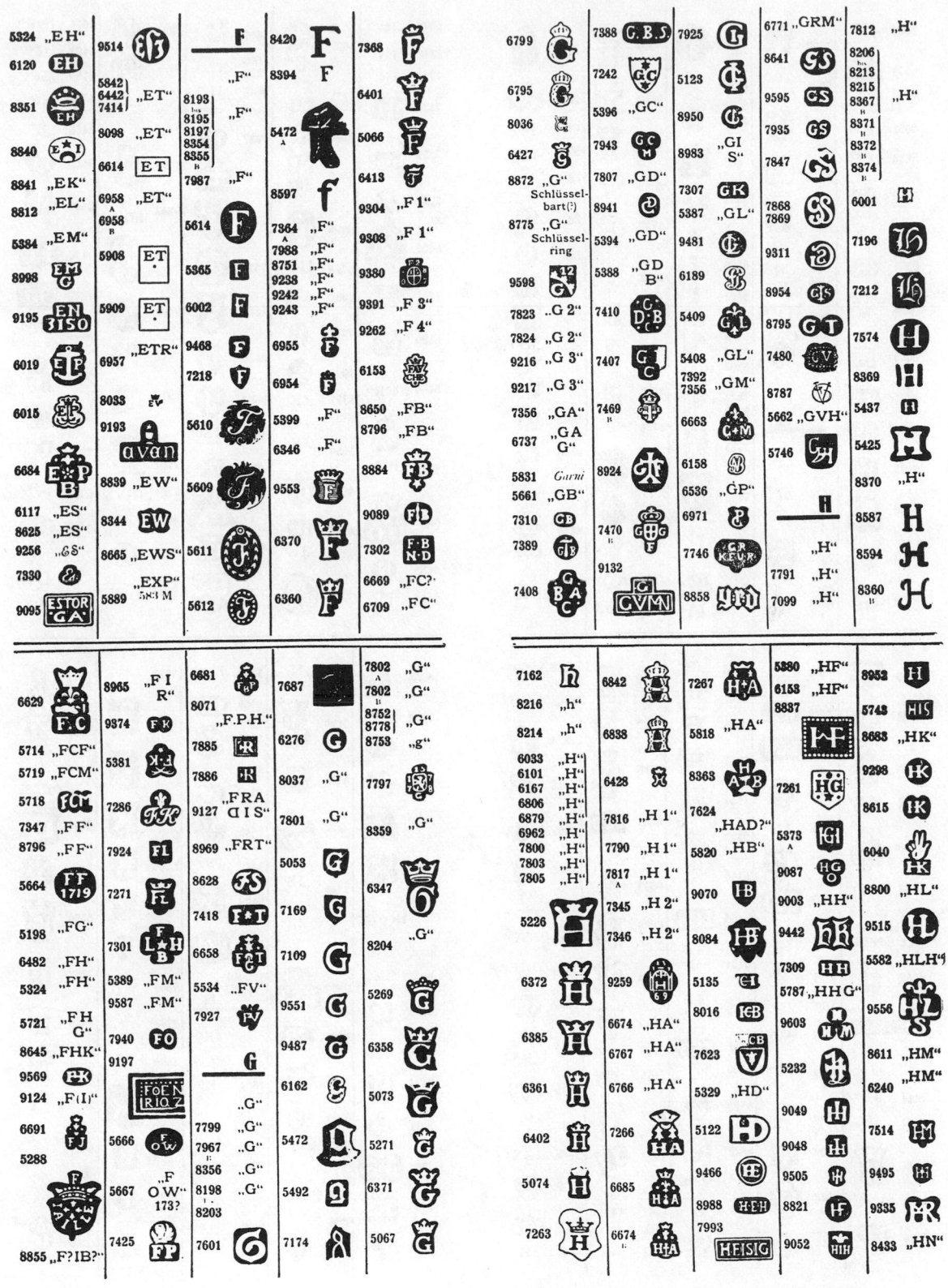

9514
5842 6442 7414 „ET“
8098 „ET“
6614 ET
6958 A 6958 B „ET“
5908 ET
5909 ET
6957 „ETR“
8033
9193 avan
8839 „EW“
8344 EW
8665 „EWS“
5889 „EXP“ 583 M

F

„F“
8193 bis 8195 8197 8354 8355 „F“
7987 „F“
5614
5365
6002
9468
7218
5610
5609
5611
5612

8420 F
8394 F
5472 A
8597
7364 A „F“
7988 „F“
8751 „F“
9238 „F“
9242 „F“
9243 „F“
6955
6954
5399 „F“
6346 „F“
9553
6370
6360

7368
6401
5066
6413
9304 „F 1“
9308 „F 1“
9380
9391 „F 3“
9262 „F 4“
6153
8650 „FB“
8796 „FB“
8884 FB
9089
7302 F·B N·D
6669 „FC?“
6709 „FC“

6799
6795
8036
6427
8872 „G“ Schlüsselbart(?)
8775 „G“ Schlüsselring
9598
7823 „G 2“
7824 „G 2“
9216 „G 3“
9217 „G 3“
7356 „GA“
6737 „GA G“
5831 *Garni*
5661 „GB“
7310
7389
7408

7388 G.B.S.
7242
5396 „GC“
7943
7807 „GD“
8941
5394 „GD“
5388 „GD B“
7410
7407
7469 B
8924
7470 B
9132 GVMN

7925
5123
8950
8983 „GI S“
7307 GK
5387 „GL“
9481
6189
5409
5408 „GL“
7392 7356 „GM“
6663
6158
6536 „GP“
6971
7746 GR KEUR
8858

6771 „GRM“
8641
9595 GS
7935 GS
7847
7868 7869
9311
8954
8795 GT
7480
8787
5662 „GVH“
5746

H

„H“
7791 „H“
7099 „H“

7812 „H“
8206 bis 8213 8215 8367 B 8371 B 8372 B 8374 B „H“
6001
7196
7212
7574
8369
5437
5425
8370 „H“
8587
8594
8360 B

6629 F.C
5714 „FCF“
5719 „FCM“
5718
7347 „FF“
8796 „FF“
5664 FF 1719
5198 „FG“
6482 „FH“
5324 „FH“
5721 „FH G“
8645 „FHK“
9569
9124 „F(I)“
6691
5288
8855 „F?IB?“

8965 „FI R“
9374
5381
7286
7924
7271
7301
5389 „FM“
9587 „FM“
7940 FO
9197 FOEN RIQZ
5666
5667 „F OW“ 173?
7425 FP

6681
8071 „F.P.H.“
7885
7886
9127 „FRA DIS“
8969 „FRT“
8628
7418
6658
5534 „FV“
7927

G

„G“
7799 „G“
7967 B „G“
8356 „G“
8198 bis 8203 „G“
7601

7687
6276
8037 „G“
7801 „G“
5053
7169
7109
9551
9487
6162
5472
5492
7174

7802 A „G“
7802 B „G“
8752 8778 „G“
8753 „g“
7797
8359 „G“
6347
8204 „G“
5269
6358
5073
5271
6371
5067

7162
8216 „h“
8214 „h“
6033 „H“
6101 „H“
6167 „H“
6806 „H“
6879 „H“
6962 „H“
7800 „H“
7803 „H“
7805 „H“
5226
6372
6385
6361
6402
5074
7263

6842
6838
6428
7816 „H 1“
7790 „H 1“
7817 A „H 1“
7345 „H 2“
7346 „H 2“
9259
6674 „HA“
6767 „HA“
6766 „HA“
7266 HA
6685
6674 B

7267
5818 „HA“
8363
7624 „HAD?“
5820 „HB“
9070
8084
5135
8016
7623
5329 „HD“
5122
9466
8988
7993 HEISIG

5880 „HF“
6153 „HF“
8887
7261
5373 A
9087
9003 „HH“
9442
7309 HH
5787 „HHG“
9603
5232
9049
9048
9505
8821
9052

8952
5743 HIS
8663 „HK“
9298
8615
6040
8800 „HL“
9515
5582 „HLH“
9556
8611 „HM“
6240 „HM“
7514
9495
9335
8433 „HN“

8637 „HN“
5148
9125 „HONDA“
8651 „HP“
8636 „HP“
9552
9332
9554
5658 „HR“ 04
8999
8817
9373
9485
8099
9035
8989

7250
9384 „HT“
8935
9475
7677
8096 „HW“
9385 „H W“
8663 HW
7228

I

„I“
6626 „I“
7817 „I“
7213
8217
8378 „J“

7740
8218 „I“
7207
7663
9428
7554
8588
9405
5988 „I“
6082 „I“
6144 „I“
6297 „J“
7821 „J“
7825 „J“
8758 „J“
7115
7189
8598
5063

6348
6354
6403
6386
6187
6183
6414
6429
7568
5774 „IA“
5187
9605
8856
7423
8060 JAR

6717
7350
5653 „JB“
8643 „JB“
6815 I & B
8801
8811
8802
8639
8620 „JB“
9536
8642
9606
6716 „JB“
6254
6705

5378 „IH“
5812 „IH“
7349 „IH“
7225
7229
7295
5665
9051
5120
5785 „I HR“
7314
5588 „IHS“
6630
5688
8017

6027
6715
6752
8866
8925
5795 „IIO“
5680 „IIS“
7957
7946
5391 „IK“
8437 „IK“
„IK“
5650
9593
6121
5769 „IK“
6180

5657 „IK“ 1697
7593
7594 „IL“
8632 „JL“
5807 „JL“
7947
5119
7533
7516
7524
5458
9591
5686 „IM“
7948
5131
9383
7257

7234
7252
7956 „IM H“
7313
9249 „I MK“
5668
7004
7005
8616
5669
7101 „INS“
7101 „INVS“
5471 „IO“
6994
5786 „I OM“

6674 „JOR“
5403 „IP“
6180 „IP“
6714 „IP“
8445 „JP“
9412
9408
7730
7299
5405 „IP“
6662
5260
7244
5325 „IP“
8432
7300
6180 „IPK“

7519
8805
6765
8857
6708
5687 „IBD“
9179 „I BENA BENTE“
6652
8901 I·BOSSARD
6716 „JB“ „P“
7444 „IC“
5677 „IC“
6196
8016 „ICB“
7534

6683
9503
7531 ICH
6999
5418 „ID“
8337
8373
9461
6701
5188 „IDC“
5793 „IDK“
8862 „ID“ „M“
9338 „ID P“
7529
7528
5651

8380 „IE“
6147 „IE“
6985
7247
7954
9517 „J.E.“
6148 „IE“
9566
6724 „IE B“
5753 „IE K“
7308
5705 „J. F“
6700
8822
8813 „IFB“
6722 „JF B“
7012

7013
7014
6689
6231
6771 „JFF“
6695
6699
6735
7010
5257 „JFS“
9583
8612
8336
5114 „IG“
6147 „IG“
6280 „IG“
8657 „IG“

6808
5766 „IG“
7235
6536
6697
6996
5791 „I GD“
5790 „IGD“
7521 „IGE“
7520
7844
6275
9337 „IG L“
5685 „IGS“
9372
9327
5147 „IH“

8962 „I PR“ *
7952 „IR“
7530
5716
6680
7243
5783 „IR(?)S“
8634 „IS“
8662 „JS“
9388
9290
8794
7951
7304
7305
7253

8635 „IS“
7278
5416
7279
5649 „IS“
5648 „IS“
7312
9531
7523
7953
5398 „IT“
9188
8823

5749 „JVH“
9560
6734
8966 „IW“
7348
7249
5413 „IW“
5199
8640

K

„K“
5589 „K“
7824 „K“
8219
8223
8226
8229 „K“
8232
8379
8391
8381 „K“

7822 „K“
7197
7214
7181
5480
8934
9521
7806
7744
8589
7190
7208
7191
6851 „K“
9214 „K“
9218 „K“

6941
5825
8652 „K“
6349
5586
5590
7653
5590
6373
5068
6057
6061
6940

6430
7282
7287
9420 „KB“
„K“
5371
„D“
7510
6180 „KI“
8137
6180 „KIP“
7016
KIRSTEIN
7008 KRUG

L

„L“
9215 „L“
8233
8238
8240
8241
8242 „L“
8244
8401
8403
8405
8406
8408

5048
7182
7689
9273
5361
6208
8595
7741
6017
8243 „l“
8239 „l“
7462 „L“
7465 „L“
8754 „L“
6953
8045 „L“
5426

6374
8042
8038
6431
5399
5402
8040
8044
8041
9602
7275
5400 „L AD“
5332 „LB“
9213 13 Adler „LB“
5081
5470 „L·D“

6179 „l.d.“
7042
9155 „lcon“
9158 LEONI
5471 „L·F“
8809 „LF“
7040
7674 „LH“
6218
8422
6761
6646
6541
6546

6547
6688 „LL“
7073
6653
5386 „LM“
6227 „L.M.“
8816
6176
5823
8399 L.M.HOLM
9136
6714 „LR“
8996 „LR“

7856 C
7394 „MDA“
7589 „ME“
8701
8605
6756
9501
8073
9255
8688 „MHB“
5737 „MHH“
9469
5745 „MI“
6770 „M JG G“
7582 MK
9310 „MK“
7515
7944 „ML“

6185
5587 „MM“
5673 „MM“ 175?
8835 MN
5250 „MO“
8252 „MO“
8062
6323
6249 MOP
6250 MOP
5459 „MP“
7809 „MP“
7764 A
8613
6263
7486

6259
8059
9573
5377 „MS“
7393 „MS“
7470 E
5748
5149 A
9161 1712 MVNOZ
8834 MZ
6234

N

„N“
7963 B „N“
8255 bis 8263
8426 „N“
8430
8436 B
8439

5049
5613
8618 „N“
5317
7171
7209
5054
8335
9406
5998 „N“
8755 „N“
8756 „N“
8916 B „N“
7406 B
9223 „N 2“
7024 B
5064

6405
6376
5069
6257
6261
9299
7985
7398 B „NA“
7409
7404
7402
7399
7403
7401

5819 „LR“
7917
6679
6714
7970 „LT“
5395 „LT“
7447
9137 LVIS
7933
7931
7932
5411 A „LW“
7006
5747
9177 LZNA
6840

6204
6844
6021
5229
8043
7512

M

„M“
5450 „M“
5744 „M“
6342 „M“
8624 „M“
8842 „M“
8245 bis 8251
8253 „M“
8254
8424
7379 B „M“
7198
5615

5180
7466 „M“
6230
5192 B „M“
5521
5275
8590
6238
8596
6225 „M“
6307 „M“
7467 „M“
7578 „M“
5322 „M?“
9601
8991 „M“
9590
6350
6375

6387
6404
5075 B
6359
7032
7036
6432
7044
6216
5576 B „M“
8602 M3
9225 „M 5“
9224 „M 5“
6220 „MA“

7315 MA
7416 MAC
9164 „MAIO RCA“
9166 MAI ORAN
9165 MAI ORID
8022
9116 MAR TIN
8608 „MB“
8607
9254
6665
7808 „MB H“
5249
5412
5781 „MD“

7400 NAP
7398 B NAPP
7398 NPL
8614
8398 NB
5128
6667
7397 B „NC“
9189 „?NCA (L)AD?“
6285
5414
6627
8409 „N.Dahl“

5696
5695
5697 „NEV“
5671 NF
7884
6346 „NG“
7926
5382 „NG“
6726
8437 „NH“
8997 „NHM“
8666
5491
8923

8434 NO
6283
6284
6979
6980
6981
6982
8963
6725 „NR D“
9544 NS
7292
7412 „NSC“
7374
9464

5525 „NV?“
8918
8919
8920

O

„O“
5011
5008
5010
8264
8323 bis 8328 „O“
8440 B
7638
7178
7210
7656
7192
7733

7691
7610 S. XVII 7608
7774 „O“
7576
6388
6406
7541
5224
6830
6834
6415
7632
8851
7659

6772
5009
8395
9121
8365
8690 „OHB"
6994
9511
8415 „O:L"
8416
8414
6988
9118 „OO"
8065
6310

7992
9174
8345

P

„P"
9401 „P"
7199
7180
9489
8265 „P"
9312
8066
8067
7764
9313
5424

7122
7120
5443
6801
7604
9434
8757 „P"
9402 „P"
6950
8068 „P"
5061
8729
6362

6407
6389
5427
5433
6133
6137
6433
6416
6436
6439
40
6441
7011
6973
9421 „P1"
9368 „P2"
9369 „P2"

9296 „P3"
9297 „P3"
9342 „P4"
9343 „P4"
8103 „P10"
9221 „P11"
9430
7273
8648 „P·A·H"
5959
6529
5251 „PB"
6252 „PB"
8807
8622
8674 Halbmond „PB"

6797
6178 „P.t."
9540
7705 „PV 1610"
7706 „P.V.1611"
7707 „P.V.1612"
7697 „P V"
7698 „P V 1606"
7700 „P V 1607"
7699
7701 „P V 1608"
7726
7704
8719
5772

Q

„Q"
7183
7692
8685
7670
8599
5070
6408
6363

R

„R"
9271 „R"
5000
8267 „R"

8266 „R"
7184
5151
6975
5057
6836
6823
6975
5233
5001
9272 „R"
6355 „R"
5707
6377
6409
6364

5062
6390
6317
6321
6417
6434
9415 „R4"
9416 „R4"
9286 „R 6"
7232
6638
7269
7738
6675 „RDC"
7303 „R DH H"

6857
6130 Lilie
6131 „RF"
7311
8814 „RH"
5616
9074
6703
7230 „RL"
5704
6671
6819
6861
6832
6815 R O A
7440 „ROMA"

6729
5653
5390 „PC"
6730 „PC"
5292 „PC"
6758
7417
9413
8891
6712
6645
7702 „PDVF 1608"
9119
9120

6690
9400
5374 „PF"
6674
5452 „PG"
6659 „PG"
6655 „PG"
7769
8689 „PH"
5689
9452
9546
8630
8723
7265
6673 „PJB"

9564
8633 „PIZ"
9247 „PI W"
9274
7627
7455
7276
7272
7277
6197
6880 „PLS"
7041
6198
6622 „PM"
5407 „PM"

5106 „PM"
6743 „PMB"
6721 „PM B"
6740
6741
5822 „PM G"
6253
9275 „PN"
5608
6983
7356 „PP"
7356
7395 „PP"
7934
6786 „PP"
6852
7356 „PPA"
7298

6786 „PP EYA"
8844 „PR"
8660 „PR"
5094
5093
8063
9444
8083
8669 „PS"
7306
PS
6977
5088 „PS"
7607 „PS"
5780
6998

6023
9125 „RONDA"
S.307 „RS"
6105
5152
7251
7030
9122 „RS" „A??"

S

„S"
S.121 „S"
7836 „S"
8949 „S"
5767 „S"
8268
8273
8275
8277
8280
8281 „S"
8283
8285
8288
8291
8442
8443
8694

7827 „S"
7848 „S"
7828
7780
7831
7830
7833
7832
7177
5050
7781
5142
7202
7203

7172
8167
8170
7829
8279 „J"
8284 „J"
7693
5482 „S"
7050 „S"
8759 „S"
6943
S.191 „S"
5225
6378
6391
5318

7785
6435
6942
6103
6107
5397 „S"
8075 „S"
9365
9366
9367
9504
8972
8973
8974

8975
8976
8977
5708 „SA"
9043
5644
7043
7045
8658 „SAUTER"
8061
7297
7296
9427
8931 „SCH"
6774

7772
8803
8804
8097 „SG"
5617
6871
6869
5784 „SH"
8085 SH
8086 „SH"
9542
8852
5775 „SI(?)"
6039
8410 SIB

8655 „SICKMAN"
5743 „SIH"
7970 „SK"
7274 SL
8619 „SL"
9607
7992 „SO"
6874 SOM
9162 „SOPU ERTA"
6020 „SP"
7437 „SP"
5645
7439 „SPQR"
7438 „SPR"
5717 SR
9407 SR
5090
6880 STSD

7294
5076 „ST"
5253 „ST"
8670 STAF HELL
7003 STAHL
5710 STEGE NW
7450 STELA
8463 „Stockholm"
7007 STRAVS
8678 „STRÖM"
5672 „STS" 1756
9425
7451 SUL
7455 SUL

7452 SUL
7453 SUL
7454 SUL
9287
9004
7284 SW
9579 SW
8638 „SY"

T

„T"
8005 „T"
9375 „T"
8292, 8298, 8696 „T"
7571
8009
8007

8008
8010
8102 „T"
7185
7688
7057
6418
7222
8591
8431
8361
6068 „T"
6115 „T"
6214 „T"
7063 „T"
8760 „T"
8964 „T"
5298 „T"
5518 „T"

8305, 8306, 8309, 8313 „V"
6343 „V"
7572
9198 „V"
7651
5522
7163
7165
7173
7186
7557
8362
6813 „V"
9199 „V"
7487

5536
5076 „V"
6366
6392
6380
7555
6419
5076 17V49
„V"
5245
5782 „VA"
9178 „VAENA"
5083 „VC"
5091 „VC"
9558
5436 „VD"

5127 „VE"
7842
7483
7919
8818
7477
7840
5699
9057 VHB
7517 VHK
7676
8629
7678
9138 „vm"

5127
7804 „VR"
7826 „VR"
9329 „VR"
9244 „VR"
7990 „VR"
8991 VRI
7883
7881
7882
5368
9076
7923
5248 „VW"
9020

W

„W"
8304, 8307, 8308, 8310, 8312, 8314, 8316, 8702, 8711, 8712, 8713, 8713 „W"
5770 „W"
7613
5058
7668
8601
7000
7001
8712 „W"
5145 „W" mit Krone

5520
5516
6365
6410
6379
7461
9437
9220 „T 2"
9423
9424
9191
5372 „TB"
8819 „T·B"
6974 „TB. fe"

7260
8064
8917 „TE"
6610
5902
5900
6608
7241
7245 TF
6989 „TF"
8960
7888
5378 „TG"
6657
7268 „TH"

7259
8680 „THOME"
7258 TI
9529
7264
9370
7034
5385 „TM"
7038
5392 „TM"
5670 TMW 1723
9175
6625 TOI
7024 TOI

9173 „TOL"
7020
7021 TOLI
7022
7023
7053
5667 T OW 173
9562 „TP"
5652 „TS"
7507
6123

U

„U"
8299, 8303, 8697, 8700 „U"

7200
7204
7664
7193
5182
7166
8600
8697
6411
8092 „U 1"
8093 „U 1"
8396 U3
8717 U4
8080 „U 4"
8094 „U 5"

V

„V"
7066 „V"

5816
5817
8992
8994
8993
9002
7851
7850
7852
7849
7853
7854
7858

7857
8024 „Warsavie"
9336 WB
6984 „WD"
5655 „WF S" 169?
8646 W HK
7270 WI
5724, 5725 Wiborg
7002 WIRZ
9608 WOO
7915
7240 WR
8626 W RB
8627 W RK

7256 WS
7255 WS
7291 W·W

X

„X"
6312 „X"
7095 „X"
5047
5059
5055
5510 „X"
7096
6945
6367
6393

5981
5977
6944
6420
8890
8914 „XID"
9334
9192

Y

„Y"
6182 „Y"
8317, 8715 „Y"
5183
7570
5274

8318 „Y"
7690
7625, 7626
7080 „Y"
9426
6381
6394
6070
6074
5545
5543
6421

9555
5546

Z

„Z“
7669
5051
9014
9013
9031
9026
9011
9010
9009
9016
9019

9012
9008
9033
9027
9015
9029
9028
9030
9032
9024
9021
9023
9018
9017
9025

9022
7960
9390
8427 „Z“
7621
5824
6368
6154
6382
6395
6156
6160

6020
6422 „3“
6352
7734
9058
7424
8030 „Z CIO PRA“
8955 „ZCT“
8338
7941
6611
5903

5966
5962
5228
8282 8286 Σ
8196 Φ
8110
8112
8115
8114
8113
8105

8108
8106
8107

8109
8111
8269 8276 Σ

8270 8272 И
8278 8287)
5144
5563
7381

6440
6438
6437

6439
5563
7478

Heavenly Bodies

7327
8039
5164 Globus

S.491 Halbmond
7227
8942

8138
8441

7658
6118

7629
7630

5130
8699
8699
6132 Globus
5126 Sonne
5291 Sonne
6486
7031
6288 Mond
8649 Halbmond

9053
5529 Halbmonde
7525
9561
7606
8961
7876
6949
6217

6289 Stern
5989 Stern
5280 Stern
5456 Stern
5286 Stern
7657
9046
9476
9496
5327 Stern D

6976
7342
7343
8987
8986
8956
8957
8958
7628

7614
5618
5619
5620
5621
7760
5622
7782
5623

5624
5625
7761

5626
5627
5628

7762
5629

5630
5632
5631

7759
S.214 Weitere Monatszeichen

Man

8135
8136
8695 Figur
5139 Figur?
6251 Madonna
7879 hl.Ambrosius
8887 St.Fridolin
9319 Wenzel
8404 Bischof
8404
7112

7146
7147
7123
7148
7149
7145
9171
8340
8159

8122
9066
5634
5723
7779
8004 Jungfrau
8160
5219
5221
8153

8150
8148
8149
8151
8152
9050 Mann CH
9088 Mann
8428
9041

9071
8696 Brustbild
5344
5244 Kopf
7605 Männerkopf
5482 Männerkopf
S.491 Kopf
6618 Merkurkopf
5466 Beginenkopf?
5291 Mohrenkopf
5864

5863, 6235, 5214, 5212, 5210, 6593, 5557, 9222, 6862, 5899, 6607, 8452, 8453

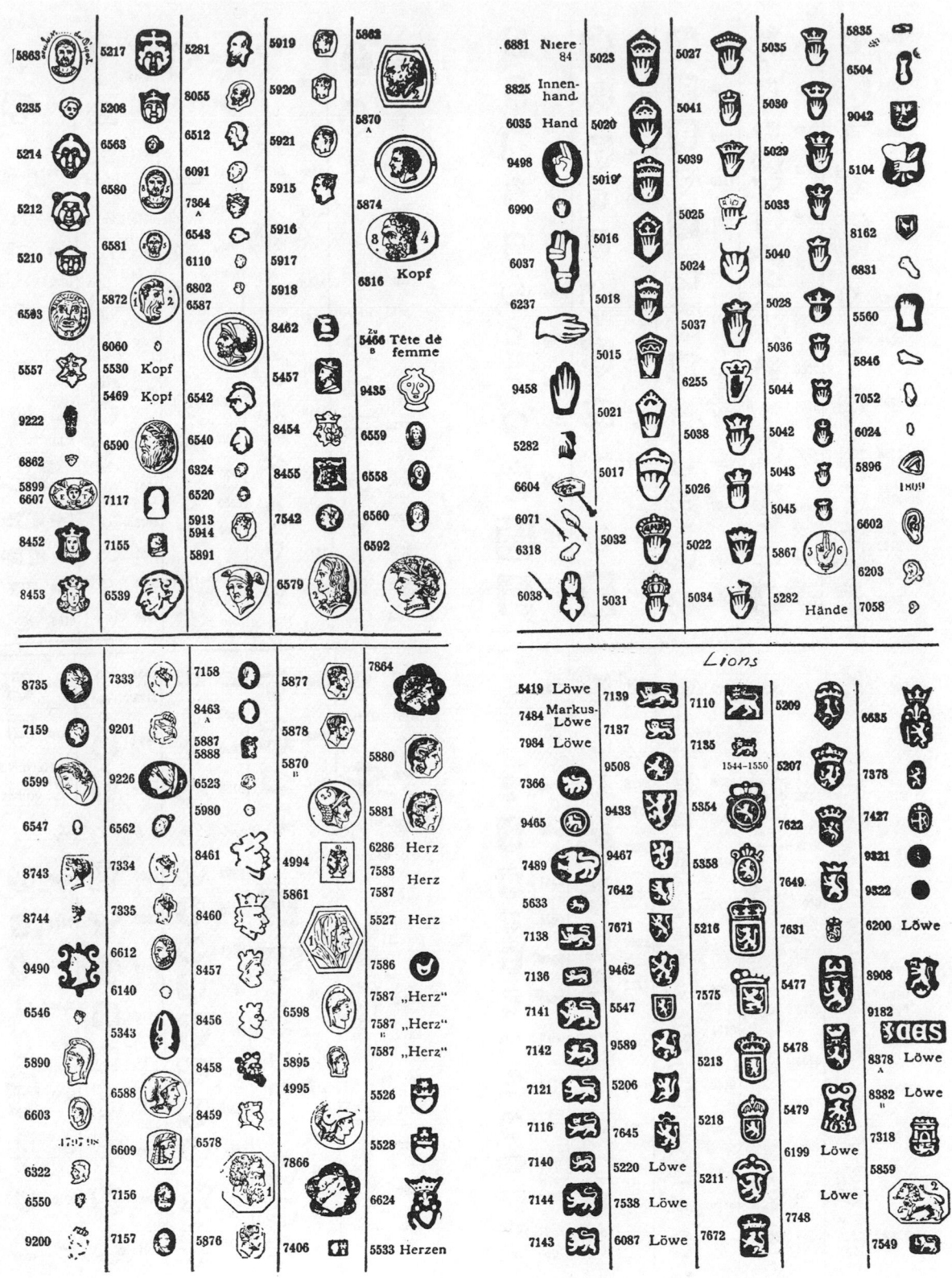

5217, 5208, 6563, 6580, 6581, 5872, 6060, 5530 Kopf, 5469 Kopf, 6590, 7117, 7155, 6539

5281, 8055, 6512, 6091, 7364 A, 6543, 6110, 6802, 6587, 6542, 6540, 6324, 6520, 5913, 5914, 5891

5919, 5920, 5921, 5915, 5916, 5917, 5918, 8462, 5457, 8454, 8455, 7542, 6579

5862, 5870 A, 5874, 6816 Kopf, Zu 5466 B Tête de femme, 9435, 6559, 6558, 6560, 6592

6881 Niere 84, 8825 Innen-hand, 6035 Hand, 9498, 6990, 6037, 6237, 9458, 5282, 6604, 6071, 6318, 6038

5023, 5020, 5019, 5016, 5018, 5015, 5021, 5017, 5032, 5031

5027, 5041, 5039, 5025, 5024, 5037, 6255, 5038, 5026, 5022, 5034

5035, 5030, 5029, 5033, 5040, 5028, 5036, 5044, 5042, 5043, 5045, 5867, 5282 Hände

5835, 6504, 9042, 5104, 8162, 6831, 5560, 5846, 7052, 6024, 5896 (1809), 6602, 6203, 7058

8735, 7159, 6599, 6547, 8743, 8744, 9490, 6546, 5890, 6603 (1797 98), 6322, 6550, 9200

7333, 9201, 9226, 6562, 7334, 7335, 6612, 6140, 5343, 6588, 6609, 7156, 7157

7158, 8463 A, 5887, 5888, 6523, 5980, 8461, 8460, 8457, 8456, 8458, 8459, 6578, 5876

5877, 5878, 5870 B, 4994, 5861, 6598, 5895, 4995, 7866, 7406

7864, 5880, 5881, 6286 Herz, 7583 Herz, 7587, 5527 Herz, 7586, 7587 „Herz", 7587 B „Herz", 7587 „Herz", 5526, 5528, 6624, 5533 Herzen

Lions

5419 Löwe, 7484 Markus-Löwe, 7984 Löwe, 7366, 9465, 7489, 5633, 7138, 7136, 7141, 7142, 7121, 7116, 7140, 7144, 7143

7139, 7137, 9508, 9433, 9467, 7642, 7671, 9462, 5547, 9589, 5206, 7645, 5220 Löwe, 7538 Löwe, 6087 Löwe

7110, 7135 (1544–1550), 5354, 5358, 5216, 7575, 5213, 5218, 5211, 7672

5209, 5207, 7622, 7649, 7631, 5477, 5478, 5479 (1682), 6199 Löwe, Löwe, 7748

6685, 7378, 7427, 9321, 9322, 6200 Löwe, 8908, 9182 (SDES), 8378 A Löwe, 8382 B Löwe, 7318, 5859, 7549

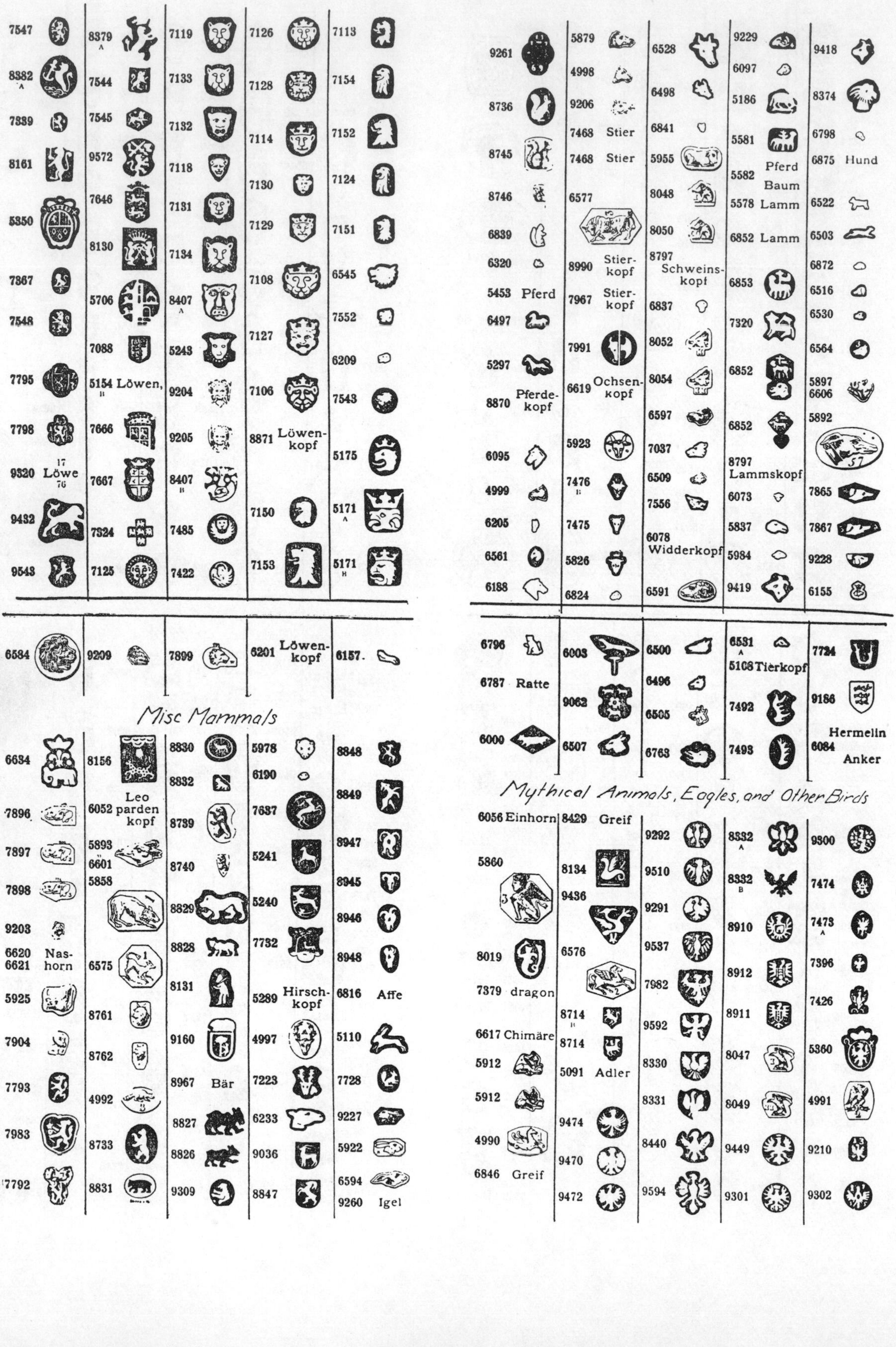
7547
8382 A
7339
8161
5350
7367
7548
7795
7798
9320 17 Löwe 76
9432
9543
8379 A
7544
7545
9572
7646
8130
5706
7088
5154 B Löwen,
7666
7667
7324
7125
7119
7133
7132
7118
7131
7134
8407 A
5243
9204
9205
8407 B
7485
7422
7126
7128
7114
7130
7129
7108
7127
7106
8871 Löwen-kopf
7150
7153
7113
7154
7152
7124
7151
6545
7552
6209
7543
5175
5171 A
5171 B
6584
9209
7899
6201 Löwen-kopf
6157.
9261
8736
8745
8746
6839
6320
5453 Pferd
6497
5297
8870 Pferde-kopf
6095
4999
6205
6561
6188
5879
4998
9206
7468 Stier
7468 Stier
6577
8990 Stier-kopf
7967 Stier-kopf
7991
6619 Ochsen-kopf
5923
7476 B
7475
5826
6824
6528
6498
6841
5955
8048
8050
8797 Schweins-kopf
6837
8052
8054
6597
7037
6509
7556
6078 Widderkopf
6591
9229
6097
5186
5581
5582 Pferd Baum
5578 Lamm
6852 Lamm
6853
7320
6852
6852
8797 Lammskopf
6073
5837
5984
9419
9418
8374
6798
6875 Hund
6522
6503
6872
6516
6530
6564
5897 6606
5892
7865
7867
9228
6155
6796
6787 Ratte
6000
6003
9062
6507
6500
6496
6505
6763
6531 A
5106 Tierkopf
7492
7493
7724
9156
Hermelin
6084 Anker
Misc Mammals
6634
7896
7897
7898
9203
6620 6621 Nas-horn
5925
7904
7793
7983
7792
8156
6052 Leo parden kopf
5893 6601
5858
6575
8761
8762
4992
8733
8831
8830
8832
8739
8740
8829
8828
8131
9160
8967 Bär
8827
8826
9309
5978
6190
7637
5241
5240
7732
5289 Hirsch-kopf
4997
7223
6233
9036
8847
8848
8849
8947
8945
8946
8948
6816 Affe
5110
7728
9227
5922
6594
9260 Igel
Mythical Animals, Eagles, and Other Birds
6056 Einhorn
5860
8019
7379 dragon
6617 Chimäre
5912
5912
4990
6846 Greif
8429 Greif
8134
9436
6576
8714 B
8714
5091 Adler
9474
9470
9472
9292
9510
9291
9537
7982
9592
8330
8331
8440
9594
8332 A
8332 B
8910
8912
8911
8047
8049
9449
9301
9300
7474
7473 A
7396
7426
5360
4991
9210
9302

9303
9379
9211
7487 A
9237
5336 A Doppel-adler
6036 Doppel-adler
7596 7597 Doppel-adler
7660
5336 B
7321
8725
9494
8121

8119
9563
9235
9236
8140
8118
9535
7661
7595
8139
8123

8117
8147
8120
7458
7457
8116
5337 Doppel-adler
5345 Doppel-adler
5338
5340
5342

5345
5347
5349
5351
5353
5355
5357
5359
7679
8865
9378
9250

9251
7237
5894
6501
5847
6494
7039 Adler-kopf
8869
8051
8053
9207
5886 Adler-kopf
6596 Adler-kopf
6595
5885
5884

5965
5869

6585
6582

7913
7900

7901
7902

9539
7609

Marine Life and Water

6488
6062
7914
7473
7553
6151 Delphin
6149 Delphin
6150 Delphine
6152 Delphine
7905
7906
7907

7908
5943
5952
7909
7910
7911
7912
9202
7446
5813 Fische
9565
8400 Fische
Krone
7611

5836
6845
5934
5924
5882
5189 A
5189 B
5946
5349
8737 Biene
5330
6997
6239

6471
5931
5940
5905
5928

5906
5907
5957
5927
5926

5883
8423
6450 Vogel
9064 Vogel
6615 Eule
5910
6252 Storch
5098 Schwan?
7745
9541
5509
6616
5911
7981
9068
7224
6978

7226
5117
6535
6475
9208
7620
5117 Vogel
5255
8353
6489
9596
5853
5849

6566
5852
6569
6574
5857
6571
6572
5855
9212
6170 Vogel
6228 Pfau

8734
7382
8741
8742
5848
6565
5856
6570
6573
5851
6568

5854
5850
6567
7035
9077
8853
8854
7054
6549
6548
6762
6586
5868
6537
5865
6508
7903

5929

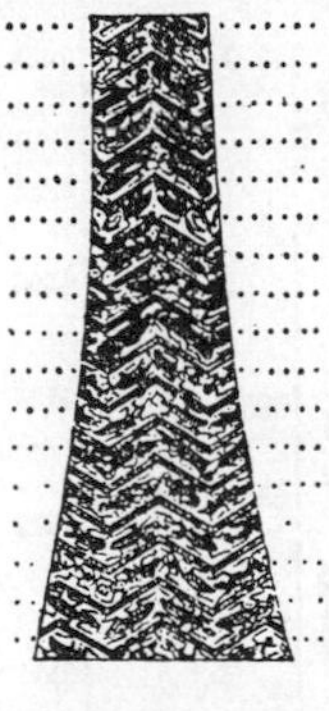

9168 Muschel
5937
6134
6177

5125
6510
6064
8979

8980
8981
8982
8132

Plants

8372
7786
7747
8346
8406
8346

7098
7639
8425 Bäume
5580
8425
6873 Laub-kranz
5102

5239 Lorbeer-zweig
6258
6818
6517
6518
6519
5765 Nesselblatt
6556

5904
6870
6108
7033
7550
7551
5277

9547
5294
7582
8978
9549
9512
9099

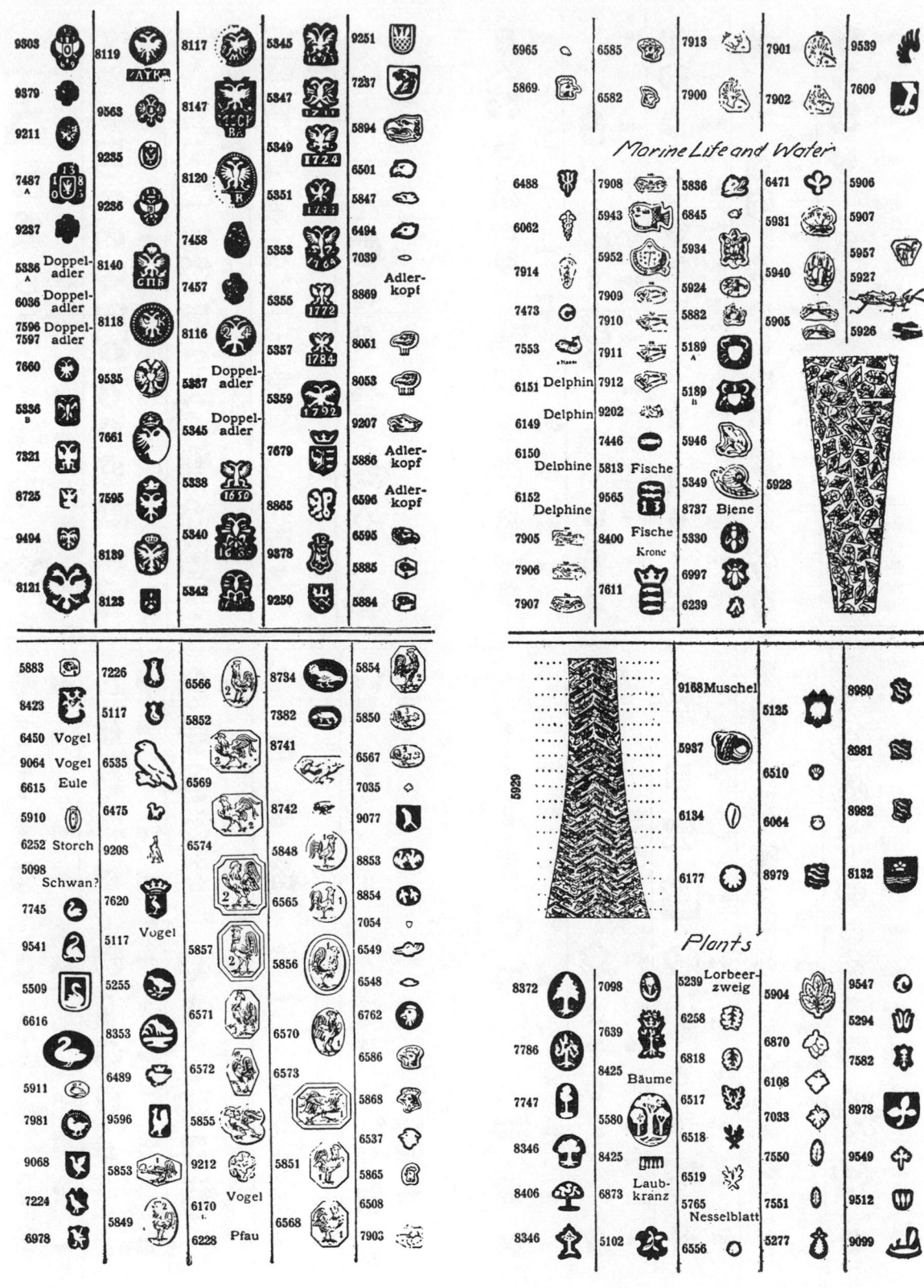

7508
9488
5196
9078
5193 Kleeblätter
7231
9518
8386
5287
5693
8355
5828 „fleur del ys"
5829 Lilie
6012 Lilie
6335 Lilie
6882 Lilie
7103 Lilie

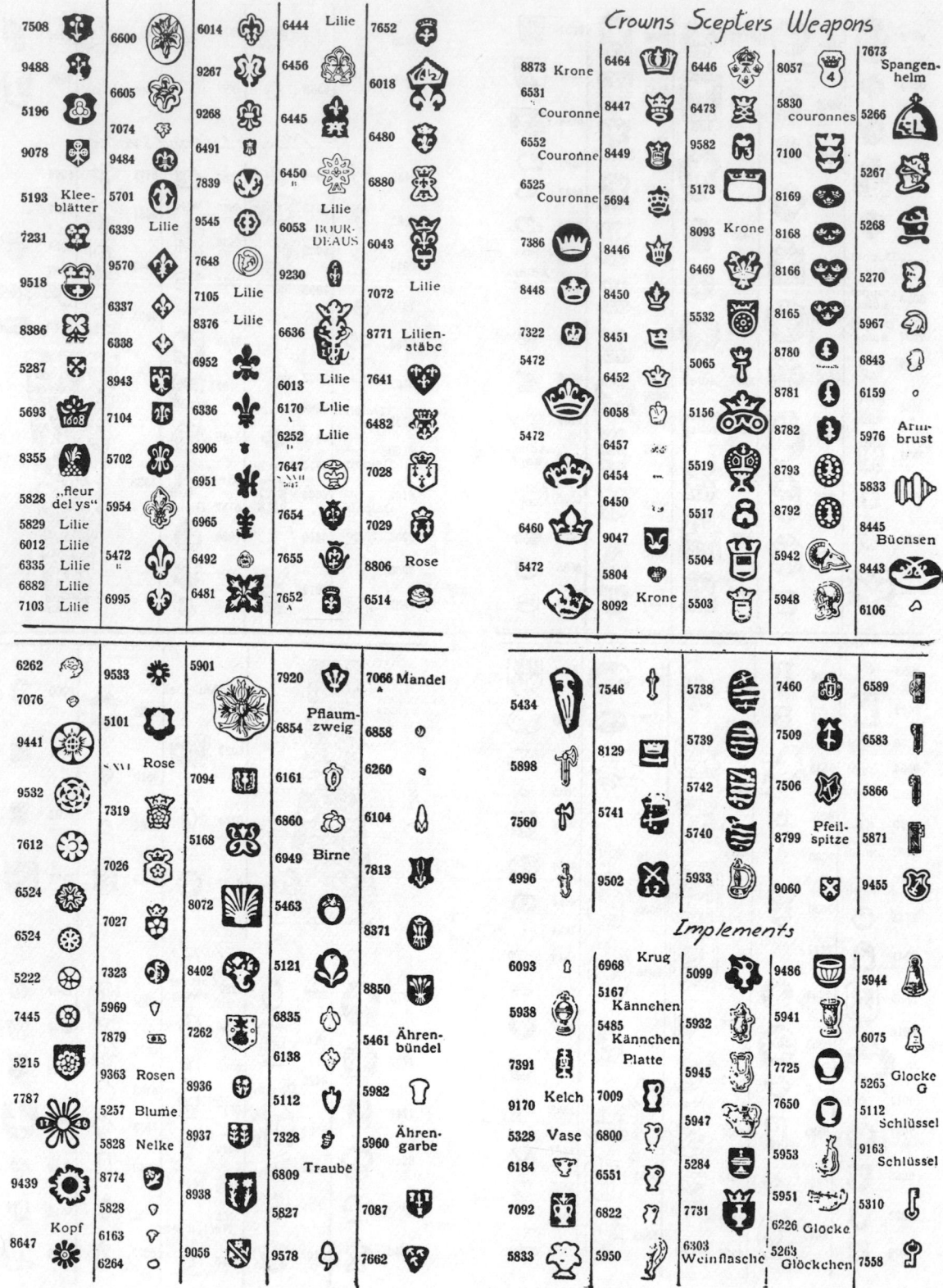

6600
6605
7074
9484
5701
6339 Lilie
9570
6337
6338
8943
7104
5702
5954
5472
6995

6014
9267
9268
6491
7839
9545
7648
7105 Lilie
8376 Lilie
6952
6336
8906
6951
6965
6492
6481

6444 Lilie
6456
6445
6450 Lilie
6053 BOURDEAUS
9230
6636
6013 Lilie
6170 Lilie
6252 Lilie
7647
7654
7655
7652

7652
6018
6480
6880
6043
7072 Lilie
8771 Lilienstäbe
7641
6482
7028
7029
8806 Rose
6514

Crowns Scepters Weapons

8873 Krone
6531 Couronne
6552 Couronne
6525 Couronne
7386
8448
7322
5472
5472
6460
5472

6464
8447
8449
5694
8446
8450
8451
6452
6058
6457
6454
6450
9047
5804
8092 Krone

6446
6473
9582
5173
8093 Krone
6469
5532
5065
5156
5519
5517
5504
5503

8057
5830 couronnes
7100
8169
8168
8166
8165
8780
8781
8782
8793
8792
5942
5948

7673 Spangenhelm
5266
5267
5268
5270
5967
6843
6159
5976 Armbrust
5833
8445 Büchsen
8443
6106

6262
7076
9441
9532
7612
6524
6524
5222
7445
5215
7787
9439
8647 Kopf

9533
5101
Rose
7319
7026
7027
7323
5969
7879
9363 Rosen
5257 Blume
5828 Nelke
8774
5828
6163
6264

5901
7094
5168
8072
8402
7262
8936
8937
8938
9056

7920
6854 Pflaumzweig
6161
6860
6949 Birne
5463
5121
6835
6138
5112
7328
6809 Traube
5827
9578

7066 Mandel
6858
6260
6104
7813
8371
8850
5461 Ährenbündel
5982
5960 Ährengarbe
7087
7662

5434
5898
7560
4996

7546
8129
5741
9502

5738
5739
5742
5740
5933

7460
7509
7506
8799 Pfeilspitze
9060

6589
6583
5866
5871
9455

Implements

6093
5938
7391
9170 Kelch
5328 Vase
6184
7092
5833

6968 Krug
5167 Kännchen
5485 Kännchen
Platte
7009
6800
6551
6822
5950

5099
5932
5945
5947
5284
7731
6303 Weinflasche

9486
5941
7725
7650
5953
5951
6226 Glocke
5263 Glöckchen

5944
6075
5265 Glocke G
5112 Schlüssel
9163 Schlüssel
5310
7558

5307
5308
9506
5750
5751
5994 Schlüssel
5312
5314
8720
5316
8721

8874 Schlüssel-stiel(?) „G"
5732 Schwert Schlüssel
8694
5730
5731
9431
8968
7997
8930
8412
8411
8412

7998
7644
7433
7434
7436
7432
7431
7499
7500
7498
7496
7497
7495
7494
7435

6111 Uhrschlüssel
6856
6272
6273
6271
6270
9034
7490
7491
9600
5293
8704
8703
8705

9387
5246 Rost
6513
6153 Sensen
5230
9040
5256 Striegel
9443
9453
9069
5433
8021
8436
7086
7443

6006 Stuhl
6181 Trag-korb
6028 Vogel-bauer

7238
6256 Destillier-Apparat

7025 Triumph-wagen
5930
7380

6089 Pflug-schar
6696
9580

5456
5472

Architecture

5200 B Haus
5195 Haus
7098
8727
8728
6029 Turm
7316 Turm
8005 Turm
6287 Turm
5278 Turm
5935
9480
8438 H

9445
7090
7056
8133
9194
5513
5472
7753
7752

7750
7751
9397
9395
9394
9396
7749 B Turm
9316
8438 A

7535
5514
7370
5441
5442
7369
5515
7372
7373

7371
9398
8101
9399
8025
7340 Türme
9451
9482
9258

8146
8145
8143
8141
8142
8144
6085 Drei-master
5711
5713
8711
5712
7994
7326
7089

5113
5810
5579
7488
7091
5838
5840
5839
5841
4993
6240 Baß-geige
5095
5490
7329
7580

7579
5449
5279 Hammer
5136
8940
8441 Hämmer
9364
8921
7059 Maurer-kelle
8843
5103
7846
5166
8341

9280
5290 Post-horn
7643
7922
5936
8158
6553
6794 Turban
6077
6833
6186
6136
6146
6119 Hand-schuh
5834
6219 Schleife

6207
6820
8125
7843
9067 Ringe
5158 Brillen-zeichen
5159
5165 Brillenz.
5157
6022
5939
5956
5993 Ball-schläger
6046 Kork-zieher
9045

5589 Türme
7083 Türme
8418 Türme
7317
7097
9567
8367
7981
7982
8418
9339
8124
5439
8860

8859
5705 Drei Türme
9219
9568
5598
5597
5599
5601
5600
5602

5603
5604
5596
5593
5594
5592
5595
5606
5605
5591
5576
8011 Stadttor

8377 Türme
8069 Tor
8012
8090
9156
8091
9340
9341
5585
9318 Staut-mauer
9315
9417

9317 Stadtmauer
9038 Gitter
9277 „Pyra-mides"
8126
9257
9278
9279
5509
9314 Staut-mauer
9604
7972
7973
9516
7815

7814
9277 „Saulen"
5963
5129
9169 Grab

Crosses

5756
5192
9478
9559
9438
5014
5013
9524
5758
9584
5759
5760
5299

5154
6754
6753
5137
6829
8747
8833
8764
8765
9457
8955
8772

8900
9086
6246 croix étoile
8959
7469 Kreuz
7471
9491
8391
9044
9085

9557
9283
9284
9285
9231
9282
5544
5542
5541

7598
7599
7561
7562
7563
7564
7566
7565

8894
8767
8769
8768
8766
8770
6227 Schild
7605 Pfahl
7608
8899
5422
5421
5421
5423
5642 3 Pfähle Kreuz

9526
7788
9574
9576
5754
5757
5755
7736
7737
9586
7472
9092
7856
6482
7665

5339
5346
5348
5352
9007
7685
7686
6888
6891
6885
6894
6900

6887
6886
6901
6884
6890
6892
6897
6889
7681
7684
7683
7682
5259

8913
9377
9376
7602
5283
7239
9479
8702
8907
9190
8861
6083 2Punkte
7397
8730
7754 Sieben Punkte

Trade Marks

8631 Hausmarke
6967
9471
8721
5086

8707
7722
9493
9447
9448

9519
9037
6970
8706
5643
9492

9460
5700
7221
8708
5641

7513
5493
9289
9459
5698

Shields and Geometrical Forms

5192 Wappenschild
6713
6882
9061
6808
7712
6883
7727

5341
8889
9082
9083
9084
9005
9081

9080
7723
9059
9233
7870
5311
5313

5309
5315
5356
7855
9294
9295

9270
9269
6226 Schild
8933
8932
8970
8971
8905

Numbers

6780 Zahlen
6780 Zahlen
8903 0,900
7463
7559
7618 2/Z
7871
7619
6793 „3 P"
7735
8056
7835 „B 4"
8095 „U 5"
6328 8
6866 8

7616 8 E
6817
6821
9093 „9 D"
7384 11
6222 12
5972 12*
7757 12
5257
7875
8867
7974
7979 „12"
7980 „13"
8020 „13"
9330 „13"

6100 13
6221 13
5970 13*
5971 13*
8995
7794
7820
7796
6898
6893
6918
6902
6896
6915

6899
6895
6905
6930
6931
6934
6933
6932
7459
6920
6912
6917

6922
6913
6923
6909
6910
6921
6924
6919
6916
6914
6908

6911	13
6906	13
6903	13
6907	13
6904	13
9582	13
7975	13 1859
8421	13
6098	14
6099	14
6280	15
8603	15 Löd
6849	16
6081	17
6847	17
6848	17
6079	18
6080	18
8174	..18 K..
6935	18/6
6143	19
6141	20
6142	20
7758	20
7878	20 A
8173	..20 K..
6936	20 K
8650	..21 K..
6049	23
8172	..23 K..
6047	24
6048	25
6086	27
7048	29
6086	30
6067	31
6086	31
6267	32
6827	33
7046	33
7047	34
6065	35
7062	35
7375	35
6066	36
6166	36
6265	37
6266	38
6825	38
6826	39
7060	40
6164	41
7061	41
6165	42
6327	43
5997	47
6114	49
6812	49
6325	50
5555	..50..
5255	..51..
5556	..51..
5227	51
6296	52
6326	52
7069	53
5995	55
6244	55
6306	56
6112	56(57)?
6810	56*(?)
5996	57
6173	57
6803	59
5256	..60..
6009	60
6113	60
6294	60
6811	60*
6878	60*
5468	61
7067	61*(?)
6032	62*
5147	..63..
6295	63
6790	64
7068	64*
5444	64
5162, 5168	..64..
6961	..65..
5077	65
6127, 6242	..66..
5257	..67..
6213	67
6304	68
6171	69
6243	69
6305	71
5163, 5169	71
5320	..72..
6172, 7079	..72..
5078	72
5321	..73..
6007	73
6865	73
6876	73 (?)
5987	75
6030	75*(?)
5445	76
6008	76
6877	76
6788	77
6959	78
6125	79
6031	79
6211	80
6780	..80..
5524	81
6789	81
6805	81
6193	82
6960	82
5446	82
6126	..83..
8023	84
5079	84
8157	84*
5276	..85..
5294	..85..
6212	..85..
7755	87
5524	87
7077	87
6863	88
5985	90
5428, 5437	..96..

7385	91·
5447	91
5429, 5437	91
7078	94
6864	95
6191	96
5986	98
7756	99
6926	XId 129
6927	XId 129
6928	XId 129
6929	IId 129
9293	17 36
5257	1760
5703	1763
7870	1774
7958	1795
7872	1798
7464	1805
7874	1824
8902	1891

Note that the marks shown on pages 373-387 are of all European countries except Germany. They have been classified according to character only, no distinction being made as to locality. However, they have been numbered according to locality and indexed accordingly, so that the marks of any locality may be ascertained by consulting the index first and then referring to the marks.

Numbers 5823-7081 are French marks and 7083-7324 are English marks. These are more completely and more specifically listed in the special tables for those countries.

5032. 1645-46
5033. 1651-52 ?
5034. 1663
5035. 1663-64
5036. 1666-67
5037. so or similar 1669-70 or 1687-88
5038. 1672-73
5039. so or similar 1686-87 or 1706-07
5040. 1688-89
5041. 1738-39
5042. 1767
5043. about 1767
5044. 1772
5045. 1784
5046. 1507-08
5047. 1524-25
5048. 1537-38
5049. 1539-40
5050. 1544-45 or 1552-53 ?
5051. 1551-52 or 1558-59 ?
5052. 1563-64
5053. 1565-66
5054. 1574-75
5055. 1581-82
5056. 1588-89
5057. 1606
5058. 1606-07
5059. 1607-08 ?
5060. 1610-11 or 1611-12
5061. 1625-26
5062. end of 17. cent.
5063. 1641-42
5064. 1645-46
5065. 1651-52 ?
5066. 1663
5067. 1663-64
5068. 1666-67
5069. 1669-70
5070. 1672-73
5072. 1685-86 or 1686-87
5073. 1687-88
5074. 1688-89
5075a. 1706-07
5075b. 1738-39
5076a. 1743-44 or 1745
5076b. 1745-49
5076c. 1749-17??
5077. 1765
5078. 1772
5079. 1784
5080. government assayer Arnold Nyst since 1869
5081. assayer Ch. Lemaire since 1869

ATH (AETH)

5154a. 1671, in changing shield form till 1788
5154b. second half of 18. cent.

OUDENAARDE

5156. about 1660
5157. 1618
5158. since 1655 and to the beginning of the 18. cent.
5159. 1771
5160. city mark early 18. cent.
5161. about 1775
5162. 1764
5163. 1771

(BRUGES)

5171a. beginning of 16. cent.
5171b-5172. about 1613, perh. 1622
5173-5174. about 1623
5175-5176. about 1660
5177. 1536-1560
5178. 1560-1584
5179. 1584-1595
5180. 1595-96
5181. 1608-09
5182. 1621-22
5183. 1630-31
5184. 1632-33
5185. 1742
5189a. Jan Crabbe, master after 1587 or
5189b. Jan Crabbe, master after 1604

BRUSSELS

5206. 15. cent.
5207-5208. beginning of 16. cent.
5209-5210. 1545 and middle of 16. cent.
5211-5212. 1553
5213-5215. about 1660
5216-5217. beginning of 18. cent.
5218-5221. 1750- about 1760
5222. since about 1760
5223. 1553
5224. 1618 ?
5225. 1624-25
5226. 1663 or perhaps 1670
5227. 1751
5228. government assayer Ch. Puttemans since 1868
5229. assayer Lelièvre since 1868

COURTRAI

5259. middle of 17.- late 18. cent.
5260. government assayer Philippeu since 1869

DINANT

5263. 1750

GHENT

5266b. about 1482
5267. second half of 16. cent.
5268-5269. about 1660
5270-5271. about 1722
5272. 1482
5273. 1557
5274. 1660
5275. 1722-26
5276. 1785

GRAMMONT

5299. about 1662

LOUVAIN

5307. late 15. cent.
5308. about 1500
5309-5310. about 1650
5311-5312. about 1712
5313-5314. about 1714
5315-5316. 1772 and 1773
5317. late 15. cent.
5318. about 1675
5319. about 1712
5320. 1772
5321. 1773

LIÈGE

5336a. 15. cent.
5336b. middle of 16. cent.
5337. 1612-1650
5338-5339. 1650-1688
5340-5341. 1688-1693
5342-5343. 1693
5344. interregnum mark, 1694, 1744, 1764, 1784
5345-5346. 1693-1705
5347-5348. 1711-1723
5349-5350. 1724-1743
5351-5352. 1744-1763
5353-5354. 1764-1771
5355-5356. 1772-1784.
5357-5358. 1784-1792
5359-5360. 1792-1797
5361. probably 1551
5362. 1745
5363. 1764
5364. or "G" 1774 or 1778
5365. 1777
5366. 1785
5367. 1788
5368. 1620-about 1640

MALINES

5421a. about 1500
5412b. 1513-37
5421c. about 1675
5421c. about 1718
5422. 1790
5423. 1791
5424. 1527-28
5425. 1592-93
5426. 1619-20
5427. 1719-20
5428. 1790
5429. 1791
5434. Jean van Campenhoudt, 1762-1791

MONS

5439. end of 15. cent.
5440. 1608-1693
5441. 17. cent.
5442. 1766
5443. about 1686
5444. 1764
5445. 1776
5446. 1782
5447. 1791

NAMUR

5477. 1505
5478. 1520
5479. 1682

NIVELLES

5490. 16. cent.
5491. 17. cent.
5492. about 1525

TERMONDE

5503. about 1713 ?
5504. about 1727

TONGRES

5509a-5509b. about 1759
5510. another comark to the inspection mark about 1764-1783

TOURNAI

5513. about 1528, if not much older
5514. 16.-17. cent.
5515-5516. 1627
5517-5518. middle of 17. cent.
5519-5520. about 1766 a n d 1781
5521. about 1606
5522. about 1615
5523. 1624 or 1627
5524a. 1781
5524b. 1787

VIRTON

5536. 1733

YPRES

5541. about 1525
5542-5543. second half of 17. cent.
5544-5545. end of 17. cent.
5546. 1701-1713
5547. 1750
5548. about 1526
5549. perhaps 1684-85
5550. 1701
5551. 1702
5552. 1703
5553. 1714
5554. 1750-51
5555-5556. 1750 and 1751

DENMARK

AALBORG, JUTLAND

5576a. 1686

AARHUS, JUTLAND

5577. inspection mark

HELSINGOER, SEELAND

5579. 1741

HOLBAEK, SEELAND

5580. 19. cent.

HORSENS, JUTLAND

5581. inspection mark

KALUNDBORG, SEELAND

5585. 17. cent.

COPENHAGEN

Inspection marks
5591. 1608
5592. 1610
5593. 1639
5594. 1645
5595. 1663
5596. 1707
5597. 1721
5598. 1725
5599. 1733
5600. 1736
5601. 1743

5602. 1747
5603. 1769
5604. 1783
5605. 1841
5606. 1851
5607. Conrad Ludolf, mint-assayer 1679-1729
5608. Pet. Nicolai von Haven, a s s a y e r, 1729-1749
5609. Christopher Fabritius, assayer 1749-1787
5610-5612. Frederik Fabritius, assayer 1787-1823
5613. Christian P e t e r Naeboe, a s s a y e r 1823-1827
5614. Jacob Greg. Graah-Fabritius, assayer 1827-1831
5615. Christian O l s e n Möller, a s s a y e r 1831-1840
5616. Pter Reimer Hin-nerup, a s s a y e r 1840-1863
5617. Sim. Chr. Sch. Groth, a s s a y e r 1863-1904

MONTH MARKS

5618. January
5619-5620. February
5621. March
5622. April
5623. May
5624. June
5625. July
5626. August
5627. September
5628. October
5629-5630. November
5631. December
5632. December
5633. June
5634. November
5635. gold since 1685
5636. gold, 18. cent.
5637. gold since 1685
5638. 18 carat gold

NAESTVED, SEELAND

5693. 1608
5694-5696. 17.-18. cent.
5697. middle of 17. cent.

ODENSE, FUENEN

5701. 1625, 1763
5702. of 18. cent.
5703. 1763

RANDERS, JUTLAND

5705. 18. cent.

RIPEN (RIBE), JUTLAND

5706. 18.-19. cent.

ROSKILDE, ZEALAND

5707. inspection mark

STEGE, ZEALAND

5710. 1750

TONDERN, SOUTH JUTLAND

5711-5712. 17. cent.
5713. 17.-18. cent.

VIBORG, JUTLAND

5723. 17.-18. cent.
5724. 1800-

ESTLAND DORPAT

5730. 17. cent.
5731. 18. cent.
5732. 18. cent.

NARVA

5738-5739. 17. cent.
5740. about 1700
5741. 17.-18. cent.
5742. 18. cent.

PERNAU

5750-5751. 18. cent.

REVAL (TALLINN)

5754. middle of 16. cent.
5755. late 17. cent.
5756. about 1690
5757. middle of 18. cent.
5758. end of 18. cent.
5759-5760. about 1780
5761. about 1716
5762. about 1796

FINLAND

FINLAND (SUOMEN TASAVALTA)

5798. 1759-1782
5799. 1783-1808
5800. 1807-1809 (10?)
5801. 1810/11-1833/34
5802. 1834/35-1857/58
5803. 1858/59
5804. since 1810

ABO

5805. 1822

HELSINGFORS

5810. inspection mark

NYSTAD

5813. inspection mark

WASA

5814. 18. and 19. cent.

WIBORG

5816. silver 18. cent.
5817. gold 18.-19. cent.

ITALY

7326-7327. 1810-1872
7328-7329. 1810-1872
7330. import mark
7331. 1818-1872
7333-7335. since 1873

AQUILA (ABRUZZI)

7336. early 15. cent.
7337. early 16. cent.

BOLOGNA

7339. 18. cent.
7340. 1811-1817
7341. inspection mark Vatican City since 1817

BOLZANO

7342. 1708
7343. middle of 18. cent.
7344. 1824-1866
7345. 1866-1872
7346. since 1872

FERRARA

7364a. 17.(?) cent.
7364b. 1815

FLORENCE

7366. 16. cent.
7367. 17.-18. cent.
7368. 18. cent.

GENOA

7369. 16. cent.
7370. 17.-18. cent.
7371. (1)720-(1)768.
7372. end of 18. cent.

LUCCA

7378. 17. cent.

MILAN

7379b. beginning of 16. cent.
7379c. middle of 16. cent.
7379d. 17.-18. cent.
7380. 1810
7381. control mark
7382-7386. master marks with comarks

MANTUA

7391. 17. cent.

MODENA

7396. 17. cent.

NAPLES

7379a. silver since 1380
7379b. gold since 1380
7398a. about 1400
7398b. 16. cent.
7399. 17. cent.
7400. 17??
7401. 1702
7402. 1716
7403. 1720
7404. 1736
7405. 1782
7406a-7406b. probably also Naples 17.-18. cent.

ASSAYER MARKS

7407. about 1700 ?
7408. about 1702
7409. about 1716
7410. about 1720
7411. about 1736
7412. about 1742

PALERMO

7426. 17. cent.

PARMA

7427. 17. cent.

ROME

7431. 17. cent.
7432-7433. end of 17. cent.
7434. 17.-18. cent.
7435. 18.-19. cent.
7436. 18.-19. cent. for gold
7437-7438. sterling, 1358-1398
7439. Bolognese standard 1508
7440. Caroline-silver 1508

SULMONA

7451. 13. and 14. cent.
7452. 14. cent. till 1406
7453. 1406-middle of 15. cent.
7454. middle of 15. cent. till ??

TRIESTE

7457-7459. 18. cent.
7460. 1805
7461. 1805
7462. 1807/09 and 1824/66
7463-7464. gold 1805
7465. 1806/07
7466. 1866-1872
7467. since 1872

TURIN

Inspection marks
7468a. 1597
7468b. 1597
7469a. since 1678
7469b. 17. cent.
7470a-7470e. 18. cent.
7471-7472. 18. cent.
7473a-7476a. about 1750
7476b. 18. cent.

VENICE

7484. 15.? cent.
7485. 17.-18. cent.
7486. 16.-18. cent.
7487a. silver since 1805
7487b. silver since 1805
7488. since 1810

LATVIA

BAUSKA

7489. inspection mark 18. cent.

GOLDINGEN

7490. 18. cent.
7491. 18.-19. cent.

MITAU

7492-7493. 17. cent.

RIGA

7494. 16. cent.
7495-7496. about 1600
7497-7498. 16.-17. cent.
7499-7500. 18. cent.
7501. 1749-56
7502. 1756-60.
7503. 1760-64
7504. 1764-68
7505. 1768-80
7514. Heinrich Meyer, 1654-1694
7516. Juergen Linden, 1674-1688
7517. Heinrich von Koelln (Kollen, Coeln), 1679-1693
7520. Joh. Georg Eben, 1703-1710
7524. Johann Abrahamsohn Lamoureux (Lamore), 1719-1744
7526. Christoffer Dey, 1729-1748
7528-7529. Johann Dietr. Rehwald, 1738-1759
7531. Joh. Christian Henck, 1750
7532. Michael Kresner the younger, 1758
7533. Joh. Friedrich Lamoureux, 1763-1797
7534. Joh. Christoph Barrowsky, 1771-1790

MEMEL

7535. mark 18. cent.

NETHERLANDS

7542. silver, since 1852
7543. gold, since 1852
7544. silver standard
7545. silver standard
7546. silver standard
7547. gold standard
7548. gold standard
7549. gold standard
7550. gold standard
7551. gold standard
7552. gold standard
7553. taxes mark till 1909
7554. inland
7555. import till 1909
7556. import till 1909
7557. since 1909
7558. export
7559. gold

AMSTERDAM

7561. about 1566
7562. 16.-17. cent.
7563. about 1606
7564. about 1608
7565. 1655
7566. about 1694
7567-7569. 18. cent.

ANNUAL LETTERS

7570. 1566
7571. 1608
7572. 1609
7573. 1655
7574. 1694
7575. 1696 and later
7576. old mark 1807

BOLSWARD

7595. mark 1725

BREDA

7598. 15.-16. cent.
7599. 16.-17. cent.
7600. 1595 or 1694

DORDRECHT

7608-7610. inspection marks with annual letters

ENKHUIZEN

7611-7613. inspection marks with annual letters

GOUDA

7614. 16. cent.

GRONINGEN

7616-7617. Cornelis Papinck,
7618-7619. master marks

THE HAGUE

7620. inspection mark
7621. inspection mark with annual letter
7622. 17. cent.

HAARLEM

7628. about 1700
7629-7630. 18. cent.
7631. middle of 18. cent.
7632. 1807

HERZOGENBUSCH

7639-7641. Aert van Muers, 1607

HOORN

7643. about 1640

LEIDEN

7644. 17. cent.

LEEUWARDEN

7645. 17.-18. cent.
7646. 1695
7652a-7652b. Johannes Lelij, 1695
7654-7656. Garbijnus van der Lelij, 1731

MAASTRICHT

7657. end of 18. cent.
7658. end of 18. cent. with annual letter

MIDDELBURG

7659. 1726
7660. middle of 18. cent.
7661-7664. inspection marks

ROTTERDAM

7665-7667. 18. cent.
7668-7669. 18. cent.
7670. 18.-19. cent.
7671. 18. cent.
7672. 18.-19. cent.

SNEEK (PROVINCE FRIESLAND)

7679. about 1770

UTRECHT

7681. about 1614
7682. 17. cent.
7683. about 1710
7684-7686. 18. cent.
7687. 1602
7688. 1614
7689. about 1650
7690. 1733 ?
7691. 1748 ?
7692. 1775 ?
7693. 1775 ? or 1802 ?

VLISSINGEN (PROVINCE ZEALAND)

7731. inspection mark

ZIERIKZEE

7734. 1600
7735. 1700

ZWOLLE

7736. 17. cent.
7737. 1721
7738. about 1726 and later
7739. 17. cent.
7740. about 1721
7741. about 1726

NORWAY

BERGEN

inspection marks
7750. 1784
7751. 1799
7752. 1812
7753. 1820
7754. 1844 (seven dots without the tower)

ANNUAL LETTERS

7755. 1787
7756. 1799
7757. 1812
7758. 1820
7759-7762. monthly marks
7763. Dimar Kahs, assayer 1763-1789
7764a-7764b. Mathias Pettersen, assayer 1796-1812
7765. Peter Michael Blytt, assayer 1812-1821

BREVIK

7771. 1779

FREDRIKSSTAD

7772. about 1687

LARVIK

7773. about 1746

OSLO (formerly CHRISTIANIA)

7774. end of 16. cent.-1624
7775. 1624
7776. 1712 ?-1781
7777. 1782-after 1814
7778. since about 1820
7779-7781. assayer mark second half of 19. cent.
7782. monthly mark April-May

SKIEN

7785. about 1781

STAVANGER

7786. first half of 18. cent.

TRONDKJEM

7787. 1746

AUSTRIA

BREGENZ

7788. about 1732
7789. since 1824
7790. 1866-68, as Vienna
7791. since 1868

GRAZ

7792. end of 16. cent.
7793. 1678
7794-7795. 1732 and 1743
7796. 1764
7797. 1778
7798. 1800
7799. 1778-1800
7800. 1807-1866
7801. 1866-1872
7802a. since 1872
7802b. since 1922
7804. 1807-1824
7805. 1810-1824

HALL (TIROL)

7810. since 1809
7811. 1809 ? 1824-1866
7812. 1866-1868

INNSBRUCK

7814. end of 17. cent.
7815. 17.-18. cent.
7816. 1868-1872
7817a. since 1872
7817b. since 1922

KLAGENFURT

7820. 1801
7821. 1807-1866
7822. 1866/67
7823. 1868-1872
7824a. since 1872
7824b. since 1922, law 1921
7825. 1806/07
7826. 1811-1824

SALZBURG

7827. 1494
7828. 16. cent.
7829. end of 16. cent.
7830. 1638
7831. 1662
7832-7833. 16.-17. cent.
7834. 1807/09
7835. 1866-72
7836a. since 1872
7836b. since 1922
7837. since 1806/07

8151. 1780
8152. about 1782-1787
8153. about 1790-1801
8154. 1816-1843
8155. beginning of 19. cent.

PSKOW (PLESKAU)

8156. 1771, 1791

TULA

8157. 19. cent.

TWER

8158. 18. ? cent.

WELIKI-USTJUG

8159. beginning of 19. cent.

WITEBSK

8160. 1873

WLADIMIR

8161. 1763

WOLOGDA

8162. 18. and 19. cent.

SWEDEN

8165. since 1752, but since 1912 only for gold
8166-8167. silver since 1912
8168. import mark since 1912 only for gold
8169-8170. import mark since 1912 for silver
8176-8328. Town Marks

ARBOGA

8330-8332a. 17.-18. cent.
8332b. about 1771
8333. since 1860 ?
8334. 1733/34, 1757/58
8335. 1771

ASKERSUND

8340a. about 1742-1765
8340b. since 1860

BORAS

8341a. 18. cent.
8341b. since 1860 ?
8342. 1694, 1718, 1742
8343. 1743 ? 1760 ?

EKSJOE

8346a. 17. cent.
8346b. 18. cent.
8347. since 1860 ?
8348. 1730, 1773

ENGELHOLM

8351. 1722-1775
8352. 1860 ?

FALKENBURG

8353. 1809-1825
8354. 1860 ?

FALUN

8355a. about 1768
8355b. since 1860 ?

GAEVLE

8356. 17.-19. cent.

GOETEBORG

8358. first half of 18. cent.
8359. since 1812
8360a. 1693 and 1717
8360b. 1724
8361. 1735
8362. 1737

HAELSINGBORG

8367a. 1702-1739
8367b. 1860 ?

HAERNOESAND

8369-8370. 18. and 18.-19. cent.

HALMSTAD

8371a. 17.-18. cent.
8371b. since 1860 ?

HEDEMORA

8372a. 18. cent.
8372b. since 1860 ?

HUDIKSVALL

8374a. 18. cent.
8374b. since 1860 ?

KALMAR

8379a. 17.-18. cent.
8379b. since 1860 ?

KARLSHAMN

8381. about 1714
8382a. end of 18. cent.
8382b. 18.-19. cent.
8383. since 1860 ?

KARLSKRONA

8384. 17. and 18. cent.
8385. since 1860 ?
8386. 1733 ?

KARLSTAD

8390a. middle of 18. cent.
8390b. since 1860 ?

KOEPING

8391a. middle of 17. cent.
8391b. since 1860 ?

KRISTIANSTAD

8392. 17. and 18. cent.
8393a. 18. and 19. cent.
8393b. since 1860 ?
8394. 1764
8395. 1820
8396. 1826

LAHOLM

8400. 17.-18. cent.
8401. since 1860 ?
8405. since 1860 ?

LIDKOEPING

8404a. beginning of 18. cent.
8404b. 18. and 19. cent.

LINDESBERG

8406a. 18. cent.
8406b. since 1860 ?

LINKOEPING

8407a-8407b. end of 18. cent.
8408. since 1860 ?

LULEA

8411. middle of 18. cent.
8412a-8412b. beginning of 19. cent.
8413. since 1860 ?

LUND

8418a. 18. cent.
8418b. 18. and 19. cent.
8419. since 1860 ?
8420. 1764
8421. about 1764

MALMOE

8423. 17.-18. cent.
8424. since 1860 ?

NORA

8425a. about 1760
8425b. about 1840-1850
8426. since 1860 ?

NORRKOEPING

8427. 17.-18. cent.
8428. 18. cent.
8429. 17. (?) and 18. cent.
8430. since 1860 ?
8431a. 1754
8431b. since 1759

NORRTAELJE

8436a. early 19. cent.
8436b. since 1860 ?

NYKOEPING

8438a. 18. cent., after 1730
8438b. early 19. cent.
8439. since 1860 ?

OEREBRO

8440a. after 1750
8440b. since 1860 ?

SCHAFFHAUSEN

8945. 16. cent.
8946. 17.-18. cent.
8947-8948. 18. cent.
8949. since 1893

SION

8956. 16. cent.
8957. 17. cent.
8958. 18. cent.

STANS (CANTON UNTERWALDEN)

8968-8969. Franz Remigius Trachser, 1724-1752

SURSEE CANTON (LUCERNE)

8970-8971. 17. and 18. cent.
8972. beginning of 17. cent.
8973-8975. 17.-18. cent.
8976. about 1680
8977. 1707

THUN

8986-8987. 17. cent.

URI

8990. inspection mark

VEVEY

8992. 16. and 17. cent.
8993-8994. 18. cent.
8995. 18. cent.

WINTERTHUR

9002. 18. cent.

ZOFINGEN, CANTON ARGAU

9005. 18. cent.

ZURICH

9007. 1545
9008. 1563
9009. 1563, 1564, 1565
9010. 1608
9011. 1621
9012-9013. early 17. cent.
9014. about 1629
9015. 1631
9016. 1633
9017. 1638
9018. 1642
9019-9029. 17. and 18. cent.
9030. 1667
9031. 1674
9032. 1752
9033. 1779
9037. Abraham Gessner, 1571-1613
9051-9052. Hans Jacob Holzhalb, 1634-1657

ZUG

9080. 1584
9081. 1620
9082. 17. cent.
9083-9084. 18. cent.

SPAIN

9092-9093. since 1881

AGUILAR, PROVINCE CORDOBA

9094. 17. cent.

ASTORGA

9095. 16. cent.

BARCELONA

9096. 14.-16. ? cent.
9097. 15. cent.
9098. 15. cent.
9099-9100. 15.-16. cent.
9101. 16. cent.
9102. late 16. cent.
9103. 16. (also 17. ?) cent.
9104-9105. 16. (also 17. ?) cent.

CERVANTES, PROVINCE LUGO, or CERVERA, PROVINCE LERIDA

9133. 15.-17. cent. ?

CORDOBA

9134. 15. cent.

MADRID

9160. 18. cent.

PALMA MALLORCA

9164. 15. cent.
9165. 15.-16. cent.
9166. 16. cent.

TOLEDO

9173. 16. cent.
9174. about 1600
9175. 17. cent.

VALENCIA

9178. 16. cent.

VALLADOLID

9179. Juan de Benavente, 1565-1609

ZARAGOZA

9180. 14. and 15. cent.
9181-9182. 16. cent.

JUGOSLAVIA

ZAGREB

9198. 1866-1872
9199. since 1872

BELGRADE

9200-9203. gold 1882-1919
9204-9207. silver 1882-1919
9208. import gold
9209. import silver

LAIBACH (LJUBLJANA)

9210. 18. cent.
9211. 1802
9212. 1806
9213. 19. cent.
9214. 1807/08 and 1824-66.
9215. 1866/68
9216. 1868/72
9217. since 1872

NEUSATZ (NUVI SAD)

9219. inspection mark
9220. 1866-1872
9221. since 1872

RAGUSA (DUBROVNIK)

9222. 17. or 18. cent.
9223. 1866/67
9224. 1868/72
9225. since 1872

CZECHOSLOVAKIA

9226. standard mark 1-4
9227-9229. standard marks
9230. import mark silver

ALTSOHL (ZVOLEN)

9231. 1657

BRUNN (BRNO)

9233-9234. till 1646
9235. 1683
9236. 1769
9237. 1806

Official marks

9238. 1807-1866
9239. 1866-1868
9240. 1869-1872
9241. since 1872
9242. 1806/07
9243. 1810-1824
9244. 1811-1824

EGER (CHEB)

9250. 17.-18. cent.
9251. beginning of 18. cent.
9252. 1868-1872
9253. since 1872

HOTZENPLOTZ (OSOBLAHA)

9257. 1769

(HUNGARIAN) HRADISCH

9258. 1608
9259. 1769

IGLAU (JIHLAVA)

9260. 1548-beginning of 18. cent.
9261. 1769 (-1776).
9262. 1807-1866
9263. 1866-1868
9264. 1869-1872
9265. since 1872

KASCHAU (KOSICE)

9267. 16. cent.
9268. 17.-18. cent.

9269-9270. 1799-1866
9271. 1866-1872
9272. since 1872

KREMNITZ (KREMNICA)

9276. inspection mark

KREMSIER (KROMERIZ)

9277. 1689
9278-9279. 1769
9280. 1769

LEUTSCHAU (LEVOCA)

9281. 1664
9282-9285. 17. cent.
9286. since 1872

MORAVIAN TRUBAU

9294. 17. cent. to 19. cent.
9295. 1813
9296. 1866-1872
9297. since 1872

NIKOLSBURG (MIKULOV)

9299. 1769

OLMUTZ (OLOMOUC)

9300. 1593, 1599
9301. 17. cent.
9302. 1755
9303. 1769-1776

Official marks

9304. 1807-1866
9305. 1866-1868
9306. 1869-1872
9307. since 1872
9308. 1810-1824 in the free mark

PRAGUE (PRAHA)

9312. 16. cent.
9313. 17. cent.
9314. second half of 17. cent.
9315-9316. 1673
9317. beginning of 18. cent.
9318. middle of 18. cent.
9319. end of 17. cent. till second half of 18. cent.
9320. since 1776
9321. 1795
9322. 1800

Official marks

9323. 1807-1813
9324. 1814-1866
9325. 1866-1872
9326. since 1872
9327. 1806/07
9328. 1810-1824
9330a. 1776-1806
9330b. import silver 1902-21

PRESSBURG (BRATISLAVA)

9364. 1576
9365. 17. cent.
9366. 17.-18. cent.
9367. 18. cent.
9368. 1866-1872
9369. since 1872

ROSENAU (ROZNAVA)

9363. 19. cent.

SCHEMNITZ

Inspection marks

9364. 1576
9365. 17. cent.
9366. 17.-18. cent.
9367. 18. cent.
9368. 1866-1872
9369. since 1872

TROPPAU (OPAVA)

9376. 16.-17. cent.
9377. 1674
9378. 1759
9379. 1789-1806

Official marks

9380. 1807-1866
9381. 1866-1868
9382. since 1872

TYRNAU (TRNAVA)

9387. 18. cent.

ZNAIM (ZNOJMO)

9389. 1727
9390. 1769
9391. official mark 1807 1866

HUNGARY

BUDAPEST

Inspection marks

9394. 17.-18. cent.
9395. 18. cent.
9396-9397. 18.-19. cent.
9398-9399. 1808, 1866
9401. 1866-1872
9402. since 1872
9403-9404. 17.-18. cent.
9405-9406. 18.-19. cent.

GRAN (ESZTERGOM)

9419. 18.-19. cent.

KECSKEMET

9418. 16. cent.

MISKOLCZ

9421. since 1872

BIBLIOGRAPHY

"English Goldsmiths and Their Marks"—Sir Charles James Jackson. Macmillan and Co. Ltd. London, 1921.

"History of Old Sheffield Plate"—Frederick Bradbury. Macmillan. 1912.

"Der Goldschmiede Merkzeichen"—Marc Rosenberg. Berlin, 1928.

"American Silversmiths and Their Marks"—Stephen G. C. Ensko. New York, 1927.

"Les Poinçons de L'Orfèvrerie Française"—Louis Carré. Paris, 1928.

"Guide de L'Amatur d'Orfèvrerie Française"—Louis Carré. Paris, 1929.

"Domestic Silver of Great Britain and Ireland"—Edward Wenham. Oxford University Press. London, 1931.

"Old English Silver"—William W. Watts. E. Benn, Ltd. London, 1924.

"Old Silver of Europe and America"—Edward Alfred Jones. B. T. Batsford, Ltd. London, 1928.

"Chats on Old Silver"—Arthur Hayden. T. F. Unwin Ltd. London, 1915.

"English Domestic Silver"—Charles C. Oman. A. C. Black Ltd. London, 1934.

"Matthew Boulton"—H. W. Dickinson. Cambridge University Press. London, 1937.

"Paul de Lamerie"—P. A. S. Phillips. B. T. Batsford, Ltd. London, 1935.

"American Silversmiths and Their Marks II"—Stephen G. C. Ensko. New York, 1937.

"Early American Silvermarks"—James Graham Jr. New York, 1936.

"American Church Silver"—Museum of Fine Arts. Boston, Mass., 1911.

"American Silver"—Introduction. R. T. H. Halsey. Museum of Fine Arts. Boston, Mass., 1906.

"American Collector"—New York, 1936 and 1937. Various.

GENERAL INDEX